The Routledge Companion to Dyslexia

The Routledge Companion to Dyslexia is a ground-breaking analysis of the whole field of dyslexia by a distinguished team of international contributors and editors engaged in literacy, inclusion and learning. Their diverse perspectives and wide expertise make this invaluable guide one of the most important additions to the field of dyslexia for over a decade.

Dyslexia is, without a doubt, the most high-profile and contentious learning difficulty, and it is a topic that has attracted a vast amount of research, opinion, professional schisms and debate. The Companion provides an invaluable overview of the field of dyslexia with vital and clear emphasis on linking theoretical perspectives with best practice. This accessible text:

- presents a survey of current and future developments in research, with a focus on how research can inform practice;
- focuses on areas such as neurobiology, phonological processing, literacy acquisition, numeracy and multilingualism;
- considers assessment and identification, with contributions on early identification, reading, spelling and mathematics;
- addresses identifying and meeting needs in an inclusive context;
- discusses inclusion and barriers to learning in a variety of different national contexts;
- includes models of instruction, direct instruction, co-operative learning and cross-curricular learning.

The Routledge Companion to Dyslexia is a superb resource for anyone interested in the subject, whether in education or related subjects such as psychology or neurology. It is ideal for those coming to the field of dyslexia for the first time as well as students and practitioners already familiar with the subject.

Gavin Reid, formerly a senior lecturer at Moray House School of Education, University of Edinburgh, is now consultant to the Centre for Child Evaluation and Teaching in Kuwait, Red Rose School in the UK and REACH Learning Center in Vancouver.

The Routledge Companion to Dyslexia

Edited by
Gavin Reid

Associate editors
Gad Elbeheri,
John Everatt,
Janice Wearmouth and
Deborah Knight

Routledge
Taylor & Francis Group

LONDON AND NEW YORK

First published 2009
by Routledge
2 Park Square, Milton Park, Abingdon, Oxon OX14 4RN

Simultaneously published in the USA and Canada
by Routledge
270 Madison Avenue, New York, NY 10016

Routledge is an imprint of the Taylor & Francis Group, an informa business

© 2009 Gavin Reid for selection and editorial matter; individual chapters, the contributors

Typeset in Bembo by
Swales & Willis Ltd, Exeter, Devon
Printed and bound in Great Britain by
TJ International Ltd, Padstow, Cornwall

British Library Cataloguing in Publication Data
A catalogue record for this book is available from the British Library

Library of Congress Cataloging in Publication Data
The Routledge companion to dyslexia/edited by Gavin Reid.
   p. cm.
   Includes bibliographical references and index.
 1. Dyslexia   2. Reading disability.   I. Reid, Gavin, 1950–
LB1050.5.R68 2009
371.91′44–dc22   2008038508

ISBN10: 0–415–43078–X (hbk)
ISBN10: 0–415–43079–8 (pbk)

ISBN13: 978–0–415–43078–4 (hbk)
ISBN13: 978–0–415–43079–1 (pbk)

Contents

2009

List of editors

Dr Gavin Reid

Dr Gavin Reid is a consultant with the Center for Child Evaluation and Teaching in Kuwait and educational psychologist at Reach Learning Center in North Vancouver, British Columbia, Canada. He was senior lecturer in the Department of Educational Studies, Moray House School of Education, University of Edinburgh, UK from 1991–2007. He is an experienced teacher, educational psychologist, university lecturer, researcher and author. He has made over 700 conference and seminar presentations world wide and has published 23 books. He wrote the first Masters course in Dyslexia in the UK in 1992 and has been external examiner to 15 universities across the world. He is a member of Dyslexia Scotland and was on the British Dyslexia Association Teacher Training Accreditation Board for ten years. He has been involved as a consultant to parent groups and charitable bodies in the UK, Europe and New Zealand and is co-founder and consultant to the Red Rose School for children with specific learning difficulties in St Annes-on-Sea, Lancashire and the international consultant for the Canadian Academy of Therapeutic Tutors.

Dr Gad Elbeheri

Dr Gad Elbeheri is the executive director of the Centre for Child Evaluation and Teaching; the premier leading centre in Kuwait which combines research and practice on learning disabilities across the Arab World. He is also the United Nations Development Programme's Country Expert on Early Childhood Challenges Programme in Kuwait. An applied linguist who obtained his PhD from the University of Durham, UK, Dr Elbeheri has a keen interest in cross-linguistic studies of dyslexia and other specific learning difficulties.

Dr John Everatt

Dr John Everatt is a researcher in literacy ability and developmental dyslexia. He lectured in psychology at the Universities of Wales and Surrey, UK, before moving to the College of Education, University of Canterbury, NZ.

Professor Janice Wearmouth

Janice Wearmouth has many years' experience of teaching, researching and publishing. Formerly she was a senior lecturer in special and inclusive education and Director of the Centre for Curriculum and Teaching Studies at the Open University in the UK, where she developed and led distance learning courses for teachers in the areas of difficulties in literacy development, behavioural issues and special educational provision in schools. Most recently she was Professor of Education at Victoria University of Wellington in New Zealand and then Professor of Pedagogical Studies at Liverpool Hope University in the UK.

Dr Deborah Knight

Dr Knight is currently serving as the Co-Director of the Rollins Center for Language and Learning at the Atlanta Speech School. She works as a partner with teachers, parents, schools and school systems to provide high quality professional development in the areas of language and literacy. Prior to assuming this position, she taught courses about struggling readers, reading methods and special education methods at the University of Delaware. Her research interests include reading disabilities, especially dyslexia; phonological and orthographic processing; and the linguistic and cognitive aspects of reading comprehension. Prior to teaching at the University of Delaware, she served as the Director for the Tennessee Center for the Study and Treatment of Dyslexia. She has taught middle school, high school, community college and university students.

Biographies of contributors

Angela Ayre, MS, is a practicing speech-language pathologist and reading specialist in the Department of Speech-Language Pathology at Massachusetts General Hospital in Boston and is conducting research examining literacy outcomes in Spanish-English bilinguals.

Manju Banerjee, PhD, is an Assistant Professor in the Neag School of Education at the University of Connecticut, Storrs, CT. She is also a Research and Education consultant for the Educational Testing Service, Princeton, NJ, and has over 20 years experience in the field of learning disabilities. She has worked as a postsecondary disability service provider, vocational rehabilitation counsellor, and research consultant for many years. Manju has published and presented widely on topics related to disability documentation, technological competencies for postsecondary transition and universal design.

Mere Berryman was a classroom practitioner for more than 20 years and now works to develop and trial programmes that will support practitioners to work more effectively with Māori students and their families. In her work she acknowledges the importance of developing relationships with Māori students and their families in ways that maintain respect for each other. This involves culturally responsive and collaborative approaches to under-standing and resolving problems, with practitioners, beginning from a position that acknowledges and supports the expertise of the child and their family, rather than from a position of perceived deficit.

Fil Came is co-founder and Director of Learning Works®. He is a respected teacher trainer, has published several books in the field of SEN and learning skills and continues to tutor individual students.

Suzanne Carreker, MS, CALT, is Vice President of Program Development at Neuhaus Education Center in Bellaire, TX, the author of several language and literacy curricula, a board member of the International Dyslexia Association, and a former classroom teacher.

Steve Chinn, BSc, PhD, AMBDA, was the founder and Principal of Mark College, UK, a specialist secondary school for dyslexic boys, awarded the elite Beacon school status by the Government in 1999. He worked in mainstream education for fourteen years, teaching physics, chemistry and mathematics before moving into special education. He was visiting

Head of a specialist school for dyslexic pupils in Baltimore USA for one year. Steve's book *The Trouble with Maths* (Routledge, 2004) won the 'Learning and Teaching Book' NASEN/TES award in 2004. *Dealing with Dyscaculia. Sum Hope* was published in 2007 by Souvenir Press. A dyscalculia and MLD diagnostic test battery co-written with John Everatt will be published by Pearson in 2009. Steve lectures and provides INSET on learning difficulties in maths and dyscalculia worldwide. www.stevechinn.co.uk

Sue Clement is currently Deputy Principal at Clyde Quay School, a primary school situated in the heart of Wellington City in New Zealand. She is also syndicate leader for senior school whanau, tutor teacher to four beginning teachers and teacher of a Year 7 and 8 composite classes in both a single cell and a shared teaching space.

Margaret Crombie has worked as a specialist teacher, manager and lecturer. She is currently tutoring for the Open University on E801, Difficulties in Literacy Development course. She has researched into dyslexia in the early years.

Kim Day is a Co-Director in the Rollins Center for Language and Learning, the professional development division of the Atlanta Speech School in Atlanta, GA. She currently works with schools, preschools and early learning centres to develop effective literacy programmes for young children through ongoing professional development with the staff and faculty members at these schools and centres. Her interests include teacher training in literacy and language development for young children as well as teacher development through mentoring and coaching practices. Dr Day has taught elementary, middle and high school students with language-based learning disabilities and was an Assistant Professor at Kennesaw State University, Atlanta, GA where she served as Graduate Program Coordinator in the Department of Special Education.

Jennifer Drysdale is a principal teacher of Learning Support with Fife Council. She has specialized in the use of ICT and is committed to developing inclusive methods for teaching children with dyslexia.

Dr Gad Elbeheri is the Executive Director of the Centre for Child Evaluation and Teaching; the premier leading centre in Kuwait which combines research and practice on learning disabilities across the Arab World. He is also the United Nations Development Programme's Country Expert on Early Childhood Challenges Programme in Kuwait. An applied linguist who obtained his PhD from the University of Durham, UK, Dr Elbeheri has a keen interest on cross-linguistic studies of dyslexia and other specific learning difficulties.

John Everatt is a researcher in literacy ability and developmental dyslexia. He lectured in psychology at the Universities of Wales and Surrey, UK, before moving to the College of Education, University of Canterbury, NZ.

Angela Fawcett is a Professor in the Centre for Child Research at the University of Swansea. She has published eight normed tests, four edited books, over 100 refereed articles and book contributions. Angela is Vice President of the British Dyslexia Association, editor of *Dyslexia: an International Journal of Research and Practice* and chaired the 2004 British Dyslexia Association International Conference.

Noel Gregg, PhD, is a Distinguished Research Professor at the University of Georgia, Director of the University of Georgia Regents' Center for Learning Disorders (Department of Psychology, Franklin College of Arts and Science) and Research Chair, Georgia Alternative Media Access Center. Her areas of specialization include adolescents and adults with learning disabilities and AD/HD, accommodations, alternative media, assessment, written language disorders and measurement validity. She has been a national expert witness for several key legal cases pertaining to accommodating adults with learning disabilities and AD/HD on high-stakes tests. She has published widely, and her new book, *Assessing and Accommodating the Adolescent and Adult Populations with Learning Disabilities and AD/HD* will be available January 2009.

Charles W. Haynes, EdD, is an associate professor of speech-language pathology and clinical supervisor at the MGH Institute of Health Professions in Boston. He is Board Member of the International Dyslexia Association, and is Research Advisor at the Center for Child Evaluation and Teaching in Kuwait City.

Brad Haynes is a journalist in Washington, DC and Fulbright Fellow in Santiago, Chile. He also serves as a researcher and translator for Spanish–English scholars at Amherst College and University of Malaga.

Vicky Hunter has been a principal teacher, Support for Learning for 20 years. She has contributed to various publications and conferences on dyslexia and ran the Edinburgh Reading Course for teachers.

R. Malatesha Joshi, PhD, is a Professor of Reading Education, ESL, and Educational Psychology at Texas A & M University, where he teaches and conducts research on assessment of and intervention for reading and spelling difficulties, as well as literacy and orthography. He is the editor of *Reading and Writing: An Interdisciplinary Journal*, which is ranked one of the top ten journals in education and educational research. Since the 1980s, he has received funding from the North Atlantic Treaty Organization (NATO) to direct international institutes in Europe. His papers have appeared in *Neuropsychologia*, the *Journal of Learning Disabilities*, the *School Psychology Review, Psychological Reports*, and the *Journal of Research in Reading*. His recent books include the *Handbook of Orthography and Literacy* (Lawrence Erlbaum Associates, 2006) and *Becoming a Professional Reading Teacher* (Paul H. Brookes Publishing Co., 2008).

Jay Kirkland's 15 years HE teaching experience, background in public relations and current role as disability adviser gave her the perspective she shares on the tensions influencing assessment of dyslexic students in HE.

Deborah Knight PhD, is currently serving as the Co-Director of the Rollins Center for Language and Learning at the Atlanta Speech School. She works as a partner with teachers, parents, schools and school systems to provide high quality professional development in the areas of language and literacy. Prior to assuming this position, she taught courses about struggling readers, reading methods, and special education methods at the University of Delaware.

Carol Leather directs the training activities of Independent Dyslexia Consultants. She provides workplace assessments and coaching for dyslexia individuals, conducts courses for trainers and provides advice to managers and employers in a wide variety of organisations. Carol is co-author *The Adult Dyslexic: Interventionss and Outcomes* (Whurr, 2002).

Neil Mackay was previously a teacher in a UK secondary school and is now an independent consultant/trainer specializing in dyslexia issues. Neil originated the concept of 'Dyslexia-Friendly Schools'. He works internationally to deliver teacher training and promote whole school dyslexia awareness and best practice.

David McLoughlin is the Director of Psychology at Independent Dyslexia Consultants and Visiting Professor of Psychology at the University of Buckingham. As well as conducting diagnostic assessments, advising individuals and organisations, he acts as an expert witness in employment tribunals concerning dyslexic employees.

Abdessatar Mahfoudhi, PhD, is a research and consultant at the Center for Child Evaluation and Teaching in Kuwait and the United Nations Development Program in Kuwait.

Brahm Norwich is Professor of Educational Psychology and Special Educational Needs at the School of Education and Lifelong Learning, University of Exeter. He has researched and published widely in these fields. His most recent books are on *Moderate Learning Difficulties and the Future of Inclusion* (Routledge 2005) and *Dilemmas of Difference, Disability and Inclusion: International Perspectives* (Routledge 2007).

Nicole Patton-Terry is an Assistant Professor in the Department of Educational Psychology and Special Education at Georgia State University in Atlanta, GA. Dr Terry received a degree in Communication Sciences and Disorders-Learning Disabilities at Northwestern University and completed postdoctoral training in Reading Research at Haskins Laboratories at Yale University. She has taught preschool and elementary school students with and without disabilities, and currently teaches courses on learning disabilities and literacy instruction for individuals with mild disabilities at the university. Dr Terry's work focuses on improving educational outcomes for children who struggle to acquire language and literacy skills, in particular children at-risk for and diagnosed with developing learning disabilities and children from culturally and linguistically diverse backgrounds.

Lindsay Peer, PhD, CBE, is a Chartered Psychologist, Speaker, Associate Fellow and a Chartered Scientist of the British Psychological Society and a Fellow of both the International Academy of Research in Learning Disabilities and the Royal Society of Arts. She holds a CBE for services to Education and Dyslexia. Lindsay held the posts of Education Director and Deputy CEO of the British Dyslexia Association until 2003.

Dr Gavin Reid, PhD, was formerly senior lecturer in the Department of Educational Studies, Moray House School of Education, University of Edinburgh. He is now consultant to the Centre for Child Evaluation and Teaching (CCET) in Kuwait. He is also consultant psychologist to REACH Learning Center in Vancouver, Canada and a director and consultant to the Red Rose School for children with specific learning difficulties in St Annes-on-Sea, Lancashire. He is also a trainer with Learning Works (International). He was senior lecturer in the Department of Educational Studies, Moray House School of Education, University of Edinburgh, UK from 1991–2007. He has made over 700 conference and seminar presentations world wide and published 23 books. He wrote the first Masters course in Dyslexia in the UK in 1992 and has been external examiner to 15 universities world wide.

Barbra Riddick is a senior lecturer in the School of Education at Durham University. She has carried out a number of important research studies on children and students with dyslexia and has published four books and numerous articles on dyslexia.

Elke Schneider received her doctorate from the University of Eichstätt, Germany specializing in foreign/second language learning and learning disabilities. She is now an associate professor and currently teaches Special Education, Literacy and English as a Second Language at Winthrop University, Rock Hill, South Carolina, USA.

Chris Singleton, PhD, is a Chartered Psychologist, senior lecturer in educational psychology at the University of Hull, UK, and Associate Editor of the *Journal of Research in Reading*.

Janice Wearmouth has many years' experience of teaching, researching and publishing. Formerly she was a senior lecturer in special and inclusive education and Director of the Centre for Curriculum and Teaching Studies at The Open University in the UK, where she developed and led distance learning courses for teachers in the areas of difficulties in literacy development, behavioural issues and special educational provision in schools. Most recently she was Professor of Education at Victoria University of Wellington in New Zealand and then Professor of Pedagogical Studies at Liverpool Hope University in the UK.

David Wray taught in primary schools for ten years and is currently Professor of Literacy Education at the University of Warwick. He has published over 40 books on aspects of literacy teaching and is best known for his work on reading and writing to learn.

Introduction

This book will provide readers with an overview of the field of dyslexia, with an emphasis on both theory and practice. We have encouraged contributors to attempt to link theoretical perspectives to practice. We are fortunate that all of the contributors in this book are experienced professionals with considerable expertise in their respective areas, whether in the classroom or in the research field. Many have experience in both.

The field of dyslexia can be complex and confusing. Much of the research on causes, identification and intervention highlight differences rather than similarities between the various theoretical and practical positions. This is not helped by the number of 'alternative' and often poorly researched innovations that claim to have a miraculous impact on intervention. This will in fact be discussed in chapter 12 of this book.

We have carefully selected the themes of this book and the chapter titles to ensure that there is a breadth of areas covered, but also that there is a clear direction to harness and enhance the reader's understanding of the key issues that impact on children, families and professionals. These themes include the state of current research, the overlap and the association between the different syndromes, issues relating to literacy acquisition and the development of language comprehension, the barriers to literacy particularly relating to the inclusive educational context, identifying needs beyond school and the need to acknowledge cultural diversity to accommodate to the learning needs of children and young people with dyslexia.

We have attempted to be 'forward thinking' and focused on areas which have not been afforded too much coverage to date, but have the promise and the potential to make an impact in the future. We have therefore moved away from the usual format of a research section heavily based on brain and genetically linked theories. While these are important they may not in themselves do much to inform the practitioner. The chapters in the research section have a focus on learning and on informing practice. An important contribution has been made by Gad Elbeheri and John Everatt who focus on the role of IQ in relation to dyslexia. They acknowledge that defining dyslexia has long been problematic not helped by the wide individual variations found in the dyslexia population as well as the issue of overlap with other syndromes. They discuss the arguments for and against the use of IQ and provide a detailed discussion on the discrepancy models. It is refreshing to read this chapter and to appreciate that despite the heated emotionally and politically fuelled debate on the role of IQ, the authors manage to provide a balanced response following a clear discussion of the various theoretical and practical influences. They provide suggestions for the way ahead and acknowledge that although there are some serious doubts and problems associated with the use of IQ–reading discrepancy in defining dyslexia, the abandonment of IQ has not gained wide acceptance. They quote Turner (1997) who points out that, it is 'dyslexia, not IQ, [that] is the focus of an assessment, and an "IQ-attainment discrepancy" is descriptive, rather than definitional, and therefore insufficient by itself for diagnostic purposes'. Reliable positive indicators of dyslexia are needed, but Elbeheri and Everatt suggest that positive diagnostic indicators for dyslexia have not been fully explored and reliably measured and until such a time as that happens the arguments for using IQ tests as a basis of indication are difficult to fully refute.

It is important that companion books, such as this one, should feature areas not fully covered in other books, yet they can make a significant contribution to our understanding of the diversity in dyslexia. This is the case in the chapter by Lindsay Peer on glue ear syndrome, which Lindsay describes as a 'sticky educational problem' and indicates at the outset concern that this area has been relatively neglected. As Dr Peer suggests, glue ear will likely have the most severe effect on children in the early years and these are the years that are the most crucial for language and literacy development. Additionally Dr Peer indicates that glue ear can be seen as 'the unrecognised cause of difficulties related to learning for so many in the education system today'. This would include those who have been undiagnosed or misdiagnosed as dyslexic. Lindsay Peer highlights the importance of this by quoting statistics on the incidence of recurrent glue ear in children that range from 8 per cent in Spain to 31 per cent in Kuwait. This chapter is also a good example of relating theory to practice as Peer provides suggestions for practical intervention.

An overview of the current research is provided by John Everatt and Gavin Reid who discuss neurobiological factors, made more evident by the advances in MRI scanning. They also discuss cognitive factors with an emphasis on the reading process and in particular how it can go wrong for some. There is therefore discussion on phonological deficit viewpoints and orthographic transparency as well as the additional consideration of dyslexia in different languages. This chapter also looks at educational research perspectives as well as issues relating to co-morbidity and overlap between different syndromes. Additionally the impact of research on practice is considered in this chapter. This section also contains a chapter by Chris Singleton who provides an illuminating discussion on the role of visual stress and dyslexia. As Singleton points out visual stress interferes with the ability to read, so consequently, children who suffer from this problem tend to avoid reading. As a result, they lack the amount of practice that is essential for the development of fluent decoding of text and good reading comprehension. He also suggests that recent studies have revealed that the prevalence of visual stress is considerably higher in children and adults with dyslexia than in the rest of the population.

The section on research is followed by the section entitled Dimensions of Dyslexia. This continues the themes of viewing dyslexia from a broader perspective as well as considering the overlap and the impact on practice. Topics covered in this section include the role of early identification from both UK and North American perspectives, a chapter on dyscalculia emphasizing the overlap between different conditions, a chapter on visual stress and chapters on reading and spelling, comprehension and assessment.

Knight *et al.* cover early identification from the North American perspective and Crombie and Reid cover the UK and Europe. Although there are differences, the rationale and the processes are similar. The key theme is that early identification does not necessarily mean early labelling, but rather the early identification of needs. It is only by identifying the child's needs at an early stage that appropriate and effective intervention can be put in place.

Assessment strategies are covered by Reid and Wearmouth who consider the broad range of assessment strategies that may be required for a teacher to assess the needs of the individual learner. This chapter also includes discussion of the current spread of cognitive measures and their relationship to diagnostic criteria for dyslexia.

It is important to see literacy development as more than merely 'cracking the code'. Certainly the acquisition of literacy is a challenge for students with dyslexia but it is important that basic literacy needs do not overshadow the broader perspectives of literacy and learning. This theme is taken up by David Wray who discusses aspects of literacy that go beyond decoding of print and for that reason this is an important chapter, as often decoding is seen as the main barrier for students with dyslexia, yet it is in fact more than that – it is about gaining a fuller appreciation of literacy.

Steve Chinn's chapter on dyscalculia is also an important one. As he points out 'I believe that a greater understanding of the ways dyslexic and dyscalculic students learn and fail mathematics will illuminate our understanding of how all children learn and fail mathematics'. This, like so many other areas developed for students with dyslexia, can often be universally applied and in many ways represent good practice. Additionally, as Chinn indicates, dyspraxia, dyslexia and dyscalculia are now grouped under the umbrella term of 'specific learning difficulties', a term that was once synonymous solely with dyslexia. This emphasizes that we need to adopt a broader perspective when dealing with dyslexia and the associated difficulties. There is little doubt that reading is related to mathematic difficulties and Chinn suggests that reading is an example of a sub-skill that suddenly becomes significant as a child moves up through the curriculum. He argues that in maths word problems are not the norm when the child is young, but when there are, some children often fail. He quotes a study in South Africa that showed a 50 per cent reduction in correct answers when a number problem was presented in words. There are other factors associated with mathematics such as short-term and working memory, emotional difficulties and self-esteem, thinking styles and sequencing, ordering and copying information – all of these can be seen in both dyslexia and dyscalculia.

Also included in this section is a chapter by Abdessatar Mahfoudhi and Charles Haynes on some general issues relating to phonological awareness in reading disability remediation. This chapter discusses a crucial area and the authors provide a very useful and detailed definition of what exactly is meant by phonological awareness. This chapter is extremely relevant for teachers and provides guidance on the role of phonological awareness for instruction in the classroom. The chapter also discusses a number of cross-linguistic studies and refers to four interacting factors: the script (orthography, or writing system) and how it represents the phonology, morphology and syntax of the language as well as the phonological, the morphological, and the syntactic structures of the language by themselves and in interaction. Mahfoudhi and Haynes suggest that these interacting factors should be taken into account when adapting research results in the more-researched languages to the less-researched languages.

This section also contains a chapter by Joshi and Carreker on spelling. The authors discuss the development of spelling with reference to a number of spelling models and conclude that learning to spell, rather than being characterized by distinct stages, should be seen as an amalgamation of phonological, morphological, and orthographic knowledge. The role of orthography in informed spelling instruction as well as the assessment of spelling and the pitfalls of both formal and informal assessment are discussed. Lastly, the authors make reference to cross linguistic studies in keeping with the international flavour of this book.

This section concludes with a critical commentary on alternative and innovative inter-ventions for Dyslexia by Gavin Reid and Angela Fawcett. They discuss the spate of alternative interventions that are available and discuss some key considerations that need to be made before their use can be justified in education. The need to obtain information on the validation of these approaches is crucial and this is highlighted in this chapter.

This section is followed by a section on inclusion and dealing with the barriers to learning. Brahm Norwich sets the scene for this section and asks how compatible the recognition of dyslexia is with inclusive education. Norwich analyses and defines inclusive education and asks whether the term 'inclusion' has become too broad and all-encompassing to be useful and meaningful. He advocates a concept of 'flexible interacting continua of provision' and discusses the models of conceptualizing disabilities, the concept of dyslexia-friendly schools, problems in literacy learning, the persistence of conceptual uncertainties and debates about dyslexia and the operational issues relating to these debates such as the response to instruction models evident in both the USA and the UK. Norwich concludes by suggesting that inclusion relates to different dimensions, such as, levels in the system (national, school, class), placement (separate to general settings), participation (academic–social) and curriculum (common–different content). He argues that 'positive assessment and identification of individual needs' is crucial and suggests that a bio-psycho-social framework should be considered for understanding the origins and causes of 'difficulties' which do not necessarily imply a single innate cause. Norwich shows that it might be possible to make links between literacy teaching for all in the general system and more specialized programmes in specialized settings and to connect the 'response to teaching' model of identification (over time and in a class teaching context) with the direct child functioning model (individual assessment of a child's profile outside the teaching context). This means that rather than being the predominant model, the direct child model can be used to supplement the 'response to teaching' model. This is an ideal chapter to head this section as it touches on many of the key factors in the conceptualization of dyslexia, criteria for identification and models of practice and provision.

This chapter is followed by one by Reid and Came which offers practical solutions to dealing with the barriers to learning within an inclusive setting. This chapter discusses barriers including cognitive (learning skills), environmental (learning experience) and progress in basic attainments (literacy acquisition), and how these can be identified and overcome. This chapter also contains a discussion on anticipating the barriers to learning and the importance of being pro-active. Empowering the learner through developing and extending learning skills is also included in this chapter as it is suggested that it is through this empowerment that students with dyslexia can progress to autonomy and self sufficiency in learning.

This theme is continued by Neil Mackay who looks at the challenges faced by students with dyslexia and indeed teachers in the secondary school. Mackay takes a whole-school perspective and discusses the need and the nature of whole-school training and provides an illuminative case study of the progress that was made by a student with dyslexia. Mackay's account also refers to a performance tracker showing individual peaks and troughs in performances. He also refers to the need for young children to become strategic learners and personalize their learning by making informed choices. It is therefore crucial to extend the learning needs and skills of learners with dyslexia and not settle for anything less than this.

The view that dyslexia has universal currency is highlighted by the chapter on raising student's literacy attainments at a school in New Zealand. It is important that good practice is disseminated and their needs to be a recognition that good practice is not necessarily culture specific but can be applied to different countries, systems and cultures. This book has sought to highlight this point by drawing on practices from different countries. A case in point is the chapter by Sue Clement on how school-wide professional development raised students' literacy levels at Clyde Quay School, Wellington, NZ. Clement shows that it is important to establish a climate of enquiry, discussion and personal reflection in schools and to encourage teachers to review and reflect on their classroom teaching practice. This chapter encourages teachers to examine their assumptions about how students are actually achieving across the school and in individual classes and Clement cites examples from the area of writing and suggests that one of the major factors that accounted for the success in the teaching of writing was the discussing and agreeing of success criteria with the classes, including those who experience literacy difficulties. It is important that this chapter is included in this book because it provides a practical model of reflective practices and through staff initiatives and practitioner research provides responses that can be applied across the whole curriculum and replicated elsewhere. The key point is that this is not a case of waiting for answers and but an example of teachers actively seeking answers though discussion, investigation and in-depth analysis of the problems experienced by students in relation to literacy.

In a book such as this readers are seeking clarification and guidance to support their professional practices. It is important that practical examples are provided and preferably by teachers who are currently experiencing the challenges of supporting students with dyslexia in the mainstream setting. The following two chapters are examples of this. Vicky Hunter tackles the issue of transition and Jennifer Drysdale provides an example of a contextual integrated approach to tackling literacy difficulties. Hunter indicates that any period of transition whether it is from primary to secondary school, school to college or from college to work has the potential to be stressful. She discusses how the potential stress can be minimized and indeed prevented. Hunter discusses the role of review meetings, transition groups, parents, careers advisors and employers all of whom can play a role in preventing transition from being a stressful period. She also points out key considerations such as self-advocacy, highlighting the view that dyslexia is not just a problem of literacy, but it can also be a problem of identity and self-esteem. This means, as Hunter points out, that children and young people have to be helped to develop a sense of identity which includes the acceptance of their dyslexia and the effect it is going to have on their life. It is important to prepare young people for transition as this will not only assist them through the potentially stressful transition period, but help to prepare them for the lifelong challenges they may face.

Jennifer Drysdale also provides practical guidance based on examples from practice. This chapter shows how literacy teaching approaches can be embedded within the themes and topics of the class work. Drysdale has developed this as a 'workshop approach' involving contextualized assessment, focused observation, phonological awareness, semantic and syntactic knowledge and reading and responding to texts. She also refers to important contributions from technology and creativity to develop the literacy skills of children with dyslexia. Drysdale paints a picture of a literacy-rich learning environment which she describes as one furnished with texts in every shape and form; on computer screens, audio tapes and MP3 players as well as books, word games and puzzles, jokes and riddles, instructions for making things, books for facts and books for fiction, ensuring that all kinds of opportunities to develop language experience are widely experienced. She also discusses some key factors in literacy acquisition such as the development of auditory and language skills, awareness of print and vocabulary, visual and motor development, grapheme/phoneme correspondence and phonic knowledge and the processing and integration of the sub-components of literacy. This comprehensive chapter also discusses the role of higher order thinking and comprehension skills and support resources.

This section concludes with a chapter by Barbara Riddick on students own personal perspectives on dyslexia. This is an extremely topical area and Riddick quotes the findings from research conducted by the National Foundation for Educational Research (2008). Recent years have witnessed a growing commitment to including young people's voice in research, evaluation and consultation, the benefits of which have been widely reported. For example, seeking the views of children and young people and involving them in decision making is reported to improve services, improve decision making, enhance the democratic process, enhance young people's skills, promote their sense of responsibility, and empower and enhance their self-esteem and this conviction is prominent in Riddick's chapter on dyslexia. She suggests that it is best for teachers to be given a detailed list of recommended practices in the classroom or to read an auto-biographical account of a child with dyslexia which may increase their empathy and understanding towards children who struggle with their literacy. As Riddick also points out, for children with dyslexia past accounts of unhappiness at school accompanied by low self-esteem scores has made improving their well-being and experience of school a priority and an important reason for listening to their perspectives. The importance of this chapter lies in that statement.

Self-advocacy and the need to listen to students' voices are also relevant in the next section on college and university students. Kirkland provides a number of good examples of best practice for supporting students in a higher education environment. She describes how protocols for supporting students in higher education can be used to diagnose disability/specific learning difficulty, establish initial competency and inform the design of an individual support programme.

This is followed by a chapter by Noel Gregg and Manju Banerjee on reading comprehension solutions for college students with dyslexia. The chapter focuses on technology and provides an integrated perspective. The authors suggest that the integration of both cognitive/metacognitive strategies and electronic tools (eTools) is essential for providing effective instruction and accommodations for college students with dyslexia and maintain that the search for a solution to access for college students may lie in the opportunities afforded by learning technologies. Traditional concepts of accommodations, they suggest, need to be re-envisioned and expanded because of the opportunities presented by eTools, e-resources and built-in scaffolds.

Dyslexia in the workplace is the focus of the following chapter. In this chapter McLoughlin and Leather discuss the issues facing both dyslexic employees and their employers. They also discuss the importance of disclosure, how employers can assist and support employees with dyslexia and how dyslexic individuals can in fact help themselves.

The next section contains chapters relating to the theme of diversity, culture and language. It commences with a comprehensive chapter by Elke Schneider who considers what the research tells us about foreign language learning and dyslexia and explains why some foreign languages are easier to learn for individuals with dyslexia than others. She also looks at teaching strategies and provides guidance on which ones are suitable for individuals with dyslexia. She suggests that the most essential factor to consider is the severity of the student's disability and the specific language processing areas most affected by the disability (letter-sound processing, pronunciation, grammar, and/or vocabulary, fluency, memory). She emphasizes the need to have a good understanding of the students' needs, abilities and learning styles.

Sociolinguistic and cultural perspectives are developed in some detail in the chapter by Abdessatar Mahfoudhi, Gad Elbeheri and John Everatt on reading and dyslexia in Arabic. They comment on a number of investigations reporting on sociolinguistic factors as a way of predicting variability in Arabic literacy learning. They emphasize the disparity between spoken Arabic (the language of communication at home) and the written Arabic of the books that form a large part of the children's school work. This, in a similar vein to chapter 26 which refers to the situation in New Zealand, also emphasizes the importance of effective links and mutual understandings between home and school. Mahfoudhi, Elbeheri and Everatt also highlight the importance of phonological processing in both Arabic and English literacy acquisition and suggest that this can provide the potential for a cross-language framework which can help to distinguish those with literacy acquisition problems (e.g., dyslexics) from those who are likely to progress at normal rates in literacy classes. But they voice some caution in relation to relying too heavily on the predictive validity of phonological processing in Arabic for identification (and intervention) by referring to the complexity of the orthography of Arabic and its variation between vowelized and non-vowelized forms, as well as the potential importance of morphology. They suggest that the interaction between orthography, morphology and syntactic awareness in the comprehension processes can influence single-word processing during text reading. This, they argue, is a highly profitable area of research, but one that has been neglected and therefore this represents an area which requires further investigation. Further research, particularly focusing on reading in context, can have implications for both identification of reading difficulties in Arabic as well as the development of teaching programmes.

This is followed by a chapter by Haynes, Ayre, Haynes and Mahfoudhi on reading acquisition and reading disabilities in Spanish and Spanish–English contexts. This chapter explores the structure of spoken and written Spanish and how it can influence the way that children acquire basic reading skills in Spanish. Additionally the chapter investigates the first language factors which influence literacy outcomes when Spanish-speaking children learn to read in English and discusses the most effective ways to teach literacy skills to Spanish English-language learners. Considering that Spanish is the third most common world language, spoken by over 330 to 400 million native speakers this is an important chapter in this book as this means a significant number of Spanish-speaking students will have dyslexia.

The book concludes with a chapter by Mere Berryman and Janice Wearmouth on responsive approaches to literacy learning within cultural contexts. The authors take a socio-cultural approach to exploring students' literacy learning at school and note the view of Vygotsky that all mental processes have social origins and the role of interpersonal and intrapersonal factors. They also emphasize the importance of the attitude of schools to the role of parents, families and community members, as prime educators of children. They also note research from the USA and New Zealand that suggests that teachers' expectations of their students are a reflection of deeply ingrained, wider societal and ideological values. They also emphasize the view that accurate identification of difficulties relate to the way the learner processes information and the importance of an awareness of the wide range of experiences that students bring with them when they come to school. They conclude with the fundamental point that how schools respond to family culture and background and the kind of teacher–student and home–school relationships that exist is crucial for an effective and positive education experience. They argue that schools must recognize these points in order to negotiate effective home–school literacy initiatives.

All the chapters in this book provide a signpost that the field of dyslexia has many obstacles to deal with and indeed has overcome many already. The path from uncertainty to eventual acceptance and moving towards a consensus is a rocky one, but it is important to note that the collaboration and consensus echoed in the pages of this book provide hope and guidance for all educators now and in the future. Major international research projects have been developed, international conferences are prevalent and collaborative products for assessment and intervention have emerged. Discussion and dissemination promoting the synthesis of ideas and perspectives are now commonplace in the many forums on dyslexia.

It is hoped that this book, by providing a range of perspectives and a broad range of information on the field of dyslexia will further this dissemination and provide readers with advice, guidance and opportunities for reflection.

References

National Foundation for Educational Research (2008) Research into pupil engagement in building schools for the future. Available at http://www.nfer.ac.uk/research-areas (retrieved 26 March 2008).

Turner, M. (1997). *Psychological Assessment of Dyslexia*. London: Whurr.

Part 1

Research: current and future developments

1

Dyslexia
An overview of recent research

John Everatt and Gavin Reid

This chapter

- discusses the significant recent advances in our understanding of dyslexia
- discusses the findings and the implications of the main research areas – neurological, cognitive and educational in the field of dyslexia
- comments on the implications for intervention
- shows how the different research areas are inter-related.

Background

There have been significant advances in research in dyslexia over the last twenty years. This has aided explanations of dyslexia and supported policy and practice. The impact has been considerable, but yet there is still no clear explanation that is universally accepted of what exactly constitutes dyslexia. Identification is still riddled with controversies despite the emergence of a number of new tests to identify dyslexia, or sub-components of dyslexia. Indeed, there is still an ongoing debate on the value of dyslexia as an identifiable syndrome (see discussions in this book). In order to provide a background for the work on dyslexia and the topics covered in this book, this chapter will discuss some of the main areas of research, with an emphasis on those currently receiving most attention, and comment on these in relation to the breadth, span and purpose of this book.

Neurobiological factors

The advances in MRI and other forms of brain imagery have been of great benefit to neuroscientists investigating factors relating to dyslexia. From these studies a number of different factors have emerged focusing on structural and functional brain-related factors. Some of these will be discussed here.

Processing speed

Breznitz (2008) presents the 'Asynchrony Phenomenon' as a means of explaining dyslexia. This implies that dyslexia is caused by a speed of processing gap within and between the various entities taking part in the word decoding process. Breznitz and colleagues devised a programme that attempted to train the brain to process information at a faster speed. Implementing this programme resulted in a substantial improvement among dyslexic children in the speed at which information was processed (Breznitz 2008). They also suggested that this improvement was successfully transferred to other material not included in the training program.

Breznitz (2008) also claims that dyslexic learners exhibit difficulties when transferring information from one hemisphere to another. These differences in inter-hemisphere transfer among dyslexics may stem from information decay in the corpus collosum, or a long non-symmetrical delay in inter-hemisphere transfer time. Shaul and Breznitz (2007) measured information transfer between the left and right hemispheres among dyslexics as compared to regular readers when performing various lexical decision tasks. They found that information arrived among dyslexics in the right hemisphere, at first, and was then transferred approximately 9 to 12ms later to the left hemisphere. Among regular readers, the information arrived in the left hemisphere first and was transferred to the right approximately 4 to 6ms later. They also supported these results from source localization of brain activity in these two reading groups during the word decoding process using Low Resolution Electromagnetic Tomography (LORETA). Comparisons between groups revealed greater activation among dyslexic readers between 110 and 140ms for words, mainly in the right temporal and perisylvian regions, as well as some activation in medial frontal regions. These findings can have significant implications for the classroom particularly in how information is presented and the pace of lessons in class.

Temporal processing

Stein (2008) argues that there is genetic, sensory, motor and psychological evidence that dyslexia is a neurological syndrome affecting the development of the brain. He also provides evidence that the development of magnocellular neurones is impaired in children with dyslexia. Stein argues that the visual system provides the main input to both the lexical and the sublexical routes for reading and therefore vision should be seen as the most important sense for reading. This view however is strongly disputed by many because they believe that acquisition of phonological skills is in fact much more crucial for successful reading (Vellutino, Fletcher *et al.*, 2004).

One of the main discoveries about the visual system made over the least 25 years according to Stein is that the different qualities of visual targets are analysed, not one after the other in series, but by separate, parallel pathways that work simultaneously moving forwards in the visual brain. Stein shows that there are two main kinds of retinal ganglion cell, whose axons project all the visual information back to the brain. Ten per cent of these are known as mangocellular cells because they are noticeably larger than the others and cover 50 times greater an area than those of the much more numerous, but much smaller, parvocells. He therefore suggests that the great variety of visual, phonological, kinaesthetic, sequencing, memory and motor symptoms that are seen in different dyslexics may arise from differences in the particular magnocellular systems that are most affected by the particular mix that each individual dyslexic inherits. This highlights the individual differences within dyslexia as well as the role of the competing or indeed complimentary theories that constitute dyslexia.

Stein (2008) argues that the most important influence in dyslexia appears to be heredity. He suggests that genetic factors likely affect the developmental migration of magnocells in utero and influence their subsequent function. Familial risk is also a useful indicator of dyslexia and is supported by prevalence rates (Molfese *et al.*, 2008). Advances during the last 20 years in the field of genetics research have brought the search for the underlying genetic basis of dyslexia to the fore (Fisher and DeFries, 2002). Innovations in neuro-imaging techniques have also driven the search for a neurobiological basis to dyslexia (Lyytinen *et al.,* 2005). These factors help to provide a number of plausible explanations for dyslexia and in some cases can point the way to intervention.

Procedural timing

The lateral zone of the cerebellum is an area that has generated interest over its apparent role in cognitive processes and for recent theoretical positions that argue for its relationship with dyslexia. In terms of its formation, the cerebellum is one of the first brain structures to begin to differentiate, yet it is one of the last to achieve maturity as the cellular organization of the cerebellum continues to change for many months after birth. According to Fawcett and Nicolson (2008) there is now extensive evidence that the cerebellum is a brain structure particularly susceptible to insult in the case of premature birth, and that such insults can lead to a range of motor, language and cognitive problems subsequently. Fawcett and Nicolson (2008) argue that the cerebellar deficit hypothesis may provide close to a single coherent explanation of the three criterial difficulties in dyslexia – reading, writing and spelling. They argue this can place dyslexia research within a meaningful context in terms of the cognitive neuroscience of learning while maintaining its position as a key educational issue. They also suggest the cerebellur deficit hypothesis provides an explanation for the overlapping factors between dyslexia and the other developmental disorders (an area that will be returned to later in this chapter).

One of the hypothesized functions of the cerebellum is in the precise timing of procedures (e.g., several motor movements) that accomplish some sort of behavioural response or task performance. This timing of sequences may play a critical role in making task accomplishment or behavioural skills automatic. Indeed, a critical aspect of learning a skill may be to make its accomplishment automatic. This means that the skill can be carried out without the individual giving it too much thought – and resources can be used to undertake other behaviours or processes. For most adults and children, the ability to walk, talk and possibly read and write may be partially or completely automatic. Consequently Fawcett and Nicolson (2008) put forward the hypothesis that dyslexic children would have difficulty in automatizing any skill (cognitive or motor). They suggest that reading is subject to automaticity and since all dyslexia hypotheses predict poor reading as a factor in dyslexia then the automatisation deficit hypothesis would be valid in relation to dyslexia. Fawcett (1989) and Fawcett and Nicolson (1992) argue that there is clear support stemming from a set of experiments in which they asked dyslexic children to do two things at once. If a skill is automatic, then the children should have been able to do two tasks at the same time. These findings strongly suggested that dyslexic children were not automatic, even at the fundamental skill of balance. For some reason, dyslexic children had difficulty automatizing skills, and had therefore to concentrate harder to achieve normal levels of performance. This has clear implications for teaching and learning in that in the classroom there will be a significant need for over-learning to be utilized with children with dyslexia.

Cognitive Processes

Researchers/theorists who concentrate on the processes that go into reading and writing typically look at these from a cognitive perspective, although many of the ideas related to cognitive theories of dyslexia also consider neurological factors and hence there is often overlap between these two general areas. For example, automaticity can be considered from the point of view of a process in learning or as a function of a particular brain area (as in the arguments of Fawcett and Nicolson, 2008). Speed of processing can be seen as an aspect of cognition (as in the views of Wolf and colleagues: Wolf and Bowers, 2000; Wolf and O'Brien, 2001) or of brain transmission (as in the views of Breznitz, 2008 and Stein, 2008, discussed above). Of the cognitive focused research that looks at processing factors, work on memory and learning may be considered as the most likely to link research with classroom practices, with a fair number of recent work either directly or indirectly relating findings to intervention (see discussions in Singleton, 2008). For example, work on cognitive style links to learning style in classrooms (Entwistle, 1981; Given and Reid, 1999; Riding and Cheema, 1991; Schmeck, 1988) and multisensory teaching methods have often been linked to the way information is stored in memory (Broomfield and Combley, 1997; Clark and Uhry, 1995). Similarly, Working Memory research has begun to inform ideas about special educational needs (Gathercole and Pickering, 2000; Jeffries and Everatt, 2004) and meta-cognitive work has focused on strategies for learning. However, perhaps the area that has linked most clearly to the teaching of literacy has been the work related to language processes.

Phonological deficit viewpoints

At present, the dominant causal viewpoint about dyslexia is the phonological deficit hypothesis. This perspective has been derived from the substantial evidence that difficulties in phonological processing, particularly when related to phonological decoding, have been a major distinguishing factor between dyslexics and non-dyslexics from early literacy learning to adulthood (see Beaton et al., 1997; Bruck, 1993; Elbro et al., 1994; Rack et al., 1992; Snowling, 2000; Stanovich, 1988) and that early phonological training (together with suitable linkage to orthography and literacy experience) improves word literacy and reduces the likelihood of literacy difficulties (see Bryant and Bradley, 1985; Cunningham, 1990; Elbro et al., 1996; Olofsson and Lundberg, 1985; Schneider et al., 1997). Children who find it difficult to distinguish sounds within verbally presented words would be predicted to have problems learning the alphabetic principle that letters represent sounds and, hence, should be those children who are most likely to be dyslexic based on the phonological deficit position. If this causal linkage is correct, then the manifestation of dyslexia may vary across languages, since languages vary in the way their orthography represents phonology. Therefore, recent research has attempted to investigate the manifestation of dyslexia across languages to assess the universality of the phonological position as well as to inform international assessment practices.

Orthographic transparency

In some languages, orthography represents phonology relatively simply: there is a close correspondence between the written symbol (grapheme) and the basic sound (or phoneme) that it represents. In other orthographies, this correspondence is less transparent. In these languages, a letter may represent several sounds and a sound may be represented by different letters. The English orthography is the best example of this less than transparent relationship between letters and sounds: consider 't' in 'thus' versus 'talk', or 'c' in 'chord' versus 'chore' or even 'receive'. There are many English words that may be considered irregular or exceptions based on the typically taught correspondence between graphemes and phonemes (e.g., 'have', 'said', 'pint', 'monk', 'yacht'). However, this level of divergence from the alphabetic principle (see Adams, 1990; Gillon, 2004) is not universal. Although most languages have some peculiarities, or complexities, in the relationship between graphemes and phonemes, most have rules that connect letters with pronunciation that are more consistent and, potentially, simpler to learn than is the case for English. Indeed, the peculiarities of the English orthography has led some theorists in the field to view English as a 'dyslexic' orthography (Spencer, 2000) or, perhaps less controversially, as an outlier in comparison to other alphabetic-type orthographies (Share, 2008).

Dyslexia in different languages

The potential importance of orthographic transparency can be seen in cross-language comparisons of reading ability that contrast scripts varying on the transparency dimension. In the majority of such studies, the rate of literacy learning, particularly word reading/decoding, has been found to increase with the level of orthographic transparency. This has been found in comparisons of different language groups (see the Cost A8 work reported in Seymour *et al.,* 2003), although differences in terms of the cultural importance of literacy learning or educational practice could also explain these effects. However, similar results have been found amongst bilinguals learning two orthographies of differing transparency (Everatt *et al.,* 2002; Geva and Seigel, 2000; Veii and Everatt, 2005). Typically, these findings point to word recognition and non-word decoding processes developing faster in the more transparent orthography. This relationship suggests that there may be fewer problems for learners of a more transparent orthography than a less transparent one, which might mean that dyslexia as a word-level literacy learning difficulty may be less evident in languages that use a relatively simple relationship between letters and sounds – i.e., the behavioural manifestation of dyslexia (such as literacy deficits) may vary across languages (see discussions in Goswami, 2000; Symthe and Everatt, 2004; Zeigler and Goswami, 2005). From a practical perspective, assessment measures used to identify dyslexia may have to vary across languages. For example, Everatt *et al.* (2004) found that although alliteration and rhyme phonological awareness tasks could distinguish groups of grade 3 children with and without literacy deficits in English, they were less reliable at distinguishing similar groups of Hungarian children. The same reduction in the ability to identify poor literacy learners from their peers has been found for decoding skills amongst German learners (see Wimmer, 1993), a measure that has often been used in English language dyslexia assessment procedures. These findings suggest the potential need to consider different tests measures in dyslexia assessments across languages, particularly those that vary on the orthographic transparency dimension. Though the same reduction in the relationship between literacy levels and pseudoword decoding can be found in a Chinese character reader (Smythe *et al.,* 2008), that is not as easily explained as being due to the level of letter-sound regularity.

This is not to say that assessments in one language may not be informative of problems in another. Research with bilingual children (e.g., Veii and Everatt, 2005) suggests that skills in one language, particularly those that focus on phonological processing, can be highly predictive of skills in the other, and that (phonological) measures developed for one language may be a useful guide for the development of appropriately translated tools in another language (see also Smythe *et al.,* 2008). However, this translation needs to be carefully considered. For example, consistent with English language work, research in Arabic has indicated that phonological processes are predictive of reading levels amongst Arabic children and that poor Arabic readers show weak phonological decoding and low levels of phonological awareness in comparison to matched normal readers (see Abu-Rabia *et al.,* 2003; Al-Mannai and Everatt, 2005; Elbeheri and Everatt, 2007). However, further work is needed to determine whether assessment procedures would be better supplemented by additional measures that focus more on the specific features of the writing system, such as an awareness of morphemic roots and patterns (see Elbeher *et al.,* 2006). In terms of theory, these data are consistent with the phonological

7

deficit viewpoint – i.e., a child with a phonological deficit is likely to show problems with learning the Arabic orthography. However, they point to a need to further investigate hypotheses derived from such causal viewpoints across languages given that the specific features of the language can lead to variations in the relationship between phonological skills and literacy levels, as well as how literacy deficits will manifest in the language.

Educational Factors

Assessment

Siegel and Lipka (2008) reviewed over 100 articles from the *Journal of Learning Disabilities* from 1968 to 2007 in order to investigate how researchers translated conceptual definitions of Learning Disabilities into operational definitions. They found that the most prevalent components were 'exclusion components' and formula components using discrepancies relating to intelligence and achievement. They concluded that exclusion components were problematic because some areas such as emotional factors cannot be objectively measured and the component of exclusion was often too vague to provide guidance on what areas to assess and the tools to use. They also concluded that the discrepancy formula component was also suspect. First, there were too many variations in the type of tests used. Siegel (1999) found that different tests of the same skill may yield different scores and she found that there was great variation in the choice different school areas/districts made when selecting tests. Second, there was debate on the cut-off point to use in the discrepancy formula, and there was even variation in the cut-off criteria for average IQ. Furthermore, Siegel and Lipka suggested that IQ scores do not appear to be predictors of the cognitive processes involved in reading, spelling, language skills and memory tasks. Therefore, they concluded that, in the analysis of children with learning disabilities, the IQ test is irrelevant. Finally, these authors argue that a diagnosis for LD should be established on the basis of achievement tests that indicate if the individual has deficits in skills compared to his or her age group. They maintain that the formula that should be used to diagnose LD in an accurate way is the grade/age vs. achievement formula. Using this formula they argue that the scores of the achievement tests should be significantly below the age or the grade level scores and this would constitute a learning disability.

Joshi and Aaron (2008) propose an alternate model for diagnosing and treating reading disability. They too are critical of the IQ–reading score based discrepancy model and argue for a model of diagnosing and instructing children with reading difficulties based on the Componential Model of Reading, which considers reading to be comprised of word recognition and comprehension aspects, which are themselves comprised of processes such as phonological awareness, decoding, listening comprehension and vocabulary. The general idea of this assessment model is to focus on the source of the reading difficulty, then target remedial instruction at this source. By looking at the components of reading, Joshi and Aaron argue that they can obtain a fruitful and accurate picture of the poor reader's strengths and weaknesses and that this has the advantage of leading to directions for remediation.

Differences between the above views focus on whether dyslexia assessments should focus purely on literacy achievement levels (the most common behavioural outcome of the condition), or whether more comprehensive cognitive assessments that identify areas of strength, as well as areas of weakness, both within the domain of literacy and outside (e.g., general language abilities) may support the identification of children with dyslexia. The more comprehensive cognitive assessments are common in Educational Psychology practice when attempting to identify learning difficulties such as dyslexia (Kaufman, 1994; Thomson, 2001; Turner, 1999).

However, their use has been questioned (e.g., Reid, 1999; Solity, 2000) and it may be that lengthy assessments are unnecessary and that resources could be better used to support learning for all children (Solity, 2000). Alternatively, it may be that more detailed assessments provide a way of distinguishing, from normal development, groups of children with different types of special educational needs, thereby informing, and hopefully leading to better, educational support and practice.

Although the above debate about assessment has focused on the difference, or lack thereof, between high IQ and low IQ poor readers, these groups are not considered to be identical. Stanovich (1988), for example, proposed that differences between high IQ and low IQ poor readers will be found in areas such as vocabulary, general knowledge, memory and compre-hension, but not in single word reading and the processes related to this area of literacy, the main area of educational deficit amongst dyslexics (British Psychological Society, 1999). Even if the same underlying phonological cause leads to these literacy deficits, it may still be important to identify IQ-related differences if they inform the assessment of compensatory strategies that the child brings to the process of acquiring literacy. For example, there is evidence that the context within which a word is placed can aid the recognition (speed and accuracy) of that word. If given the sentence context of 'The skiers were buried in the . . .', an individual will name the next word presented faster if it is an appropriate ending to that sentence, such as SNOW, rather than an incongruous or neutral word (Stanovich and West, 1983). Such context priming effects have been found to be greater amongst dyslexics than reading-age matched controls (see Nation and Snowling, 1998) despite the usual finding that dyslexics present poorer phonological-based decoding skills than these controls (Frith and Snowling, 1983). The use of semantic/syntactic features may provide a compensatory process for poor phonological decoding skills (see also Bishop and Snowling, 2004). If this is the case, behavioural mani-festations of dyslexia (such as reading performance) may be as much a factor of these compensatory strategies as the underlying deficit. A similar argument can be made in terms of the strategy-based influence of vocabulary, which may explain findings indicating the use by dyslexics of known word analogies to read unfamiliar letter strings (non-words) compared to the attempts of low IQ poor readers to apply faulty phoneme correspondences to read the same unfamiliar items (Spagna, 1996). Additional compensatory strategies may be used by dyslexics with proficient visual processing skills (Snowling, 2000) and, indeed, there is evidence for differences in effective strategies used by high IQ and low IQ children with literacy acquisition deficits in learning spellings (Brooks and Weeks, 1998). Brooks and Weeks (1998) found that high IQ poor spellers learned more effectively through methods that emphasized visual and semantic strengths whereas the low IQ children learned best when provided with carefully structured procedures focusing on phonic skills. The assessment of factors such as vocabulary level and appreciation of semantics, as well as visual skills, should inform assessors of such potential areas of compensation, thereby clarifying observed reading behaviours and potential strategies for learning. Research identifying areas of strength, either relative to individual areas of weaknesses or relative to normal development, may prove as vital as that which highlights skills in need of remediation.

Comorbidity and learning difficulties overlap

If the purpose of assessment is to inform appropriate methods for remediation or strategies for learning, then assessments that distinguish between children with different learning problems may be more useful than those that simply focus on the behavioural/educational outcomes of the learning difficulty (see Everatt et al., 2008). One of the challenges for such differential assessments, though, is the level of overlap between supposedly different learning difficulties. This overlap is probably a feature of our current understanding of the conditions; however, it could also be a factor of comorbidity between learning disabilities. The latter term refers to the likelihood of two or more learning disabilities co-occuring within the same individual. An individual with a learning difficulty is more likely to be assessed as having a second disability than would be expected based on the incidence of the disability in the normal population. Indeed, there is a growing body of evidence to suggest that comorbidity may be highly prevalent (see, for example: Bishop and Snowling, 2004; Caron and Rutter, 1991; Kaplan *et al.*, 2001; Semrud-Clikeman *et al.*, 1992; Visser, 2003). The challenge, then, is to produce assessment procedures that reliably separate different learning disabilities, or related conditions, so as to allow the optimal education plan to be implemented. An individual with dyslexia and an attention deficit, for example, may require different teaching interventions compared to an individual with dyslexia alone.

In the UK, children with generally lower IQ levels are typically referred to as children with moderate learning difficulties (MLD) and would include the low IQ poor readers discussed in previous paragraphs and, therefore, will potentially overlap with dyslexics in a number of areas (Ellis *et al.*, 1996; Share, 1996; Stanovich, 1988), including the cause of their mutual reading (and spelling) problems. However, dyslexic and MLD children may differ in the development of areas that may support compensatory strategies (Brooks and Weeks, 1998) suggesting, therefore, that the differential assessment of dyslexia and MLD against normal performance may be educationally important.

Due to the relative weaknesses in phonological processes described above, dyslexia may be regarded as a sub-type of general language difficulties (see discussions in: Bishop and Snowling, 2004; Catts *et al.*, 2002; Snowling, 2000). Children with specific language impairments (SLI) may well show the same weaknesses in phonological processing shown by dyslexics and, hence, similar literacy acquisition difficulties may be found amongst groups of dyslexic and SLI children (though contrast Bishop and Snowling, 2004; Gillon, 2004). However, in contrast to dyslexics, those with SLI are likely also to present with broader problems in language areas such as vocabulary, syntax and comprehension (Stackhouse and Wells, 1997). Therefore, the overlap presented by mutual literacy and phonological deficits would coincide with differences in areas that may provide potential for compensatory strategies (vocabulary and semantics) and, therefore, optimal educational plans may differ across these two related conditions.

Dyspraxia has been less researched than dyslexia, but may be regarded as including people with central processing weaknesses in visual and motor skills, or a non-verbal learning deficit (Portwood, 1999; Rourke, 1989). However, some individuals with dyspraxia may also show relative weaknesses in their phonology and verbal memory (Stackhouse and Snowling, 1992) and there are individuals who have been assessed as dyslexic who show relative visual/non-verbal weaknesses (Rack, 1997; Ramus *et al.*, 2003). Consequently, there is an overlap between dyspraxia and dyslexia in terms of our current understanding of their cognitive and literacy development (see also Visser, 2003). However, the most likely causal pathway that leads to literacy difficulties in these groups may vary. In dyslexia, phonological deficits seem the most likely precursor to poor literacy, which may manifest particularly in the area of decoding letters to sounds or sounds to letters. If we consider Developmental Verbal Dyspraxia as a special case of language disability (for example, see discussions in Gillon, 2004), the most likely causal pathway for the majority of dyspraxic individuals would seem to be from visual-spatial/motor deficits to coordination deficits that may be more pronounced in spelling and text processing. These may subsequently lead to poor literacy skills due to a general lack of motivation to learn following experience of failure, in addition to a lack of reciprocal support provided across

10

different aspects of literacy. Such differences in causal pathways may lead to the need to consider different intervention methods.

Overlaps have also been identified between dyslexics and children with attention or behavioural difficulties, such as attention deficit (hyperactivity) disorder (AD(H)D) or emotional/behavioural difficulties (EBD). Again, evidence of poor educational achievement, including literacy acquisition deficits, can be found amongst children assessed as having behavioural problems (Barkley, 2006). Similarly, dyslexics have been found to present evidence of poor attention, possibly due to low levels of educational success or a common causal pathway (see discussions in Capute et al., 1994; Everatt, 1999). Additionally, the consequences of poor educational achievement amongst dyslexics may be low levels of self-esteem and accompanying increases in anxiety and depression (Huntington and Bender, 1993; Miles and Varma, 1995). Although this may suggest some level of overlap between dyslexic, AD(H)D and EBD groups, the literacy deficits found amongst these groups may be due to differing causes. The phonological deficits that seem to accompany the poor reading skills of dyslexic individuals may not manifest in the AD(H)D child (see Pennington et al., 1993). Those assessed as having attention, emotional and/or behavioural problems may show poor reading skills due to educational disadvantages produced by the incompatibility of the child's behaviour and the school's teaching procedures. For the child with these attention/emotion/behaviour problems, there may be a need to produce an education plan that overcomes these areas of difficulty in addition to (or even prior to) interventions targeted at literacy.

All the groups discussed above (dyslexia, MLD, SLI, dyspraxia, ADD/EBD) may show evidence of literacy weaknesses (Everatt et al., 2008), yet they may need different interventions to support learning. Assessments that differentially distinguish these groups from normal functioning should provide the basis on which to make appropriate recommendations for practice. Further research informing assessment practices that can specifically distinguish such groups is still needed.

Intervention

If dyslexia is considered as an educational problem, with difficulties that focus on weaknesses in the acquisition of literacy skills, then the main focus of intervention will be educational and concentrate on improving literacy skills. On the other hand, views that see dyslexia as more than a weakness in literacy acquisition may see intervention as requiring work in areas beyond those directly related to literacy, which may involve non-educational interventions.

At one extreme, dyslexia simply represents the lower end of a normal distribution of reading (and spelling) ability. Therefore, teaching methods should be based on the same ideas as for all children. Dyslexics may take longer to acquire literacy skills, but learning should be based on the usual teaching methods used in schools. Hence, an effective way of teaching literacy to any child should be appropriate for the dyslexic too. Norwich and Lewis (2005) propose the view that teaching approaches themselves should be seen as on a continuum and that children with dyslexia do not need anything different, or special, but they can be placed at a different point on the continuum. This would imply that the pedagogy and the curriculum are the same for all although there may be a greater degree of adaptation in some cases.

However, this view is controversial as many of the specialized approaches that have been developed for children with dyslexia rely to a great extent on the opportunity to pull the child out of class and implement approaches on a one-on-one basis (Henry 2003). Sawyer and Bernstein (2008), however, argue that 'pull-out' programmes cannot 'offer sufficient in-school time to learn, apply, and master the complexity of skills that are essential for continuous and appropriate progress toward competent literacy performance' (page 324). At the same time, Coffield, Riddick, Barmby and O'Neill (2008) suggest that the development of 'dyslexia friendly standards' for all schools within a local authority can provide a useful tool for developing effective in-class intervention.

Sawyer and Bernstein (2008) discuss the effects of two or more years of school-based interventions among 100 students with phonological dyslexia. Although norm-referenced measures indicated that all children made significant grade-level gains in word reading, spelling and reading comprehension, standard scores revealed a different pattern. When compared to peers of the same age, the gap in achievement was essentially unchanged for word reading and actually increased for spelling. Only reading comprehension showed a substantial gain of about six standard score points, on average. The authors concluded that although these students had not closed the achievement gap with their peers neither had they fallen further behind and they did benefit from the intervention.

Consistent with the view of the importance of phonological processing for early literacy development, the most comprehensive data related to teaching literacy to those with literacy difficulties, including those diagnosed with dyslexia, revolves around the benefits of phonological training methods, particularly if performed early in the literacy learning process (see discussions in Blachman, 1997 and Torgesen, 2002). The dominant phonological deficit hypothesis is compatible with the success of these methods. Teaching methods that develop skills in grapheme–phoneme translation, as well as provides a basis for building a sight vocabulary, may be successful because they overcome the problems associated with the phonological deficits (see, for example, Hatcher et al., 1994). However, one of the problems with these general intervention procedures is that they can be resource-heavy, particularly in staff/student time, and that there is evidence that not all dyslexics benefit from intervention methods that focus purely on phonics training. For example, Torgesen and colleagues (see review in Torgesen, 2004) concluded from a series of relatively large studies in the USA that phonological-based literacy remediation needs to be long and intensive with, potentially, 150 hours of one-to-one tuition being needed to bring a typical poor reader in these studies up to average ability levels. Even with such intensive intervention, the same studies found that between 5 and 25 per cent of children with poor literacy skills did not show reliable gains in literacy. One of the main factors that predicts successful intervention is how early this occurs. The earlier the intervention, the better the chance of a positive outcome. The later it is left, the harder it is for such methods to be successful. However, the initial abilities of the child seem to influence successful outcome too. Although there is also some evidence that those with generally low levels of ability show poor intervention outcome (Wise et al., 1999), the main finding seems to be that those with severe and specific deficits in phonological skills seem to show least benefits from phonological interventions (Lundberg, 1988; Torgesen and Davis, 1996). For example, Lundberg (1988) discusses findings indicating that children in the lowest quartile on phonological awareness tasks did not show a great deal of benefit from phonological training. Similarly, even though the eight-week phonological training programme used in a study by Torgesen, Morgan and Davis (1992) proved effective with the majority of children, still some 30 per cent of the sample of at-risk kindergartners failed to show reliable gains in phonological awareness skills. These findings suggest that the more severe the phonological deficit, the harder it is to remediate.

The evidence of treatment resistors has meant that many interventions for literacy learning problems related to dyslexia have focused on more than the phonological remediation tactic. For example, positive results have also been found following literacy teaching methods that have focused on whole-word or look-and-say methods (see Brooks and Weeks, 1998). This can be explained from the same causal position as the phonological training interventions. The argument here is that dyslexics have problems with converting letters into sounds, which should not be affected by methods that focus on sight vocabulary development. The use of visual features may also support memory, and avoid the problems with verbal memory associated with dyslexia. Also, intervention programmes that are argued to train fluency in word identification have been found to improve the exception word reading skills of reading disabled children, particularly those with specific naming deficits (Lovett et al., 1994; 2000; see also Wolf et al., 2000). Similar arguments can be provided for methods that focus on more semantic strategies, which may involve the use of pictures to support understanding, or the use of rhymes or songs to support memory, as well as mnemonic strategies (see Scruggs and Mastropieri, 1990). As with the whole-word/look-and-say methods, the idea here is to support learning through strategies that focus on the abilities of the child and circumnavigate the areas of deficit (i.e., the phonological decoding weaknesses). Similar strategies may involve motor movements or the kinaesthetic senses to support recall. Such strategies might involve using letter shapes that can be touched and felt by the child, or may get the child to use exaggerated hand movements when writing a letter or word to help the child remember the shape of the letter and the spelling of the word. Alternatively, they might involve getting the child to think about the shape and movement of the mouth when pronouncing words or producing letter-sounds. Although there is not a great deal of evidence to support these specific methods, often they have been incorporated into multisensory methods for which there are data supportive of effectiveness (for example, see Reason et al. 1988). Connor (1994), in reviewing studies on the teaching of literacy skills, concluded that a 'scattergun' approach is needed. The view here was that, since dyslexia is multifactorial, it is inappropriate to use a single-intervention style. This approach included a consideration of factors in addition to multisensory teaching, such as emotional wellbeing and family support, but recognizes one of the potential benefits of the multisensory procedures – that of targeting lots of areas so that something will sink in, even if one area is weak. However, despite the long history behind multisensory methods, and their clear influence on teaching approaches used within the learning disabilities field, there is a surprising lack of formal research evidence for their efficacy (see Joshi et al., 2002).

Given that many different literacy-specific teaching methods have been found useful with dyslexics, a problem arises when deciding which one to use. The majority of evidence supports the view that a phonological-based intervention/teaching strategy will work for most children. However, alternative methods may be better for some children and a procedure for identifying who will benefit from what would be valuable. One way to do this is to monitor progress in the intervention and change the teaching method if the expected improvements are not occurring. For example, current Response to Intervention procedures use smaller-scale interventions within schools for the majority of those with poor literacy progress and only focus more intensive remediation processes on those who are not showing improvements with the less intense methods (see discussions in Bradley et al., 2005; Burns et al., 2005; Justice, 2006). Thus, children who are showing poor scores on literacy measures (most likely within the first year or two of formal education) will be given special help within the school, most likely by a school teacher trained in using the less intensive intervention procedures. This will form part of normal school practices, and most likely will focus on basic phonological-related training procedures to attempt to improve early literacy, or word level decoding, skills. Improvements during this intervention should then be monitored. If, after an appropriate time period for intervention (which is variable across different Response-to-Intervention methods and may be ten weeks or a whole school year), improvements have not been made, or fall below a designated threshold, then further interventions will be needed under special educational

13

provisions. The idea is that the majority of children with weak literacy skills will benefit from the first level of intervention to such a degree that they do not require the more intensive intervention provided by the special provisions. The latter, more resource-heavy and longer intervention (as suggested by the work of Torgesen, 2004) can then be focused on those who require them, and may involve further phonological training or additional support. This process has developed out of views that not all children with poor levels of literacy acquisition have dyslexia (see, for example, discussions in Vellutino *et al.*, 1996) and can provide an argument against those who argue that current literacy-focused interventions are too costly and time-inefficient as it has the potential to reduce the number of children requiring more intensive special education (Burns *et al.*, 2005). However, such procedures rely on reliable initial literacy assessment and intervention monitoring tools, as well as teachers trained in using these tools and identifying those who are not showing appropriate levels of success with the intervention. There is also not a great deal of data showing that this two-level intervention process is any better than a one-off assessment followed by intervention process (though see Vellutino *et al.*, 2006) and some have criticized the process for being too phonologically-based and ignoring other areas of strength and weakness that can support individual intervention identification (Fiorello *et al.*, 2006).

Relatively recent remediation methods that have moved away from the literacy-based interventions discussed above have focused on visual- or motor-related problems. The visual deficit hypothesis has been the traditional alternative to the phonological position (for reviews see: Everatt, 2002; Stein, 2001, 2008). As such there have been a great many remediation programmes developed around the idea of changing the way the dyslexic sees the world or the written page: from training eye movements through text to covering one eye. However, few have lasted long as viable remediation procedures. One that has lasted some time, and for which there is still research activity, is the use of coloured overlays or tinted lenses (see Wilkins, 2004). Research has suggested that visual filters (coloured lenses that are worn, or coloured overlays that are placed over the page, when reading) may be effective for alleviating (at least some) reading difficulties (see Wilkins *et al.*, 1994). However, despite the research and practitioner evidence, the theoretical rationale for such visual filters lacks specification and is often contradictory (eg, the requirement for precise hew specification when making lenses, but not for changes in lenses when moving between lighting conditions, such as a normal bulb versus the sun, that will change the perceived colour of the same object). Some of the original ideas for this method were derived from the view that dyslexia may be associated with Scotopic Sensitivity Syndrome (Irlen, 1991). However, the diagnosis of Scotopic Sensitivity Syndrome is controversial (see Lopez *et al.*, 1994) and it is unclear what mechanism is responsible for the hypothesized sensitivity (see discussions in Wilkins, 2004). Additionally, the normal intervention practice of allowing dyslexics to choose the filter that they feel improves their reading is open to placebo effects. Indeed, the one study that has attempted to control potential placebo effects (Wilkins *et al.*, 1994) did not find reliable improvements in reading amongst the individuals provided with correct filters compared to a placebo filter. However, dramatic improvements have been claimed for this treatment and it is a pity that this is one of the weakest visual-based areas in terms of research and theory.

Another intervention procedure that has developed from the research of those investigating visual-related deficits amongst dyslexics, and for which there are still research programmes ongoing, is that related to the use of food supplements that contain appropriate levels of complex (long chain or polyunsaturated) fatty acids (see Stordy and Nicholl, 2000, for a review of this intervention procedure). The use of such supplements has been argued to improve visual processing, particularly hand–eye coordination, motion perception and the processing of low contrast visual stimuli (ie, those areas of visual processing often associated with magnocellular pathway functioning). Supplementation is argued to be important due to the lack of these fatty acids in the modern diet and their hypothesized importance in the rapid transmission of ions across cell membranes. This may slow down processing, leading to many of the features associated with speed of processing deficits amongst learning disabled children. However, the deficits in fatty acid uptake described also argue for dyslexics showing the physical features of such a deficiency. These include skin and hair problems that are not typically associated with dyslexic individuals (though see arguments in Richardson and Puri, 2000). Therefore this particular intervention procedure has yet to be shown to be appropriate for use with dyslexic individuals (see also the evidence reported by Voight *et al.*, 2002, for a lack of efficacy of such supplementation procedures for children with behavioural difficulties).

The traditional third general remediation area focuses on motor deficiencies that have been identified amongst dyslexics. These typically focus on training motor movements to develop interactions between and processes within different brain areas. In the case of the Fawcett and Nicolson work (discussed above), the brain area of focus has been the cerebellum (Fawcett and Nicolson, 2001). Recent work by Reynolds and colleagues (Reynolds and Nicolson, 2007; Reynolds *et al.*, 2003) has claimed improvements in motor movement, as well as literacy skills, following an intervention programme (referred to as DDAT since it focuses on dyslexia, dyspraxia and attention-deficit treatment) which is argued to focus on the functioning of the cerebellum. However, this particular work has been criticized due to its design (see commentaries in same journal issues as the papers) with many researchers arguing that these weaknesses make it impossible to make appropriate conclusions about the intervention's effectiveness (see Rack *et al.*, 2007). Despite this controversy, the motor training method has been around for some time (see discussions in Everatt, 1999; Goddard, 1996). Such methods have the attractive feature that the remediation is typically independent of school teaching; meaning that it will not disrupt conventional teaching processes or require extra teaching resources. The child is remediated so that he/she can benefit from normal teaching methods with the rest of his peers. The main problem with such motor-based interventions is that it is difficult to see how they relate to reading difficulties and spelling problems that are not due to poor hand-movement control, since the primary focus of the intervention is usually training in gross motor movement control (crawling or remaining steady on a moving surface) or basic reflexive movements. Additionally, prior to the DDAT study and the work of McPhillips and colleagues (McPhillips *et al.*, 2000), much of the evidence from such remediation techniques was equivocal or negative (see Cratty, 1997). Hence, although such intervention procedures are used by practitioners, there are major weaknesses with both the theories and research evidence associated with this work.

Tying the strands

Given the focus of the book on research and practice, this chapter will end by relating the research discussed to practice. The aim of special education practice is to lead to appropriate learning and/or intervention. Hence, much of the work covered in this chapter leads to issues related to intervention. Overall, the evidence argues against accepting one method and rejecting all others. The main methods used by practitioners seem to focus on multisensory teaching; although typically this involves improving phonological skills and linking these to literacy via multisensory strategies, and hence such methods can be subsumed within the phonological deficit viewpoint – and as discussed above, the evidence for the efficacy of this approach is far from conclusive. Similarly, although intervention studies have been conducted in several different language contexts (particularly European/Scandinavian languages, although some Asian languages as well), much of the data presented have been derived from studies of English-speaking children. Given the recent increase in research on cross-language comparisons (as discussed earlier in this chapter), there seems to be an opportunity to assess intervention methods across languages, thereby providing evidence for the efficacy of those methods and potentially informing practice about likely cases where the intervention may or may not be successful. Currently, the main recommendation from the research evidence is that an intervention should target literacy – i.e., the method should be embedded in an understanding of the processes in literacy. Given that there may be differences across languages in literacy acquisition, there is a clear need to assess this viewpoint across those differing language contexts – research discussed in this chapter will, hopefully, provide a basis on which to conduct such cross-language work.

However, other research evidence discussed in this chapter argues that literacy may not be the only area where children with dyslexia may struggle. Although more controversial than the data for literacy weaknesses, evidence for slow processing speeds (or temporal processing deficits), motor sequencing/automaticity deficits and even visual problems may be one of the reasons for practitioners considering a range of intervention methods when dealing with different children. Clearly, considering aspects of performance beyond literacy is an important part of the practitioner's role. One of the most useful aspects of multisensory instructional methods is that they are often more interesting than alternatives, thereby reducing problems due to boredom or fatigue, and, as discussed above, such methods may target a number of areas of deficit. Despite this, there are children who struggle even with these methods (particularly those identified when older, after several years of poor literacy acquisition) leading to many dyslexia practitioners considering a range of intervention methods, and potentially relying on a trial-and-error approach to identify the best for a particular child. Clearly, there is a need for further research informing practice to reduce the need for such an approach. The most likely would seem to be to relate assessment practices to intervention outcomes, and further research here would seem to be appropriate.

Overall, the main theme of such intervention work for present purposes is that it should develop from work with, and research into, dyslexia. As our understanding of literacy learning problems and dyslexia increases, so we should get closer to identifying the best method to support the learning of the individual. Whether this will be one method used for all, or a multi-method approach has yet to be determined, but the research work and theoretical development should inform and improve practice.

References

Abu-Rabia, S., Share, D. and Mansour, M. (2003). Word recognition and basic cognitive processes among reading disabled and normal readers in the Arabic language. *Reading and Writing*, 16, 423–440.

Adams, M.J. (1990). *Beginning to Read*. Massachusetts: MIT Press.

Al-Mannai, H.A. and Everatt, J. (2005). Phonological processing skills as predictors of literacy amongst Arabic speaking Bahraini school children. *Dyslexia*, 11, 269–291.

Barkley, R.A. (2006). *Attention Deficit Hyperactivity Disorder*. New York: Guilford.

Beaton, A., McDougall S. and Singleton, C. (eds) (1997). Dyslexia in literate adults. *Journal of Research in Reading*, 20 (1).

Bishop, D.V.M. and Snowling, M.J. (2004). Developmental dyslexia and specific language impairment: same or different. *Psychological Bulletin*, 130, 858–886.

Blachman, B.A. (ed.) (1997). *Foundations of Reading Acquisition and Dyslexia: Implications for Early Intervention*. Mahwah, NJ: LEA.

Bradley, R., Danielson, L. and Doolittle, J. (2005). Response to intervention. *Journal of Learning Disabilities*, 38, 485–486.

Breznitz, Z. (2008). The origin of dyslexia: the asynchrony phenomenon. In G. Reid, A. Fawcett, F. Manis and L. Siegel (eds) *The Sage Dyslexia Handbook*. London: Sage Publications.

British Psychological Society (1999). *Dyslexia, Literacy and Psychological Assessment*. Report of a Working Party of the Division of Educational and Child Psychology. Leicester: British Psychological Society.

Brooks, P. and Weeks, S. (1998). A comparison of responses of dyslexic, slow learning and control children to different strategies for teaching spellings. *Dyslexia*, 4, 212–222.

Broomfield, H. and Combley, M. (1997). *Overcoming Dyslexia: A Practical Handbook for the Classroom*. London: Whurr.

Bruck, M. (1993). Word recognition and component phonological processing skills of adults with childhood diagnosis of dyslexia. *Developmental Review*, 13, 258–268.

Bryant, P. and Bradley, L. (1985). *Children's Reading Problems*. Oxford: Blackwell.

Burns, M.K., Appleton, J.J. and Stehouwer, J.D. (2005). Meta-analytic review of response-to-intervention research: examining field-based and research-implemented models. *Journal of Psychoeducational Assessment*, 23, 381–394.

Capute, A.J., Accardo, P.J. and Shapiro, B.K. (eds) (1994). *Learning Disabilities Spectrum: ADD, ADHD, and LD*. Baltimore: York Press.

Caron, C. and Rutter, M. (1991). Comorbidity in child psychopathology: concepts, issues and research strategies. *Journal of Child Psychology and Psychiatry*, 32, 1063–1080.

Catts, H.W., Fay, M.E., Tomblin, J.B. and Zhang, X. (2002). A longitudinal investigation of reading outcomes in children with language impairments. *Journal of Speech, Language and Hearing Research*, 45, 1142–1157.

Clark, D.B. and Uhry, J.K. (1995). *Dyslexia: Theory and Practice of Remedial Instruction*. Baltimore: York Press.

Coffield, M., Riddick, B., Barmby, P. and O'Neill, J. (2008). Dyslexia friendly primary schools: what can we learn from asking the pupils? In G. Reid, A. Fawcett, F. Manis and L. Siegel (eds) *The Sage Handbook of Dyslexia*. London: Sage Publications.

Connor, M. (1994). Specific learning difficulty (dyslexia) and interventions. *Support for Learning*, 9, 114–119.

Cratty, B.J. (1996). Coordination problems among learning disabled children. In B.J. Cratty and R.L. Goldman (eds) *Learning Disabilities: Contemporary Viewpoints*. Amsterdam: Harwood.

Cunningham, A.E. (1990). Explicit versus implicit instruction in phonemic awareness. *Journal of Experimental and Child Psychology*, 50, 429–444.

Elbeheri, G. and Everatt, J. (2007). Literacy ability and phonological processing skills amongst dyslexic and non-dyslexic speakers of Arabic. *Reading and Writing*, 20, 273–294.

Elbeheri, G., Everatt, J., Reid, G. and Al Mannai, H. (2006). Dyslexia assessment in Arabic. *Journal of Research in Special Educational Needs*, 6, 143–152.

Elbro, C., Nielsen, I. and Petersen, D.K. (1994). Dyslexia in adults: evidence for deficits in non-word reading and in the phonological representation of lexical items. *Annals of Dyslexia*, 44, 205–226.

Elbro, C., Rasmussen, I. and Spelling, B. (1996). Teaching reading to disabled readers with language disorders: a controlled evaluation of synthetic speech feedback. *Scandinavian Journal of Psychology*, 37, 140–155.

Ellis, A.W., McDougall, S.J.P. and Monk, A.F. (1996). Are dyslexics different? *Dyslexia*, 2, 31–58.

Entwistle, N. (1981). *Styles of Learning and Teaching*. Chichester: Wiley.

Everatt, J. (ed.) (1999). *Reading and Dyslexia: Visual and Attentional Processes*. London: Routledge.

Everatt, J. (2002). Visual processes. In G. Reid and J. Wearmouth (eds) *Dyslexia and Literacy: Theory and Practice*. Chichester: Wiley.

Everatt, J., Smythe, I., Ocampo, D. and Veii, K. (2002). Dyslexia assessment of the bi-scriptal reader. *Topics in Language Disorders*, 22, 32–45.

Everatt, J., Smythe, I., Ocampo, D. and Gyarmathy, E. (2004). Issues in the assessment of literacy-related difficulties across language backgrounds: a cross-linguistic comparison. *Journal of Research in Reading*, 27, 141–151.

Everatt J., Weeks, S. and Brooks, P. (2008). Profiles of strengths and weaknesses in dyslexia and other learning difficulties. *Dyslexia*, 14, 16–41.

Fawcett, A. (1989) Automaticity: A New Framework for Dyslexic Research. Paper presented at the First International Conference of the British Dyslexia Association, Bath 1989.

Fawcett, A.J. and Nicolson R. (1992). Automatisation deficits in balance for dyslexic children. *Perceptual and Motor Skills*, 75, 507–529.

Fawcett, A.J. and Nicolson, R.I. (2001). Dyslexia: the role of the cerebellum. In A. Fawcett (ed.), *Dyslexia: Theory and Good Practice*. London: Whurr.

Fawcett, A. and Nicolson, R. (2008) Dyslexia and the cerebellum. In G. Reid, A. Fawcett, F. Manis and L. Siegel (eds) *The Sage Handbook of Dyslexia*. London: Sage Publications.

Fiorello, C.A., Hale, J.B. and Snyder, L.E. (2006). Cognitive hypothesis testing and response to intervention for children with reading problems. *Psychology in the Schools*, 43, 835–853.

Fisher, S.E. and DeFries, J.C. (2002). Developmental dyslexia: genetic dissection of a complex cognitive trait. *Neuroscience*, 3, 767–780.

Frith, U. and Snowling, M.J. (1983). Reading for meaning and reading for sound in autistic and dyslexic children. *British Journal of Developmental Psychology*, 1, 329–342.

Gathercole, S.E. and Pickering, S.J. (2000). Working memory deficits in children with low achievements in the national curriculum at 7 years of age. *British Journal of Educational Psychology*, 70, 177–194.

Geva, E. and Siegel, L. (2000). Orthographic factors in the concurrent development of basic reading skills in two languages. *Reading and Writing: An Interdisciplinary Journal*, 12, 1–30.

Gillon, G.T. (2004). *Phonological Awareness: From Research to Practice*. New York: Guilford Press.

Given, B.K. and Reid, G. (1999). *Learning Styles: A Guide for Teachers and Parents*, St Annes-on-Sea: Red Rose Publications.

Goddard, S. (1996). *A Teacher's Window Into the Child's Mind*. Eugene: Fern Ridge Press.

Goswami, U. (2000). Phonological representations, reading development and dyslexia: Towards a cross-linguistic theoretical framework. *Dyslexia*, 6, 133–151.

Hatcher, P.J., Hulme, C. and Ellis, A.W. (1994). Ameliorating early reading failure by integrating the teaching of reading and phonological skills: the Phonological Linkage Hypothesis. *Child Development*, 65, 41–57.

Henry, M.K. (2003) *Unlocking Literacy: Effective Decoding and Spelling Instruction*. Maryland, Baltimore, USA: Paul Brookes Publishing Co.

Huntington, D.D. and Bender, W.N. (1993) Adolescents with learning disabilities at risk? Emotional well-being, depression, suicide. *Journal of Learning Disabilities*, 26, 159–166.

Irlen, H. (1991). *Reading by the Colors*. Garden City Park, NY: Avery Publishing Group.

Jeffries, S. and Everatt, J. (2004). Working memory: its role in dyslexia and other learning difficulties. *Dyslexia*, 10, 196–214.

Joshi, R.M. and Aaron, P.G. (2008) Assessment of literacy performance based on the Componential Model of Reading. In G. Reid, A. Fawcett, F. Manis and L. Siegel (eds) *The Sage Handbook of Dyslexia*. London: Sage Publications.

Joshi, R.M., Dahlgren, M. and Boulware-Gooden, R. (2002). Teaching reading through multi-sensory approach in an inner city school. *Annals of Dyslexia*, 53, 235–251.

Justice, L. (2006). Evidence-based practice, response to intervention and the prevention of reading difficulties. *Language, Speech and Hearing Services in the Schools*, 37, 284–297.

Kaplan, B.J., Dewey, D.M., Crawford, S.G. and Wilson, B.N. (2001). The term comorbidity is of questionable value in reference to developmental disorders: data and theory. *Journal of Learning Disabilities*, 34, 555–565.

Kaufman, A.S. (1994). *Intelligent Testing with the WISC-III*. New York: Wiley.

Lopez, R., Yolton, R.L., Kohl, P., Smith, D.L. and Sexerud, M.H. (1994). Comparison of Irlen Soctopic Sensitivity Syndrome test results to academic and visual performance data. *Journal of the American Optometric Association*, 65, 705–713.

Lovett, M.W., Borden, S.L., DeLuca, T., Lacerenza, L., Benson, N.J. and Brackstone, D. (1994). Treating the core deficits of developmental dyslexia: I Evidence of transfer of learning after phonologically and strategy based reading training programs. *Developmental Psychology*, 30, 805–822.

Lovett, M.W., Steinbach, K.A. and Frijters, J.C. (2000). Remediating the core deficits of developmental reading disability: a double-deficit hypothesis. *Journal of Learning Disabilities*, 33, 334–358.

Lundberg, I. (1988). Preschool prevention of reading failure: does training in phonological awareness work? In R.L. Masland and M.W. Masland (eds), *Prevention of Reading Failure*. Parkton, MD: York Press.

Lyytinen, H., Guttorm, T.K., Huttunen, T., Hämäläinen, J., Leppänen, P.H.T., and Vesterinen, M. (2005). Psychophysiology of developmental dyslexia: a review of findings including studies of children at risk for dyslexia. *Journal of Neurolinguistics*, 18, 167–195.

McPhillips, M., Hepper, P.G. and Mulhern, G. (2000). Effects of replicating primary-reflex movements on specific reading difficulties in children: a randomised, double-blind, controlled trial. *The Lancet*, 355, 537–541.

Miles, T.R. and Varma, V. (eds) (1995). *Dyslexia and Stress*. London: Whurr.

Molfese, V.J., Molfese, D.L., Barnes, M.E., Warren, C.G. and Molfese, P.J. (2008). Familial predictors of dyslexia: evidence from preschool children with and without familial dyslexia risk. In G. Reid, A. Fawcett, F. Manis and L. Siegel (eds) *The Sage Handbook of Dyslexia*. London: Sage Publications.

Nation, K. and Snowling, M.J. (1998). Individual differences in contextual facilitation: Evidence from dyslexia and poor reading comprehension. *Child Development*, 69, 996–1011.

Norwich, B. and Lewis, A. (2005) How specialized is teaching pupils with disabilities and difficulties? In A. Lewis and B. Norwich (eds) *Special Teaching for Special Children? Pedagogies for Inclusion*. Maidenhead: Open University Press.

Olofsson, A. and Lundberg, I. (1985). Evaluation of long-term effects of phonemic awareness training in kindergarten: illustrations of some methodological problems in evaluation research. *Scandinavian Journal of Psychology*, 16, 21–34.

Pennington, B.F., Groisser, D. and Welsh, M.C. (1993). Contrasting cognitive deficits in attention deficit hyperactivity disorder versus reading disability. *Developmental Psychology*, 29, 511–523.

Portwood, M. (1999). *Developmental Dyspraxia: Identification and Intervention*, second edition. London: David Fulton Publishers.

Rack, J.P. (1997) Issues in the assessment of developmental dyslexia in adults: Theoretical perspectives. *Journal of Research in Reading*, 20, 66–76.

Rack, J.P., Snowling, M.J. and Olson, R.K. (1992). The nonword reading deficit in developmental dyslexia: a review. *Reading Research Quarterly*, 27, 29–53.

Rack, J.P., Snowling, M.J., Hulme, C., and Gibbs, S. (2007). No evidence that an exercise-based treatment programme (DDAT) has specific benefits for children with reading difficulties. *Dyslexia*, 13(2), 97–104.

Ramus, F., Pidgeon, E. and Frith, U. (2003). The relationship between motor control and phonology in dyslexic children. *Journal of Child Psychology and Psychiatry*, 44, 712–722.

Reason, R., Brown, P., Cole, M. and Gregory, M. (1988) Does the 'specific' in specific learning difficulties make a difference to the way we teach? *Support for Learning*, 3(4), 230–236.

Reed, P. (1999). Managing dyslexia is understanding dyslexia: implicit functional and structural approaches in the articles by Cameron and his critics. *Educational and Child Psychology*, 16, 51–69.

Reynolds, D. and Nicolson, R.I. (2007). Follow-up of an exercise-based treatment for children with reading difficulties. *Dyslexia*, 13(2), 78–96.

Reynolds, D., Nicolson, R.I. and Hambly, H. (2003) Evaluation of an exercise: based treatment for children with reading difficulties. *Dyslexia*, 9(1), 48–71.

Richardson, A.J. and Puri, B.K. (2000) The potential role of fatty acids in attention deficit/hyperactivity disorder (ADHD). *Prostaglandins Leukotrienes Essential Fatty Acids*, 63, 79–87.

Riding, R. and Cheema, I. (1991). Cognitive styles: an overview and integration. *Educational Psychology*, 11, 193–215.

Rourke, B.P. (1989). *Nonverbal Learning Disabilities: The Syndrome and the Model*. New York: Guilford Press.

Sawyer, D.J. and Bernstein, S. (2008) Students with phonological dyslexia in school-based programs: insights from Tennessee schools. In G. Reid, A. Fawcett, F. Manis and L. Siegel (eds) *The Sage Handbook of Dyslexia*. London: Sage Publications.

Schmeck, R.R. (ed.) (1988). *Learning Strategies and Learning Styles*. New York: Plenum Press.

Schneider, W., Küspert, P., Roth, E., Visé, M. and Marx, H. (1997). Short-and long-term effects of training phonological awareness in kindergarten: evidence from two German studies. *Journal of Experimental Child Psychology*, 66, 311–40.

Scruggs, T.E. and Mastropieri, M.A. (1990). The case for mnemonic instruction. *Journal of Special Education*, 24, 7–29.

Semrud-Clikeman, M., Bierderman, J., Sprich-Buckminster, S., Lehman, B.K., Faraone, S.V. and Norman, D. (1992). Comorbidity between ADHD and learning disability: A review and report in a clinically referred sample. *Journal of the American Academy of Child and Adolescent Psychiatry*, 31, 439–448.

Seymour, P.H.K., Aro, M. and Erskine, J.M. (2003). Foundation literacy acquisition in European orthographies. *British Journal of Psychology*, 94, 143–174.

Share, D.L. (1996). Word recognition and spelling processes in specific reading disabled and garden-variety poor readers. *Dyslexia*, 2, 167–174.

Share, D.L. (2008). On the Anglocentricities of current reading research and practice: the perils of overreliance on an 'Outlier' orthography. *Psychological Bulletin*, 134, 584–615.

Shaul, S. and Breznitz, Z. (2007). Asynchrony of Cerebral Systems Activated During Word Recognition: A Comparison of Regular and Dyslexic Readers. Manuscript submitted for publication.

19

Siegel, L.S. (1999). Issues in the definition and diagnosis of learning disabilities: a perspective on Guckenberger v. Boston University. *Journal of Learning Disabilities*, 32, 304–319.

Siegel, L. and Lipka, O. (2008) The definition of learning disabilities: who is the individual with learning disabilities? In G. Reid, A. Fawcett, F. Manis and L. Siegel (eds) *The Sage Handbook of Dyslexia*. London: Sage Publications.

Singleton, C. (2008). Visual stress and dyslexia. In G. Reid, G. Elbeheri, J. Everatt, D. Knight and J. Wearmouth (eds) *The Routledge Companion to Dyslexia*. London: Routledge.

Smythe, I. and Everatt, J. (2004). Dyslexia: a cross-linguistic framework. In I. Smythe, J. Everatt and R. Salter (eds) *The International Book of Dyslexia*, 2nd edition. London: Wiley and Sons.

Smythe, I., Everatt, J., Al-Menaye, N., He, X., Capellini, S., Gyarmathy, E. and Siegel, L. (2008). Predictors of word level literacy amongst Grade 3 children in five diverse languages. *Dyslexia*, 14, 170–187.

Snowling, M.J. (2000). *Dyslexia* (second edition). Oxford: Blackwell.

Solity, J. (2000). The Early Reading Research: applying psychology to classroom practice. *Educational and Child Psychology*, 17, 46–55.

Spagna, M.E. (1996). All poor readers are not dyslexic. In B.J. Cratty and R.L. Goldman (eds), *Learning Disabilities: Contemporary Viewpoints*. Amsterdam: Harwood Academic Publishers.

Spencer, K. (2000). Is English a dyslexic language? *Dyslexia*, 6, 152–162.

Stackhouse, J. and Snowling, M.J. (1992). Barriers to literacy development in two cases of developmental verbal dyspraxia. *Cognitive Neuropsychology*, 9, 273–99.

Stackhouse, J. and Wells, B. (1997). *Children's Speech and Literacy Difficulties: A Psycholinguistic Framework*. London: Whurr.

Stanovich, K.E. (1988). Explaining the difference between the dyslexic and the garden-variety poor reader: the phonological–core variable–difference model. *Journal of Learning Disabilities*, 21, 590–612.

Stanovich, K.E. and West, R.F. (1983). On priming by a sentence context. *Journal of Experimental Psychology: General*, 112, 1–36.

Stein, J.F. (2001). The magnocellular theory of developmental dyslexia. *Dyslexia*, 7, 12–36.

Stein, J.F (2008) The neurobiological basis of Dyslexia. In G. Reid, A. Fawcett, F. Manis and L. Siegel (eds) *The Sage Handbook of Dyslexia*. London: Sage Publications.

Stordy, B.J. and Nicholl, M.J. (2000). *The LCP Solution: The Remarkable Nutritional Treatment for ADHD, Dyslexia and Dyspraxia*. New York: Ballantine Books.

Thomson, M. (2001). *The Psychology of Dyslexia*. London: Whurr.

Torgesen, J.K. (2002). The prevention of reading difficulties. *Journal of School Psychology*, 40, 7–26.

Torgesen, J.K. (2004). Preventing early reading failure. *American Educator*, Fall.

Torgesen, J.K. and Davis, C. (1996). Individual difference variables that predict response to training in phonological awareness. *Journal of Experimental Child Psychology*, 63, 1–21.

Torgesen, J.K., Morgan, S. and Davis, C. (1992). The effects of two types of phonological awareness training on word learning in kindergarten children. *Journal of Educational Psychology*, 84, 364–370.

Turner, M. (1999). *Psychological Assessment of Dyslexia*. London: Whurr.

Veii, K. and Everatt, J. (2005). Predictors of reading among Herero–English bilingual Namibian school children. *Bilingualism: Language and Cognition*, 8, 239–254.

Vellutino, F.R., Scanlon, D.M., Sipay, E.R., Pratt, A., Chen, R. and Denckla, M.B. (1996). Cognitive profiles of difficult-to-remediate and readily remediated poor readers: early intervention as a vehicle for distinguishing between cognitive and experiential deficits as basic causes of specific reading disability. *Journal of Educational Psychology*, 88, 601–638.

Vellutino, F.R., Fletcher, J.M., Snowling, M.J. and Scanlon, D.M. (2004). Specific reading disability (dyslexia). What have we learned in the past four decades? *Journal of Child Psychology and Psychiatry*, 45, 2–40.

Vellutino, F.R., Scanlon, D.M., Small, S. and Fanuele, D.P. (2006). Response to intervention as a vehicle for distinguishing between children with and without reading disabilities: evidence for the role of kindergarten and first grade intervention. *Journal of Learning Disabilities*, 39, 157–169.

Visser, J. (2003). Developmental coordination disorder: a review of research on subtypes and comorbidities. *Human Movement Science*, 22, 479–493.

Voight, R.G., Llorente, A.M., Jensen, C.L., Fraley, J.K., Berretta, M.C. and Heird, W.C. (2002). A randomized double-blind, placebo-controlled trial of docosahexaneoic acid supplementation in children with attention-deficit/hyperactivity disorder. *Journal of the American Academy of Child and Adolescent Psychiatry*, 41, 139.

Wilkins, A. (2004). *Reading Through Colour*. Chichester: Wiley.

Wilkins, A.J., Evans, B.J.W., Brown, J.A., Busby, A.E., Wingfield, A.E., Jeanes, R.J., and Bald, J. (1994). Double-masked placebo-controlled trial of precision spectral filters in children who use coloured overlays. *Ophthalmic and Physiological Optics*, 14, 365–370.

Wimmer, H. (1993). Characteristics of developmental dyslexia in a regular writing system. *Applied Psycholinguistics*, 14, 1–33.

Wise, B.W., Ring, J. and Olson, R. (1999). Training phonological awareness with and without explicit attention to articulation. *Journal of Experimental Child Psychology*, 72, 271–304.

Wolf, M. and Bowers, P.G. (2000). Naming speed processes and developmental reading disabilities: an introduction to the special issue on the double-deficit hypothesis. *Journal of Learning Disabilities*, 33, 322–324.

Wolf, M. and O'Brien, B. (2001). On issues of time, fluency and intervention. In A. Fawcett (ed.) *Dyslexia: Theory and Good Practice*. London: Whurr.

Wolf, M., Miller, L. and Donnelly, K. (2000). Retrieval automaticity, vocabulary elaboration, orthography (RAVE-O): a comprehensive fluency-based reading intervention programme. *Journal of Learning Disabilities*, 33, 375–386.

Zeigler, J.C. and Goswami, U. (2005). Reading acquisition, developmental dyslexia, and skilled reading across languages: A psycholinguistic grain size theory. *Psychological Bulletin*, 131, 3–29.

2

Dyslexia and IQ
From research to practice

Gad Elbeheri and John Everatt

This chapter

- provides an understanding of the role of IQ in defining dyslexia
- analyses the theoretical debate on IQ and dyslexia
- discusses the practical and theoretical implications on the role of IQ in identification and definitions.

Introduction

This chapter provides the reader with a general overview of the role of IQ in dyslexia definitions, identification and assessment. In addition to providing the theoretical background for the debate over the role of IQ in dyslexia identification, the chapter also considers the potential implications of employing IQ in the field of dyslexia assessment with reference to practical, as well as more political, viewpoints. Both sides of the debate are presented in terms of this practical emphasis with the conclusion arguing for a consideration of components of IQ tests and issues for intervention.

Defining dyslexia

The explanation of developmental dyslexia has long been problematic leading some to conclude that "defining dyslexia has remained an elusive business" (McLoughlin *et al.*, 2002: 10). A precise definition is elusive because dyslexia is a condition that can vary widely in severity (Singleton 2002), making statements of incidence based on level of difficulty problematic, and, as with any human condition, is subject to individual differences, meaning that characteristics of dyslexia need to be separated from normal variation in a population. Complicating this is the fact that the condition often does not exist alone but may occur together with one or more of the three other major clinical entities that have been considered within the framework of learning disabilities: i.e. (i) motor-perceptual dysfunction syndromes, (ii) language delays and (iii) the syndrome of distractibility, hyperactivity and decreased attention span (Malatesha and Aaron 1982). This potential confusion may be related to differing viewpoints about what dyslexia is. For example, in contrast to a purely literacy-focused viewpoint (the definition of the British Psychological Society, 1999), Hornsby (1995) claims that dyslexia can show itself in a number of ways, including inadequate spatial orientation, poor verbal naming, poor reading and writing, organizational and notational skills, and can equally result from various causes. These multi-cause definitions can be contrasted with those which focus on a single (e.g., phonological) cause of the literacy deficits associated with dyslexia (Snowling, 2000; Stanovich, 1988). Yet, focusing purely on literacy weaknesses too may be problematic. Snowling (2000) claims that difficulties in attempting to define dyslexia are due to the confusion of whether to describe or explain a particular type of reading problem – i.e., simply stating that a weakness exists, against some norm, versus explaining the reason why the weakness exists by looking for additional features over and above the literacy problem. What to look for in terms of additional features typically depends on theoretical viewpoints that can differ widely. For example, the IQ–reading achievement discrepancy method (the focus of this chapter) is often seen as determining what the reading weakness is not (i.e., it is not due to low intelligence), whereas the phonological deficit viewpoint attempts to explain the poor reading levels in terms of a specific underlying (cognitive) weakness. The potential alternative causal viewpoints led a working group of educational and child psychologists in the UK to propose a definition of dyslexia that returns to the simple description position: i.e., that dyslexia is simply a difficulty in the acquisition of reading and spelling (British Psychological Society, 1999).

Reid (2002) argues that the various types of dyslexia definitions support the view that dyslexia is representative of a broad range of difficulties associated with 'literacy and learning, that individual differences will be present, that some students with dyslexia can have positive attributes and that any difficulties are only part of the overall picture' (Reid 2002: 69). Reid and Kirk (2001) also observe that there is a tendency for definitions of dyslexia to reflect broader conceptual frameworks while at the same time acknowledge the individuality of the dyslexic learner. They also confirm that one of the key resulting issues is that people with dyslexia 'will not all exhibit the same characteristics nor to the same degree' (Reid and Kirk 2001: 3). However, the term dyslexia is sometimes avoided in educational practice because of its overwhelming emphasis on the causative factors that are within the child, in addition to its perceived effects on social policy. In other words, it is sometimes avoided because of its resulting risks of unequal distribution of public resources that are often limited.

The term dyslexia and its common usage

The British Psychological Society (1999) claim that the UK general public have been formulating their own theories concerning the underlying reasons as to why some individuals fail to acquire literacy and have marked and persistent problems in their reading and writing abilities. The report concludes that as a result, the definition of dyslexia has somehow lost its technical status and is no longer regarded as a specialist term confined within the fields of cognitive psychology or special education alone. The term, the report elaborates, has acquired wide use in societal circles and is being constantly used in popular daily language to refer to various cases of specific reading-disabled individuals who have, by their very nature, individual differences amongst them. It is within this context that the perceived links between reading abilities, intelligence and privilege, which may well be still current today, are well rooted in the educational and social history of dyslexia research and practice in the UK (British Psychological Society, 1999).

However, this popular and political link with intelligence (normally referred to as IQ) has remained an important feature in dyslexia practice. Despite the debate surrounding this link (see below), IQ and dyslexia have been associated in such a way that it is often impossible to

23

disconnect the two in social/political discourse. Even for those who have argued against using IQ in definitions/diagnosis of dyslexia have often felt it important to make statements/arguments along the lines of 'dyslexics are not stupid'. In the past, such statements have been related to important policy debates and advocacy for the recognition of dyslexia as an important component of educational practice. Yet dissociating IQ from dyslexia, and the recognition of individual differences amongst dyslexics, means that if such a thing as 'stupid' exists, it must exist as much in the dyslexic population as in the non-dyslexic population. The term 'stupid' is used here, of course, for purely emotive emphasis – to show that arguments in the field of dyslexia and its relationship to IQ can lead to strong feelings. When it comes to practice, just as in research, such emotive views need to be tempered. However, their influence on advocacy and policy have left an imprint on definition and hence identification. Therefore, they need to be recognized and considered carefully, particularly when dealing with societal/political positions. This is not to say that IQ-based definitions need to be retained because of an historical, political and/or emotional link. Rather, they are described herein to show how the arguments for and against IQ-based identification procedures can become emotional in themselves and to show how, despite evidence against IQ-based diagnostic procedures in the identification of dyslexia, they are still highly prevalent around the world.

Dyslexia and IQ–reading discrepancy: the debate

The connection between IQ and dyslexia has been crystalized most obviously by the traditional method of identifying dyslexia. This compares reading ability with IQ-predicted ability. If there is a discrepancy between IQ-predicted reading level and actual reading level, such that the latter is considered significantly lower than the former, then the individual is assessed as dyslexic. The basis of this discrepancy view is that low IQ leads to poor functioning in various skills, including reading, and, under exclusionary criteria, those with poor reading skills due to similarly low IQ should be rejected from the group with specific reading difficulties. This view has a long history and is based on definitions of dyslexia such as that of the World Federation of Neurology which proposed that dyslexia is 'a disorder in children who, despite conventional classroom experience, fail to attain the language skills of reading, writing and spelling commensurate with their intellectual abilities' (World Federation of Neurology, 1968, cited in Critchley, 1970). Therefore, the IQ–reading discrepancy method requires the use of IQ tests in the identification of dyslexic individuals: 'Among exclusionary factors, intelligence has been given the most attention by practitioners' (Catts and Kamhi, 1999: 60).

In this context, IQ is taken to represent a statement of a person's overall intellectual ability, which is based, most commonly, on an arithmetic average of a person's scores on several tests of ability. In order to be diagnosed with dyslexia, an individual had to demonstrate a significant difference between general mental abilities, as measured by this average on the intelligence test, and reading achievement. Hence, this discrepancy approach is said to distinguish between dyslexics, who have reading skills at a level much lower than expected, and common-or-garden poor readers, whose reading skills are exactly as expected based on their intellectual abilities. IQ has often been used in this context because, as Turner and Nicholas (2000) argue, IQ is a well-established predictor of academic success. According to this view, IQ may allow practitioners to know about who will not succeed in education due to low intellectual ability and those who may fail in education purely because of poor literacy skills. The argument, in this case, would be that if we remediate the literacy skills of the low IQ individuals, they will still fail in education, whereas remediating literacy for those with a discrepancy between reading level and intellectual ability should lead to them succeeding in education. A slight alternative to this is that remediating literacy should bring educational achievement up to the level predicted by intellectual functioning (IQ). For example, reading may not be poor against norms on a reading measure, but is weaker than predicted based on the individual's level of intelligence. Remediating literacy in this latter case will allow the individual to do better in education, by removing barriers to achievement due to poor reading and writing. This may be most obviously seen at higher education levels (e.g., university level), where intellectual functioning may be key to success. A poor reader with a low IQ score may not be able to access the university level curriculum whether their literacy skills are remediated or not. However, a higher IQ dyslexic individual may be able to make use of the curriculum to a high level if the literacy learning problems can be overcome. Hence, the arguments go, identification of dyslexia under this IQ–reading discrepancy formula is the best way to identify those who will benefit from literacy-based intervention procedures.

However, Siegel (1989) questions the usefulness of IQ in the diagnosis of dyslexia. The discrepancy diagnosis uses an IQ test such as the Wechsler Intelligence Scale of Children (WISC) in order to work out a person's expected reading ability. The WISC, as argued by Siegel (1989), includes subtests that are either irrelevant to the types of abilities required to predict reading or taps abilities that would be impaired by having the learning disability. Ellis (1993) also questions such definitions when trying to find out what constitutes 'normal intelligence' or how much difficulty in learning to read and write has to be manifested before a child can be called dyslexic (Ellis 1993: 94). Berninger (2001) also argues that IQ-achievement discrepancy is based typically 'just on accuracy measures of reading achievement and not measures of reading rate or spelling that may tap the kinds of persisting problems dyslexics experience' (Berninger 2001: 39).

Aaron (1994) supports Siegel's (1989) views and argues that IQ–reading discrepancy is based on two assumptions related to the nature of the relationship between IQ and reading achievement. The first assumption is that the relationship between IQ and reading achievement is unidirectional; in other words IQ determines reading achievement and not vice-versa. The second is that the degree of correlation between IQ and reading achievement is high enough to predict reading achievement from IQ. In his reference to what Stanovich (1991) called the 'Matthew Effect', Aaron (1994) argued that the IQ–reading achievement relationship is not unidirectional. There are well documented observations which confirm that poor readers read less than good readers and as a result 'fail to develop sufficient language and vocabulary skills which, in turn, can lower their verbal IQ' (Aaron 1994: 5–6). Similarly, Stanovich (1991, 1994) argues against the second assumption that there exists a high correlation between IQ and reading. Stanovich listed numerous studies where researchers find very low correlations between IQ and reading, which include Tunmer et al. (1988) ($r = 0.10$), Lundberg, Olfsson and Wall (1980) ($r = 0.19$), Tonneus (1984) ($r = 0.24$), Stanovich et al. (1984) ($r = 0.25$), Zifcak (1981) ($r = 0.27$), Jule et al. (1986) ($r = 0.34$), Vellutino and Scanlon (1987) ($r = 0.34$), Helfgott (1976) ($r = 0.41$) and Share et al. (1984) ($r = 0.47$). Although, maybe the best conclusion here is that the relationship is variable across studies, potentially due to the use of different measures, since some theorists have used some of the same data to argue for a relationship between IQ and reading. Torgeson (1989), for example, concludes that reading ability is generally correlated with intelligence and that intelligent people tend to be good readers while less intelligent people tend to be poorer readers. Additionally, Torgeson (1989) claims that IQ is not irrelevant to reading ability and points out that even in Siegel's (1989) data, good readers tended to have higher-IQ scores while poor readers tended to have lower-IQ scores.

Torgeson (1989), Turner (1997), Thomson (2001), Doyle (2002) and others agree that IQ testing, if administered correctly, can be a useful tool to differentiate between dyslexia and poor reading ability due to underachievement or to otherwise general poor reading abilities. Thomson (2001) claims that 'the evaluation of intelligence is an important element of the assessment of dyslexia' (Thomson 2001: 34), a claim which seems perhaps the 'most common justification for the use of the IQ-achievement discrepancy' in defining dyslexia (Catts and Kamhi 1999: 61). Turner and Nicholas (2000) quote Neisser's argument that:

> The relationship between [intelligence] test scores and school performance seems to be ubiquitous. Wherever it has been studied, children with high scores on tests of intelligence tend to learn more of what is taught in school than their lower-scoring peers . . . intelligence tests. . .are never the only influence on outcomes, though in the case of school performance they may well be the strongest.
>
> (Neisser *et al.*, cited in Turner and Nicholas 2000: 70)

Another area where the IQ–reading discrepancy model has been criticized is the lack of difference between high-IQ poor readers (dyslexics under the model) and low-IQ poor readers (the common-or-garden sort). Samuelson (2002) concluded that the IQ-achievement discrepancy definition of dyslexia 'does not distinguish between readers with dyslexia and other poor readers on tasks measuring phonological processing skills' (Samuelson 2002: 51). Share (1996) did find differences between high-IQ and low-IQ poor readers in one out of 26 separate reading-related measures, but concluded that this difference was more likely to be due to a type I error than an actual difference. Stanovich (1991) points to research which indicates that there is little evidence that dyslexic children differ from poor readers without an IQ–reading discrepancy in terms of performance on literacy, or literacy-related measures such as phonological processing, as well as on heritability and neuro-anatomy factors that have been associated primarily with literacy learning problems. In the report of the National Institute of Child Health and Human Development (NICHD) in the USA, Lyon (2003) asserts that the process of distinguishing between disabled readers with an IQ–reading achievement discrepancy and those without such a discrepancy reflects in fact an invalid practice at the beginning stages of reading and he argues that children with and without such a discrepancy do not differ in their information processing skills (both on their phonological and their orthographic coding) which are necessary requirements for accurate and rapid single word reading. Lyon (2003) argues that genetic and neuro-physiological (Functional Magnetic Resonance Imaging) studies did not indicate differential aetiologies for reading disabled children with and without discrepancies. Lyon (2003) has concluded that converging data from several NICHD sites also indicate that the 'presence and magnitude of IQ–reading achievement discrepancies are not related significantly to a child's response to intervention'. A conclusion supported by Catts and Kamhi (1991) who argue that research has generally failed to find reading differences between subgroups based on IQ-achievement discrepancy. They further asserted that 'IQ based subtypes have also failed to show expected differences in response to intervention' (Catts and Kamhi 1991: 74).

Indeed, despite the link between IQ and educational achievement being used as a reason for considering IQ in dyslexia assessments, there is an argument that using the IQ–reading discrepancy method is not outcome based at all (see Aaron, 1994). Flowers, Meyer, Lovato and Wood (2000) report Thorndike's (1963) caution that 'IQ scores are only appropriate as estimates of current levels of functioning, not as estimates of future potentials' (Flowers *et al.*, 2000: 52). Similarly, as Crombie (2001) points out, since reading and writing are skills that a child would not be expected to master before starting school, the IQ–reading discrepancy criteria seem to rule out any attempts or benefits of early identification and intervention. Moreover, according to such a criterion, dyslexia can only be identified after the child has been taught for some time, which means that an IQ–reading discrepancy diagnosis has to wait for children to fail, which ultimately results in the severe loss of motivation and the consequent low self-esteem and frustration sometimes associated with dyslexics. Smythe and Everatt (2000) argue that this frustration might lead to disruptive behaviour at school or indifference to educational demands, leading to further complications in the process of learning to read and write and thus 'producing a spiral of cognitive and emotional difficulties' (Smythe and Everatt 2000: 12–21). Berninger (2001) also argues that this discrepancy method is less than optimal since it is easier to prevent severe reading problems than remediate them. Overall, the earlier that intervention can be implemented, the more likely it is to be successful (Blachman, 1997; Torgeson, 2004).

Dickman (2001) considers the IQ–reading discrepancy as partially responsible for a more serious condition known as the aptitude-achievement discrepancy formula, which according to Dickman, will only declare a child eligible for special education if they fail to achieve, as predicted, in reference to other children who share similar intellectual potentials. Dickman (2001) opposes such a view and argues that it is effectively rewarding those who cure, and overlooks those who prevent, simply because prevention is not quantifiable. This, he concludes, implicitly sends the wrong signal to the already counter-productive prevalent system of special education. Flowers et al. (2000) conclude that employing the ability–achievement discrepancy construct 'contributes little to our understanding of dyslexia . . . in fact it may be harmful as it promotes a "wait to fail" approach rather than one of early identification and early intervention' (Flowers et al. 2000: 67).

In defence of the use of IQ, Thomson (2001), nevertheless, argues that 'it is quite clear that it is possible to examine the relationship between intelligence, however imprecisely measured, and reading' (Thomson 2001: 49), although he fails to elaborate on what intelligence means and what constitutes intelligence in this context or what are the best tests available to measure it. Friedenberg (1995) disagrees and argues that intelligence, by its very nature, is a construct; i.e., it is not a physical characteristic like height which can be measured directly and it is not simple to develop a test to measure a level of intelligence. Friedenberg (1995) explains that because intelligence is a construct, psychologists must identify behaviours that reflect intelligence and develop tests of these behaviours. To be certain that these really measure the desired characteristics, psychologists must reverse the process and examine the relationship between scores on the tests and other independent measures. Friedenberg (1995) concludes that 'without additional data to confirm that the tests measure intelligence, it is impossible to know what the tests really measures' (Friedenberg 1995: 252).

Other researchers however share Thomson's argument and consider measures of IQ to be indispensable in dyslexia assessment and diagnosis (Gardner, 1994; Stein, 2001; Turner and Nicholas, 2000). Turner and Nicholas insist that the IQ component of any dyslexia assessment test 'though sometimes a distraction has a serious statistical utility' (Turner and Nicholas 2000: 21), while Gardner claims that a high number of research studies which have been carefully planned do in fact support the use of intellectual abilities tests and their usefulness in predicting children's successes either at school or in higher education. However, Gardner confirms that the latter do not 'of themselves take account of other factors important in determining success, such as motivation and perseverance' (Gardner 1994: 89). For basic psychometric and other important statistical reasons those in favour of the use of an IQ component in dyslexia assessment have argued that one needs a general mental abilities factor, often referred to as 'G', which is considered a higher order general factor in intelligence. This view of intelligence is based on a theory which was originally proposed by Spearman in 1927 (cited in Doyle, 2002) who had hypothesized that intelligence consists of two parts he called factors. The first part is the general factor which he referred to as the general mental ability and the second part is made up of various specific factors. Spearman claimed that there is only one general factor which, he argued, is found in almost all the population. Specific factors are the various abilities required for different kinds of mental tasks, which explains why some individuals are good in verbal abilities while poor in mathematical skills and vice versa (Doyle, 2002). The general factor is the primary point of argument in the dyslexia field. Arguing for its use, Turner (1997) and Doyle and Nicholas (2002) maintain that minimal intelligence or general cognitive and/or mental abilities must be assessed in order to distinguish between underachievers and dyslexics. Without such a critical differentiation, no dyslexia diagnosis will be reliable. Turner and Nicholas (2000) argue that researchers uncomfortable with cognitive discrepancy have based their criticism for the use of IQ in dyslexia testing on a 'precise analysis of diagnostic methodology, rather than on generalized objections to the measurement of individual differences in ability' (Turner and Nicholas 2000: 24).

However, IQ testing is often saturated in verbal instructions, potentially making it counter-productive when assessing language-related learning problems. Reid and Kirk (2001) explain that the nature of the conventional IQ test means that some subtests are challenging for dyslexic individuals and that the aggregate score may not represent the individual's real intellectual ability. Miles (1996) also makes this point, arguing that dyslexics are 'strong on some tasks and relatively weak on others' (Miles, 1996: 177). Therefore, combining scores to produce a global IQ may mean that we underestimate the potential of the child and conclude that the child is not dyslexic, but rather is presenting reading skills commensurate with their intellectual abilities. Miles (1996) worries that some researchers take the concept of global IQ for granted, uncritically citing IQ figures without paying any attention to the sub-skills that make up the IQ figure.

Additionally, Frith (1997) also disputes the use of IQ in developmental dyslexia definitions and claims that for a discrepancy to be found, the child has to have a relatively high IQ test score, which introduces a bias against less able dyslexics. Siegel, who had started the whole debate, maintained that 'calculating an IQ–discrepancy seems an illogical way of calculating whether or not there is a learning disability' (cited in Thomson 2001: 49). Siegel argued that various measures of IQ do not measure intelligence, but rather measure factual knowledge as well as other skills such as expressive language ability and short-term memory, which may be improved through literacy experience. Siegel concluded that the implications of this for dyslexic children would be that 'their scores in relation to factual knowledge, expressive language and short-term memory will provide an artificially depressed IQ score' (cited in Reid 1998: 36–37).

Bakker and Satz (1970) claimed that defects in experimental design and methodology implemented to identify and diagnose dyslexia are responsible for causing confusion over the disorder. They reported that there are various studies based on heterogeneous clinical samples including children from socially and educationally deprived areas. In their opinion, these children, by definition, are unrepresentative of developmental dyslexia. Catts and Kamhi (1999) investigated the methodological issues used in identifying dyslexics, and indicated the specific issue of statistical regression. They concluded that because of regression towards the mean, calculation of IQ–achievement discrepancy 'results in the over identification of dyslexia in students with high IQs and under identification of students with low IQs' (Catts and Kamhi 1999: 61). Siegel and Himel (1998) provided evidence that IQ is related to socio-economic status, which is a measure, at least in part, of the individual's environment. Consequently, individuals from more disadvantaged environments would be expected to achieve lower scores on IQ tests. Vellutino (1979) was of the same opinion and he noted that if the theory of dyslexia is that children are characterized by basic deficiency in visual–spatial orientation, then it might be counterproductive to employ, for selection criteria, an IQ test highly saturated with demands requiring spatial reasoning and visual orientation. On the other hand, Frith (1997) claimed that while the behavioural definition of dyslexia as an unexpected reading failure (a discrepancy between the attainment and abilities of individuals) has been frequently attacked on theoretical and statistical background, it has, in fact, been extremely helpful. She maintained that, 'objectively measured performance elevates discussion of dyslexia from an unspecified complaint that may be in the mind of the beholder to a reality that is there for all to see' (Frith 1997: 1).

To sum up, researchers who argued forcefully against the IQ–reading discrepancy criteria view such a discrepancy as based on an outdated and indefensible construct (IQ) which does not differentiate between the reading skills of different groups of poor readers and which has no obvious implications for differential teaching strategies. As such, there is no reason to maintain the IQ-based diagnostic process. However, those who have supported the use and validity of IQ measurements, and their application in dyslexia assessments, point to data indicating that psychometric assessment generally, and IQ measurement in particular, have made great progress and many studies have replicated the validity and the reliability of employing IQ measures when identifying dyslexia. Removing IQ measurement from the assessment process will lead to less reliable procedures.

Dyslexia and IQ–reading discrepancy: the way ahead

Although a large number of researchers now view the use of IQ–reading discrepancy criteria in dyslexia definition and assessment as inappropriate, not every one has the same opinion regarding the use of non-verbal reasoning and reading discrepancy in dyslexia testing. Doubts which have been cast on the role of intelligence tests 'have resulted in some controversy on their use in a diagnosis of dyslexia' (Reid 1998: 3). A large number of researchers now reject the use of IQ in dyslexia assessment (Vellutino 1979; Siegel 1989; Stanovich 1996; Reid 1998; Peer and Reid 2000; Smythe et al., 2004). Mather (1998) argues that our knowledge of cognitive correlates of dyslexia has increased to the extent that the 'practice of using aptitude–achievement discrepancy formula as the sole determining criterion for the identification of individuals must be discontinued' (Mather 1998: 7). Frith (1999) suggests that 'it is time to move away from the restricting definitions of reading failure by reference to arbitrary cut off points on behavioural tests and arbitrary discrepancies between test scores' (Frith 1999: 199).

However, Miles (1994) argues that 'tests of reading and of intelligence and the use of discrepancy and exclusionary criteria are not so much wrong as in need of modifications' (Miles 1994: 105). Berninger (2001) indicates that just because IQ–achievement discrepancy is not adequate, it does not mean that it is irrelevant to learning differences (Berninger 2001). Tonnessen (1995) claims that a discrepancy can be informative when it suggests a specific difficulty, although absence of a discrepancy should not be used to exclude the possibility of a difficulty. Nicolson (2001), on the other hand, suggests that the advantage of the label 'dyslexia' is that it has 'no intrinsic meaning, for it does not in itself provide information on causes or whether it describes visual, phonological, motor or any combination' (Nicolson 2001: 5). Although it is now clear that there are some serious doubts and problems associated with the use of IQ–reading discrepancy in defining dyslexia, the abandonment of IQ as an exclusionary criterion has not gained wide acceptance. This, as Catts and Kamhi argue, is not surprising given that 'normal or above normal intelligence has always been a defining characteristic of dyslexia' (Catts and Kamhi 1999: 62). This is, of course, in addition to the fundamental role IQ tests play in eligibility for special education. What has helped this view of intellectual abilities tests is the 'overwhelming success in their practical application' (Gardner 1994: 89).

Another reason for the continued use of IQ in dyslexia assessments is the lack of consensus about an alternative. For example, some have suggested that it might be possible to replace or supplement traditional IQ-discrepancy with other types of more relevant discrepancies such as single word reading and listening comprehension (see Joshi and Aaron, 2008). However, such alternative discrepancy methods have rarely been accepted in educational circles. The main alternative, therefore, which has gained some level of acceptance is to continue to use the IQ test, but rather than using it as a way of simply measuring global IQ, utilizing it as a way of measuring sub-skills that may be diagnostically related to dyslexia and hence to arrive at a better understanding of the areas of strengths and weaknesses of the individual being assessed. Probably the best known of these is the assessment of sub-skill from the WISC to produce the ACID Profile (see Vargo et al., 1995). This IQ-based sub-skill profiling method is based on the assumption that dyslexics will show poor performance in the sub-tests of Arithmetic, Coding, Information and Digit Span, whereas they will show average or good scores on other sub-tests. However, other profiles of sub-tests, such as ACID and SCAD, have also been suggested (Thomson, 2001), as well as different combinations of sub-tests scores (e.g., Kaufman, 1994). However, such methods have been criticized since they may not identify all dyslexics (see Frederickson, 1999, for problems with the ACID profile) as well as because the sub-skills are suggested as being related to the underlying problem associated with dyslexia, rather than a direct measure of the deficit and it would be more reliable to measure the deficit directly. For example, the Arithmetic sub-test is seen as indicative of underlying working memory deficits. But, if this is the area of deficit to be identified, why not use direct measures of working memory functioning, rather than measures that rely on ability in mathematics? This leads to a difference in view about using IQ tests as a well-standardized measure of related skills versus using less well-standardized measures of direct skills. One solution here would seem to be to increase the availability of well standardized alternatives. Snowling (2000) proposes that for the sake of clinical utility, the discrepancy criteria needs to be substituted by positive diagnostic indicators in order to allow practitioners to identify children who 'show early or residual signs of dyslexia that require intervention and do not depend solely on the extent of the child's reading problem' (Snowling 2000: 25). However, until these positive diagnostic indicators are fully explored and reliably measured, the arguments for using IQ tests as a basis of indication will be difficult to fully refute. As Turner (1997) points out, it is 'dyslexia, not IQ, [that] is the focus of the assessment and an IQ-attainment discrepancy is descriptive, rather than definitional, and insufficient by itself for diagnostic purposes' (Turner 1997: 37).

References

Aaron, P. (1994). Deferential diagnosis of reading disabilities. In G. Hales (ed.), Dyslexia Matters (pp. 3–18). London: Whurr.

Bakker, D.J. and Satz, P. (1970). Specific Reading Disability. Advances in Theory and Method. Rotterdam: Universitaire Pers Rotterdam.

Berninger, V. (2001). Understanding the 'lexia' in dyslexia: A multidisciplinary team approach to learning disabilities. Annals of Dyslexia, 51, 23–48.

Blachman, B.A. (ed.) (1997). Foundations of Reading Acquisition and Dyslexia: Implications for Early Intervention. Mahwah, NJ: Lawrrence Erlbaum Associates.

British Psychological Society (1999). Dyslexia, Literacy and Psychological Assessment. Report of a Working Party of the Division of Educational and Child Psychology of the British Psychological Society. Leicester: British Psychological Society.

Catts, H. and Kamhi, A. (1999). Language and Reading Disabilities. Massachusetts: Allyn and Bacon.

Critchley, M. (1970). *The Dyslexic Child*. London: Heinemann.

Crombie, M. (2001). Dyslexia: its early days. *Dyslexia Contact, 20* (2), 9.

Dickman, E. (2001). Dyslexia and the aptitude-achievement discrepancy controversy. *Perspectives, 27* (1), 23–27.

Doyle, J. (2002). *Dyslexia: An Introductory Guide 2nd edition*. London: Whurr.

Ellis, A. (1993). *Reading, Writing and Dyslexia: a Cognitive Analysis*. East Sussex: Psychology Press.

Flowers, L., Meyer, M., Lovato, J. and Wood, F. (2000). Does third grade discrepancy status predict the course of reading development? *Annals of Dyslexia, 50*, 49–71.

Frederickson, N. (1999). The ACID test – or is it? *Educational Psychology in Practice, 15*, 2–8.

Friedenberg, L. (1995). *Psychological Testing: Design, Analysis and Use*. Massachusetts: Allyn and Bacon.

Frith, U. (1997). Brain, mind and behaviour in dyslexia. In C. Hulme and M. Snowling (eds), *Dyslexia: Biology, Cognition and Intervention* (pp. 1–19). London: Whurr.

Frith, U. (1999). Paradoxes in the definition of dyslexia. *Dyslexia, 5* (4), 192–214.

Gardner, P. (1994). Diagnosing dyslexia in the classroom: A three stage model. In G. Hales (ed.) *Dyslexia Matters*. London: Whurr.

Hornsby, B. (1995). *Overcoming Dyslexia: A Straightforward Guide for Families and Teachers*. London: Martin Duntiz.

Joshi, M. and Aaron, P.G. (2008). Assessment of literacy performance based on the Componential Model of Reading. In G. Reid, A. Fawcett, F. Manis and L. Siegel (eds) *The Sage Dyslexia Handbook*. London: Sage Publishing.

Kaufman, A.S. (1994). *Intelligent Testing with the WISC-III*. New York: Wiley.

Lyon, G. (2003). *The NICHD research programme in reading development, reading disorders and reading instructions*. Retrieved 04/01/2004, from http://www.ncld.org/research/keys99_nichd.cfm

Malatesha, R. and Aaron, P. (1982). *Reading Disorders: Varieties and Treatments*. London: Academic Press.

Mather, N. (1998). Relinquishing aptitude–achievement discrepancy: the doctrine of misplaced precision. *Perspectives*, 4–7.

McLoughlin, D., Leather, C. and Stringer, P. (2002). *The Adult Dyslexic: Interventions and Outcomes*. London: Whurr.

Miles, T. (1994). Towards a rationale for diagnosis. In G. Hales (ed.), *Dyslexia Matters* (pp. 101–108). London: Whurr.

Miles, T. (1996). Do dyslexic children have IQs? *Dyslexia, 2* (3), 175–178.

Nicolson, R. (2001). Developmental dyslexia into the future. In A. Fawcett (ed.), *Dyslexia: Theory and Good Practice* (pp. 1–35). London: Whurr.

Peer, L. and Reid, G. (2000). *Multilingualism, Literacy and Dyslexia: A Challenge for Educators*. London: David Fulton.

Reid, G. (1998). *Dyslexia: A Practitioner's Handbook* (Second ed.). Chichester: Wiley and Sons.

Reid, G. (2002). Definitions of dyslexia. In M. Johnson and L. Peer (ed.), *The Dyslexia Handbook 2002* (pp. 68–74). Reading: The British Dyslexia Association.

Reid, G. and Kirk, J. (2001). *Dyslexia in Adults: Education and Employment*. Chichester: Wiley and Sons.

Samuelson, S. (2002). Reading disabilities among very-low-birthweight children: Implications for using different exclusion criteria in defining dyslexia. In C. Von Euler and E. Hjelmquist (eds), *Dyslexia and Literacy* (pp. 39–53). London: Whurr.

Share, D.L. (1996). Word recognition and spelling processes in specific reading disabled and garden-variety poor readers. *Dyslexia, 2*, 167–174.

Siegel, L. (1989). Why we do not need intelligence test scores in the definition and analyses of learning disabilities. *Journal of Learning Disabilities, 22* (8), 514–518.

Siegel, L. and Himel, N. (1998). Socioeconomic status, age and the classification of dyslexics and poor readers: The dangers of using IQ scores in the definition of reading disability. *Dyslexia, 4* (2), 90–103.

Singleton, C. (2002). Dyslexia: Cognitive factors and implications for literacy. In G. Reid and J. Wearmouth (eds), *Dyslexia and Literacy: Theory and Practice* (pp. 115–129). Chichester: Wiley and Sons.

Smythe, I. and Everatt, J. (2000). Dyslexia diagnosis in different languages. In L. Peer and G. Reid (eds), *Multilingualism, Literacy and Dyslexia: A Challenge for Educators* (pp. 12–21). London: David Fulton.

Smythe, I., Everatt, J. and Salter, R. (eds) (2004). *The International Book of Dyslexia: A Cross-language Comparison and Practice Guide* (second edn). Chichester: Wiley and Sons.

Snowling, M. (2000). *Dyslexia* (second edn). Oxford: Blackwell.

Stanovich, K.E. (1988). Explaining the difference between the dyslexic and the garden-variety poor reader: The phonological-core variable–difference model. *Journal of Learning Disabilities*, 21, 590–612.

Stanovich, K.E. (1991). Discrepancy definitions of reading disability: Has intelligence led us astray? *Reading Research Quarterly, 36*, 7–29.

Stanovich, K.E. (1994). Phenotypic profile of children with reading disabilities: A regression-based test of the phonological-core variable–difference model. *Journal of Learning Disabilities, 21*, 590–612.

Stanovich, K.E. (1996). Towards a more inclusive definition of dyslexia. *Dyslexia*, 2 (3), 154–66.

Stein, J. (2001). The magnocellular theory of developmental dyslexia. *Dyslexia*, 7 (1), 12–36.

Thomson, M. (2001). *The Psychology of Dyslexia: A Handbook for Teachers*. London: Whurr.

Tonnessen, F.E. (1995) On defining dyslexia. *Scandinavian Journal of Educational Research* 39, 139–56.

Torgeson, J.K. (1989). Why IQ is Relevant to the definition of learning disability. *Journal of Learning Disabilities, 22* (8), 484–486.

Torgesen, J.K. (2004). Preventing early reading failure. *American Educator*, Fall.

Turner, M. (1997). *Psychological Assessment of Dyslexia*. London: Whurr.

Turner, M. and Nicholas, A. (2000). From assessment to teaching: Building a teaching program from a psychological assessment. In J. Townend and M. Turner (eds), *Dyslexia in Practice* (pp. 67–91). New York: Kluwer Academic and Plenum Publishers.

Vargo, F.E., Grosser, G.S. and Spafford, C.S. (1995). Digit span and other WISC-R scores in the diagnosis of dyslexia in children. *Perceptual and Motor Skills*, 80, 1219–1229.

Vellutino, F. (1979). *Dyslexia: Theory and Research*. Massachusetts: MIT Press.

3

Dyslexia and glue ear
A sticky educational problem

Lindsay Peer

This chapter

- provides a working definition of dyslexia and indicates its links and overlap with glue ear, investigates the impact of glue ear on language development
- discusses its on-going links into education
- highlights the most effective provision for teaching.

Introduction

Little has been done over the years to investigate the impact which glue ear might have on educational success of children in the early years – the years which are so crucial for language learning and subsequent literacy acquisition. This has possibly been due to the limitations imposed on funding regimes which in many countries separated education from speech and language, restricting research. Now that cross-disciplinary work and research is being undertaken, it is my view that there is a need to investigate the impact of glue ear on language development and its on-going links into education – and then make provision for teaching.

Whilst it is clear within the dyslexic cohort that there is a high percentage who suffered from glue ear as children, the sub-group of bi/multilingual children within this grouping has not generally been identified, due to the misperception that 'other' language(s) have caused any difficulties in learning. By default, these students are often ignored, fall within low achieving groups of learners and unnecessarily end up on Special Needs registers.

Other authors in this textbook write about dyslexia in great depth. In this chapter I intend to establish my working definition of dyslexia and show its links and overlaps with glue ear – the unrecognised cause of difficulties related to learning for so many in the education system today.

Dyslexia

Understanding of the term 'dyslexia' has altered considerably since it was first recorded in the *British Medical Journal* of November 1896 by the General Practitioner, Dr Pringle-Morgan. For the purposes of this chapter, I will use the British Psychological Society definition (1999) which is as follows: 'Dyslexia is evident when accurate and fluent word reading and/or spelling develops very incompletely or with great difficulty.' There are some researchers today who consider dyslexia to be solely a reading problem, but very many see it is a wider issue. Studies have been carried out investigating areas related to cognitive development, phonological deficits, magnocellular deficits, automisation deficits, developmental and educational psychology, genetics and neuroscience to name but a few. Some work has been carried out on bilingual learners where consideration must be given as to the cultural and linguistic background of the dyslexic child and an understanding of the impact of additional languages has to be made for those functioning in more than one language. It is clear that the aetiology of dyslexia is complex and that there is still much to learn.

Glue ear (Otitis media)

In different areas of the world and even within the same country, there has been no standard use of one definition (Daly, 1997). For the purposes of this chapter, as it encompasses all the diseases of the Otitis Media continuum, I will use a common definition which is 'Otitis media: An inflammation of the middle ear.' In a healthy child, the area in the middle ear is filled with air allowing for the flow of sound to the middle ear. When a child has glue ear it is either partially or completely filled with a sticky fluid which reduces the transmission of sound resulting in fluctuating hearing. It can be observed in children who show no signs of illness as well as in those who do; this is a concern as it could be that a child's hearing is significantly impaired without anyone – parent, teacher or psychologist – being aware of the loss.

Friel-Palti and Finitzo (1990) suggest that hearing loss during the first two years of life may result in a delay in emerging receptive or expressive language or both. Gravel and Wallace (1995) maintain that although communication skills may appear normal for this group of children on entry to school, other auditory-based deficits may emerge in the classroom situation. They, and others, suggest that there are weaknesses associated with listening comprehension, academic achievement and even attention and behavioural difficulties.

Glue ear is an on-going condition for large numbers of children, meaning that they experience significant hearing loss as well as extreme discomfort and/or pain in the ears over a lengthy period of time. In cases of those experiencing recurrent episodes, weeks, if not months, of life will be affected. It may also lead to a lack of concentration as well as an inability to process the fine sounds that are necessary for auditory perception and speed of processing which is a major key to language learning. Tallal (1999) states that: 'Timing cues present in the acoustic waveform of speech provide critical information for the recognition and segmentation of the on-going speech signal.' It would appear that in children under one year of age, the length of resolution of glue ear is longer than it is for older children. It has been suggested by some researchers that significant problems with glue ear at such a young age are likely to lead to chronic problems at a later stage (Marchant et al., 1984).

As it is so often treated solely as a medical condition, the longer term educational implications for some children are not understood and hence not acted upon. Even when medical tests show that levels of hearing have returned to normal limits, the former presence of glue ear may have a direct impact on learning, particularly on the development of language and literacy throughout early childhood, adolescence and into adulthood.

Very often children who have suffered glue ear and have undergone ventilation of the middle ear by the insertion of grommets, experience hearing levels that return to normal very soon after the operation. Teachers and psychologists often assume that the learner no longer experiences difficulty with auditory processing once treatment has taken place and medical readings appear normal. However, deficits in complex auditory processing may well persist long after hearing has returned to normal (Hall *et al.*, 1997).

Anecdotal discussion with head teachers, teachers and parents of dyslexic children in specialist dyslexia and other schools, has highlighted vast numbers of children reported to have suffered from serious bouts of ear infections leading to glue ear – one specialist school reported over 90 per cent. The effects of these weaknesses are even more apparent in the bi/multilingual child where specific sounds of different languages need fine hearing and acuity if learning and functioning are to be successful experiences.

There is an identifiable weakness for listeners with a history of glue ear, as opposed to normal listeners, when trying to identify sounds within complex auditory processes (Schilder, Snik, Straatman *et al.*, 1994). It is therefore reasonable to suggest that children experiencing such weakness are at a potential disadvantage in the average classroom. Trying to hear words spoken by the teacher whilst there are sounds being made by other learners in different places in the classroom will lead to an inability to process that which is being spoken. Glue ear appears to lead to a significant loss of auditory function for some people.

Even compensated dyslexic adults often find decoding of the written word a laborious task; throughout their lives, reading often remains troublesome. They are neither fluent nor automatic in their ability to identify words and report being tired and very slow at functioning when performing roles that require those skills. Many dyslexic people have a problem with speed of processing information which contributes to poorer functioning within the learning process. Stresses upon the system that supports speed of processing are exacerbated by a bilingual background and in some cases by residual glue ear.

A single bout of glue ear is a widespread condition in young children many of whom grow out of it and suffer little long term damage. When investigating numbers of children affected by repetitive bouts of the condition, Daly (1997) noted that when investigating school-based incidence, the numbers are as follows:

- Japan – 4 per cent – 15 per cent
- USA – 12 per cent
- Denmark – 16 per cent – 22 per cent
- UK – 20 per cent – 30 per cent
- Spain – 8 per cent
- Kuwait – 31 per cent

It must be remembered that definitions will influence statistics. However, compared with evidence internationally, within the dyslexic population, there is a significantly higher number than would be expected. Research (Peer, 2002) recorded that of 1000 people identified as dyslexic, 703 had experienced the condition to such a serious extent, that they had undergone surgery.

Personal experience of numerous cases over the years has led me to believe that there is a significant overlap between allergies, glue ear and dyslexia. Work with a speech, language and communication therapist to identify strengths and weaknesses and to provide a programme of intervention is most worthwhile.

Symptoms of glue ear in relation to learning

A cluster of the following should trigger referral; a child does not need to experience all of them in order for this to happen:

- Early speech, language or communication difficulties
- Confusion of letters and/or words especially when young
- Mishearing words in speech
- Difficulty in following a conversation/lesson/lecture when background noise is present
- Difficulties learning additional languages
- Spelling difficulties – omission of letters/sounds or phonetically spelled words
- Reading weaknesses – single word, pseudoword, comprehension
- Poor pragmatic language – children missing nuances of language, e.g. question mark
- Poor written expression
- Omission of words
- Incomplete multisyllabic words or sentences
- Confusion of tenses
- Poor use and understanding of words, expressions and terminology
- Delay in understanding subject specific terminology
- Weak general knowledge
- Tiredness and weariness
- Distractibility
- Lack of concentration
- Frustration
- Feelings of insecurity
- Difficulty following instructions
- Social isolation and loneliness
- Lack of understanding of playground rules.

Furthermore, there appears to be a strong link with co-existing allergies, particularly to milk, highlighting a possible weakness in the auto-immune system (Geschwind and Behan, 1982).

Medical treatment

Parents and/or schools will sometimes refer children to medical practitioners due to the difficulties outlined above. Treatments may include 'watchful waiting,' decongestants, anti-biotics or surgery.

Children who have had bouts of glue ear of such significance that it has led to the insertion of grommets have been deprived of much of the input needed for normal development in areas of language and literacy. Some children have required the insertion of several sets of grommets over the years due to a recurring problem. Such loss of hearing has the effect of causing a chain of difficulties in the development of phonological awareness, ultimately leading to difficulties with reading and spelling.

Medical practitioners should be apprised of the link between the condition and its potential ramifications on speech, language and education (Peer, 2005).

Processing speech

Speech is sometimes unclear and spoken at an inconsistent speed. Use of the vernacular, emphasis and so on will vary as will the level of sound production amongst speakers. There are additional influences which have the effect of altering perception and understanding, e.g. background noise, acoustics. If language becomes too difficult to follow, sufferers will often ignore a considerable amount of auditory information. Some children, as a result of glue ear, encode information incorrectly. So that they can appreciate that which is going on around them, high levels of concentration must be employed which may need to be maintained over a prolonged period of time; this is stressful. There are also other associated behaviours such as weariness, retreat, tiredness and clinging behaviour which are not unusual.

Auditory perception

There is undoubtedly a link between auditory perception, speed of processing and phonological skills which affects functioning in many dyslexic learners. Furthermore, there may be a negative influence leading to poor motivation, self-esteem and behaviour.

There are many children with dyslexia who have subtle difficulties in hearing, such as a high frequency hearing loss like 's' or a low frequency loss leading to difficulty recognising vowel sounds or consonants such as 'b.' However 'auditory perception' does not refer to hearing or acuity problems but to levels of auditory discrimination and coding. Wepman (1960), whose tests are still used by some today, suggested that auditory discrimination difficulties are due to developmental lags of speech perception and are partly dependent upon auditory acuity. Typically a child might find difficulties discriminating between 'pin' and 'pen.' Imagine the problems for a bilingual child whose first language has only one sound for the three soft vowels: a, e, u. We need to consider therefore, whether incorrect encoding is a problem of learning disability, auditory perception or linguistic confusion?

Phonological awareness and glue ear

Phonology is the part of language that underlies speech perception and speech production. It is the link between semantic, syntactic and morphological information. In order to acquire phonological awareness, a child must be able to perceive, store and analyse the characters of speech and language. A large body of evidence has shown a relationship between phonological awareness and reading ability. Studies such as that by Bradley and Bryant (1985) showed that performance on phonological tasks predicted reading skill. Goswami and Bryant (1990) asserted that both the segmentation factor and an awareness of rhyme in words causally relate to reading development and are in fact pre-requisites for it. Muter et al. (1998) agreed that the ability to segment contributes significantly to the ability to acquire reading but believe that it is the combination of this together with letter knowledge that is the best predictor of later reading ability. Studies showed that tasks such as verbal short-term memory (Jorm et al., 1984), speech rate (McDougall et al., 1994) and rapid automised naming (Bowers, 1995) are significant too. Whatever the underlying debates relating to phonological awareness, it is clear that there is a direct connection between it and the acquisition of literacy and language.

When auditory input is impaired, there is a significant link to educational failure. It would appear that this is exacerbated when there are bouts of glue ear. There are further significant issues when the child is learning to acquire fluency in more than one language. A child will then have to process sets of sounds and understand and apply rule systems which differ from language to language. Children with a history of glue ear seem eventually to acquire the phonology of their mother tongue. There may however be specific and detailed aspects of phonology which have not been researched which remain residual deficits and therefore problematic for individuals. Schwatrtz et al. (1997) suggest that there is still a significant amount of work to be done in the areas of speech perception, speech production and morphological acquisition if there is to be greater understanding of the effect of glue ear on phonological acquisition. They believe that many children who go on to exhibit speech and language disorders have a history of glue ear.

Tallal (1999) related the difficulties dyslexic individuals have in speech perception, phonological processing and phonological awareness to lower level auditory processing impairment. Studdert-Kennedy and Mody (1995) suggested that weak readers have poorly represented phonemic categories – the phoneme being the smallest meaningful segment of language and a fundamental element of the linguistic system.

Shaywitz (1996) noted that before words can be identified, understood, stored in memory or retrieved from it, they must first be broken down into their phonemic units by the phonological module of the brain. The process occurs automatically in spoken language, at a preconscious level, once people have been exposed to it. Reading reflects spoken language and must be learned at a conscious level. The task becomes one of transferring graphemes into their corresponding phonemes. The ability to do this depends initially upon the individual's understanding of the phonological structure of spoken words and then the understanding that the orthography represents the phonology. In some dyslexic children it is this last stage that is impaired supporting the phonological deficit hypothesis. In practice, this impairs the decoding of words preventing word identification. This in turn prevents access into the higher-order linguistic processes necessary for the comprehension of meaning from text. In some cases, it can also affect speech.

Speed of processing

For many dyslexic learners, but especially for those who use more than one language, weakness in speed of processing is often evident. It stems from a range of sources including:

- the stress of the overload of language exacerbated by short-term memory weaknesses, e.g. translation, information demanded at speed;
- the stress of attempting to remember the shape and patterns of letters which are specific to particular languages and then producing them at speed;
- the sequencing weaknesses which will be affected by differing language structures;
- the inability to 'hear' specific sounds which are new and poor auditory perception – leading to problems with speech and spelling;
- organizational weaknesses exacerbated by demands from differing linguistic codes;
- motor skill weakness exacerbated when languages are written in an unfamiliar way, e.g. letters not joined, words written in opposite directions.

It is now clearly established that children with dyslexia suffer difficulties in processing speed (Nicolson and Fawcett, 1994), in working memory (Gathercole and Baddeley, 1990) and in automisation of the skill (Nicolson and Fawcett, 1990). Whatever the academic debate surrounding phonological deficits, the question still remains to be answered as to why the problem exists. In view of the significant link between children who have poor functioning in language and literacy (not due to low cognitive levels) and the incidence of a history of glue ear within that cohort, I maintain that the existence of glue ear could be the root cause (Peer, 2002).

Poor short-term memory

McNamara and Wong (2002) identified that dyslexic students found significant difficulty both in reading and in comprehending text. Beyond difficulty related to phonological tasks, they noted that learners had significant difficulty retrieving everyday information. They hypothesized that this was due to poor working memory processing. Gathercole and Pickering (2000) also concluded that complex working memory skills are closely linked with children's academic performance in the early years of school. This will have clear implications both across the academic curriculum as well as daily living. Many researchers have noted a clear association between short-term memory weaknesses and dyslexia. Chasty (1989) analysed four main functions in the process of working memory:

- the provision of short-term memory in strategy dependent systems related to the five major senses which may be used in learning, but particularly auditory, motor and visual information processing;
- the facilitation of the encoding of incoming information for effective storage and retrieval in long-term memory using the strategies preferred by the learner;
- enabling the recall of already learned material from long-term memory and facilitating perception and problem-solving using the child's past experience;
- facilitating the automatic control of a previously learned skill, while other incoming or recalled information is processed simultaneously in the alternative sub-systems.

Research has shown that children with dyslexia and glue ear experience difficulties with short-term memory recall (Peer, 2002). They often find rote learning very difficult indeed. Poor perception of sound, slow processing of information, poor phonological weakness and a poor short-term memory will combine to have a direct and negative effect upon language and learning.

Glue ear leading to frustration

There is no doubt that when children cannot clearly hear that which is going on around them they may feel left out. At times, they are likely to either 'switch off' and withdraw from the situation or 'act out.' This can be very frustrating and disorientating for parents and teachers – as well as peers – as no-one quite knows when the child can and can't hear due to the fluctuating nature of the condition. The child him/herself may not even be aware when they are missing something.

It was suggested to me by an audiotometrist that children such as these could lose a substantial part of their hearing for up to eight weeks after a heavy cold. In such circumstances, weeks of work may be lost at school as a child struggles to follow – or gives up. Whilst an adult may develop strategies for dealing with such situations it may be that a child does not; they may even act out in rebellion in the classroom.

Children have told me that they been shouted at by adults for not listening and not following instructions when in fact they had not heard, could not remember or felt that everything had been spoken too quickly for them to follow. I was told that, at times, they had missed out on social activities as they had not heard them or had not grasped the rules of games in the playground. These people live with on-going frustration on a daily basis in whatever circumstances they find themselves. Children and adults have also reported experiencing on-going and varying levels of pain which interfere with the ability to cope with learning and daily functioning.

Particular challenges facing bi/multilingual speakers

Different parts of the brain are used according to the demands of the language. For example, when reading Chinese, children need to use visual memory in order to memorise hundreds of symbols representing words. This is processed by using a different part of the brain to that used by children learning a non-visually based language. However, it may still be that Chinese children experience specific difficulties in their own language, e.g. following speech spoken at speed and following instructions; they may also experience considerable difficulty learning a language such as English even if they appear to experience less difficulty in Chinese. Although they present in a non-conventional way, investigation still needs to take place. When bilingual children do not appear to be functioning effectively in school, questions need to be asked. All too often there are preconceived notions about the ability (or lack of ability) of specific cultural groups; or decisions are made about individuals without an attempt to understand the effects of linguistic background. As documented by (Peer and Reid, 2000):

> Teachers and psychologists have tended to ignore the difficulties in learning experienced by these students, because of the multiplicity of factors which are apparently relevant: a non-supportive home background resulting in different or impoverished language skills; unusual learning profile; apparently low intelligence (which sometimes arises out or insensitive testing); unbalanced speech development; and restricted vocabulary in one of more languages. These are assumed to be the relevant factors; that there might be a biological basis for children's reading, writing and spelling retardation is sometimes overlooked, with disastrous consequences.

Furthermore, it is clear that when these children are affected by a history of recurrent episodes of glue ear, even more strain is placed upon the processing system. Parents should be asked questions about hearing and ear infections which may have occurred many years previously in order to establish a history. They are unaware that they should report this to teachers as they feel that it is a medical problem, something that affected the child in the past and is therefore now irrelevant. Until we understand the full impact of glue ear on learning, children will be limited in their potential to achieve.

Conclusions

The combination of glue ear and dyslexia is as relevant to monolingual learners as it is to those who are bi/multilingual. The loss of consistent hearing at a young age may well lead to lack of normal development in language and literacy. It has the effect of causing a chain of difficulties in the development of phonological awareness, leading to reading and spelling difficulties. Bouts of ear infections may also lead to difficulties with balance, leading, e.g. to travel sickness, and may possibly cause ocular motor difficulties. It may be that glue ear, occurring at a time when auditory and vestibular skills are developing rapidly, may of itself be sufficient to lead to the symptoms of dyslexia.

It is important to add the issue of behaviour to the discussion. It is quite common for dyslexic children to display signs of anxiety and often poor behaviour (Peer, 2000). This is often a reaction due to the frustration felt by that learner when demotivation and low self-esteem set in. Add to this the discomfort and exclusion that so many of them feel over the course of time and the problems outlined above are exacerbated.

There is a need to identify and provide for those children experiencing dyslexic-type difficulties as early as possible if they are to make the greatest progress in their language and learning. The same is necessary for those who have experienced glue ear. The medical diagnosis when the child is very young could be seen as an indicator of possible impending difficulties, particularly if it is known that other members of the family have experienced difficulties in areas of reading, spelling, writing, speaking or mathematics. In such cases, pro-active steps should be taken to prepare the child in the pre-requisites for learning such as phonological skills, development of language and listening and memory skills. Should it happen that the child does not have difficulties with learning, additional training will do no harm.

Contact needs to be made with those who understand the range of languages that our learners experience so that we can understand the structures and demands of each and their correlation. Also, explanation to parents, teachers and medical professionals should be given, listing the early signs of glue ear and dyslexia and the potential link between the two, to enable children to be referred for assessment and support to be put in place as early as possible. Research needs to take place so that the co-morbidity of conditions is further investigated and so that tests are developed and provision is put in place.

References

Bowers, P.G. (1995). Tracing symbol naming speed's unique contributions to reading disabilities over time. *Reading and Writing, 7*, 189–216.

Bradley, L. and Bryant, P.E. (1985). *Rhyme and Reason in Reading and Spelling*. Ann Arbour: University of Michigan Press.

Chasty, H. (1989). Lecture, *Dyslexia Institute*, London.

Daly, K.A. (1997). Definition and epidemiology of Otitis media. In J.E. Roberts, I.F. Wallace and F.W. Henderson (eds) *Otitis Media in Young Children: Medical, Developmental and Educational Considerations* (pp. 14–15). Baltimore, Maryland: Paul Brookes Publishing Company Inc.

Friel-Palti, S. and Finitzo, T. (1990). Language learning in a prospective study of Otitis media with effusion in the first two years of life. *Journal of Speech and Hearing Research, 33*, 188–194.

Gathercole, S.E. and Baddeley, A.D. (1990). Phonological memory deficits in language disordered children: Is there a causal connection? *Journal of Memory and Language, 29*, 336–360.

Gathercole, S.E. and Pickering, S.J. (2000). Working memory deficits in children with low achievements in the national curriculum at 7 years of age. *British Journal of Educational Psychology, 70*, 177–194.

Geschwind, N. and Behan, P.O. (1982). Left-handedness: Association with immune disease, migraine and developmental learning disorder. *Proceedings of the National Academy of Sciences, 799*, 5097–5100.

Goswami, U. and Bryant, P.E. (1990). *Phonological Skills and Learning to Read*. London: Erlbaum.

Gravel, J.S. and Wallace, I.F. (1995). Early Otitis media, auditory abilities and educational risk. *American Journal of Speech-Language Pathology*, 4, 89–94.

Hall, J.W., Grose, J.H. and Drake, A.F. (1997). Effects of Otitis media with effusion on auditory perception. In F.W. Henderson (eds) *Otitis Media in Young Children: medical developmental, and educational considerations*. Baltimore, MD: Paul Brookes Publishing.

Jorm, A.F., Share, D.L., MacLean, R. and Matthews, R. (1984). Phonological confusability in short-term memory for sentences as a predicator of reading ability. *British Journal of Psychology, 36*, 355–362.

McDougall, S., Hulme, C., Ellis, A.W. and Monk, A. (1994). Learning to Read: The role of short-term memory and phonological skills. *Journal of Experimental Child Psychology, 58*, 112–133.

McNamara, J. and Wong, B. (2002). Memory for Everyday Information in Students with Learning Disabilities. Presentation to the 26th Conference of the International Academy for Research in Learning Disabilities. Washington.

Marchant, C.D., Shurin, P.A., Turczyk, V.A., Wasikowski, D.E., Tutuhasi, M.A. and Kinney, S.E. (1984). Course and outcome of Otitis media in early infancy: A prospective study, *Journal of Paediatrics, 104*, 826–831.

Muter, V., Hulme, C., Snowling, M. and Taylor, S. (1998). Segmentation, not rhyming predicts early progress in learning to read. *Journal of Experimental Psychology, 73*, 139–158.

Nicolson, R.I. and Fawcett, A.J. (1990). Automaticity: A new framework for dyslexia research? *Cognition, 30*, 159–182.

Nicolson, R.I. and Fawcett, A.J. (1994). Reaction times and dyslexia. *Quarterly Journal of Experimental Psychology, 47A*, 29–48.

Peer, L. (2000). Dyslexia and its manifestations in the secondary school. In L. Peer and G. Reid (eds) *Dyslexia: Successful Inclusion in Secondary Schools.* London: David Fulton.

Peer, L. (2002). *Dyslexia, Multilingual Speakers and Otitis Media.* PhD thesis, University of Sheffield.

Peer, L. (2005). *Glue Ear.* London: David Fulton.

Peer, L. and Reid, G. (2000). Dyslexia in adults and university students. In L. Peer and G. Reid (eds) *Multilingualism, Literacy and Dyslexia: A Challenge for Educators* (Section 4 pp. 153–202) London: David Fulton.

Schilder, A.G.M., Snik, A.D.M., Straatman, H. and van den Broek, P. (1994). The effect of Otitis media with effusion at pre-school age on some aspects of auditory perception at school age. *Ear and Hearing, 15*, 224–231.

Schwartz, R.G., Mody, M. and Petinou, K. (1997). Phonological acquisition and Otitis Media. In J.E. Roberts, I.F. Wallace and F.W. Henderson (eds) *Otitis Media in Young Children: Medical, Developmental and Educational Considerations* (pp. 126–127). Baltimore, Maryland: Paul Brookes Publishing Company Inc.

Shaywitz, S.E. (1996). Dyslexia. *Scientific American*, November, 99.

Studdert-Kennedy, M. and Mody, M. (1995). Auditory temporal perception deficits in the reading-impaired: A critical review of the evidence. *Psychonomic Bulletin and Review*, 2(4), 508–514.

Tallal, P. (1999). Lecture entitled *Language Impairments and their remediation* at the Center for Molecular and Behavioural Neuroscience, Rutgers University – JHU Cognitive Science Colloquium Series.

Wepman, J.M. (1960). Auditory discrimination, speech and reading. *The Reading Teacher, 14*, 245–247.

4

Visual stress and dyslexia

Chris Singleton

This chapter

- describes the characteristics of visual stress
- discusses the impact of visual stress on the ability to develop fluent reading skills
- discusses the causes of visual stress and how to identify it
- refers to different theoretical perspectives
- provides guidance for intervention.

Introduction

Visual stress is the subjective experience of unpleasant visual symptoms when reading (especially for prolonged duration) and in response to some other visual stimuli. This is a surprisingly common condition: although reported rates of prevalence vary according to the criteria and type of sample used, incidence of visual stress in unselected samples is generally accepted to be about 20 per cent (Jeanes *et al.*, 1997; Kriss and Evans, 2005; Wilkins *et al.*, 1996). The symptoms of visual stress fall into two categories: first, discomfort (e.g. sore, tired eyes; headaches; photophobia); second, visual–perceptual distortions and illusions (e.g. illusions of shape, motion and colour in the text; transient instability of focus; double vision). These symptoms were first independently noted by Meares (1980) and Irlen (1983), who also both observed that the unpleasant effects can usually be alleviated by using colour, either in the form of acetate sheets placed over the text ('coloured overlays'), or tinted spectacles. Since its discovery, the condition has been given various labels, inclduing 'Meares–Irlen syndrome', 'visual discomfort', 'visual dyslexia' and 'scotopic sensitivity syndrome' (some of which are less suitable than others) but 'visual stress' is increasingly recognised as being the most appropriate term (Evans, 2001; Singleton and Henderson, 2007a; Wilkins, 2003).

Visual stress interferes with the ability to read for any reasonable duration and consequently children who suffer from this problem tend to avoid reading. As a result, they lack the amount of practice that is essential for the development of fluent decoding of text and good reading comprehension (Tyrell *et al.*, 1995). Practice enables decoding to become automatic, reading eye movements to become smooth and disciplined, and the brain to cope with processing and understanding large amounts of text. Consequently, although visual stress can occur in normal readers it is more often observed in poor readers (Jeanes *et al.*, 1997). If visual stress is not identified and dealt with early on, children are at risk of remaining unskilled readers, particularly when trying to understand longer and more complex texts. Adults who suffer from visual stress tend to steer clear of activities involving reading, which can have implications for education and employment. In higher education visual stress has been noted to be an increasingly common problem that interferes with students' studies (Grant, 2004).

Recent studies have revealed that the prevalence of visual stress is considerably higher in children and adults with dyslexia than in the rest of the population (Singleton and Trotter, 2005; Singleton and Henderson, 2006). Whiteley and Smith (2001) estimated the prevalence of visual stress in dyslexics to be in the region of 50 per cent, a figure that has turned out to be not very far from those reported in several recent studies. Using percentage increase in rate of reading with a coloured overlay as the criterion for assessing susceptibility to visual stress, Kriss and Evans (2005) found that 45 per cent of dyslexic children read 5 per cent faster with an overlay, compared with 25 per cent of non-dyslexic control children; when a more conservative criterion of 8 per cent increase in reading speed with an overlay was applied, these figures dropped to 34 per cent and 22 per cent, respectively. Using ViSS, a computer-based screening tool for visual stress, Singleton and Henderson (2007b) found that 41 per cent of dyslexic children in their sample showed high susceptibility to visual stress; the corresponding figure for the non-dyslexic control group was 23 per cent. White *et al.* (2006) found that 35 per cent of their sample of dyslexic children aged 8–12 years met criteria for visual stress while only 18 per cent of the non-dyslexic control group matched for non-verbal IQ met criteria for visual stress. Grant (2004) reported that of a sample of 377 university students referred for psychological assessment for dyslexia, 42 per cent showed strong evidence of visual stress and a further 34 per cent reported some visual stress symptoms.

These findings raises several important issues that will be the focus of this chapter, including theoretical issues regarding the relationships between dyslexia and visual stress, and professional issues regarding how visual stress can most efficiently be identified and treated, especially in dyslexics.

Causes of visual stress

The most widely supported theory of visual stress is that it is the result of a general over-excitation of the visual cortex due to hypersensitivity to contrast or pattern glare (see Evans, 2001; Wilkins, 2003). Wilkins's theory is that the visual cortex functions normally until strong physiological stimulation results in stimulation of neurons that are close together. These neurons share inhibitory neurons and hence normal inhibitory processes will be compromised if they all fire together because the availability of inhibitory neurotransmitter is reduced. The outcome is the triggering of other neurons that signal movement or colours, which are consequently experienced as illusions or hallucinations. In other words, the visual cortex works normally until stimulation is too strong, whereupon a catastrophic non-linear failure of inhibition occurs, which spreads to other neurons (Wilkins, 1995; Wilkins *et al.*, 2004b).

Potentially, any stimulus that creates square-wave on–off signals in the visual cortex can trigger these neural effects. Perhaps the most obvious examples are high contrast, rapidly flashing or flickering illumination such as strobe lighting, fluorescent lighting, CRT computer monitors with low refresh rate, and bright sunlight viewed through trees when moving in a vehicle. All these stimuli cause headaches in many people, especially those who suffer from migraine, and they also trigger seizures in people with photosensitive epilepsy (Wilkins, 1995). The most dramatic case of flashing stimuli on TV triggering epileptic seizures in children occurred in Japan in 1997, when a 'Pokemon' cartoon transmitted on TV resulted in 685 people (most of them children) being admitted to hospital. Of these, 560 were found to have had epileptic seizures and of these 76 per cent of these had no previous history of epilepsy. The epileptic seizures experienced by these children were subsequently shown to be attributable to intense, rapidly flashing red/blue colour changes (Harding, 1998). The same cartoon, when viewed in black-and-white did not provoke seizures (Tobimatsu *et al.,* 1999) Compared with non-affected children, significantly more affected children reported that they had been viewing very close to the screen and in an unlit or dimly lit room – i.e. under conditions of high contrast (Furusho *et al.*, 2002). After the Pokemon incident was understood, guidelines on the use of coloured flashing images on TV were revised (see Binnie *et al.*, 2002).

Similar effects have been reported with some computer and video games, which, in cases of photosensitive epilepsy, are often associated with the first reported epileptic seizure (Wilkins *et al.*, 2004a). About 80 per cent of epilepsy patients between the age of 7 and 19 years were found to spend greater than one hour per day playing videogames (Quirk *et al.*, 1995). Unlike TV, there are no guidelines regarding flashing images in computer games, but Nintendo and some other computer game manufacturers put warnings on their programs that they may be harmful if used by people who suffer from photosensitive epilepsy.

Geometric repetitive patterns, such as stripes, create square-wave on–off neural signals similar to those causes by flashing lights, which explains why such patterns can cause unpleasant somatic and perceptual side effects (McKay, 1957; McKay, Gerrits and Stassen, 1979; Wilkins and Nimmo-Smith, 1987). A proportion of people who suffer from photosensitive epilepsy also report that stationary gratings, stripes or checkered patterns, can trigger seizures, especially when there is a strong light/dark contrast in the pattern (Fisher *et al.*, 2005). Harding and Jeavons (1995) found that about 30 per cent of photosensitive patients were also sensitive to patterns. The incidence of a family history of migraine in children who benefit from coloured filters has been found to be twice that in children who do not (Maclachlan *et al.*, 1993).

Since text can resemble a pattern of stripes with visually stressful characteristics, this explains why it can provoke perceptual distortions and cause headaches. The visual grating created by moving the eyes across lines of print, especially where the pattern is glaring, can generate similar physiological effects to those created by flashing lights. These findings suggest a continuum of photosensitivity for people suffering from photosensitive epilepsy, migraine and visual stress. Individuals who suffer from visual stress (but not photosensitive epilepsy or migraine) would be regarded as 'moderately photosensitive', so that their symptoms are not as extreme as those of individuals who suffer from photosensitive epilepsy or migraine, and these symptoms are less easily triggered. Wilkins (1995, 2003) suggests that because the wavelength of light is known to affect neuronal sensitivity, the use of colour could reduce over-excitation, redistributing cortical hyperexcitability and thus reducing perceptual distortion and headaches.

Visual stress and the magnocellular system

An alternative perspective on visual stress comes from researchers investigating the magnocellular visual system. There are two types of cells found in the neural tracts between the retina and the visual cortex: *magnocells* are large cells that code information about contrast and movement; *parvocells* are smaller and code information about detail and colour. (The magno-cellular system is also sometimes known as the *transient system*, and the parvocelluar system as the *sustained system*.) Cooperation between these two systems enables us to perceive a stationary image when we move our eyes across a scene or a page of text. When reading, the eyes do not move smoothly across the page but in a series of very quick jumps (saccades) in order to fixate successive portions of the text. During saccades, which typically take about 20–40 milliseconds, vision is suppressed.

The magnocellular system plays several important roles in visual functioning, including control of eye movements, selective attention and visual search (Facoetti *et al.,* 2000; Iles *et al.,* 2003; Stein and Walsh, 1997; Steinman *et al.,* 1997; Vidyasagar, 1998; Vidyasagar and Pammer, 1999). Consequently it has generally been assumed that it is the magno system which suppresses information coming in via the parvo system during saccadic movements of the eyes, thus facilitating clear perception of text in successive visual fixations (Breitmeyer, 1993; Breitmeyer and Ganz, 1976). However, accumulating evidence suggests the opposite, i.e. that the *magno pathway* is suppressed during saccades, which would explain why we do not experience visual movement when moving the eyes from one fixation to another (Burr *et al.,* 1994; Parke and Skotton, 1999; Ross *et al.,*).

Many studies have reported deficits in magnocellular functioning in poor readers and dyslexics. For example, Cornelissen *et al.* (1995) found dyslexics to be significantly poorer than controls in perception of moving stimuli. Talcott *et al.* (1998) found dyslexics to have significantly higher thresholds for perceiving random dot kinematograms. Eden *et al.* (1996) found that dyslexics did not show activation of certain critical areas of the visual cortex that are normally activated by moving stimuli. Evans *et al.* (1994) reported a number of anomalies in the magnocellular processing of dyslexics, including in contrast sensitivity. These studies, and others like them, have provided the basis for the magnocellular deficit theory of dyslexia (Stein, 2001). However, reviewing 22 different studies of magnocellular functioning in dyslexics, Skottun (2000) found that only four were clearly in support of the hypothesis that dyslexia could be attributed to magno deficits. Deficits in motion perception are certainly not found in all dyslexics (e.g. Everatt *et al.,* 1999) or with all motion-perception tasks (e.g. Raymond and Sorensen, 1998). White *et al.* (2006) found that magnocellular tasks did not significantly discriminate dyslexic from control children; only two out of 23 dyslexic children showed deficits in visual motion while three out of 22 control children showed deficits in visual motion. Thus while it remains a possibility that a minority of dyslexics have deficits in magnocellular functioning, the evidence for the magnocellular theory of dyslexia is not convincing (Skottun, 2005).

However, deficits in the magnocellular visual system have also been suggested as the cause of visual stress. For example, Lovegrove and his colleagues (Lovegrove, 1991; Lovegrove *et al.,* 1986; Lovegrove *et al.,* 1990) hypothesized that an abnormality in the magnocellular subsystem causes visual stress by diminishing the inhibition of the parvocellular system after each saccade and thus the capacity to erase the previous visual image. While this might account for some of the symptoms experienced in visual stress (e.g. blurring of text, illusions of movement and eye strain) it is not clear how magno deficits could cause illusions of colour, nor how coloured overlays might work as a treatment. Nevertheless, Lovegrove's hypothesis has a number of supporters (e.g. Chase *et al.,* 2003; Cornelissen *et al.,* 1994; Livingstone *et al.,* 1991; Robinson and Foreman, 1999).

Threshold shift theory

The evidence reviewed in this chapter so far suggests that dyslexia and visual stress are probably quite different conditions. The magnocellular deficit theory (Stein, 2001) proposes a causal link between dyslexia and visual stress mediated by the visual system but, as we have seen in the previous section, this theory is undermined by conflicting evidence on impairment in visual motion processing amongst dyslexics and by probable misunderstanding of the inhibitory mechanisms in saccadic eye movements. Against this, a more convincing explanation is provided by the theory that visual stress is due to hyperactivation in the visual cortex caused by contrast or pattern glare (Wilkins, 1995, 2003). As far as dyslexia is concerned, the greatest weight of evidence is consistent with the phonological deficit theory (Farmer and Klein, 1995; Ramus, 2001; Ramus et al., 2003; Snowling, 2000; Vellutino et al., 2004; White et al., 2006). According to the phonological deficit view, the problems of the dyslexic arise not because of difficulties in visual processing but because of difficulties in mapping graphemic representations (letters and words) on to phonological representations (sounds) and in holding phonological information in working memory.

However, if we accept that dyslexia and visual stress are different conditions, an explanation still has to be found for the increased prevalence of visual stress amongst dyslexics compared with the general population. Singleton (2008b) has suggested that the link between dyslexia and visual stress may not necessarily be causal. Visual stress discourages inclination to practice reading, which will create a 'Matthew effect' (Stanovich, 1986), i.e. the gap between good and poor readers will progressively widen as a function of differences in reading experience. It is likely that the dyslexic person's lack of automaticity in word recognition (e.g. due to underlying deficits in phonology or memory) forces them to adopt techniques for processing text (e.g. detailed scrutiny of individual 'problem' words) that increase their sensitivity to the physical characteristics of the print. In turn, this will naturally tend to make symptoms or effects of visual stress worse.

Susceptibility to visual stress varies from person to person: the majority of the population is only mildly susceptible (i.e. they have a *high threshold*), but nevertheless most people will experience visual stress under certain conditions, e.g. when viewing a particular visual pattern or seeing flashing lights. At the extreme end of the spectrum, individuals who suffer from photosensitive epilepsy or from migraine tend to be highly susceptible to visual stress (i.e. they have a *low threshold*). Singleton (2008b) has hypothesized that there is a continuum of physiological excitation (sensitivity) to visually stressful stimuli from low sensitivity to high sensitivity, which may be assumed (for the time being, at least) to be approximately normally distributed. All individuals will lie at a point somewhere on this continuum of physiological sensitivity as a consequence of genetically determined cortico-visual functioning. This point is their *physiological threshold for visual stress*. Individuals who suffer from migraine or photosensitive epilepsy will be near to the upper (high sensitive) end of this distribution and hence will have a low threshold. Singleton also posits another point on the continuum of physiological sensitivity that constitutes a *clinical threshold for visual stress*, i.e. a point above which individuals find that symptoms of visual stress interfere significantly and substantially with everyday functioning such that aversive action to mitigate symptoms is called for. For any given individual, there will be a difference (on the continuum of physiological sensitivity) between their physiological threshold for visual stress and their clinical threshold for visual stress. This difference is the amount to which the threshold for visual stress has been shifted as a result of non-physiological factors. It is anticipated that in almost every person the clinical threshold will be lower than the physiological threshold, because various factors will tend to increase sensitivity. The degree of *threshold shift* will be determined by the following factors:

1 *Cognitive factors* (e.g. dyslexia, reading problems; working memory) The greater the difficulty in decoding text and in holding the information in working memory while deriving meaning, the greater the sensitivity and lower the threshold.
2 *Demand factors* (e.g. demands created by education or employment circumstances) The greater the amount of reading the person has to do and the higher the cognitive load placed

on the person by that reading, the greater the sensitivity and lower the threshold.

3 *Ophthalmic and orthoptic factors* (e.g. amblyopia, astigmatism, diplopia, hypermetropia, nystagmus, detached retina, cataracts) The presence and severity of these visual problems will tend to increase sensitivity and lower the threshold.

4 *Optical factors* (e.g. lighting conditions, font type and size, line spacing, contrast, glare, flicker) The more that these factors diverge from the ideal, the greater the sensitivity and lower the threshold.

5 *Subjective factors* (e.g. personal tolerance of discomfort).

This theory of the relationship between dyslexia and visual stress can be called *threshold shift*. In a nutshell, this view is that dyslexia tends to increase a person's susceptibility to visual stress, because the effect of dyslexia is to shift the threshold for visual stress from higher to lower. The threshold shift theory is consistent with much of the current evidence on visual stress. It predicts that visual stress will be more prevalent in dyslexics and in other poor readers than in the rest of the population, which has been shown in many studies (e.g. Kriss and Evans, 2005; Singleton and Henderson, 2007b; White *et al.*, 2006). Connah (2008) tested undergraduate students with dyslexia using ViSS (Singleton and Henderson, 2007c) and found that the average increase in visual search time for this group on visually stressful items compared to that on non-visually stressful items was 33 per cent; the corresponding figure for non-dyslexic controls was 11 per cent.

The threshold shift theory also predicts that the more severe the reading/dyslexic difficulties, the greater the sensitivity to visual stress and the lower the threshold. This prediction has some support, Connah (2008), for example has found that severity of dyslexia accounts for a significant proportion (11 per cent) of the variance in severity of visual stress. The threshold shift theory also predicts that in situations where intensive reading is called for (e.g. at university), visual stress will be more prevalent. Evans and Joseph (2002) studied 113 unselected university students and found that 89 per cent reported beneficial perceptual effects of a chosen coloured overlay and these students read significantly faster with an overlay than without it. Eighty-one of the students experienced headaches, of which 44 per cent said they were associated with reading. These figures are higher than in studies of school children. In addition, the threshold shift theory predicts that people with ophthalmic and orthoptic problems are more likely to display symptoms of visual stress, which has been reported (Evans, 2001; Garzia and Nicholson, 1990).

Optical factors have also been found to influence susceptibility to visual stress. Hughes and Wilkins (2000) not only found that children's reading speed is a function of font size and characteristics of the text, but those children who were susceptible to visual stress were disproportionately affected by font size and text characteristics. Wilkins (2002) has observed that the levels of illumination often found in classrooms is up to four times that recommended by European standards, with the result that contrast is increased and children become more vulnerable to visual stress.

A further prediction of the threshold shift theory is that the distribution of reported symptoms of visual stress in unselected samples would not be normal, but would be positively skewed (i.e. an elongated right tail with mode<median<mean) because the non-physiological factors listed above will shift the threshold and extend the number of cases in the right (higher) tail of the distribution. There is some evidence for this: Singleton and Trotter (2005) and Singleton and Henderson (in preparation) found that the distribution of reported symptoms of visual stress in unselected samples [number of symptoms × severity of symptoms] has a positive skew. However, the threshold shift theory raises some unanswered questions. For example, we do not

know whether the use of coloured tints (a) *lowers the physiological threshold* making the person less sensitive and less likely to experience symptoms of visual stress, or (b) *lowers the clinical threshold*, thus reducing threshold shift and bringing the clinical threshold closer to the physiological threshold, or (c) a combination of these two effects.

Identifying visual stress

The techniques most commonly used for identifying visual stress rely either on the person reporting symptoms of visual stress or on them making a judgement that text is easier to read with a certain colour rather than another. Both these approaches carry the disadvantage of subjectivity, which, in turn, can result in unreliability of the measures.

The use of symptom questionnaires (e.g. Irlen, 1991; Conlon and Hine, 2000) has more justification when assessing adults (Evans and Joseph, 2002; Singleton and Trotter, 2005) than when assessing children, who can be suggestible and/or unreliable in their reports of symptoms (Northway, 2003). Children who suffer from the condition do not necessarily know they have a problem, and if they do report symptoms these may not always be accurate. Many adults who suffer from visual stress fail to appreciate why they find reading so tiring, or notice particular symptoms, and may not realise that this problem affects their work efficiency.

Assessment of whether colour makes reading more comfortable may be carried out using either overlay screening or an *Intuitive Colorimeter*, which is an apparatus in which the optimal colour of illumination for reading can be determined from the whole colour range (Wilkins *et al.*, 1992). In overlay screening, which is the most widely-used method to identify visual stress (Tyrrell *et al.*, 1995; Wilkins, 1995; Wilkins *et al.*, 2001), pairs of overlays from a set of about 10–12 are successively compared in order to determine the colour (or, if necessary, combination of colours) that is perceived to be most comfortable for reading. The number of colours is therefore restricted to probably fewer than 30, compared with the full range in the case of the colorimeter. However, whichever tool is used, the main snag with this approach is that – given the choice – most children, as well as adults, will select a colour, even though many of them don't really need it. Furthermore, while colour is an effective treatment for most people with visual stress, it does not work for all (Evans and Joseph, 2002; Singleton and Trotter, 2005), so not everyone with visual stress will be detected in an overlay screening. Wilkins *et al.* (2001) found that of a normal sample of children aged 8–11 years, 60 per cent chose an overlay. Using a slightly wider age range (5–11 years) Jeanes *et al.* (1997) found that 53 per cent of children chose an overlay. Evans and Joseph (2002) found that 88 per cent of an unselected sample of university students chose an overlay. In most studies, however, after two to eight months, voluntary sustained use is generally found to have dropped to between 20–30 per cent. For an adult that may not be of great concern – we can safely assume that if they stop using an overlay then that is probably because they don't feel any real benefit –although if tinted lenses have been prescribed and then just left in a drawer this is a significant waste of money. But where children are concerned, parents and teachers don't know if the child has just forgotten to use the glasses or the overlay, or is just being lazy, or whether they simply don't need them after all.

In order to ascertain the impact of a coloured overlay or tinted lenses Wilkins devised the *Rate of Reading Test* (Wilkins *et al.*, 1996), which can be administered to check that a chosen overlay makes a discernible difference to reading speed. This test requires speeded oral reading of a short passage of text comprising 15 high frequency words (which are familiar to children from 7 years) that are repeated in random order. The test is administered first with an overlay placed over the text, two times without an overlay and finally with an overlay again, to test for an immediate benefit in rate of reading with an overlay. This test reveals that improvements in reading speed are not seen in all those who choose an overlay. Wilkins *et al.* (1996) found that of an unselected sample of 77 children aged 8–11 years, 49 per cent selected an overlay and 20 per cent were more than 5 per cent faster on the rate of reading test with their chosen overlay than without it. In the Wilkins *et al.* (2001) study, 36 per cent read more than 5 per cent faster with their chosen overlay than without it, and in the Evans and Joseph (2002) study of adults, 34 per cent read more than 5 per cent faster with their chosen overlay than without it. But, as we have seen earlier, by no means all these individuals persist in using an overlay – suggesting that their difficulties were not sufficiently serious to merit treatment – so how is the effectiveness of this approach to be evaluated? One method is to calculate the sensitivity and specificity of the 5 per cent criterion for these various studies, as Kriss and Evans (2005) have done. *Sensitivity* can be calculated as the percentage of the sample who chose an overlay and continued to use it and who had initially showed an improvement of >5 per cent in rate of reading with an overlay. *Specificity* can be calculated as the percentage of the sample who either did not choose an overlay or did not continue to use it, and who had not showed an improvement of >5 per cent in rate of reading with an overlay. In the Wilkins *et al.* (1996) study, sensitivity was 73 per cent and specificity 90 per cent, and in the Wilkins *et al.* (2001) study the figures were 68 per cent and 79 per cent, respectively.

Another way of representing those data is in terms of classification errors. *False positives* are errors of classification where individuals who have been judged to have visual stress (on the basis of overlay screening and rate of reading test) but who *did not* turn out to have the condition (on the basis of sustained voluntary use). *False negatives* are errors of classification where individuals who have been judged *not* to have visual stress (on the basis of overlay screening and rate of reading test) but who actually turned out to have the condition (on the basis of sustained voluntary use). In the studies quoted above, the average incidence of false positives was 16 per cent and of false negatives was 30 per cent. Although the 16 per cent false positive rate is within commonly accepted limits, the 30 per cent clearly is not (see Glascoe and Byrne, 1993; Grimes and Shultz, 2002; Kingslake, 1982; Potton, 1983; Singleton, 1997). In fact, the use of the criterion of 'greater than 5 per cent increase in reading speed with an overlay' for diagnosis of visual stress is limited in applicability because of interaction with reading accuracy, as Singleton and Henderson (2007a) have shown. Children with average or above average reading accuracy often show increases of less than 5 per cent with an overlay despite suffering from visual stress. Of course, the criterion percentage of increase in reading rate with an overlay could be altered, which would have the effect of reducing one type of classification error, but only at the expense of increasing the other (Bland, 1999; Singleton, 1997). In summary, overlay screening can result in unacceptably large numbers of false positives and false negatives.

There are other unsatisfactory aspects of this general approach. One of the problems with the Rate of Reading Test is that it only evaluates the impact of an overlay on reading speed over a short time, which may well be why it doesn't always predict overlay usage in the long term very well. None of these techniques establishes objectively that the person definitely has visual stress and therefore needs an overlay or other treatment. One could, of course, give a person an overlay and wait and see. If they continue to use it over the long term it is probably safe to conclude that they suffer from visual stress. But if they stop using it, and the individual in question is a child, then the conclusion may not be so sure. And as a technique for identifying visual stress, 'waiting to see' is clearly a non-starter because of the unacceptably long delay in knowing the result.

In order to ensure that children and adults who need overlays or tinted lenses are identified promptly, objective evidence is required on whether the person actually suffers from visual stress or not. To this end, Singleton and Henderson (2007a, 2007b) researched an objective method of screening for visual stress based on visual search. There is evidence that individuals with visual stress are impaired by visually stressful stimuli during visual search (Conlon *et al.*, 1998; Conlon and Hine, 2000; Tyrell *et al.*, 1995). In the task devised by Singleton and Henderson, individuals were required to locate a randomly generated three-letter word in a matrix of distractor three-letter words presented on a computer screen. The background on which the matrix is superimposed is either visually unstressful (grey) or visually stressful (alternating black/white horizontal stripes of equal duty cycle). In various studies, with children from age 7 upwards and adults, Singleton and Henderson (2007a) found that if there is a significant difference between search times in the visually unstressful and visually stressful conditions, this is a strong predictor of visual stress. Using this method, called ViSS (Visual Stress Screener), to screen unselected samples of children aged 7–17 years, it was found that children classified as having high susceptibility to visual stress had significantly larger increases in reading rate with a coloured overlay compared with those classified by ViSS as having low susceptibility to visual stress. Individuals classified by ViSS as having susceptibility high visual stress also reported more symptoms, although there were indications that reports of symptoms were less reliable in the younger age group. Subsequent studies showed that ViSS also had the same predictive value when used with adults (Singleton and Henderson, 2007c). The objectivity of ViSS not only makes it more accurate than other methods currently available, but Singleton and Henderson (2007b) also showed that the program is equally capable of identifying susceptibility to visual stress in children with dyslexia, because it is not significantly influenced by reading ability. In this study, visually stressful stimuli were found to cause significantly more disruption of visual search in the dyslexic sample than in the control sample, but on visually unstressful stimuli there were no differences between the groups. This not only demonstrates the effectiveness of ViSS for objective screening for visual stress in dyslexic as well as non-dyslexic children, but also indicates that ViSS is not simply measuring other cognitive abilities, such as memory or attention, which are clearly required for visual search but which may also be deficient in dyslexia.

Treatment of visual stress

The symptoms of visual stress can be alleviated by various techniques, including enlargement of print or use of a typoscope, which is a reading mask that covers the lines of text above and below the lines being read, thus reducing pattern glare (Hughes and Wilkins, 2000). However, the most widely used treatment is that of coloured tints, either in the form of acetate overlays or tinted lenses (Wilkins, 2003). Irlen was the first to use this technique systematically, but until the 1990s members of the medical, psychological and educational professions remained sceptical. Following the landmark studies of visual stress in the 1990s by Wilkins and colleagues, using rigorous double-masked randomised placebo-controlled trials (Wilkins *et al.,* 1994; Evans *et al.,* 1994, 1996), it is now generally accepted that coloured tints can reduce symptoms of visual stress and improve reading speed, fluency, accuracy and comprehension. Accurate specification for optimal tints for lenses ('precision tints') can be determined using the Intuitive Colorimeter (Wilkins *et al.,* 1992). Precision tinted lenses are usually found to afford the greatest benefits because they are easier to use (e.g. with white boards and when writing) and because the colour can be precisely prescribed from the full range of possible colours. Alternative systems offering limited ranges of tints (e.g. Chromagen and Harris filters) are used by some optometrists, but the effectiveness of these in comparison with precision tints has yet to be properly determined and they have been criticized by Wilkins (2003).

Precision tinted filters have also been shown to reduce headaches in patients who suffer from migraine. About 40 per cent of patients with migraine report that headaches are triggered by visual stimuli (Hay *et al.*, 1994). Wilkins *et al.* (2002) found that the frequency of migraine headaches was reduced 50 per cent on days when patients wore precision tinted lenses compared with days when they wore other lenses that were similar but not their optimal tint. This finding is consistent with the hypothesis that coloured filters are beneficial because they reduce cortical hyperexcitability (Wilkins, 1995, 2003).

Many studies have demonstrated the benefits of coloured overlays, including symptom reduction, gains in rate of reading (Bouldoukian *et al.,* 2002; Jeanes *et al.*, 1997; Whiteley and Smith, 2001; Wilkins and Lewis, 1999) and improvements in reading accuracy and comprehension (Robinson and Foreman, 1999). In a study of children aged 8–16, Tyrrell *et al.* (1995) found that differences between reading with and without a chosen overlay began to emerge after about 10 minutes in book reading. After this point, children who suffered from visual stress started to tire and experience unpleasant symptoms such as eyestrain when not using their chosen coloured overlay. But when using the overlay these children were able to continue reading unaffected. Those children who did not suffer from visual stress did not slow down or experience unpleasant symptoms, and using an overlay made no difference to their reading.

In a study of 426 children aged 6–8 years in 12 schools, Wilkins *et al.* (2001) found that initially 60 per cent of the children selected an overlay and after 8 months, 31 per cent of the children were still using their overlays. The average gain in reading speed of those using regularly overlays was 13.3 per cent compared with 2.5 per cent of the rest of the children. Although children who did choose overlays reported significantly more symptoms of visual stress than those who did not choose overlays, there was no significant difference in the frequency or type of symptoms reported by those who continue to use overlays compared with those who ceased to use overlays. This latter point underlines the need for objective methods of identifying visual stress (such as ViSS) as opposed to relying just on subjective methods such as overlay screening, as it is not clear whether those who ceased using overlays should have been encouraged to continue in their use.

Coloured overlays are normally supplied in A4 size, but these can be cut down if required. Recently, however, a range of inexpensive small overlays called *Reading Rulers* [www.cross boweducation.com] has been introduced which are proving popular in schools. These are about the width of an A4 page but only 60 mm high, with a black horizontal stripe across the middle to assist keeping on the line of text. Reading rulers have the advantage that they are conveniently sized and will fit easily into a pocket or pencil case, or can be kept in the pages of a book as a bookmark. They are more discreet than whole sheets of coloured acetate and hence may be more acceptable to older children and adults who might be embarrassed about using larger sheets of acetate. Smith and Wilkins (2007) compared Reading Rulers with conventional overlays and found that children with visual stress did not show any significant increase in reading speed using Reading Rulers whereas using the conventional overlays they did. This effect was not due to the smaller size of the Reading Rulers but, rather, to the limited range of colours in the set which dramatically reduced the chances of coming close to the optimal tint for any given child. As a direct result of this research, the range of colours available in Reading Rulers has now been increased from five to ten, which should address this particular problem although unlike conventional overlays, Reading Rulers are only for use singly and are not suitable for use in combination. However, there remain concerns about the way in which Reading Rulers may be used in the classroom, as children are often permitted to select colours by idiosyncratic preference on a day-by-day basis rather than by systematic pair-wise comparison in a screening situation so that the teacher can ensure that the most effective colour is being used by the child. There is a real danger that if, by chance, children choose a colour that is not effective for them, they may decide that colour, *per se*, does not help their reading when they have not had a proper opportunity to determine the most effective colour.

Unfortunately, few controlled studies of use of coloured filters or overlays have been carried out with adults. Robinson and Conway (2000) reported positive benefits of coloured filters in a small-scale study of adults, and Evans and Joseph (2002) studied 113 university students of whom 100 chose an overlay as improving their perception of text. These students were significantly more likely to report visual stress symptoms than those who did not choose an overlay, and they read 3.8 per cent faster with their chosen overlay than without it. This gain seems much lower than that typically found in comparable studies with children. Again, objective assessment would have helped to clarify whether those that chose an overlay really suffered from visual stress; some of these university students may have heard or read that coloured overlays improve reading and this may have affected their subjective judgement.

Singleton and Trotter (2005) compared university students who reported high frequency and intensity of visual stress symptoms with those who did not report visual stress symptoms. These participants were selected so that half of the group had dyslexia and the other half had no literacy difficulties. It was found that only the dyslexic students with high visual stress significantly improved reading rate with an overlay (average improvement of 16 per cent); the dyslexic without visual stress showed a non-significant 3 per cent gain and both groups of non-dyslexic participants (high visual stress and no visual stress) had non-significant gains of 4 per cent. Although all groups had similar reading accuracy scores, the non-dyslexic students read significantly faster than the dyslexic students in all conditions. It is notable that the average reading speed of the dyslexic high visual stress group in the optimal colour condition was essentially the same as that of the dyslexic low visual stress group when reading without colour. Thus while the benefits of colour were not sufficient to raise their reading speed to similar levels as those shown in the non-dyslexic group, nevertheless, effectively, it did bring them up to the same level as other dyslexic students who do not suffer from visual stress.

In the Singleton and Trotter (2005) study, the failure to find a significant improvement in reading speed in the non-dyslexic high visual stress group when using an overlay should not be over-interpreted. Compared to the Evans and Joseph (2002) study, this was a small-scale experiment with a high-ability adult sample, specifically designed to examine the effects of visual stress in combination with dyslexia. In addition, classification of susceptibility to visual stress was based on reported symptoms rather than any objective method. However, it should be noted that although coloured tints are usually beneficial, this is not the case for everyone who displays symptoms of visual stress. In the Evans and Joseph study, 32 per cent of participants did not read any faster with their chosen overlay than without it, and only one-third of their sample demonstrated a significant benefit of overlays, despite 88 per cent of the sample having chosen overlays. It is also clear from the Evans and Joseph study that many adults benefit from using coloured overlays when reading, despite not reporting any symptoms of visual stress. In small-scale studies such individual differences in response can mask general trends.

People who suffer from visual stress often find that reading or writing on a computer can be visually irritating, leading to headaches and eyestrain. When children or adults are writing using a word processor, they should be encouraged to work in a font size, viewing size and colour that they find most comfortable. There are now several programs available that address this problem and which make using computers less tiring. These products enable an easy choice of colours, fonts, size and spacing to be made (see Singleton, 2008a for further discussion).

Conclusions

The results of the Singleton and Trotter (2005) study suggest that identifying visual stress on the basis of a person's choice of a coloured overlay (and possible improvements in reading speed when using the overlay) is likely to be unreliable. Similar conclusions can be drawn from the study by Singleton and Henderson (2007a). Objective determination of susceptibility to visual stress would seem to be much more satisfactory (Singleton, 2008b). Unlike the studies by Singleton and Trotter (2005) and Singleton and Henderson (2007b), previous studies of visual stress have not distinguished between participants who have, or do not have, dyslexia. In the light of recent findings, this would seem to be a methodological oversight that may have clouded our understanding of visual stress. We now know that considerably more dyslexics than non-dyslexics suffer from visual stress, and thus it is possible that the presence of (undetected) dyslexics in participant samples in visual stress studies may have contributed disproportionately to the reported effects.

Several important educational conclusions can be drawn from recent research on visual processes in reading (Cornelissen and Singleton, 2007; Singleton, 2008b; Singleton and Henderson, 2006). The efficient organisation of the various components involved in reading – including eye movements, word recognition, working memory, and comprehension – develop and become integrated as an efficient system as a result of the experience of learning to read. This underlines the educational requirement for adequate and appropriate practice in text reading in order to discipline eye movements, attain fluency in decoding and provide a firm basis for competent reading comprehension. Visual factors, such as visual stress, that disrupt the reading process will have detrimental effects on the development of fluency and comprehension. Where individuals also have dyslexia as well as suffering from visual stress there is likely to be a multiplicative detrimental effect on reading. The threshold shift theory (Singleton, 2008b) maintains that, for dyslexics, as a combined result of lack of reading experience and the reading style that they are forced to adopt, the sensitivity threshold for visual stress is shifted, making them more sensitive to the physical characteristics of text (such as contrast, glare, stripedness and font size) and increasing their risk of experiencing the unpleasant symptoms of visual stress. Hence there is a strong case for screening for visual stress in all children, but especially in those who are already known to have dyslexia, since not only is their risk of visual stress much greater than that found in other individuals but, also, if they do suffer from visual stress, the repercussions of remaining untreated are likely to be of much greater educational significance. The availability of objective computer-based screening using ViSS [www.visual-stress.com] now makes reliable identification of visual stress in schools a realistic proposition, and the availability of a variety of efficacious treatments using coloured tints provides cost-effective solutions that are easy to use in the classroom and at home.

References

Binnie, C.D., Emmett, P., Gardiner, G.F.A., Harding, D., Harrison, D. and Wilkins, A.J. (2002) Characterizing the flashing television images that precipitate seizures. *SMPTE Journal*, July–August 2002, 323–329.

Bland, M. (1999) *Introduction to Medical Statistics* (2nd edn). Oxford: Oxford Medical Publications.

Bouldoukian, J., Wilkins, A.J. and Evans, B.J.W. (2002) Randomized controlled trial of the effect of coloured overlays on the rate of reading of people with specific learning difficulties. *Ophthalmic and Physiological Optics*, 22, 55–60.

Breitmeyer, B.G. (1993) Sustained (P) and transient (M) channels in vision: a review and implications for reading. In D.M. Willows, R.S. Kruk and E. Corcos (eds) *Visual Processes in Reading and Reading Disabilities*. Hillsdale, NJ: Lawrence Erlbaum Associates Inc., pp. 95–110.

Breitmeyer, B.G. and Ganz, L. (1976) Implications of sustained and transient channels for theories of visual pattern masking, saccadic suppression, and information processing. *Psychological Review*, 83, 1–36.

Burr, D.C., Morone, M.C. and Ross, J. (1994) Selective suppression of the magnocellular visual pathway during saccadic eye movements. *Nature*, 371, 511–513.

Chase, C., Ashourzadeh, A., Kelly, C., Monfette, S. and Kinsey, K. (2003) Can the magnocellular pathway read? Evidence from studies of colour. *Vision Research*, 43, 1211–22.

Conlon, E. and Hine, T. (2000) The influence of pattern interference on performance in migraine and visual discomfort groups. *Cephalagia*, 20, 708–713.

Conlon, E., Lovegrove, W., Hine, T., Chekaluk, E., Piatek, K. and Hayes-Williams, K. (1998) The effect of visual discomfort and pattern structure on visual search. *Perception*, 27, 21–33.

Connah, A. (2008) *Investigating the Relationship between Dyslexia and Visual Stress in Adults*. Unpublished research project report, Department of Psychology, University of Hull.

Cornelissen, P.L. and Singleton, C.H. (eds) (2007) *Visual Factors in Reading*. Oxford: Blackwell.

Cornelissen, P., Richardson, A., Mason, A. and Stein, J.F. (1995) Contrast sensitivity and coherent motion detection measured at photopic luminance levels in dyslexics and controls. *Vision Research*, 35, 1483–1494.

Eden, G.F., VanMeter, J.W., Rumsey, J.W., Maisog, J. and Zeffiro, T.A. (1996) Functional MRI reveals differences in visual motion processing in individuals with dyslexia. *Nature*, 382, 66–69.

Evans, B.J.W. (2001) *Dyslexia and Vision*. London: Whurr.

Evans, B.J.W. and Joseph, R. (2002) The effect of coloured filters on the rate of reading in an adult student population. *Ophthalmic and Physiological Optics*, 22, 535–545.

Evans, B.J.W., Drasdo, N. and Richards, I. (1994) An investigation of some sensory and refractive visual factors in dyslexia. *Vision Research*, 34, 1913–1926.

Evans, B.J.W., Wilkins, A.J., Brown, J., Busby, A., Wingfield, A.E., Jeanes, R. and Bald, J. (1996) A preliminary investigation into the aetiology of Meares–Irlen Syndrome. *Ophthalmic and Physiological Optics*, 16, 286–296.

Everatt, J., Bradshaw, M.F. and Hibbard, P.B. (1999) Visual processing and dyslexia. *Perception*, 28, 243–254.

Facoetti, A., Paganoni, P. and Lorusso, M.L. (2000). The spatial distribution of visual attention in developmental dyslexia. *Experimental Brain Research*, 132, 531–538.

Farmer, M. and Klein, R. (1995) The evidence for a temporal processing deficit linked to dyslexia: A review. *Psychonomic Bulletin and Review*, 2, 460–493.

Fisher, R.S., Harding, G., Erba, G., Barkley, G.L. and Winkins, A.J. (2005) Photic-and pattern-induced seizures: a review for the Epilepsy Foundation of America working group. *Epilepsia*, 46, 1426–1441.

Furusho, J., Suzuki, M., Tazaki, H., Yamaguchi, K., Iikura, Y., Kumagi, K., Kubagawa, T. and Hara, T. (2002) *Pediatric Neurology*, 27, 350–355.

Garzia, R.P. and Nicholson, S.B. (1990) Optometric factors in reading disability. In D.M.Willows, R.S.Kruk and E. Corcos (eds) *Visual Processes in Reading and Reading Disabilities*. Hillsdale, NJ: Lawrence Erlbaum Associates Inc., pp. 419–434.

Glascoe, F.P. and Byrne, K.E. (1993) The accuracy of three developmental screening tests. *Journal of Early Intervention*, 17, 368–379.

Grant, D. (2004) *From Myths to Realities: Lessons to be Drawn from Over 600 Student Assessments*. Paper presented at the 6th International Conference of the British Dyslexia Association, University of Warwick, March 2004.

Grimes, D.A. and Shultz, K.F. (2002) Use and misuse of screen tests. *Lancet*, 359, 881–884.

Harding, G.F.A. (1998) TV can be bad for your health. *Nature Medicine*, 4, 265–267.

Harding, G.F.A. and Jeavons, P.M. (1995) Photosensitive epilepsy. *Clinics in Developmental Medicine, No. 133*. Cambridge: Cambridge University Press.

Hay, K.M., Mortimer, M.J., Barker, D.C., Debney, L.M. and Good, P.A. (1994) 1044 women with migraine: the effect of environmental stimuli. *Headache*, 34, 166–168.

Hughes, L.E. and Wilkins, A.J. (2000) Typography in children's reading schemes may be suboptimal: Evidence from measures of reading rate. *Journal of Research in Reading*, 12, 314–324.

Iles, J., Walsh, V. and Richardson, A. (2000) Visual search performance in dyslexia. *Dyslexia*, 6, 163–177.

Irlen, H. (1983) *Successful treatment of learning difficulties*. Paper presented at the Annual Convention of the American Psychological Association, Anaheim, California.

Irlen, H. (1991) *Reading by the Colours*. New York: Avery.

Jeanes, R., Busby, A., Martin, J., Lewis, E., Stevenson, N., Pointon, D. and Wilkins, A. (1997) Prolonged use of coloured overlays for classroom reading. *British Journal of Psychology*, 88, 531–548.

Kingslake, B. (1982) The predictive (In) Accuracy of On-entry to school screening procedures when used to anticipate learning difficulties. *Special Education*, 10 (4), 23–26.

Kriss, I. and Evans, B.J.W. (2005) The relationship between dyslexia and Meares–Irlen syndrome. *Journal of Research in Reading*, 28, 350–364.

Livingstone, M., Rosen, G.D., Drislane, F. and Galaburda, A. (1991) Physiological evidence for a magnocellular deficit in developmental dyslexia. *Proceedings of the New York Academy of Science*, 88, 7943–7647.

Lovegrove, W.J. (1991) Is the question of the role of visual deficits as a cause of reading disabilities a closed one? Comments on Hulme. *Cognitive Neuropsychology*, 8, 435–441.

Lovegrove, W.J. Martin, F. and Slaghuis, W.L. (1986) A theoretical and experiental case for a visual deficit in specific reading disability. *Cognitive Neuropsychology*, 3, 225–227.

Lovegrove, W.J., Garzia, R.P. and Nicholson, S.B. (1990) Experimental evidence of a transient system deficit in specific reading disability. *Journal of the American Optometric Association*, 61, 137–146.

McKay, D.M. (1957). Moving visual images produced by regular stationary patterns. *Nature*, 180, 849–850.

McKay, D.M., Gerrits, H.J.M. and Stassen, H.P.W. (1979). Interaction of stabilized retinal patterns with visual noise. *Vision Research*, 19, 713–716.

Maclachlan, A., Yale, S. and Wilkins, A.J. (1993). Open trials of precision ophthalmic tinting: 1-year follow-up of 55 patients. *Ophthalmic and Physiological Optics*, 13, 175–178.

Meares, O. (1980) Figure/ground brightness contrast and reading disabilities. *Visible Language*, 14, 13–29.

Northway, N. (2003) Predicting the continued use of overlays in school children – a comparison of the Developmental Eye Movement test and the Rate of Reading test. *Ophthalmic and Physiological Optics*, 23, 457–464.

Parke, L.A. and Skotton, B.C. (1999) The possible relationship between visual deficits and dyslexia: Examination of a critical assumption. *Journal of Learning Disabilities*, 32, 2–5.

Potton, A. (1983) *Screening*. London: Macmillan.

Quirk, J.A., Fish, D.R. and Smith, S.J. (1995) First seizures associated with playing electronic screen games: a community-based study in Great Britain. *Annals of Neurology*, 37, 733–737.

Ramus, F. (2001) Outstanding questions about phonological processing in dyslexia. *Dyslexia*, 7, 197–216.

Ramus, F., Rosen, S., Dakin, S.C., Day, B.L., Castellote, J.M., White, S. and Frith, U. (2003) Theories of developmental dyslexia: Insights from a multiple case study of dyslexic adults. *Brain*, 126, 1–25.

Raymond, J.E. and Sorensen, R. (1998) Visual motion perception in children with dyslexia: normal detection but abnormal integration. *Visual Cognition*, 5, 389–404.

Robinson, G.L. and Conway, R.N.F. (2000) Irlen lenses and adults: a small-scale study of reading speed, accuracy comprehension and self-image. *Australian Journal of Learning Disabilities*, 5, 4–12.

Robinson, G.L. and Foreman, P.J. (1999) Scotopic sensitivity/Irlen Syndrome and the use of coloured filters: a long-term placebo-controlled and masked study of reading achievement and perception of ability. *Perceptual and Motor Skills*, 88, 35–52.

Ross, J., Burr, D. and Morrone, C. (1996) Suppression of the magnocellular pathways during saccades. *Behavioural Brain Research*, 80, 1–8.

Singleton, C.H. (1997) Screening early literacy. In J.R. Beech and C.H. Singleton (eds) *The Psychological Assessment of Reading*. London: Routledge, pp. 67–101.

Singleton, C.H. (2008a) Visual stress and dyslexia. In C.H. Singleton (ed.) *The Dyslexia Handbook 2008–9*. Bracknell, Berks: British Dyslexia Association.

Singleton, C.H. (2008b) Visual factors in reading. *Educational and Child Psychology*, 25(3), 9–20.

Singleton, C.H. and Henderson, L.M. (2006) Visual factors in reading. *London Review of Education*, 4, 89–98.

Singleton, C.H. and Henderson, L.M. (2007a) Computerised screening for visual stress in reading. *Journal of Research in Reading*, 30, 316–331.

Singleton, C.H. and Henderson, L.M. (2007b) Computerised screening for visual stress in children with dyslexia. *Dyslexia*, 13, 130–151.

Singleton, C.H. and Henderson, L.M. (2007c) *Lucid Visual Stress Screener (ViSS)*. Beverley, East Yorkshire: Lucid Research Ltd.

Singleton, C.H. and Henderson, L.M. (in preparation) Symptomatology of visual stress: a factorial study.

Singleton, C.H. and Trotter, S. (2005) Visual stress in adults with and without dyslexia. *Journal of Research in Reading*, 28, 365–378.

Skottun, B.C. (2000) On the conflicting support for the magnocellular-deficit theory of dyslexia. *Trends in Cognitive Science*, 4, 211–212.

Skottun, B.C. (2005) Magnocellular reading and dyslexia. *Vision Research*, 45, 133–134.

Smith, L. and Wilkins, A. (2007) How many colours are necessary to increase the reading of children with visual stress? A comparison of two systems. *Journal of Research in Reading*, 30, 332–343.

Snowling, M.J. (2000) *Dyslexia* (2nd edn). Oxford: Blackwell.

Stanovich, K. E. (1986) Matthew effects in reading: Some consequences of individual differences in the acquisition of reading. *Reading Research Quarterly*, 21, 360–407.

Stein, J.F. (2001) The magnocellular theory of dyslexia. *Dyslexia*, 7, 12–36.

Stein, J.F. and Walsh, V. (1997) To see but not to read: The magnocellular theory of dyslexia. *Trends in Neuroscience*, 20, 147–152.

Steinman, B., Steinman, S., and Lehmkuhle, S. (1997) *Vision Research*, 37, 17–23.

Talcott, J.B., Hansen, P.C., Willis-Owen, C., McKinnell, I.W., Richardson, A.J. and Stein, J.F. (1998) Visual magnocellular in adult developmental dyslexics. *Neuro-Ophthalmology*, 20, 187–201.

Tobimatsu, S., Zhang, Y.M., Yomoda, T., Mitsudome, A. and Kato, M. (1999) Chromatric sensitive epilepsy. *Annals of Neurology*, 45, 790–793.

Tyrrell, R., Holland, K., Dennis, D. and Wilkins, A.J. (1995) Coloured overlays, visual discomfort, visual search and classroom reading. *Journal of Research in Reading*, 18(1), 10–23.

Vellutino, F. R., Fletcher, J. M., Snowling, M. J. and Scanlon, D. M. (2004) Specific reading disability (dyslexia): what have we learned in the past four decades? *Journal of Child Psychology and Psychiatry*, 45, 2–40.

Vidyasagar, T.R. (1998) Gating of neuronal responses in macaque primary visual cortex by an attentional spotlight. *NeuroReport*, 9, 1947–1952.

Vidyasagar, T.R. and Pammer, K. (1999) Impaired visual search in dyslexia relates to the role of the magnocellular pathway in attention. *NeuroReport*, 10, 1283–1287.

White, S., Milne, E., Rosen, S., Hansen, P., Swettenham, J., Frith, U. and Ramus, F. (2006) The role of sensorimotor impairments in dyslexia: a multiple case study of dyslexic children, *Developmental Science*, 9:3, 237–269.

Whiteley, H.E. and Smith, C.D. (2001) The use of tinted lenses to alleviate reading difficulties. *Journal of Research in Reading*, 24, 30–40.

Wilkins, A.J. (1995) *Visual Stress*. Oxford: Oxford University Press.

Wilkins, A.J. (2002) Coloured overlays and their effects on reading speed: a review. *Ophthalmic and Physiological Optics*, 22, 448–454.

Wilkins, A.J. (2003) *Reading Through Colour*. Chichester, Sussex: Wiley.

Wilkins, A.J. and Lewis, E. (1999) Coloured overlays, text and texture. *Perception*, 28, 641–650.

Wilkins, A.J., and Nimmo-Smith, M.I. (1987) The clarity and comfort of printed text. *Ergonomics*, 30, 1705–1720.

Wilkins, A.J., Nimmo-Smith, I. and Jansons, J. (1992) A colorimeter for the intuitive manipulation of hue and saturation, and its application in the study of perceptual distortion. *Ophthalmic and Physiological Optics*, 12, 381–385.

Wilkins, A.J., Evans, B.J.W., Brown, J., Busby, A., Winfield, A.E., Jeanes, R. and Bald, J. (1994) Double masked placebo controlled trials of precision spectral filters in children who use coloured overlays. *Ophthalmic and Physiological Optics*, 14, 365–370.

Wilkins, A.J., Jeanes, R. J., Pumfrey, P.D. and Laskier, M. (1996) Rate of Reading Test: its reliability and its validity in the assessment of the effects of coloured overlays. *Ophthalmic and Physiological Optics*, 16, 491–7.

Wilkins, A.J., Lewis, E., Smith, F., Rowland, E. and Tweedie, W. (2001) Coloured overlays and their benefit for reading. *Journal of Research in Reading*, 24, 41–64.

Wilkins, A.J., Patel, R., Adjamian, R. and Evans, B.J.W. (2002) Tinted spectacles and visually sensitive migraine. *Cephalagia*, 22, 711–719.

Wilkins, A.J., Bonanni, P., Porciatti, V. and Guerrini, R. (2004a) Physiology of human photosensitivity. *Epilepsia*, 45 (Supplement 1), 1–7.

Wilkins, A.J., Huang, J. and Cao, Y. (2004b) Visual stress theory and its application to reading and reading tests. *Journal of Research in Reading*, 27, 152–162.

Part 2

Dimensions of Dyslexia

5

Preventing and identifying reading difficulties in young children

Deborah F. Knight, Kim Day and Nicole Patten-Terry

This chapter

- examines the nature of early intervention
- examines in detail the implications of the Response to Intervention (RTI) process
- describes the role and the challenges of screening and continuous progress monitoring, including preventative measures.

Although the field of early childhood education is increasingly emphasizing pre-literacy skills, three- and four-year-olds are not generally expected to be readers. Because dyslexia by definition describes an impairment in the ability to read, it is neither possible nor desirable to diagnose and label a young child not expected to be reading as dyslexic. However, as early as three years of age, some young children display behaviors that indicate that they are not developing oral language, phonological awareness, and motor skills as one would expect. Some of these children will be diagnosed with dyslexia, while others need intervention to allow them to have the necessary experiences to become readers. Children in both groups are at-risk for developing reading difficulties. The needs of both groups can be supported by the same identification and intervention process, starting at a very early age. Identifying the children in need of supplemental instruction, providing targeted instruction, monitoring their progress carefully, and adjusting instruction according to their needs are keys to helping young children become readers. This chapter describes Response to Intervention (RTI), a process gaining popularity in the United States that strives to intervene early when children experience reading difficulties.

Literacy in the United States

Thirty-three percent of fourth graders and twenty-six percent of eighth graders read below a minimum level of comprehension in the United States. Students who are eligible for free and reduced lunch programs (an indicator of low socioeconomic status (SES)) perform lower than students who are not eligible. Students who attend schools in urban areas perform lower than those who attend schools in towns, rural areas, and suburbs. Black, Hispanic, and American Indian/Native Alaskan students have lower reading achievement than Whites and Asian/Pacific Islanders (Planty, M. *et al.*, 2008).

Unfortunately, these achievement differences are often present before children begin formal schooling. Findings from numerous research studies indicate that many young children in the United States, particularly those from low SES backgrounds, begin school at-risk for reading failure because of weak oral language skills (Bardige, 2005; Brown and Bogard, 2007; Hart and Risley, 2003; Horowitz, Kaloi and Petroff, 2007; Lee and Burkam, 2002; Neuman, 2006; Snow, Burns and Griffin, 1998). As an example, in their seminal study Hart and Risley (2003) found that by age three, children who came from higher SES families had vocabularies twice the size of those coming from lower SES families. This difference in vocabulary development was predictive of the children's performance on language and literacy measures through grade three, with the children from higher SES families continuing to out-perform their peers from lower SES families.

Similarly, data reported from the U.S. Department of Education's Early Childhood Longitudinal Study, Kindergarten Cohort (ECLS-K) on more than 20,000 children from across the United States, provides additional evidence of the negative impact this achievement gap has on the reading performance of both low SES and culturally and linguistically diverse children into grade five (Princiotta et al., 2006). While the underachievement that many of these children experienced may be attributed to dyslexia, many of them struggle with reading because of poor oral language skills. Early identification of reading difficulty along with targeted, research-based interventions can improve children's chances of becoming more effective readers (Henry et al., 2004; Lamy et al., 2005; Lynch, 2007; Reynolds et al., 2001; Schweinhart, 1993; Southern Education Foundation, 2007, 2008). The RTI process may be an effective mechanism for both identifying children who struggle to acquire reading skills and implementing appropriate interventions to help them succeed in school.

Response to Intervention

Identification of learning disabilities and dyslexia has been problematic from the beginning of the field. Issues with IQ-achievement discrepancy, the "wait-to-fail" model rather than a prevention model, disproportionate identification of minorities, and failure to consider the quality of a student's instruction have plagued the field (see chapter 2). Recently, researchers and professional educators have been developing and implementing RTI processes as an alternative approach to identifying and intervening with children with learning disabilities. The 2004 reauthorization of the Individuals with Disabilities Act, the United States law that addresses the educational needs of children with disabilities from birth to the age of 21, allowed states to use RTI processes to identify and intervene on behalf of students performing below the expected level of achievement. In addition, the reauthorization encourages the development of early intervening services (EIS). These two new concepts result in general and special education being more closely aligned. Alexa Posny, the Director of the Office of Special Education Programs, stated, "RTI and EIS are absolutely the future of education—not the future of special education, but of education" (Burdette, 2007).

RTI offers the promise of early identification of students whose progress is below the established benchmark, regardless of the reason. RTI can result in a seamless process, integrating the services of special, remedial, and general education (National Association of State Directors of Special Education, Inc. [NASDSE], 2006). Appropriate and effective interventions for students can result in either successful progress or early pre-referral services for students with more serious learning difficulties. This approach is especially encouraging in the field of early childhood education because it results in child-centered instruction and intervention without the need for identification of a disability, thus alleviating the "wait-to-fail" model.

Although there are variations of the RTI process, certain key components are present in all variations:

1 Universal screening
2 Progress monitoring
3 High quality, research-based instruction for all students in the general education classroom (Tier 1)
4 Tiers of intervention targeting students who do not demonstrate adequate progress on screening or progress monitoring measures (Mellard and Johnson, 2008).

These components have been studied more extensively in school-age populations. Preschool variations of the RTI process are just now being studied. For instance, Coleman *et al.* (2006) have created an RTI process for preschool children called Recognition and Response that includes four essential components: an intervention hierarchy; screening, assessment, and progress monitoring; research-based curriculum, instruction, and focused interventions; and a collaborative problem-solving process for decision-making. These investigations are expected to provide critical information on how best to implement RTI in preschool classrooms in a developmentally appropriate manner. Although the research evidence is forthcoming, the following sections describe the essential components of RTI and the implications for an early childhood model.

Universal screening

The goal of universal screening is to identify students who are at-risk for, in this case, reading difficulties. Typically, universal screening is conducted three times during the school year, and it is often administered by the classroom teacher. This screening is accomplished by administering to all students measures that accurately and efficiently evaluate key skills that predict reading success. The screening is not meant to measure all possible aspects of a skill, but rather samples the skill with an indicator that is predictive of reading achievement (Kaminski *et al.*, 2008).

Continuous progress monitoring (described below) can also play a role in screening. After initial screening to identify students at-risk for reading difficulties, progress monitoring can be used to provide data on the actual achievement growth of students. While Stecker *et al.* (2005) found that research supports weekly monitoring, Speece and Walker (2007) suggested that progress monitoring on all children weekly may be unacceptable for practical reasons. Mellard and Johnson (2008) report emerging studies that indicate that progress monitoring once every three weeks may adequately identify progress. Frequency of monitoring is an area that will require further investigation.

The challenge of universal screening is to balance accuracy (i.e., not identifying children as at-risk when they are not or failing to identify children who are at-risk) with efficiency. Accuracy can be improved by adding more tasks to the assessment, but only at the expense of efficiency. Speece and Walker (2007) recommend testing the efficacy of competing screening models, such as teacher ratings, continuous progress monitoring, screening measures, and teacher ratings plus screening measures to determine empirically the most effective tools to screen students.

Universal screening for preschool students

In the context of the preschool setting, universal screening procedures can be used to identify children at-risk for reading failure or underachievement and should include measures of phonological skills, print and word awareness, alphabet knowledge and oral language development, particularly vocabulary skills (Dickinson et al., 2003; Kirby, Desrochers, Roth and Lai, 2008; Kirby et al., 2003; Purcell and Rosemary, 2008). A very real challenge for preschool teachers will be locating formal and informal tests appropriate for measuring these skills in young children. The use of informal observations, checklists of developmental benchmarks, curriculum-based measures (CBM), work sampling and/or formal or standardized measures (e.g., *Phonological Awareness Literacy Screening: Pre-Kindergarten* [PALS-P, Invernizzi et al., 2004] and *Peabody Picture Vocabulary Test – IV* [PPVT-IV, Dunn and Dunn, 2007]) should occur within the first three months of entering a preschool program as a pre-measure and again mid-year and end of year to determine children's progress or response to instruction around language and literacy skills (Coleman et al., 2006). Of importance, is that teachers utilize authentic measures that are reliable and valid to ensure that *how* and *what* is being measured is accurate and provides information on what children know and need to know regarding literacy concepts (Bryan et al., 2008).

Progress monitoring

Progress monitoring involves administering frequent CBM and evaluating children's progress. Recommendations for frequency vary from daily to once every three weeks (National Research Center on Learning Disabilities, 2006). The student's current levels of performance are determined and learning goals are identified. Progress is measured by comparing the student's actual achievement to the rate of progress necessary to reach the targeted goal. Both the student's initial level of achievement as well as the rate of growth are considered in progress monitoring. If a student fails to make adequate progress as defined by the rate of growth necessary to reach the goal, instruction is adjusted. Progress monitoring is a well researched and validated tool for measuring progress to inform instruction and improve student achievement (see Stecker et al., 2005 for a review of research).

Progress monitoring can be used to determine if a student is responding to intervention. Decisions based on progress monitoring data can result in adjustment to instruction, termination of intervention, or referral to a more intensive intervention. Decision rules about when to move a student into or out of an intervention should be determined in advance. A generally accepted guideline is to change an intervention when three consecutive data points fall below the goal line (Fuchs, 1989).

Monitoring the progress of preschool students

Much like universal screening, teachers in preschool programs may have difficulty identifying appropriate ways to monitor young children's progress on language and literacy concepts and skills. Often, student portfolios are developed in which work samples, observational notes, benchmark checklists and curriculum evaluation measures are organized for progress monitoring (e.g., the Work Sampling System developed by Meisels, et al., 1995). The use of portfolios provides multiple sources of information to help identify individual student's responses to instruction and/or the need for additional support or specialized intervention for an individual student or group of students. This type of progress monitoring can also be useful in reporting to parents and other professionals throughout the school year. Portfolios, however, are reliable and valid only when teachers clearly understand what language and literacy concepts and skills are meaningful and developmentally appropriate for preschool children (Purcell and Rosemary, 2008). While many states are working to develop guidelines and standards for portfolio development, additional research and teacher training needs to occur in order for progress monitoring to be most effective (Coleman *et al.*, 2006).

High quality, research-based literacy instruction for all students

For RTI to be successful, all students must receive high quality, research-based literacy instruction and supports in Tier 1. Tier 1 is intended to be preventive (NASDSE, 2006). One goal is to reduce the number of referrals to special education by providing high quality instruction to all students using research-based curricula delivered by highly qualified general education teachers. Tier 1 includes the following features: whole class instruction using a research-based methodology for a minimum of 90 minutes daily, use of flexible groups within the general education classroom, mastery of content (ideally determined by progress monitoring), and universal screening at least three times per year (Mellard and Johnson, 2008; NRCLD, 2006; Vaughn, 2003). High quality instruction in Tier 1 will result in an integrated system in which curriculum, instruction, intervention, assessment, and professional development support the learning of all students. Approximately 80 per cent of students should achieve adequately at Tier 1 if the core instruction is effective (NASDSE, 2006). If fewer than 80 per cent of students are meeting the benchmark on the universal screening, the quality of the Tier 1 instruction must be evaluated.

High quality, research-based literacy instruction in preschool

Early childhood educators have, for many years, recognized the importance of oral language development in young children's acquisition of literacy skills (Hymes, 1965). More recent studies have further validated the significance of oral language development as a key component in helping children learn to read and subsequently, read to learn (Christie, 2008; Dickenson and Smith, 1994; Hart and Risley, 2003; Horowitz *et al.*, 2007; Kalmar, 2008; Karweit, 1989; Morrow, 1985; National Reading Panel, 2000; Neuman, 2006; Phillips, Clancy-Menchetti, and Lonigan, 2008; Snow *et al.*, 1998; Vasilyeva, Huttenlocher and Waterfall, 2006). These studies have also provided insights about how to successfully implement language-based programs for young children using direct, systematic instructional approaches with particular attention given to teacher and student interactions and differentiated instruction within the classroom (Early *et al.*, 2007; Purcell and Rosemary, 2008). Classrooms also need to be language- and literacy-rich environments that promote classroom discourse so that students are actively engaged in developing language skills and learning how to learn (Bogard and Takanishi, 2005; Mashburn *et al.*, 2008; Pianta and Hadden, 2008). The specific language-based skills young children need to acquire through their preschool experience are:

- oral expressive and receptive language skills that support vocabulary development, syntactic development and inferential thinking,
- print awareness,
- phonological awareness skills such as rhyming, alliteration, word and syllable segmentation and phoneme awareness,
- alphabet knowledge.

Tiers of intervention

Tier 2

RTI is conceived as a process in which students move in and out of several tiers. When students are identified as at-risk on a universal screening, they might be identified for Tier 2 instruction or be monitored to determine if they make progress in Tier 1 instruction. Vaughn (2003) describes Tier 2 instruction as small-group supplemental instruction provided in addition to the core reading instruction of Tier 1. Approximately 15 per cent of students might fall in this tier (NASDSE, 2006). Programs, strategies, and procedures are intended to supplement and support Tier 1 instruction. Vaughn identifies these features of Tier 2: small groups (up to five students), 30 minutes of intervention in addition to 90 minutes of core (Tier 1) instruction using a research-based program or approach, progress monitoring, and intervention either within or outside of the classroom. Vaughn's research supports 10 to 12 weeks of instruction, at which time a decision must be made about a student's needs. Students might exit Tier 2 instruction, remain in Tier 2 instruction for another session, move to Tier 3 instruction, or be referred to determine special education eligibility.

One goal of Tier 2 is to reduce the number of referrals to special education. The concept of determining how students respond to intervention is not new. Most schools have an interdisciplinary team (e.g., student instructional team, school support team, or building assistance team) to develop a plan to modify the curriculum for a targeted student. The teams use a problem-solving approach to design an individual instructional intervention. When these teams work within an RTI process, they continue to use a problem-solving approach that clearly identifies the problem, collects data in the general education class, and evaluates the data objectively. An intervention plan is designed that directly addresses the student's needs, and the student's progress is monitored regularly. The team meets to determine if the intervention is effective, what adjustments need to be made, and whether further evaluation is warranted (Gersten and Dimino, 2006; NRCLD, 2006). RTI may strengthen this team problem-solving process by providing a clear process with identified assessments and decision rules about what constitutes research-based interventions, adequate response to the intervention, and next steps. In an RTI process, the intervention is an integral part of the identification process. Teams will need to link RTI data from assessment and intervention to referral and eligibility decisions in special education. Gersten and Dimino (2006) suggest that the RTI process has the potential to provide the Student Study Team with "hard" data from progress monitoring, interventions attempted, and diagnostic tests. These data are quantitative and dynamic, reflecting the student's performance over time.

Tier 3

Tier 3 can be thought of as synonymous to special education. As stated above, some RTI processes include four or five tiers. Those intervention tiers would fall between 2 and 3, as they are described in this chapter. If students make inadequate progress in Tiers 1 and 2, they would be considered for a comprehensive evaluation to determine if a disability is present. Services in Tier 3 are designed for an individual and include more intensive instruction in smaller groups, modifications, accommodations, and remediation. Although students can move in and out of Tier 3, the duration of Tier 3 will likely be longer, perhaps months or years (Vaughn, 2003; NRCLD, 2006). NASDSE (2006) estimates that approximately 5 per cent of students will fall in this category. Ideally, those students who are truly in need of special education would be identified, allowing targeted instruction for students with dyslexia and other specific learning disabilities.

Tier 2 and Tier 3 instruction for preschool children

Through either a process of screening or progress monitoring, individual students may be identified who are not responding adequately to Tier 1 instruction. In the case of preschool children this may indicate a need to modify the curriculum or instructional practices in the classroom. Teachers may want to provide a range of developmentally appropriate tasks for small groups of students to engage in, allow for repeated practice or opportunities to demonstrate language and literacy-based concepts or skills and/or utilize an array of instructional strategies that allow for active engagement of children in whole-group and small group instruction (Coleman *et al.*, 2006). As teachers modify the language and literacy curriculum and instruction, they will need to continue to stay focused on research-based practices which will more than likely improve instruction for all students.

In the case of a student failing to respond to Tier 2 modifications more intensive, targeted intervention in a 1:1 situation may be necessary. It will be imperative for teachers to work with other educational professionals such as speech/language pathologists, psychologists, reading specialists and early childhood special educators in order to recognize and respond appropriately to these children. This collaborative approach, along with data from progress monitoring or screening instruments will help guide decisions about the kind of intervention needed and if or when a formal evaluation is considered necessary to determine the need for special education services. Currently, more research is needed to help guide teachers in determining appropriate and effective Tier 2 and Tier 3 interventions for preschool children (for example, recent funding from the US Department of Education awarded to Charles Greenwood and Judith Carta to direct and conduct research at the Center for Response to Intervention in Early Childhood, Juniper Gardens Children's Project at Kansas University; see http://www.jgcp.ku.edu/~jgcp/news/2008/April_Greenwood_Carta.shtml).

Early identification of the young student with dyslexia

Prior to the 1990s, the assessment measures used to identify school readiness had very little predictive validity (Gersten and Dimino, 2006). With current measures of phonological awareness and naming speed (Kirby *et al.*, 2003) children can be identified as early as preschool as exhibiting characteristics that indicate that they might be at-risk for difficulties in reading. In kindergarten, tests of phonemic awareness, letter and sound knowledge, and decoding can be used to identify students who need interventions, regardless of the underlying cause of their difficulty. By first grade, oral reading fluency can be included to identify students struggling to read on level (Torgesen, Foorman, and Wagner, 2008). With effective universal screening, progress monitoring, and early referral for diagnosis as part of an RTI process, students with dyslexia may be more likely to be identified early and appropriately. Although dyslexia cannot be cured, its severity can be ameliorated by early intervention targeted to address the specific difficulties which the student encounters.

Conclusion

As Gersten and Dimino (2006) stated, we have come up with yet one more way to think about identifying and intervening on behalf of students with learning disabilities such as dyslexia. RTI processes encourage early identification and intervention; integration of special, remedial, and general education; research-based instruction; and data driven decisions about instruction. However, the success of RTI depends on faithful implementation of well researched methods of instruction and intervention, careful use of assessment and progress monitoring data to inform the instruction and intervention, and highly effective teachers. The hope is that students needing intervention, but not special education, will receive effective support early. As a result, there will be fewer inappropriate referrals to special education, permitting more targeted instruction for those who do qualify for special services.

The field of early childhood education has traditionally embraced the differences that children bring to school as a catalyst for growth and learning. Just as children show social and emotional variation, they can also be expected to show academic variation, even at the age of three or four. As the field continues to incorporate more intentional language and literacy instruction into the classroom, teachers will need resources to help children who struggle to acquire reading skills. RTI processes can be aligned with many of the traditional goals of early childhood education, including attending to the needs of individual children and providing developmentally appropriate instruction. When implemented well, these processes may help to identify young children who struggle to learn to read, determine appropriate interventions for these children, and ultimately provide support for children with dyslexia early and effectively.

References

Bardige, B. (2005). *At a Loss for Words: How America is Failing our Children and What We Can Do About It.* Philadelphia: Temple University Press.

Bogard, K. and Takanishi, R. (2005). PK-3: An aligned and coordinated approach to education for children 3 to 8 years old. *SRCD Social Policy Report, 19* (3).

Brown, B.V. and Bogard, K. (2007). Pre-kindergarten to 3rd grade (PK-3) school-based resources and third grade outcomes. *Cross Currents* (Child Trends DataBank), *5,* 1–7.

Bryan, T., Ergul, C. and Burstein, K. (2008). Curriculum-based measurement of preschoolers' early literacy skills. In L.M. Justice and C. Vukelich (eds), *Achieving Excellence in Preschool Literacy Instruction* (pp. 317–338). New York: Guilford Press.

Burdette, P. (2007). *Response to Intervention as it Relates to Early Intervening Services: Recommendations.* Retrieved August 10, 2008, from http://www.projectforum.org/docs/RTIasitRelatestoEIS.pdf.

Christie, J. F. (2008). The scientifically based reading research approach to early literacy instruction. In L.M. Justice and C. Vukelich (eds), *Achieving Excellence in Preschool Literacy Instruction.* (pp. 25–40). New York: Guilford Press.

Coleman, M.R., Buysse, V. and Neitzel, J. (2006). *Recognition and Response: An Early Intervening System for Young Children At-risk for Learning Disabilities.* Retrieved August 8, 2008, from www.fpg.unc.edu/~randr/pdfs/2006Synthesis_RandR_ES.pdf.

Dickinson, D. and Smith, A. (1994). Long-term effects of preschool teachers' book readings on low-income children's vocabulary and story comprehension. *Reading Research Quarterly, 29*: 104–122.

Dickinson, D.K., McCabe, A., Anastasopoulos, L., Peisner-Feinberg, E.S. and Poe, M. (2003). The comprehensive language approach to early literacy: The interrelationships among vocabulary, phonological sensitivity, and print knowledge among preschool-aged children. *Journal of Educational Psychology, 25,* 465–481.

Dunn, L.M., and Dunn, L.M. (2007). *Peabody Picture Vocabulary Test – IV.* Circle Pines, MN: American Guidance Service.

Early, D., Maxwell, K., Burchinal, M. *et al.* (2007). Teachers' education, classroom quality, and young children's academic skills: Results from seven studies of preschool programs. *Child Development, 78,* 558–580.

Fuchs, L.S. (1989). Evaluating solutions: Monitoring progress and revising intervention plans. In M.R. Shinn (ed.), *Curriculum-based Measurement: Assessing Special Children* (pp. 153–181). New York: Guildford.

Gersten, R. and Dimino, J.A. (2006). RTI (Response to Intervention): Rethinking special education for students with reading difficulties (yet again). *Reading Research Quarterly, 41 (1),* 99–108.

Hart, B. and Risley, T. (2003). The early catastrophe: The 30 million word gap by age 3. *American Educator* (Spring). Online: www.aft.org/pubs-reports/American_educator/spring2003/catastrophe.html.

Henry, G., Rickman, D., Ponder, B., Henderson, L., Mashburn, A. and Gordon, C. (2004). *The Georgia Early Childhood Study: 2001–2004 Final Report*, Georgia State University: Andrew Young School of Policy Studies.

Horowitz, S. H., Kaloi, L. and Petroff, S. (2007). *Transition to kindergarten: Policy implications for struggling learners and those who may be at risk for learning disabilities.* New York: National Center for Learning Disabilities.

Hymes, J.L. (1965) Early reading is a very risky business. *Grade Teacher, 82,* 88–92.

Invernizzi, M., Sullivan, A., Meier, J. and Swank, L. (2004). *Phonological Awareness Literacy Screening: Pre-Kindergarten.* Charlottesville, VA: University of Virginia.

Kalmar, K. (2008). Let's give children something to talk about: Oral language and preschool literacy. *Young Children,* 88–92.

Kaminski, R., Cummings, K.D., Powell-Smith, K.A. and Good, R.H.III (2008). Best practices in using Dynamic Indicators of Basic Early Literacy Skills for formative assessment and evaluation. In A. Thomas and J. Grimes (eds), *Best Practices in School Psychology V.* Bethesda, MD: National Association of School Psychologists.

Karweit, N. (1989). The effects of a story-reading program on the vocabulary and story comprehension skills of disadvantaged prekindergarten and kindergarten students. *Early Education and Development, 1,* 105–114.

Kirby, J.R., Parrila, R.K. and Pfeiffer, S.L. (2003). Naming speed and phonological awareness as predictors of reading development. *Journal of Educational Psychology, 95,* 453–464.

Kirby, J.R., Desrochers, A., Roth, L. and Lai, S. (2008). Longitudinal predictors of word reading development. *Canadian Psychology, 49,* 103–110.

Lamy, C., Barnett, W.S. and Jung, K. (2005). *The effects of Oklahoma's early childhood four-year-old program on young children's school readiness.* National Institute for Early Education Research, Rutgers University.

Lee, V.E. and Burkam, D.T. (2002). Inequality at the starting date: Social background differences in achievement as children begin school. Washington, DC: Economic Policy Institute.

Lynch, R. (2007). Enriching children, enriching the nation: Public investment in high-quality prekindergarten. Economic Policy Institute (Executive Summary) Retrieved August 12, 2008, from http://www.epi.org.

Mashburn, A., Pianta, R., Hamre, B., Downer, J., Barbarin, O., Bryant, D., Burchinal, M., Early, D. and Howes, C. (2008). Measures of classroom quality in prekindergarten and children's development of academic, language, and social skills. *Child Development, 79,* 732–749.

Meisels, S., Marsden, D., Dichtelmiller, M. and Jablon, J. (1995). *The Work Sampling System.* Pearson Education, Inc.

Mellard, D. F. and Johnson, E. (2008). *RTI: A Practitioner's Guide to Implementing Response to Intervention.* Thousand Oaks, CA: Corwin Press.

Morrow, L. (1985). Retelling stories: A strategy for improving young children's comprehension, concept of story structure, and oral language complexity. *The Elementary School Journal, 85,* 646–661.

National Association of State Directors of Special Education, Inc. (NASDSE) (2006). *Response to Intervention: Policy Considerations and Implementation.* Alexandria, VA: Author.

National Reading Panel (2000). *Report of the National Reading Panel: Teaching Children to Read.* Washington, DC: U.S. Department of Health and Human Services.

National Research Center on Learning Disabilities (NRCLD) (2006). *A tiered service delivery model.* Retrieved July 23, 2008 from www.fpg.unc.edu/~randr/pdfs/2006Synthesis_RandR_ES.pdf.

Neuman, S. B. (2006). The knowledge gap: Implications for early education. In Dickenson, D.K. and Neuman, S.B. (eds), *Handbook of Early Literacy Research, Volume 2* (pp. 29 – 40). New York: Guilford Press.

Phillips, B., Clancy-Menchetti, J. and Lonigan, C.J. (2008). Successful phonological awareness instruction with preschool children: Lessons from the classroom. *Topics in Early Childhood Special Education, 28:* 3–17.

Pianta, R. and Hadden, D.S. (2008). What we know about the quality of early education settings: Implications for research on teacher preparation and professional development. University of Virginia: National Center for Research on Early Childhood Education.

Planty, M., Hussar, W., Snyder, T., Provasnik, S., Kena, G., Dinkes, R., Kewal-Ramani, A. and Kemp, J. (2008). *The Condition of Education 2008* (NCES 2008–031). Washington, DC: U.S. National Center for Education Statistics, Institute of Education Sciences, U.S. Department of Education.

Princiotta, D., Flanagan, K.D. and Hausken, E.G. (2006). *Findings from the fifth-grade follow-up of the Early Childhood Longitudinal Study, Kindergarten Class of 1998–99 (ECLS-K).* (NCES 2006–038) U.S. Department of Education. Washington, DC: National Center for Education Statistics.

Purcell, T. and Rosemary, C.A. (2008). Differentiating instruction in the preschool classroom: Bridging emergent literacy instruction and developmentally appropriate practice. In L.M. Justice and C. Vukelich (eds), *Achieving Excellence in Preschool Literacy Instruction* (pp. 221–241). New York: Guilford Press.

Reynolds, A., Temple, J., Robertson, D. and Mann, E. (2001). Long-term effects of an early childhood intervention on educational achievement and juvenile arrest. *The Journal of the American Medical Association, 285 (18).* Retrieved July 13, 2008, from http://jama.ama-assn.org.proxyremote.galib.uga.edu:2048/cgi/content/full/285/18/2339.

Schweinhart, L. (1993). *What the High/Scope Perry Preschool study reveals about developmental transitions and contextual challenges of ethnic males.* Paper presented at the Annual Meeting of the American Psychological Association, Toronto, Ontario, Canada.

Snow, C.E., Burns, M.S. and Griffin, P. (eds) (1998). *Preventing Reading Difficulties in Young Children.* Washington, CD: National Academy Press.

Southern Education Foundation (2007). *Pre-Kindergarten in the South: The Region's Comparative Advantage in Education.* Atlanta, Georgia.

Southern Education Foundation (2008). *Time to Lead Again: The Promise of Georgia Pre-K.* Atlanta, Georgia.

Speece, D.L. and Walker, C.Y. (2007). What are the issues in response to intervention research? In D. Haager, J. Klingner and S. Vaughn (eds), *Evidence-Based Reading Practices for Response to Intervention* (pp. 287–301). Baltimore: Brookes.

Stecker, P.M., Fuchs, L.S. and Fuchs, D. (2005). Using curriculum-based measurement to improve student achievement: Review of the research. *Psychology in the Schools, 42 (8),* 795–819.

Torgesen, J.K., Foorman, B.R. and Wagner, R.K. (2008) *Dyslexia: A Brief for Educators, Parents, and Legislators in Florida.* Retrieved August 15, 2008, from Florida State University, Florida Center for Reading Research Web site: http://www.fcrr.org/TechnicalReports/Dyslexia_Technical_Assistance_Paper-Final.pdf.

Vasilyeva, M., Huttenlocher, J. and Waterfall, H. (2006). Effects of language intervention on syntactic skill levels in preschoolers. *Developmental Psychology, 42* (1), 164–174.

Vaughn, S. (2003, December). *How Many Tiers Are Needed for Response to Intervention to Achieve Acceptable Prevention Outcomes?* Paper presented at the National Research Center on Learning Disabilities Responsiveness-to-Intervention Symposium, Kansas City, MO.

6

The role of early identification
Models from research and practice

Margaret Crombie and Gavin Reid

This chapter

- highlights the importance of early identification
- discusses the at risk factor associated with early identification
- looks critically at the wait to fail model
- discusses the intervention that can be used as a follow-through from early identification
- discusses the role of parents in early identification.

Introduction

The responsibility for early identification should not rest solely on the teacher or school, but it should be a planned and integrated activity involving parents and professionals working together in the context of both home and school. The legislation *Every Child Matters* (England and Wales) (CWDC, 2007) and *Getting it Right for Every Child* (Scotland) (Scottish Executive, 2005) implies that this is the most desirable method and the common assessment framework (CAP) which is incorporated into the above legislation can help to make early identification a reality (Came and Reid, 2008).

The school should not be the only agency involved in early identification. If integrated assessment is to be effective structured and collaborative planning is necessary. This collaboration needs to involve teachers, parents, community workers and other professionals such as home teachers, occupational therapists, psychologists and speech and language therapists.

It is also important that early identification of children who are at risk of literacy failure is accompanied by appropriate opportunities for intervention. This can be more challenging with pre-school children as the difficulties with literacy learning may not be too obvious at this stage. Yet if early identification is to be effective then it is important that it focuses on pre-school children as well as children in the early years of primary school.

Identification through failure

It is often the case, in a local authority context, that a child has to *fail* to learn to read and write before difficulties are recognised, and certainly before the term 'dyslexia' can be used. This means there is a delay in providing effective provision (Crombie, 2002; Lipsett, 2007; Reid *et al.*, 2005). This failure, with its detrimental effects on self-esteem, motivation, and often classroom behaviour, exerts not only an unacceptable burden on the dyslexic child, but also affects teachers and parents who must cope with the subsequent social, emotional and developmental effects of the child's early frustrations (Frith, 1999). We have not yet been able to measure the exact extent to which failure to tackle early difficulties may lead to later social problems, mental health issues and/or loss of potential, but we do know that these are significant issues (Daniel *et al.*, 2006; Miles and Stipek, 2006; Rack, 2005; Reid and Kirk, 2001; Trzesniewski *et al.*, 2006). We also know that there are early indications which can tell us that later failure to learn to read and write are more likely (Bradley, 1989). With this knowledge, it is therefore possible that we can prevent, or at least minimise the later damaging effects of reading failure.

Dyslexia and early identification – the 'at risk' factor

Early identification of potential difficulties is not the same as early identification of dyslexia. The two may go together, but they are distinctly different, and only time will tell if it is appropriate to apply the term 'dyslexia'. For that reason many of the screening tests for dyslexia only claim to identify children 'at risk' of dyslexia and do not offer a definitive diagnosis. An example of this is the battery of Dyslexia Screening Tests (Fawcett and Nicolson, 1996a, 1996b). Fawcett and Nicolson suggest that each screening test, the Dyslexia Early Screening Test (4.5 to 6.5 years), the Dyslexia Screening Test (6.5 to 16.5), the Dyslexia Adult Screening Test (16.5 to 65) and the Pre-school Screening Test (3.5 to 4.5), was designed as the first of a series of stages in a structured Screening–Assessment–Support procedure. These tests were intended to be used by teachers in schools and, as such, were deliberately designed to be quick, cheap and effective in providing the 'positive indicators' for dyslexia, and attractive to pupils as they were 'fun, varied, and non-threatening'.

Early identification of potential later literacy difficulties can be made from the earliest stages in a child's life or indeed from early screening. For example we may see lack of co-ordination and sequencing skills as the baby struggles to learn to crawl (or simply does not bother to crawl), or we may be aware that the nursery-age child is unable to pick up the skills of rhyming and alliteration that the other children do (Viholainen *et al.*, 2002; Molfese *et al.,* 2008). The child derives no pleasure from playing sound 'games'. Some children seem unable to recall the names of familiar objects and seem to jumble up the syllables in their words. When we see a pattern of concerns, sometimes coupled with a known family history of dyslexia, we have identified a child at possible 'risk' of the later frustration and humiliation which may result from failure to gain skills related to literacy. It is at this stage that timely appropriate interventions can make a huge difference to the child's prospects (Vellutino *et al.*, 2006). At this stage, there is no need to label to give the appropriate help, but there is an obligation on the adults around to ensure that everything that can be done, is done to prevent the likely de-motivation that will result from failure to learn. The label may be important in time, but at the early pre-school stage, it is the identification of concerns and the accompanying appropriate interventions that are vital.

The 'wait to fail' model

Wagner (2008) however suggests that the traditional approach to identification does not identify poor readers in the United States until second grade on average. There are significant shortcomings on this approach and this model is often referred to as the 'wait to fail' model. Wagner however argues that new developments in understanding of early literacy may eliminate or reduce the 'wait to fail' nature of approaches that compare reading achievement to expectations based on performance in other areas. He argues that emergent print awareness can provide the means for earlier identification. Reading is a developmental phenomenon that builds on a range of skills and these can be noted in pre-school children. Wagner suggests that print awareness can be reliably assessed in children as young as three, and is highly predictive of later decoding. Print awareness measures can be used to identify preschool-age children whose early literacy development is lagging behind that of their peers (Lonigan *et al.*, 2007).

In the United States the Response to Intervention (RTI) model is now used comprehensively. The RTI approach begins with the provision of effective reading instruction in a regular classroom, ideally in first grade. Progress monitoring is carried out and additional help is provided after documenting a failure to respond to effective instruction in the regular classroom. The next step is to add small-group based tutoring and resume progress monitoring for an additional period of several months. If however this process doesn't begin until formal reading instruction is underway usually in the first grade, it is not likely that children with learning disabilities will be identified earlier than they have been using the traditional approaches. Wagner however suggests that an alternative and more desirable approach would be to implement an RTI approach for preschool-age children, using progress monitoring of print awareness. Wagner also suggests that a hybrid model of identification that combines elements of the traditional and RTI approaches might make the most sense through identifying measures of phonological processing and rapid naming as these are among the best predictors of which children are likely to be non-responders in an RTI model. The model suggested by Manis *et al.* (2000) uses measures that consist of phonological processing, rapid naming and print awareness – all of which are predictive of reading performance.

Early identification and family history

Molfese *et al.* (2008) argues that increasing attention is now paid to identifying the characteristics of young children that place them 'at risk' for difficulties in developing literacy skills even before they show evidence of poor reading. They suggest that the 'risk' of dyslexia and reading-related skill deficits can be due to a family history in which one or more close relative has been assessed with dyslexia and this information can be utilised for early identification. There is a large body of research on children with a family history of dyslexia, including seven longitudinal studies covering age ranges from preschool/kindergarten through 2nd, 4th or 6th grade (Elbro *et al.*, 1998; Pennington and Lefly 2001; de Jong and van der Leij 1999, 2003; Lyytinen *et al.*, 2001, 2004; Scarborough, 1990; Snowling *et al.*, 2003; Wagner *et al.*, 1997). These studies report early differences in letter knowledge, naming speed, specific phonological skills (e.g., rhyming, short-term memory), and some language skills (e.g.. vocabulary, grammar) as markers of group differences at preschool age or kindergarten. Molefese *et al.* (2008) report on a longitudinal study where 38 per cent of Finnish children who had family histories of dyslexia developed reading disabilities, compared to 12 per cent of children with no known familial risk.

Early identification and intervention

In a longitudinal study conducted with young children in New York, Vellutino and his colleagues (Vellutino *et al.*, 2006) investigated the effects of implementing early intervention for children identified on entry to kindergarten as potentially 'at risk' of reading failure. All children in the study were given a test of letter-name knowledge and roughly 30 per cent were identified as being 'at risk for early reading difficulties' on the basis of the findings. Tests of phonological awareness (sensitivity to rhyme and alliteration), rapid automatised naming, counting by ones and number identification were also included. The 'at risk' group were given an hour's training each week during their kindergarten year, split into two sessions, from specially trained staff. The sessions, conducted in small groups of two or three children, focused on activities such as concepts of print, letter recognition, letter identification, phonological awareness, letter–sound matching, sight word learning, shared and guided reading and listening to stories. From their results, Vellutino and his colleagues concluded that early intervention made at the kindergarten stage can significantly improve early skills and prepare the children for more formal reading instruction.

All children, dyslexic or not, can benefit from the targeted focus on literacy development, so additional strategies do not need to be individual or specific to one particular child at this early stage, but should be aimed to encourage a small group at least. The inclusion of children 'at risk' in group learning situations could bring benefits for the whole group. Though some children may not need the focused intervention, it will do no harm, and is likely to make them more confident.

Early identification and social and community factors

Young children are affected by social circumstances and factors in the home. This includes parenting practices, family activities, language spoken at home, exposure to books and magazines and socioeconomic status (SES) variables such as parental education and occupation. According to Molfese and Molfese (2002) these factors alone will not cause dyslexia, but they may exacerbate it. Examples of this can be seen in the practice in one Scottish Education Authority – East Renfrewshire – where home tutors have been employed to work with targeted families at the pre-school stage. Community activities also featured in the desire to heighten the awareness of books and the need for a literacy-rich culture. It is accepted however that early identification and intervention are important 'for preventing early and long-term reading difficulties in most "at risk" children' whatever the home background (Vellutino et al., 2006).

Early intervention – follow through

Torgesen (2000) argues that even with appropriate intervention at an early stage, not all children will reach an age-appropriate level of reading when they proceed into the more formal learning situation. There is an ever-increasing desire to increase literacy levels and countries can be easily embarrassed by international studies and 'league tables' that identify those countries that are failing in literacy (Shiel, 2002). Substantial amounts of money and government intervention are common to attempt to secure a rise in literacy levels (Rose, 2006; Reid-Lyon, 2003). On both sides of the Atlantic recent studies have revealed that systematic, structured programmes for teaching reading can benefit huge numbers of children. In the United States the National Institute of Child Health and Human Development (NICHD) with the U.S. Office of Education, and in the UK, Klynveld Peat Marwick Goerdeler (KPMG) with the University of London and the Department for Education and Skills (DfES) have been conducting research studies with large numbers of children into the effectiveness of various programmes for intervening early in a child's reading career with the lowest achieving children (Burroughs-Lange, 2006; Gross, 2006; Rose, 2006; Torgesen et al., 2006). While it is important to appreciate that reading involves a number of different skills, both decoding and comprehension of written words are vital. If children cannot decode, they are unlikely to be able to comprehend what has not been decoded. If verbal skills are weak and the children have poor vocabulary knowledge, then even teaching the children to decode will not result in a high level of comprehension, so results on reading comprehension tests are likely to vary according to levels of oral understanding (Torgesen, 2000), not necessarily decoding ability.

However, even when this has been taken into account, progress can be made by early intervention for the lowest achieving readers using methods such as Reading Recovery and Synthetic Phonics. However for a very small percentage of children, those that Torgesen (2000) calls 'treatment resisters', perhaps appropriately also called 'dyslexic', more targeted and systematic multisensory programmes will be required over a longer period to achieve success. It is for these children too that a range of other strategies will be required to ensure that boredom through repeated use of the same material does not reinforce a sense of failure. While reading interventions are to be welcomed before the sense of failure becomes embedded, it is desirable to be able to identify and target these potential 'treatment resisters' even earlier. If not, these children will remain vulnerable throughout their school lives.

Identifying a profile

Early identification is more than identifying the lowest performing reading grouping in order for them to receive help, though this strategy will increase the reading skills of many children. For many however, it is about identifying a 'dyslexic profile' early on using the indicators such as – letter and sound knowledge, short-term and working memory skills, alliteration and rhyming abilities, speedy naming of objects, sequencing often along possible difficulties in accessing known words for objects, possible organisation skills often along with a genetic component. While motor skills difficulties and balance often co-occur with dyslexia, they do not always, and seem to correlate to the severity of the dyslexic difficulties (Haslum and Miles, 2007). With this knowledge, a protocol can be developed to ensure we do not allow children to fail to learn without intervening to prevent that failure before it happens.

Transition

There are various transition points in a child's life when they are particularly vulnerable. Moving from the relative informality of the nursery or kindergarten to the more formal primary school years is likely to start to highlight weaknesses in literacy where these exist. Moving from one teacher to another, again with varying levels of formality of classroom organisation can in itself cause problems, and then the change from primary to secondary where the pupils have a different format to their day, but a different range of subjects can have both positive and negative effects on the pupil. At all stages including the move to college or work, it is important that any difficulties are understood and that the pupils know this. Hunter (this volume, Chapter 17) suggests that parents can harbour considerable concern that their children's challenges will go unnoticed at school especially when they are changing school or moving from one sector to another. Parents according to Hunter can be concerned about the child not being able to copy homework down accurately, not keeping up with reading and other copying tasks and perhaps being at a disadvantage in class assessments. There is also the concern that school staff may see the parents as undue 'worriers' and consider them over-anxious parents.

Conflicting perspectives: research and practice

Different perspectives held by researchers and practitioners somehow need to be reconciled and converted into practice to satisfy the demands of legislation, policy makers, school management, teachers, psychologists, parents and, above all, to support all pupils in engaging in learning both within educational institutions and outside.

Singleton has utilised cognitive psychology and current theories on dyslexia to produce a computer based cognitive profiling system which attempts to identify children at high risk of literacy failure at 4 years of age. The theoretical basis of the Cognitive Profiling System (CoPS) (Beech and Singleton, 1996) is that some cognitive factors such as visual/verbal memory, auditory/verbal memory associations, phonological awareness and colour discrimination correlate with the development of early literacy. This would mean that children who have difficulty in these cognitive tasks will very likely have difficulty acquiring literacy. The CoPS, therefore, according to Singleton, should have a predictive value for the teacher. It is crucial, however, that parents are directly involved in research studies in order to identify the best practice in collaborative activities between home and school.

Education policy

The early literacy intervention strategy in East Renfrewshire in Scotland is an example of an integrated strategy that represents a deliberate attempt on the part of the local educational authority to make equitable provision for the literacy education of young children from diverse backgrounds. Simultaneously, they make provision for the special learning needs of those students who experience particular difficulties in literacy acquisition. The East Renfrewshire approach to fostering children's early literacy development considers the following factors: family background, the promotion of a literacy-rich environment for all children, current knowledge to address early literacy acquisition for every child, the integration of school and community resources and staff ability to address early identification and intervention through teacher professional development. This approach emphasizes the importance of promoting an integrated policy which is supported through carefully planned funding, distributed across community services.

Role of parents

Parents have a key role to play in early identification. In many cases it is the parent who may alert the school of concern over the child's literacy development. In some cases the parent may be aware of concern before the child even commences school, particularly if there are other children in the family or relatives who have dyslexia. Parents usually know their child well and can be alerted to signs of anxiety or stress when the child is learning new material. Parents can often feel the sense of frustration from their child and can usually work out if the frustration is stemming from the challenges of the task (Reid, 2004). This is reflected in some formal assessment tools such as the *Special Needs Assessment Profile* (SNAP) (Weedon and Reid, 2002) which asks 32 questions of parents in order to collect information at the starting point of the assessment. This includes information relating to medical, social, emotional and educational areas as well as the child's learning habits and preferences.

Most schools now accept, or at least they should, that parents have a key role to play in the assessment process. In fact some schools and educational authorities go further, as was seen in the area of Fife in Scotland when they produced a policy on dyslexia called *Partnership: Professionals, Parents and Pupils* (Fife Education Authority, 1995). This emphasizes the key role parents of children with dyslexia can play in collaboration with schools.

There is also a role for parental participation as part of the assessment process. The information that parents can provide on early pre-school development, the age at which key milestones were reached since birth, e.g. when their child started talking and walking, the reasons why the parents feel that their child may have dyslexia, and any other reason for a possible difficulty in learning, such as problems at birth, factors such as behaviour, lack of interest in learning and what type of activities motivate their child. These are all crucial for the assessment and need to be considered at an early stage in the process.

Conclusion

It needs to be acknowledged that early identification does not necessarily mean early labelling. Early labelling can be misleading and perhaps unnecessary, but early identification of 'at risk' children is essential. This chapter has supported the view that if early identification is to be successful then collaborative processes need to be in place. This collaboration should see early identification being embedded into the system and used widely across all schools. Ideally early identification should stem from the daily business of teaching and the 'at risk' children should be noted from the monitoring of children's responses to individual tasks. It is crucial that early identification is seen as an everyday part of the role of a teacher and not a 'one-off' special occurrence. Every child needs to be part of an early identification policy. This will pave the way for curriculum and teaching procedures that can identify 'at risk' children and importantly provide the means of intervention that can prevent early difficulties from restricting progress in literacy.

References

Beech, J.R. and Singleton, C. (1996) *The Psychological Assessment of Reading*. London: Routledge.

Bradley, L. and Bryant, P.E. (1983) Categorising sounds and learning to read: A causal connection. *Nature, 310*, 419–421.

Burroughs-Lange, S. (2006) *Evaluation of Reading Recovery in London Schools: Every Child a Reader 2005–6*. University of London Institute of Education.

Came, F. and Reid, G. (2008) *CAP it All: Concern, Assess and Provide. Practical tools and techniques to identify and assess individual needs*. Marlborough, Wiltshire: Learning Works International.

Children's Workforce Development Council (CWDC) (2007). *Every child matters: Common assessment framework*. Leeds: CWDC.

Crombie, M. (2002) Dyslexia – The New Dawn: Policy, Practice, Provision and Management of Dyslexia from Pre-five into Primary. (Doctoral thesis, University of Strathclyde).

Dale, P.S., Price, T.S., Bishop, D.V.M. and Plomin, R. (2003) Outcomes of early language delay: Predicting persistent and transient language difficulties at 3 and 4 years. *Journal of Speech, Language and Hearing Research, 46*, 544–560.

Daniel, S.S., Walsh, A.K., Goldston, D.B., Arnold, E.M., Reboussin, B.A. and Wood, F.B. (2006) Suicidality, school dropout, and reading problems among adolescents. *Journal of Learning Disabilities, 39*, 6, 507–514.

deJong, P. and van der Leij, A. (1999) Specific contributions of phonological abilities to early reading acquisition: Results from a Dutch latent variable longitudinal study. *Journal of Educational Psychology, 91*, 450–476.

deJong, P.F. and van der Leij, A. (2003) Developmental changes in the manifestation of a phonological deficit in dyslexic children learning to read a regular orthography. *Journal of Educational Psychology, 95*, 22–40.

Dickinson, D.K. and Tabors, P.O. (1991) Early literacy: Linkages between home, school and literacy achievement at age five. *Journal of Research in Childhood Education, 6*, 1, 30–46.

Elbro, C., Borstrom, I. and Petersen, D.K. (1998) Predicting dyslexia from kindergarten: The importance of distinctness of phonological representations of lexical items. *Reading Research Quarterly, 33*, 36–60.

Farver, J.M., Nakamoto, J. and Lonigan, C.J. (2007) Assessing preschoolers' emergent literacy skills in English and Spanish with the Get Ready to Read! screening tool. *Annals of Dyslexia, 57*(2), 161–178.

Fawcett, A. and Nicolson, R. (1996a) *Dyslexia Early Screening Test*. London: The Psychological Corporation, Harcourt Brace and Company Publishers.

Fawcett, A. and Nicolson, R. (1996b) *Dyslexia Screening Test*. London: The Psychological Corporation, Harcourt Brace and Company Publishers.

Frith, U. (1999) Paradoxes in the definition of dyslexia. *Dyslexia, 5*(4), 192–214.

Gross, J. (2006) *The Long Term Costs of Literacy Difficulties*. London: KPMG Foundation.

Haslum, M.N. and Miles, T.R. (2007) Motor performance and dyslexia in a national cohort of 10-year-old children. *Dyslexia, 13*, 4, 257–275.

Hatcher, P.J., Hulme, C. and Ellis, A.W. (1994) Ameliorating early reading failure by integrating the teaching of reading and phonological skills: The phonological linkage hypothesis. *Child Development, 65*, 1, 41–57.

Hulme, C., Hatcher, P., Nation, K., Brown, A., Adams, J. and Stuart, G. (2002) Phoneme awareness is a better predictor of reading skill than onset-rime awareness. *Journal of Experimental Child Psychology, 82*, 2–28.

Lipsett, A. (2007, 5 December) MP proposes new law to help children with dyslexia. *Education Guardian*, Retrieved 3 January 2008, from http://education.guardian.co.uk/sen/story/0,2222302,00.html.

Lyytinen, P. and Lyytinen, H. (2004) Growth and predictive relations of vocabulary and inflectional morphology in children with and without dyslexia. *Applied Psycholinguistics, 25*, 2, 397–411.

Lyytinen, H., Aro, M., Eklund, K., Erskine, J., Guttorm, T., Laakso, M.-L. *et al.* (2004). The development of children at familial risk for dyslexia: birth to early school age. *Annals of Dyslexia, 54*, 184–220.

Lyytinen, P., Eklund, K. and Lyytinen, H. (2005) Language development and literacy skills in late-talking toddlers with and without familial risk of dyslexia. *Annals of Dyslexia, 55*, 2, 166–192.

McCardle, P., Scarborough, H.S. and Catts, H.W. (2001) Predicting, explaining, and preventing children's reading difficulties. *Learning Disabilities Research and Practice, 16*, 4, 230–239.

Manis, F.R., Doi, L.M. and Bhadha, B. (2000) Naming speed, phonological awareness and orthographic knowledge in second graders. *Journal of Learning Disabilities, 3*(4), 325–333.

Miles, S.B. and Stipek, D. (2006) Contemporaneous and longitudinal associations between social behavior and literacy achievement in a sample of low-income elementary school children. *Child Development, 77*, 1, 103–117.

Molfese, V.J. and Molfese, D.L. (2002) Environmental and social influences on reading skills as indexed by brain and behavioural responses. *Annals of Dyslexia, 52*, 121–137.

Molfese, D.L., Molfese, V.J., Barnes, M.E., Warren, C.G. and Molfese, P.J. (2008) Familial predictors of dyslexia: evidence from preschool children with and without familial dyslexia risk. In G. Reid, A. Fawcett, F. Manis and L. Siegel (eds) *The Sage Dyslexia Handbook*. London: Sage Publications.

Paul, R. (2000) Predicting outcomes of early expressive language delay: Ethical implications. In D.V. Bishop and L.B. Leonard (eds) *Speech and Language Impairments in Children. Causes, characteristics, intervention and outcome* (pp. 195–209). Hove, UK: Psychology Press.

Pennington, B.F., Filipek, P.A., Lefly, D.L., Churchwell, J., Kennedy, D.N. and Simon, J.H. (1999). Brain morphometry in reading-disabled twins. *Neurology, 53*, 723–729.

Rack, J. (2005) *The Incidence of Hidden Disabilities in the Prison Population*. Egham: Dyslexia Institute.

Reid, G. (2004) *Dyslexia: A Complete Guide for Parents*. Chichester: Wiley.

Reid, G. and Kirk, J. (2001) An examination of the relationship between dyslexia and offending in young people and the implications for the training system. *Dyslexia: An International journal of research and practice, 7*, 2, 77–84.

Reid, G., Shaywitz, S.E. and Shaywitz, B.A. (2003) Defining dyslexia, comorbidity, teachers' knowledge of language and reading: A definition of dyslexia. *Annals of Dyslexia, 53*, 1–14.

Reid, G., Deponio, P. and Petch, L.D. (2005) Identification, assessment and Intervention: implications of an audit on dyslexia policy and practice in Scotland. *Dyslexia, 11*(3), 203–216.

Rescorla, L. (2002) Language and reading outcomes to age 9 in late-talking toddlers. *Journal of Speech, Language and Hearing Research, 45*, 360–371.

Rose, J. (2006) *Independent Review of the Teaching of Early Reading*. Nottingham: DfES Publications.

Scarborough, H. (1990) Very early language deficits in dyslexic children. *Child Development, 61*, 1728–1743.

Scottish Executive (2005) *Getting it Right for Every Child: Proposals for Action*. Edinburgh: Scottish Executive.

Shiel, G. (2002) Literacy standards and factors affecting literacy: what national and international assessments tell us. In G. Reid and J. Wearmouth (eds) *Dyslexia and Literacy*. Chichester: Wiley.

Snowling, M.J., Gallagher, A. and Frith, U. (2003) Family risk of dyslexia is continuous: Individual differences in the precursors of reading skill. *Child Development*, 74, 358–373.

Torgesen, J.K. (2000) Individual differences in response to early interventions in reading: The lingering problem of treatment resisters. *Learning Disabilities Research* and *Practice*, 15, 1, 55–64.

Torgesen, J.K., Myers, D., Schirm, A., Stuart, E., Vartivarian, S., Mansfield, W., Stancavage, F., Durno, D., Javorsky, R. and Haan, C. (2006) *National assessment of title 1 interim report to Congress: Volume II: Closing the reading gap, first year findings from a randomized trial of four reading interventions for striving readers.* Washington, DC: U.S. Department of Education, Institute of Education Sciences.

Trzesniewski, K.H., Moffitt, T.E., Caspi, A., Taylor, A. and Maughan, B. (2006) Revisiting the association between reading achievement and antisocial behavior: New evidence of an environmental explanation from a twin study. *Child Development*, 77, 1, 72–88

Vellutino, F.R., Scanlon, D.M., Small, S. and Fanuele, D.P. (2006) Response to intervention as a vehicle for distinguishing between children with and without reading disabilities: Evidence for the role of kindergarten and first-grade interventions. *Journal of Learning Disabilities*, 39, 2, 157–169.

Viholainen, H., Ahonen, T., Cantell, M., Lyytinen, P. and Lyytinen, H. (2002) Development of early motor skills and language in children at risk for familial dyslexia. *Developmental Medicine* and *Child Neurology*, 44, 761–769.

Wagner, R. (2008) Rediscovering Dyslexia: New Approaches for Identification, Classification and Intervention. In G. Reid, A. Fawcett, F. Manis and L. Siegel (eds) *The Sage Dyslexia Handbook*. London: Sage Publications.

Wagner, R.K., Torgesen, J.K., Rashotte, C.A., Hecht, S., Barker, T., Burgess, S. and Garon, T. (1997) Causal relations between the development of phonological processing and reading: A five-year longitudinal lstudy. *Developmental Psychology*, 33: 468–479.

Weedon, C. and Reid, G. (2002) *Special Needs Assessment Profile* (SNAP). London: Hodder Murray.

7

Identification and assessment of dyslexia and planning for learning
Gavin Reid and Janice Wearmouth

This chapter

- is concerned with the complex challenge facing teachers who are responsible for assessing difficulties in literacy development in order to plan effective programmes to address dyslexic pupils' learning needs
- includes discussion of the broad range of assessment strategies that may be required for a teacher appropriately to assess the characteristics of the individual pupil within and without the context of the classroom
- includes discussion of the current spread of cognitive measures and their relationship to diagnostic criteria for dyslexia
- covers some of the issues raised by the growing expectation that the perspectives of the 'users' of the system, that is both students and their parents or carers, will be taken into account in the assessment process
- assesses ways in which the learning environment potentially creates barriers to, or facilitates, literacy development and the implications for effective planning of learning
- establishes links between assessment and classroom practice.

Introduction

There have been a number of developments in the understanding of learning and, therefore, difficulties in learning, and also in the area of children's and parents'/carers' rights in recent years that have had important repercussions for assessment and planning of teaching and learning in the area of dyslexia. These developments have included a move away from the solely 'medical' model of difficulties in learning to one that recognizes the interactive nature of difficulties in learning (Wedell, 2000) and a broader concept of what specially 'needs' to be done to address such difficulties. In this 'interactive model', the barriers to pupils' learning arise as a result of the interaction between the characteristics of the student and what is offered through the pedagogy and supporting resources. Further, as a result of the implications of current models of learning which emphasize the agency of the learner (Vygotsky, 1987), the issue of pupil self advocacy has assumed an increasing significance. Legal and moral considerations (Gersch, 2001) have supported this emphasis on greater pupil involvement and have, additionally, created the need to take seriously the right of parents and carers not just to be consulted over the formal process of educating young people, but also to be actively engaged in the decision-making processes.

Overall, there is no golden formula for addressing the special learning needs of every student who experiences difficulties of a dyslexic nature. As noted by Wearmouth (in press), there are a number of general considerations in relation to addressing individual student's special educational needs in the area of dyslexia. For example:

- every student who experiences difficulties of a dyslexic nature is different;
- every situation is different.

Addressing difficulties is a question of problem-solving:

- find out about the learner, the difficulties s/he experiences and his/her views;
- find out about the views of the learner's family;
- assess barriers to the student's learning in the classroom environment and in the particular curriculum area;
- think about the requirements of the particular curriculum area;
- reflect on what will best address those barriers to help the learner to achieve in the classroom.

Finding out about the learner

The use of tests: points to ponder

Assessment is a powerful educational tool for promoting learning. However, assessment activities should be appropriate to the aims of the assessment, to the objectives of the curriculum, and to the individual students (Caygill and Elley, 2001; Clarke et al., 2003). Dyslexia is a difficulty with information processing, so when carrying out an assessment it is important to identify the processing skills of the child. Often the reasoning and understanding are unaffected, but the actual processing of information can be challenging. Areas such as accessing print, decoding and encoding print, processing speed and memory as well as written output are all involved in the processing activities necessary for literacy acquisition.

Reid (2003) suggests that assessment for dyslexia should consider three aspects – discrepancies, difficulties and differences. Discrepancies become apparent when we make comparisons between decoding and reading/listening comprehension, between oral and written responses and between performances within the different subject areas of the curriculum. The central difficulty is usually related to the decoding or the encoding of print, and this may be the result of different contributory factors. For example, some difficulties may include phonological processing, visual-processing difficulties, memory factors, organizational and sequencing difficulties, motor and co-ordination difficulties, language problems or perceptual difficulties of an auditory or visual nature. It is also important to acknowledge the differences between individual learners. This particularly applies to dyslexic children. An assessment, therefore, should also consider learning and cognitive styles as well as the learning and teaching environment. This also helps to take the child's preferences for learning into account, which, in fact, should be one of the aims of an assessment.

Cognitive measures

One of the most well used practices in the assessment procedures for dyslexia is to obtain a measure of intellectual functioning as part of the investigation into discrepancies. Often the

WISC is used as an ability measure as it is well standardized and translated in a number of languages (WISC-1V) (Wechesler, 2004). The use of ability measures, however, such as the WISC, according to Siegal (1989, 1992), rests on all or some of the following assumptions:

- that tests of ability or IQ are valid and reliable measures, so that there is some virtue in examining discrepancies between ability and achievement;
- particular subtests are valid instruments in the assessment of specific cognitive subskills;
- distinctive patterns may emerge that can be reliably correlated with learning difficulties;
- and that IQ and reading share a causal dependency, with IQ factors influencing reading ability.

Some authors (for example Siegel, 1989, Siegel and Lipka, 2008), however, argue that the evidence in relation to these points is inconsistent. IQ tests do not necessarily measure intelligence, but in fact measure factual knowledge, expressive language ability, short-term memory and other skills related to learning. The stages within the information-processing cycle are important in relation to dyslexia. Often children with dyslexia have difficulty in actually receiving the information—input—particularly if it is provided verbally. This can have implications for the use of standardized tests, which are often administered verbally, and the child has to process the information using the auditory modality. Similarly, there is much evidence that children with dyslexia can have difficulties in relation to cognition. Cognition essentially involves how children think and process information in order to understand it, to relate it to previous knowledge and to store it in long term memory. Since these cognitive factors can represent difficulties often associated with dyslexia there is a tendency to focus an assessment principally on these cognitive factors. The other factor associated with dyslexia and information-processing is the output of information. It is interesting to note that often children with dyslexia do not perform to their best in tests because responding to test items involves immediate responses, many of which are in written form and all of which have to be delivered without any help from the examiner. Yet, children with dyslexia more often than not respond well to cues and with assisted assessment can often reveal skills and aptitudes that are concealed in traditionally administered psychometric tests. Siegel and Lipka (2008) argue that recent studies have demonstrated the limitation of IQ in assessing students with learning disabilities. Further, they suggest that IQ is irrelevant, except possibly to define the border between learning disabilities and retardation.

Assessment of processing skills

The principal method of identifying specific difficulties in processing skills has been the use of instruments that measure intellectual functioning such as the WISC. A significant breakthrough in terms of process assessment, however, has emerged from the revision of the Process Assessment of the Learner (PAL-11) diagnostic assessment for reading and writing (Berninger 2007). Berninger suggests that intelligence tests such as the WISC-1V may offer correlation data with measures of academic achievement, but do not explain why a child is experiencing poor learning outcomes or how to intervene to improve learning outcomes. It may indicate that a child needs intervention but it does not tell us precisely what kind of intervention would be the most effective. The Process Assessment (PAL-11) materials developed by Berninger offers clues to why a child may be underachieving in reading or writing and provides guidance on how such difficulties can be tackled.

The sub-tests of the PAL target those neuro-developmental processes most relevant to reading and writing. These include orthographic skills, phonological skills, morphological and syntactic skills, rapid automatic naming, silent reading fluency, word specific spellings and narrative compositional fluency. The test is very specific and extremely well conceptualized. The reading related sub-tests are in the form of domains such as orthographic coding, phonological coding, morphological/syntactic coding, verbal working memory, and rapid automatic naming. For each of these domains there are at least two to four specific subtests. For example orthographic coding contains subtests on receptive coding and expressive coding. The receptive coding subtest is used to measure the processes involved in coding written words into memory and analysing units of the written word without having the child writing or pronouncing them. This suite of tests can provide an alternative, or at least reduce the dependency on the use of measures of intellectual functioning.

Similarly the Wechsler Individual Achievement Test (WIAT-11) provides comprehensive insights into literacy acquisition and the scores can be correlated with the measures on the WISC. While there is a range of skills taken into account in the WIAT-11 it is still up to the examiner to attempt to use the data diagnostically. Essentially the results inform us on the extent of the child's difficulties but do not provide guidance on the areas within the reading process that can precisely account for these difficulties. The WIAT-11 does provide composite measures on key aspects such as reading, mathematics, written and oral language, and although, for example, the reading composite includes a test on pseudoword decoding, it does not inform us of the reasons for the child's difficulties. Difficulties in pseudoword reading, for example, can suggest difficulties in applying phonetic decoding skills, but it does not tell us what kind of phonological difficulty the child experiences.

This emphasizes the need to use tests selectively and purposefully. It is important to obtain measures of the extent of the difficulty, but equally it is important to obtain evidence of the nature of the difficulties experienced and the reasons for these difficulties. This information is necesary if appropriate and effective intervention is to be put in place.

There are more specific tests that can accompany some of these mentioned above and can provide diagnostic criteria as well as age/grade related measures. One such example of this is the Comprehensive Test of Phonological Processing (CTOPP) (Wagner et al., 1999). The authors have placed the test within a theoretical framework that pinpoints three types of phonological processing relevant for mastery of written language – phonological awareness, phonological memory and rapid naming. Phonological awareness refers to an individual's awareness of and access to the sound structure of oral language. It is important to assess phonological awareness as this is often seen as one of the principal difficulties in dyslexia and, furthermore, studies show that children who are weak in phonological awareness show improved reading performance after being given intervention designed to improve their phonological awareness (Torgeson et al., 1992; Torgeson et al., 1997).

The other areas in the CTOPP theoretical model are phonological memory and rapid naming. Phonological memory refers to coding information phonologically for temporary storage in working or short term memory. This is often referred to as the 'phonological loop' (Baddeley, 1986; Torgeson, 1996). Difficulties in this area can restrict a child's abilities to learn new material. Phonological coding in working memory, according to Wagner, Torgeson and Rashotte (1999), therefore plays an important role in decoding new words, particularly multisyllabic words.

The third aspect of the model underpinning the CTOPP is rapid naming. This relates to the efficiency with which young readers are able to retrieve phonological codes associated with individual phonemes, word segments and entire words. This is important as it has been shown that individuals who have difficulty in rapid naming usually have difficulty in reading fluency and that individuals who have difficulty in both rapid naming and phonological awareness (double deficit) will have greater difficulty in learning to read than individuals with deficits in either rapid naming or phonological awareness (Bowers and Wolf, 1993).

This type of test not only provides precise diagnostic information but also can be used as a means of monitoring and evaluating a child's progress with the intervention that is being used.

A similar process is used in the Woodcock Reading Mastery Tests – revised (Woodcock, 1998). There are three main areas to the model used in this test battery. These are reading readiness, basic skills and reading comprehension. For readiness, therefore, visual/auditory learning and letter identification are included; for basic skills, word identification and word attack are included; and for reading comprehension, word comprehension and passage comprehension are included. This provides a comprehensive model using dimensions of reading that can lead to a diagnostic understanding of the child's difficulties. Additionally there is a word attack error inventory which records the child's errors on target sounds and target syllables. This type of reading inventory is formal and structured. There is also some benefit in using more informal measures to record precise reading errors such as the system of recording miscues. The Gray Oral Reading Tests (GORT-4) does precisely that. This particular test looks at both bottom-up and top-down processes. It includes the recording of errors in graded passages to obtain accuracy scores and timed reading for fluency as well as questions on the passage for the reading comprehension component. Additionally, however, it includes a miscue analysis system to record miscues. The miscues are divided into five types:

- meaning similarity – word error in relation to the meaning of the story;
- function similarity – word error in regard to the grammatical correctness of the word substituted in the sentence;
- graphic/phonemic similarity – the appropriateness of the word error as to its similarity to the look and sound of the printed word;
- multiple sources – word error that has a combined meaning, function and graphic-phonemic similarity to the word;
- self-correction – when a word error is immediately corrected by the student (Wiederholt and Bryant, 2001).

This system will provide useful diagnostic information that in itself can inform planning.

Contextualizing assessment with a view to intervention

It is important to ensure that the assessment process and results from any tests used are contextualized in relation to the curriculum and the nature of the child's learning situation. Sometimes factors within the classroom and the materials that are being used may account for the difficulties the child is displaying as much as the child's own attributes. Came and Reid (2008) tackle the issue of assessing literacy from the view of identifying concern and empowering the teacher to be in a position to do this. In their publication *Concern, Assess, Provide (CAP) it all* Came and Reid (2008) the authors provide a range of materials that can be used in the classroom context and focus directly on the student's current work.

They ask the key question 'What is literacy?' and suggest that the answer to that question will determine selection of information to undertake an assessment. This can mean addressing the functional aspects of literacy (technical) or the purpose of literacy (meaning). One of the important aspects of this is to have efficient and effective monitoring mechanisms in place to ensure that all aspects of the reading process are addressed. They suggest a number of such mechanisms. Figure 7.1 sets out the complete process. Unlike some other tests, they include

1 **Background information**: a summary of the pupil's reading-related information based on scores of standardized achievement tests, criterion referenced tests and basal end-of-book tests. The current reading status of the pupil is indicated as is any supplementary help he/she is receiving.

2 **Purpose of Referral**: a synopsis of the reasons for the request for diagnostic evaluation. Included are comments of specific reading concerns expressed by classroom teachers, resource personnel, school psychologists, parents, etc.

3 **Testing**: a brief description of the pupil's behaviour and displayed attitude during the testing battery. Also stated are the specific areas of reading that were tested.

4 **Diagnostic Summary**: an explanation of the results of tests administered in each reading skill area:

A Emergent/Readiness Skills Checks for: beginning reading skills

Deficiency suggests: difficulty understanding and following directions

B Auditory Skills Checks for: hearing and remembering sounds in words

Deficiency suggests: difficulty understanding and following oral directions, instructions, class discussions and establishing sound/symbol relationships necessary for phonic instruction

C Visual Skills Checks for: seeing and remembering printed or written material

Deficiency suggests: difficulty remembering letters in words – consequently writing words with letters reversed or jumbled or perceiving words incorrectly for decoding

D Word Recognition Skills Checks for: recognizing and applying the sounds for the symbols such as phonic generalizations and syllabic principles

Deficiency suggests: difficulty reading fluently with many mispronunciations

E Language and Vocabulary Development Checks for: understanding and expressing adequate language and the concepts of written words

Deficiency suggests: difficulty understanding written material and understanding classroom instructions

F Oral Reading/Comprehension Checks for: decoding ability, fluency, accuracy and comprehension

G Silent Reading/Comprehension Checks for: understanding of vocabulary and comprehension

H Listening Comprehension Checks for: processing information presented orally and comparing listening to oral/silent reading ability

5 **Interpretation of Diagnosis**: the tester's opinion of what might be blocking the pupil's reading growth – the reading weaknesses and the strengths the teacher must take into consideration in adjusting the curriculum to meet the pupil's needs.

6 **Learning Goals**: a concise list of goals the tester has devised to improve the pupil's learning to read.

7 **Teaching Recommendations**: specific suggestions and methods to aid in providing appropriate instruction in order for the pupil to attain the goals.

8 **Learning Activities**: Suggestions are designed to help in understanding and assisting the pupil in coping.

Figure 7.1 Assessing reading ability and skills

Source: reproduced with permission Learning Works, Came and Reid, 2008.

assessment of children's inferential understanding of text as well as the literal meaning of the passage. Identifying the inferences in texts is an important element for developing higher order thinking and processing skills and particularly important for children with dyslexia, as often their main focus tends to be on mastering the bottom-up sub-skills of reading and the inferential meanings of the text are sometimes lost.

This emphasizes their view that assessment should not be carried out in isolation. It needs a context, a purpose and appropriate linkage with intervention. Similarly, teaching reading should not be carried out in isolation. Assessment therefore is the starting point but it is important that the time allocated to assessment is used appropriately and productively. That is why they suggest that a range of materials be used and that the teacher needs to be empowered to take some responsibility for the assessment process – to observe, to diagnose, to monitor and to plan appropriate intervention based on a solid and sound framework.

On-going assessment that enhances learning

'There is no evidence that increasing the amount of testing will enhance learning' (Assessment Reform Group, 1999, p. 2). In many countries there has been a shift in emphasis in recent years from assessment methods that serve only summative or 'assessment of learning' purposes. Results from externally-imposed summative tests, especially where there are very high stakes attached to these results in countries such as England, can have very negative effects on students. Teachers often feel that they have to devote considerable time to practise test-taking rather than to use assessment to support learning. Where this is the case, students, especially lower achievers, tend to become over-anxious and demoralized, seeing assessment as something that labels and stigmatizes them among their peers. As the Assessment Reform Group comment, to be successful, learners need to:

- understand the goals for which they are aiming;
- be motivated;
- possess the skills to achieve success.

In a seminal piece of work that synthesized research on assessment and classroom learning, Black and Wiliam (1998) demonstrated clearly that student achievement, particularly that of lower achievers, can be raised through formative assessment in the classroom. Improving learning through assessment depends on five, 'deceptively simple', factors:

- the provision of effective feedback;
- the active involvement of students in their own learning;
- adjusting teaching to take account of the results of assessment;
- a recognition of the profound influence assessment has on the motivation and self-esteem of students, both of which are crucial influences on learning;
- the need for students to be able to assess themselves and understand how to improve.

(Assessment Reform Group, 1999, p. 5)

Black and Wiliam's research synthesis takes the view that learners have active agency in learning. They must, ultimately, be responsible for their own learning. They do it for themselves. Assessment that supports learning must therefore involve students so that they have information about how well they are doing that guides subsequent learning. Much of this information will come as feedback from the teacher. Some may also result from assessment of their own work in a constructive way that shows them what they need to do, and can do, to make progress.

The shift in emphasis in the purpose of day-to-day assessment in classrooms has resulted in a focus on 'Assessment for Learning' (AfL) in some places.

Principles of formative assessment in practice

AfL is:

> the ongoing day-to-day formative assessment that takes place to gather information on what a child or group of children understand or do not understand and how future teaching will be adapted to account for this. Effective ongoing day-to-day assessments would include effective questioning; observations of children during teaching and while they are working; holding discussions with children; analysing work and reporting to children; conducting tests and giving quick feedback and engaging children in the assessment process.
>
> (http://www.standards.dfes.gov.uk/primary/features/
> primary/1091819/1092063, accessed 7 May 2008)

On-going continuous formative assessment can therefore provide teachers with formal and informal opportunities to:

- notice what is happening during learning activities;
- recognise where the learning of individuals and groups of students is going;
- see how they can help to take that learning further.

Teachers who do this are sometimes called 'reflective practitioners' (Schön, 1983, 1987). Reflective practitioners notice what is different or unusual about patterns of progress in student learning. They think carefully and deeply about what assessment information is telling them about student understandings, and also more particularly about their own teaching and what they should or can do differently to connect to and respond to the thinking of each student.

Feedback to students is most effective when it:

- focuses on the tasks and the associated learning, not the student;
- confirms for the student that he or she is on the right track;
- includes suggestions that help the student (that is that scaffold their learning);
- is frequent and given when there is opportunity for the student to take action;
- is in the context of a dialogue about the learning.

Feedback that connects directly to specific and challenging goals related to students' prior knowledge and experience helps those students to focus more productively on new goals and next learning steps.

Criterion referencing: use of exemplars to illustrate work at particular levels

In order to enable teachers to engage in conversations that link back to and promote students' learning outcomes, some schools use authentic examples of students' work that illustrate what the criteria related to the levels described in each of the National Curriculum statements look like in practice. Using a wide range of authentic examples of students' work, exemplars can illustrate key features of learning, achievement and quality at different stages of student development. They can be used by students and teachers to identify next learning steps and also, to guide teachers in their interpretation of the descriptive criteria for each curriculum level.

If teachers annotate the students' work samples to highlight important features of the work this can exemplify learning, achievement and quality in relation to the levels described in the national curriculum documents. Teachers can use the exemplars in a number of different ways to further the learning of students:

- To compare a student's work sample with the exemplars in order to identify specific strengths and weaknesses, identify individual teaching and learning needs and prioritize new learning goals.
- To collaborate with students to review learning outcomes by comparing the progress they have made in relation to the samples of work. In so doing, teachers can exemplify the next learning steps while also raising expectations and collaboratively working towards raising performance and achievement.
- For students' self and peer review, once they are familiar with this process. In this way, they can learn to evaluate their own work and development and reflect on the next steps in their learning.
- As the basis for a discussion about the work of their students with parents and caregivers. By discussing and exemplifying a child's achievement and progress in relation to selected samples of work, parents and caregivers can be better informed about what work at a particular curriculum level looks like and how they too can better support the next learning steps.

Students' views

If we assume that students are active agents in their own learning we have to try to understand how they feel about difficulties related to dyslexia, and what they know will support them most effectively. Otherwise there is a serious question about how we can know what will best fit what they need. This does not mean, of course, that we have to provide everything a student asks for in a school.

There are a number of philosophical and practical issues surrounding students' self-advocacy, however. For example, student self-advocacy may conflict with professionals' values and assumptions both about themselves with the responsibility for maintaining control and direction in the classroom, and the school as a whole, and also about students' rights and abilities to express their own views (Garner and Sandow (1995). There are no easy solutions to this issue. It represents, essentially, conflict between the roles of the participants within the system of the school.

The assessment of students' perceptions of, and feelings about, the difficulties they experience depends on very finely-tuned listening skills as well as suspension of judgmental responses on the part of professionals. In terms of practice it is important to recognize that:

> True listening is an art; children will make decisions about people they can talk to and trust, and those they cannot. We know from the counselling literature that good listeners offer time, support, non directive questions, acknowledgement of feelings, reflecting back, and such non-verbal behaviour as eye contact, sitting next to (rather than opposite,

behind a desk), and a basically trusting atmosphere which communicates that it is all right to speak honestly.

These are not easy situations to create in school.

(Gersch, 1995, p. 48)

Engaging with parents' or carers' perspectives

Schools have a lot of power to affect the lives of children and their families and carers through the kind of assessment and provision that they make. Some families are in a good position to advocate for their children and contribute to the assessment and planning process. Others may feel far less comfortable. The following are suggestions for professionals dealing with parents in schools which have been adapted from Friend and Cook (1996, p. 232):

- create an environment that is welcoming;
- schedule the meeting at the convenience of the parent;
- provide an advance summary of the topics to be covered and a list of questions that the parent might want to ask;
- suggest the parent brings to school copies of work the child has done at home;
- let the parent be seated at the meeting table first;
- provide the parent with a file folder containing copies of the information that the professionals have in their folders;
- use your communication skills to structure the meeting so that the parent has opportunities to provide input throughout the meeting.

These suggestions and advice from Friend and Cook (1996) highlight the need for reciprocity and mutual respect between teachers and parents, whereby each acknowledges the expertise and competencies of the other.

Assessment of the learning environment

Understanding how the learning environment can contribute to barriers to pupils' learning is complex. There are a number of ways of conceptualising the interactional relationship between the learning environment and the learner. For example, from an ecosystemic perspective Bronfenbrenner (1979) identifies four levels that influence student outcomes:

- microsystem, the immediate context of the student – school, classrooms, home, neighbourhood;
- mesosystem, the links between two microsystems, e.g. home–school relationships;
- exosystem, outside demands/influences in adults' lives that affect students;
- macrosystem, cultural beliefs/patterns or institutional policies that affect individuals' behaviour.

Walberg's (1981, 1982) multi-factor psychological model of educational productivity holds that learning is a multiplicative, diminishing-returns function of student age, ability and motivation; of quality and quantity of instruction; and of the psychosocial environments of the home, the classroom, the peer group and the mass media. Any factor at zero-point will result in zero learning because the function is multiplicative. Empirical probes of the educational productivity model (Walberg, 1984) showed that classroom environment is a strong predictor

89

of both achievement and attitudes even when a comprehensive set of other factors was held constant. In this regard, the DfES (2004, p. 38) has produced a classroom environment checklist to assist teachers to consider the optimal classroom environment for learning:

- the classroom is attractive and inviting
- adequate lighting
- appropriate temperature and ventilation
- adequate acoustics
- furniture arranged to best effect
- there is a seating plan which is known by the children
- clearly defined pathways with sufficient space for children to move freely between activities
- routines to foster a calm and positive atmosphere
- routines to encourage children to make choices
- chalk board, whiteboard, etc. easily seen
- quiet area available
- differing learning areas are clearly delineated
- room organisation meets differing curriculum needs
- materials easily accessible and visibly labelled to support children's independent learning
- materials/resources match the learning styles of a wide range of individuals
- provision and organisation of materials/activities support the development of social, emotional and behavioural skills.

The planning process

Curriculum planning for any learner or group needs to incorporate an overall long-term plan based on a global view of the learner and an awareness of the context within which the plan must take effect. A longer term vision of a range of possibilities for a learner that can be shared between the learner, the parent/carer and the professionals is important to give a sense of direction to the whole planning process. From this long-term plan it is possible to draw up medium- and short-term plans. At the meeting to review the student's progress a considerable amount of revision and amendment to a pupil's programme might be needed in the light of current achievement and personal development, changes in the learning environment and the stage reached in the National Curriculum. The review cycle does not detract from the need to think about possible routes for learners over a much longer period than this. Individuals' needs change over time. It is very important to retain flexibility of thinking so that the planning process is facilitative of learning rather than restrictive.

Planning a curriculum to meet particular special learning needs of individual dyslexic students should take place within the context of the same decision-making processes that relate to teaching and learning for all students in a school. In addition it must take account of any formal and informal individual assessment of student learning that has taken place, and this should address any statutory requirements. Effective planning means setting out to work from strengths and interests. Staff attitudes and students' view of themselves as able to learn (or not!) make for potent interactions for good or ill. When planning for students who experience difficulties in literacy, we first need to know whether the student or group can, with appropriate access, strategies and teaching styles, work on the same learning objectives as the rest of the class. Getting this right will depend on accurate assessment of what the student knows, understands and can do. For many dyslexic students it is highly likely that what is needed is adaptations to teaching styles and the use of access strategies, rather than different learning objectives.

If a student cannot work on the same objectives as the class as a whole the teacher might want to choose learning objectives that are linked to the topic on which the whole class is working, but earlier in a learning progression. If working in literacy it will be possible to 'track back' through the objectives in the National Strategy Frameworks to locate earlier learning objectives.

Planning will also need to be informed by the individual priorities for students. Normally it will be appropriate for them to work on objectives that are similar and related to the whole class topic. However, at other times teachers will also have to consider whether the students have other priority needs that are central to their learning, for example a need to concentrate on some key skills such as communication, problem solving, working with others, managing their own emotions and so on. These needs may be detailed in the student's Individual Education Plan (IEP) or a Statement of SEN. They can often be met within the whole class learning. What the teacher wants the student to learn may be distinct and different from the learning objectives for the class, but the activities designed for the class as whole can encompass the student's individual priority need.

Some students may have additional needs which cannot easily be met through class activities. For these students alternative objectives may be needed to meet specific needs for identified periods of time. For example, a student might be withdrawn for a time-limited number of weeks for a one-to-one literacy intervention programme. Such alternative activities are legitimate as long as they are in the context of ensuring that, over time, all students receive a broad and balanced curriculum.

This process begins by ensuring students receive appropriate learning goals related to the appropriate stage of learning with the National Curriculum guidelines, and are engaged in interactive learning conversations throughout their learning activities within a well-informed understanding of what constitutes an appropriate curriculum for the age group and the students' peers in the first place. Lessons may be planned to facilitate understanding of content, develop concepts or skills, practise problem solving, or encourage students' personal interests. Sometimes it happens that barriers are created to children's learning simply by the way in which material designed to facilitate understanding of a concept is presented. Where students experience literacy difficulties, it is essential to tease out whether the problem lies at the level of conceptual understanding or is the result of the mode of communication, especially when this is reliant on written text.

In some institutions there may be a difference of opinion over the level of detail required for the targets that are set for students. There is the possibility that an 'over-reliance on task components can lead to a rigid application of prescriptive teaching, which takes no account of the knowledge a child brings to any given task or the specific strategies that a child utilizes' (Dockrell and McShane, in Open University, 1993, pp. 196–197). In addition, some areas lend themselves to this approach more easily than others. This might be addressed by considering the purpose of the IEP or individual profile which, as Tod et al. (1998) note, is to facilitate student learning by means of the effective negotiation and planning of learning goals as well as the nature of the assessment it reflects.

Targets for Individual Education Plans need to be embedded in the regular cycle of classroom activity integrated with the learning experience offered to the child through the curriculum. In lesson planning, teachers and classroom assistants need to be aware of which pupils have IEPs and be conversant with their content so that they can take adequate account of individual pupils' needs. Interventions designed, for example, to address problems associated with dyslexia should take account of the student's sensitivities, fit in with the curriculum offered to peers, and also be compatible with the school's policy towards supporting the personal wellbeing and development of its students. Differentiation of lesson activities, tasks and resources would need to take account of the full range of learning needs among children in the classroom and any requirements on individual education plans. This includes current reading levels, consideration of possible visual and auditory difficulties, interest level of the poems that are used, considerations of student grouping in the classroom, prior experiences of students, the potential range of applications of ICT that might support learning, and so on. Resources include the human as well as the material. In a primary classroom, discussion and preparation with teaching assistants and any other adults prior to the sequence of lessons is vital.

Summary

There is no golden formula for identifying and addressing the special learning needs of every student who experiences difficulties of a dyslexic nature. Addressing difficulties is a question of problem-solving the inter-relationship and interaction between the characteristics of the individual learner, the requirements of the curriculum and factors related to the learning environment and teachers' pedagogies.

Dyslexia should not *only* be identified through the use of a test. The identification of dyslexia is a process and that 'process' involves much more than the administration of a test or a group of tests. Specifically identification should consider three aspects in particular – discrepancies, difficulties and differences, and these should relate to the classroom environment and the curriculum, as well as the learning preferences of the child. The assessment therefore needs to consider classroom and curriculum factors, the learning preferences of the child, as well as the specific difficulties and strengths. Essentially it needs to consider the task and the curriculum, as well as the learning environment and the learning experience.

References

Assessment Reform Group (1999) *Assessment for Learning: Beyond the Black Box*, Cambridge: University of Cambridge School of Education.

Baddeley, A. (1986) Working Memory, *Science*, 255, 556–559.

Berninger, V.W. (2007) *Process Assessment of the Learner (PAL-11) Assessment for Reading and Writing*. San Antonio, TX: Psychological Corporation.

Black, P. and Wiliam, D. (1998) 'Assessment and Classroom Learning', *Assessment in Education*, 5(1), 7–74.

Bowers, P. G. and Wolf, M. (1993). 'Theoretical links among naming speed, precise timing mechanisms and orthographic skill in dyslexia'. *Reading and Writing: An Interdisciplinary Journal*, 5, 69–85.

Bronfenbrenner, U. (1979) *The Ecology of Human Development*, Cambridge, MA: Harvard.

Came, F. and Reid, G. (2008) *CAP It All: Concern, Assess and Provide: Practical Tools and Techniques to Identify and Assess Individual Needs*. Marlborough, UK: Learning Works International.

Caygill, R. and Elley, L. (2001) 'Evidence about the effects of assessment task format on student achievement'. Paper presented at the British Educational Research Association, University of Leeds.

Clarke, S., Timperley, H. and Hattie, J. (2003) *Unlocking formative assessment: Practical strategies for enhancing students' learning in the primary and intermediate classroom*. Auckland: Hodder Moa Beckett.

Department for Education and Skills (DfES (2004) *Behaviour in the Classroom: A Course for Newly Qualified Teachers*, London: DfES.

Dockrell, J. and McShane, J. (1993) *Children's Learning Difficulties: A Cognitive Approach*, Oxford: Blackwell.

Friend, M. and Cook, L. (1996, 2nd edn) *Interactions: Collaboration Skills for School Professionals*, White Plains, NY: Longman.

Garner, P. and Sandow, S. (1995) *Advocacy, Self Advocacy and Special Needs*, London: Fulton.

Gersch, I. (1995) 'Involving the child', in *Schools' Special Educational Needs Policies Pack*, London: National Children's Bureau.

Gersch, I. (2001) 'Listening to Children', in J. Wearmouth (ed.) *Special Educational Provision in the Context of Inclusion*, ch. 12, pp. 228–244, London: Fulton.

Reid, G. (2003) *Dyslexia: A Practitioners Handbook* (3rd edition). Chichester: Wiley.

Schön, D. (1983) *The Reflective Practitioner: How Professionals Think in Action*, New York: Basic Books.

Schön, D. (1987) *Educating the Reflective Practitioner*. London: Jossey-Bass.

Siegel, L.S. (1989). 'Why we do not need intelligence test scores in the definition and analyses of learning disabilities'. *Journal of Learning Disabilities, 22* (8), 514–518.

Siegel, L.S. (1992) 'An evaluation of the discrepancy definition of dyslexia'. *Journal of Learning Disabilities*, 25, 618–629.

Siegel L.S. and Lipka, O. (2008) 'The definition of learning disabilities: who is the individual with learning disabilities?' In G. Reid, A. Fawcett, F. Manis and L. Siegel (eds) *The Sage Handbook of Dyslexia*. London: Sage Publications.

Tod, J., Castles, F. and Blamires, M. (1998) *Implementing Effective Practice*. London: Fulton.

Torgeson, J.K. (1996) A model of memory from an informational processing perspective: the special case of phonological memory. In G.R. Lyon and N.A. Krasnegor (eds) *Attention, Memory and Executive Function.* (pp. 157–184). Baltimore, MD: Brookes.

Torgeson, J.K., Morgan, S.T. and Davis, C. (1992) 'Effects of two types of phonological training on word learning in kindergarten children'. *Journal of Educational Psychology*, 84, 364–370.

Torgeson, J.K., Wagner, R.K., and Rashotte, C.A. (1997) 'Prevention and remediation of severe reading disabilities: keeping the end in mind'. *Scientific Studies of Reading*, 1, 217–234.

Vygotsky, L.S. (1987) *The Collected Works, Vol 1. Problems of General Psychology*, NY: Plenum.

Wagner, R. K., Torgesen, J. K. and Rashotte, C. A. (1999). *Comprehensive Test of Phonological Processing.* Austin, TX: PRO-Ed.

Walberg, H.J. (1981) 'A psychological theory of educational productivity', in F. Farley and N. Gordon (eds) *Psychology and Education*, Berkeley, CA: McCutchan.

Walberg, H.J. (1982) 'Educational productivity: Theory, evidence and prospect', *Australian Journal of Education, 26*, 115–122.

Walberg, H.J. (1984) 'Improving the productivity of America's schools', *Educational Leadership, 41*, 19–30

Wearmouth, J. (in press) *A New Teacher's Guide to Special Educational Needs*, Buckingham: Open University Press.

Wechsler, D. (2004) *Wechsler Intelligence Scale for Children – 1V*. San Antonio, TX: Psychological Corporation.

Wedell, K. (2000) Interview transcript in *E831 Professional Development for Special Educational Co-ordinators*, Milton Keynes: Open University.

Wiederholt, J.L. and Bryant, B.R. (2001) *Gray Oral Reading Tests – Fourth Edition (GORT-4)*. Austin, TX.

Woodcock, R.W. (1998) *Woodcock Reading Mastery Tests – Revised*. Circle Pines, MN: American Guidance Service.

8

Extending literacy skills
Issues for practice

David Wray

This chapter:

- emphasises the need to think about extending literacy skills as well as developing basic literacy skills
- looks at the nature of extended literacy skills
- discusses some classroom strategies for teaching such skills
- considers some common features of the effective teaching of these skills.

Introduction

The standard of literacy achieved by primary school children, in particular in reading, is an issue which attracts perennial media and professional attention. Current media reports in the UK (e.g. Curtis, 2008) draw attention to the fact that, in England around 20 per cent of children emerge from their primary school experience without the basic levels of attainment expected of them in literacy. This is in spite of a 10-year intensive focus on literacy teaching by the UK government, and what is termed 'the stubborn 20 per cent' are apparently resistant to the huge amount of effort and resource which has been poured into primary literacy teaching over this 10-year period. Interestingly, however, the bulk of the attention given to literacy teaching in the past few years, in the UK and in other countries, has been on initial literacy skills (currently, in many countries, the focus is on the teaching of reading through systematic, synthetic, phonics programmes). Yet the achievement scores which draw the attention tend to be those of 11- year-old children, at the conclusion of their primary or elementary school experience. It might be considered that, by the age of 11, attention in literacy might not be best placed simply on initial skills, but rather on the uses to which these skills are put in terms of wider learning, and on the nature of the skills that learners need to cope with the diversifying curriculum of the later primary years and of secondary schooling. Yet such 'extended literacy skills' have always, it seems, received less attention, in the literature as well as in classrooms, than initial literacy skills.

Concern about this area is not new. In their 1978 survey of primary schools in England (DES, 1978), Her Majesty's Inspectors of Schools (HMI) found 'little evidence that more advanced reading skills were being taught' (para. 5.30). Their 1990 report on the teaching of reading in English primary schools made almost the identical statement.

Relating to the teaching of writing, the 1978 HMI report's comments again raised important issues in its identification of the lack of range of writing set by upper primary school teachers (para. 5.36) and the extensive use of copying rather than original composition (para. 5.33). Work in Australia (Martin, 1985; Littlefair, 1991) was suggesting that much more attention needed to be given to the issue of genre in children's reading and writing, and that there was a body of linguistic knowledge with which teachers needed to familiarise themselves if they were successfully to help children cope with the reading and writing demands of schooling and of the world beyond school.

Responding to these concerns, we began, in 1992, a major programme of research and curriculum development in the area of extending literacy skills (the EXEL project). The outcomes of this project (Wray and Lewis, 1997: Lewis and Wray, 1995) had a major impact on the 1998 National Literacy Strategy, implemented in England by an incoming government intent on making education one of its main priorities. Our main thrusts were, first, an emphasis upon strategies for developing comprehension in reading, especially of non-fiction texts, and, second, the development of pedagogic practices in extending and developing writing, again especially of non-fiction. For a few years, our two best known outcomes (an approach to developing extending literacy dubbed the EXIT (extending interactions with texts) model, and an approach to scaffolding children's writing through the use of 'writing frames') were widely used in both primary and secondary schools throughout the UK.

Times change, however, and the emphasis today in literacy teaching is very much back once again on initial skills. Yet this does not mean that the need to extend literacy skills has gone away. On the contrary, I would argue that it is precisely an over-emphasis on initial skills which might actually create some of the literacy problems that teachers later have to deal with. We know that, for many children, the problem they have with literacy is related more to their engagement with it (or lack of) than it is to their potential to learn the requisite skills (Baker *et al.*, 2000). One thing which is potentially extremely engaging for children (particularly the boys, whose literacy achievement always seems to lag behind that of the girls) is using literacy to engage with a whole series of interesting facts and ideas — in other words the use of literacy to encounter, react to and record 'the stuff of the world', as Arthur Eddington termed it. Extending literacy is essential, therefore, partly because it is a crucial way (and maybe for some the only way) of giving children an insight into what literacy is good for. It is also, of course, functionally essential, since the reading and writing that most of us do every day tends to be done in order to get something done. Reading our newspapers, our information manuals, our market reports, our computer screens and writing our notes, our letters of application, our complaints, our reports — all of these are vital to our working lives and they all require a lot more than simply a knowledge of phonics to accomplish.

There is an imperative, therefore, for us to ensure that children are taught literacy beyond the basic skills. It may even be the case that a focus on extending literacy skills is something that might enable children who struggle with basic literacy to engage with it in real purposeful ways. I hope to give some examples of this later in the chapter.

My aims in this chapter are first to explore the nature of what we might term 'extended literacy skills' and second to draw out some principles for the teaching of such skills. I will try to achieve these aims through a presentation and analysis of some of the encounters with extended literacy that we observed during our EXEL project research. The chapter is centred around four classroom episodes, or cameos, each involving primary school children with some significant difficulties in basic literacy. I will try to show through these cameos that these literacy difficulties were not a bar to the exercise of extended literacy — they simply required some thoughtful and effective teaching.

Cameo 1: Zoe and the dolphins

Zoe is a 10-year-old with some reading problems. Her learning support teacher works individually with her for three lessons a week. On this occasion, the teacher arrives in the classroom to find that Zoe, along with the rest of the class, has been asked to 'find out about whales'. The child is working diligently. The outcome of her 'research' is the writing given in Figure 8.1.

She cannot read this work back to her support teacher and has only the vaguest understanding of what she has written. Of course, we all recognise what has happened. Zoe has copied, word for word, from a book. Why is this? Our research (Wray and Lewis, 1992) has suggested that most children are aware that they should not copy directly from books. Many can give sound educational reasons for this (e.g. 'you learn more if you put it in your own words'), and yet they continue to do so. There appear to be several reasons underlying this but figuring largely amongst them must be the nature of the task the child has been given to do and the type of text with which they are asked to engage when reading for information.

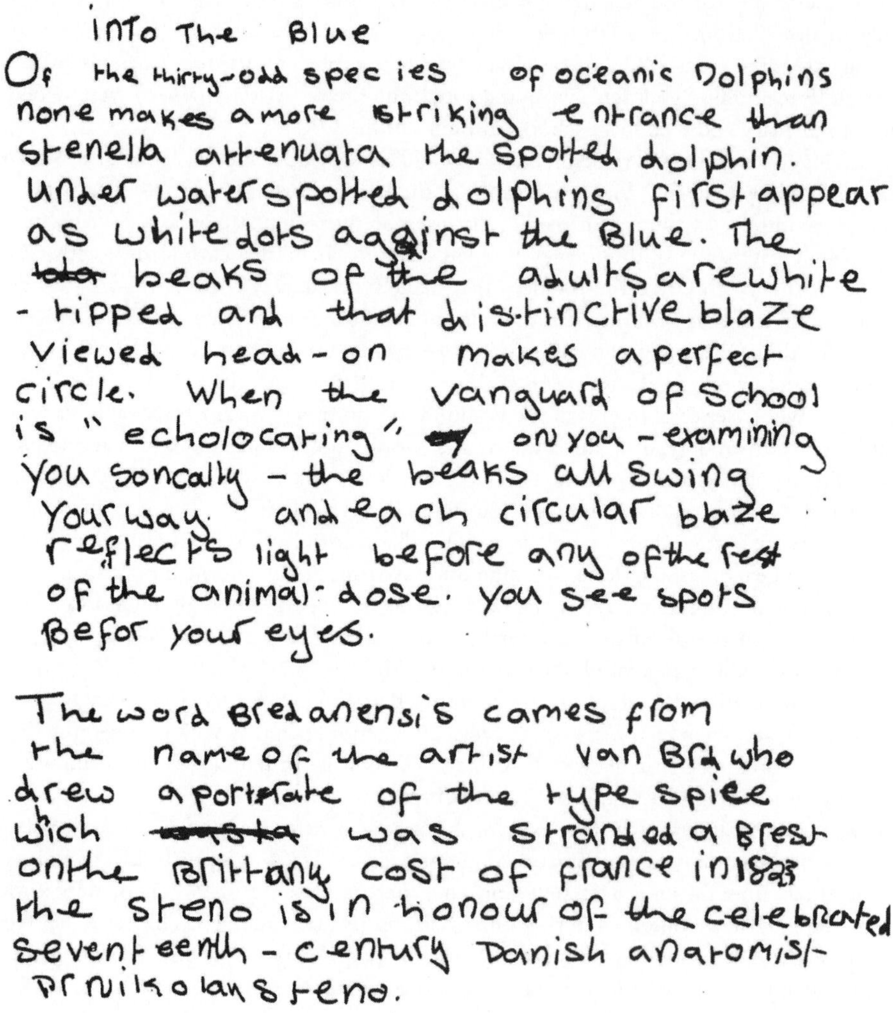
Into The Blue
Of the thirty-odd spec ies of oceanic Dolphins none makes amore striking entrance than stenella attenuata the spotted dolphin. under waterspotted dolphins first appear as white dots aggainst the Blue. The ~~tota~~ beaks of the adults arewhite - tipped and that distinctive blaze viewed head-on makes a perfect circle. When the vanguard of school is "echolocating" ~~ey~~ on you - examining you soncally - the beaks all swing your way and each circular blaze reflects light before any of the rest of the animal dose. you see spots Befor your eyes.

The word Bredanensis cames from the name of the artist van Brd who drew a portrate of the type spiee wich ~~was ta~~ was stranded a Brest onthe Brittany cost of france in 1823 the steno is in honour of the celebrated seventeenth - century Danish anatomist Dr nikolans teno.

Figure 8.1 Zoe's original dolphin writing

The purpose for 'finding out' may not be clear to the child and how to begin to 'find out' may seem difficult and daunting. Having located a book on the required topic the child might still find the text difficult to deal with. Children in primary classrooms tend to lack experience of the different genres of non-fiction and their organizational structures (Winograd and Bridge, 1986; Littlefair, 1991). They find the linguistic features (vocabulary, connectives, cohesion, register) more difficult to comprehend than those of the more familiar narrative texts (Halliday and Hasan, 1976; Perera, 1984; Anderson and Armbruster, 1981; Littlefair, 1991) and this textual inexperience affects their writing of non-fiction as well as their reading. In the case of Zoe, the problem was further compounded by the child's poor literacy skills (relative to her age). Her diligent copying was the only strategy she had for coping with the demands of the task.

Zoe's support teacher has been working with the EXEL project and she decided to introduce Zoe to a different way of approaching her task. At the end of their hour together Zoe had produced a different piece of writing about dolphins (see Figure 8.2).

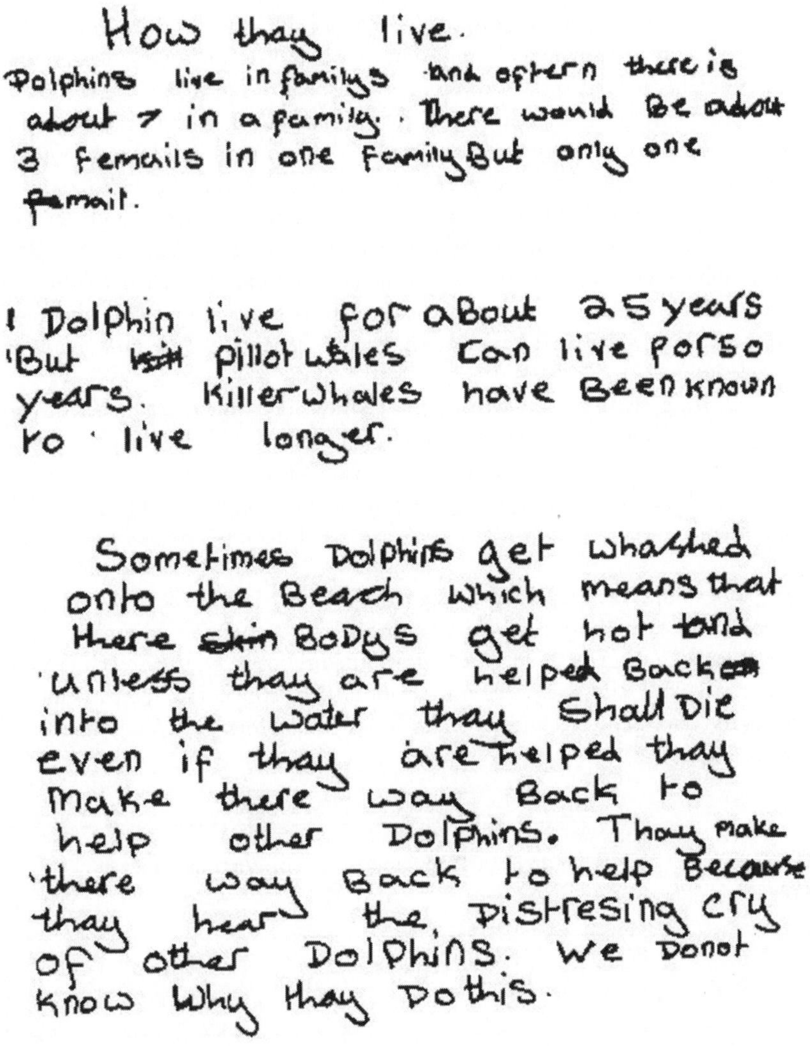

> How thay live.
> Dolphins live in familys and oftern there is about 7 in a family. There would be about 3 femails in one family But only one femail.
>
> I Dolphin live for about 25 years But pillot wales can live por 50 years. Killer whales have been known ro live longer.
>
> Sometimes Dolphins get whashed onto the Beach which means that there skin Bodys get hot and unless thay are helped Back into the water thay shall Die even if thay are helped thay make there way Back to help other Dolphins. Thay make there way Back to help Because thay hear the Distresing cry of other Dolphins. We Donot know why thay Do this.

Figure 8.2 Zoe's final dolphin writing

Let us examine how this support teacher moved Zoe on from passive copying to undertaking her own research.

The first step was to close Zoe's library book. Zoe was then taken through two of the stages in our EXIT model (see Wray and Lewis (1997) for a full description of this) and taught strategies to help her use these stages before she returned to looking for information in books. These stages were:

- activating prior knowledge
- establishing purposes.

There is considerable research underpinning each of these mental activities.

Activating Prior Knowledge (what do I know?)

There is a great deal of research which indicates the importance of children's prior knowledge in their understanding of new knowledge (e.g. Anderson and Pearson, 1984; Keene and Zimmerman, 2007)). Furthermore it appears to be important that this prior knowledge needs to be brought to the forefront of the learner's mind, that is, made explicit, if it is to be useful (Bransford, 1983). Schema theory suggests that our brains are not a random ragbag of knowledge but that knowledge is structured and categorised into schema, organised cognitive 'maps' of the parts of the world we know about. The concepts that constitute a schema can be said to 'provide slots that can be instantiated with specific information' (Wilson and Anderson, 1986). When we encounter new knowledge we incorporate it into our existing schema either by accretion (adding detail to the map) or restructuring (altering the map to fit the new information). If we have already activated our prior knowledge (schema) we are more ready to deal with new knowledge.

Many teachers already use discussion to activate prior knowledge, but research has shown that this can be an ineffective way of enhancing comprehension unless it is undertaken carefully (Alvermann et al., 1987). If prior knowledge is to be made explicit, it may be helpful to record it in some way. This has the added advantage of giving the teacher some record of the child's knowledge and, importantly, access to gaps in that knowledge and any misconceptions the child may hold.

The KWL grid was developed as a teaching strategy in the USA (Ogle, 1986, 1989) and is a simple but effective strategy which both takes children through the steps of the research process and also records their learning. It gives children a logical structure for tackling research tasks in many areas of the curriculum and it is this combination of a simple but logical support scaffolding that seems to be so useful to children with learning difficulties. A KWL grid consists of three columns (see Figure 8.3).

What do I KNOW about this already?	What do I WANT to know?	What did I LEARN

Figure 8.3 KWL grid

Zoe's support teacher introduced her to the strategy by drawing a KWL as three columns in Zoe's jotter. She then asked Zoe what she already knew about whales and acted as a scribe to record Zoe's responses. What Zoe knew can be seen in the K column of Figure 8.4. In the introductory stages of teaching the strategy, as for most new strategies and skills, teacher modelling is very important. Only when the child is thoroughly familiar with the strategy should they be encouraged to attempt it independently.

Not only does the activation of prior knowledge have a vital role to play in helping Zoe comprehend the texts she was to read, but it also gave her an active personal engagement in the topic right from the beginning. By asking her what she knew, her self-esteem and sense of 'ownership' of knowledge was enhanced instead of her being faced instantly with the (for her) negative experience of tackling a text without knowing quite how she was to make sense of it.

The discussion between Zoe and her teacher was crucial at this stage and the activation of prior knowledge should always be an active social process. Some times we do not actually know what we know until it is triggered for us by discussion. This discussion could, of course, also take place in partnership with another child or in groups with other children rather than with a teacher.

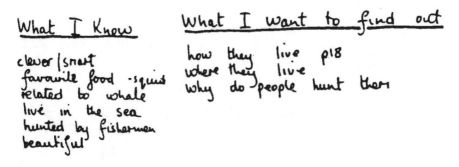

Figure 8.4 Zoe's KWL grid

Establishing purposes (what do I want to know?)

The next stage helps focus the subsequent research. The usual formulation of the task, as in 'find out about', is far too broad to be useful and can be read as requiring enough information to fill a postcard or to fill a book. Discussing and recording what she already knew was enough to generate further questions for Zoe – questions which she would be interested in researching. These were again scribed by the teacher (see the L column of Figure 8.4). It is tempting here to talk about giving the child some ownership of the work she is to undertake.

It might sometimes be necessary for the teacher to set questions at this stage. If, for example, there was incorrect information in the 'what I know' column then the teacher would wish to direct a question to lead to further investigation in that area. There may be content details that the teacher regards as vital to include and these could form the focus of questions. There is the opportunity at this stage for the teacher to intervene as little or as much as their professional judgement deems appropriate.

On this occasion Zoe and her teacher decided to focus on just one question (they had only one hour together) and she was encouraged to brainstorm around her 'How do they live?' question. Again her teacher scribed and the resultant concept map can be seen in Figure 8.5.

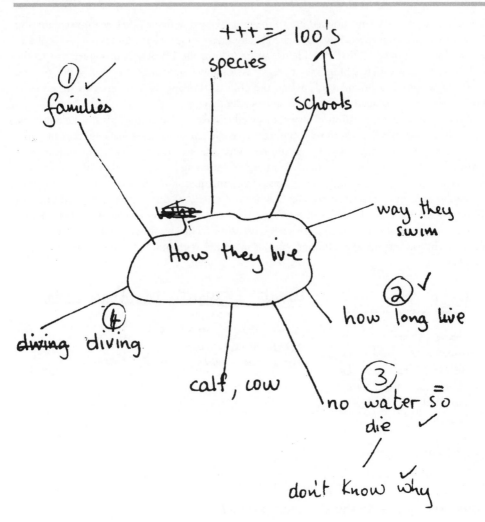

Figure 8.5 Zoe's concept map

The sub-questions generated by this procedure were numbered to keep the process clear and manageable and at this point Zoe was ready to return to her library books to try to find the answers to her questions. Now Zoe also had key words which she could use to search the index and list of contents, etc. Sometimes her teacher wrote the word on a piece of card for her so that she could run it down the index/page and match the word. This gave her practice in scanning. We can see from the writing she had completed by the end of the session (Figure 8.2) that she was working her way logically through the questions (she had completed 1 and 2) and not only had she learnt something about dolphins but she had also had a powerful lesson on how to begin research.

Cameo 2: James and the Ancient Greeks

Perhaps the effectiveness of making such strategies as the KWL accessible to less able children can be judged by whether the children, having been introduced to it by their support teacher, choose to use it spontaneously when their support teacher is not with them. Baker and Brown (1984) have suggested that students do not gain any long term benefits from study strategies until they start to incorporate these strategies spontaneously for themselves, signalling that they understand how and why they work.

An example of this happening is the case of James. He, like Zoe, was introduced to the two process stages and the use of KWL by his support teacher. This time the context was some work on the topic of Ancient Greece. Notice how his listing of what he knows (Figure 8.6) also enables his teacher to see his misconceptions (medals were not given at the Olympic Games in Ancient Greece) as well as things he does know. His KWL grid, scribed by his teacher, then acted as the basis for his subsequent writing on the topic (see Figure 8.7) which was a very extensive piece of work for James.

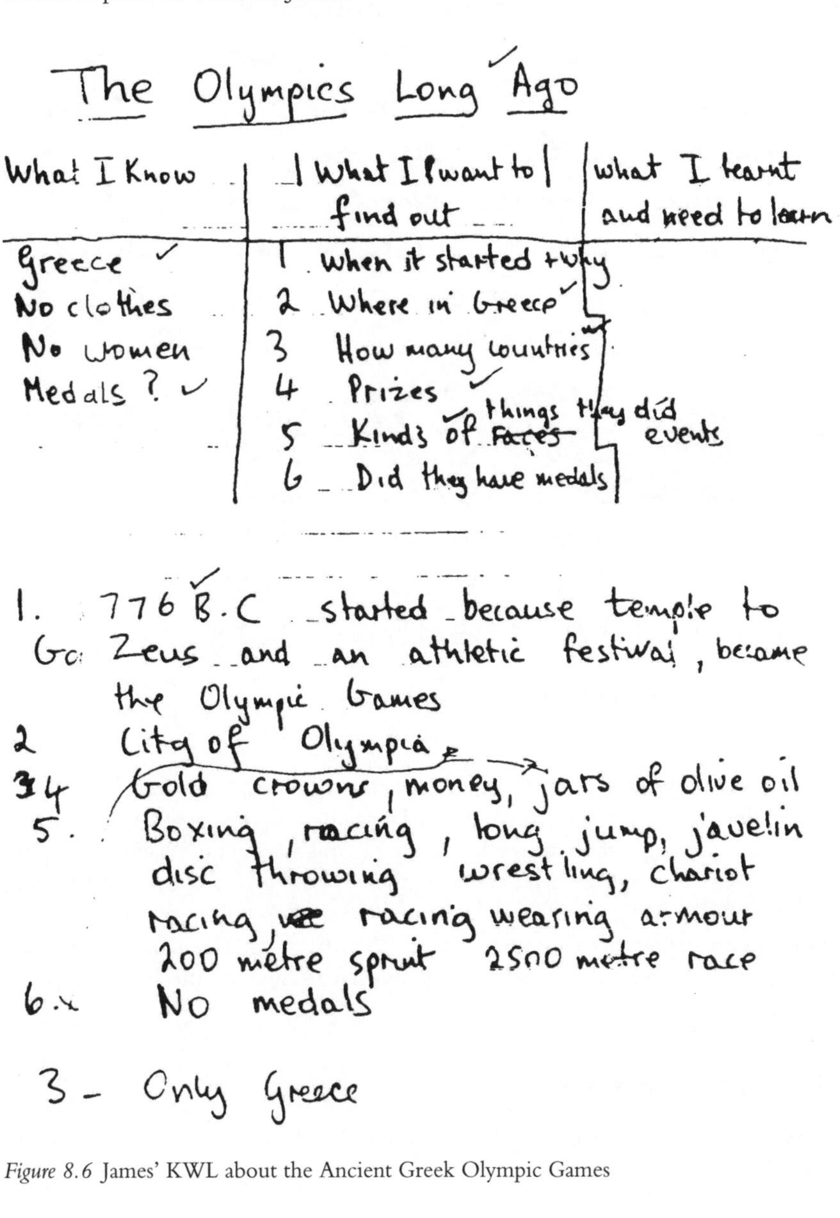

The Olympics Long Ago

What I Know	What I (I want to) find out	what I learnt and need to learn
Greece ✓	1 when it started +why	
No clothes	2 Where in Greece ✓	
No women	3 How many countries	
Medals ? ✓	4 Prizes — things they did	
	5 Kinds of Races — events	
	6 Did they have medals	

1. 776 B.C started because temple to Go Zeus and an athletic festival, became the Olympic Games

2 City of Olympia

3 4 Gold crowns, money, jars of olive oil

5. Boxing, racing, long jump, javelin disc throwing wrestling, chariot racing, racing wearing armour 200 metre sprint 2500 metre race

6. No medals

3 — Only Greece

Figure 8.6 James' KWL about the Ancient Greek Olympic Games

101

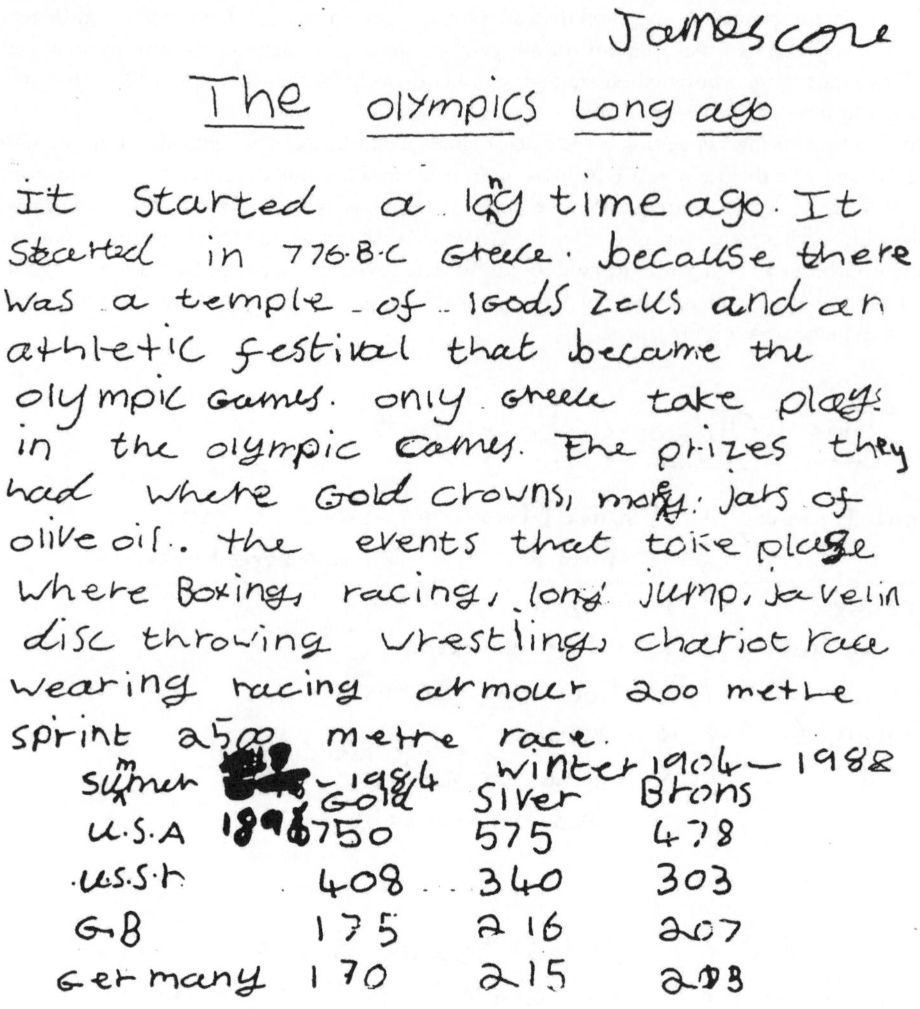

James core

The olympics long ago

It started a long time ago. It started in 776 B.C Greece. because there was a temple - of Goods Zeus and an athletic festival that became the olympic Games. only Greece take plays in the olympic Games. The prizes they had where Gold crowns, many. Jars of olive oil.. the events that toke place where Boxing, racing, long jump, javelin disc throwing wrestling, chariot race wearing racing armour 200 mette sprint a 500 mette race.

	summer 1984 Gold	winter 1904 – 1988 Silver	Brons
U.S.A	1896 750	575	478
.u.S.S.h	408	340	303
G.B	175	216	207
Germany	170	215	208

Figure 8.7 James' writing about the Ancient Greek Olympic Games

James had obviously found the strategy useful because the following week his support teacher returned to find that he had spontaneously used it again in his next piece of topic work. This time the class was finding out about the home life of Athenians. James had drawn three columns in his jotter and although he hadn't labelled them – why give yourself extra writing if writing is a problem? – he had used the middle column to set himself four questions and was ticking these off as he gathered the information to answer them (see Figure 8.8). His subsequent writing indicates how the questions may also have suggested the structure of the finished piece (Figure 8.9)

Cameo 3: Kim and the cress seeds

One of the major issues which has been identified in terms of children's writing of non-fiction (Wray and Lewis, 1997) is the tendency to write in recount style when another form of writing

Figure 8.8
James' questions
about Ancient
Greek home life

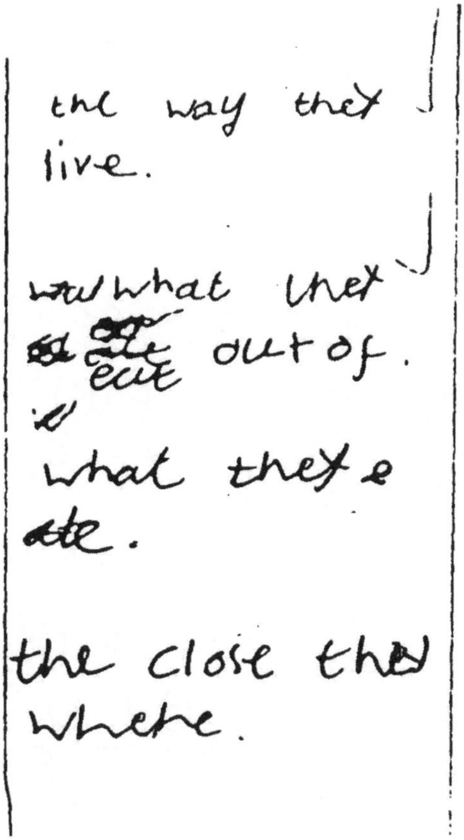

the way they J
live.

wuwhat they J
eat out of.

what they e
ate.

the close the
where.

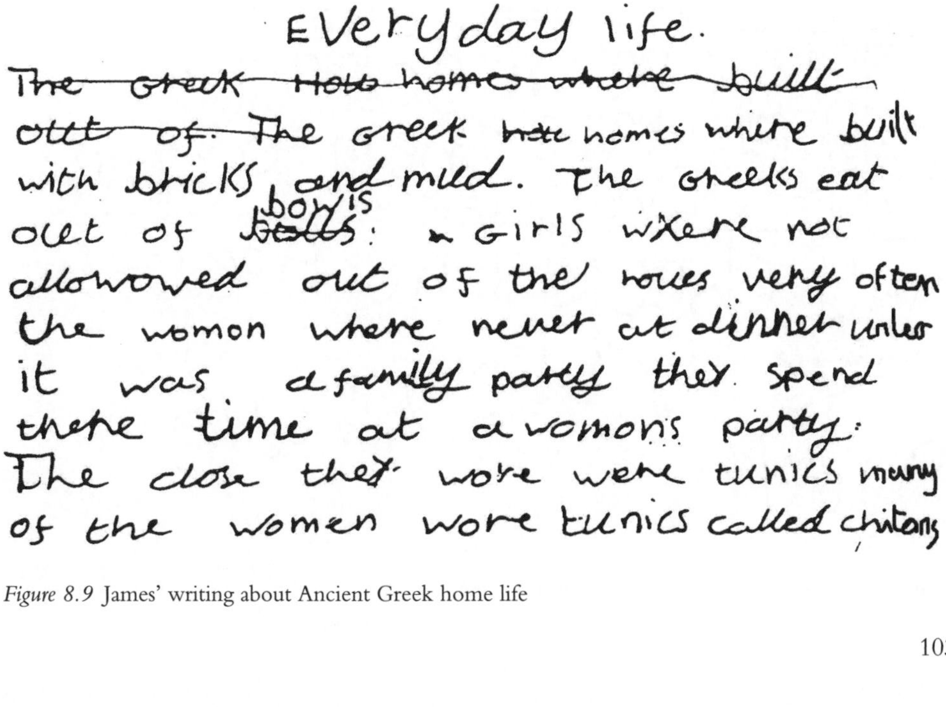

EVeryday life.

The Greek Hold homes where built
out of. The greek tree homes where built
with bricks, and mud. The Greeks eat
out of bolls: boyis Girls where not
allowowed out of the houes very often
the womon where never at dinner unles
it was a family party they spend
there time at a womons party.
The close they wore were tunics many
of the women wore tunics called chitons

Figure 8.9 James' writing about Ancient Greek home life

might help them achieve their purpose more effectively. This was a major claim of the group of Australian researchers who became known as 'genre theorists' (e.g. Kress, 1988; Johns, 2001). The writing of 6-year-old Kim (Figure 8.10) is a very good example of this. Having planted some cress seeds in class, Kim had made her own packet of cress seeds in order to take some seeds home to sow for herself. She had looked at some examples of seed packets and discussed the kind of information that was written on the back of these and the ways in which it was written. However, on her own packet she wrote a straightforward recount of the planting activity she had just completed. The inclusion of other factual information shows she had

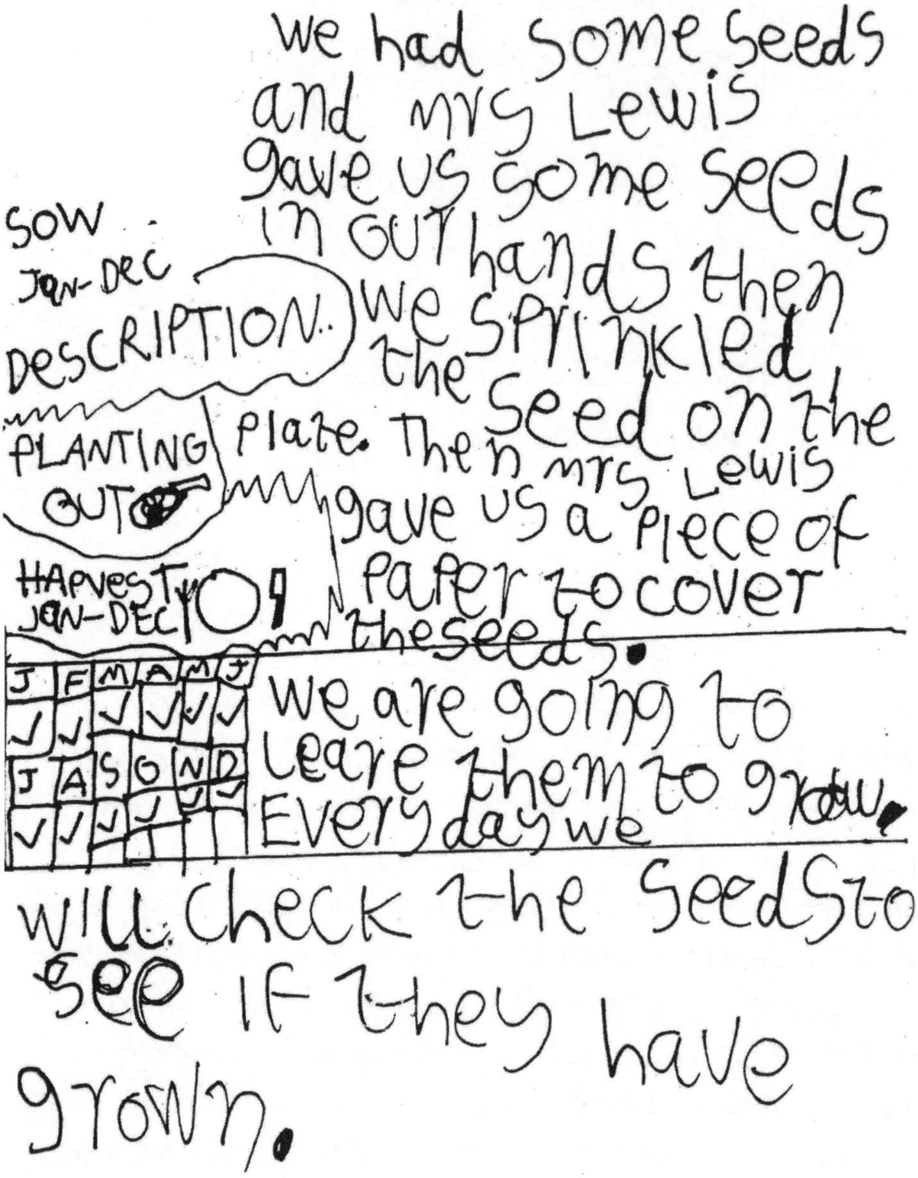

Figure 8.10 Kim's original instructions for planting cress seeds

studied the backs of the seeds packets carefully but she had not adopted the most appropriate written form for conveying sowing instructions.

In this case Kim had been asked to write the instructions she would need to follow when she took the seeds home. It would seem that Kim had failed to recognise the appropriate generic form (procedural) that would have made her writing more effective in achieving its aim of giving directions for planting. She is not alone in this. Most teachers will recognise occasions when children write a recount of what they did rather than offer an explanation or give instructions or write a report. This response springs from the well established, well-understood and important tradition of offering children 'real experiences' and then asking them to write about them. Such a request invites a personal retelling. It is of course very important that children write in this way but we also need to encourage children to move from always giving a personal recount to the more formal and abstract writing demanded to write a report, an explanation, a procedure, an argument and a discussion.

Kim's teacher responded to her inappropriate genre use by offering a more structured approach to the writing. She presented Kim with a writing grid to encourage awareness of the structure of the text Kim was trying to write. She also did some direct modelling of language form by dictating the first few words of the 'How to sow' section of the grid – 'get a plate'. With these two forms of support, Kim was then able to go on to produce the text shown in Figure 8.11, which is clearly much more like instructional writing than was her first attempt.

Cameo 4: Scott and the Egyptians

As we have seen, some children appear to find non-fiction writing problematic compared to writing narrative. Children, it is claimed, lack experience of the different genres of non-fiction and their organizational structures (Winograd and Bridge, 1986; Littlefair, 1991). They find the linguistic features (vocabulary, connectives, cohesion, register) more difficult to comprehend and write than those of the more familiar narrative texts (Halliday and Hasan, 1976; Perera, 1984; Anderson and Armbruster, 1981). This textual inexperience affects their writing (Gallagher, 2000). One of the main strategies we have developed to support the writing of such children is the scaffolding technique known as the writing frame.

A writing frame consists of a skeleton outline to scaffold children's non-fiction writing. The skeleton framework consists of different key words or phrases, according to the particular generic form. The template of starters, connectives and sentence modifiers which constitute a writing frame gives children a structure within which they can concentrate on communicating what they want to say, rather than getting lost in the form. However, by using the form, children become increasingly familiar with it.

With some children, a writing frame not only helps them write in an appropriate form and style, it helps them write, full stop. In addition to the problem of knowing about writing structures, we have identified three other problems in writing which are significant for many children, especially those with learning difficulties.

a) The blank page

Most writers will agree that the most difficult part of writing is the first line or two. Getting started can be so difficult, even for experienced writers, that they invent a number of 'delaying tactics' (sharpening pencils, making coffee, etc.) to put off the awful moment. A blank page can be very daunting and for many less experienced writers it can result in abandoning the writing task.

When to sow	any time in the year
Where to sow	inside
How to sow	get a Plate, Three tissues, a Jug of water and seeds. fold Tissue's in half ontop of ~~each~~ each over. put on the Plate and Put on ~~water~~ Water. sprinckle Seeds on. cover with Paper. when it is acm Long take Paper off andwhen it isready cut off.
When to eat	When it is about 5cm high. It takes about ~~b days~~

Figure 8.11 Kim's final instructions for planting cress seeds

b) Writing and talking

When talking to another person, the language user receives constant support for his/her language. In a dialogue one person says something, prompting the other person to say something, which in turn prompts the first person to reply, and so on. Talkers receive continual prompts for their language. Writers, on the other hand, get no such prompts. They are alone, forced to produce language without support from another.

c) The 'and then' syndrome

Inexperienced writers tend to have a limited range of ways of joining together ideas in writing. Most teachers will recognise this by the prevalence of 'and then' in their pupil's writing, as if this were the only way of linking ideas. Young writers need support to broaden their range of connectives.

Nine year old Scott was a writer just like those we have described. When asked to write, his response would usually be active avoidance. Writing was clearly a chore for him, and it was rare that he would produce more than a line or two in response to any request to compose.

On this occasion, however, something different happened. Scott's class had watched a video about the Ancient Egyptians. This time, instead of asking Scott to write his responses to the video on a blank sheet of paper, the teacher gave him a writing frame to guide him. The frame she used was the following:

> Before I began this topic I thought that
> But when I read about it I found out that
> I also learnt that
> Furthermore I learnt that
> Finally I learnt that

As well as simply presenting Scott with the writing frame, the teacher also, and this is important, began by talking him though the sequence of sentence starters, and discussing together the kinds of things he might write in response to each. His final piece of writing can be seen in Figure 8.12. Without personal knowledge of Scott it is difficult to realise how significant this piece of writing was to him. He was asked to read it aloud to his classmates, who responded with spontaneous applause. Perhaps for the first time in his school career so far, Scott saw himself as a successful writer.

Features of effective teaching

The four cameos just described have a number of elements in common, which, I would argue, are characteristic of effective teaching, particularly of children with learning difficulties. These can briefly be summarised as:

1 engaging content
2 teacher modelling
3 scaffolding
4 expectation of success.

I will try to unpick each of these features a little more.

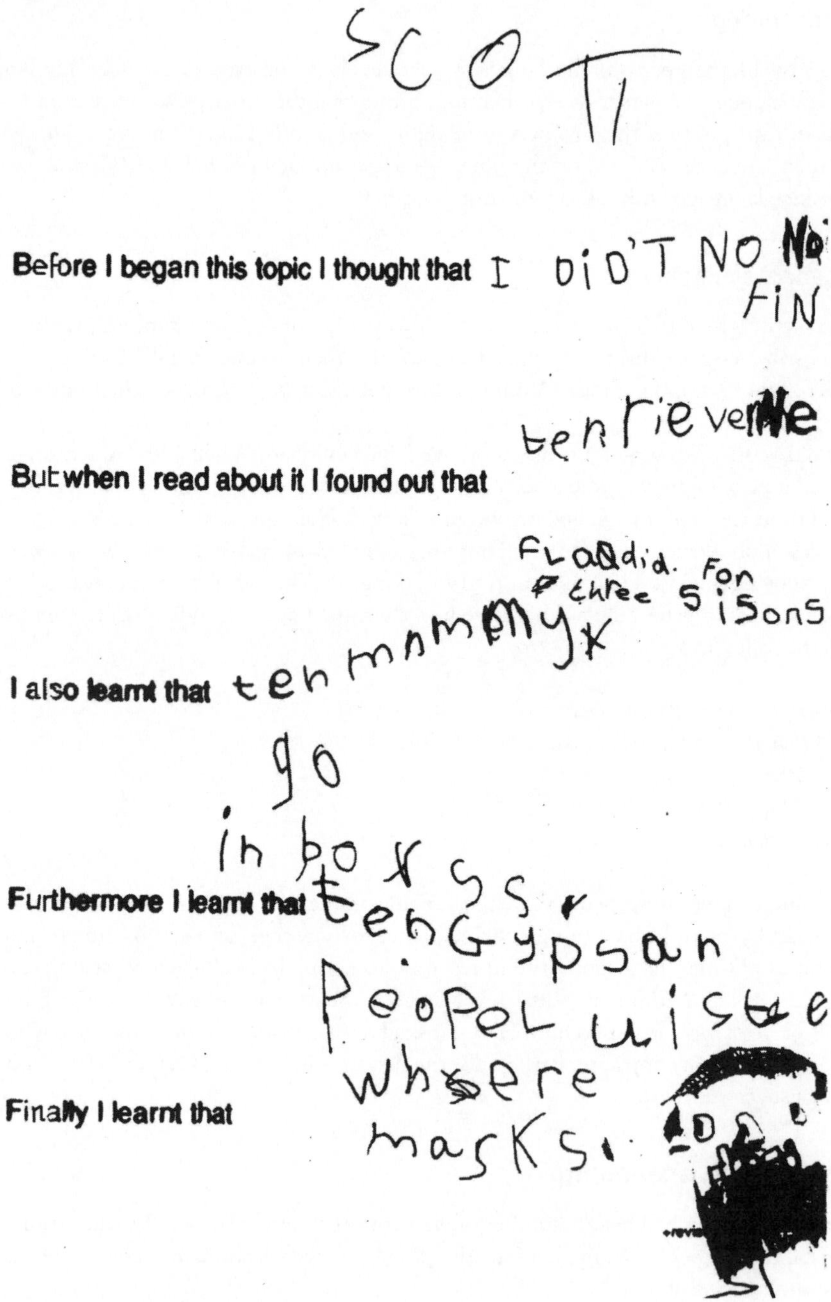

SCOTT

Before I began this topic I thought that I DiD'T NO NO FiN

But when I read about it I found out that ten rie ver Ne

I also learnt that t e h mnmmy x FL aNdid. For three s iSonS

Furthermore I learnt that ten Gypsan go in bo x s s r

Finally I learnt that PeoPeL wiste whsere masks.

Figure 8.12 Scott's framed writing
Crib sheet
Before I began this topic I thought that I didn't know nothing.
But when I read about it I found out that the river Nile flooded for three seasons.
I also learnt that the mummies go in boxes.
Furthermore I learnt that the Egyptian people used to wear masks.
Finally I learnt that

108

Engaging content

In each of the cameos, the material which formed the focus of the reading and writing shown by these children was interesting in its own right. It concerned aspects of the world which the children would have wanted to explore even had they not been within a classroom context. It was relatively easy to engage them with the content about which they were reading and writing, because that content was intrinsically engaging.

One of the main findings to emerge from research into reading achievement has been that engaged readers tend to be achieving readers (Baker *et al.*, 2000). This link is not surprising at all – most adults can think of activities that engage them, and at which they make much more effort. And the opposite is also true. I find gardening rather an uninteresting activity. Consequently the garden at my house would never be assessed as of high quality. I don't enjoy the activity enough to do much of it. This is not too serious for me (except when neighbours begin to comment adversely about the unkempt nature of my garden), but if I were to substitute reading or literacy in the above statements, the significance of engagement becomes much greater. Children who are not engaged are reluctant to take part in these activities: because they avoid taking part they do not get the levels of practice which might help them improve; because they do not improve, they carry on struggling. The only way to break into this vicious circle is to try to ensure that children do find the reading activities they are asked to participate in engaging. The ability to do this is a strong characteristic of effective teachers. As Baker *et al.* (2000) put it: 'children in the classrooms of outstanding teachers experience classroom environments that facilitate intense literacy engagement' (p. 12).

Teacher modelling

Another feature of the cameos described above is the role the teacher takes within them. Zoe, James, Kim and Scott each experienced a teacher who not only told them what they had to do but also joined in and did it with them. By doing this, the teacher not only offered each child support, but she also provided them with a direct model of how to act like an expert in reading and writing.

What these teachers were doing was teaching in a very similar way to what Palincsar and Brown (1984) described as 'reciprocal teaching'. This teaching procedure is based upon the twin ideas of 'expert scaffolding' and what Palincsar and Brown refer to as 'proleptic' teaching: that is, teaching in anticipation of competence (Oczkus, 2006). This model arises from the ideas of Vygotsky (1978), who put forward the notion that children first experience a particular cognitive activity in collaboration with expert practitioners. The child is first a spectator as the majority of the cognitive work is done by the expert (parent or teacher), then a novice as he/she starts to take over some of the work under the close supervision of the expert. As the child grows in experience and capability of performing the task, the expert passes over greater and greater responsibility but still acts as a guide, assisting the child at problematic points. Eventually, the child assumes full responsibility for the task with the expert still present in the role of a supportive audience. Using this approach to teaching, children learn about the task at their own pace, joining in only at a level at which they are capable – or perhaps a little beyond this level so that the task continually provides sufficient challenge to be interesting. The approach is often referred to as an apprenticeship approach, and there is a substantial research literature which suggests it is a very effective means of developing skills (see Braunger *et al.* (2004) for applications of the apprenticeship approach to extending literacy).

Scaffolding

An essential corollary to teacher modelling is the concept of scaffolding. The modelling of an activity or skill by an expert practitioner (teacher) is a crucial element in successful teaching and learning, but by itself it does not guarantee that the learner takes over the activity independently. What is needed is an intervening period in which the learner can be offered support but in which this support is gradually reduced as independence is gained.

Lawson (2002) describes scaffolding as 'a process by which a teacher provides students with a temporary framework for learning. Done correctly, such structuring encourages a student to develop his or her own initiative, motivation and resourcefulness. Once students build knowledge and develop skills on their own, elements of the framework are dismantled. Eventually, the initial scaffolding is removed altogether; students no longer need it.'

In the cameos described above, both the KWL grids and the writing frames used were forms of scaffolding. These devices acted to support the children in their literacy activities, making it possible that each child could achieve more than he/she would have done without the support. In our work on the Exel project (Wray and Lewis, 1997), we have always made the point strongly that scaffolding devices such as writing frames are not intended to be static teaching supports. We have argued that the use of a writing frame should always begin with discussion and teacher modelling before moving on to joint construction (teacher and learner(s) together) and then to the child undertaking writing supported by the frame. This oral–teacher–modelling, joint construction pattern of teaching is vital for it not only models the generic form and teaches the words that signal connections and transitions but it also provides opportunities for developing children's oral language and their thinking. Some students, especially those with learning difficulties may need many oral sessions and sessions in which their teacher acts as a scribe before they are ready to attempt their own writing.

Later, when children are becoming familiar with the writing structures with which frames provide them, the teacher needs to begin deliberately to 'wean them off' the frames. At this stage, when children begin to show evidence of independent usage, the teacher may need only to have a master copy of the frames available as help cards for those occasions when children need a prompt. A box of such help cards could be a part of the writing area in which children are encouraged to refer to many different aids to their writing. Such a support fits with the general 'procedural facilitation' strategy for students' writing suggested by Bereiter and Scardamalia (1987). It also seems to be a way into encouraging children to begin to make independent decisions about their own learning.

Expectation of success

The final common feature of all the cameos described is that in every case the teacher made her interactions with each child in the confident expectation that a successful outcome would result. Beginning with *Pygmalion in the Classroom* (Rosenthal and Jacobson, 1968), an extensive body of research has described how teachers' expectations can influence their learners' performance. While it would be misleading to state that teacher expectations determine a child's success, the research clearly establishes that teacher expectations do play a significant role in determining how well and how much children learn.

For all four of the children described in these cameos, it would have been almost forgivable for their teachers to have fairly low expectations about their likely success. Yet in each case, the teacher not only expected success to come, she also put in sufficient support to ensure it did. Such a positive approach to children with learning difficulties seems essential if these difficulties are ever to be overcome.

110

Conclusion

I have tried in this chapter to do a number of things. My main aim has been to make, and exemplify, the case that children with literacy difficulties do not always just need more initial literacy teaching – they need this literacy extending, that is, they need guided opportunities to use and apply their literacy to achieve something which both they and their teachers consider worthwhile. Literacy in itself is not much use: it is what it enables you to do that is the crucial thing.

I have also tried, through the classroom episodes I have presented, to elaborate a little on the nature of extended literacy skills, and, along the way, to present some classroom strategies for teaching such skills. Finally I have tried to unpick some common features in the effective teaching of these skills.

References

Alvermann, D., O'Brien, D. and Dillon, D. (1987) *Using Discussion to Promote Reading Comprehension.* Newark, DE: International Reading Association

Anderson, R.C. and Pearson, P.D. (1984) 'A schema-theoretical view of basic processes in reading comprehension' in P.D. Pearson (ed.) *Handbook of Reading Research.* New York: Longman.

Anderson, T.H. and Armbruster, B.B. (1981) *Content Area Textbooks.* (Reading Education Report no. 24). University of Illinois: Center for the Study of Reading.

Baker, L. and Brown, A. (1984) 'Metacognitive skills and reading', in D. Pearson (ed.) *Handbook of Reading Research.* New York: Longman

Baker, J., Dreher, M. and Guthrie, J. (2000) *Engaging Young Readers.* New York: Guilford

Bereiter, C. and Scardamalia, M. (1987) *The Psychology of Written Composition.* Hillsdale, New Jersey: Lawrence Erlbaum.

Bransford, J. (1983) 'Schema Activation – Schema Acquisition'. in R.C. Anderson, J. Osborn and R.J. Tierney (eds) *Learning to Read in American Schools.* Hillsdale, NJ: Lawrence Erlbaum.

Braunger, J., Donahue, D., Evans, K. and Galguera, T. (2004) *Rethinking Preparation for Content Area Teaching: The Reading Apprenticeship Approach.* San Francisco, CA: Jossey Bass.

Curtis, P. (2008) 'Education: Primary pupils without basic skills highlight Labour's biggest failure, says schools minister', *Guardian*, Thursday 21 August (http://www.guardian.co.uk/education/2008/aug/21/primaryschools.earlyyearseducation).

Department of Education and Science (DES) (1978) *Primary Education in England.* London: HMSO.

Gallagher, C. (2000) 'Writing across genres', *The Language Teacher*, 24 (7), 14.

Halliday, M.A.K. and Hasan, R. (1976) *Cohesion in English.* London: Longman.

Johns, A. (2001) (ed.) *Genre in the Classroom: Multiple Perspectives.* London: Routledge.

Keene, E. and Zimmerman, S. (2007) *Mosaic of Thought: The Power of Comprehension Strategy Instruction.* Portsmouth, NH: Heinemann.

Kress, G. (1988) *Communication and Culture: An Introduction.* Kensington, NSW: New South Wales University Press.

Lawson, L. (2002) 'Scaffolding as a Teaching Strategy', paper available on the *Scaffolding Website*, http://condor.admin.ccny.cuny.edu/~group4/, accessed 14 July 2008.

Lewis, M. and Wray, D. (1995) *Developing Children's Non-fiction Writing.* Leamington Spa: Scholastic.

Littlefair, A. (1991) *Reading all Types of Writing* Milton Keynes. Open University Press.

Martin, J. (1985) *Factual Writing: Exploring and Challenging Social Reality.* Oxford: Oxford University Press.

Oczkus, L. (2006) *Reciprocal Teaching at Work.* Newark, DE: International Reading Association.

Ogle, D.M. (1989) 'The Know, Want to Know, Learn strategy' in K.D. Muth (ed.) *Children's Comprehension of Text.* Newark, DE: International Reading Association.

Ogle, D.M. (1986) 'A teaching model that develops active reading of expository text'. *The Reading Teacher*, 39 (6), 564–571.

Palincsar, A. and Brown, A. (1984) 'Reciprocal teaching of comprehension-fostering and comprehension-monitoring activities', *Cognition and Instruction*, 1 (2), 117–175.

Perera, K. (1984) *Children's Reading and Writing.* Oxford: Blackwell.

Rosenthal, R. and Jacobson, L. (1968) *Pygmalion in the Classroom.* New York: Rinehart and Winston.

Vygotsky, L. (1978) *Mind in Society: The development of Higher Psychological Processes*. Cambridge MA.: Harvard University Press.

Wilson P.T. and Anderson R.C. (1986) 'What they don't know will hurt them: the role of Prior Knowledge in Comprehension' in J. Orasanu (ed.) *Reading Comprehension: from Research into Practice*. Hillsdale, NJ: Lawrence Erlbaum.

Winograd, P. and Bridge, C. (1986) 'The comprehension of important information in written prose' in J. Baumann (ed.) *Teaching Main Idea Comprehension*. Newark, DE: International Reading Association.

Wray, D. and Lewis, M. (1992) 'Primary children's use of information books', *Reading*, 26 (3), 19–24.

Wray, D. and Lewis, M. (1997) *Extending Literacy: Reading and Writing Non-fiction in the Primary School*. London: Routledge.

9

Spelling
Development, assessment and instruction

R. Malatesha Joshi and Suzanne Carreker

This chapter

- looks at the development of spelling in children
- discusses the role of phonology, morphology and orthography in spelling
- discusses the assessment of spelling
- looks at spelling instruction
- examines cross linguistic studies of spelling.

Even though good spelling is critical for literacy, spelling today does not receive as much attention as reading, both in terms of research and instructional recommendations that follow from research findings. Many more research studies have addressed how children learn to read than how they learn to spell. According to the ISI Web of Science, 10,235 articles were published from 2003 to 2008 on reading but only 896 on spelling. Perhaps there is a mistaken notion that when reading is taught, spelling is also learned rather automatically, and therefore no separate teaching of spelling principles is needed. On the contrary, when spelling skills are mastered, perhaps reading will be easier, at least in the English language, as virtually every good speller is a good reader. In fact, early American books used for teaching reading were called spellers and as Noah Webster stated as early as 1773, "spelling is the foundation of reading and the greatest ornament of writing" (as cited in Venezky, 1980). In this chapter, we will briefly outline the development of spelling, nature of spelling, assessment of spelling, instructional procedures for spelling, cross-linguistic studies on spelling, and some recommendations.

Development of spelling

Dyslexia is marked by inaccurate single-word decoding, lack of fluency, and poor spelling. With explicit and systematic instruction and sufficient practice, individuals with dyslexia can gain proficiency in single-word decoding and fluency. On the other hand, deficits in spelling tend to be more tenacious. Difficulties with spelling persist long after reading deficits have been ameliorated.

An understanding of how spelling skills are acquired heightens awareness of why spelling may be so difficult for individuals with dyslexia and can better inform the instruction for these

113

individuals. The acquisition of spelling skills generally follows a gradual sequence that has been described by several models of stages or phases (e.g., Ehri, 1989, 1992, 2000; Frith, 1985; Gentry, 1982).

Frith (1985) proposed a model of reading and spelling development that included three stages: 1) *logographic*—children recognize words for reading by how they look with little regard to letters or sounds, 2) *alphabetic*—children understand the relationships between letters and sounds and can sound out words for reading and spelling, and 3) *orthographic*—children begin to read and spell words as whole orthographic units. According to Frith's model, very young children spell words by sounding them out, and this skill transfers to the ability to sound out unfamiliar words when reading. Eventually, children recognize recurring orthographic patterns for reading that are then transferred to spelling (Davis and Bryant, 2006).

The five stages proposed by Gentry (1982) were specific to spelling. At the *precommunicative* stage, children demonstrate an understanding that writing represents spoken language through scribblings or random letters or strings of random letters. Children demonstrate the use of a sound-base strategy and include some of the salient sounds of a word (e.g., *en* for *enough*) at the *semi-phonetic* stage. At the *phonetic* stage, all sounds are present and marked by some letter or group of letters (e.g., *enuf* for *enough*). Every sound and prominent orthographic feature of a word is present (e.g., *enughf* for *enough*) at the *transitional* stage. The *correct* stage is the production of the conventional spelling of the word.

Ehri (2000) combined the models of Frith (1985) and Gentry (1982) and other researchers who proposed similar models (e.g., Beers and Henderson, 1977; Henderson, 1981; Templeton and Bear, 1992). Ehri outlined four distinct levels that capture the essences of the different models, and explain the progression in which spelling skills are acquired: *prealphabetic, partial alphabetic, full alphabetic,* and *consolidated alphabetic*. The first three level of this model suggest as the previous models do that children's spellings become more informed as the children's alphabetic knowledge increases. In the final level, children become aware of units for spelling—syllables, prefixes, and suffixes—and are better able to spell or invent multisyllabic words.

The spellings of young children provide valuable information about their awareness of sounds and relationships among sounds. Children's grasp of the alphabetic principle progresses from rudimentary levels (e.g., *f* or *frd* for *friend*) to complete representations of every phoneme in a word (e.g., *frend* for *friend*). Increasingly, spelling relies more on children's knowledge of recurring orthographic patterns.

There is variability in spelling development among children. Rarely will children move through the stages in a distinct progression. Ehri (1992) cautioned that stages are not tied to a maturation timetable but are inextricably tied to instruction. As Moats (2005) has stated, "Rather than a developmental progression characterized by distinct stages, learning to spell is more accurately described as a continual amalgamation of phonological, morphological, and orthographic knowledge" (p.14).

Nature of spelling

Because spelling is an amalgamation of phonological, morphological, and orthographic knowledge, we shall briefly outline the roles of each one of these in spelling acquisition. Given the persistence of spelling problems with individuals with dyslexia, appropriate spelling instruction is of particular importance.

Role of phonology in spelling

It has been recognized that phonology plays an important role in the acquisition of spelling skills by children. This conclusion is primarily based on the works of Read (1975) and Treiman (1993). Read analyzed the data from spontaneous production of spelling by precocious preschoolers and concluded that, similar to learning to talk, learning to spell is a creative process. Read also noticed that spelling errors committed by children were not random errors but reflected the influence of phonology that underlies spelling. For instance, children often omitted nasal sounds such as /n/ because nasal consonants are acquired much later than other concomitants. Hence, children had a tendency to leave out *n* in words like *pant* and *snow* but not in *nose*. Since the study by Read (1971) showed that phonology plays an important role in spelling, several studies have shown the influence of pronunciation or spoken language on spelling. For instance, Treiman *et al.* (1997) analyzed the spelling errors of 6- to 7-year-old children from the US and England and found that the US children spelled *car* as *cr* or as *kr* while the British children spelled it as *ca* or as *ka* and *hurt* was spelled as *hrt* by the US children and as *hut* by the British children. Further, the dialect influence on spelling was observed even among adults. University students in the UK spelled *leper* as *lepa* while such kind of errors (rhotic *r* or *r* intrusions) were not observed among university students in the US (Treiman and Barry, 2000). Treiman (2004) found similar results among speakers of African American Venacular English (AAVE) and Standard Academic English. Further, it has been shown that training in phonemic awareness improves a child's spelling ability (Arra and Aaron, 2001; Ball and Blachman, 1991; Lundberg, Frost, and Petersen, 1988).

Role of morphology in spelling

In addition to phonology, morphological knowledge also plays an important role in spelling. According to Carlisle (1995), morphological awareness "focuses on children's conscious awareness of the morphemic structure of words and their ability to reflect on and manipulate that structure" (p. 194). Morphology refers to the units of language that carry meaning. Base words, roots, combining forms, prefixes, inflectional endings, and suffixes are morphemes, units that carry meaning. Some morphemes can stand alone (i.e., free morphemes), and some morphemes must be combined with other morphemes (i.e., bound morphemes). The understanding of morphemes for spelling is as basic as understanding that /z/ at the end of the word *pins* represents an inflectional ending that denotes the plural form and, therefore, should be spelled *s* and not *z*. Similarly, the two words *fox* and *rocks* are a good example of morphemic word structures. A one syllable word with one morpheme that ends with the /ks/ sound will be usually spelled with *x* as found in the word *fox*. A one-syllable word with two morphemes (one the meaning and the other signaling number) is usually spelled with *ks* as in the word *rocks*. More complex understanding involves the idea that English is a morphophonemic language, and the spelling of a root morpheme may be preserved to emphasize meaning over pronunciation. For example, *sign* is the root of *signature* or *know* is the root of *knowledge*. While the pronunciations of the words in each pair differ, the spellings of the roots do not (Aaron *et al.*, 2008).

Derivatives are formed with a root or base word and one or more affixes. Knowledge of affixes (i.e., prefixes, suffixes, inflectional endings) supports the correct spelling of words. There are three reliable rules that dictate the spelling of base words when a suffix or an inflection ending (i.e., a suffix that denote number, tense, voice, mood, or comparison) is added. The spelling of the base word may change through the doubling of the final consonant, the dropping of a final silent *e*, or the changing of a final *y* to *i*. Each rule has several determinants that must

115

be present for the spelling of the base word to change. Table 9.2 presents the rules and the determinants. The addition of a prefix does not change the spelling of the root or base word, but the spelling of the prefix may change. In the word *attracted*, there are three morphemes – *ad, tract, ed*. The spelling of the final letter in the prefix *ad-* changes to match the first letter of the root *tract*. This is done for euphony, to ease the pronunciation. Knowledge of prefixes that may change spelling helps students spell words that may contain doubled consonants. Prefixes that may change spelling are presented in Table 9.1.

Henry (1988) reported that fluent readers looked first at the morphemes, second at the syllables and only lastly at the phonemic breakdown of a word. A series of studies by Bryant and colleagues (Bryant *et al.*, 2006; Nunes *et al.*, 1997), led them to conclude that knowledge of morphemes may play a causal role in the spelling. Since both phonological as well as morphological knowledge is required to spell well, English is referred to as a morphophonemic language. Terry (2006), after analyzing the spelling of speakers of African American Vernacular English (AAVE), found that the ability to spell inflected morphemes correctly is related to students' elicited oral production and understanding of these standard forms, and AE speakers outperformed AAE speakers in both these skills.

Role of orthography in spelling

Henderson (1984) defined orthography as "graphemic patterns of a written language and their mapping onto phonology, morphology, and meaning" (p. 1). In short, orthography is the visual representation of a spoken language. The orthographic depth hypothesis suggests that the depth of a language's orthography influences the rate at which it is learned for reading and spelling (Seymour, 2006). Shallow or transparent orthographies (e.g., Finnish, Italian) tend to have

---

Table 9.1 Spelling rules adding suffixes

The doubling rule

When a base word ends in one vowel, one consonant, and one accent (all one-syllable words are accented) and a vowel suffix (a suffix that begins with a vowel) is being added, double the final consonant of the base word before adding the suffix.

 hop + ed = hopped
 star + ing = starring
 begin + ing = beginning

The dropping rule

When a base word ends in a final *e* and a vowel suffix is being added, drop the final *e* in the base word before adding the suffix.

 hope + ed = hoped
 blue + ish = bluish
 complete + ing = completing

The changing rule

When a base word ends in one vowel and a final *y* and a suffix that does not begin with *i* is being added, change the *y* to *i* before adding the suffix.

 try + ed = tried
 silly + ness = silliness
 penny + less = penniless

Table 9.2 Eight prefixes that may change spelling

---

ab- (a-, abs-)
ad- (a-, ac-, af-, ag-, al-, an-, ap-, ar-, as-, at-)
con- (co-, col-, com-, cor-)
en- (em-)
ex- (e-, ec-, ef-)
in- (il-, im-, ir-)
ob- (oc-, of- op-)
sub- (suc-, suf-, sup-, sur-, sus-)

Source: adapted from Carreker (2005a), p. 269.

nearly perfect grapheme–phonemes correspondences, essentially one phoneme for each grapheme (i.e., spelling unit) and one grapheme for each phoneme. Deep or opaque orthographies (e.g., French, Danish) have multiple graphemes that represent one phoneme or multiple phonemes that represent a single grapheme. A language with a shallow orthography is learned much faster than a language with a deep orthography.

English falls into the category of deep orthographies, with between 40–45 phonemes and 26 letters. The 26 letters can represent single graphemes that represent one or multiple phonemes (e.g., *j* = /j/ vs. *s* = /s/, /z/, /sh/) or can be combined to form multi-letter graphemes (e.g., *sh, ch, tch, dge*) that can represent one or more phonemes (e.g., *sh* = /sh/ vs. *ch* = /ch/, /k/, /sh/). In total, there are some 70 common letters and letter combinations (Ehri, 2000) and close to 250 graphemes in English (Caravolas, 2006). Additionally, single phonemes can be represented by multiple graphemes (e.g., /k/ = *k, c, ck, ch,* or /j/ = *j, g, dge*). English orthography is indeed very complex (Venezky, 1999). The goal of spelling instruction is to make the orthography of the language explicit by heightening awareness of sounds in words and the frequently recurring patterns that spell those sounds (Carreker, 2005b).

Assessment of spelling

While reading and spelling are closely interrelated (the coefficient of correlation ranges from 0.68 to 0.86; Ehri, 2000), reading and spelling are not simply inverse operations. Reading is highly influenced by the context and, therefore, is a recognition skill. Every letter in an unfamiliar word does not need to be remembered for reading. As Ehri noted, "it is easier to read words accurately in English than to spell them. Failure to remember one or two letters dooms a perfect spelling but not necessarily an accurate reading" (p. 24). Spelling demands complete recall not only of all the letters in a word but also the correct order of the letters, which makes spelling more difficult to remediate than reading. However, the need for exact recall also may make spelling a more accurate indicator of literacy than reading.

Problems with formal and informal spelling assessments

The dualist and finite assessment of spelling words as *right* or *wrong* is counter to the nature of spelling development and masks the predictable progression of spelling development. As previously mentioned, spelling proficiency unfolds in gradual sequence. The progression of the sequence relies on specific underlying phonological and orthographic knowledge that is ultimately consolidated to form conventional spellings. Informal assessment of spelling (i.e., weekly spelling tests) and formal assessment of spelling using standardized measures often fail to capture an individual's true spelling ability or proficiency (Joshi and Aaron, 2005).

117

Formal, standardized spelling tests score words as *right* or *wrong*, and often fall short in discriminating good and poor spellers (Moats, 1994). For example, a frequently used standardized spelling measure, *The Test of Written Spelling-3* (Hammill and Larsen, 1996) includes words that may be considered as regular and irregular. Supposedly, regular words on the test can be sounded out while irregular words need to be spelled from memory. The inability of the test to discriminate good and poor spellers is that it uses words that may not be familiar to students. If a student has never seen a word, he or she is not likely to hold that word in memory; hence, he or she will spell the word phonetically regardless of whether the word is regular or irregular. The error is not necessarily indicative of a poor speller.

On informal assessments such as weekly spelling tests, scoring written spelling as *right* or *wrong* does not give credit for the patterns that have been learned. For example, a student who spells *hospital* as *hospitle* has greater knowledge of the patterns of the language than the student who spells *hospital* as *hostl*. A qualitative analysis of errors can provide insights as to the progress of an individual understanding of the patterns of language. This understanding not only enhances spelling performance, the understanding also enhances decoding performance (Joshi, 1995; Moats, 2005/2006).

Qualitative assessment

Qualitative analysis of spelling requires the scorer to have in-depth phonological, orthographic, and morphological knowledge and knowledge about spelling development. The creation of a scale or rubric can delineate more basic spellings from more informed spellings. For example, Tangel and Blachman (1995) devised a seven-point scale, with a 0 for spellings with no alphabetic representation and 6 for the correct spelling. The scores 1–5 represented spellings with increasing accuracy of phonological and/or orthographic elements. This type of qualitative analyses can also guide instructional programs. For instance, a child who spells *cat* as *KT* needs a different kind of instruction than a child who spells *cat* as *MB*. The first child has some knowledge of letter–sound correspondence while the second child does not know the letter–sound correspondence, hence the instruction has to be tailored accordingly. A word of caution: Even though Tangel and Blachman's spelling error analysis is novel, a much more refined assessment instrument as well as scoring rubric may be needed. The reason being, in this analysis, a word like *cat* spelled correctly receives 6 points and a more difficult word spelled correctly like *elephant* also receives 6 points. The word *elephant* is a much more complex word in terms of its phonological and orthographical structure while the word *cat* is a much simpler word compared to the word *elephant*. A solution to this problem could be to have a separate scoring scale for each word as devised by Treiman and colleagues in many of their research studies (Treiman and Barry, 2000).

Considerations with qualitative assessment

Qualitative assessment must take into account an individual's dialect or primary language. The extent to which individuals understand one another distinguishes a dialect from a language. Individuals speaking a different dialect can be understood; individuals speaking a different language cannot be understood (Aaron *et al.*, 2008). A common English dialect is African American Vernacular English (AAVE). There are phonological variations in AAVE that can influence spelling. For example, speakers of AAVE do not differentiate /ĭ/ and /ĕ/, omit /r/ before a vowel or consonant, omit /l/ in final position, and may alter the sequence of phonemes. English Language Learners (ELL) may substitute or confuse phonological or orthographic elements from the primary language or have difficulty with phonological elements that do not exist in the primary language (see Joshi and Aaron, 2006).

Informed spelling instruction

Spelling instruction is often a postscript to reading instruction, and frequently involves the memorization of words for a weekly test. The words are memorized but promptly forgotten once the test is over. Rote memorization suggests that visual memory is the primary basis for spelling. Although rote memorization is a common practice in many classrooms, visual memory is not the primary basis. For example, if visual memory were the primary basis for spelling, words with reliable spelling patterns (i.e., regular words) and words with unexpected spelling patterns (i.e., irregular words) that are similar in length and frequency should be misused equally often; however, children misspell irregular words more often than regular words (Treiman, 1993). Additionally, children learning English misspell vowels more often than consonants, a consistency that would not occur if visual memory were the primary basis for spelling (Caravolas *et al.*, 2005; Kessler and Treiman, 2001). While some words must be memorized because of orthographic irregularities (e.g., *said, enough, ocean*), spelling instruction should not be limited solely to the rote visual memorization of words. Rote memorization constrains the benefits of the reliable nature of English orthography (Joshi, Treiman, Carreker, and Moats, 2008).

English spelling is less chaotic than often thought (Kessler and Treiman, 2003; Treiman, 2006). In fact, Chomsky and Halle (1968) claimed that English spelling is a "near optimal system for lexical representation" (p. 49). Hanna *et al.* (1966) estimated that the spellings of nearly 87 per cent of English words are predictable based on letter–sound correspondences or almost predictable except for one sound (e.g., *gnat, match*). Additionally, knowledge of word origins and word meanings reduces the percentage of English words that are truly irregular to about 4 per cent. While the 87 per cent reliability of English orthography seems to imply that learning to spell English words should be fairly simple, the high reliability is somewhat deceptive (Carreker, 2005a). Learning to spell in English is not an easy task. Learning to spell is primarily a linguistic task that requires simultaneous integration of phonological, orthographic, morphological, semantic, and syntactic knowledge (Frith, 1980; Moats, 1995). English adds to the task a reliable but complex orthography. Therefore, spelling instruction should be linguistically based (Joshi *et al.,* 2008) and should make the reliability of English obvious (Carreker, 2005a).

There are some rules or constraints in English orthography that govern grapheme sequences, position, and usage. For example, the sequence *skr* does not occur within a syllable; *ck* does not appear in the initial position of words; *v* and *j* do not occur in the final position of words; and *j, y, v,* and *w* rarely or never double in English words. Beginning spellers often intuit these constraints without instruction; for instance, beginning spellers are more likely to choose *nuss* as a possible spelling and not *nnus* and are not likely to spell *cake* as *ckak* (Treiman, 1993, 1997). Students with dyslexia usually do not intuit these constraints and need explicit attention to the constraints.

The orthographic depth of English requires the explicit teaching of recurring spelling patterns that represent specific phonemes. The choice of graphemes to represent phonemes may be determined by the frequency with which a specific grapheme represents a specific phoneme. The grapheme-to-phoneme translations in decoding are more dependable than the phoneme-to-grapheme translations in spelling (Adams, 1990). Context when decoding makes the translation of a spelling that has multiple pronunciations more apparent. Carreker (2005a) explained:

When a letter or group of letters has more than one possible pronunciation (e.g., *ea* can be pronounced /ē/, /ĕ/, or /ā/), the reader affirms his or her pronunciation choice by determining whether the chosen word makes sense in the sentence (e.g., one nods one's /hēd/, /hĕd/, or /hād/). (p. 258)

Spelling lacks the aid of context. The translation of a phoneme with more than one grapheme choice is problematic (e.g., /ā/ can be spelled *a*-consonant-*e*, *ai*, *ei*, *eigh*, *ea*). As Carreker (2005a) noted, "After all the word pronounced /tām/ (*tame*), spelled incorrectly as *taim*, *teim*, *teighm*, or *team*, would share the same context" (p. 258). Initially, grapheme choice may need to be determined by frequency. Of all possible choices, one recurs more often (e.g., in initial or medial position of a one-syllable word, *a*-consonant-*e* as in *cake* is the most frequent choice for /ā/; Hanna *et al.*, 1966). Introducing the most frequent grapheme choices first in spelling instruction increases the likelihood that a high percentage of words will be spelled correctly. The focus on one pattern for spelling a specific phoneme increases awareness of other patterns.

The choice of graphemes may also be determined by the position of the phoneme in a word (e.g., final /ā/ is usually spelled *ay*), the length of the word (e.g., final /ē/ at the end of a one-syllable word is usually spelled *ee* and *y* at the end of a multisyllabic word), or the influence of surrounding phonemes (e.g., /ŏ/ after /w/ is usually spelled *a* as in *wash*, *water*, *want*). There can be one determinant for a grapheme choice or there may be multiple determinants for grapheme choice (e.g., final /j/ after a short vowel in a one-syllable word is usually spelled *dge*). A selection of reliable patterns of grapheme choices are presented in Table 9.3.

In general, less frequent patterns do not need to be taught. Less frequent patterns are presented in Table 9.4. Words that contain the infrequently used patterns can be taught as exception words. These words and words with striking orthographic irregularities (e.g., *yacht*, *ocean*) need to be memorized. Memorization is aided by the use of spelling-based pronunciations, which build a memory of a word's orthography (e.g., the pronunciation of *yacht* as /y/ /ă/ /ch/ /t/). A second strategy is to have a student trace and copy the word several times, saying the word each time and naming each letter while writing. Tracing, copying, and naming build words in memory.

Cassar *et al.* (2005), in a study of students with and without dyslexia, concluded that:

> The similarities between children with and without dyslexia suggest that the two types of children do not need qualitatively different kinds of spelling instruction. Children with dyslexia clearly require more direct assistance to develop their phonological and spelling skills. But good instruction that focuses on the kinds of difficulties that are experienced by typical children should help all children.
>
> (p. 46).

Further information about patterns and instructional techniques of teaching spelling can be found in Aaron et al. (2008), Bear *et al.* (2005), Carreker (2005a), Henry (2003), and Moats (2005).

Cross-linguistic studies on spelling

Spelling development has been examined in several orthographies such as French, (Fayol *et al.*, 1999; Jaffre and Fayol, 2006; Pacton *et al.*, 2001), Spanish (Justicia *et al.*, 1999), Greek (Porpodas, 2006), Danish (Juul and Elbro, 2004) and Kiswahili (Alcock, 2006). The above-mentioned languages incorporate alphabetic orthography, hence to spell, graphemes have to be

Table 9.3 Reliable spelling patterns

Initial and Medial consonant sounds:
/k/ before *e, i,* or *y* is spelled *k* (*keep, kite, sky*)
/k/ before *a, o, u,* or any consonant is spelled *c* (*cat, cot, cut, clap, crash*)
/j/ before *e, i,* or *y* is spelled *g* (*gem, giant, gym*)
/j/ before *a, o,* or *u* is spelled *j* (*jam, joke, junk*)
/s/ after a vowel and before *e, i, or y* is spelled *c* (*grocer, recede*)

Final consonant sounds:
/k/ after a short vowel in a one-syllable base word is spelled *ck* (*pack, sock*)
/k/ after a short vowel in a word with two or more syllables is spelled *c* (*music, public*)
/k/ after a vowel pair or consonant is spelled *k* (*peek, milk*)
/j/ after a short vowel in a one-syllable base word is spelled *dge* (*badge, fudge*)
/j/ after a vowel pair, long vowel, or consonant is spelled *ge* (*scrooge, cage, bulge*)

Initial and medial vowel sounds:
/ā/ before a final consonant sound is spelled *a-consonant-e* (*cake, rotate*)
/ā/ at the end of a syllable is spelled *a* (*table, canine*)
/ē/ is spelled *ee* (*eel, meet, green*)
/ē/ at the end of a syllable is spelled *e* (*even, equal*)
/ū/ before a final consonant sound is spelled *u-consonant-e* (*use, cube*)
/ū/ at the end of a syllable is spelled *u* (*unit, music*)
/oi/ is spelled *oi* (*joint, appoint*)
/ou/ is spelled *ou* (*round, astound*)

Final vowel sounds:
/ā/ is spelled *ay* (*day, decay*)
/ī/ is spelled *y* (*try, reply*)
/ō/ is spelled *ow* (*show, window*)
/ē/ in a one syllable word is spelled *ee* (*see, free*)
/ē/ in a word of two or more syllables is spelled *y* (*candy, ugly*)
/ŭ/ at the end of a word is spelled *a* (*tuba, sofa*)
/oi/ is spelled *oy* (*boy, destroy*)
/ou/ is spelled *ow* (*cow, endow*)

Source: adapted from Carreker (2005b), p. 22.

used to represent phonemes of the spoken language. However, the mapping of the graphemes to phonemes varies among different orthographies. For instance, while Spanish and Czech have almost one-to-one correspondence between graphemes and phonemes, English orthography uses approximately 250 graphemes to represent 40–45 phonemes. Thus, spelling acquisition and development may vary among different orthographies. For instance, a series of studies conducted by Caravolas and colleagues (Bruck *et al.*, 1998; Caravolas *et al.*, 2003), has shown that even though phoneme awareness is important for spelling development in both English and French, phoneme awareness is more important for English than for French. Further, it has been shown that French- and German-speaking children develop better spelling skills in their third and fourth years of spelling than English-speaking children (Caravolas, 2006; Landerl, 2006; Wimmer and Landerl, 1997). Oney and Durgunoglu (1997) found that Turkish Kindergartners performed significantly better than English Kindergartners and first graders on a syllable tapping task. This finding was attributed to the agglutinative nature of the Turkish language. It appears that just as the transparent orthographies make it easier to decode words and non-words, spelling may also be easier to acquire in shallow orthographies.

Table 9.4 Infrequent spelling patterns

/ǎ/	=	*la<u>ugh</u>, pl<u>ai</u>d*
/ā/	=	*caf<u>e</u>, st<u>ea</u>k, matin<u>ee</u>, r<u>ei</u>n, <u>ei</u>ght, th<u>ere</u>, th<u>ey</u>, ball<u>et</u>*
/au/	=	*c<u>augh</u>t, br<u>ough</u>t, br<u>oa</u>d*
/ĕ/	=	*h<u>ea</u>d, s<u>ai</u>d, <u>a</u>ny*
/ē/	=	*c<u>ei</u>ling, monk<u>ey</u>, sk<u>i</u>, pet<u>ite</u>*
/g/	=	*<u>gh</u>ost, catalo<u>gue</u>*
/ĭ/	=	*for<u>fei</u>t, en<u>gi</u>ne*
/ī/	=	*<u>ai</u>sle, ka<u>ya</u>k, h<u>eigh</u>t, t<u>ie</u>, l<u>igh</u>t, d<u>ye</u>, b<u>uy</u>*
/k/	=	*Ira<u>q</u>, mar<u>qu</u>ee, anti<u>qu</u>e*
/ō/	=	*b<u>eau</u>, t<u>oe</u>, d<u>ough</u>*
/ōō/	=	*s<u>ou</u>p, d<u>o</u>, sh<u>oe</u>, s<u>ui</u>t*
/sh/	=	*<u>s</u>ure*
/ŭ/	=	*s<u>o</u>n, bl<u>oo</u>d, t<u>ou</u>ch*
/ū/	=	*<u>Eu</u>rope*
/w/	=	*s<u>u</u>ede*
/y/	=	*gen<u>i</u>us*
/z/	=	*<u>X</u>erox*

Source: adapted from Carreker (2005b), p. 267.

Phonemic awareness and knowledge of the alphabetic principle, morphology, and orthographic structure of words assist in developing accurate spelling. Boulware-Gooden (2004) administered tests that tap phonology, morphology, and orthography of children in Grades 4 and 6 in the US and Russia. Multiple regression analyses showed that phonology and morphology subtests contributed more for spelling of English words while orthography and morphology subtests contributed more for spelling of Russian words. The results are explained in terms of the orthographic nature of English and Russian languages. There are very few studies examining the nature of spelling in different orthographies as well as among bilinguals. Certainly more controlled studies are needed.

Conclusion

Spelling has been a neglected area of study even though it is a fundamental skill in becoming a literate person. We have briefly outlined the nature of spelling and how the current procedure of assessment is not helpful in informed instruction of spelling. Explicit spelling instruction must be distinct from reading instruction. As Ehri (2000) noted, "the acquisition of spelling skill can be left to the work of reading instruction and practice because the memory requirements for spelling English words accurately exceed the memory requirements for reading words accurately" (p. 33). The memory requirements needed for spelling are not satisfied through rote memorization. Rather as Joshi et al. (2008) explained:

> . . . memory for orthographic patterns relies on and is facilitated by an understanding of linguistic concepts, including speech sounds, sound–symbol correspondences, word origins, and meaningful parts of words. The primary mechanism for word memory is not a photographic memory, as many believe; it is insight into why the word is spelled the way it is. It is recommended that more studies on systematic instruction of spelling as well as cross-linguistic studies are needed.

References

Aaron, P. G., Joshi, R. M., and Quatroche, D. (2008). *Becoming a Professional Reading Teacher: What to Teach, How to Teach, Why it Matters*. Baltimore: Paul H. Brookes Publishing Co.

Adams, M. J. (1990). *Beginning to Read: Thinking and Learning about Print*. Cambridge, MA: MIT Press.

Alcock, K. (2006). Literacy in Kishwahili. In R. M. Joshi and P. G. Aaron (eds), *Handbook of Orthography and Literacy* (pp. 405–419). Mahwah, NJ: Lawrence Erlbaum Associates.

Arra, C.T. and Aaron, P.G. (2001). Effects of psycholinguistic instruction on spelling performance. *Psychology in the Schools, 38*, 357–363.

Ball, E.W. and Blachman, B.A. (1991). Does phoneme awareness training in kindergarten make a difference in early word recognition and developmental spelling? *Reading Research Quarterly 26*, 49–66.

Bear, D. R., Invernizzi, M., Templeton, S., and Johnston, F. (2005). *Words their Way: Word Study, Phonics, Vocabulary, and Spelling Instruction* (3rd edn). Upper Saddle River, NJ: Merrill Publishing.

Beers, J., and Henderson, E. (1977). A study of developing orthographic concepts among first graders. *Research in the Teaching of English, 2*, 133–148.

Boulware-Gooden, R. (2004). *The Role of Phonology, Morphology, and Orthography in English and Russian Spelling*. Unpublished doctoral dissertation, Texas A & M University, College Station.

Bruck, M., Treiman, R., Caravolas, M., Genesse, G., and Cassar, M. (1998). Spelling skills of children in whole language and phonics classrooms. *Applied Psycholinguistics, 19*, 669–684.

Bryant, P., Deacon, H., and Nunes, T. (2006). Morphology and spelling: what have morphemes to do with spelling? In R.M. Joshi and P.G. Aaron (eds), *Handbook of Orthography and Literacy* (pp. 545–579). Mahwah, NJ: Lawrence Erlbaum.

Caravolas, M. (2006). Learning to spell in different languages: how orthographic variables might affect early literacy. In Joshi, R.M. and Aaron, P.G. (eds), *Handbook of Orthography and Literacy* (pp. 424–449). Mahwah, NJ: Lawrence Erlbaum.

Caravolas, M., Bruck, M., and Genesse, F. (2003). Similarities and differences between English and French-speaking poor spellers. In N. Goulandris (ed.), *Dyslexia in Different Languages*, (pp. 157–180). London: Whurr.

Caravolas, M., Kessler, B., Hulme, C., and Snowling, M. (2005). Effects of orthographic consistency, frequency, and letter knowledge on children's vowel spelling development. *Journal of Experimental Child Psychology, 92*, 307–321.

Carlisle, J. F. (1995). Morphological awareness and early reading achievement. In L. Feldman (ed.), *Morphological Aspects of Language Processing* (pp. 54–78). Hillsdale, NJ: Lawrence Erlbaum.

Carreker, S. (2005a). Teaching spelling. In J. R. Birsh (ed.), *Multisensory Teaching of Basic Language Skills* (2nd edn, pp. 217–256). Baltimore: Paul H. Brookes Publishing Co.

Carreker, S. (2005b). Spelling instruction: foundation of reading and ornament of writing. *Perspectives, 31*(3), 22–25.

Cassar, M., Treiman, R., Moats, L., Pollo, T. C., and Kessler, B. (2005). How do the spellings of children with dyslexia compare with those of nondyslexic children? *Reading and Writing: An Interdisciplinary Journal, 18*, 27–49.

Chomsky, N., and Halle, M. (1968). *The Sound Pattern of English*. New York: Harper and Row.

Davis, C., and Bryant, P. (2006). Causal connections in the acquisition of an orthographic rule: A test of Uta Frith's developmental hypothesis. *Journal of Child Psychology and Psychiatry, 47*, 849–856.

Ehri, L. C. (1989). The development of spelling knowledge and its role in reading acquisition and reading disability. *Journal of Learning Disabilities, 22*, 356–365.

Ehri, L. C. (1992). Review and commentary: stages of spelling development. In S. Templeton and D. Bear (eds), *Development of Orthographic Knowledge and the Foundations of Literacy: A Memorial Festschrift for Edmund H. Henderson* (pp. 307–332). Hillsdale, NJ: Lawrence Erlbaum Associates.

Ehri, L. C. (2000). Learning to read and learning to spell: two sides of a coin. *Topics in Leaning Disorders, 20*, 19–49.

Fayol, M., Hupet, M., and Largy, P. (1999). The acquisition of subject-verb agreement in written French: from novice to expert errors. *Reading and Writing: An Interdisciplinary Journal, 11*, 153–174.

Frith, U. (ed.). (1980). *Cognitive Processes in Spelling*. London: Academic Press, Inc.

Frith, U. (1985). Beneath the surface of developmental dyslexia. In K. Patterson, J. Marshall, and M. Coltheart (eds), *Surface Dyslexia* (pp. 287–295). Baltimore: University Park Press.

Gentry, J. R. (1982). An analysis of developmental spelling in GYNS at WRK. *The Reading Teacher, 36*, 192–200.

Hammill, D., and Larsen, S. (1996). *Test of written spelling*. Austin, TX: ProEd.

Hanna, P. R., Hanna, J. S., Hodges, R. E., and Rudorf, E. H., Jr. (1966). *Phoneme-grapheme correspondences as cues to spelling improvement.* Washington, DC: U. S. Department of Health, Education, and Welfare.

Henderson, E. (1981). *Learning to Read and Spell: The Child's Knowledge of Words.* DeKalb, IL: Northern Illinois University Press.

Henderson, L. (1984) *Orthographies and Reading*, London: Lawrence Erlbaum.

Henry, M.K. (1988). Beyond phonics: Integrated decoding and spelling instruction based on word origin and structure. *Annals of Dyslexia, 38,* 259–275.

Henry, M.K. (2003). *Unlocking Literacy: Effective Decoding and Spelling Instruction.* Baltimore: Paul H. Brookes.

Henry, M. K. (2005). A short history of the English language. In J. R. Birsh (ed.), *Multisensory Teaching of Basic Language Skills* (2nd edn, pp. 119–139). Baltimore: Paul H. Brookes Publishing Co.

Jaffre, J-P., and Fayol, M. (2006). Orthography and literacy in French. In R. M. Joshi and P. G. Aaron (eds), *Handbook of Orthography and Literacy* (pp. 81–103). Mahwah, NJ: Lawrence Erlbaum Associates.

Joshi, R. M. (1995). Assessing reading and spelling skills. *School Psychology Review, 24,* 361–375.

Joshi, R. M., and Aaron, P. G. (2005). Spelling assessment and instructional recommendations. *Perspectives, 31*(3), 38–41.

Joshi, R. M., Treiman, R., Carreker, S., and Moats, L. C. (2008). Isn't spelling just memorizing words? Answers to some common questions about spelling. *American Educator, 32* (4), 6–16, 42–43.

Justicia, F., Defior, S., Pelegrina, S., and Martos, F. (1999). Sources of error in Spanish writing. *Journal of Research in Reading, 22,* 198–202.

Juul, H., and Elbro, C. (2004). The links between grammar and spelling: a cognitive hurdle in deep orthographies? *Reading and Writing: An Interdisciplinary Journal, 17,* 915–942.

Kessler, B., and Treiman, R. (2001). Relationships between sounds and letters in English monosyllables. *Journal of Memory and Language, 44,* 592–617.

Kessler, B., and Treiman, R. (2003). Is English spelling chaotic? Misconceptions concerning its irregularity. *Reading Psychology, 24,* 267–289.

Landerl, K. (2006). Reading acquisition in different orthographies: evidence from direct comparisons. In R. M. Joshi and P. G. Aaron (eds), *Handbook of Orthography and Literacy* (pp. 513–530). Mahwah, NJ: Lawrence Erlbaum Associates.

Lundberg, I., Frost, J., and Petersen, O.P. (1988). Effectiveness of an extensive program for stimulating phonological awareness in preschool children. *Reading Research Quarterly, 23,* 263–284.

Moats, L. C. (1994). Assessment of spelling in learning disabilities research. In G. R. Lyon (ed.), *Frames of Reference for the Assessment of Learning Disabilities* (pp. 333–349). Baltimore: Paul H. Brookes Publishing Co.

Moats, L. C. (1995). *Spelling: Development, Disability, and Instruction.* Baltimore: York Press.

Moats, L. C. (2000). *Speech to Print: Language Essentials for Teachers.* Baltimore: Paul H. Brookes Publishing Co.

Moats, L. C. (2005). *Spellography for Teachers: How English Spelling Works (Language Essentials for Teachers of Reading and Spelling [LETRS], Module 3).* Longmont, CO: Sopris West.

Moats, L. C. (2005/2006). How spelling supports reading: And why it is more regular and predictable than you think. *American Educator, 12–22,* 42–43.

Nunes, T., Bryant, P.E. and Bindman, M. (1997) Morphological spelling strategies: developmental stages and processes. *Developmental Psychology, 33,* 637–649.

Oney, B., and Durgunoglu, A. Y. (1997). Beginning to read in Turkish: a phonologically transparent orthography. *Applied Psycholinguists, 18,* 1–15.

Pacton, S., Perruchet, P., Fayol, M., and Cleeremans, A. (2001). Implicit learning out of the lab: the case of orthographic regularities. *Journal of Experimental Psychology: General, 130,* 401–426.

Porpodas, C. (2006). Literacy acquisition in Greek: research review of the role of phonological and cognitive factors. In R. M. Joshi and P. G. Aaron (eds), *Handbook of Orthography and Literacy* (pp. 189–199). Mahwah, NJ: Lawrence Erlbaum Associates.

Read, C. (1971). Pre-school children's knowledge of English phonology. *Harvard Educational Review, 41,* 1–34.

Read, C. (1975). *Children's Categorization of Speech Sounds in English.* Urbana, IL: National Council of Teachers of English.

Seymour, P. H. K. (2006). Theoretical framework for beginning reading in different orthographies. In R. M. Joshi and P. G. Aaron (eds), *Handbook of Orthography and Literacy* (pp. 441–480). Mahwah, NJ: Lawrence Erlbaum Associates.

Tangel, D. M., and Blachman, B. A. (1995). Effect of phoneme awareness instruction on the invented spelling of first-grade children: a one-year follow-up. *Journal of Reading Behavior, 27*, 153–185.

Templeton, S., and Bear, D. (eds). (1992). *Development of Orthographic Knowledge and the Foundations of Literacy: A Memorial Festschrift for Edmund H. Henderson*. Hillsdale, NJ: Lawrence Erlbaum Associates.

Terry, N.P. (2006) Relations between dialect variation, grammar, and early spelling skills. *Reading and Writing, 19*, 907–931.

Treiman, R. (1993). *Beginning to Spell*. New York: Oxford University Press.

Treiman, R. (1997). Spelling in normal children and dyslexia. In B. Blachman (ed.), *Foundations of Reading Acquisition and Dyslexia: Implications for Early Intervention* (pp. 191–218). Mahwah, NJ: Lawrence Erlbaum Associates.

Treiman, R. (2004). Spelling and dialect: comparison between speakers of African American vernacular English and White speakers. *Psychonomic Bulletin and Review, 11*, 338–342.

Treiman, R. (2006). Knowledge about letters as a foundation for reading and spelling. In R. M. Joshi, and P. G. Aaron (eds), *Handbook of Orthography and Literacy* (pp. 581–599). Mahwah, NJ: Lawrence Erlbaum.

Treiman, R., and Barry, C. (2000). Dialect and authography: some differences between American and British spellers. *Journal of Experimental Psychology: Learning, Memory, and Cognition, 26*, 1423–1430.

Treiman, R., Goswami, U., Tincoff, R., and Leevers, H. (1997) Effects of dialect on American and British children's spelling. *Child Development, 68*, 229–245.

Venezky, R.L. (1980). From Webster to Rice to Roosevelt. In U. Frith (ed.), *Cognitive Processes in Spelling*. (pp. 9–30). London: Academic Press.

Venezky, R. L. (1999). *The American Way of Spelling: The Structure and Origins of American English Orthography*. New York: Guilford Press.

Wimmer, H., and Landerl, K. (1997). How learning to spell German differs from learning to spell English. In C. Perfetti, L. Rieben, and M. Fayol (eds), *Learning to Spell: Research, Theory, and Practice Across Languages* (pp. 81–96). Mahwah, NJ: Lawrence Erlbaum Associates.

10

Dyscalculia and learning difficulties in mathematics

Steve Chinn

This chapter

- discusses the range of difficulties that can arise in maths
- looks at the prevalence of dyscalculia, its causes and intervention
- examines the issue of comorbidity
- looks at why some children fail mathematics
- provides suggestions for success in mathematics.

Introduction

Learning difficulties in mathematics is not a new phenomenon. I suspect that mathematics learning difficulties for many children and adults existed years ago. However, in terms of popular usage, using the term dyscalculia is a relatively new phenomenon in the learning disabilities field. Research into this construct is minimal and a consensus on a definition and an aetiology has yet to be achieved. In a survey of the literature on maths learning difficulties compared to language difficulties Murphy, *et al.* (2007) found only 231 articles on maths learning difficulties compared to 1077 articles on dyslexia over a 21-year period.

Most teachers in schools and many lecturers in both further education and higher education will have met children and students who present as totally helpless in maths. But what combination of reasons creates this situation? And is there a pattern or a coherence in those difficulties? The answers to both questions will be complex, not least because every learner is such an individual mix of abilities, deficits and emotional factors.

In schools, which we can assume are the first environments where the problem is likely to be recognised, we have three major interlinking factors: the subject itself, mathematics, the child and the teacher. Each has a part to play and each interacts with the other two factors. The interactions will be labile. Consequently, there will be no simple answers or solutions. For example, give one child a calculator and he may cease to have significant maths difficulties yet for another child the calculator may make no difference at all or may even handicap true understanding of number. Give another child a set of word problems and suddenly he has serious maths difficulties. Some problems are learner specific, some are topic specific and some are created by inappropriate programmes or teaching methods.

Mathematics makes demands on many skills from the learner, including mathematical memory, working memory and the ability to generalise and see patterns and links. Emotions can compound the problems created by these cognitive skills. If learning fails then there will come a point where the child reduces his input and learning becomes even less effective. It is our obligation as educators to ensure that this does not happen.

Difficulties that arise from mathematics itself are about curriculum, the teaching style it advocates, what aspects of mathematical intelligence it demands and the expectations it has of mathematical long-term and working memory. For example, in England we modify our National Numeracy Strategy so that we expect children to memorise multiplication facts at ever earlier ages. In Ireland, prior to 1999, the mathematics curriculum was very prescriptive only allowing children, for example, to use one method for subtraction. There is evidence that mathematics is still presented in English schools as an exercise in recall with the 2006 Ofsted evaluation of mathematics provision for 14–19 year old students observing, 'Mathematics became an apparently endless series of algorithms for them, rather than a coherent and inter-connected body of knowledge.'

Difficulties that may arise from teaching are the teacher's teaching style, the speed of delivery, the use, or not, of concrete and visual materials, the relating of mathematics to real life and the extent to which the teaching prevents the child from uncontrolled failure.

Even from this summary it should be clear that there are enough factors, with enough variation in levels of impact for each factor, to make a single answer to the problem virtually impossible, or in truth, totally impossible.

So is a dyscalculic child unable ever to grasp maths? If we work on a spectrum of difficulties, where, as for dyslexia, dyscalculia is viewed like obesity (that is as a continuum) rather than measles (you have it or you do not) (Ellis, 1985) then where we define the cut-off could well, in the economic realities of education, be entirely arbitrary and not related to diagnosis.

However, working from the concept of the spectrum of difficulties, I believe that a greater understanding of the ways dyslexic and dyscalculic students learn and fail mathematics will illuminate our understanding of how all children learn and fail mathematics. One extrapolation from this belief is that many, if not all of the methods which are found to be efficacious for disabled learners will also help many non-MLD students to learn mathematics more securely and successfully.

Dyscalculia

The publication of Brian Butterworth's screening test for dyscalculia (2003) and the inclusion of dyscalculia as a specific learning difficulty on the UK government website are helping to push dyscalculia into the educational spotlight (see also Butterworth and Yeo, 2004) in the UK. However, as stated in the Introduction, dyscalculia is a complex concept, not least because there is unlikely to be a single reason behind the problem of the many, many people who fail to master maths, not all of whom will be diagnosed as dyscalculic.

The UK Department for Education and Skills booklet (DfES, 2001) *The National Numeracy Strategy: Guidance to Support Learners with Dyslexia and Dyscalculia* defines dyscalculia as;

Dyscalculia is a condition that affects the ability to acquire mathematical skills. Dyscalculia learners may have difficulty understanding simple number concepts, lack an intuitive grasp of numbers and have problems learning number facts and procedures. Even if they produce a correct answer or use a correct method, they may do so mechanically and without confidence.

127

Very little is known about the prevalence of dyscalculia, its causes or treatment. Purely dyscalculic learners who have difficulties only with numbers will have cognitive and language abilities in the normal range and may excel in non-mathematical subjects. It is more likely that difficulties with numeracy accompany the language difficulties of dyslexia.

Kosc (1974), a pioneer in the study of dyscalculia, defined dyscalculia in terms of brain abnormalities:

Developmental dyscalculia is a structural disorder of mathematical abilities which has its origin in a genetic or congenital disorder of those parts of the brain that are the direct anatomico-physiological substrate of the maturation of the mathematical abilities adequate to age, without a simultaneous disorder of general mental functions.

Recent work from University College, London (Kadosh et al., 2007) looking at brain imaging, suggests that the right parietal lobe is responsible for dyscalculia. There is an increasing tendency to use brain imaging to study dyscalculia.

If dyscalculia, like other specific learning difficulties has a spectrum or continuum of levels of difficulty, then one of the questions one could and should ask is 'When does the difficulty become significant enough to earn the label "dyscalculia".' This brings us back to the match between the learner, the curriculum and the teacher. There is research on the prevalence of dyscalculia (see later) but prevalence does depend on the definition chosen. In a sense it is a cyclic argument.

There is also the issue of comorbidity which is alluded to in the UK definition above. Comorbidity is a term which is used to describe the co-existence of two or more disorders in the same individual. Some of the early work on specific mathematics learning difficulties was carried out with dyslexic learners (for example, Miles and Miles, 2004; Chinn and Ashcroft 1998) and with dyspraxic learners (Yeo, 2003). In the UK dyspraxia, dyslexia and dyscalculia are now grouped under the umbrella term of 'specific learning difficulties', a term that was once synonymous solely with dyslexia.

In terms of comorbidity, Joffe's much-quoted, pioneering paper (1980) on maths and dyslexia included a statistic that has been applied over-enthusiastically and without careful consideration of how it was obtained, that is, '61 per cent of dyslexics are retarded in arithmetic' (and thus, many have since assumed, 39 per cent are not). The sample for this statistic was quite small, some 50 dyslexic learners. The maths test on which the statistic was largely based was the British Abilities Scales Basic Arithmetic Test which is primarily a test of arithmetic skills. Although the test was untimed, Joffe noted that the high attainment group would have done less well if speed was a consideration. She also stated extrapolations from this paper would have to be cautious. Other writers seem to have overlooked Joffe's own cautions and detailed observations, for example, 'Computation was a slow and laborious process for a large proportion of the dyslexic sample.' The results from mathematics tests can depend on many factors. Not surprisingly, speed of working will be one of the most influential factors for a population that is often slow at processing written information.

The prevalence of learning difficulties in mathematics depends on the label and the definition of that label. Many of the research papers originating from the USA define MLD as pertaining to the bottom quartile of attainment, whereas research into dyscalculia suggests it occurs in about 6 per cent of the population. At the most severe end of the spectrum, and probably at very low prevalence, is a total loss of any ability to do mathematics, called acalculia.

Perhaps it is not surprising, given that we do not have a clear and agreed definition of dyscalculia, that there is a range of figures given for the prevalence of dyscalculia and/or specific mathematics difficulties. For example, in a study by Lewis *et al.* (1994) of 1200 children aged 9 to 12, only 18 were identified as having specific mathematics difficulties in the absence of language difficulties. Lewis *et al.* did not find any one pattern or reason why the difficulties occurred, but the study did focus on a difficulty only in mathematics, not a comorbid condition with language difficulties. The same distinction is made by Ramaa and Gowramma (2002) in a fascinating study of children in India. Ramaa and Gowramma used both inclusionary and exclusionary criteria to determine the presence of dyscalculia in primary school children. Both experiments suggest that the percentage of children identified as potentially dyscalculic was between 5.5 and 6 per cent. Ramaa and Gowramma also list thirteen observations from other researchers about the nature and factors associated with dyscalculia, including persistent reliance on counting procedures and extra stress, anxiety and depression. Sutherland (1988) states that on the basis of his study, few children have specific problems with number alone. Miles (Miles and Miles, 1992) suggests that mathematical difficulties and language difficulties are likely to occur concurrently. Badian (1999) has produced figures for the prevalence of persistent arithmetic, reading or arithmetic and reading disabilities, from a sample of over 1000 children, suggesting that for grades 1 to 8, 6.9 per cent qualified as low in arithmetic, which included 3.9 per cent low only in arithmetic.

We should be careful not to confuse acalculia with dyscalculia. Some educators tend to take a pessimistic line which is basically viewing the problem with mathematics as perseverant, whereas, if one views dyslexia and dyscalculia as similar in nature, then it would follow that many of the problems of learning mathematics can be circumvented. However, the underlying problems can still persist into adulthood. There is always the danger of regression if hard–won skills are not regularly practised. A more optimistic view would not preclude success in maths for some 'dyscalculics' in the same way that dyslexia has not held back some great writers and actors. Of course, any skill which is based solely on recall is more likely to regress than a skill which is based on understanding as well as recall.

So, if dyscalculia infers lack of success in mathematics, what factors contribute to failure and what does it take to be successful at mathematics. Krutetskii (1976) listed the following components as contributors to success in mathematics:

- the ability for logical thought in the sphere of quantitative and spatial relationships, number and letter symbols; the ability to think in mathematical symbols;
- the ability for rapid and broad generalisation of mathematical objects, relations and operations;
- flexibility of mental processes in mathematical activity;
- striving for clarity, simplicity, economy and rationality of solutions;
- the ability for rapid and free reconstruction of the direction of a mental process, switching from a direct to a reverse train of thought;
- mathematical memory (generalised memory for mathematical relationships), and for methods of problem solving and principles of approach.

These components are closely interrelated, influencing one another and forming in their aggregate a single integral syndrome of mathematical giftedness.

Why some children fail mathematics

To provide a fully comprehensive list of the reasons why children may fail to learn mathematics would be arrogant and most likely reveal a lack of understanding of the diversity of children. Unlike my experiments when I was a physicist, the variables in any study of people are too many and too unpredictable to control, even if one was able to identify them all in the first place. Some of the key factors are:

Mathematical memory

It is likely that the concept of multiple intelligences (Gardner, 1993) applies to memories. There is research (Geary, 2000; Mabbott and Bisanz, 2008) to suggest that dyscalculics and students with MLD have poor long-term mathematical memories. Some compensate by using strategies (Ackerman *et al.*, 1986), but however gifted a pupil is at working things out from basics, there have to be some facts and procedures retrievable from memory. The skill for educators is to be realistic in understanding what a pupil can and can't learn and then to find the truly key facts for the pupil to learn if limited retrieval is the issue. As stated above, a total reliance on memory is not likely to produce enduring skills in mathematics for any learner.

Speed of working

This is a classic example of the demands of the subject creating the problem. The culture of mathematics is that it is to be done quickly. For example, children are timed for recall of basic facts. Speed is not, in my opinion an intellectual demand. In fact, I think it is a demand that encourages impulsivity, inefficiency and certainly anxiety (Chinn, forthcoming) in many learners. Because speed is part of the culture of mathematics it is hard to change the perceptions and expectations about working quickly which are held by many teachers and parents. The dyslexic and the dyscalculic learners I have taught are frequently slow processors of mathematical information and tasks. If a learner perceives the demand for speed to be beyond his capabilities then he will not attempt the task. We all assess risk (at different levels of acceptability) and we all withdraw when we think the task involves too much risk.

Reading and writing

The other two R's. Reading is an example of a sub-skill that suddenly becomes significant as a child moves up through the curriculum. There are no word problems to read when the child is young, then there are and some children fail. I suspect this is an international problem. Certainly a study in South Africa showed a 50 per cent reduction in correct answers when a number problem was presented in words. A further issue is that the world of maths word problems is frequently bizarre and rarely meaningful to a child (Polya, 1990).

Some children find writing and/or documenting their work a problem. Again, the child may well perform at mental arithmetic when the demands are within his skill range, but he may fail when the new skill of documenting is introduced (and, for some children, vice-versa).

Thinking styles

I often explain thinking style in maths in my lectures by asking delegates to do some carefully selected mathematics questions. I then explain that how each question is solved will illustrate the delegates' thinking styles. Usually the split between the two thinking styles, which I will describe below, is close to 50–50. This suggests that teachers, in terms of thinking style, are as varied as their students.

Thinking styles have been studied by a number of researchers (for example, Skemp 1986; Marolda and Davidson, 2000). Work by my two American colleagues and myself in the 1980s led to us describing 'inchworms' as sequential, procedural, literal thinkers, who often do not have a good 'feel' for numbers and operations. Inchworms like to document, to the point that their paper and pen acts almost like a comfort blanket. 'Grasshoppers' are intuitive, flexible in methods used, have a good sense of numbers and operations and their inter-relationships, are answer-oriented and often do not document their methods.

There are several consequences of thinking styles for learners and for teachers (Chinn, 2004) but teachers need to be aware that their meticulous, step-by-step explanation of a new topic may not resonate with the grasshopper learner or that a sweeping overview loses the inchworm, who fails to see the necessary connections to other ideas and concepts.

A further consequence may be the teacher's appraisal of the pupil and his work is coloured by his own thinking style and that a mismatch between teacher and student thinking style may have a detrimental effect on the learner/teacher relationship.

Although it may be tempting to think that dyslexic learners are more likely to favour grasshopper strategies, this may be overwhelmed by a tendency to take instructions literally and to feel safer with the consistency of procedures and algorithms.

Short-term and working memory

Dyslexic learners often have poor short-term and working memories (Mabbott and Bisanz, 2008). This, as with so many other factors, is not a characteristic which is unique to dyslexic learners.

The use of short-term and working memory is pervasive in mathematics, not just in mental arithmetic. It affects the ability to do any part of any calculation 'in your head'. It affects how you analyse data. For example, in the series abcdeabcdeabcdeab . . ., a pupil tried to analyse it in chunks of three, abc, dea, bcd, eab, which was as much as he could hold in his memory at one time. It was not surprising that he failed to see the pattern.

Pupils with weak short-term memories find it challenging to copy information. For example, if copying from a board they have to look up at the board, track to the correct place, memorise as many items as they can, transfer their gaze to a notebook and write the information in the correct place, then back to the board and then search for the right place. A consequence may be that, if copying maths questions, they mix up the questions as set and create a new set of their own unique questions!

The affective domain

This domain includes anxiety, expectations, beliefs, attributions, self-esteem and self-concept. These are factors that are difficult to measure, but that does not diminish their capacity to influence learning.

> Over and above common cognitive demands and neurological representations and functions, performance in reading and arithmetic is influenced by a number of motivational and emotional factors such as need of achievement, task orientation, helplessness, depression, anxiety, self-esteem, self-concept, locus of control
>
> (Lundberg and Sterner, 2006)

Recent research has shown that working memory becomes less effective if the learner is anxious (Ashcraft *et al.*, 1998). Although a little anxiety may enhance performance, usually it is a condition that diminishes performance.

Maths anxiety may well be a consequence of another maths culture issue. We are judgmental in maths. Indeed, maths itself is judgmental. Work and answers are 'Right' or 'Wrong'. This judgment is not always delivered empathetically, so the learner becomes anxious that he may be wrong (again) and avoids further risk of failure by withdrawing from the task.

The ethos of the classroom will have a huge affect on anxiety levels in the pupils. Anxiety may result in pupils not taking risks. A good learning classroom teaches and encourages pupils how to evaluate and take risks. Pupils who avoid risk are often avoiding learning.

A recent survey of maths anxiety in pupils from mainstream schools and from specialist dyslexia schools (Chinn, forthcoming) showed that tasks which made demands of memory, such as traditional 'long' division and examinations, created the most anxiety in all pupils, irrespective of age, sex, or dyslexia.

Children enter maths classrooms with a set of beliefs that will colour their attitude to maths. For example, many children (and adults) believe that only very clever (and boring) people are good at maths. Others may believe, as a consequence of this, that they can never be clever enough to be good at maths. That can make teaching a challenge.

Children are surrounded by expectations. For example, one of the expectations that affects many dyslexic learners is that pupils will rote learn basic multiplication facts by a certain age. There is evidence that suggests this is not realistic for many dyslexic learners (Chinn, 2003). The impact of failure to meet this particular expectation can be demotivating for the child and distressing for the parent and possibly detrimental to their relationship.

Persistent failure, whether real or perceived can affect self-esteem and self-concept. The decline of these in a child leads them to not being involved in trying to learn maths. One of my most successful, mathematically, ex-pupils told me how much he hated the words, 'Never mind, you did your best.' His argument was, that if he had done his best then he didn't want failure. If he judged that failure was a possibility, then he would not try his 'best' and then failure would not be such a blow to self-esteem.

Most influential of all is attribution, the way a pupil attributes his reasons for success and failure. These attributions colour the way each new learning experience is approached. It is not always easy to predict when a child is about to become 'learned helpless' (Seligman, 2006) in maths, but certain maths topics often create a sense of failure, for example, a pupil may come to assume that because he failed at long division, he will fail at all future maths topics. This is a pervasive attribution. He may begin to believe that he is just too stupid to be able to do maths. This is a personal attribution. He may think that because he can't do the maths lesson today that he will not be able to do tomorrow's lesson or any other lesson ever again. That is a permanent attribution and the child presents as learned helpless.

With all of these affective dimensions, the child with a learning difficulty will be more susceptible to making negative interpretations of feedback, or pay more heed to the negative partly due to the frequency of the negative feedback and partly due to their fragile self-esteem.

Finally, it should be remembered that an insecure learner values consistency. This characteristic must be linked to automaticity, in that automaticity allows the brain to devote more capacity to what is different or an extension of a known procedure. Consistency will also reduce anxiety.

Diagnosis of dyscalculia and mathematics learning difficulties

There are combinations of the factors described above that may lead to mathematics learning difficulties and to dyscalculia. These combinations can form the framework for a diagnostic protocol (Chinn and Everatt, 2009).

1 An extreme grasshopper who does not/will not document his methods. This may well be the major reason why 'A' level students fail. They have the ability to solve the problem, but lack of documentation will result in failure in exams.
2 An extreme and inaccurate grasshopper, probably impulsive, will fail.
3 An extreme inchworm who is a very slow processor may fail.
4 An extreme inchworm with poor short-term memory will fail in mental maths and be slow in written maths (see also 3, as slow processing may not be entirely due to poor short-term memory).
5 An extreme inchworm with poor long-term mathematical memory for basic facts and procedures will fail as the memory demands that maths makes as they progress up through school exceed their capabilities. Bizarre errors on a multiple choice x test will provide additional evidence.
6 Over-reliance on counting strategies, a poor understanding of place value and procedural errors will create maths learning difficulties.
7 Poor retrieval of basic facts without compensatory strategies could create maths learning difficulties, especially in rigid teaching environments.
8 High anxiety may prevent a learner from engaging in maths activities. A high incidence of 'no attempt' errors on any short screener and subsequent criterion tests would confirm this.
9 Poor documenting/layout skills can lead to failure.
10 An inability to see the patterns and generalisations and develop concepts (move from the concrete to the abstract) will result in failure.

Characteristic behaviours of learners with mathematics difficulties

The factors above may manifest themselves in actual classroom behaviours. Learners may demonstrate some, many or all of the behaviours listed below.

Learners with mathematics difficulties:

- have difficulty remembering basic addition facts
- cannot count objects accurately and lack the ability to make 'one-to-one correspondence' when counting
- cannot 'see' that four objects are four without counting (or three, if a young child)
- count on for addition facts, as for 7 + 3, counting 8, 9, 10
- count all the numbers, 1, 2, 3, 4, 5, 6, 7, 8, 9, 10 (which would be a stronger indicator of dyscalculia than the above item)
- use tally marks for problems, rarely grouping the tallies (for example in fives or tens)
- find it *much* harder to count backwards instead of forwards
- cannot fluently count less familiar sequences, such as: 1, 3, 5, 7, 9, 11 . . . or 14, 24, 34, 44, 54, 64 . . .
- can only access the 2×, 5× and 10 × multiplication facts
- count on to access the 2× and 5× facts

- may be able to learn the other multiplication facts, but will forget them overnight
- make bizarre errors for multiplication facts, such as $6 \times 7 = 67$ or $6 \times 7 = 13$
- cannot write numbers which have zeros within them, such as, 'three hundred and four' or 'four thousand and twenty one'
- write 51 for fifteen or 61 for sixteen (and all teen numbers)
- cannot judge whether an answer is right, or nearly right
- cannot estimate
- are weak at mental arithmetic
- forget the question asked in mental arithmetic
- like to use formulas, but use them mechanically
- cannot remember mathematical procedures, especially as they become more complex, such as decomposing, renaming or borrowing for subtraction and almost certainly any long division
- find it difficult to make the cognitive progress from the materials (counters, blocks) to symbols
- are unable to relate algebra to the arithmetic they met earlier
- have poor organisation of written work, for example columns of numbers are not lined up
- have poor skills with money, for example, they are unable to calculate change from a purchase
- 'see' numbers literally and not inter-related, for example, counts from 1 to get 9, rather than subtracting 1 away from 10
- think an item priced at £4.99 is '£4 and a bit' rather than almost £5
- are very anxious about doing *any* mathematics
- do not recognise patterns or generalisations, especially ones that are new to them, for example that ½, ⅓, ¼, ⅕ is a sequence that is getting smaller
- do not 'see' that $7 + 5$ is the same as $5 + 7$ or that 7×3 is the same as 3×7
- are impulsive when doing maths, rather than analytical. They start at the first information rather than over-viewing all the information
- they rush to get any task over with, *or* they avoid the task by not starting it.

This list can be used as a basic screening tool and also as a diagnostic tool for highlighting areas for intervention.

How more children can succeed in mathematics

Dr Harry Chasty, a great pioneer and advocate for dyslexics said, 'If the child doesn't learn the way you teach, can you teach her the way she learns?' In this deceptively simple sentence lies a challenge. Certainly that challenge was not an issue for the teachers who taught me back in the 1950s. I had to learn the way that they taught. That adaptation is not a possibility for most dyslexic, dyspraxic and dyscalculic pupils.

Hopefully now we accept a more enlightened view. It is a matter of who takes responsibility for the learning. In the first stages of learning a new topic, it has to be the teacher. Later in the process the responsibility transfers in part to the pupil. Judging the moment for that transition to occur is part of the skill of working with all children or adults, but especially for those with specific learning difficulties.

So, what did Harry Chasty mean? He meant, 'Can you adjust the way you present material for that learning experience so that communication with each student is effective?' In maths this may mean that I use a visual model for the concept I am trying to explain. Perhaps this will be Base Ten blocks to explain long multiplication or quadratic equations. There are a range of adjustments that can be made to reduce the number of occasions when pupils fail. In order to reach the way a child or adult learns we have to know how they can learn and what creates failure (Holt, 1969, 1970; Chinn, 2004).

There are a number of examples of a first stage or level of adjustment. They do not require teachers to do anything particularly onerous, they just help to make sure communication is as effective as possible. There is an additional benefit in that it is likely that these considerations will be helping several other pupils who do not have an identified learning difficulty.

The next stage or level requires a reconsideration of some beliefs and a restructuring of some aspects of the maths curriculum, again based on 'Can I teach the way she learns?' The major acknowledgment here is that some learners have weak memories for basic facts and procedures in maths. This deficit is compounded if the learner has little understanding of mathematical concepts and relationships. The combination of poor memory and poor understanding of concepts is devastating in maths.

Of course, students have to learn some facts. The challenge is for teachers to work with the learner to maximise the benefits of knowing those facts. For the students, learning to extend the use of and build on key facts will provide them with a secure base for building concepts and the continual return to and use of key facts will reinforce the retention and retrieval of those facts. There is a strong coherence between many maths topics, facts and skills which many learners do not recognise. The foundations for understanding many of the topics which are perceived as difficult can be taught very early in schools.

Let me give two examples.

The number bonds for 10

When working with students who have an attainment deficit, a key question is 'What else are you teaching?' If an intervention can have multiple and linked objectives then the outcome will be more efficacious, especially if the students need to catch up with their peers. The developmental nature of mathematics means that even at the first stages concepts are being (or should be) introduced with an awareness of where they lead mathematically.

For example, the number bonds for 10 are key facts. They can be extended and used in many topics in maths, for example in calculating means or in understanding decimals or in learning how to estimate. These facts emphasize the key role of 10 and can be instrumental in taking children away from the very low level skill of counting.

It would be inappropriate in this chapter to explain exactly how this collection of facts is taught and how related concepts are developed, but the programme would cover some of the aspects below:

- explaining conservation by explaining the conservation of 10 (perhaps using a bead string)
- creating an image of one of the addends becoming smaller as the other increases (as you progress from $0 + 10$ to $1 + 9$ to $2 + 8$ and so on); perhaps using Cuisenaire rods to illustrate this
- the subtraction facts for 10, presented as $7 + \square = 10$ (which introduces algebra) as well as $10 - 7 = \square$; perhaps using the Cuisenaire rods to show comparison between the 10 rod and the 7 rod and how that comparison can be represented in more than one way with symbols
- demonstrating the number bonds for 9 as they relate to the number bonds for 10, which would include visualising 9 as close to 10 and using 10 as an estimate for 9 (very applicable when shopping. . .£9.99, etc.)

135

- adding on to 10 (and being aware of the irregular pattern of 11 and 12 and of the reversed language for the 'teen' numbers)
- adding on to 9, by adding 10 (as an estimate) and subtracting 1 (refining the estimate)
- number bonds for 100 (10 + 90, 20 + 80 . . .), which also reinforces the concept of place value
- number bonds for 10 and 100 (46 + 54, 73 + 27)
- number bonds for 1 (0.3 + 0.7) which again illustrates place value
- adding a column of numbers by casting out tens, which also encourages learners to overview a problem before starting to compute
- subtracting by counting on; bridging 10s and 100s as in pre-computer shop checkout days when change was counted on, which also links subtraction to addition and is of particular benefit to learners who find counting back a problem

In each of these examples 10 is the focus. In each of these examples the same key facts are rehearsed. The list is not exhaustive but illustrates how far one set of facts can be taken, conceptually as well as for aiding recall/retrieval. This learning model also allows pupils to return time and time again to the same key facts. Each exposure should enhance the ability to retain in memory and retrieve from memory these facts.

Although this programme advocates the use of materials to demonstrate concepts we must realise that the learner should be involved in the choice of material. Hart (1989) warned that materials may not necessarily generate the same links and learning images in the teacher and the learner.

Basic multiplication facts

Within the confines of this particular chapter, again this can only be a summary of the principles underlying this learning model.

A large number of pupils fail to achieve mastery in the retrieval of times table facts. This persists into adulthood and even 12- or 13-year-old pupils may have forgotten what they so assiduously learned when they were 8 or 9 years old.

This particular body of facts is subject to some strong beliefs. For example, those who succeeded with the task say words to the effect, 'I learned them when I was at school. Why can't you?' A quick appraisal of those words will reveal the total lack of logic behind them. The expectation will cause great anguish for many children and their parents. The failure for the child in this task is likely to result in money being spent on all manner of guaranteed 'fun' ways of learning the tables, including singing them.

Yet, like the number bonds for 10, if taught wisely, these facts can open the door to many concepts. Rote learning is, obviously an efficacious method, if the learner can do it, but successful rote learning may disguise a lack of understanding of numbers and numeracy.

Times tables give the opportunity to teach:

- the link between addition and multiplication
- a way of using the 'easy' facts (1×, 2×, 5×, 10×) to access all other facts (The 'easy' facts are also the values we choose for our coinage)
- the area model for any xy calculation from 6×7 to $(3x + a)(5x - b)$
- an alternative (and, I would argue, a more logical) algorithm for long multiplication and thus long division
- division facts and factors
- multiplying fractions.

The materials that are most effective for illustrating these ideas are Cuisenaire rods, coins and Base Ten blocks. Each material will have a strength for a range of concepts. For example for basic facts strategies such as deriving 6 x 6 from 5×6 plus 1×6, Cuisenaire rods can illustrate the repeated addition of 6 rods via the grouping of five of the rods as an efficient partial product to which one more 6 is added. The algebra here is

$$6a = a + a + a + a + a + a = 5a + a$$

This might develop, via the use of Base Ten rods to illustrate the area model, to partial products in long multiplication

$$21 \times 46 = 20 \times 46 + 1 \times 46$$

or a four-way partial product model, which will lead to

$$(x + a)(y + b).$$

The model suggested was developed by recognising that not every learner can master learning all of the basic facts. The model makes a positive benefit of this issue by introducing strategies that address the problems and teach the underlying links, patterns and concepts of mathematics. It looks at the development of a concept both from the beginning early number facts and by working back from the procedures of algebra. It builds in the consistency and constant reviews of facts and procedures that insecure learners so desperately need.

Finally

Students and adults who have difficulty in learning maths, whether they are labelled as dyscalculic, dyslexic or not labelled at all, obviously need an alternative approach. This chapter suggests an alternative approach, based on the characteristics of the learner and an adjustment in the way mathematical content is structured and presented. It does not advocate 'the method' but acknowledges that all children are individuals and will benefit from the responsive flexibility that comes from acknowledging the learning characteristics of that individual.

The chapter also suggests that there will not be just one profile of dyscalculia and that some profiles will be hidden possibly all through the school years, hence the need to be proactive and address the issues at all times and for all learners.

References

Ackerman, P.T., Anhalt, J.M. and Dykman, R.A. (1986) Arithmetic automatization failure in children with attention and reading disorders: associations and sequela. *Journal of Learning Disabilities* 19 (4): 222–232.

Ashcraft, M., Kirk, E.P. and Hopko, D. (1998) On the cognitive consequences of mathematics anxiety. In C. Donlan (ed.) *The Development of Mathematical Skills*. Hove: The Psychological Corporation.

Badian, N.A. (1999) Persistent arithmetic, reading or arithmetic and reading disability. *Annals of Dyslexia* 49: 45–70.

Butterworth, B. (2003) *The Dyscalculia Screener*. London: NFER-Nelson.

Butterworth, B., Yeo, D. (2004) *Dyscalculia Guidance*. London: David Fulton.

Chinn, S.J. (2003) Multiplication table facts . . . a quest. *Dyslexia Review* 15 (1): 18–21.

Chinn, S.J. (2004) *The Trouble with Maths*. London: RoutledgeFalmer.

Chinn, S.J. and Ashcroft, J.R. (1998) *Mathematics for Dyslexics*. 1st edn. London: Whurr.

Chinn, S.J. and Everatt, J.M. (forthcoming) *A Diagnostic Test Battery for MLD and Dyscalculia*. London: Pearson.

DfES (2001) *The National Numeracy Strategy: Guidance to Support Learners with Dyslexia and Dyscalculia*. London: DfES.

Gardner, H. (1993) *Multiple Intelligences: Theory into Practice*. New York: Basic Books.

Geary, D.C. (2000) Mathematics and learning disabilities. *Journal of Learning Disabilities* 37 (1): 4–15.

Hart, K. (1989) There is little connection. In P. Ernest (ed.) *Mathematics Teaching: The State of the Art*. Lewes: Falmer Press.

Holt, J. (1969) *How Children Fail*. Harmondsworth: Pelican.

Holt, J. (1970) *How Children Learn*. Harmondsworth: Pelican.

Holt, J. (1984a) *How Children Learn*. Harmondsworth: Pelican.

Holt, J. (1984b) *How Children Fail*. Harmondsworth: Pelican.

Joffe, L. (1980) Dyslexia and attainments in school mathematics: Part 1. *Dyslexia Review* 3 (1): 10–14.

Kadosh, R.C., Kadosh, K.C., Schuhmann, T., Kaas, A., Goebel, R., Honik, A. and Sack, A.T. (2007) Virtual dyscalculia induced by parietal-lobe TMS impairs automatic magnitude processing. *Current Biology*, 17(8), 689–693.

Kosc, L. (1974) Developmental dyscalculia. *Journal of Learning Disabilities* 7(3), 46–59.

Krutetskii, V.A. (1976) *The Psychology of Mathematical Abilities in School Children*. Chicago: University of Chicago Press.

Lewis, C., Hitch, J.G. and Walker, P. (1994) The prevalence of specific arithmetical difficulties and specific reading difficulties in 9 to 10 year old boys and girls. *Journal of Child Psychology and Psychiatry*, 33 (2): 283–292.

Lunberg, I., Sterner, G. (2006) Reading, arithmetic and task orientation – how are they related? *Annals of Dyslexia*, 56 (2): 361–377.

Mabbott, D.J. and Bisanz, J. (2008) Computational skills, working memory and conceptual knowledge in older children with mathematics learning difficulties. *Journal of learning Disabilities* 41 (1): 15–28.

Marolda, M.R. and Davidson, S.D. (2000) Mathematics learning profiles and differentiated teaching strategies. *Perspectives* 26 (3): 10–15.

Miles, T.R. (1992) Some theoretical considerations. In T.R. Miles and E. Miles (eds) *Dyslexia and Mathematics*. London: RoutledgeFalmer.

Murphy, M., Mazzocco, M., Hanich, L. and Early, M. (2007) Cognitive characteristics of children with mathematics learning disability (MLD) vary as a function of the cut off criterion used to define MLD. *Journal of Learning Disabilities* 40 (5): 458–478.

Polya, G. (1990) *How to Solve It*. London: Penguin.

Ramaa, S. and Gowramma, I.P. (2002) Dyscalculia among primary school children in India. *Dyslexia* 8(2): 67–85.

Seligman, M.E.P. (2006) *Learned Optimism*. New York: Random Books.

Skemp, R.R. (1986) *The Psychology of Learning Mathematics* (2nd edn). Harmondsworth: Pelican.

Sutherland, P. (1998) Dyscalculia. Sum cause for concern? *Times Educational Supplement*. 18 March.

Yeo, D. (2003) *Dyslexia, Dyspraxia and Mathematics*. Chichester: Wiley.

11

Phonological awareness in reading disabilities remediation
Some general issues

Abdessatar Mahfoudhi and Charles W. Haynes

This chapter

- defines what is meant by phonological awareness
- discusses principles related to phonological awareness relevant to teachers
- provides guidance on the role of phonological awareness in instruction
- refers to issues that concern teachers of languages other than English
- describes cross-linguistic research evidence of the role of phonological awareness in the development of reading from both developing and dyslexic readers.

Introduction

There is now robust evidence that explicit, structured phonics instruction—teaching of rules that link speech information with letters and letter patterns—improves word recognition skills and contributes to spelling, decoding fluency, and reading comprehension in typically developing children as well as children with dyslexia and related language learning difficulties (e.g., National Reading Panel (NRP), 2000).

Reading theories and remediation programs for students with dyslexia have been based primarily on research done in English, and researchers and practitioners working in other languages have relied on this literature for the development of their remediation programs. This reliance on research in English has been useful, but not sufficient, for understanding the roles of phonological awareness in learning to read in different language systems.

When adapting a remedial program that has proven effective in English to any language where research is not abundant, one is faced with difficult decisions. One decision regards what elements of language instruction to emphasize. For example, within the literature on initial reading instruction in English, there is no total agreement on what to teach and when to teach it. Some studies prescribe that phonological awareness (PA) training—instruction that develops awareness of and capacity to manipulate speech sounds—should begin prior to formal instruction in reading, while other researchers recommend that PA be taught as part of phonics instruction (Lindamood and Lindamood, 1998; Lundberg *et al.*, 1988). Another issue is that methods for English might not work for other languages due to the differences in culture and script. Independent of the language of instruction, factors that influence the efficacy of PA instruction include the learner's profile of neuro-cognitive strengths and weaknesses, as well as the learner's age (an indicator of previous language experience), motivation, and linguistic background (quality of their instruction, monolingual versus bi-/multilingual status).

The present chapter first discusses principles related to phonological awareness that apply to all practitioners, including those working with English-speaking learners and then moves to issues that concern persons teaching in other languages and cultures. While most of the evidence cited in this chapter is based on English, we have made sure to include evidence from other language families and scripts. The chapter is organized as follows. The first section includes a definition of phonological awareness illustrated with sample tasks from English. The second section provides cross-linguistic research evidence (with a bias for English) of the role of phonological awareness in the development of reading from both typically developing and dyslexic readers. The role of phonological awareness in (remediation) instruction is the subject of the third section. The fourth and the fifth sections deal with principles that should guide the adoption or adaptation of a phonological awareness-based remediation program. While the fourth section focuses on general principles that are relevant to most educational, linguistic and cultural contexts, the fifth section raises issues that are language and culture-specific.

1 Phonological awareness in theory: Definition and representative tasks

Scarborough and Brady (2004) define phonological awareness as "the broad class of skills that involve attending to, thinking about, and intentionally manipulating the phonological aspects of spoken language, especially the internal phonological structure of words" (p. 7). Phonological awareness is an umbrella term that includes awareness and manipulation of speech at the word, syllable and phoneme levels. This latter ability to analyze and manipulate speech at the phoneme level is known as "phonemic awareness." Corresponding examples of tests/tasks that are often used to measure or teach phonological awareness may include: word level activities, like identifying the number of words in a given phrase or sentence; syllable tasks, such as syllable counting or syllable blending; rhyme tasks, such as identifying or producing a rhyme; phoneme segmentation tasks, such as counting, tapping, or identifying phonemes; sound blending tasks, in which the student joins isolated sounds or syllables to make words; and phoneme manipulation (identify, delete, add, substitute, or transpose phonemes or syllables) (for additional examples, see Adams, 1990).

Phonological awareness is believed to develop from the global to the small and more subtle, that is from the rhyme to the syllable, to intra-syllabic units, such as onset [first consonant in a syllable and rime (the vowel and consonant sound(s) that make up the middle and end of a syllable)], to the phoneme level (for reviews, see Muter, 2003, Chapter 2; Goswami, 2005). The most difficult of the above-mentioned phonological awareness tasks, at least in English, seems to be phoneme manipulation (deletion, addition, substitution) (Goswami, 2002; Goswami and Bryant, 1990; Muter, 2003). The difficulty of phonemic awareness derives in part from the fact that we speak in overlapping vocal movements that blur distinctions between individual phonemes (Liberman and Mattingly, 1985). Table 11.1, provides examples of typical syllable, rhyme, rime and phoneme awareness activities used to help children develop abstract, or "meta," awareness of the sound structure of words.

Phonological processing is a superordinate category that includes phonological awareness as well as other phonology-related skills often mentioned in relation to learning to read, reading instruction, and dyslexia. Scarborough and Brady (2004) define phonological processing as the

Table 11.1 *Some typical phonological awareness activities*

Unit	Type	Example (answer)
Syllable typically contains an onset (a consonant or more), a nucleus (a vowel or a diphthong) and coda (a consonant or more)	Isolation Blending Deletion Segmentation/Counting	"Tell me the first syllable in 'forget'." (for) "What word is, /'ex/ – /er/ – /cise/?" (exercise) "What is 'teacher' without /er /?" (teach) "Sound out (clap hands; tap knee; count on fingers) number of syllables in the word 'remember'." (re/mem/ber, = 3 syllables)
Rhyme refers to the stressed vowel and the phoneme(s) that follow it, which could be a rime of a syllable as in 'bin' and 'tin' or more than one part of a syllable as in 'perfection' and 'affection')	Identity recognition Production	"Tell me which two words among these rhyme 'forget, remember, bet'?" "Tell me two words that rhyme." (e.g, look, book)
Onset and Rime the 'onset' is the first consonant of a syllable while the 'rime' is the vowel and the consonants that follow it in a syllable, the rime could just be a vowel as in 'bee'	Isolation Categorization	"Which one sounds different – jug, ram, bug?" "Which ones sound the same – rib, bib, jag?"
Phoneme i.e. individual sound	Identity recognition Isolation Categorization Blending Segmentation Deletion	"Tell me the sound that is the same in far, flow, and France." (/f/) "Tell me the first sound in 'car'." (/k/) "Which word does not belong? man, morning, friend?" (friend) "What word is, /f/ – /i / – /f / – /t /–/i/?" (fifty) "How many sounds in cat?" (3 – /k / +/a / + /t /) "What is 'train' without /t /?" (rain)

formation, retention, and/or use of phonological codes [mental representation of speech elements] or speech while performing some cognitive or linguistic task or operation such as speaking, listening, remembering, learning, naming, thinking, reading, or writing. In contrast with phonological awareness, most phonological processes do not require conscious awareness; they can be, and often are, carried out without our attending to them.

(p. 23)

Researchers employ a variety of cognitive and linguistic tasks to tap phonological processing. In addition to phonological awareness probes like the activities described in Table 11.1, tasks may include but are not limited to: speech perception, decoding of phonetic non-words, phonological memory (storage and recall of phonological representations in tasks such as non-word repetition), and naming speed/rapid automatized naming (RAN, also known as rapid serial naming) of familiar stimuli like letters, digits, colors, or objects. Before we resume our focus on phonological awareness, it is important to note that there is evidence that to varying degrees, performance on any of these phonological processing tasks correlates with as well as predicts word recognition skills (for a review, see Muter, 2003, Chapter 3).

2 Phonological awareness and reading development

In this section, we briefly discuss patterns of research evidence regarding the role of phonological awareness in the development of reading in typically developing and dyslexic readers.

There are three main hypotheses as to the relationship between reading and phonological awareness:

1 Phonological awareness precedes decoding and encoding, and aids their development.
2 The process of learning to decode and encode develops the awareness of speech sounds.
3 There is a reciprocal relationship between learning to decode or encode and development of phonological awareness.

The preponderance of evidence supports the third hypothesis, that is, while phonological awareness predicts reading development, there is evidence that learning to read and spell also helps develop phonological awareness (cf. development of phonemic awareness when learning an alphabetic language like English).

Goswami and Bryant (1990) found a correlation between awareness of alliteration and rhyming in English in preliterate children (aged 4 or 5) and their reading (and spelling) development in the following three years (also see reviews by Snowling, 2000). Studies indicating that rhyme awareness, syllable awareness, and onset and rime awareness can develop in the pre-literacy period lend support to the first hypothesis, that this awareness may be a prerequisite for learning to read. Nevertheless, research suggests that awareness at the phoneme level develops with the onset of literacy when children start to use letters (e.g., Goswami and Bryant, 1990). For example, when children are well trained in sound symbol correspondence skills, their performance in phoneme (deletion) tasks improves as well. Perfetti et al. (1987) also report that English-speaking first graders show evidence that phonemic awareness develops conjointly with formal reading instruction. Interestingly, this finding is further supported by a study of adults in Portuguese, a language that, like English, has less consistent sound symbol relationships. Performance on tasks of phoneme addition and deletion was much better among participants who were illiterate and then learned to read in an adult literacy program than was awareness in a group of untaught illiterate adults (Morais et al., 1979).

There is ample evidence in English that beginning readers rely on correspondence between phonology and graphemes for reading new words (for a review, see Goswami and Bryant, 1990). Typically developing readers employ grapheme to phoneme correspondence more in beginning stages of reading and rely on identification of orthographic (word shape) analogies more in later reading. Goswami and Bryant (1990) argue that children have a preliterate awareness of onsets and rimes, which helps them in later stages of reading when they rely more on analogy for recognizing letter groups such as word endings. Nevertheless, there is compelling evidence showing that across all levels of readers grapheme-to-phoneme correspondence skills as measured by tasks like non-word reading are robust predictors of a range of reading abilities (Snowling, 2000, Chapter 4).

Thus, phonological awareness plays an important role in the development of reading among typically developing readers. There is also a consensus among researchers now that dyslexia, also termed "reading disabilities," is primarily characterized by deficits in phonological awareness and phonological processing in general. Following most researchers in the field, we take dyslexia to be a syndrome, whose main symptoms are problems in word recognition and spelling, short-term phonological memory, as well as other possible problems in sequencing of tasks and attention (Lyon et al., 2003). Students with dyslexia most frequently display problems in reading words and pseudo-words. While the most frequently used criterion for identifying dyslexia has been a discrepancy between reading ability and IQ, there is an increasing consensus that symptoms of dyslexia can be present without this criterion being met (e.g., Stanovich and Siegel, 1994).

While much of the evidence regarding dyslexia is based on studies of English, research in other languages has generally lent support to the view that phonological deficits, problems with the representation and use of phonological information, are the predominating, if not universal, characteristic of dyslexia. Thus, children with dyslexia mainly display difficulties with phono-logically based tasks such as word and pseudo-word reading, rapid naming, and phonemic awareness. This theory regarding the phonological basis of dyslexia, has come to be known as the Phonological-Deficit Hypothesis (e.g. Snowling, 2000).[1]

While there is general agreement that persons with dyslexia have difficulty manipulating and processing phonological elements and relating them to orthographic symbols, there is less agreement as to which phonological awareness skills are at the core of learning to read. The role of phonemic awareness seems to be a central factor in reading development and disabilities in alphabetic languages such as English, however, research is needed to determine the potentially differing contributions of phonological processes, and phonological awareness in particular, in different language families and orthographies. Which aspect(s) of phonological awareness should be addressed teaching reading in different languages? How much training is needed? We will address these and related questions in the following section.

3 Teaching phonological awareness to dyslexic and at risk readers

In this section, we first describe the main principles on which most phonological-awareness-based remediation programs are founded and then briefly review what research has told us about what works best and in which settings.

Several PA-based programs have been designed to prevent or remedy the reading problems in learners with dyslexia and related language learning difficulties. Most of these programs derive from the pioneering work/program of Anna Gillingham and Bessie Stillman (1997, first appeared in 1936) based on the ideas of Samuel Orton and Anna Gillingham. A few examples of programs in English in the UK and the USA: Sound Linkage (Hatcher, 1994) in the UK and the Phonological Awareness Training Programme (Wilson, 1993); the Multisensory Teaching System for Reading (Johnston *et al.*, 1999) in the US. These are fixed programs in the form of a kit that the teacher adapts to their students' needs. Other programs have been developed as approaches that train the teacher to develop and execute their own individual educational plans; examples of these are the training programs given by the Canadian Association of Therapeutic Tutors, or the Academy of Orton Gillingham Practitioners (U.S.). The International Multisensory Structured Language Education Council (IMSLEC) was formed to set standards and provide support for phonological awareness-based teacher-training programs.

All of these programs, whether in kit form or emphasizing training of teachers, are based on the following principles regarding what to teach and how to teach it. These kits and approaches address at least the following:

- phonological awareness instruction (see Table 13.1)
- grapheme–phoneme and syllable-shape to syllable-sound correspondence skills (linking letter shapes with corresponding sound(s), linking orthographic shapes of syllables to their pronunciations)
- segmentation and blending for word identification or spelling (breaking written words into phonemes and/or syllables and blending the sounds back together into a spoken word or the reverse process for spelling)
- structural analysis—recognizing or recalling orthographic patterns of morphemes for word identification or spelling (e.g. *sub* + *marin-* are morphemes that make up sub-marine)
- automaticity and fluency (speed plus accuracy) of decoding and encoding (spelling) at the word, phrase, sentence, and text levels.

While the primary deficits in dyslexia pertain to the above phonologically related areas of language learning, some structured language teaching programs also include vocabulary development and language comprehension strategies to aid students with concomitant difficulties in these areas.

The above skills are taught following these principles:

- Teaching and learning activities are multi-sensory, employing visual, auditory, tactile and kinesthetic (related to motor movement) feedback. The teacher and learner use learning modalities of listening, speaking, reading and writing simultaneously as much as possible to strengthen memory and retrieval.
- Inductive, metacognitive strategies are employed to help the learner discover and become aware of how language works instead of relying on rote learning.
- Teaching is direct. While teaching relies on discovery on the part of the learner, the teacher also confirms that concepts and rules are understood explicitly with no room left for ambiguity.
- Teaching is structured and cumulative: Language is taught in a hierarchical way from smaller to larger units and from the simple to more complex structures.
- Teaching to success is emphasized. The learner does not progress to another skill until they have mastered prerequisite skills.
- Teaching is empirical in nature, and based on data from diagnosis and continuous testing. An individualized teaching plan is developed based on the diagnosis of the learner's needs and progress is monitored periodically to fill in the gaps before moving to later stages in the plan/curriculum.

Some of the structured, phonology-based programs have been tested for their efficacy and most of their authors have attempted to make them "research-based," incorporating the research results about what methods work best.

The efficacy of phonological awareness teaching

The U.S. National Reading Panel (NRP, 2000) conducted a meta-analysis of efficacy studies in various components of reading. The NRP examined studies of phonemic awareness because research in English had indicated that phonemic awareness, along with letter knowledge, appeared to be the strongest predictor of reading development in the early grades. Their meta-analysis resulted in a number of conclusions with direct implications for instruction. Phonological awareness-based instruction:

- works significantly better than other forms of instruction for improving spelling, reading accuracy, and comprehension;
- when used with accompanying letters, phonological awarness helps typically developing and at-risk children develop their phonemic awareness better than phonological awareness training without manipulation of letters;
- when incorporated in programs of between 5 to 18 hours, it results in better progress than when taught in programs of shorter or longer duration. Note, however, that after the NRP's report in 2000, a long, intensive program (+/− 80 hours) of phonological awareness and phonics was shown to result in significant and lasting improvement in the word recognition and comprehension skills of younger grade school children with severe reading disabilities (Torgenen et al., 2001);
- is effective when taught by either teacher or computer;
- best results in transfer to reading when: training is coupled with manipulating letters, the focus is on segmenting and blending, and the instructional group size is small (as opposed to individual or large groups);
- aids reading disabled learners up to grade 6;
- helps to develop word and non-word reading well after the period of the training and it also improves reading comprehension, although to a lesser extent.

With respect to the effects of PA-related training on spelling, the NRP determined that when manipulation of letters was accompanied by phonemic awareness training, this training contributed to a greater effect size than did any other moderator variable. Kindergartners' spelling benefited more from PA instruction than did first graders', while reading-disabled children's spelling benefited minimally from PA intervention.

These results should be taken into consideration when adopting or adapting a phonological awareness-based remediation program at least in English.

In addition to benefiting learners who are at risk of dyslexia in English, phonological awareness instruction also benefits readers with dyslexia in languages other than English. For instance, Lundberg (1994) who trained a group of at-risk "pre-school" Danish children in phonological awareness found that they had a typical reading ability three years after the training and did better than the control group in reading. The finding of a positive relationship between phonological awareness instruction and improved word recognition skills obtains across languages studied to date, though variation has been found in the influence of "grain size" (phoneme, syllable, word, letter, syllabary symbol, ideograph), syllable structure complexity of the language, as well as transparency of relationships between the orthographic and spoken forms of the language (see Ziegler and Goswami, 2005, 2006).

145

4 General principles for adopting or adapting a PA-based remediation program

In this section, we consider what instructors and curriculum developers should take into account when adapting or adopting a PA-based intervention program regardless of their cultural-linguistic context.

Research-based intervention

At every stage, instuctions should be informed by research results from available efficacy studies. The results by NRP (2000) summarized above give important guidelines especially for English, and practitioners should of course remain attentive to new and emerging research. Those of us working on languages that are under-researched (e.g., Arabic, Japanese, Chinese) need to adhere to foundational findings that pertain cross-linguistically, for instance: the importance of early intervention, the benefit of structured, explicit teaching–learning, and the importance of establishing automaticity of symbol–sound connections in the early stages of the training.

It is also important to be informed by research into how reading develops. As previously noted for English, there is evidence that phoneme awareness develops much better than rhyme awareness when schooling starts, due to the teaching of the alphabetic orthography (see Seymour et al., 1999).

Learning to read is more than learning to decode, and therefore we need to incorporate PA instruction within a larger structured program that accounts for the component reading skills in addition to phonological awareness (structural analysis, automaticity/fluency, vocabulary, comprehension). Lastly, research has shown that, in addition to displaying deficits in phonological awarnesss, readers with dyslexia also display deficits in morphology and syntax (Siegel and Ryan, 1988; Rispens et al., 2004); performance in these latter two language areas predicts both decoding and comprehension, (e.g. Tunmer, 1989) as well as spelling in general (e.g. Lyster, 2002). We will return to the importance of morphology and syntax in our later discussion of adapting instruction to different languages.

Learner/reader variation

One also needs to take into account the heterogeneity of readers, who present with a variety of different learning and cognitive profiles. Research identifying categories of reading difficulties can lead us to strategies for tailoring instruction to students' specific needs. For instance, Castles and Coltheart (1993) as well as Manis et al. (1996) divided dyslexics into two groups, surface and phonological dyslexics on the basis of their performance on reading pseudo-words and exception words. Surface dyslexics have difficulty in the recognition of exception words and phonological dyslexics have problems in reading pseudo-words. Seymour (1986) identified two other major types of dyslexics: readers with phonological problems and others with morphological deficits. By identifying students' patterns of performance in these ways, we can identify children who may particularly need help with phonological awareness and sound-symbol instruction versus students who might benefit more from approaches emphasizing memorization of larger morphological shapes in words.

Aaron et al. (1999) identified three types of reading disability: 1) problems with decoding/encoding (dyslexia) but no listening comprehension problems, 2) difficulties with listening comprehension (hyperlexia), and 3) deficits in both decoding/encoding and comprehension (language learning disability). While students with dyslexia may benefit more from phonological

awareness training combined with sound-symbol instruction, students with primary comprehension deficits would likely benefit more from instruction emphasizing vocabulary development and comprehension strategies. It follows that children with language learning disabilities
(deficits in decoding as well as underlying language problems) would most likely benefit from
forms of instruction suited for students with dyslexia or students with comprehension deficits.

Another sub-categorization of reading disability, the Double Deficit Hypothesis, is based on
decoding speed versus phonological coding accuracy (Wolf *et al.*, 1994). Research supporting
this hypothesis has divided readers with dyslexia into those who have a deficit in decoding
(phonological awareness and decoding), those who have only a rapid naming deficit (speed of
phonological retrieval and visual-to-verbal transfer), and a third group who have both deficits
at the same time. While the former group typically benefits from phonological awareness
training coupled with decoding instruction, the students with deficits in coding speed usually
benefit from drills targeting word-level automaticity and as well as text-level decoding fluency.
Students with a double deficit would show more severe deficits, would need both forms of
instruction, and would typically make slower progress. The double deficit hypothesis
underscores the importance of knowing the type and severity of the reading disability in order
to vary treatment accordingly (Wise and Olson, 1998; Nelson *et al.*, 2003).

In the same way that learners with reading disabilities differ in the type and severity of their
reading and spelling problems, these same students also differ in their patterns of strengths
(Snowling, 1987). It follows that students' cognitive assets can be developed into compensation
strategies for overcoming their deficits. For example, Campbell and Butterworth (1985)
describe the case of a student who succeeded using visual strategies of analogy to aid word
recognition. Similarly, comprehension problems can be addressed in part by exploiting strengths
in top-down psycholinguistic guessing strategies when students are in the reading fluency stage
(Frith and Snowling, 1983; Muter, 2003). While compensatory strategies alone are not sufficient
for teaching reading skills, they can be a helpful adjunct.

In addition to establishing and exploiting individual patterns of strengths and weaknesses, it
is important to recognize the age of the learner(s). While dyslexia in both children and adults
shows the characteristic deficits in phonological awareness and nonword reading, young adults
with dyslexia may exhibit difficulties with inferential comprehension related to their problems
with fluency and phonological working memory (Gottardo *et al.*, 1997; Hanley, 1997; Everatt,
1997). There is sparse research on the remediation in adult population, so some caution should
be exercised when applying intervention findings based on research with children. Regardless
of the need for more research, the content and the instructional methods of an intervention
program should be adapted to older students' maturity levels.

Non-cognitive predictors of reading

Socio-economic status (SES) may seem irrelevant to the cognitive bases of dyslexia, however,
SES can directly influence the success of an intervention program. SES—an indicator of parent
education, access to educational resources, and family literacy practices—correlates positively
with word reading, print knowledge, and phonological awareness even when IQ is controlled
for (see Muter, 2003, Chapter 5). Torgesen and colleagues (1999) found that parent education,
a key factor defining SES, was among the best predictors of students' response to reading
instruction.

In a review of a series of studies conducted in India, Patel (2004) reports that children in
deprived areas showed similar cognitive-linguistic development to their peers in "mainstream"
schools, but were well behind in literacy performance. On the basis of these results, Patel

questions the usual practice of excluding economic and socially disadvantaged children from reading services simply because they do not meet the criterion for "pure" dyslexia. Thus, phonological awareness instruction, and structured reading intervention in general, should be provided for all children with reading difficulties, but should be tailored to each student's profile of strengths and weaknesses.

Recently, a rather inclusive approach to reading disability intervention and assessment has emerged under the name of Response to Intervention (RTI) (Berninger *et al.*, 2001; Berninger *et al.*, 2006; Shores and Bender, 2007). RTI is a system of organizing intervention into a three-tiered system that varies in intensity of instruction and allows the student to move dynamically from tier to tier depending on the level of success:

- Tier 1: Research-based classroom literacy instruction for all students in the class;
- Tier 2: Research-based small group instruction within the classroom for students grouped by common needs;
- Tier 3: Intensive individualized tutorial-type research-based literacy instruction for students who fail in response to Tier 1 and Tier 2 instruction.

Shores and Bender define RTI as

a process of implementing high-quality, scientifically validated instructional practices based on learner needs, monitoring student progress, and adjusting instruction based on the student's response. When a student's response is dramatically inferior to that of his peers, the student may be determined to have a learning disability

(2007, p. 7).

In its ideal form, the benefits of RTI include early intervention that does not wait for the child to fail, continuous monitoring of progress and efficiency of intervention, and inclusion of students within the school. Criticisms of RTI within the U.S. are the lack of consensus on what comprises "research-based instruction" as well as the lack of regular education teachers with the knowledge and skills to implement research-based literacy teaching within their classrooms.

While RTI may represent a helpful advance, cognitive profiling (learning style, strengths and weaknesses) of the student is still useful for evaluating the effects of instruction and adapting it to the individual learner's needs; there remains a need to combine RTI with the cognitive approaches to diagnosis and intervention (Fiorello *et al.*, 2006).

Implementation issues

Schuele and Boudreau (2008) identified the following issues that are necessary to address when developing and/or implementing a phonological awareness-based program: 1) when in child's development to initiate instruction, 2) duration and intensity of instruction, 3) scope of skills and instructional sequence (what to teach and in which order), and 4) teaching methods. We add to these an additional issue: 5) evaluation of the efficacy of the program/training.

Issue 1 When in children's development to initiate phonological awareness instruction

There is evidence in English that in kindergarten the skills of rhyme and alliteration tasks develop and by late kindergarten and early first grade children start to display phoneme segmentation and blending (for example, see Good and Kaminski, 2002). The NRP report

(2000) suggests that the sooner in schooling phonological awareness training starts, the better, because after grade 3, it is difficult for at-risk children to narrow the gap between their skills and the skills of their typically developing peers.

Issue 2 Duration (length of session), intensity (degree of individualized, rigorous focus on skills), as well as frequency of instruction (number of sessions per week).

These factors are critical to address in constructing and implementing a PA-based literacy intervention program, and need to be adapted to the individual needs of the student. The program should be flexible and allow for the reading specialist to determine the duration and the intensity, depending on the response of the child/ren to the intervention. Of course the evaluation and the plan of action for the training will depend in part on the context of the program—whether it is done in an individual tutoring-basis, administered to a small group of learners or to a whole class. Intensity needs to vary according to how the child responds to the intervention (Byrne, 1998; Byrne and Fielding-Barnsley, 1995).

Issue 3 Scope and sequence

These will depend on the research with the target language/context, which as noted above is sparse in languages other than English.

Issue 4 Teaching methods

Methods employed should be based on available efficacy studies, clinical observation and should optimally be married with the teaching practices in the school context as well as teachers' experience (Birsh, 2005). Lesson plans should articulate long- and short-term goals, specific learning objectives, tasks, strategies and procedures. The lesson plans should also include scenarios about what to do in response to error (e.g. Schuele and Boudreau 2008, pp. 12–15). Lyon and Moats (1997) underscore the importance of considering age as well as intensity and length when matching methods with the child's needs.

Issue 5 Testing the efficacy of the program

It is necessary to make sure the program has benefits that generalize and extend beyond the training period (e.g., Torgesen *et al.*, 1999). Given that PA-based training does not work with all learners, the cognitive and psychological tests that predict intervention resistors should be identified (see discussion in Niemi *et al.*, 1999).

5 Language-and culture-specific principles for adopting or adapting a PA-based remediation program

Cross-linguistic variation in orthography, phonology, morphology and syntax

Cross-linguistic variation is due to at least four interacting factors: the script (orthography, or writing system) and how it represents the phonology, morphology and syntax of the language as well as the phonological, the morphological, and the syntactic structures of the language by themselves and in interaction. This variation should be taken into account when adapting research results in the more researched languages to the less-researched languages.

The development or delay of reading in English differs from the development of reading in other languages mainly because of the nature of writing systems (scripts). English has an alphabetic system that is rather opaque, or deep. Other languages that share the alphabetic system like German or Spanish are more transparent, or shallow (see Frost *et al.*, 1987). Transparent orthographies have a one-to-one relationship between sounds/phonemes and letters like Spanish, Finnish, or Serbo-Croatian. Other languages are less transparent such as German and French. Of the languages with opaque orthographies, English perhaps provides the most extreme example of opacity: for example, a given sound can be represented by many different letters or letter combinations (/s/ = *ce* in cent, *ci* as in pencil, *s* as in sip, *ss* as in brass, *sc* as in scent) or a letter can be pronounced in numerous ways, i.e. an individual letter may represent many different sounds (*a* = /eI/ in baby, /"uh"/ in sofa, /a/ in father, /ae/ in dad).

The opacity of English comes at a cost to rate of learning basic reading skills. In a study that examined development of word reading accuracy and decoding pseudo-words in the first grade in 14 European languages, English learners lagged at least one year behind children who were learning languages with highly transparent orthographies such as Greek, Finnish, German, Italian and Spanish (Seymour *et al.*, 2003).

Reading difficulties in German, a highly transparent orthography, are most evident at the decoding fluency level and are best predicted with tests of phonological retrieval speed such as rapid serial naming (Wimmer, 1993). In contrast, reading deficits in English, first appear in word-level decoding inaccuracies, and are best predicted by measures of phonological awareness, specifically segmentation tasks. These findings suggest that the nature of reading difficulties varies in relationship to the degree of transparency of the orthography (see discussion in Muter, 2003, Chapter 3).

Ziegler and Goswami (2005) argue in support of a "psycholinguistic grain size theory" to explain how readers' differences in accuracy and speed of decoding across languages reflects a difference in the strategies learners have acquired in response to the structure of their language. In languages with highly regular orthographies and simple syllable structure, such as Spanish or Italian, the most efficient strategy for word recognition is grapheme-to-phoneme decoding. In English by contrast, the smaller units (graphemes) have inconsistent symbol–sound correspondences while larger units like rimes are more consistent and thus developing readers learn that matching these latter units with their sounds through rime analogies (eg. Goswami, 1986), is more efficient. Thus, English readers tend to develop two strategies—one for regular words and another for irregular words—unlike children learning a transparent orthography like German or who tend to rely only on grapheme to phoneme decoding (Goswami *et al.*, 2001; Ziegler and Goswami, 2005). Still another example of the variations between reading and language structure is Brahmi script, in which the minimal written unit is based on a conception of the syllable different from English; in Brahmi the rime is not recognized, but the body is and so is the coda (onset and nucleus) (see Patel, 2004).

The strategies that children learn as they process and manipulate language have implications for the methods that we employ for teaching them. With respect to teaching English for instance, Goswami (2005) calls for a "balanced" approach to teaching word recognition that takes into account the dual characteristics of the syllable structure. While this might work for English, teachers of other languages/orthographies have to decide which approach(es) to use based on research results in their languages. In the absence of research, they might rely on research findings for languages with similar structures and examine the efficacy of approaches that appear to be appropriate.

Since phonemic awareness is developed in the process of learning an alphabetic script, children whose languages do not represent phonemes typically display weak phonemic awareness. For example, first grade children learning to read in Japanese display syllable awareness in response to learning to read in highly regular kana syllabaries (hiragana and katakana) while, as noted previously, learners acquire phonemic awareness in response to learning to read in largely alphabetic orthography such as English (Perfetti, 2003; Mann, 1986). Examples such as these suggest that caution should be employed when adopting or adapting an English-based phonological awareness instruction to orthographies that differ from English.

Reading is also affected by the interaction of the script with the morphology and syntax of a language. For example, Chitiri (1991) studied the reading processes of monolingual adolescents in English and Greek, two languages that differ in their structure (Greek is a highly inflected language while English grammar depends more on word order) and found that the Greek monolingual readers recognize endings of content words more efficiently than their English-speaking peers do. Another language with rich morpho-syntactic characteristics is Arabic (see Ferrando, 2004). The highly agglutinative feature of Arabic morpho-syntax is manifested in its script which makes reading quite challenging: while reading within a larger syntactic context the reader must rapidly unpack morphemes from words that often contain densely layered morphological structures (see Abu-Rabia, 2007). Compared to more agglutinative languages like Greek or Arabic, English's pattern of roots with prefixes and suffixes is comparatively simple. Thus, morphological complexity is a factor that may be important to consider when adapting English-centered methods to other languages.

Socio-linguistic factors (diaglossia, bilingualism and multilingualism)

In addition to the script and its interaction with the language, there are other socio-linguistic factors that should be taken into account in developing and implementing a PA-based program. These factors are relevant in the development, adoption, or adaptation of intervention programs to L1 contexts other than English as well as to contexts where English is an additional language.

In the Arabic context, for instance, there is a serious problem of diaglossia that affects literacy development. All Arabic speakers have to learn Modern Standard Arabic, a variety that is different from the dialect they speak at home. Given that there are numerous dialects of spoken Arabic, preschool home exposure to Modern Standard Arabic is a key predictor of development of reading (e.g. Abu-Rabia, 2000; Saiegh-Haddad, 2003). The implication here is that in diaglossic contexts, the standard dialect for literacy must be addressed early and intentionally.

In second language and multilingual contexts, it is usually difficult to identify reading disabled learners due to the lack of sensitive diagnostic instruments and the paucity of trained testers with adequate bilingual skills (Cline, 2002; see also Everatt et al., 2000). Most of the research on bilinguals or multilinguals has been on those learning English as an additional language. An excellent collection of meta-analyses of the available literature on biliteracy was compiled by the U.S. National Literacy Panel on Language-Minority Children and Youth ("NLP"; August and Shanahan, 2006). Some of the central conclusions of this report follow.

The predictors of word recognition skills in English L2 are the same as found in monolingual learners of English, and include the key components of phonological processing: phonemic awareness, rapid naming, phonological memory. Predictors of L2 reading comprehension are also similar to what has been found in L1: namely background knowledge, vocabulary, story structure, and home literacy. Like L1 readers, L2 learners with dyslexia have difficulties mainly in phonological awareness and working memory (Lesaux et al., 2006).[2]

Oral language proficiency in L2 correlates more with reading comprehension rather than with word or pseudo-word reading (Geva, 2006). There is also evidence that performance on such skills as word reading, reading comprehension, spelling and writing are very much correlated with the learners' performance in their first language, that is literacy skills transfer across L1 and L2 (Dressler and Kamil, 2006).

The findings regarding second language or foreign language literacy training converge with findings for monolingual learners of English: structured training in the core components of literacy (phonemic awareness, decoding, fluency, vocabulary, reading comprehension and writing) leads to improvement in literacy development (Shanahan and Beck, 2006). The areas that the NLP report suggest need to be addressed in L2 English literacy instruction are:

1 The linguistic and typological differences between the L1 and the L2 such as the sounds that exist in L2 but do not exist in L1.
2 The development of oral language skills in English, a skill that is apparently overlooked, the need to teach oral comprehension as well as the traditional core components of literacy (Shanahan and Beck, 2006).
3 Building on literacy skills that are similar in L1 and L2 which are likely to be transferable.

Conclusion

Phonological awareness, the meta-linguistic capacity to reflect on the sound structure of the language, is a robust predictor of beginning reading skills in English and in most other languages studied to date. Given the findings that support phonological awareness-based teaching in English and some European languages (e.g., Danish, Finnish), it is worthwhile adapting this methodology to less-researched language contexts. Principles for teaching that are likely to pertain across languages include general emphases on explicit, structured, linguistically informed instruction that introduces skills systematically and ensures that students have automatized rote skills. As we have illustrated in this chapter, languages vary in their phonological, morpho-syntactic and orthographic characteristics as well as socio-linguistic contexts in which they are learned. Assessment and instruction should be adapted to the unique characteristics of the host language and culture and should factor in the child's cognitive-linguistic strengths as well as response to different levels of instructional intensity. In the absence of research on a given language, it may be productive for teacher educators and practitioners to approach the challenge by basing their assessment and teaching on what has been learned from research in other languages that share similar characteristics.

Notes

1 There are other less evidence-substantiated definitions that are based on different explanation of what the source of the deficit is. These include mainly the following hypotheses: (i) temporal processing deficit hypothesis (e.g. Tallal, 1980) which argues that the phonological deficits in dyslexia are secondary to more general deficit in sensory deficit in processing auditory information, (ii) the cerebellar deficit hypothesis (Nicolson et al., 2001) and (iii) visual processing deficit (e.g. Stein and Talcott, 1999).
2 It is noteworthy this meta-analysis included other languages other than English (e.g. Hebrew learned by minority Arabs in Israel; Swedish in a Finnish majority in Finland, Nahuatl native Americans learning Spanish in Mexico) as well as English as a Foreign Language (whose first language varied from French, to Chinese, or Persian, etc.

References

Aaron, P.G., Joshi, M. and Williams, K.A. (1999). Not all reading disabilities are alike. *Journal of Learning Disabilities, 32* (2), 120–137.
Abu-Rabia, S. (2000). Effects of exposure to literary Arabic on reading comprehension in a diaglossic situation. *Reading and Writing: An Interdisciplinary Journal, 13*, 147–157.

Abu-Rabia, S. (2007). The role of morphology and short vowelization in reading Arabic among normal and dyslexic readers in grades 3, 6, 9, and 12. *Journal of psycholinguistic research*, 36(2), 89–106

Adams, M.J. (1990). *Beginning to Read Thinking and Learning about Print*. Cambridge, MA: MIT Press.

August, D., and Shanahan, T. (2006). *Developing Literacy in Second-Language Learners. Report of the National Literacy Panel on Language-Minority Children and Youth*. Mahwah, NJ: Lawrence Erlbaum Associates.

Bailey, C.E., Manis, F.R., Pedersen, W.C., and Seidenberg, M.S. (2004). Variation among developmental dyslexics: Evidence from a printed-word-learning task. *Journal of Experimental Child Psychology*, 87, 125–154.

Bell, S.M., McCallum, R.S., and Cox, E.A. (2003). Toward a research-based assessment of dyslexia: Using cognitive measures to identify reading disabilities. *Journal of Learning Disabilities*, 36 (6), 505–516.

Berninger, V.W., Stage, S.A., Smith, D.R., and Hildebrand, D. (2001). Assessment for reading and writing intervention: A three-tier model for prevention and remediation. In J. Andrews, D. Saklofske, H. Janzen, and G. Phye (eds), *Handbook of Psychoeducational Assessment* (pp. 195–223). New York: Academic Press.

Berninger, V.W., Rutberg, J.E., Abbott, R.D., Garcia, N., Anderson-Youngstrom, M., Brooks, A., and Fulton, C. (2006). Tier 1 and Tier 2 early intervention for handwriting and composing. *Journal of School Psychology*, 44, 3–30.

Birsh, J.R. (ed.) (2005). *Multisensory Teaching of Basic Language Skills* (2nd edn). Baltimore: Paul H. Brookes Publishing Co.

Byrne, B. (1998). *The Foundation of Literacy: The Child's Acquisition of the Alphabetic Principle*. Hove, UK: Psychology Press.

Byrne, B., and Fielding-Barnsley, R. (1995). Evaluation of a program to teach phonemic awareness to young children: A 2- and 3-year follow-up and a new pre-school trial. *Journal of Educational Psychology*, 87, 488–503.

Campbell, R., and Butterworth, B. (1985). Phonological dyslexia and dysgraphia in a highly literate subject: A developmental case with associated deficits of phonemic processing and awareness. *Quarterly Journal of Experimental Psychology*, 37A, 435–475.

Castles, A., and Coltheart, M. (1993). Varieties of developmental dyslexia. *Cognition*, 47, 149–180.

Chitiri, H-F. (1991). *The influence of language and writing system characteristics on the reading process*. Unpublished PhD Dissertation, University of Toronto, Department of Education, Canada.

Cline, T. (2002). Issues in the assessment of children learning English as an additional language. In G. Reid, and J. Wearmouth (eds.), *Dyslexia and Literacy* (pp. 201–212). Chichester, UK: John Wiley and Sons Ltd.

Dressler, C., and Kamil, M. (2006). First- and second-language literacy. In August and Shanahan (eds.) (pp. 197–238).

Everatt, J. (1997). The abilities and disabilities associated with adult developmental dyslexia. *Journal of Research in Reading*, 20(1), 13–21.

Everatt, J., Smythe, I., Adams, E., and Ocampo, D. (2000). Dyslexia screening measures and bilingualism. *Dyslexia*, 6, 42–56.

Ferrando, I. (2004). The phonology and morphology of Arabic. *Journal of Semitic Studies*, 49, 175–178.

Fiorello, C.A., Hale, J.B., and Snyder, L.E. (2006). Cognitive hypothesis testing and response to intervention for children with reading problems. *Psychology in the Schools*, 43(8), 835–853.

Frith, U., and Snowling, M.J. (1983). Reading for meaning and reading for sound in autistic and dyslexic children. *British Journal of Developmental Psychology*, 1, 329–342.

Frith, U., Wimmer, H., and Landerl, K. (1998). Differences in phonological recoding in German and English-speaking children. *Scientific Study of Reading*, 2, 31–54.

Frost, R., Katz, L., and Bentin, S. (1987). Strategies for visual word recognition and orthographical depth: A multilingual comparison. *Journal of Experimental Psychology: Human Perception and Performance*, 13, 159–180.

Geva, E. (2006). Second-language oral proficiency and second-language literacy. In August and Shanahan (eds.) (pp. 123–140).

Gillingham, A., and Stillman, B. (1997). *The Gillingham Manual. Remedial training for children with specific disability in reading, spelling, and penmanship* (8th Edition). Cambridge and Toronto: Educators Publishing Service.

Good, R.H., and Kaminksi, R.A. (eds.) (2002). *Dynamic indicators of basic early literacy skills*. (6th ed.). Eugene, OR: Institute for the Development of Education Achievement.

Goswami, U. (1986). Children's use of analogy in learning to read: A developmental study. *Journal of Experimental Child Psychology, 42*, 73–83.

Goswami, U. (2002). Phonology, reading development and dyslexia: A cross-linguistic perspective. *Annals of Dyslexia, 52*, 1–23.

Goswami, U. (2005). Synthetic phonics and learning to read: A cross-language perspective. *Educational Psychology in Practice, 21*(4), 273–282.

Goswami, U., and Bryant, P. (1990). *Phonological Skills and Learning to Read*. Hove, UK: Psychology Press.

Goswami, U., Gombert, J., and de Barrera, F. (1999). Children's orthographic representations and linguistic transparency: Nonsense word reading in English, French and Spanish. *Applied Psycholinguistics, 19*, 19–52.

Goswami, U., Ziegler, J.C., Dalton, L., and Schneider, W. (2001). Pseudohomophone effects and phonological recoding procedures in reading development in English and German. *Journal of Memory and Language, 45*(4), 648–664.

Gottardo, A., Siegel, L.S., and Stanovich, K.E. (1997). The assessment of adults with reading disabilities: what can we learn from experimental tasks? *Journal of Research in Reading, 20*(1), 42–54.

Hanley, J.R. (1997). Reading and spelling impairments in undergraduate students with developmental dyslexia, *Journal of Research in Reading, 20*(1), 22–30.

Hatcher, P.J. (1994). *Sound Linkage*. London: Whurr.

Holm, A., and Dodd, B. (1996). The effect of first written language on the acquisition of English literacy. *Cognition, 59*, 119–147.

Johnston, M., Philips, S., and Peer, L. (1999). *Multisensory Teaching System for Reading Special Educational Needs Centre*. Manchester Metropolitan University: Didsbury School of Education.

Lesaux, N., Koda, K., Siegel, L., and Shanahan, T. (2006). Development of literacy. In August and Shanahan (eds.) (pp. 75–122).

Liberman, A., and Mattingly, I. (1985). The motor theory of speech perception, revised. *Cognition, 1*, 1–36.

Lindamood, C.H., and Lindamood, P.C. (1998). *The Lindamood Phoneme Sequencing Program for Reading, Spelling, and Speech*. Austin, TX: Pro-Ed.

Lundberg, I. (1994). Reading difficulties can be predicted and prevented: A Scandinavian perspective on phonological awareness and reading. In C. Hulme, and M.J. Snowling (eds.), *Reading development and dyslexia* (pp. 180–199). London: Whurr.

Lundberg, I., Frost, J., and Petersen, O. (1988). Effects of an extensive program for stimulating phonological awareness in preschool children. *Reading Research Quarterly, 23*(3), 263–284.

Lyon, G.R., and Moats, L.C. (1997). Critical conceptual and methodological considerations in reading intervention research. *Journal of Learning Disabilities, 30*(6), 578–588.

Lyon, G.R., Shaywitz, S., and Shaywitz, B. (2003). Part I. Defining dyslexia, comorbidity, teachers' knowledge of language and reading. *Annals of Dyslexia, 53*(1), January, 1–14.

Lyster, S.A.H. (2002). The effects of morphological versus phonological awareness training in kindergarten on reading development. *Reading and Writing: An Interdisciplinary Journal, 15*, 261–294.

Lyytinen, H., Ronimus, M., Alanko, A., Poikkeus, A-M., and Taanila, M. (2007). Early identification of dyslexia and the use of computer game-based practice to support reading acquisition. *Nordic Psychology, 59*(2), 109–126.

Manis, F.R., Seidenberg, M.S., Doi, L.M., McBride-Chang, C., and Petersen, A. (1996). On the bases of two subtypes of developmental dyslexia. *Cognition, 58*, 157–195.

Mann, V. (1986). Phonological awareness: The role of reading experience. *Cognition, 24*, 65–92.

Miles, E. (2000). Dyslexia may show a different face in different languages. *Dyslexia, 6*, 193–201.

Morais, J., Cary, L., Alegria, J., and Bertelson, P. (1979). Does awareness of speech as a sequence of phones arise spontaneously? *Cognition, 7*, 323–331.

Muter, V. (2003). *Early Reading Development and Dyslexia*. London: Athenaeum Press.

Nelson, J.R., Benner, G.J., and Gonzalez, J. (2003). Learner characteristics that influence the treatment of effectiveness of early literacy interventions: A meta-analytic review. *Learning Disabilities Research* and *Practice, 18*(4), 285–267.

National Reading Panel (NRP) (2000). *Teaching Children to Read: An evidence-based assessment of the scientific research literature on reading and its implications for reading instruction*. http://www.nationalreading panel.org/Publications/subgroups.htm, accessed 26/10/08.

Nicolson, R.I., Fawcett, A.J., and Dean, P. (2001). Developmental dyslexia: The cerebellar deficit hypothesis. *Trends in Neurosciences, 24*, 508–511.

Niemi, P., Kinnunen, R., Poskiparta, E., and Vauras, M. (1999). Do pre-school data predict resistance to treatment in phonological awareness, decoding and spelling? In I. Lundberg, F.E. Tonnessen, and I. Austad (eds), *Dyslexia: Advances in Theory and Practice* (pp. 245–254). Dordrecht: Kluwer Academic Publishers.

Nikolopoulos, D.S. (1999). *Cognitive and linguistic predictors of literacy skills in the Greek language. The manifestation of reading and spelling difficulties in a regular orthography.* Unpublished PhD Dissertation: University College London.

Pan, N., and Chen, L. (2005). Phonological/phonemic awareness and reading: A crosslinguistic perspective. *Journal of Multilingual Communication Disorders, 3* (2), 145–152.

Patel, P.G. (2004). *Reading Acquisition in India: Models of reading and dyslexia.* New Delhi: Sage Publications.

Perfetti, C.A. (2003). The Universal Grammar of reading. *Scientific Studies of Reading,* 7(1), 3–24.

Perfetti, C.A., Beck, I.L., Bell, L.C., and Hughes, C. (1987). Phonemic knowledge and learning to read are reciprocal: A longitudinal study of first grade children. *Merrill-Palmer Quarterly, 33,* 283–319.

Rispens, J., Roeleven, S., and Koster, C. (2004). Sensitivity to subject–verb agreement in spoken language in children with developmental dyslexia. *Journal of Neurolinguistics, 17,* 333–347.

Saiegh-Haddad, E. (2003). Linguistic distance and initial reading acquisition: The case of Arabic diaglossia. *Applied Psycholinguistics, 24,* 431–451.

Scarborough, H.S., and Brady, S.A. (2004). Toward a common terminology for talking about speech and reading: A glossary of the "phon" words and some related terms. In *Dyslexia: Myths, Misconceptions, and Some Practical Applications* (pp. 1–49). The International Dyslexia Association (reprinted version of Scarborough and Brady (2002) paper by the same title in *Journal of Literacy Research,* 34, 299–334).

Schuele, C.M., and Boudreau, D. (2008). Phonological awareness intervention: Beyond the basics. *Language, Speech, and Hearing Services in Schools, 39,* 3–20.

Seymour, P.H.K. (1986). *A Cognitive Analysis of Dyslexia.* London: Routledge and Kegan Paul.

Seymour, P.H.K, Duncan, L.G., and Bolik, F.M. (1999). Rhymes and phonemes in the common unit task: Replications and implications for beginning reading. *Journal of Research in Reading,* 22(2), 113–130.

Seymour, P., Aro, M., and Erskine, J.M. (2003). Foundation literacy acquisition in European languages. *British Journal of Psychology, 94,* 143–174.

Shanahan, T., and Beck, I. (2006). Effective literacy teaching for English-Language Learners. In August and Shanahan (eds) (pp. 415–488).

Shores, C., and Bender, W.N. (2007). Response to intervention. In W.N. Bender and C. Shores (eds.), *Response to Intervention: A Practical Guide for Every Teacher* (pp. 1–19). Thousand Oaks, CA: Council for Exceptional Children and Crown Press.

Siegel, L.S., and Ryan, E.B. (1988). Development of grammatical sensitivity, phonological, and short term memory skills in normally achieving and learning-disabled children. *Developmental Psychology, 24,* 28–37.

Simmons, F., and Singleton, C. (2000). The reading comprehension abilities of dyslexic students in higher education. *Dyslexia, 6* (3), 178–192.

Snowling, M.J. (1987). *Dyslexia: A Cognitive Developmental Perspective.* Oxford: Blackwell.

Snowling, M.J. (1996). Contemporary approaches to the teaching of reading. *Journal of Child Psychology and Psychiatry, 37,* 139–148.

Snowling, M.J. (2000). *Dyslexia,* 2nd edn, Oxford: Blackwell Publishers.

Stanovich, K.E., and Siegel, L.S. (1994). Phenotypic performance profile of children with reading disabilities: A regression-based test of the phonological-core variable-difference model. *Journal of Educational Psychology, 86,* 24–53.

Stein, J., and Talcott, J. (1999). Impaired neuronal timing in developmental dyslexia—the magnocellular hypothesis. *Dyslexia: An International Journal of Research and Practice, 5,* 59–77.

Tallal, P. (1980). Auditory temporal perception, phonics, and reading disabilities in children. *Brain and Language, 9,* 182–198.

Torgesen, J.K., Wagner, R.K., Rashotte, C.A., Rose, E., Lindamood, P., Conway, T. *et al.* (1999). Preventing reading failure in young children with phonological processing disabilities: group and individual responses to instruction. *Journal of Educational Psychology, 91,* 579–593.

Torgesen, J.K., Alexander, A.W., Wagner, R.K., Rashotte, C. A. *et al.* (2001). Intensive remedial instruction for children with severe reading disabilities: immediate and long-term outcomes from two instructional approaches. *Journal of Learning Disabilities, 34* (1), 33–58.

Tunmer, W. E. (1989). The role of the language-related factors in reading disability. In D. Shankweiler, and I.Y. Liberman (eds.), *Phonology and Reading Disability: Solving the Reading Puzzle, IARLDM* (pp. 91–131). Ann Arbor, MI: University of Michigan Press.

Wilson, J. (1993). *Phonological Awareness Training Programme*. University College London: Educational Psychology Publishing.

Wimmer, H. (1993). Characteristics of developmental dyslexia in a regular writing system. *Applied Psycholinguistics, 14*, 1–34.

Wise, B.W., and Olson, R.K. (1998). Studies of computer-aided remediation for reading disabilities. In C. Hulme and R. M. Joshi (eds.), *Reading and Spelling: Development and Disorders* (pp. 473–487). Mahwah, NJ: Lawrence Erlbaum Associates.

Wolf, M., Pfeil, C., Lotz, R., and Biddle, K. (1994). Towards a more universal understanding of developmental dyslexias: The contribution of orthographic factors. In V. Berninger (ed.), *The Varieties of Orthographic Knowledge* (pp. 137–172). Boston: Kluwer Academic Publishers.

Ziegler, J.C., and Goswami, U. (2005). Reading acquisition, developmental dyslexia, and skilled reading across languages: A psycholinguistic grain size theory. *Psychological Bulletin, 131*(1), 3–29.

Ziegler, J.C., and Goswami, U. (2006). Becoming literate in different languages: Similar problems, different solutions. *Developmental Science, 9* (5), September, 429–436.

12

Dyslexia and alternative interventions for dyslexia

A critical commentary

Angela Fawcett and Gavin Reid

This chapter

- provides background to the current situation in the field of dyslexia that has made it possible for alternative interventions to obtain a 'foothold'
- discusses what is meant by 'alternative' interventions
- discusses these against the background of the 'multiple perspectives' on what constitutes dyslexia
- places these alternative 'treatments' within the range of traditional and established approaches used in classrooms and clinics
- engages in the current debate in relation to scientific criteria for the utilisation of a new or alternative approach
- suggests a way forward for dealing with new interventions and particularly on how to provide informed and impartial advice to schools and parents.

Introduction

The syndrome of dyslexia has been hotly debated, and in some quarters hotly disputed, for many years. There now does appear to be some consensus that there are a number of key characteristics that constitute dyslexia, but there is still considerable disagreement on the particular emphasis of these characteristics in both identification and intervention. It can be argued that this situation of uncertainty and disagreement has permitted alternative interventions to mushroom and grow in popularity, often without the research support that is seen as essential for classroom intervention approaches.

Background

Although dyslexia has been recognised for many years there is still no real agreement on the most effective way to remediate dyslexia, and as we shall discuss, even traditional phonological based interventions have not proved as successful in developing reading fluency as one might hope (National Reading Panel, 2001a). In addition there is now a growing body of opinion, significantly from the adult area (McLaughlin and Leather, 2008), to suggest that we should be

157

focusing on support rather than remediation and enhancing the understanding of those in contact with people with dyslexia (teachers and employers) in addition to identifying more effective learning methods. From a parent's viewpoint, they may be concerned not only for their child's progress in literacy, but also for their dwindling self-esteem. All of these issues make alternative interventions appealing, particularly as many promise to complement the traditional teaching received in school by improving the child's ability to learn.

Intervention can be divided into a number of broad priorities and perspectives and the specific and individual approaches discussed in this chapter usually fall into one of these categories. Broadly speaking there are four main avenues by which all approaches are influenced. These are:

- the neurological/neurophysiological and pharmaceutical approach (what the child has/has not);
- the cognitive and learning approach (what the child can do /can't do);
- the child centered classroom 'hands on' approach (how the child actually performs and how this can be improved);
- the curriculum and dyslexia-friendly approach which includes the learning environment (what the system can do to make the learning experience more effective and efficient for learners with dyslexia).

It might be argued that the ideal would be a menu of perspectives and approaches and that schools and parents can select that which is most appropriate for their child, such as for example a system of benchmarking.

This however raises a number of issues.

- Not all the approaches are currently evaluated.
- Not all the evaluations that have been carried out use the same criteria for identifying how successful the approach is.
- Some approaches may have an advantage over others because of a heavy commercial thrust and a vigorous marketing approach that makes them well known. Some consumers can misinterpret and be influenced into thinking that 'well known' means 'well used' and 'well used' means 'successful'.
- There are variations on the approaches suggested, or advocated, by educational authorities/school districts and this can lead dissatisfied parents to believe there is something different and 'better' available and that they should attempt to seek it out.
- The current thrust towards inclusive schools can mean that interventions based on individual programmes, for example involving one-to-one interaction, are not practical and there can be a perception that what is on offer from the school does not meet the individual needs of the child.
- The disparity in provision and training among education authorities and individual schools can provide an opportunity for astute commercial interests to capitalise on the insecurities that may arise from this. For example a headline in the national New Zealand newspaper 'Dyslexia to be Recognised in New Zealand' was actually all about an alternative approach that was making some headway in New Zealand and in fact this approach seemed to be the catalyst for this headline.

The problem therefore may not actually lie in the development and availability of alternative approaches, but more due to the state of 'unreadiness' of the current administrative and school system to provide informed and consistently applied identification and classroom based intervention focusing on individual needs. If provision and practice was informed and consistent then alternative approaches would not be so welcomed nor met with the current mix of excitement. But often this excitement is intermingled with anxiety, uncertainly, concern, controversy and dilemmas. But this is in fact the situation and this is the reality for parents wishing to capitalise and use the precious window of opportunity for their child when time is of the essence. Some will even risk financial hardship to seek out the best for their children. It is important that if they are to do this then we, as responsible educators, should have information on these alternative approaches ready for them. Educators need to know how these approaches compare, or indeed complement, the methods used in school. That way educators can help parents make informed decisions.

What do we mean by alternative approaches?

Usually, 'alternative approaches' refer to those approaches which are first very individual and second not available in the mainstream classroom. Schools tend to use mainstream approaches which have been tried and tested over a period of time or are recommended by government reports. For example in the UK the Rose Report (Rose, 2007) suggested that schools should be using synthetic phonics following a number of research studies that had been conducted which highlighted the merits of this approach. In the USA the *No Child Left Behind Act* also advocated a number of established practices (see http://www.ed.gov/nclb/overview/intro/reauth/successstories/index.html for a number of intervention success stories). When any approach is advocated in a wholesale manner it tends to be for the majority and not all. Success stories therefore tend to be selective and this can pave the way for enterprising individuals to develop an alternative to what is being offered in schools. Moreover, even these well evaluated tradional therapies are not proving as successful as had previously been hoped, despite the development of costly long term studies by the National Institute for Child Health and Human Development (NICHD) in the USA to help children with dyslexia and other reading difficulties. The problem is that training leads to improvements in the area which has been trained, but it is much more difficult to ensure that this generalises to reading skill overall. The most difficult task is to improve children's standard scores in literacy, because these take age into account, and are often based on irregular words which do not improve with phonological training. Therefore the results from the US National Reading Panel (2001b) show improvement in phonological skills, but this has not always generalised into accurate reading, nor typically has this improvement generalised into more fluent reading.

It is against this background of partial success that the alternative therapies in this chapter should be evaluated. Before we can do this, we need a better understanding of what a satisfactory evaluation involves. We should start with a caveat to the reader, when trying to understand whether or not interventions work. It is particularly important to be aware that there are differences in the quality of material presented. We are all aware that advertisements try to persuade us to buy a product, and although they are monitored it is possible to make claims which are not backed up by research. This is even more likely when we read material presented on a website, which is not monitored in any way. We can read reports in the media, but these are often based on personal opinon, and the media sometimes have a vested interest in presenting material in a controversial fashion. We can read reports or books, but again these may be partly based on opinion rather than fact, and will not be peer reviewed. The most reliable information we can obtain should be from research published in a peer reviewed journal, although even here there is a hierarchy, with some journals having a higher impact than others and these are likely to be the sources on which we can best rely. It is important to be aware that some of the material quoted has been more stringently evaluated than others. To make it more difficult to evaluate interventions effectively, alternative evaluations which have been evaluated by the promoters are easily dismissed, but it is difficult to persuade independent researchers to undertake a properly controlled evaluation, which can be not only expensive and lengthy but also involve them in controversy.

Controlled studies: the issues

The gold standard experimental design for evaluating interventions is the double blind placebo controlled study, taken from the medical field where it is widely used to evaluate how effective new drugs are, and whether or not they have harmful side effects. A double blind approach means that neither the experimenter, nor the child, the teacher or the family know which approach the child is receiving, the therapy which the study is testing, or whether they have been given an alternative known as a placebo. It is important to make sure that studies are double blind, to overcome any tendency for performance to improve simply because the child or the experimenter expects this. In some studies, a cross-over technique is used. This means that half the children receive the placebo in the first set of trials and in the second set of trials they receive the intervention. This is held to be ethically sound, because no one is deprived of an intervention thought to be beneficial. A stringent and well-controlled system would mean that the trial supervisor was not aware of who received placebo and who received treatment. This approach is relatively easy within a medical setting, but is less easy to adhere to in an experimental setting. There has been considerable debate on whether or not the approaches typically used in the education system, for both traditional and alternative interventions are stringent enough. It is common for teachers who are administering an intervention to know which approach they are delivering to each child, and any improvements may reflect the commitment the teacher has rather than the effectiveness of the intervention. For a review of some of the issues arising in the methodology of interventions see the special issue of *Dyslexia*, 2007, 13 (4), pages 231–256.

Currently there is quite a range of alternative approaches and these will be discussed here.

The Dore programme

This has been arguably the most controversial approach over the previous few years, based on a published controlled study with a cross over design, which meant that the control group received a delayed intervention, and a later published follow-up, where of course there were no longer any controls, but the children's progress was compared with their progress over the preceding years, and with their achievements in standardized NfER tests which were given to all the children annually, and SATs performance at the end of the study (Reynolds and Nicolson, 2007). The children tested showed mild deficits on a screening test, and they were matched on their overall performance on that test, rather than their reading age. This meant there were individual differences within each group, with some children diagnosed with dyslexia, dyspraxia or ADHD, some with relatively mild problems in speed, and the groups overall were not well matched for reading. The second article, looking at effects over time, clearly states that there was little improvement for the children after the intervention in their scores on speeded tests of reading and spelling, although there were significant improvements in NfER reading, and on phonological skills. The problem here was not simply the content and the methodology of the two articles, which were rigorously reviewed and had been deemed appropriate for publication in an academic journal, but the associated hype in the media and the inflated claims of cures on the company website. These factors, plus the cost of the intervention and uncertainty about the effectiveness of the approach in improving reading, led a number of academics to resign from the editorial board of the publishing journal. The Dore approach has largely been based on the cerebellar deficit of dyslexia (Nicolson and Fawcett, 1995, 2001), which claims that the problems in learning to read are part of a brain-based problem in learning to become automatic in any skill, originally identified in balance (Nicolson and Fawcett, 1990) which can be traced to differences in the cerebellum in dyslexia. Converging evidence from a number of groups has supported this theory, with incidence of deficits ranging from 50–80 per cent dependent on the age group tested and the task used, and evidence from neuroscience that the cerebellum is involved in reading and language. However, the theory does not suggest that balance training would improve reading, and indeed the cerebellar circuits for language are different from the motor circuits which would be affected by training. The Dore approach as originally instantiated was expensive to deliver, employing psychologists and medically trained personnel and using large-scale technical equipment to measure progress. Dore also promised to continue training until the children and adults involved were 'cured' in terms of their balance and eye movements in return for an inclusive fee. Many of the children attending had complex problems, they had already received traditional intervention without much success, and their treatment was lengthier than Dore had originally anticipated. As this volume goes to press, Dore has run into financial difficulties, closing his centres, and fuelling controversy in the media further, amidst fears that parents will lose the money they have paid out. Dore has agreed to provide web-based support for families undertaking the training, and promised to provide a free service to non-profit making organisations. Nevertheless, it is not clear whether public confidence in the approach can ever be restored.

Other movement approaches

There has been long-standing interest in exercise and therapies based on movement for children with dyslexia and other associated conditions. Fitts and Posner (1967) provided an account of the learning stages in motor skill development and, particularly, the development of automaticity. Denckla and Rudel (1976) found that children with dyslexia had a deficit in rapid, automatised naming, and Denckla (1985) suggested that children with dyslexia are characterised by a 'non-specific developmental awkwardness' that is irrespective of athletic ability. In terms of intervention, Doman and Delacato (see Tannock, 1976) through a series of exercises related motor development to the development of other cognitive skills, although it is important to note that this approach is itself controversial and has not been scientifically evaluated. The work of Ayres (1979) has been developed considerably by Blythe (1992), Blythe and Goddard (2000), Goddard Blythe and Hyland (1998), Dobie (1996), Goddard Blythe (2005). A series of exercises have emerged from the Institute of Neuro Developmental Physiological Psychology (INPP) based in the UK. According to Blythe the term NDD or Neuro Developmental Delay describes the omission or arrest of a stage of early development. Blythe established INPP to investigate the links between physical development and problems with reading, writing, spelling, coordination, behaviour and emotional functioning in both children and adults. It is based on the view that every normal, full-term baby is born with a set of primitive or survival reflexes that are inhibited or controlled by higher centres in the brain during the first year of life. If these are not inhibited at the correct time, they remain active in the body and can interfere with balance, motor control, eye functioning, eye–hand coordination and perceptual skills and this can result in behavioural symptoms such as frustration, hyperactivity and hypersensitivity, and failure to match performance to ability. Blythe and Goddard Blythe (Goddard Blythe, 2005) suggest that sympoms such as difficulty learning to ride a bicycle, mixed laterality (preferred foot, hand, ear, eye, etc.) above the age of 8 years, and a range of literacy difficulties can be accounted for by neuro-developmental delay.

For many years evidence for this approach was based on anecdotal reports and case histories, all of which indicated success but which did not constitute scientific evidence. In her recent book, Goddard Blythe (2005) investigated the extent of this in a study with 810 children with special educational needs in order to assess whether neurological dysfunction was a significant factor underlying academic achievement.

The progress of 339 children aged 4 to 5 years of age was tracked through the school year to see whether children with higher scores on the INPP Developmental Test Battery (indications of neurological dysfunction) performed less well academically at the end of the school year and 235 children aged 8–10 years undertook a specific programme of developmental exercises (the INPP Schools' Developmental Exercise Programme) for 10 minutes a day under teacher supervision over the course of one academic year. The results showed that the children who participated in the daily INPP exercises made significantly greater improvement on measures for neurological dysfunction, balance and coordination when compared to a control group. Children who had scores of more than 25 per cent on tests for neurological dysfunction and whose reading age was less than their chronological age at the outset also showed small but significantly greater progress in reading than children who did not take part in the programme. Goddard Blythe and Bythe have published a considerable amount of data to support the programme and have engaged heavily in training programmes and the recipients of this training are actively engaged in implementing this form of treatment in clinics and in schools. Peer reviewed articles however would further help to support these impressive claims.

The most rigorous approach adopted to NLP has been from McPhillips and his colleagues, who ran a double blind randomised controlled study of the effects of NLP intervention in children with specific reading difficulties (McPhillips et al., 2000). Sixty children matched on age, sex, verbal IQ and persistent assymetric tonic neck reflex, with problems on a sentence reading test were identified in the school system. Children were then given further standardized tests of reading, and randomly assigned to experimental, motor skill placebo or control group. At the post-test 12 months later, the experimental group had significantly improved in their reflexes, and made substantially greater gains in reading than the two control groups. The approach was then extended to include groups of children at the bottom, middle and top 10 per cent of readers age, aged 9–10, with 41 in each group (McPhillips and Sheehy 2004). Persistent reflexes were checked by an experimenter blind to reading levels and an association with poor reading identified. In a further example of the approach in a study in Western Australia, Taylor (2002), following the approach of Blythe and Goddard Blythe, examined the effects of retention of primitive reflexes in children diagnosed as ADHD. Her results supported the evidence of the importance of this area for cognitive development and learning and, in fact, suggested 'cumulative associations between high stresses, atypical brain lateralization and uninhibited reflexes on scholastic competency' (pp. 216–217).

Brain Gym

Brain Gym or educational Kinesiology is a good example of an alternative approach that has become very mainstream. It is based on the work of Dennison (Dennison, 1981; Dennison and

Hargrove, 1985), Dennison and Dennison (1997, 2001) and Hannaford (1995, 1997) on the importance of dominance and laterality and, particularly, the influence of dominance patterns on learning have also been influential in classrooms, especially with children with specific learning difficulties. Information provided on the website gives a broad range of academic studies, many of them published in the Brain Gym journal. However, a more recent review of the research in the area (Hyatt, 2007) concludes that both the theory and the experimental evidence provided do not support the current wide use in the school environment.

Conclusions on motor skill training.

There has been considerable interest over the years in the concept of motor skills training in schools, and there is considerable anecdotal evidence to support the beneficial effects of these approaches. We are becoming more aware that our children need the opportunity for exercise to improve their health and their congitive functioning. The approaches which have been evaluated in peer reviewed published studies include the Dore programme, and NLP, but there remains considerable controversy over the Dore approach and more research is clearly needed, funded by someone with no interest in the outcomes. It is interesting to note that around two thirds of children in Northern Ireland now receive regular training to eliminate retained reflexes, in 10-minute whole class sessions based on McPhillips work. Training is provided by a charity for one teacher in each school at a reasonable cost, but there have been no claims that retained reflexes are associated with dyslexia, indeed they seem to be found in all poor readers, and there has been no associated controversy.

Visual approaches

There are a number of different visual treatments that have been specifically marketed for treating dyslexia. Most are commercially operated and run by private companies although some have close links with universities and other research establishments.

Scotopic sensitivity

This term was first used in 1983 when Helen Irlen presented a paper on Scotopic Sensitivity Syndrome at the annual meeting of the American Psychological Association. She proposed that tinted glasses would improve the reading ability of dyslexic children and following that paper the treatment became popularised and sensationalised before there was time for sufficient control studies to be carried out to verify the claims (Silver, 2001). Scotopic sensitivity, which is now more commonly referred to as Meares–Irlen Syndrome, refers to the presence of a visual defect that can be related to difficulties with light source, glare, wave length and black and white contrast. Irlen (1994) in fact reported on a number of areas of difficulty, such as:

- eye strain
- poor visual resolution
- reduced span of focus
- impaired depth perception
- poor sustained focus.

The assessment procedures for the above are usually carried out though a screening process by people who have undergone courses to become screeners. Some optometrists also carry out such screening. During the screening the individual is asked a series of questions after being shown pages containing different patterns, musical notes, geometric figures and words. Observations are then made on how he/she responds to these. For example observations will be made on the length of concentration span, whether the figures jump, run off the page, merge and if vision is blurred when concentrating on complex visual images. The colour of any lenses that are prescribed are usually determined by the responses to these factors as well as some additional and more sophisticated laboratory procedures.

It was initially difficult to establish a scientific basis for the Irlen approach, and in view of the high cost of the lenses there were some concerns that any positive effects of coloured lenses might be based on a placebo effect. Much of the supporting evidence for the success of visual treatments is anecdotal. At the same time the treatment has been very popular and many recipients of the treatment have claimed it has been successful. Arnold Wilkins, a scientist with the Medical Research Council (Wilkins, 2002), clearly supports the notion of visual stress and produced a sophisticated screening device which he called the Intuitive Colorimeter that measures the degree of therapeutic tint. Wilkins has performed a number of controlled scientific studies to examine the effectiveness of the use of tinted glasses following assessment using the Intuitive Colorimeter (Wilkins *et al.*, 1996; Scott *et al.*, 2002). Double-masked placebo controlled studies by Wilkins, based on the use of the Colorimeter, have reduced any concerns on the scientific basis of the lens. The Colorimeter allows a child to select the colour which they find most useful in reducing any effects of glare, which can be used as a coloured overlay or built into a pair of glasses. Using the Colorimeter, the child cannot see which colour they have chosen, and they are then tested with that colour (which is helpful) and the opposite colour (which is not helpful). If the effects were based on placebo, then using either overlay should be helpful, but the effects are specific to using the correct overlay. Wilkins also demonstrates the benefits of coloured lenses in individuals with migraine headaches (Evans *et al.*, 2002), and suggests that the lenses work by cutting down glare and cortical hyperexcitability. The approach adopted now to validate the use of the lens, is to look for immediate improvements (typically more than 5 per cent) on the Wilkins Rate of Reading test. In a review of the syndrome (Kriss and Evans, 2005) studies suggest a prevalence rate of 20–34 per cent, and identify two rigorous double blind studies, Wilkins *et al.*, 1994, and Robinson and Foreman, 1999. These studies explain why results differ between studies, because the colour needs to be defined very precisely in order to be effective.

In the following section we describe two types of filter, based on the work of Wilkins, using information derived from their websites The cost of the lens is around £350, but a cheaper option to consider is the use of coloured overlays which can also be beneficial in terms of reading speed and reduced stress for some children.

ChromaGen

ChromaGen™ is a range of precision tinted Haploscopic Filters of a specific density and hue – individually prescribed for patients – that are worn as either contact lenses or spectacles. ChromaGen™ according to the website http://www.dyslexia-help.co.uk/chromagen_helps_ dyslexia.html has been clinically proven to dramatically improve accuracy of reading, writing and comprehension. According to their website recent study by one of their own practitioners involving over 400 children found that over 90 per cent of the subjects reported a significant improvement in reading, writing and comprehension levels when wearing ChromaGen™ coloured glasses and contact lenses and showed a minimum 45 per cent improvement in their reading, writing and handwriting skills over a six-month assessment period. Tests covered reading speed and accuracy, and handwriting accuracy and presentation. The performance of each child was measured throughout the six-month period. They also suggest that ChromaGen™ is not a cure for either reading disorders including visual dyslexia or colour vision problems. ChromaGen™ is only a management system that can assist in both applications to break barriers and help transform lives. It is heartening to read a statement such as this in a climate of mass cures and exaggerated claims for miracle treatment of dyslexia.

Tintavision

TintaVision is a commercial outlet for a company that offers testing and treatment to identify the best colour of overlay or filter for individuals. TintaVision has designed a process using computer software that can identify the colour of filter that maximises the rate of reading and edge detection for individual learners. Once identified, the appropriate filter is selected and learners use the filter as much as possible. Learners are also given colour coordinates to use as a background colour on a computer. This has the same effect as the filter when working on screen. After six to eight weeks, users are re-tested and, if necessary, a change of filter is provided. According to Irons (2007 personal communication) Tintavision is a company which has been set up to develop an understanding of 'access to text' from a purely biological angle. He maintains that their original work was based on research from the Medical Research Council on the link between colour and reading. Most of their activities have been mainly confined to dyslexic undergraduates. They have also applied the protocols with FE and school students with outstanding success. Over the last two years we have seen and worked with over 700 clients who have been diagnosed as dyslexic by educational psychologists and in over 90 per cent of cases the outcomes have been very positive. They claim that all of the work is objective/quantitatively based (http://lists.becta.org.uk/pipermail/senco-forum/2000-May/009344.html).

Conclusions – visual approaches and coloured lens

The evidence suggests that scotopic sensitivity is a recognised problem which can be ameliorated by the use of the appropriate coloured lens, but that it is found in the general population as well as in dyslexia. Interestingly, Kriss and Evans show that the difference in prevalence between dyslexic and non-dyslexic readers is not significant, although they suggest that children who have dyslexia and the Meares–Irlen Syndrome are likely to be particularly impaired. Recent analyses of the visual processing characteristics of children with Meares–Irlen (Kruk *et al.*, 2008) suggest that these children differ from those with traditional dyslexic difficulties in visual processing, that Meares Irlen may represent a problem in visual spatial attention, and that it can be associated with any type of dyslexia. Use of lens or overlays cuts down glare and improves the speed of reading in crowded text.

Pharmaceutical/dietary approaches

Richardson (2001) suggests that there is a wide spectrum of conditions in which deficiencies of highly unsaturated fatty acids appear to have some influence. Further, Richardson argues that fatty acids can have an extremely important influence on dyslexia, dyspraxia and ADHD. Richardson argues that it is not too controversial to suggest that there is a high incidence of overlap between these three syndromes. In fact, she suggests that overlap between dyslexia and ADHD can be around 30–50 per cent and even higher in the case of dyspraxia. Richardson also argues that the truly essential fatty acids (EFA), which cannot be synthesized by the body, must be provided in the diet – these are linoleic acid (omega-6 series) and alpha-linoleic acid (omega 3 series). She suggests that the longer chain highly unsaturated fatty acids (HUFA) that the brain needs can normally be synthesized from EFAs but, this conversion process can be severely affected and limited by dietary and lifestyle factors. Some of the dietary factors, for example, which can block the conversion of EFA to HUFA include excess saturated fats, hydrogenated fats found in processed foods, deficiencies in vitamins and minerals as well as excessive consumption of coffee and alcohol, and smoking. Richardson suggests that the claims connecting hyperactivity and lack of EFA are not new. Colquhoun and Bunday (1981) noted various clinical signs of possible EFA deficiency in a survey of hyperactive children, and Richardson reports on further studies that support these early claims (Stevens *et al.,* 1996; Richardson and Puri, 2000). Furthermore, studies on dyspraxia have highlighted the possibility of links with EFA and suggested that fatty acids supplements can be beneficial (Sordy, 1995, 1997). In relation to dyslexia and ADHD, Richardson suggests that fatty acid supplements have also shown to be successful, and supplementation has been associated with improvements in reading. She further reports on school-based trials, indicating that this intervention can be realistically applied in schools (Richardson, 2002; Portwood, 2002). The most recent evidence emerging on fatty acids and dyslexia in adults by Richardson and her colleagues (Cyhlarova *et al.,* 2007) shows that reading performance in both dyslexics and controls is linked to higher total Omega-3 concentration, and that for dyslexic subjects was negatively related to Omega-6 concentration, suggesting that it is the balance between the two which is relevant to dyslexia.

Conclusions on fatty acids

Research on fatty acids by Richardson and her colleagues has been undertaken carefully, and the group have not promoted their findings until their research was well-developed, despite the inevitable pressure from the manufacturers of the fatty acids who have funded the research. It is interesting to note that the levels recommended involve higher concentrations than normally recommended for supplementation and that the cost of daily supplementation is therefore relatively higher. John Stein (2003) now promotes the importance of fish in improving Omega-3 levels, linking this to his theoretical research on the magnocellular deficit in dyslexia, and presenting his research in conjunction with cookery demonstrations by his brother Rick Stein.

Approaches using new technology

Tallal and her colleagues (1998) have claimed that, like language disordered children, children with dyslexia take longer to process sounds which change rapidly. This is tested with high and low tones, or the sounds *ba* and *da*, which are only different in the first few milliseconds. Children with dyslexia (and Specific Language Impairment) cannot tell the difference between the sounds if they are presented close together, and this means that they are likely to have problems with phonological awareness. This theory has been under development for the last 30 years.

In terms of intervention, the Fast ForWord programme has been designed to train children in just those changes which prove most difficult for them. In order to help them to be successful, the sounds they hear are drawn out by 50 per cent so that they sound like whale noises, and with this prolonged presentation children learn to complete the task.

Two different sequences are used:

1 Circus sequence: based on perceptual identification
2 Phonetic recognition which one of two phonetic elements was first presented (e.g. /be/ . . . /de/)

The program starts at an easy level with slowed down onset and as the children progress the onsets become faster and faster. Children are asked to complete around 10 hours' practice a week in 20 minute sessions for six to eight weeks, which leads to significant improvements in their ability on the games and also on the Tallal test. Note that children are pretested and retested with natural sounds, and so training with acoustically modified sounds leads to improvements in dealing with natural language.

This intervention has been highly controversial amongst researchers and educators. This is largely because not enough research was done or published on the effects of the intervention before it was marketed. Moreover, although Paula Tallal is careful to explain that much of her research is with Specific Language Impaired children, and that only a proportion of dyslexic children show deficits of this type, the Haskins lab, a highly reputable speech lab in the US with whom Paula was formerly associated were particularly keen to refute her claims (see Mody *et al.*, 1997). Even dyslexic children showing characteristic difficulties in phonology do not necessarily show problems with rapid auditory processing. Consequently, although Paula Tallal is an eminent researcher and a good cognitive psychologist, the negative response to her claims has meant that at one stage her work was excluded from main stream conferences on dyslexia.

Criticisms include the following:

1 A control group is needed who receive some alternative training to control for Hawthorne effects.
2 Studies need to show that this helps reading or phoneme identification rather than just language.
3 Most researchers would expect that intensive training on a particular task would lead to improvements!

In a controlled study Hook *et al.* (2001) found that their Fast ForWord group showed significant gains in phonemic awareness following intensive training, but after two years, gains in spoken language and reading were no greater than a control group which received no intervention, and not as good as children undertaking a more traditional intervention. It is claimed that a major drawback is the lack of flexibility in the Fast ForWord system, which means that it is not possible to vary the program systematically to check which aspects are helpful. A new programme currently under evaluation, Fast ForWord Language to Reading has now been developed as a second stage to improve reading, based on the use of normal consonants.

Most recent evaluations of the suite of Fast ForWord products, drawn from the IeS US Department of Education website (July, 2007) have identified five studies from the 115 which they reviewed which meet their stringent criteria for evidence standards, based on randomised controlled trials. More than half of the studies reviewed were reports from Scientific Learning Corporation, who distribute Fast ForWord. These studies, including 587 children from kindergarten to 3rd grade show that there were positive effects on alphabetics (mean an improvement of 8 percentile points) and mixed effects on comprehension (mean an improvement of 1 percentile point), but the website considers the evidence for improvement to be small. None of the studies meeting the criteria address fluency or general reading achievement.

Conclusions on Fast ForWord

It would be fair to say that there is still some controversy over the effectiveness of Fast ForWord, although Merzenich and colleagues (e.g Temple *et al.*, 2000) are now showing evidence of changes in the brain following completion of training which suggest a normalisation of the processing underlying reading. Moreover, there have been extensive studies of the effectiveness, and although only five studies here meet the criteria for a double blind placebo controlled study, there are a range of studies which would be judged satisfactory under less stringent criteria. Fast ForWord is used widely in the USA, with over 570,000 students using the programme in 3700 schools nationwide. Schools taking part buy a licence for use of the programme, with costs ranging from $500–$900 depending on the programme, and no discount for quantity.

Measuring progress: The techniques

In order to evaluate change, a range of parameters need to be measured, which include the effectiveness and cost effectiveness of the change, that is how much effect the therapy has and how much money it cost to achieve that level. There are important issues here in terms of the types of change, is it a general rather than a specific change, and should this be seen as a primary or a secondary effect. One of the more difficult aspects to measure is whether the changes reflect the Placebo, Hawthorne, or Pygmalion effects. A placebo effect is based on the expectation of change, so that even a sugar pill will produce the effects which have been described. A Hawthorne effect is based on the extra interest taken in the children, which leads them to blossom under the positive input. Finally, the Pygmalion effect was found when teachers were simply told to expect great things from certain children, and their re-evaluation of the potential of the children did indeed lead to improvements. The causes of the change are therefore critical in evaluating therapies – have they led to changes in the brain, to changes in cognitive behaviour or is it simply the environment which has changed thus allowing a child the possibility of greater success. Finally, how valuable is the change, will it transfer to other skills, lead to permanent improvements, and what efforts will be needed to maintain progress?

What can we learn from studying alternative approaches

It may be seen from the questions above that it can be difficult to evaluate therapies objectively, and that how useful they seem may be critically dependent on who is evaluating them, theorist, policy maker, parent or practitioner. It is important to recognise here that there different parameters for success and failure. Parents and their children seek immediate effects, and may not really be concerned as to why an intervention works, only whether it does. Indeed, for most parents, happiness is a more salient criterion than literacy. It seems that most one-to-one interventions will be fairly effective, even if only via generalised factors. Alternative therapies remind us that there are issues to consider beyond the reading and spelling approach adopted by traditional interventions, which are concerned with how the child is achieving within the school environment. Clearly we would not wish to underestimate the importance of becoming literate for the child in realising their potential. Nevertheless, alternative therapies are focused more on the whole child, rather than on their achievements. Many of these approaches would claim that they are equipping the child to become a more successful learner, and there are a number of very real issues here. Improving the child's self-esteem, improving the child's health with dietary supplements, improving the child's language processing, or cutting down the aversive glare which affects their ability to concentrate, all these can have potent and lasting

168

effects on progress. The issue of whether or not these therapies are affecting the brain and making real changes has not been fully proven and further research is needed. It is important to remember here that we are dealing with individual children who have been damaged by their failure to acquire the literacy skills which others take for granted. For many of these children, traditional interventions mean many further hours of trying to struggle with the skills they find most difficult. Any therapy which allows them to approach these tasks with renewed vigour could be said to have some contribution to make.

Traditional approaches: Does 'old' mean 'bad'?

According to Reynolds (2008) part of the difficulty is that there is an absence of proof of validity of the existing treatments. He suggests for example that in relation to conventional phonics-based interventions the effect is minimal and will 'wash out six to nine months after the intervention ceases'. Therefore according to Reynolds phonics is not a powerful intervention.

The technique used to measure improvements in intervention studies is called an 'effect size'. These allow comparisons to be made between different studies, to see which is the most successful. This is particularly important in intervention studies, where significant differences between the techniques are unusual although there may be subtle differences between the groups. Effect sizes are worked out by taking the mean performance of the control group from the mean performance of the intervention group, and dividing this by the standard deviation of the two groups. This allows any differences between the two groups to be measured, taking into account the variability within the group at the start. Note that this makes no attempt to measure the amount of time which was needed to achieve the effect (cost-effectiveness will be discussed later in the chapter). In terms of an equation an effect size would be as follows:

(Mean intervention − Mean control)/(Mean of standard deviation intervention + standard deviation control).

An effect size of 0 means that the two groups are the same. An effect size of + or − 1 means that the intervention group is around 1 standard deviation better/worse than the control group. In terms of the statistical significance of effects sizes, 0.20 is considered low, 0.50 is moderate and 0.80 is high (Cohen, 1969). Remember that if the group used is small with little variability within it, effect sizes will be artificially larger, because the standard deviation − the number used for division − will be smaller.

In order to illustrate how difficult it can be to make any difference with an intervention, it is useful to understand that even well designed interventions based on 35 hours extra teaching over a year using a well-tried method, the Orton-Gillingham approach, can achieve an effect size of as little as 0.04 improvement in reading in comparison with a control group who received normal teaching. An analysis of the 100 effect sizes derived from the National Reading Panel's meta-analysis suggests that high effect sizes of 0.8 and over are found in around a third of the studies reported there (32/100) whereas effect sizes of 2.0 and over were comparatively rare (6/100).

In working out the effects of intervention it is also important to take into account the natural development with age, which should mean that the control group have made some progress without intervention. If the effect size for the corresponding control groups is subtracted from that for the intervention groups, the 'added value' effect size for the intervention can be seen. This allows a check to be made on the difference between the control group and the intervention group, and provides a measure of improvement beyond that expected in the natural process of development. This technique is not routinely adopted, although it is held to be good practice.

When considering outcomes from an intervention study, it would be hardly surprising if children improved on the skill in which they had been directly trained. However, there may also be evidence of near transfer or far transfer. Near transfer means that there are improvements in skills only indirectly related to the skill trained. Intervention studies seek evidence of far transfer, so that a skill held to be unrelated to the trained skill, is improved. Naturally, this is the most difficult to achieve, and so most studies of phonological intervention look at near transfer to reading, and possibly far transfer to spelling. Note that the alternative interventions which are not based on phonological intervention are by definition evaluated on far transfer. Finally, it is useful to establish that improvements are not just a general Hawthorne effect of the greater interest taken in the child. This means that evidence should be specific to the skill in question, rather than just a generalised improvement (good as this might be!).

In this section and the sections which follow, the effect sizes of each intervention will be included in brackets. Data from the National Reading Panel (2001a) including all published studies from which sufficient data was available to compute effect sizes, showed that phonemic awareness training is effective in improving skills such as segmenting (0.87), blending (0.61) and deletion (0.82), but has only low impact on reading skills (0.33) So the intervention has improved the skills targeted, but there is less evidence of near transfer to reading. Intervention is most successful if not given for too long, with a moderate effect of training for 1–4 hours and high effect size for five hours plus. Surprisingly, effects decline if training is given for more than 20 weeks, possibly because children become bored with the repetition once they have mastered the concepts. Training of this type is effective with all ages but most strikingly with pre-school children (with an exceptional effect size of 2.37), when delivered in a group (1.38), by teachers researchers or computers, and with high or low SES children. These skills have been shown to be important predictors of reading success and it is encouraging to note that they are remarkably easy to teach to young children.

In terms of transfer to reading however, as noted above, there is only a low impact on reading on standardized tests (0.33), although there is a larger effect on experimenter's word lists (0.61). This is largely because standardized tests often include irregular words, for which phonemic training is really no help, whereas experimenter's lists will typically contain words which have been included in aspects of the training. Transfer to comprehension is similar (0.32). Again, impact is greatest in preschool children (1.25), and those who are at risk (0.86). Interestingly, the findings on phonemic awareness training suggest that it is most effective when combined with letters (0.67 around twice as effective as without letters), which makes it essentially *phonics* training.

More recent evaluations drawn from the IES website (July 2007) allow comparisons to be made between different reading programmes. The approach adopted is to measure the improvement in terms of an index of improvement, based on comparison of the improvement for the average student in the intervention group, with the average student in the control group, with scores ranging from +50 to −50, The most difficult task is to improve children's standard scores in literacy, because these take age into account, and are often based on irregular words which do not improve with phonological training. It is important to note therefore that control children typically fall back over the time course of an intervention, because their performance does not improve, but they get older. Effectiveness is rated in terms of the quality of the research design, the statistical difference, the size of the difference, and the consitency in findings across studies. The extent of the evidence tells readers how much evidence was used, based on the number and size of the studies. Looking at 887 studies which reviewed 153 reading programmes up to grade 3, only 27 studies met evidence standards, and a further 24 met standards with reservations. Of the acceptable approaches, Early Intervention in reading shows improvements of +36, but the evidence base is small, Reading Recovery shows improvement of +34, again with a small evidence base, whereas Ladders to Literacy shows less improvement at +25, but is based on a medium to large evidence base. If we search expressly for phonics interventions, there are no studies which yet meet the IES standards.

The IES system is laudable to produce a proper benchmarking system, but there are a number of issues missing here. First, there is no attempt to measure the persistence of effectiveness over time, and the 'wash-out' effect cited by Reynolds is well known in the literature – that once the intervention stops the effects dissipate. In a really useful bench-marking system we would need some measure of effectiveness over time, so we would be interested in studies with a follow-up. We also need some measure of cost-effectiveness, how many hours of teacher time are needed in order to achieve the improvements noted. It is well-known for example that Reading recovery is very cost-intensive, and it might well be that similar gains could be obtained with group interventions over a shorter time scale. Finally, do we really need to to dismiss all the published studies which do not meet these criteria, or should we have a sliding scale, where we could perhaps see studies as working towards achieving validation.

The way forward

It is clear that in order to evaluate alternative interventions, we need to set up a system of benchmarking. Here we need to consider a number of ways to measure change, which show whether or not intervention has proved successful:

a) Improvement in literacy and skills
   - Standardized tests
   - Curriculum based tests
   - Underlying skills
b) Improvement in engagement
   - Quality of life – self-esteem and confidence
   - Behaviour and motivation
   - Attention
c) Costs
   - Financial
   - Time parent/child
   - Time teacher
d) Persistence over time
   - Effects after six months
   - Effects after one year
   - Continuous improvement
e) The strength of the evidence
   - Anecdotal
   - Case studies
   - Pre- and post-group evaluation
   - Controlled cross-over
   - Double blind placebo controlled.

The IES system as currently instantiated looks only at improvement on standardized tests following double blind placebo controlled studies. In the system we are proposing, all the aspects above should be included in this evaluation, remembering that standardized tests may be the last to show positive effects. It is clear that there are a range of interventions available – and there may be different reasons why they work. If the particular aspect of these therapies which differ from traditional interventions are considered, it seems that they all allow children a fresh start. Rather than exposing them to literacy where they expect to fail (again!), each child is pitted against himself in improving his performance in a series of relatively novel tasks. In adopting these techniques, both parent and child are subscribing to a belief system, which holds that this particular intervention is the answer to their difficulties. The effect on self-esteem and motivation to succeed must account for at least a proportion of the success of these alternative techniques.

Conclusion

In this chapter we have considered a range of alternative therapies, and why they may be gaining ground. We have considered the strengths and weaknesses of these approaches, and cautioned against uncritically accepting claims based on anecdotal evidence and published on websites. We have discussed the issues arising around methodologies for evaluating interventions, and discovered that the majority of studies on which we base our thinking do not satisfy the most stringent criteria. We have discussed the differences in outlook between researchers, practitioners and parents, and how these differences may affect the type of support sought. We have advocated a system of benchmarking which can identify whether there is any evidence for the usefulness of alternative therapies, and which type of child might benefit, in order to provide information to parents. It is important to bear in mind that children show different profiles of difficulty, within the syndrome of dyslexia, dyslexia plus ADHD and dyspraxia. Research indicates that early interventions are the most effective in 'accelerating' literacy for many children, but those children who are resistant to intervention will show entrenched problems and need intensive 1:1 support such as provided by standard reading therapy. A combination of traditional teaching and alternative therapy might well prove the most effective, producing truly multi-sensory teaching for some children with severe and complex difficulties. However, overall, if a choice must be made between alternative and traditional approaches, we would only ever see alternative therapy as complementary to the tried and tested traditional interventions with which we are all familiar.

References

Ayres, A.J. (1979) *Sensory Integration and the Child*. Los Angeles, CA: Western Psychological Services.

Blythe, P. (1992) *A Physical Approach to Resolving Specific Learning Difficulties*. Chester: Institute for Neuro-Physiological Psychology.

Blythe, P. and Goddard, S. (2000) *Neuro-Phsysiological Assessment Test Battery*. 4 Stanley Place, Chester, England: INNP.

Cohen, J. (1969) *Statistical Power Analysis for the Behavioral Sciences*. New York: Academic Press.

Colquhoun, I. and Bunday, S. (1981) A lack of essential fatty acids as a possible cause of hyperactivity in children. *Medical Hypothesis*, 7, 673–679.

Cyhlarova, E., Bell, J.G., Dick, J.R., Mackinlay, E.E., Stein, J.F. and Richardson, A.J. (2007). Membrane fatty acids, reading and spelling in dyslexic and non-dyslexic adults. *European Neuropsychopharmacology*, 17, 116–121.

Denckla, M.B. (1985) Motor co-ordination in dyslexic children: Theoretical and clinical implications. In F.H. Duffy and N. Geschwind (eds) *Dyslexia: A Neuroscientific Approach to Clinical Evaluation*. Boston, MA: Little Brown.

Denckla, M.B. and Rudel, R.G. (1976) Rapid 'automatised' naming (RAN): Dyslexia differentiated from other learning disabilities. *Neuropsychologia*, 14, 471–479.

Dennison, G.E. and Dennison, P.E. (1997) *The Brain Gym © Handbook*. California: Edu-Kinesthetics Inc.

Dennison, G.E. and Dennison, P.E. (2000) *Educational Kinesiology Brain Organisation Profiles. Teachers Training Manual*, 3rd edition. California: Edu-Kinesthetics Inc.

Dennison, G.E. and Dennison, P.E. (1989) *Educational Kinesiology Brain Organisation Profiles*. California: Edu-Kinesthetics Inc.

Dennison, G.E. and Dennison, P.E. (2001) *Brain Gym © Course Manual*. California: Edu-Kinesthetics Inc.

Dennison, P.E. (1981) *Switching On: The Holistic Answer to Dyslexia*. California: Edu-Kinesthetics Inc.

Dennison, P.E. and Hargrove, G. (1985) *Personalized Whole Brain Integration*. California: Edu-Kinesthetics, Glendale.

Dobie, S. (1996) Perceptual motor and neurodevelopmental dimensions in identifying and remediating developmental delay in children with specific learning difficulties. In G. Reid (ed.), *Dimensions of Dyslexia*. Edinburgh: Moray House Publications.

Evans, B.J.W., Patel, R. and Wilkins, A.J. (2002) Optometric function in visually sensitive migraine before and after treatment with tinted spectacles. *Ophthalmic and Physiological Optics*, 22, 2, 130–142.

Fitts, P.M. and Posner, M.I. (1967) *Human Performance*. Belmont, CA: Brooks Cole.

Goddard Blythe, S. (2005) Releasing educational potential through movement. *Child Care in Practice, 11* (4), 415–432.

Goddard Blythe, S. and Hyland, D. (1998) Screening for neurological dysfunction in the specific learning difficulties child. *British Journal of Occupational Therapy*, 61 (10), 459–464.

Hannaford, C. (1995) *Smart Moves. Why Learning is Not All in Your Head*. Virginia: Great Ocean Publishers.

Hannaford, C. (1997) *The Dominance Factor. How Knowing Your Dominant Eye, Ear, Brain, Hand and Foot Can Improve Your Learning*. Virginia: Great Ocean Publishers.

Hook, P.E., Macaruso, P. and Jones, S. (2001) Efficacy of Fast ForWord training on facilitating acquisition of reading skills by children with reading difficulties. *Annals of Dyslexia*, 51, 73–96.

Hyatt, Keith J. (2007) Brain Gym®: Building stronger brains or wishful thinking? *Remedial and Special Education*, 28, 117–124.

IES What works clearing house (2007) http://ies.ed.gov/ncee/wwc/reports. Institue of Education Sciences, US Department of Education.

Irlen, H. (1994) Scotopic sensitivity/Irlen syndrome: Hypothesis and explanation of the syndrome. *Journal of Behavioural Optometry*, 5, 62–65.

Kriss, I. and Evans, B.J.W (2005) The relationship between dyslexia and Meares–Irlen syndrome. *Journal of Research in Reading*, 28, 350–364.

Kruk, R., Sumbler, K. and Willows, D. (2008) Visual processing characteristics of children with Meares–Irlen syndrome. *Opthalmic and Physiological Optics*, 28, 35–46.

McLaughlin, D. and Leather, C. (2008) Dyslexia: Meeting the needs of employers and employees in the workplace. In G. Reid (ed.) *The Routledge Companion to Dyslexia*. London: Routledge.

McPhillips, M., Hepper, P.G. and Mulhern, G. (2000) Effects of replicating primary-reflex movements on specific reading difficulties in children: A randomised, double blind, controlled trial. *The Lancet*, 355, 537–541.

McPhillips, M. and Sheehy, N. (2004). Prevalence of persistent primary reflexes and motor problems in children with reading difficulties. *Dyslexia*, 10 (4), 316–338.

Mody, M., Studdert Kennedy, M. and Brady, S. (1997) Speech perception deficits in poor readers: Auditory processing or phonological coding? *Journal of Experimental Child Psychology*, 64 (2), 199–231.

National Reading Panel (2001a) *National Reading Panel Report*. Washington, DC: US Government.

National Reading Panel (2001b) *Teaching Children to Read: An evidence-based assessment of the scientific research literature on reading and its implications for reading instruction*. Washington, DC: US Government.

Nicolson, R.I. and Fawcett, A.J. (1990) Automaticity: a new framework for dyslexia research. *Cognition*, 30, 159–182.

Nicolson, R.I., Fawcett, A.J. and Dean, P. (1995) Time estimation deficits in developmental dyslexia: Evidence for cerebellar involvement. *Proceedings of the Royal Society: Biological Sciences*, 259, 43–47.

Nicolson, R.I., Fawcett, A.J. and Dean, P. (2001) Developmental dyslexia: the cerebellar deficit hypothesis, *Trends in Neurosciences*, 24, 508–512.

Portwood, M. (2002) School based trials of fatty acid supplements. Paper presented at Education Conference Durham County Council, June.

Reynolds, D. (2008) *Support for People with Dyslexia in Wales*. Report of the Enterprise and Learning Committee, available at www.assemblywales.org.

173

Reynolds, D. and Nicolson, R.I. (2007) Follow-up of an exercise-based treatment for children with reading difficulties. *Dyslexia, 13* (2), 78–96.

Richardson, A.J. (2001) *Dyslexia, Dyspraxia and ADHD – Can Nutrition Help?* Paper presented at 4th Cambridge Conference, Helen Arkell Dyslexia Association, March, Cambridge.

Richardson, A.J. and Puri, B.K. (2000) The potential role of fatty acids in Attention deficit/hyperactivity disorder (ADHD). *Prostaglandins Leukotr Essent Fatty Acids,* 63, 79–87.

Richardson, A.J. and Puri, B.K. (2002) A randomized double-blind, placebo-controlled study of the effects of supplementation with highly unsaturated fatty acids on ADHD-related symptoms in children with specific learning difficulties. *Progress in Neuro-Psychopharmacology and Biological Psychiatry, 26* (2), 233–239.

Robinson, G.L., and Foreman, PJ. (1999) Scotopic sensitivity/Irlen syndrome and the use of coloured filters: A long term placebo controlled and masked study of reading achievement and perception of ability. *Perceptual and Motor Skills,* 89, 83–113.

Rose, J. (2007) Rose Report on Reading. London: DfES.

Scott, L., McWhinnie, H. and Taylor, L. (2002) Coloured overlays in schools: orthoptic and optometric findings. *Ophthalmic and Physiological Optics, 22,* 156–165.

Silver, L. (2001) Controversial therapies. *Perspectives* 27 (3) 1,4. The International Dyslexia Association, Baltimore, MD, USA.

Stein, J. (2003) Visual motion sensitivity and reading , *Neuropsychologia, 41* (13), 1785–1793.

Stevens, L.J., Zentall, S.S., Abate, M.L., Kuczek, T. and Burgess, J.R. (1996) Omega-3 fatty acids in boys with behaviour, learning and health problems. *Physiology and Behaviour,* 59, 915–920.

Stordy, B.J. (1995) Benefit of docosahexaenoic acid supplements to dark-adaptation in dyslexics. *Lancet, 346,* 8971, 385–385.

Stordy, B.J. (1997) Dyslexia, attention deficit hyperactivity disorder, dyspraxia: Do fatty acids help? *Dyslexia Review,* 9 (2).

Tallal, P., Merzenich, M.M., Miller, S. and Jenkins, W. (1998) Language learning impairments: integrating basic science, technology, and remediation. *Experimental Brain Research,123,* 210–219.

Tannock, R. (1976) Doman-Delacato method for treating brain injured children. *Physiotherapy,* 28 (4).

Taylor, M.F. (2002) Stress-induced atypical brain lateralization in boys with attention-deficit/hyperactivity disorder. Implications for scholastic performance. Unpublished PhD thesis, University of Western Australia, Perth, Australia.

Temple, E., Poldrack, R.A., Protopapas, A., Nagarajan, S., Salz, T., Tallal, P., Merzenich, M. and Gabrielim J.D. (2000) Disruption of the neural response to rapid acoustic stimuli in dyslexia: Evidence from functional MRI. *Proceedings of the National Academy of Sciences,* 97, 13907–13912.

Wilkins, A. (2002) Coloured overlays and their effects on reading speed: a review. *Ophthalmic and Physiological Optics, 22,* 5, 448–454.

Wilkins, A.J., Evans, B.J.W. and Brown, J.A (1994) Double maked placebo-controlled trial of precision spectral filters in children who use coloured overlays. *Opthalmic and Physiological Optics,* 14, 365–370.

Wilkins, A.J., Jeanes, J.R., Pumfrey, P.D. and Laskier, M. (1996) *Rate of Reading Test R: its reliability, and its validity in the assessment of the effects of coloured overlays.* MRC Applied Psychology Unit, 15 Chaucer Road, Cambridge.

Part 3

Identifying and meeting needs in an inclusive concept

Inclusion and the barriers to learning

13

How compatible is the recognition of dyslexia with inclusive education?

Brahm Norwich

This chapter makes the following points:

- dyslexia and inclusive education have to be analysed for their background meaning and use
- inclusion is analysed in terms of *flexible interacting continua of provision*
- bio–psycho–social framework required for understanding the origins and causes of 'difficulties' in literacy
- general literacy teaching can be connected to specialized programmes through a 'wave' model: 'response to teaching' model of identification complements direct child functioning model
- well-formulated ideas about more inclusive school provision depend on recognising specific learning difficulties (preferred term).

Introduction

Addressing the question of whether recognising dyslexia is compatible with the principles of inclusive education raises questions about two concepts which have usually been kept apart that have belonged to different, some would argue, conflicting perspectives. Inclusive education has often been associated with a critique of a deficit model of learning difficulties, sometimes referred to as the medical model (Thomas and Loxley, 2001). The notion of developmental dyslexia has its origins in medical thinking and practice in which some children's reading difficulties are separated out as different from general reading difficulties. (The term dyslexia will be used in this chapter to refer to developmental dyslexia). This chapter addresses these issues and aims to analyse various perspectives on these concepts and principles and to synthesise a position that links specific literacy difficulties with a model of inclusive provision based on a wave model.

Inclusive education

It is a commonplace that there are problems with existing concepts of inclusion and inclusive education. This arises partly because the term is used to do different things for different purposes. Given its policy significance, this is a serious matter that even the House of Commons Select Committee identified when urging that the: 'The Government should work harder to define exactly what it means by inclusion' (House of Commons, 2006: section 64).

The Government department, responded by trying to clarify its understanding of the term with the following: 'The Government shares the Committee's view that inclusion is about the quality of a child's experience and providing access to the high quality education which enables them to progress with their learning and participate fully in the activities of their school and community' (DfES, 2006: section 28).

This multi-faceted definition makes reference to (a) the quality of a child's experience (b) access to high quality education (c) progress in learning, and (d) participation in school activities and community. However, as a definition it is still vague as there is no clarification of what is involved in participating 'fully in the activities of their school'. It could mean participate in a separate school for children with dyslexic difficulties and not a typical school. This Government definition is consistent with an emphasis on an inclusive school system, where participation is not necessarily in local ordinary schools. This systems view of inclusion diverges from another influential concept of inclusion, for example: 'Participation in the cultures, curricula and communities of *local* schools' (Inclusion Index, Booth *et al.,* 2000).

The Inclusion Index definition implies a presence in local general schools that provide for a diversity of children from different social, ethnic and religious backgrounds. Though participation, in the latter definition, involves various kinds of participation, including social and academic, it is also does not clarify whether 'participation in local schools' requires that children with difficulties in learning be in ordinary classrooms for all or most of lesson time. The Centre for the Study of Inclusive Education (CSIE), which has promoted a strong form on inclusive education, stated in its inclusion charter that:

> Time spent out of the ordinary classroom for appropriate individual or group work on a part-time basis is not segregation. Neither is removal for therapy or because of disruption, provided it is time-limited, for a specified purpose . . . Any time-out from the ordinary classroom should not affect a student's right to full membership of the mainstream.
>
> (Thomas and Vaughn, 2004, page 137)

This kind of concession about class withdrawal raises boundary questions about whether time-limited withdrawal with specific purposes to an off-site setting managed by ordinary schools or federations of ordinary schools might be acceptable as 'inclusive'. It also raises questions about whether withdrawing from an ordinary classroom, for a substantial period, say up to about 60 per cent, is consistent with being 'inclusive'.

There are also other positions that reject inclusion as necessarily being about location, placement or presence. Mary Warnock, for example, has recently rejected educational inclusion as 'all children under the same roof'. She prefers a common curriculum concept of inclusion: 'including all children in the common educational enterprise of learning, wherever they learn best' (Warnock, 2005: p. 14). 'Full membership of the mainstream'- the CSIE phrase – might mean in her position, simply engaging in the 'common educational enterprise of learning'.

This is where we find that those defending a particular view about inclusion like to distinguish between inclusion and integration, so that any gaps and difficulties in provision are seen as 'bad integration', not inclusion which means 'changing schools so all children can flourish' (CSIE, 2003) Along these lines, Mittler (2000) has indicated that inclusive schools involve:

178

i   all children attending neighbourhood schools (in regular classes with appropriate support);

ii   all teachers accept responsibility for all pupils (receiving appropriate support and opportunities for professional development);

iii   schools rethinking their values (restructuring their organisation, curriculum and assessment arrangements, overcoming barriers to learning and participation and catering for the full range of pupils in their school and community).

Mittler's definition is clear, though it differs from the one promoted recently by Warnock and the Government department. However, a definition is one thing, another is providing specific indications of how far ordinary schools can be transformed in these ways and whether literally all children will learn and progress in such transformed settings. There is a risk that transformation and overcoming barriers can be presented as fairly unproblematic school processes.

Inclusive education: going beyond generalities

From the above analysis, we might ask whether the term 'inclusion' has become too broad and all-encompassing to be useful and meaningful. I have argued elsewhere (Norwich and Gray, 2006), that inclusive educational provision may be better framed within a set of 'flexible and interacting continua'. These continua or dimensions arise from the above analysis of differing conceptions of inclusion. The continuum idea arises from the idea that there is a range of options along each dimension which represent various balances between common aspects (that meet inclusive values) and differentiated aspects (that meet individual needs and requirements) (Norwich, 2007). Some options on the continua represent high levels of commonality and low levels of differentiation, while others represent the reverse balance. This set of *flexible interacting continua of provision* includes the following:

1 Positive assessment identification of learners individual needs:
   - the general system of monitoring and assessing learning progress and establishing individual or 'personalised' needs
   - a wider group of those at risk of social exclusion with additional needs
   - generic groups of those with disabilities (functionally defined – e.g. specific learning difficulties)
2 Kinds of participation:
   - in programmes and practices
     - academic
     - technical/vocational
     - creative/social rituals
   - social and cultural membership/belonging
     - organizational
     - group/class
     - inter-personal
3 Location in:
   - separate school (special school) linked to ordinary school
   - same class (varying degrees of withdrawal)
   - same learning group
4 Curriculum and teaching:
   - same general aims, different pathways/teaching approaches

- same areas and pathways/programmes, different teaching approaches
- same general teaching approaches with some differentiation

5 Governance and responsibility of separate settings (under national regulations):
  - regional system of governance
  - local authority governance
  - schools and clusters/federations of schools governance.

This conception of *flexible interacting continua of provision* differs from the conventional placement continuum of special provision in several respects. It operates in terms of key dimensions that are seen as distinct but related. It also sets limits to these options in each range; some conventional and current practices are not included. For example, in the location dimension, separate special schools without links to ordinary schools are not included, as these do not represent a balance between common and separate provision. Nor are curriculum aims that are distinct from general common curriculum aims included in the curriculum aspect, as they also do not represent enough of a balance between common and differentiated curriculum content. What makes this framework inclusive is that progress in developing educational provision in terms of these dimensions is towards greater commonality. This reflects a political-ideological position and commitment; in a democratic society others might take a different position. However, using this framework does imply that all five dimensions are taken into account, not just one or two dimensions, such as, the curriculum/teaching and the social membership/belonging aspect of participation (to be contrasted with the position in Warnock, 2005).

Dyslexia-friendly schools

The British Dyslexia Association (BDA) initiated the notion of 'dyslexia-friendly schools' (DFS), which has conceptual and value links to the idea of inclusive schools. The BDA issued a DFS resource pack (BDA, 1999) that used a checklist to specify a DFS. The model of DFS is as follows:

A all teachers:
  1 are appropriately trained
  2 aware of the impact of cognitive difficulties on teaching their subject
  3 aware of the strengths and weaknesses of individuals with dyslexia
  4 practice appropriate assessment which focuses on content rather than presentation
  5 make an effort to raise self esteem and enable the child to develop her/his strengths
  6 accept that parents have anxieties and are to be responded to positively
  7 seek advice when they face problems in responding to child with dyslexia
B the school system:
  8 enables children to learn how best to learn
  9 gives access to specialist teaching (balance between withdrawal and in-class support)
  10 gives access to appropriate ICT to support learning.

Mackay (2001) argues that seeking to build a school culture of dyslexia friendliness involves empowering the learner, acceptance of dyslexia and clarity of objectives (to enable assessment of what is to be learned; beyond literacy/presentation). His practical principles: help rather than hinder, support rather than confuse, open rather than close doors, indicate that the notion of DFS has its origins in a 'whole school SEN approach' which has been promoted since the 1980s across all areas of SEN, and as such included specific areas, such as specific learning difficulties/ dyslexia (Thomas and Feiler, 1988). For this reason the principles of DFSs represent the application of this whole school approach to the field of dyslexia. There have also been links since the 1980s between the central principles of the 'whole school SEN approach' – schools should accommodate and respond positively to diverse learning needs – and the more recent notion of inclusive schools. This continuity is evident in the fact that some leading proponents of the older notion continue to be proponents of the more recent one (Thomas and Loxley, 2001). However, despite these continuities, the notion of DFS departs from the more general 'inclusive schools' term by focusing on those with dyslexia. Inclusive schools are not just about accommodating children with a specific area of SEN, e.g. dyslexia, nor even all children with SEN/disabilities, but all children including those with additional needs; who are also seen as at risk or vulnerable (see Inclusion Index – Booth *et al.,* 2000). There is therefore a tension between an all-encompassing and a specific kind of inclusiveness. This tension represents different movements, one that focuses on a broad group (focused on the 'socially excluded', 'vulnerable' or with 'additional needs'), the other associated with specific interest groups that focus on medically defined areas of difficulties, e.g. dyslexia, dyspraxia, AD/HD and autism.

This analysis of 'school friendliness' or inclusiveness at three levels (specific SEN/disability, e.g. dyslexia – SEN/disability overall – 'additional needs' overall) raises questions about the justification and benefits of working only at the disability-specific level. What do notions like DFS contribute over and above broader concepts like inclusive schools? This is an important question when the main policy developments over the last 30 years in this country have been about the range of SEN and more recently about an even wider diversity overall. One view is that the promotion of specific SEN/disability developments by disability interest groups and associations, like the BDA, represents a sectional interest. This can detract from broader developments relevant to a wider group of children with additional needs. The implication is that DFS needs to be connected to the idea of inclusive schools by showing where there are common elements and where there are specific aspects not covered by general inclusive principles and practices. This balance between common and specific SEN/disability aspects of inclusiveness has clear implications for the direction of policy and practice for schools, local authorities and voluntary organisations. It is notable that proponents of DFSs argue that schools that are friendly to children with dyslexia also support learning for other children with literacy difficulties and wider SENs (Mackay, 2001). However, this point itself reinforces the position in this chapter that 'dyslexia-friendly' is too narrow a movement for enhancing school provision.

Social and medical models

It is often argued that inclusion depends on assuming the social model of disability (CSIE, 2003). In this view barriers to learning are seen to arise from 'the interactions between learners and the learning environment and the setting itself' (CSIE, 2003: page 138). This is seen to contrast with a medical model in which 'difficulties and disabilities are attributed to "deficits" in individuals to be identified and treated as "abnormal" in segregated settings' (CSIE, 2003: page 138). Criticisms of the medical model have focused on the identification of a single thing – a within-child deficit – that has gone wrong and needs to be put right (Thomas and Loxley, 2001). These authors recognise that medical models are fine in their place (e.g. with infectious diseases), but not where there is an interplay between the individual and organisations. Other proponents of the social model have assumed that individuals can have impairments, but that these impairments are not contributory causes of disabilities; impairments are transformed into disabilities by the negative attitudes of society (Oliver and Barnes, 1998).

The social model is associated with assumptions that disabled people are disabled by prejudice and discrimination not their impairments (Riddick, 2001). In terms of the social model, disability is therefore a form of social oppression and not an individual personal tragedy, a view that social model theorists attribute to a medical model. Riddick applies these ideas to dyslexia by suggesting that the phonological impairment associated with dyslexia can lead to a disability 'because of society and particularly schools' attitudes to literacy' (Riddick, 2001: page 226). From a social model perspective the key issue is society's inflexible norms and standards about literacy and how these are applied. English is identified as an irregular and complex language which particularly disadvantages children with dyslexic difficulties. These norms and standards are criticized as they become the grounds on which children and students who struggle with literacy are made to feel deficient and demoralized.

There are aspects of the social model which have been used to protect human rights and defend those who struggle with literacy or experience other learning difficulties. The social model also alerts us to the social and historical contexts in which literacy difficulties arise. But what is involved exactly in the social model, as summarised above, is unclear and whether disability can be defined only as socially determined is questionable. To argue that society transforms an impairment, like a phonological impairment, into a disability, like dyslexia, is to assume that only social factors are active and that a phonological impairment has no influence on the processes of learning to read and write. The social model does redress the balance away from an over-emphasis on the determining influence of impairments that ignores contextual factors. But, it goes too far in then denying such influences altogether. The problem is that the terms 'impairment' and 'disability' are used in vague and different ways in different contexts. Some proponents of the social model define 'impairment' as a physical difference or defect, which is relevant to sensory and motor impairments, but not other impairments (Oliver, 1986). Others talk about phonological difficulties as impairments (Riddick, 2001), which indicates that impairments are functional descriptions. If an impairment can be a difficulty in some function, then it is likely that it can also be influenced by environmental factors and not just physical structural ones. This implies that an impairment might itself be the outcome of a causal interaction and cannot be separated from social factors. This suggests a wider concept of impairment that includes physiological and psychological functions of body systems as well as body structures (anatomical parts of the body such as organs, limbs and their components). (International Classification of Functioning, ICF: WHO, 2002). According to the ICF, impairments are 'problems in body function or structure such as a significant deviation or loss' (page 10).

Critiques of medical or deficit models often do not distinguish between the 'deficit' as i) a functional difficulty which arises from an interaction of child and environmental factors and, ii) as an inherent difficulty (perhaps innate). For example, Riddick (2001) is uncomfortable with 'deficit models' and following a social model approach, refers to phonological impairments as leading to a disability 'because of society'. (page 226). But, later on in the same paper, she clearly talks about dyslexia as a child's difficulty – when she refers to false attributions to intellectual and motivational factors for children with reading and writing difficulties and criticises those who express scorn towards someone who cannot spell. In these cases she is assuming that some people *have* functional difficulties.

What is needed here is greater clarity about the bases for identifying and responding to difficulties. Table 13.1 sets out some key questions about conceptualising different approaches to functional difficulties. The first question is about the social expectations or norms used in evaluating different levels and kinds of functioning. We can envisage societies where there are no literacy norms. Some may even hope for a modern suspension of such norms; a hope expressed when dyslexia is sometimes described as a 'difference' (Singleton, 1999). However, it is assumed widely that modern society will have literacy norms.

However, we can envisage a range of literacy norms: reading and writing may be evaluated strictly in terms of high general standards in some societies. Towards this end of the range, there would be more clear-cut literacy difficulties. At the other end of the range, there may be diverse norms across different groups in society, where literacy expectations vary and what counts as literacy may be evaluated loosely. Towards this end of the range, there would be a lower incidence of difficulties. With respect to this first question, the social model of dyslexia reminds us of the significance of social norms and their role in what counts as literacy and therefore literacy difficulties. Nevertheless, a social model assumes that there are norms, even if they are diverse and less stringent.

Though the extent of literacy difficulties depends on the kind and level of social norms, their presence leads to a second question – what is the extent of the 'difficulty'? One response may be that there is nothing wrong as the literacy level is not of a kind and level to count as a difficulty. The implication is that nothing is wrong; norms are being met. However, when a 'difficulty' is identified, it may vary from severe to mild. The third question can then be asked – what is the cause of the 'difficulty'? The origin can be attributed either to broad single factors (person or social context) or to multiple interactive factors (person and social context). Social model proponents tend to polarise the causal factors into person versus social context ones, and opt for the latter factors and ignore that some models, such as the ICF, assume an interaction of factors (WHO, 2002). It may be that one of the reasons that the causal question becomes polarised is because the social model conflates the causal question with a question about responsibility for the 'difficulty' – the fourth question.

Assuming a 'difficulty' is identified, questions can come to be asked about control of it, which have moral responsibility and blame implications. One option is to avoid the controllability

Table 13.1 Ways of conceptualising functional difficulties

Questions	Options
What is socially expected? (norms)	*Norms*: few, high level, general tightly interpreted norms (more clear-cut difficulties) ↔ many, varied levels, loosely interpreted norms (fewer difficulties) versus *No norms*
What is extent of 'difficulty'?	*Difficulty*: Severe ↔ mild versus *Difference* (no difficulty)
What is/are cause/s of 'difficulty'?	*Single broad causes* (within person or social context) versus *Multiple interactive* (within person and social context)
Who is responsible for 'difficulty'?	*Controllable difficulty*: lack of effort (blame person) ↔ lack of help (blame society/schools) versus *Controllability not applicable*
How respond?	*Remediate / recover/ develop functioning*: (high intervention capacity ↔ low/no intervention potential/capacity) versus Accommodate

question – see it as not applicable – and focus on the causal questions, as a way of avoiding attributions of blame. The other alternative involves a range of positions about controllability. At one end of the range, responsibility is attributed to the person with literacy difficulties in the form of blame for a lack of effort, while at the other end it is attributed to those in authority in schools, home and wider society for a lack of help. Although the social model is not explicitly presented as about responsibility attributions, advocates of the social model seem to assume that it is, because it diverts moral blame away from those with difficulties. And, in focusing blame on those in authority, this provides the basis for political action. However, it is also relevant that the concept of 'dyslexia' has functioned to divert blame from individual children who struggle with literacy learning (Miles and Miles, 1999). It has done this by its focus on recognising difficulties and their causes rather than asking responsibility questions.

Assuming that there is a 'difficulty', questions also come to be asked about the response to these difficulties. One option is to accommodate different levels and kinds of literacy and not to focus on developing or remediating conventional literacy levels. For instance, Lacey et al. (2007) have suggested that few students with severe learning difficulties (disabilities) are likely to learn to read and write conventionally (i.e., read for pleasure, work and study) and that it may be useful to explore alternative media to provide 'inclusive literacy experiences'. Alternatively, the prospect of some development, recovery or remediation of literacy functioning may be judged as viable. But this depends on the potential of the intervention (suitability/effectiveness) to bring about these literacy changes. This intervention capacity can range from low (where current interventions have limited but some potential to develop literacy) to high (where interventions have more potential to develop literacy).

This analysis of questions about problems in literacy learning shows that positions usually associated with pure versions of the social or medical (individual deficit) models are overly simplified. What is needed is a broader and more encompassing model that takes more account of the interaction of social and individual factors in the identification, causal analysis and intervention of problems in literacy learning. This is the sort of functional model associated with the International Classification of Functioning (WHO, 2002) which assumes a range of social, psychological and biological factors. This approach goes beyond the over–socialised assumptions of the social model and the over-individualised assumptions of the individual or medical model.

Problems in literacy learning

Parallels can be drawn between the relationship of dyslexia-friendly schools to inclusive schools and between the two traditions of approaching problems in literacy learning. One focuses on a specific group with dyslexia and another focuses on all learners, an inclusive approach to literacy. These traditions have had different starting points and often have neither confronted nor conferred with each other.

Starting with the specific group: Dyslexia

This tradition has a long history of disputes about defining the specific group, which have continued through the twentieth into the twenty-first century. When problems in literacy learning are framed as a developmental disorder, this brings teaching problems into a medical framework of diagnosis and treatment. In this perspective dyslexia was seen as a syndrome of neurological origin. This led to considerable debate about the definition of dyslexia, an issue bearing on questions of identification and intervention. Even fairly recent medical definitions, such as that of the World Federation of Neurology (Critchley, 1970), have fallen into disrepute as they defined the difficulty in learning to read by exclusion (not instruction, not low intelligence and no lack of opportunity). Not having positive identification criteria, with its origins in clinics and not whole populations, and with the uncertainty about the usefulness of general exclusionary causal factors, this definitional approach was bound to fail. However, epidemiological approaches were developed to examine readers with low reading levels who were designated as having specific reading difficulties and general learning difficulties (Rutter and Yule, 1975). Specific reading difficulties were identified when reading was significantly lower than would be expected based on predictions in terms of age and cognitive abilities. From this method arose the *discrepancy* model of identifying children as having a specific reading difficulty. Children identified with specific difficulties might read at the same level as other children whose reading levels were expected from their lower cognitive abilities; what is sometimes called in the UK mild/moderate general learning difficulties.

One of the advantages of the discrepancy model of specific reading difficulties was that it did not necessarily confine the identification of a specific group to those with high cognitive abilities. Children with lower cognitive abilities could also be identified if their reading levels were significantly below individually predicted levels. However, the distinction between low reading associated with individual defined higher cognitive abilities (specific difficulty) and that associated with lower cognitive abilities (general difficulty) critically depends on where the cut-off is drawn in terms of the difference between actual and predicted reading. The incidence of specific difficulties has also been shown to be influenced by socio-economic conditions (more in less advantaged settings) and to be unstable over time (Snowling, 2000). Some children with specific reading difficulties also responded well to teaching to the extent that they were no longer identified as having specific difficulties (Vellutino *et al.,* 1996). The limitation of the discrepancy model was also evident in findings that specific difficulty and general difficulty groups differed only in terms of cognitive ability scores.

One now widely accepted response to the problems of defining a specific group has been to include a positive criterion about inadequate phonological processing abilities. This cognitive developmental model sees dyslexia as a phenomenon in literate societies, where the literacy difficulties (behaviour level) are analysed in terms of the interaction between biological, cognitive and behavioural levels all in interaction with environmental factors (Frith, 1997). Literacy difficulties are seen to arise in this causal model from the interaction of phonological processing difficulties (cognitive level) and environmental factors. The biological basis is seen in terms of a brain-based disposition that can lead to the phonological difficulties. This cognitive developmental approach still assumes a disorder, though unlike the earlier medical model (e.g. Critchley, 1970), involves the interaction of bio-psycho-social factors.

The cognitive developmental model contrasts with the more functional definition provided by a working party of the British Psychological Society (BPS, 1999), which defined dyslexia as 'evident when accurate and fluent word reading and/or spelling develops very incompletely or slowly'. This definition has been presented as not providing a causal explanation for incomplete/slow literacy development. The authors of the BPS definition see it as the basis for a staged process of assessment through teaching and realise that it requires further specifying to make it operational. However, it is notable that though the BPS definition does not refer to underlying cognitive difficulties, it does exclude 'appropriate learning opportunities' as a causal explanation of the 'severe and persistent' difficulties. But, more important its version of dyslexia broadens the meaning of the term well beyond that of its origins as a specific rather than a general learning difficulty. According to the BPS version, dyslexia as a term could apply to any child whose literacy development is incomplete/slow. It could therefore be used to describe the literacy difficulties of those with severe general learning difficulties/disabilities (Lacey *et al.,*

185

2007). It is clear that this extended meaning is not what most people mean by the term, as shown by the fairly recent Government definition of dyslexia as a form of specific learning difficulty: 'Pupils with dyslexia have a marked and persistent difficulty in learning to read, write and spell, despite progress in other areas' (DfES, 2003b). The phrase 'despite progress in other areas' indicates that dyslexia is still seen as a specific rather than a general difficulty, in keeping with its historic meaning.

This critique of the BPS approach is focused more on how the difficulties in learning are conceptualized than on the 'response to teaching' model. The persistence of conceptual uncertainties and debates about dyslexia has been evident in recent media led interest in the field (Elliott, 2005). Elliott questioned whether clear distinctions can be made between dyslexic/non-dyslexic groups (conceptual question), whether identification of dyslexia had implications for appropriate interventions (teaching question) and whether identification should result in additional resourcing (resourcing question). His position was not to deny that some children have difficulties in literacy learning, but to question whether some of these difficulties can be validly and usefully identified (in teaching terms) as distinct from other literacy difficulties. He argued for a move away from assessment and identification in terms of direct assessment of dyslexia in favour of assessment of individual needs in teaching terms. Critics of Elliott's approach point to the difficulties experienced by parents in getting appropriate additional provision for their children. Dyslexia is seen as providing access to additional teaching resources. Elliott counters this by arguing that identifying dyslexia is inefficient and inequitable (in implying that others with difficulties in learning do not have access to addition resources), and that what is needed is a description of individual needs. The crux of his argument is that the 'power of the label is rooted in its ability to foster a more positive conception of self and its leverage with teachers and gatekeepers to resources'. This positive self conception arises from a key aspect of the historic meaning of dyslexia, which excludes low intellectual abilities as a cause of the literacy difficulties. This forms the positive social identity of parents and children around the dyslexia label; having dyslexia does not mean low intelligence.

Though Elliott does not deny that some children have literacy difficulties, his position does not elaborate on how we conceptualise difficulties in learning. This is shown by his ignoring of the concept of specific learning difficulties and the way he claims that assistance and support requires a 'clear description of need' and not the label of dyslexia. 'Need' is a coded word which is sometimes used as a more positive way of referring to difficulties. Its use can sometimes be associated with an attempt to avoid a deficit model (see discussion above about social model) and as an alternative to a deficit model. However, these moves are hard to justify as additional resourcing (to what is generally provided) requires identifying additional needs and these additional needs depend on there being a difficulty in learning. 'Additional needs' implies difficulties beyond some cut-off, so even if the dyslexia label is neither valid nor useful, additional resourcing requires the identification of a 'difficulty', whether called specific learning, literacy or reading difficulties, reading disabilities or disorders.

Following this argument, it is also worth examining the position that there is no clear distinction between specific reading difficulties and other reading difficulties. In terms of the argument for equity in resource allocation, all children with reading difficulties (specific and non-specific difficulties) would require additional provision. This would involve setting a cut-off in terms of the average reading level; all children below this cut-off would have additional provision. However, there remains the question of additional provision for children whose reading is *above* this cut-off but *well below* their own attainment levels in other areas of learning (see cut-off in Figure 13.1). Assuming that there are some children with this pattern of attainments, it can be seen that this question is a policy one about resources. This question is

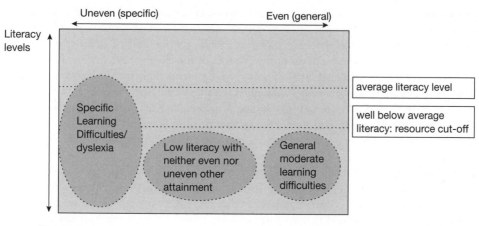

Notes:
1. Specific and general learning difficulties are assumed to lie on continuum: some learners may have below cut-off literacy levels, but not a low (even) attainment profile as do the moderate learning difficulty group: those who fall in the middle of the three groups in the figure.
2. The dotted lines for the two groups represent uncertain boundaries of these groups

Figure 13.1 Literacy levels for learners with general-specific difficulties

whether to additionally resource low reading levels as defined by national average reading levels only or to also take account of individuals' other curriculum attainment levels. Seen in these resource terms, it follows that identifying a specific learning difficulty group is ultimately a policy decision about resource worthiness. It is not primarily about whether this group requires specific teaching approaches nor only about engendering a positive social identity.

Figure 13.1 assumes that some learners with specific literacy difficulties have above average literacy levels. If additional literacy teaching is provided only to all those below a general cut-off, then some learners with specific difficulties will not receive additional provision. Additional provision will be only for learners whose literacy and other attainments are well below average (general learning difficulties), those with specific difficulties below literacy cut-off and those between these groups.

Starting with the teaching of literacy: Literacy for all

The tradition which starts with the general teaching of literacy is located in ideas and practices associated with teaching literacy in primary and secondary schools, quite distinct from special education. Though this brief account is based on the English system, the analysis illustrates more generally applicable issues. The introduction of the National Curriculum in 1988 was aimed not only at bringing consistency in teaching and learning across schools in the country, but at raising national levels of attainment, the standards agenda. Literacy standards have been monitored when pupils were aged 7, 11, 14 and 16 with national tests, including literacy tests. The initial version of the National Curriculum (NC) promised entitlement for all children and was welcomed as such for its inclusive purposes, but not for its standardized and inflexible approach to the range of children's educational needs. As some commentators noted at the time, the NC design barely took account of special educational needs, except for permitting some exemptions from the programmes of study and assessment arrangements (SEN Policy Options Group, 1998).

Political pressure grew in the early 1990s to protect the interests of children with SEN, particularly those in ordinary schools in the context of the changes in schools following the introduction of the NC and market style funding arrangements. The first SEN Code of Practice (DfE, 1994) amongst other guidance, established the role of the SEN co-ordinator, the staged process of identifying children prior to the issuing of Statements and individual educational plans (IEPs). The Code also recognised specific learning difficulties as an area of SEN. However, the Code's individualised planning procedures did not align well with the whole school planning required to implement the NC. Experience of the NC also led to questioning of the constraints posed by the supposed entitlements for all children, for example, having programmes that were designed for their age range and not functional level. The changes introduced to the NC in 2000 with the introduction of an inclusive statement (QCA, 2000) reflected how the general system was starting to respond to a diversity of needs. These changes were influenced by the development of ideas and models about inclusive education that were relevant to SEN but went beyond to other areas of additional need.

Wave model

Further moves that led to the general system becoming more responsive to a diversity of needs was evident in the introduction of the Literacy and Numeracy Strategies in primary schools leading to the Primary Strategies (DfES, 2003b). These Strategies included guidelines on classroom teaching of literacy and led to the development of additional literacy programmes for those with low literacy attainments. These small group additional programmes formed the basis for the introduction of the 'wave' model (NLS, 2003), which connected the general system of literacy teaching to one which provided for those with significant literacy difficulties. The wave model operates at 3 levels:

- Wave 1: the effective inclusion of all children in high quality differentiated literacy programme,
- Wave 2: additional small-group intervention in addition to wave 1, for children who can be expected to catch up with their peers as a result of the intervention,
- Wave 3: specific targeted approaches for children identified as requiring SEN support in terms of the graduated system (School Action, School Action Plus or with a Statement of special educational needs; NLS, 2003).

The wave model owes its origins to a public health framework involving primary, secondary and tertiary prevention (Adelman and Taylor, 2003) which has influenced mental health and psychological intervention frameworks. In school education it has been used to link general to special education with more specific links to the US 'three tiered' model – where primary intervention consists of the general education programme, secondary intervention involve fixed duration, intensive programmes and tertiary intervention involves special education programmes (Vaughn and Fuchs, 2003). Using this three tiered model there have been US attempts to reconceptualise specific learning disability (often referred to in the USA just as learning disability, a term that corresponds to specific learning difficulties in the UK). This has been based on the idea of 'response to instruction' rather than what has been called the 'wait to fail' model where identification does not derive from nor is linked to teaching and learning settings. The principle underlying the 'response to instruction' model is that if those showing early signs of not progressing in their literacy learning (considered as 'at risk') *respond* to an intensive fixed duration programme, then they return to the general programme. *Non-responding* is used as the criterion for identifying a learning disability that requires special educational programming.

There are conceptual and operational issues about this 3 tiered model as there are with its derivative three wave model (Vaughn and Fuchs, 2003). There are various aspects to be clarified: what is the extent of adaptations made in tier/wave 1 for those not progressing in literacy learning in the general classroom, are tier/wave 2 programmes part of general or special education programmes and how intensive do tier/wave 1 and 2 programmes have to be for valid identification? There is also the question of whether inadequate literacy learning in response to instruction or teaching (to use UK term) is equivalent to a specific learning disability/difficulty? What about other associated difficulties, such as attentional, language and behaviour difficulties? What about inadequate literacy learning associated with consistent inadequate learning across the curriculum? And, what about children whose literacy levels/rates of literacy learning are not discrepant enough from the general school/class mean, but whose level/rate are still below the mean and highly discrepant from their own level/rate in other curriculum areas? In the USA Vaughn and Fuchs (2003) recognise that these questions indicate the value of further assessment and identification procedures beyond a simple 'response to instruction' model.

It is evident that the BPS definition of dyslexia is influenced by the US 'response to instruction' model (BPS, 1999) as are aspects of the DfES SEN classification (DfES, 2003b). (The 'response to instruction' model will now be called the 'response to teaching' model when applied in the UK.) However, the BPS goes further than corresponding US development in using the model to redefine dyslexia rather than redefine specific learning difficulties; the counterpart of the US learning disability concept. In doing so this influential UK definition has ignored the need, recognised by Vaughn and Fuchs (2003), for further assessment and identification procedures than 'severe and persistent' literacy difficulties. Nevertheless, the 'response to teaching' model does provide a bridge between the historically separate traditions – starting from the general systems versus starting with services for those with significant literacy difficulties. But, it is also important to note that the 'response to teaching' model does not deny that some children have 'difficulties' just because it does not assess cognitive difficulties directly. The 'response to teaching' model focuses on teaching to eliminate contextual factors as accounts of the literacy problems: the inadequate response is taken to indicate a difficulty.

Conclusions

This chapter has explored the much-used but evidently complex and vague concepts of inclusion and dyslexia. In addressing the starting question of whether recognising dyslexia is compatible with the principles of inclusive education, it has been argued that these terms have to be analysed for their background meaning and use. Seeking clarification reveals the tensions associated with inclusion; that inclusion in one dimension might imply exclusion in another and that being more inclusive in a particular dimension might still involve some exclusion. This arises because inclusion relates to different dimensions, for example, levels in the system (national, school, class), placement (separate to general settings), participation (academic–social) and curriculum (common–different content). It also arises because educational provision has to balance common with differentiated provision in aiming to provide for individual needs in equitable and shared ways. So, it was proposed that inclusion be seen in terms of multiple dimensions of provision, *flexible interacting continua of provision,* where there are various options which reflect varying balances between common and differentiated aspects.

One of the proposed dimensions in this model of inclusion was the 'positive assessment and identification of individual needs'. Three options that balanced common–differentiated assessment and identification in different ways were represented;

i) a general system of monitoring and assessing learning progress to establish individual or 'personalised' needs for all
ii) general system as in (i) plus differentiating a wider group of those 'at risk' of social exclusion (said to have additional needs)
iii) general system as in (i) plus a wider differentiated system as in (ii) plus differentiating groups of those with disabilities (functionally defined – e.g. specific learning difficulties).

This analysis was reinforced by a critique of the social model, as often understood and proposed, based on an analysis of the underlying questions that arise in assessment and identification. This led to a rejection of the medical (individual) and social models in favour of a bio-psycho-social framework for understanding the origins and causes of 'difficulties'. In this framework social norms are central to recognising 'difficulties', but such attributions do not necessarily imply a single innate cause.

The chapter then focused on how literacy problems have been conceptualized as a separate group in terms of dyslexia. Weaknesses in the traditional medical models and the discrepancy cognitive ability based models were discussed. The developmental disorder model with its focus on phonological factors within a bio-psycho-social model was also discussed. The dyslexia denial debate was re-visited in order to show that the assessment net had to be cast beyond literacy levels and rates of progress to avoid missing some specific literacy difficulties. This linked to the critique of the influential BPS model of 'assessment through teaching' and its problematic redefinition of dyslexia. The influence of the US development ('response to instruction' model) on UK development was evident in recent UK positions about 'dyslexia' but also about teaching literacy in the general school system through the wave model.

The chapter shows that it might be possible to make links between literacy teaching for all in the general system and more specialized programmes perhaps in separate settings for short periods through the wave model. It might also be possible to connect the more recent 'response to teaching' model of identification (over time and in a class teaching context) with the direct child functioning model (individual assessment of child's profile outside teaching context). Rather than being the predominant model, the direct child model can be used to supplement the 'response to teaching' model. This chapter veers more towards the concept of specific learning difficulties, as this can in principle be put into practice through monitoring attainments, in the general system and through the wave model. The term 'specific learning difficulty' is relevant in terms of resource worthiness; there is no necessary acceptance that its use implies specialized and distinctive teaching approaches (Reid, 2004). In this use it also needs operational definition as part of a wider system of additional resource allocation, a very important consideration not dealt with fully in this chapter.

The chapter recognizes that there are 'difficulties' in literacy learning, despite problems in the practical use of the concept 'difficulties'. It is concluded that well-formulated and clear ideas about more inclusive school provision depend on recognising specific learning difficulties. Given the underlying issues raised in this chapter, it is suggested that 'dyslexia' is best seen as a term of convenience, an alerting term, a short-hand that draws our attention and reminds us about significant literacy difficulties. In the same way inclusive education is a term of convenience that draws our attention to a commitment to provide those experiencing literacy and other difficulties with respect, sensitivity and suitable quality educational experiences.

'Dyslexia' and 'inclusion' are terms to be used cautiously, not as terms that can do as much for us either conceptually or practically as some believe.

References

Adelman, H.S. and Taylor, L. (2003) Rethinking school psychology (commentary on public health framework series). *Journal of School Psychology, 41*, 83–90.

Booth, T., Ainscow, M., Black-Hawkins, K., Vaughn, M. and Shaw, L. (2000) *Index for Inclusion: developing learning and participation in schools.* Bristol: CSIE.

British Dyslexia Association (BDA) (1999) *Achieving Dyslexia Friendly Schools.* Reading: British Dyslexia Association.

British Pyschological Society (BPS) (1999) *Dyslexia, Literacy and Psychological Assessment.* Leicester: BPS.

Centre for the Study of Inclusive Education (CSIE) (2003) *Reasons Against Segregated Schooling.* Bristol: CSIE.

Critchley, M. (1970) *The Dyslexic Child.* London: Heineman Medical Books.

DfE (1994) *Code of Practice on the identification and assessment of special educational needs.* London: DfE.

DfES (2002) *SEN Code of practice.* London: DfES.

DfES (2003a) *Excellence and Enjoyment: A Strategy for Primary Schools.* London: DfES DfES0377/2003.

DfES (2003b) *Data collection by type of SEN.* Guidance: LEA/0220/2003. London: DfES.

DfES (2006) *Response to Select Committee Report on SEN.* London: DfES.

Elliott, J.G. (2005) Dyslexia: diagnoses, debates and diatribes. *Special Children, 169,* 19–23.

Frith, U. (1997) Brain, mind and behaviour in dyslexia. In C. Hulme and M.J. Snowling (eds.) *Dyslexia, Biology, Cognition and Intervention.* London: Whurr Publishers.

House of Commons (2006) *SEN Report: Education Select Committee.* House of Commons.

Lacey, P., Layton, L., Miller, C., Goldbart, J. and Lawson, H. (2007) What is literacy for students with severe learning difficulties? Exploring conventional and inclusive literacy. *Journal of Research in Special Educational Needs,* 7, 3 149–160.

Mackay, N. (2001) Dyslexia friendly schools. In Peer, L. and Reid, G. (eds.) *Dyslexia: Successful Inclusion in the Secondary School.* London: David Fulton.

Miles, T.R. and Miles, E. (1999) *Dyslexia a Hundred Years On.* 2nd edn. Buckingham: Open University Press.

Mittler, P. (2000) *Working Towards Inclusive Education: Social Contexts.* London: David Fulton Publishers.

NLS (2003) *Targeting Support: choosing and implementing interventions for children with significant literacy difficulties.* National Literacy Strategy. London: DfES 0201/2003.

Norwich, B. (2007) *Dilemmas of difference, inclusion and disability: international perspectives and future directions.* Abingdon, Oxon: Routledge.

Norwich, B. and Gray, P. (2006) Special schools in the new era: conceptual and strategic perspectives, in SEN Policy Paper: *Special schools in the new era: how do we go beyond generalities? Journal of Research in Special Educational Needs,* 7, 2 71–89.

Oliver, M. (1986) Social policy and disability, *Disability, Handicap and Society,* 1, 5–17.

Oliver, M. and Barnes, C. (1998) *Disabled People and Social Policy.* London, Longmans.

QCA (2000) *Inclusion Statement of the National Curriculum.* London: QCA.

Reid, G. (2004) Dyslexia. In A. Lewis and B. Norwich (eds.) *Special Pedagogy for Special Children: Pedagogies for Inclusion.* Maidenhead: Open University Press.

Riddick, B. (2001) Dyslexia and inclusion: time for a social model of disability perspective? *International Studies in Sociology of Education, 11,* 3, 223–234.

Rutter, M. and Yule, W. (1975) The concept of specific reading retardation. *Journal of Child Psychology and Psychiatry, 16,* 187–197.

SEN Policy Options Group (1998) *Future policy for SEN: Response to the Green Paper.* Tamworth: NASEN.

Singleton, C. (1999) *Dyslexia in Higher Education: policy, provision and practice.* Hull: The National Working Party on Dyslexia in Higher Education.

Snowling, M.J. (2000) *Dyslexia.* Oxford, Blackwell Publishers.

Thomas, G. and Feiler, A. (1988) *Planning for Special Needs: A Whole School Approach.* Oxford: Blackwell.

Thomas, G. and Loxley, A. (2001) *Deconstructing Special Education and Constructing Inclusion.* Buckingham: Open University Press.

Thomas, G. and Vaughn, M. (2004) *Inclusive Education: Readings and Reflections.* Maidenhead: Open University Press.

Vaughn, S. and Fuchs, L.S. (2003) Redefining learning disabilities as inadequate response to instruction: the promise and potential problems. *Learning Disability Research and Practice*, 18(3), 137–146.

Vellutino, F.R., Scanlon, D.M., Sipay, E., Small, S., Pratt, A., Chen, R. and Denckla, M. (1996) Cognitive profiles of difficult to remediate and readily remediated poor readers: towards distinguishing between constitutionally and experientially based causes of reading disability. *Journal of Educational Psychology*, *88*, 601–638.

Warnock, M. (2005) *Special Educational Needs: A New Look*. London: Impact.

World Health Organisation (WHO) (2002) *International classification of functioning, disability and health: towards a common language for functioning, disability and health*. Geneva: WHO.

14

Identifying and overcoming the barriers to learning in an inclusive context

Gavin Reid and Fil Came

This chapter

- highlights the barriers experienced by learners with dyslexia
- indicates how and why these barriers should be anticipated and prevented
- shows how learners with dyslexia can be accommodated within an inclusive school and
- emphasizes the importance of taking a holistic perspective when planning for learning and anticipating and dealing with the barriers for learners with dyslexia.

The two key phrases in the title of this chapter 'barriers to learning' and 'inclusive context' are of considerable significance in meeting the needs of learners with dyslexia. Most education systems throughout the world are attempting to include children with dyslexia within the mainstream curriculum. This can only be really effective if additional support, or training for teachers is available. It is also important to shift from the 'mind set' of viewing dyslexia as a 'disability' or a 'deficit' to a more positive and pro-active perspective.

Barriers to learning

When identifying the barriers to learning it is important to look at students' holistic needs. This would include: cognitive (learning skills), environmental (learning experience) and progress in basic attainments (literacy acquisition) (see Figure 14.1). These factors highlight a number of key factors relating to the learner, the task and the learning experience. This highlights the need not to solely focus on the child, and what he or she can or cannot do, but to look at the task that is being presented, the expectations being placed on the learner and the learner's readiness for the task. From that premise the first step is to identify those factors – cognitive, educational, environmental and social/emotional that can be presenting barriers to the learner acquiring competent literacy and other skills. It is important that learners with dyslexia gain some success as this will help to develop a positive self-esteem. This is crucial for successful learning. Success can usually be acquired if the learner achieves so it is important to ensure that the task is achievable.

Cognitive Factors

Differences in information processing:

- Visual-orthographic processing
  Phonological processing
- Limited capacity working memory
- Poor sequencing
- Weak spatial awareness
- Lacking coordination/dexterity

Educational Factors

Challenges that derive from cognitive differences:

- Reading
- Spelling
- Writing
- Proofreading
- Numeracy
- Organisation
- Social communication
- On-task behaviour
- Planning
- Time keeping

Interrelated factors, issues and outcomes for the dyslexic pupil

Social/Emotional Factors that give rise to:

- Lack of confidence
- Low self-esteem
- Isolation
- Anxiety
- Stress
- Lack of understanding from peers and adults
- Lack of hope due to history of failure
- Inappropriate labelling
- Family history and context

Environmental Factors that are a mis-match with learning needs:

- Literacy demands
- Aural demands
- Restictions in movement
- Lack of visiual aids/prompts
- Undue time pressures
- Peer and social expectations
- Limited access to technology
- Too much stimulation and lack of structure to information
- Noise levels
- Formal learning situations create dis-comfort, stress, poor concentration

Figure 14.1 A holistic view of the barriers to learning

Dealing with difficulties experienced by the learner

It is important to obtain an understanding of the type of difficulties experienced by learners with dyslexia and to identify how these difficulties can be minimised. Some of the potential difficulties are discussed below.

Understanding

Often the learner with dyslexia may not actually understand the task. This can in fact offer a reason why they can answer a seemingly different question to the one intended. Understanding the task therefore can be a barrier that confronts the student with dyslexia in most subjects. It is not because they do not have the necessary cognitive skills to understand the task but it is because the task is presented in a manner that makes it very challenging for the dyslexic student.

Identifying the key points

Dyslexic students may have difficulty in recognising what the task, or the text, is suggesting because they have not been able to identify the key issues. They may pick up some tangential issues that side-track them into a different path and this can lead to a different type of response from that intended. It is crucial to highlight the key points rather than expect learners with dyslexia to identify these themselves.

Processing information

Two of the key components that need to be considered in relation to identifying and dealing with the barriers for learners with dyslexia relate to the distinction between processing and reasoning.

Often the person with dyslexia will have good reasoning ability – given that the barriers have been removed they will be able to access thinking skills and show good comprehension. The processing of information, however, which is often noted in the output – that is the written work – may be more challenging. Processing involves the following aspects noted below.

Comprehending the task

This means that the learner has to be able to access the vocabulary and the purpose of the task. For some learners with dyslexia this can be demanding. This highlights the importance of pre-task discussion. During that time the teacher would discuss the task, the vocabulary, the concepts and the purpose of the task with the learner. This is essential to ensure that learner has an appropriate schema for the task as this will assist in the access and utilisation of background knowledge and existing skills. This indicates that one of the key issues is not the 'what' question but the 'how' question: How do I do this? In other words: What information do I need and what do I do first. This means that the learner with dyslexia needs support in the actual learning process. This will be time well spent as it has been indicated that often learners with dyslexia can have low metacognitive awareness (Tunmer and Chapman, 1996) indicating that they find the process of learning challenging and once they receive support in this area they can usually deal with the task more competently.

Implementation of the task

This means being able to use the information provided to assist in finding the answer to the question. This would have implications for being able to identify the key points and focusing on the actual task. It is possible for learners with dyslexia to be side tracked and look at issues which may be important, but may not directly relate to the task.

Autonomous learning

It is often the case that students with dyslexia become dependent on a teacher or support teacher when they are tackling questions. This means that they are leaning towards a dependency culture and becoming too dependent on another person. This in the short-term may be exactly what they need, but it has dangers. One danger inherent in this can be gleaned from 'Attribution Theory'. This would imply that if learners become dependent on support they will attribute their success to the presence of the teacher. It is important that this attribution is shifted in order that they attribute success to their own efforts. This is the first and essential step to becoming an independent learner.

Reporting on the task

This is an important factor as this is the final component of learning that is often seen as a measure of competence. Yet learners with dyslexia can often have competence but not be able to display that either in written form or indeed orally. This can be frustrating so it is important

	Individual Pupil Factors	Task Factors	Teaching Style & Class Management	Resources & Support
Teacher Input/Content	Slower processing Limited capacity stm and working memory Poor sequencing Weak spatial awareness			
Pupils Process/Work	Lacking coordination/ dexterity Poor sense of timing Lack of confidence			
Pupils Respond/Produce	Low self-esteem Isolation Anxiety Stress History of failure Inappropriate			

Figure 14.2 Planning framework

that support is available to help with organising, sequencing and structuring the key points to assist in the reporting process.

Anticipating and dealing with the barriers

Some key points

- *Balance* Try to ensure that teaching and planning incorporates a range of learning and teaching styles and that there are activities that can accommodate visual, auditory, kinesthetic and tactile learners. It is also important to identify different areas of the classroom that can be accommodated to the different learning preferences of the students. This is particularly important for students with dyslexia as often they are not as flexible or versatile as some other learners and may need to use their preferred learning style more often, particularly with new learning.
- *Planning* Meeting the needs and dealing with the barriers need to be identified at the planning stage. This is crucial and the important factor in this is knowledge of the child. Planning should not take place in isolation but needs to be contextualized to the learning environment, the anticipated learning experience and the actual learner. It is important therefore to have pre-knowledge of the individual learner when engaged in planning (see Figure 14.2). This can also be achieved through developing an observation schedule or framework that can help to inform both planning and teaching.
- *Differentiation* Differentiation is really about good teaching and advanced planning. If the curriculum is effectively differentiated to take account of the task, the input, output and the resources that are to be used then it is likely that all students will be catered for in some way. Differentiation is about supporting the learner and guiding him/her from where they are now to where they should be. In other words it is about helping to make all curricular materials accessible. It is also important to look at the assessment materials as these may also have to be differentiated for learners with dyslexia. Differentiation therefore needs to consider the learner, the task and the outcome as well as the resources (see Figure 14.3 'reframing your view of the dyslexic learner').

Can't/Negative	Can/Positive
Difficulty	Difference
Finish work	Enthusiastic starter
Work with others	Good at working on own
Keep on task	Good multi-tasker
Doesn't get the detail straight away	Good powers of visualisation
Slow to catch on	Good practical ideas
Poor at writing down thoughts	Artistic talents, particularly where good visuospatial skills are required
Stick to rules	Creative problem-solving skills
Complicates situations	A 'big picture' approach to problem solving

Figure 14.3 Refraning your view of the dyslexic learner

197

- *Learner awareness/ learning style* It is worth-while spending time with the leaner so that he/she will be aware of their own learning preferences. It will be useful to help them understand that there are advantages and disadvantages to every learning style and help them to identify their own particular style of learning and how they can use that style effectively.
- *Acknowledging creativity* There has been a great deal written on creativity and dyslexia (West, 1997). While a number of students with dyslexia will have natural creative abilities this will not apply to all. At the same time it is important that every student is provided with opportunities and support to develop and utilise creativity and individual ways of using information. Healy (1992) provides ideas to develop creativity through talk. She believes that talk is the basis of intelligent thinking and the development of creativity and skills in learning. Some of the talk tactics described by Healy are shown below.
- Acknowledging
  - That's a new idea
  - I see
  - Interesting point
- Restating
  - You want to know . . .?
  - Does that mean . . .?
  - Are you saying . . .?
  - So you are disagreeing with . . .?
  - You think . . .?
- Clarifying
  - Why do you say that?
  - I don't quite understand what you mean
  - What are we really discussing here?
  - That seems to relate to . . .?
- Disagreeing
  - You make an interesting point, have you considered . . .?
  - Is it possible that . . .?
  - Here's another thought . . .
- Challenging thinking
  - I wonder how we know . . .?
  - Can you give some reasons for . . .?
- Redirecting
  - How does that relate to . . .?
  - Good point, but have we finished discussing . . .
- Expanding
  - I wonder what else this could relate to . . .?

(Adapted from Healy, 1992)

Planning

- *Knowledge of the child's strengths and difficulties* This is essential particularly since not all children with dyslexia will display the same profile. This is therefore the best starting point as often strengths can be used to help deal with the weaknesses. For example dyslexic children often have a preference for visual and kinesthetic learning and a difficulty with auditory learning. Therefore phonics which relies heavily on sounds, and therefore the auditory modality, needs to be introduced together with visual and experiential forms of learning. The tactile modality involving touch and feeling the shape of letters that makes them specific should also be utilised, as well as the visual symbol of these letters and letter/sound combinations.

■ *Consultation* The responsibility for dealing with children with dyslexia within the classroom should not solely rest with the class teacher. Ideally it should be seen as a whole school responsibility. This means that consultation with school management and other colleagues is important, and equally it is important that time is allocated for this. Information from previous teachers, support staff, school management and parents are all important and such joint liaison can help to ensure the necessary collaboration to provide support for the class teacher. Importantly this should be built into the school procedures and not be a reaction to a problem that has occurred – such collaboration can therefore be seen as preventative and proactive.

■ *Current level of literacy acquisition* An accurate and full assessment of the child's current level of attainments is necessary in order to effectively plan a programme of learning. The assessment should include listening comprehension as well as reading accuracy and fluency. Listening/reading comprehension can often be a more accurate guide to the abilities and understanding of dyslexic children than reading and spelling accuracy. Indeed it is often the discrepancy between listening or reading comprehension and reading accuracy that can be a key factor in identifying dyslexia. Information on the level of attainments will be an instrumental factor in planning for learning.

■ *Cultural factors* Cultural factors are important as these can influence the selection of books and whether some of the concepts in the text need to be singled out for additional and differentiated explanation. Cultural values are an important factor. It has been suggested that the 'big dip' in performance noted in some bilingual children in later primary school may be explained by a failure of professionals to understand and appreciate the cultural values, and the actual level of competence of the bilingual child, particularly in relation to conceptual development and competence in thinking skills. In order for a teaching approach with bilingual students to be fully effective it has to be comprehensive which means that it needs to incorporate the views of parents and the community. This requires considerable preparation and pre-planning, as well as consultation with parents and community organisations.

Developing learning skills

Learning is a developmental process that takes place over time. There is evidence that learners with dyslexia do need more time to consolidate new learning. The key word here is 'developing' as this encapsulates that learning is a process and for learners with dyslexia that process may need to be individualised.

Bransford *et al.* (2000) suggest that the word 'development' needs to be more firmly understood in educational terms. They maintain this term is critical to the understanding the changes to children's conceptual growth. This implies that cognitive development does not result from the gathering of knowledge, but from the processes involved in cognitive reorganisation. One of the underlying points from their expanded edition of *How People Learn* (Bransford *et al.*, 2000) is that we do not give young children enough credit for their ability to develop metacognitive skills. They suggest that children can develop metacognitive skills very early on and are able to plan and monitor their success and correct errors when necessary. These abilities however need to be nurtured and are dependent on mediation from the teacher. This

199

is important in relation to dyslexia. The role of the teacher in promoting and developing metacognitive learning is crucial. Often competence in learning can only be fully acquired when learners are able to transfer what they have learned to new situations. In order to facilitate transfer of learning students need to monitor their own learning and actively consider how they are progressing with the task, and the strategies which they are using. Many students with dyslexia may be unable to do this and will need monitoring and guidance to achieve this.

The key question, therefore, for the student with dyslexia in relation to developing learning competencies is 'How do I know this?' This is the question the learner needs to ask him/herself throughout the learning experience. This can help to develop self-awareness and metacognitive skills. This will help learners transfer learning and assist them in finding out about themselves as learners. It is this self-knowledge that will provide the most useful and effective tool in future learning for students with dyslexia as it will promote learner independence.

Brown and Campione (1994) highlight this when discussing the key principles of effective teaching and learning. They suggest that students should be encouraged to be self-reflective. The environment, they argue, should be designed to foster intentional learning to encourage student reflection and should focus on the students' ability to discover and use knowledge. Again this is crucial for learners with dyslexia as often they are not able to utilise previous learning without guidance and support from the teacher. This means that every learning situation is in fact a new one. This can cause fatigue and certainly necessitates additional time to be spent on the new learning.

The role of schema

It is important that children with dyslexia are supported to develop new concepts and ideas and to incorporate these into their existing understanding. This is essentially the development of schema which is a conceptual framework that can help the learner organise information into a meaningful context. This can aid understanding and recall. This can also aid comprehension and recall as the new knowledge is being assimilated into the student's current schema or re-framed and accommodated into a new schema.

When children read a story or a passage, they need to relate this to their existing framework of knowledge – i.e. their own schema. So when coming across new knowledge, learners try to fit it into their existing framework of knowledge based on previous learning. The development of a schema can help the learner:

- attend to the incoming information;
- provide a scaffolding for memory;
- make inferences from the passage which also aid comprehension and recall;
- utilise his/her previous knowledge.

When considering the barriers to learning experienced by children with dyslexia it is important to acknowledge the importance of developing concepts and recognizing the level of the child's schema for the new learning.

Scaffolding

It is important to consider the scaffolds that will be used to assist the learner develop new schema. When considering the needs of learners with dyslexia it is also important to recognise multi-sensory principles and practices. Ideally a range of learning modalities should be used

---

Learning Toolkit

General 'learning to learn' strategies leading to independence

Planning and managing information

Memorisation techniques

Motivation techniques

Student responsibility over learning

Time and personal organisation

Communication and interpersonal skills

Thinking and drafting skills and techniques

Goal and target setting

Reflecting on personal learning styles

Figure 14.4 Learning toolkit

when developing scaffolds. It is important to see these not as a special form of provision, but as a learning toolkit that can be utilised by most learners as well as those with dyslexia. This toolkit will be seen as a vehicle for enhancing learning skills (see Figure 14.4).

Dyslexia, learning and self-esteem

A positive self-esteem is crucial for learning as this can provide the learner with confidence and motivation enabling learners to utilise learning approaches, such as those mentioned earlier in this chapter. A child with dyslexia with a low self-concept will very likely have a cautious approach to learning and will have an over-reliance in the structure provided by the teacher. It is unlikely that such learners will develop a risk taking approach to learning as they will not have the confidence to take responsibility for their own learning. Yet it is important that students with dyslexia assume responsibility for their own learning and in time develop their own strategies and structures and eventually have the skills to assess their own competencies in tasks.

It is important that tasks, indeed all learning and learning experiences are directed to developing the student's self-esteem. In order to develop self-esteem the learner with dyslexia must have some perception of success. It is obvious that if a learner is continually in a failure situation this will in turn have some influence on the learner's self-esteem. It is crucial that tasks are developed to ensure that the learner will succeed. This will require tasks to be broken down into manageable units for the learner. This would ensure that the child with dyslexia will achieve some early success when undertaking a task and this will provide motivation for subsequent learning.

Burden (2002) refers to Kelly's Personal Construct theory (Denicolo and Pope, 2001) as a means of helping students develop an awareness of their own perception of themselves as learners. This relates to how the individual sees him/herself as a learner and importantly the attributions that they make for their successes and failures in learning. If learners constantly fail at learning they will attribute this failure to themselves and their lack of ability. In fact they may be failing because the task or the learning environment is not conducive to the learner's current level of knowledge or his/her learning style. The attributions, that is the reasons children give for failure are important and can provide useful information on the learner's self-perception and self-esteem. If learners have negative perceptions of their learning abilities this can giver rise to feelings of low self-worth and any repeated failure can result in situation that can be referred to as 'learned helplessness' (Smiley and Dweck, 1994). This means that the student loses motivation to learn as a result of an accumulation of failures.

It is important that this situation is prevented for learners with dyslexia. It is for that reason that the barriers to learning need to be identified at an early stage and strategies are in place to prevent failure. One of the main means of doing this is by ensuring the student has some early success. A base line assessment is crucial for that and Came and Reid (2008) have developed a set of materials that can help to identify both concern and need. They suggest that it is crucial for teachers in the classroom to be the first to identify concern. This can be done through observation and from checklists and other proforma materials looking at skills and attainments and checking on progress in the sub skills of literacy and in other areas of learning.

This point is further highlighted in the results of the 'say no to failure' project (Xtraordinary People, 2008) which published an interim report in March 2008. This report indicated that overall 55 per cent of all pupils who failed to reach expected targets for national Standard tests (SATs) in the UK were found to be at risk of dyslexia. The sample size was 1341 taken from Years 3 to 7 in 20 schools across three different authorities in England. The participating authorities included a large London inner city borough with a wide ethnic mix, a rural community in the south west of England and an authority in the North of England that included towns and a widespread rural community. The research also highlighted that a relatively greater proportion of 'at-risk' children in Year 7 had more severe difficulties compared to those at risk in Year 3. This highlights the need to identify children at risk at an early stage to first identify the nature of their difficulties and second to minimise the potential for failure.

Identifying at-risk children requires planning for both assessment and intervention. This can help the teacher recognise if there are concerns and pinpoint precisely which aspect of learning should be prioritized in a learning programme. This helps to both identify and deal with the barriers to learning – crucial if all students with dyslexia are going to be equipped to deal with the challenges of learning effectively in an inclusive educational setting.

References

Bransford, J.D., Brown, A.L. and Cocking, R.R. (eds) (2000) *How People Learn: Brain, Mind, Experience and School.* Commission on Behavioural and Social sciences and Education, National Research Council. Washington DC: National Academy Press.

Brown, A.L. and Campione, J.C. (1994) Guided discovery in a community of learners. In K. McGilly (ed.) *Classroom Lessons: Integrating Cognitive Theory and Classroom Practice* (pp. 229–270). Cambridge MA: MIT Press.

Burden, R.L. (2002) A cognitive approach to dyslexia: Learning styles and thinking skills. In G. Reid and J. Wearmouth (eds) *Dyslexia and Literacy.* Chichester: Wiley.

Denicolo, P. and Pope, M. (2001) *Transformational Professional Practice: Personal Construct Approaches to Education and Research.* London: Whurr.

Healy, J. (1992) *How to have Intelligent and Creative Conversations with Your Kids.* New York: Doubleday.

Tunmer, W.E. and Chapman, J. (1996) A developmental model of dyslexia. Can the construct be saved? *Dyslexia,* 2(3), 179–89.

West, T. (1997) *In the Mind's Eye: Visual Thinkers, Gifted People with Dyslexia and Other Learning Difficulties, Computer Images and the Ironies of Creativity* (updated edition). New York, Prometheus Books.

Xtraordinary People (2008) *Say No to Failure Project.* www.notofailure.com. March.

15

Dyslexia in the secondary school
Improving whole school achievement through dyslexia-aware best practice

Neil Mackay

This chapter

- acknowledges the need for a paradigm shift in perceptions of dyslexia among teachers
- suggests it is not beneficial to view dyslexia as a disability
- argues for the distinction between achievement and attainment to be made clear
- looks at whole school perspectives on developing achievement for learners with dyslexia
- discusses the need for personal learning choices for dyslexic learners.

Introduction

The creation of a dyslexia-aware secondary school initially depends on a common understanding among all staff of what dyslexia is and how it manifests as a learning and teaching issue. A key issue is to arrive at a description of dyslexia that resonates with classroom practitioners. Presenting dyslexia as a specific learning difficulty is not helpful – in secondary schools this often leads to it being seen as a problem which is the responsibility of someone with "special training". Consequently during whole school training the writer always refers to dyslexia as a specific learning difference. Subject specialists have related well to this, especially when challenged to identify students who have "unexpected difficulties" in reading and recording aspects of the subject in comparison to ability appropriate understanding of themes and concepts. Now, as teachers strive to adopt new techniques such as personalised learning and assessment for learning, a new description – dyslexia as a learning preference – is beginning to have a significant impact internationally.

The paradigm shift

The case for this paradigm shift is seductive and compelling; if dyslexia is a learning preference it means that there is nothing intrinsically "wrong" with the student as implied through terms such as specific learning difficulty or even disability. Instead student learning needs are defined by preferred ways to access, process and present knowledge, skills and concepts.

Having delivered hundreds of hours of whole school dyslexia training to secondary schools in the UK and abroad the writer is very clear about one thing – experienced and pressured teachers do not value or appreciate training which focuses on identification through checklists and their "responsibilities" to a small group of dyslexic students with severe learning needs. For better or for worse, what they do want is to know how to identify and respond effectively to individual learning needs within whole class settings in order to improve achievement and attainment.

They also appreciate guidance on how to make use of readily available data that has been "collected once and used lots". In other words they are looking for strategies and responses which fit seamlessly into current whole school imperatives based around monitoring, tracking and adding value though effective learning and teaching. This is not to marginalise the needs of severely dyslexic students; rather it is to acknowledge the current reality that most dyslexic students in secondary schools around the world spend most, if not all, of their time in mainstream classes being taught by subject specialists with little awareness of or interest in the reasons behind their specific learning needs. The final objective of effective whole school training is to support all staff to develop their "dyslexia radar", not to label students but to identify those who will benefit from being taught as if they are dyslexic. Getting it right means more needs met through Quality First teaching resulting in higher quality intervention being available for smaller numbers of students.

Interestingly, one impact of effective whole school training is a definite interest in causation. It is as if effective training removes scales from the eyes of previously cynical teachers who, now they understand, somehow feel better able to "notice" dyslexic type learning needs and "adjust" their teaching accordingly, especially when they are shown how close best practice is to what they are currently doing. Indeed it is often the most suspicious teachers who end up as champions of their dyslexic students.

So being dyslexic in a secondary school can be a rewarding experience; it can also be extremely uncomfortable. The determining factor seems to be the commitment and vision of the Senior Management Team (SMT) and experience shows that this may be even more important to the educational and emotional well-being of dyslexic learners than a lead person with a specialist qualification. The ideal scenario, of course, is to have the specialist backed by the senior management. However a specialist without support can only influence a small number of students whereas a strong management team communicates a message that all learners are important, institutes rigorous monitoring to identify a "stuck" pupil, plans inter-vention to move them on and tracks to make sure the movement continues. This style of management embodies the principle of "no learner left behind" which is an appropriate mantra for an aspiring dyslexia-aware secondary school. Effective whole school training offers directions for senior managers as well as subject teachers especially with regard to criteria for lesson observations and performance management interviews and also the way subject/team leaders manage by walking about – "learning walks" with clearly understood and communicated criteria for the observation of dyslexia-aware best practice are very effective in identify and promoting desired learning and teaching outcomes.

The challenge

The challenge is always to justify changing the way a school works on behalf of the 10 per cent or so of learners who are dyslexic to some degree. "What about the rest?" is a common refrain, especially from staff who feel it is their job to teach the syllabus, rather than secure learning. Appreciating this subtle distinction between teaching and learning is at the heart of developing a dyslexia-aware school, a distinction which is very current in the UK in particular and also likely to be a major issue in countries like New Zealand, where a new National Curriculum has just been launched, and in Hong Kong where changes are being implemented to public examinations to include more dyslexic learners. Ironically, it is the flawed UK national curriculum which is leading to exciting and intrinsically dyslexia-aware developments as teachers struggle to come to terms with prescriptive syllabi, programmes of study which assume that all learners are ready to move to the next stage at the same time and a culture which places a premium on the acquisition and recall of knowledge rather than the development of skills. Effective responses to pressures to deliver the undeliverable have included initiatives to personalise learning and to assess through and during learning as well as at the end of a sequence of instruction. Although these measures were not put in place with the needs of dyslexic learners in mind they both epitomise dyslexia-aware best practice, offering significant opportunities to improve achievement and attainment.

It is important at this time to distinguish between achievement and attainment; achievement is about a learner's journey from where they were to where they are now and can be measured by, for example, comparing work done in September with work done in March. The sample of work in Figure 15.1 is an example of student achievement in the form of a learning journey over a period of some seven months for a 12-year-old learner.

While there can be little doubt that the dyslexic student whose work is shown in Figure 15.1 is achieving, actual attainment may be harder to measure, especially in terms of norm-based results and/or the sorts of "level descriptors" that can typify a national curriculum approach. In these contexts student performance is measured against either a large age-related sample or an arbitrary statement about what "should be" achievable at a given age. Both contexts embody a traditional view of attainment and tend to discriminate against dyslexic students because few are traditional learners. Interviews with high-achieving dyslexic adults tend to support this view – Richard Branson is reported to have found school a "nightmare" before going on to found the Virgin group while Einstein's teachers apparently considered him to be "mentally slow"! In consequence both highly successful individuals needed to get out of compulsory education in order to achieve their potential, something which is often still the case today, especially in schools which find it difficult to establish a culture in which achievement is valued as much as attainment.

In reality the situation is not a black-and-white case of either attainment or achievement – dyslexia-aware schools acknowledge that facilitating achievement is the first step towards attainment, especially as success breeds success. Students who work in a culture of achievement soon cast off the baggage of years of perceived failure to attain and, as self image and confidence improve, they begin to make progress against a variety of measures. This is one benefit that a dyslexia-aware school brings to a wider range of students –the measures that are put in place to ensure that no dyslexic student is left behind seem to improve the opportunities of students with a range of learning needs, including those with Attention Deficit/Hyperactivity Disorders (ADHD), Asperger's Syndrome and Dyspraxia/Developmental Coordinational Disorder. In the case of the writer's school, as dyslexia-aware best practice became common practice, measurable improvements were recorded in a number of areas, including exam results, attendance and, evidenced by the number of new families choosing to move into the school catchment area, parental confidence.

All too often teachers with management responsibilities for student progress find themselves trying to do everything for everybody, with inevitable compromises in terms of quality and efficiency. On the other hand, the only way to eat an elephant is to take one bite at a time. Beginning with a focus on the achievement and attainment of dyslexic students offers a manageable opportunity to develop effective monitoring, tracking and response strategies within a clearly defined target group. Then, as confidence and expertise develop, the focus can be

205

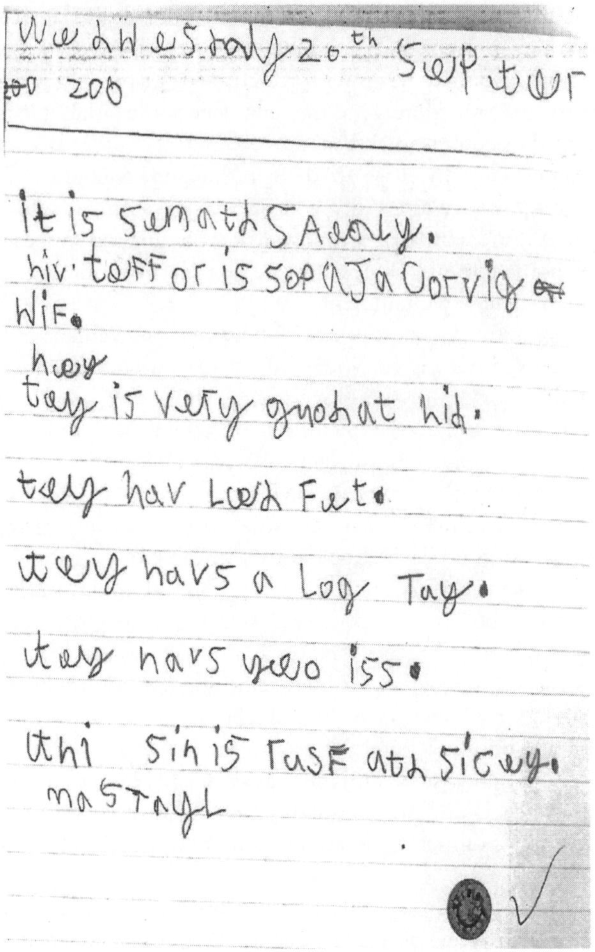

Figure 15.1
An example of student
achievement in the form
of a learning journey
over a period of some
seven months

extended across a range of target learners – perhaps more able and talented or those failing to make expected progress – using techniques developed with dyslexic learners. Also, as schools "drill down" through the layers of data relating to dyslexic students and respond to findings, the seismic vibrations inevitably influence other groups. So, almost by default, a focus on one group can secure tangible benefits for all. Why then begin with dyslexic learners? Simply because they are the largest definable group of vulnerable students within any school and their learning needs respond well to the types of fine tuning of lesson preparation, materials and delivery that represent the very best of current and future classroom practice. In other words, defining and delivering a basic curricular entitlement for dyslexic students sets the standard for all.

The basic entitlement

There are two key questions that must be addressed by any school aspiring to improve whole school achievement and attainment through a focus on dyslexia-aware best practice.

1 Which students may not be benefiting enough from their education?

Figure 15.1
Continued

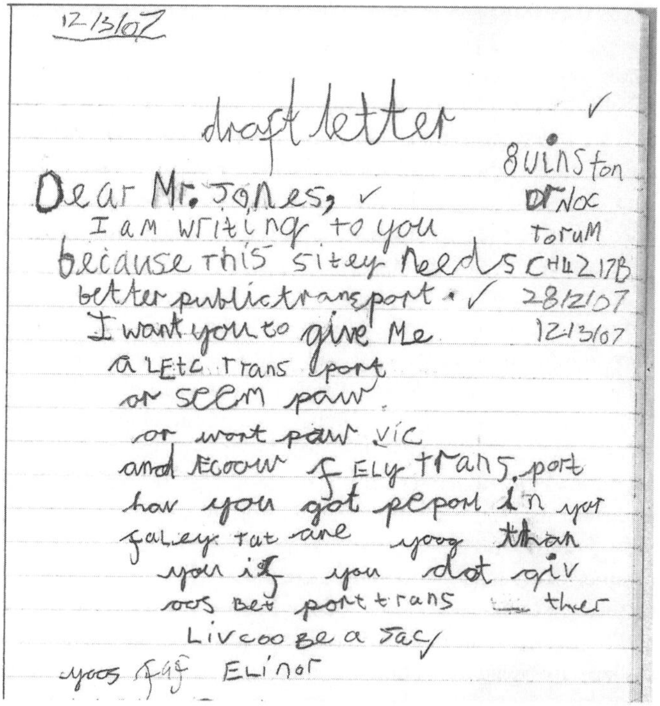

The only way to answer this question is to have measures of ability and achievement as well as current attainment. To rely on measures of current attainment alone, for example public examination scores passed on from primary school, is likely to be ineffective and potentially damaging. Some secondary schools in the UK use the scores from the SATs public examinations taken in primary school to set pupils on entry. In a dyslexia-aware school this is an inappropriate use of such data for various reasons:

- it is unlikely that the results are a true reflection of the true ability of dyslexic learners, leading to underestimations of ability and subsequent placement in low sets
- it gives far too much importance to an artificial assessment procedure which has little to do with the education of students but everything to do with inspecting and assessing schools
- the assessments create unhealthy levels of stress in students, parents and teachers.

This is not to dismiss information gained by these assessments but the effects of the current process on the emotional and mental health of students is a growing concern in the UK and also in Hong Kong, where examinations to get into Band 1 schools are causing similar high levels of stress. In the UK it would make a tremendous difference if secondary schools stopped using primary SATs results as the basis for setting after transition.

The use of data to establish "expected progress" is proving to be very useful in the UK and, it is fair to say, results of public examinations taken at age 11 and 14 contribute greatly to this. Once this benchmark is in place student progress can be monitored very easily. However the process is perhaps rather "blunt" for dyslexic learners as current weaknesses in some aspects of basic literacy and numeracy may artificially depress a student's expectation of progress and also fail to take into account age/ability appropriate conceptual development. One solution is to ensure that all data used to establish expected progress for dyslexic learners is supplemented with a measure of non-verbal reasoning, either via an individual test or as part of a group test such as NFER's CATs test which includes this element. Like all assessments, non-verbal reasoning tests are only a snapshot of performance at that moment in time, but they do give a measure of how a student thinks and reasons, skills which are essential for the achievement of potential. Therefore a student with weak basic skills but age appropriate non-verbal reasoning is clearly not a "slow learner" – s/he will definitely learn some aspects of literacy and/or numeracy slowly but learning in other areas can be in line with national expectations.

When dyslexic students transfer from primary to secondary schools or move between year groups they often experience "transition dip" – their achievement and attainment dips while they adjust to new teachers and different course requirements. A simple but effective technique to monitor this is the "Arrow Tracker". The example in Figure 15.2 is using English National Curriculum English levels as the basis for monitoring.

When a teacher receives the levels for a new class they are recorded on the tracker as in the example. Student names are recorded under the attainment level they achieved prior to transition. In October and February informal assessment of current levels are made and arrows used to indicate "where students are now". It can be clearly seen that the attainment of a number of students has deteriorated following transfer to the new group. However, when a further assessment was carried out in February some are now making good progress.

The tracker indicates the following individual peaks and troughs in performance for SpLD students following transition and then later in the academic year:

- Jodie lost ground briefly on transition but is now making good progress.
- Luke was at Level 2C on transfer but slipped back a sub level in October. However he then found his feet and made good progress. A specific intervention triggered this progress (see group provision map (Figure 15.3)).

2B	2B	3A	3B	3C	4A	4B	4C
	Jodie						
	Luke						
	Carmel						
			Millie				
			Harry				
			Alysha				
				Danny			

October	———————➤
February	- - - - - - - - ➤

Figure 15.2 'Arrow Tracking' Year 7 reading

	Speech and language support		Learning mentor		Phonic programme		Teaching assistant support	
	Sep	Feb	Sep	Feb	Sep	Feb	Sep	Feb
Jodie	#	#						#
Luke						#		
Carmel					#		#	
Millie				#				
Harry					#			
Alysha							#	#
Danny				#	#			

Figure 15.3 SpLD group provision map

- Carmel had no problems on transition and continued to make progress.
- Millie went back by three sub-levels on transition and, by February, had only managed to catch up to her original transition level.
- Alysha lost ground but has more than caught up and is now doing fine following successful intervention (see group provision map (Figure 15.3)).
- Danny went back nearly three sub levels on transition and has still not caught up in February.

So this tracker suggests that Millie and Danny are not benefiting enough from their education.

It can also be interesting to compare performance on the arrow tracker with the group's provision map (the plan of interventions provided for individual students) (Figure 15.3).

When viewed with the Arrow Tracker this provision map demonstrates the impact of certain interventions. For example, having noticed that Luke was losing ground, the school adjusted his education by building in a phonic programme. The impact has been very positive. The situation is rather different for Alysha. She did well during her final year in primary school and it was decided that she no longer needed support from a Teaching Assistant (TA) in the secondary school. As can be seen from the arrow tracker, Alysha lost ground until the TA was reinstated in late September. Since then she has continued to progress. Danny is an interesting case – despite having the support of a Learning Mentor and starting on a phonic programme, he is not making expected progress so it is time to re-visit his provision. Perhaps TA support may have more impact? One intervention which can have a major impact on the achievement of dyslexic students in the secondary school is anger management. In some cases this can be more effective than traditional learning support.

2. How are we responding to specific learning needs without underestimating intellect?

The monitoring and tracking strategies used to identify those dyslexic learners who may not be benefiting enough from their teaching also help schools respond to specific learning needs without underestimating intellect. Dyslexic students tend to think faster and more effectively than they read, write and spell. Consequently it can be depressingly easy to underestimate their ability and make unsafe judgements about groupings and sets based on solely on weak basic skills. This is compounded when secondary schools make decisions based on performance in national examinations and/or fail to liaise effectively with primary schools in order to assess achievement as well as attainment.

A characteristic of a dyslexia-aware secondary school is a willingness to place dyslexic learners in ability appropriate groups and sets despite current weaknesses in basic literacy and/or numeracy. It is important to view these weaknesses as current rather than in any way permanent – with quality first teaching, reasonable adjustments and effective intervention as required, dyslexic learners can achieve their potential and go on to be the best they can be. However this will only occur if schools have measures of ability to set alongside data on achievement and attainment. Therefore dyslexic learners of high intellectual ability will be placed in appropriate sets and supported with reading and recording while developing conceptual abilities alongside their intellectual peers. This accommodation will apply to dyslexic learners of all abilities who are receiving support with basic skills to enable them to access lessons at ability appropriate levels.

Another important characteristic is the willingness of the school to take a flexible view of the curriculum. UK inspectors are keen that all students have the right to a broad balanced curriculum which can be a major problem for some dyslexic students because it causes subject overload. So rather than being a right, being subject to a broad balanced curriculum can be a tyranny! The issue of curricular overload is reported to be compounded by a message from School Improvement Partners that everything must be taught to everybody; to fail to do so is somehow unprofessional. In a dyslexia-aware school, the curriculum is driven by local perceptions of individual student needs, with subject managers empowered by the SMT to look carefully at the programmes of study and "ignore, adapt, pick and mix" aspects of content. To put this in context, it would be reasonable to find dyslexic students with a good understanding of Science being supported to function in ability appropriate sets while much of their English time is spent on "catch up" to improve basic skills to a functional level. Also it may be necessary to consider reducing the number of subjects studied, especially for public examinations, to allow for consolidation of learning and the explicit teaching of revision and study skills.

The quality of learning, teaching and awareness available to a student with dyslexia should not be a "timetable lottery" – a student should be able to move from lesson to lesson and be completely confident that every teacher has a basic understanding of dyslexia, knows how to address dyslexic-type learning needs in general and has been properly briefed regarding specific issues for individual students. A whole school approach is the obvious answer and this is best secured through whole school training, preferably committing a full day to the issue. Although the focus is on teaching dyslexic students, the most effective training also concentrates on subject based "notice and adjust" strategies within the context of on-going school improvement targets rather than going in to exhaustive detail about causation and neurology. Basically what teachers and teaching assistants seem to appreciate from training is a rationale to justify the fine tuning of current practice and to find out what they can do slightly differently next lesson in order to be more effective.

Effective whole school dyslexia-aware training has the potential to pull together a range of current educational imperatives into one coherent strategy. In the UK for example, the impact of three important initiatives, mind-friendly learning, assessment for learning and personalised learning has been significantly reduced by a lack of joined-up thinking and communication between implementing agencies. In consequence the measures are often seen as separate entities rather than sides of the same coin. Schools which are able to accept dyslexia as a learning preference are already open to the notion that students do not learn according to curriculum manuals or national decrees. Therefore responding to the "non-traditional" preferences of dyslexic learners in terms of the ways they prefer to access, record and provide evidence of learning becomes a normal part of what the school does. "If they don't learn the way we teach them, we'll teach them the way they learn." Unfortunately the key message of mind-friendly learning, that it is about improving opportunities for achievement and attainment, has somehow become lost due to a lack of rigour in terms of outcomes.

Part of the problem has been the use of the phrase "intelligences" which can label students in an unhelpful way and restrict the ways they feel able to organise and present their learning. Indeed it is not unusual for students to challenge an assignment because "I am a kinaesthetic learner and I can't be expected to do it like that." Substituting "preferences" for "intelligences" creates an important paradigm shift for students and teachers alike and introduces the important concept of comfort zones. So students may well prefer to produce evidence in one way but appreciate that they can also do so in a variety of less comfortable ways in order to achieve a result – effectively becoming strategic learners. Dyslexic students in secondary schools are particularly appreciative of opportunities to "show they know" in creative and eclectic ways which minimise current basic skill issues and capitalise on a range of strengths.

If dyslexia is a learning preference it is important to qualify the position; dyslexic students do not prefer to acquire aspects of basic skills slowly and definitely do not prefer to have to deal with typical memory and information processing issues. On the other hand, a learning preference is just that – a preference to acquire and demonstrate knowledge, skills and concepts in certain ways. So, just as a student with a strong mathematical sequential preference may use flow charts and bullet points rather than mind maps, a dyslexic student may prefer to use a core strategy based on the use of colour, visual imagery/metaphor and mind maps within an overarching kinaesthetic format. The concept of dyslexia as a preference was recently presented informally to psychologists and teachers in the UK and Asia and received guarded approval as an idea worthy of further discussion and debate; what is certain is that it definitely strikes a chord with non-dyslexia specialist subject teachers in secondary teachers since it offers notice and adjust strategies without the need to label or assess.

Once mind-friendly teaching and learning is cut loose from the confines of VAK (visual, auditory, kinaesthetic) and embraces seven or eight preferences, the stage is set for a significant contribution to classroom and examination performance. From this position it is but a small step to personalising learning.

Like mind-friendly, personalised learning has suffered from the way it has been introduced and arguably has failed to regain the credibility lost through mixed messages communicated during the initial roll out. The message often received by teachers is that they are somehow expected to plan for an individual approach for each student, a message which has not been helpful. However, students are perfectly capable of personalising their learning when given the opportunity to make informed choices within a framework of metacognition (understanding how to learn) and strategic learning preferences. Lesson planning based around the personalisation of learning through student choice is a very different process to attempting to personalise by effectively differentiating for each member of the class – definitely not recommended.

Personalising learning through choice can work like this:

1   Use a learning preferences questionnaire (try, for example, the free questionnaire available through www.acceleratedlearning.com or other free web resources) to identify two or three preferences for each student. This cluster becomes a student's "core learning strategy" and forms the basis of preferential approaches to the organisation and presentation of learning.

2 Demonstrate how to use each learning preference within the core as an organizational and processing tool within a given subject and provide safe, stress-free opportunities to develop personalised strategies. Challenging students to "show they know" or requiring homework tasks to be presented within certain preferences are effective ways of developing preferential strategies in real classroom situations. The keys to success include:

■ well-planned teaching and learning opportunities to gain mastery at a range of preferential organizational techniques
■ consistent opportunities to make choices in the formative and summative presentation of work.

Recent work in Wales with infant children offers insights into effective personalisation techniques with older students. An innovative learning project organised in conjunction with Powys Children's Service challenged an experienced teacher to lead her class to develop mastery of three organizational strategies, mind mapping, story boarding and flow charting. The strategies were built in to the current class project on pirates and, having been taught each one, the children used templates as scaffolding tools to develop mastery.

It was when the children were invited to choose a preferred strategy to deliver a piece of work that the power of personalised learning became clear. The children chose their template, gave reasons for their choice and went to work. Several interesting things happened – Josh, who had not finished a piece of work all year, was one of the first to complete his task and other "poor completers" were soon to follow. Also the teacher expressed surprise both at the quiet and effective way the class settled to work and the choices made by some students. She observed that a significant number of students chose to work outside of their normal preference or comfort zone because, as they explained, they thought they would do better another way. So pupils perceived as strongly preferring to draw and organise work with storyboards may have chosen, instead, a very linear flow chart for the activity in hand. There were clear examples of a significant number of students choosing to work out of apparent comfort zones in order to gain perceived advantages through another strategy.

In the context of the chart, these very young students had been supported to move out of their comfort zone by being challenged to attempt different planning approaches. Having become competent in a range of approaches they found themselves in the zone of confidence, happily doing whatever was necessary, even to work in relative "discomfort" in order to plan and deliver a good piece of work (see Figure 15.4). The teacher also observed that, had she differentiated the task by outcome – allocated planning scaffolds to pupils based on her knowledge of preferred learning strategies, she would not have been able to predict with any accuracy actual preferred choices – individuals made strategic choices based on personal reasons which actually defied teacher predictions. If this result can be informed by future research it may call into question a great deal of conventional wisdom about the value of teacher planned differentiation, especially differentiation by task, where the teacher allocates tasks to individual groups based on a perception of ability, aptitude and interest. It would appear, from this example, that the concept of differentiation by task may be flawed, especially with regard to the allocation of tasks involving information processing and/or the organising of writing.

Applying this to the secondary setting, it becomes clear that, if young children are capable of becoming strategic learners and personalising their learning by making informed choices, the potential of this approach with older students is huge. Once students are empowered to work effectively across a range of information processing and presentation strategies the teacher can challenge them to personalise their responses by setting assessment challenges as follows (with key words emphasized):

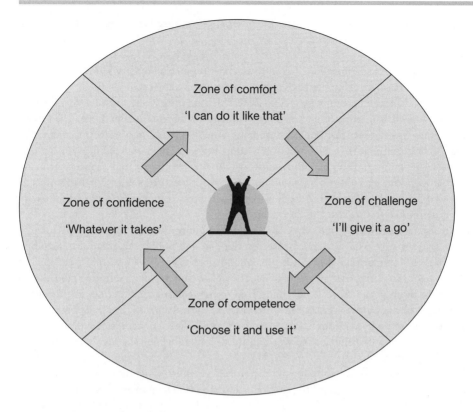

Figure 15.4 Learning through the zones

Your *challenge* is to show me what you know/have learned about . . . Here is the mark scheme/list of assessment criteria. You have the *right* to choose any way that you think is appropriate for the task. Here is a list of possible way: (mind map, flow chart, story board, play script, video diary, model, power point presentation, recorded interview, etc). You have the *responsibility* to choose a method of presentation that will generate a *markable outcome*. I have to be able to give you marks for what you do, using the criteria we have discussed. Off you go.

An understandable concern, which is invariably voiced during whole school training, is that students cannot use mind maps or flow charts as evidence of learning in public examinations. While this is sad but true, it is to miss the point that these techniques are actually springboards or stepping stones to the production of traditional evidence of achievement. Marking and celebrating alternative evidence of achievement is a positive and motivating force; students remember what has touched their emotions and success is a powerful thing. However the required next step and one which is all too rarely emphasized in current writing on mind friendly or personalised learning techniques, is to carefully and explicitly teach the process of turning the alternative into the traditional. An effective way is to require students to:

- teach and talk through their alternative strategy with a talking partner
- use visualisation techniques to "photograph" the strategy with their mind

- during the test/exam recall and draw the alternative strategy very quickly as a planning exercise before starting to write.

The approach needs to be developed as soon as students enter secondary school and utilised consistently by all teachers using methods appropriate to their subjects.

This idea was challenged recently by secondary teachers in Hong Kong, who felt that dyslexic students were already failing to complete public examinations during the time limit. The feeling was that if they spent time planning the students would actually answer fewer questions. However once the principle of planning for writing was explained and discussed it became apparent that five minutes planning and twenty-five minutes writing would probably generate a more thorough and perhaps longer response than trying to write solidly for half an hour. Students writing from a plan would be less likely to become blocked and would generally communicate more effectively in the time available.

These techniques are equally effective when used to support dyslexic students to personalise their study and revision skills for school-based assessments and public examinations, including GCSE, A level, International Baccalaureate, and degree courses. The same principle of establishing a core learning strategy applies, except that the students need sensitive guidance to cut loose from the baggage of years of failure from trying to learn via "traditional" means; as stated earlier, dyslexic students tend not to be traditional learners and attempts to apply standard revision solutions to non-traditional dyslexic learners are unlikely to succeed. Leading dyslexic students to a realisation that they actually can "learn to remember" as effectively as their peers is one of life's great pleasures!

Almost by definition personalised learning approaches require similarly eclectic approaches to assessment, especially with regard to securing alternative evidence of achievement. This can present a problem in secondary schools where well-established assessment procedures, quite understandably, are carefully designed to mirror the requirements of public examinations. Breaking free from the artificial constraints of examinations, while ensuring that students are equipped to deal with them, is a juggling act which a growing number of secondary schools are managing through their commitment to assessment for learning. At its most simple, assessment for learning is the formative process of working out where students are during a lesson or unit of work, working out where they need to go and how to get there. This is a very different process from formative "end of unit/end of year" assessments which can result in students failing to achieve for significant periods of time before problems are noticed. Secondary schools which fully embrace assessment for learning are dyslexia-aware in all sorts of ways before they even begin to think about the specific needs of dyslexic students. This is because all teachers are already changing what they do, lesson by lesson, in response to their students and are actively encouraged to modify schemes of work and units of study to meet learning needs. Add to this sound procedures for tracking, monitoring and responding to individual difficulties, linked to individual responsibility for noticing and adjusting to learning needs, and no dyslexic student need ever be left behind again.

16

School-wide professional development to raise students' literacy levels at Clyde Quay School, Wellington, New Zealand

Sue Clement

This chapter

- provide examples of literacy achievement
- shows how the performance of those who experience the most difficulty in literacy, can be improved where teachers engage in collaborative professional development around literacy acquisition which supports them in:
    - reviewing and reflecting on their classroom teaching practice and sharing their understandings of the level of their students' skills and needs;
    - determining precise goals for themselves and precise achievement goals for all their students;
    - exploring changes they could make in their own classrooms and school-wide and committing themselves to actioning new ideas;
    - opening up their classrooms to their colleagues within the school and beyond, allowing themselves to be observed and thus establishing a climate of enquiry, discussion and personal reflection.

Introduction

This chapter outlines a whole-school approach to raising the literacy levels of its students, including those who experience specific difficulties in literacy acquisition, at Clyde Quay School, Wellington, New Zealand. In it, the author describes how she and a colleague together with the whole staff negotiated a series of literacy initiatives through an action research approach embedded in professional development around literacy acquisition. She comments on how the changes that she and her colleagues actively embraced were those where they explored, both individually and collectively, aspects of their own teaching practice. The very clear focus on individual student achievement as well as the achievement of whole cohorts enabled the teachers to evaluate what they were doing and establish a clear rationale for initiating particular projects year on year to improve overall literacy achievement in the school. It also enabled them to scaffold support for individual students' learning from teacher aides (teaching assistants) and teachers very effectively to enable those students to aim for the same literacy goals as their peers.

Background

In 2000, the New Zealand Ministry of Education funded a teacher professional development initiative in Literacy Leadership that was intended to raise students' achievement in literacy. This initiative sought to support teachers with strong professional leadership in their schools, through on-going access to quality professional development opportunities, and with appropriate classroom materials. Research by the New Zealand Education Review Office in 2000[1] had indicated that the most effective school improvement through professional development was focused within schools on groups of teachers working and planning together. They also noted that the transfer into classrooms of professional learning undertaken during in-service work is more likely to take place if in-service:

- is school based;
- deals with issues relevant to teachers' daily working lives;
- is within a school culture where collaboration and collegiality are the norm.

Central to the Literacy Leadership Initiative was teacher action research that was intended to provide schools with a framework for planning and carrying out their own literacy projects.

The school

Clyde Quay School is a multi-cultural, inner city, 'full' primary school (new entrants to Year 8) in central Wellington, New Zealand. It is a decile 7 school[2] with a roll of 240 students. Except for the new entrant class, the remaining eight classes are composite, each made up of students from two year levels: years 1 and 2, years 3 and 4, years 5 and 6, and years 7 and 8.

Our students are from a range of family backgrounds, socio-economic and cultural groups with approximately 61 per cent of the students identifying as New Zealand European; 13 per cent as Maori; 12 per cent as Chinese and other Asian; 7 per cent as Pacific nations and 7 per cent as Other. Parents from outlying suburbs choose Clyde Quay for a variety of reasons including the school being a full primary school, its proximity to their place of work, the after-school care programme and because our students come from such diverse backgrounds. In 2005, at the instigation of the Ministry of Education, the school's Board of Trustees prepared and implemented an enrolment policy to restrict the number of students enrolling in the school and ensure places were available for students living within our designated enrolment zone. Approximately 50 percent of our students come from homes within our local suburb of Mount Victoria.

We are very proud of the diverse nature of the school. We believe the diversity of our school community enables children, staff, and parents/caregivers to learn more about the way each of us live and what each of us values, so reflecting the world our students will live in as adults.

As a school we aim to produce creative thinkers who are highly:

- competent in reading, writing, maths and social science
- literate in information communication technology
- actively involved in the arts
- enthusiastic about sports
- knowledgeable and talented
- aware of the value of diversity.

'Literacy Leadership' initiative at Clyde Quay

At Clyde Quay School (CQS) the action research approach that was central to the Literacy Leaders' Initiative provided us with a process by which we could examine our teaching practices and find out what was actually happening in our rooms rather than what we imagined to be happening.

My colleague Kerry and I accepted the roles of co-literacy leaders. I was Deputy Principal and senior teacher of the senior school (years 5 – 8) and Kerry was Assistant Principal and a senior teacher in the junior school (new entrants – year 4).

As literacy leaders we were responsible for developing and supporting a professional learning community at CQS by:

- helping teachers to gather and analyse classroom data on student progress;
- facilitating the action research model;
- planning and then leading professional development sessions for the whole staff team and for our two syndicates[3] separately;
- sourcing and introducing new teaching material to staff;
- purchasing new reading material for our students;
- enabling teachers to reflect on the dimensions of effective literacy teaching practice in relation to the teaching of reading;
- observing teaching practice and providing constructive feedback to our colleagues individually and to the staff group as a whole;
- helping teachers integrate new approaches and ideas into their classroom practice;
- providing on-going discussion opportunities at whānau/syndicate and whole staff meetings for on-going reflection, for sharing progress, for discussing next steps and for making future plans.

First literacy focus: Reading comprehension (2002)

Staff collectively agreed in 2002 to undertake their professional development for that year as a whole school. Across the school we had begun the school year in February assessing our students in a number of curriculum areas including reading, spelling, and mathematics, using a variety of assessment tools. We all had taken and analysed a running record in literacy on each student in our class. These running records gave us information on how fluently each student read, their accuracy and self-correction rates, and how well the student comprehended the text they were reading.

Very early on in our professional development focus we realised that as a staff group we did not have a common understanding of how to administer and then analyse a running record. It was important that we addressed this quickly to ensure our reading assessments of our students were all completed in a consistent way. We agreed that we expected students to read with an accuracy of at least 95 per cent and score at least 70 per cent in answering the comprehension questions for a passage. If a student read with accuracy at over 95 per cent but their comprehension score was below 70 per cent we deemed that that particular passage was too hard for them and we had them read the passage below this one to confirm their reading age.

Teachers shared this assessment data with our principal and the senior management team. In analysing the data the senior management team noted that in the middle and senior years there were significant numbers of students who were decoding text well and had high accuracy rates; however, their reading comprehension scores were poor. We therefore agreed that our first professional development focus would be on strengthening our students' reading comprehension skills. Using this assessment data as the baseline, we launched our first school-wide literacy focus on reading comprehension. For the most part all students remained with their peer groups for literacy teaching. However, clearer identification of which students were experiencing difficulties enabled individual and small group tuition that was organised at times when students' engagement in class activities would be least disrupted.

Kerry and I saw our roles as co-literacy leaders to empower, support and steer our colleagues to look critically at the content (the what) of their classroom programmes and the processes (the how) of learning and teaching in their rooms. We undertook this work with individual teachers, in whānau meetings and in whole staff meetings.

Outcomes

Student achievement

As the school year ended in December 2002 we reassessed our students' reading skills and were able to make comparisons with the assessment data we had collected at the start of the school year. The end of year data showed that:

- teachers were now seeking 70 per cent comprehension and were more accurately administering the running records and accompanying comprehension analysis for each passage a student read;
- 73 per cent of students were now reading at or above their chronological age in comparison with 34 per cent of our students at the start of the school year.

At the start of our school year in 2003 we again assessed our students' reading and noted that 70 per cent of students were reading at or above their chronological age. We continued to embed the reading practices we had adopted the year before in addition to aligning our reading and writing programmes.

Our end-of-year reading assessment results in December 2003 showed that 85 per cent of students were now reading at or above their chronological age at year's end.[4]

Changes in teachers' practices

Kerry and I together undertook in-class observations of all our colleagues teaching a reading lesson. These in-class observations allowed us to observe each teacher's classroom practice in relation to our school-wide professional development work. We were able to make clear links between recently explored and observed practices and new approaches, allowing for action, reflection and evaluation. Following these in-class observations Kerry and I were able to share with the staff as a whole:

- effective teaching practices observed;
- observations of student engagement and progress;
- evaluations of our progress to date;
- recommendations for future professional development, including planning our next learning steps.

It was our experience during 2002 at CQS that implementing the action research model brought about goal-focused classroom change across the school. It provided a framework for teachers to work together towards identified goals and to monitor their progress as they changed their strategies, techniques and approaches in the teaching of reading. Through reflection we all became more aware of our own practices. We became more willing to reflect on new knowledge that had an impact on our thinking and actions in the teaching of reading.

Lessons learned from the first initiative

The lessons we felt we learned from the first initiative related both to ways of understanding difficulties in literacy acquisition experienced by particular groups of students, and also to the process of professional development itself.

Understanding professional development

A key factor in ensuring our literacy foci took shape and that the new initiatives did not lose momentum was having two staff members jointly responsible for leading the year's professional development focus. Kerry and I provided perspectives from the junior and senior ends of the school. We were able to take into consideration what we knew about our colleagues, their teaching styles and strengths, and what we knew, too, about the students in our whānau (syndicates).

There were, we believe, other factors that ensured the success of this first school-wide literacy initiative. These factors also laid the foundation for the following two years' focus on the teaching of writing. We believe those factors were that:

- the professional development focus was agreed upon by all the teaching staff
- the focus was chosen as a result of an identified student need highlighted through our analysis of our assessment data
- the entire teaching team were committed to participating in this professional development focus together
- the professional development focus was tailored to meet our school's specific needs (the identified needs of both our students and our staff team)
- in planning the professional development focus the staff's range of experiences were taken into account and an agreed starting point was always from the team's least experienced member
- the ownership of the professional development focus remained with the staff team and was lead by two senior staff who understood both their colleagues' and students' needs.

In reflecting on our first literacy initiative we knew that in planning to lead our writing professional development focus for the following year we would agree with staff:

- more whole-school goals as opposed to the more individual or syndicate goals staff had chosen during our reading comprehension focus in 2002
- a more consistent approach to trialling and adopting new teaching practices across the school. We would seek evidence of these practices in our in-class observations of all teachers. Such an approach we were sure would also provide consistency for our students across the school.

219

Second literacy focus: the teaching of writing (2003–4)

As noted in the school's annual curriculum plan prepared by the senior management team 'school-wide assessment and analysis continues to provide a solid overview of student progress and assists in identifying curriculum priorities and resourcing requirements'. This school-wide assessment data was shared with all staff and our parent Board of Trustees (Board of Governors). Collectively we reflected upon and evaluated our current practices, our students' successes and set goals for the following year.

At the end of 2002 we identified through our end-of-year assessments that many of our senior students' writing skills were at level 2.[5] Ideally we would want to see our year 8 students in their final year of primary school writing confidently at at least level 3. We had had a concerted school-wide focus on reading comprehension during 2002 and now we felt our students' writing skills did not reflect our students' reading abilities.

As a staff group we agreed we wanted to plan for and implement in 2003 a focus for our professional development that highlighted writing and used a similar process to the professional development we had undertaken in the preceding year. At the onset we agreed we wanted to:

- share how we currently taught writing in each of our rooms
- share what was currently working for each of us when we taught writing
- have a consistent way of editing and proof-reading our students' writing across the school
- have a consistent use of exercise books by our students across the school
- explore a structured approach to teaching writing
- have the support of outside facilitators in addition to the work of the school's co-literacy leaders
- include in-class observations in all classes by the co-literacy leaders
- release staff to be able to observe a colleague teach writing
- collect and analyse data on our students' progress with a formative and summative writing sample for each writing focus
- devise a matrix for staff to use in marking, moderating and levelling our students' writing samples using the work undertaken by the Ministry of Education's writing exemplars as the basis.

In deciding each of our school-wide writing foci we agreed to focus on a specific genre for an extended period of time. Writing foci have varied from ten to fifteen weeks depending on the genre chosen. In each instance we began the writing focus with introducing and orientating teaching staff to the particular genre of writing chosen. We agreed collectively what we expected students to demonstrate at each level of writing. We also agreed the learning outcomes we would be seeking for each writing focus after identifying what makes a quality piece of writing in the chosen genre.

During this stage of our writing focus we used the English writing exemplars created by the Ministry of Education. These exemplars are examples of students' work that are annotated to illustrate learning, achievement, and quality in relation to levels 1 to 5 of the English curriculum statement in New Zealand. For example, there are exemplars for poetic and transactional writing. The exemplars help to answer the question 'What do we mean by "quality work"?' Although they are not norm-referenced, they provide reference points that help teachers and students to make decisions about the students' current achievement and progress and about the next steps for teaching and learning. Staff then collectively agreed to write their own matrix to moderate and level the writing samples taken at the start and then again at the end of the writing focus.

Writing sample conditions and how a writing focus would be introduced to all students was agreed by all the teaching staff in an effort to ensure we were comparing apples with apples once we began to assess the level of our students' pre-unit writing skills and identify what pre-knowledge of a particular genre our students had. Having collected a writing sample from each student, classroom teachers used the agreed matrix to level their students' writing samples before meeting with colleagues in their whānau. Our writing matrix covered four levels of writing and each level could be further broken down into three sub-levels: low, mid or high. Staff as a whole team then met to moderate examples of writing at each level. A collection of levelled pieces of writing for that specific genre was then collated after staff had collegially assessed writing samples from across the school. The English writing exemplars provided staff with a reference for pieces of writing already levelled. We considered our writing samples alongside those of *The New Zealand Curriculum Exemplars*. Staff and students were then able to refer to this collated document of levelled writing throughout the writing focus. It provided staff and students alike with a shared understanding of the writing criteria we were seeking, a shared language to describe students' writing work and a shared focus for teachers and teacher aides together to work out how best to design and implement interventions for those individuals who experienced the most difficulties in writing within the overall goals that we set for all students.

In order to make our writing purposeful and authentic we linked our chosen writing focus closely to our reading programmes and to other curriculum areas. For example, we chose a persuasive writing focus when as a school we undertook an environmental unit Reduce, Reuse and Recycle; we chose personal experience writing when we undertook a Social Studies unit where students shared family treasures (taonga) and the history/story behind each object; and later we chose explanation writing linked to our science units on the Night Sky and on the processes of decomposition and composting.

Once a writing genre was underway across the school the maintaining of this professional development and subsequent pedagogical changes took place through frequent whānau and staff meetings. It has been our experience at CQS that at these meetings staff were able to offer each other support, stimulation and encouragement to understand students' achievement as well as barriers to their progress, and in the implementation of new teaching practices to promote students' learning. At both whānau and whole staff meetings teachers were able to share their success stories, share teaching resources which had proved useful in their lessons, seek guidance and advice from their colleagues and discuss the progress of students of concern. Throughout the writing focus teachers contributed to the building up of resources that could be used by others in their classrooms. In addition to sharing those ideas at our whānau and staff meetings we also had a resource box in the staffroom into which teachers could put any supporting material that they thought was particularly useful in teaching a feature or specific aspects of the chosen focus or in teaching individual students or small groups.

Alongside our focus on strengthening our writing skills we adopted a model of incorporating in our reading programmes deliberate links to our writing focus. In both our guided reading sessions and shared reading sessions (either with the whole class or with a group of students) we select text to support our students' extend their understandings of the writing genre we are learning to have mastery over. This approach allowed us to:

- focus on specific literacy devices used by writers for each genre of writing
- focus on the purpose of a text
- focus on the characteristics and text features of different text forms
- encourage the students 'to read as writers'.

221

We believe our students have experienced success as writers during our ten to fifteen week writing foci as we have planned a minimum of four to six literacy sessions a week based around our writing focus. These literacy lessons have been both writing and reading lessons. They have included whole-class and small group approaches, shared reading lessons, and guided reading lessons. Our students have had the opportunity to be immersed in the text type we have been focusing our writing intentions on.

In order to meet the range of skills and abilities in our senior classes we were required to differentiate our programmes to ensure we were meeting the needs both of our learning support students and also our more able students. This meant that we at times cross-grouped students in the four senior classes, targeted our use of teacher aides (teaching assistants) and additional teaching support, and provided enrichment opportunities, including workshops for students. These enrichment opportunities have been led by published authors, directors, actors and teachers and have covered writing from personal experience, writing and performing a monologue, script writing for short film making, poetry and play writing.

Outcomes

Student achievement

Data from in-class observations undertaken by both our principal and by Kerry and me, as the two literacy leaders, over our two-year writing focus suggested that there were strong links between writing, reading and oral language in each classroom.

Across the school we noted that a significantly large proportion of writing sessions were oral language based. They were also clearly purposeful. Anecdotal evidence suggested that the substance of students' discussions had improved significantly. Students were:

- finding out about the features of a particular genre of writing;
- processing information prior to using it in their writing (in particular transactional writing genre including explanation writing);
- discussing the technical or topic specific vocabulary needed in their explanations.

Teachers and students together clarified, extended and supported developing usage of the structures or features of the genre and/or grappled with key vocabulary of the specific writing topic, and/or allowed a rehearsal before actually committing pen to paper and beginning to write.

In the junior school teachers were introducing to their students not only genres they previously had not taught their years 0–2 students before but they were also explicitly introducing their students to the deeper features of a genre.

We set out to make the learning processes transparent to students, including the sharing of exemplary work and success criteria, agreeing what is expected of the task and allowing students to evaluate themselves against the agreed success criteria. We noticed students' increased skill at using the criteria to make judgements about the quality of writing they produced and that they became more adept at discussing their work, editing, recrafting and critiquing their own and others' writing. Overall, students became more able to:

- articulate what they were learning;
- identify what they had done well;
- set themselves specific personal goals; and
- engage actively in the learning process.

Our goal was to have most of our students reach level 3 or 4 by years 7 and 8, and at the end of a writing focus students undertook a second writing sample which provided staff with summative data on each of their students' writing progress. Students could move a level or within a level. Our increased attention to detail enabled us to notice that students could perform at different levels/sub-levels on different components of each writing genre. For example in transactional writing (writing an explanation) we assigned a level for four components – impact, ideas, sentence structure and vocabulary. The majority of students moved sub-levels or remained static at the end of a writing focus. In 2003 95 per cent of our students moved or remained static compared to 93 per cent in 2004, 92 per cent in 2005 and 92 per cent in 2006. Our students have shown over the past five years that the majority of them remain at level 1 or 2 until they are in years 4 or 5 when students start separating out with a few moving to level 3.

Changes in teachers' practices

As noted in the *Best Evidence Synthesis: Quality Teaching for Diverse Students in Schooling* "quality teaching is optimized when there is a whole school alignment" (Alton-Lee, 2003, p. 91). Our experience at Clyde Quay School during our two year focus on the teaching of writing has borne this out. It resulted in a much sharper focus by teachers on their practices in the teaching of writing, in particular their understanding and use of assessment to support improved literacy achievement.

At CQS we have collectively experienced and benefited from assessment in writing which has focused us on:

- examining our assumptions about how students are actually achieving across the school and in individual classes in writing;
- the desire to improve the quality of teaching and learning in writing school wide;
- creating a shared understanding about the teaching of writing including best practices;
- establishing a shared culture for the teaching of writing across the school.

Our assessment analysis school-wide has resulted in staff deciding collectively annual professional development foci; altering our teaching practice; and identifying very specifically the reading and writing achievements of our students. Cross-grouping for literacy provided learning support and extension opportunities on a daily basis for students in our years 5–8 classes. Teacher aide support became much more focused and involved teacher aides moving away from a withdrawal model of working with students to a more inclusive one of working with students in their classes.

Assessment in writing is an

on-going process aimed at understanding and improving student learning. It involves making our expectations explicit and public; setting appropriate criteria and high standards for learning; systematically gathering, analysing, and interpreting evidence to determine how well performance matches those expectations and standards; and using the resulting information to document, explain, and improve performance.

(Angelo, 1995 as cited by The Assessment Network, www.nsac.ns.ca)

Assessment in writing is now an integral and key component of our writing programmes. We assess at the beginning of a writing focus to determine what prior skills and knowledge students have of a writing genre by undertaking a school-wide writing sample. These samples of writing inform our future teaching. The information these samples provide is used by both students and teachers alike. In the middle and senior classes teachers and students set individual and class goals for writing. Students are better able to assess their own work as a writing focus progresses after being included in the diagnostic assessment stage of a new writing genre.

Alton-Lee's *Best Evidence Synthesis* iteration, *Quality Teaching for Diverse Students in Schooling* (2003) notes that gathering and analysing of high-quality student achievement data and using externally referenced benchmarks can be powerful tools in facilitating changes in teachers' practices and, consequently, higher achievement for students. A key shift for me personally in the teaching of writing has been in the discussing and agreeing of success criteria with all the students in my classes, including those who experience difficulties. This has coincided with more focused and specific feedback to students on their progress in writing. Students are better able, as result of these changes to my teaching practice, to evaluate their own work as they review what they have done, identify their strengths and accomplishments, and decide on areas where they need support.

Effect of focus on assessment

We have moved, as a staff group, to seeing assessment during our literacy focus as 'something we do with and for students not something we do to them' (Wiggins cited in AToL Assess to Learn seminar notes, April 2002). In providing formative feedback to students we have adopted Cook's model of feedback (as cited in McInerney and McInerney, 2002, p. 9) which notes that students need to receive feedback while they are learning to master a skill/concept not only to keep them on task but to avoid them practising mistakes for too long. Cook notes that feedback should be specific, communicated positively, specify what is correct and/or incorrect and state what the student needs to do to rectify the problem.

Our experience at CQS has been that our students have become better writers because they have been encouraged to reflect and act on the constructive feedback they have received. It is our experience that our students are able to act on teacher and peer feedback as it has been:

- directly linked to the learning intentions for a specific lesson or skill being explored by the class or that particular student;
- linked to the agreed writing criteria we had developed and used in our writing matrix.

We have also noted that as the students were able to use a common language to discuss their writing, a language used by both staff and students alike, they actively sought feedback about their writing from both the teacher and their peers to help ensure their writing was clear, met the lesson brief, and had impact.

Lessons learned from the second initiative

The lessons we felt we learned from the second initiative related both to our growing understanding and application of the model of students as active learners in the process of literacy acquisition, and also, again, to our awareness of important issues in school-wide professional development.

Students' active agency in learning

Our chosen model of professional development has created a culture and structure within the school that clearly links "on-going teacher learning to the enhancement of student learning"

(Young, as cited by Lingard and Mills, 2002, p. 66). As we reflected on how we approached the teaching of writing we gained an understanding that as teachers we needed to:

- see learning as a process of co-construction between teacher and students and between students and students – actively engaged learners building their understandings of writing;
- activate the prior knowledge of students (MOE, 2003, p. 13) and acknowledge that what the learner brings to the learning task is as important as what the teacher teaches (MOE, 2003, p. 27);
- use effective scaffolding where "teachers challenge and enable students to move beyond what they can do independently by providing structural assistance" (Alton-Lee, 2003, p. 91);
- use "effective feedback, as formative assessment" (Alton-Lee, 2003, p. 92) that is specific, constructive and regular as it can be one of the strongest influences on student learning. "Assessment should be an inherent part of the literacy programme, not something that is 'done' after teaching and learning" (MOE, 2003, p. 50);
- actively involve students in their own learning by making the learning outcomes and the relevance of learning activities transparent. This includes setting a purpose for the lesson and each activity. In making our "own criteria explicit, public, and open to discussion, teachers provide instructive and illuminating models of how judgements are made" (Preece, 1995, p. 33);
- have the students actively engaged in discussing in the learning taking place including asking questions about the content and processes of their learning. These discussions include students being encouraged to think and talk about their own learning. "Being able to articulate what they know and can do helps students to set themselves new goals and meet new challenges" (MOE, 2003, p. 26);
- explicitly and systematically teach skills and strategies (MOE, 2003, p. 14) in order to meet a particular purpose so that students develop their knowledge, strategies, and ability to think critically when writing;
- enable students to integrate their knowledge, awareness and repertoire of strategies in using and creating texts (MOE, 2003, p. 14);
- model the processes of being an effective writer (MOE, 2003, p. 14);
- make explicit the links between reading and writing.

In introducing and implementing a new writing genre in our classrooms we based much of our classroom practice on Westwood's research (as cited by McInerney and McInerney, 2002, p. 8) which notes that effective teachers:

- have high expectations;
- impose a structure on the content to be covered;
- present new material in a step-by-step manner;
- use a variety of resources;
- employ direct (explicit) teaching procedures;
- frequently demonstrate appropriate task-approach strategies;
- adjust instruction and reteach where necessary;
- provide frequent feedback to students;
- use high rates of questioning to motivate students and to check understanding.

We work from an assumption that learning is an active process and that the knowledge of a new genre is constructed cumulatively. Students need to be able to make connections to prior

225

knowledge and with ideas covered in earlier sessions. As teachers, our experience of teaching writing at CQS confirms the work of Nuthall and Alton-Lee (1994) which notes that students need to "encounter a new idea or concept on at least four different occasions" that are no more than two days apart so that effective learning can take place.

Like Gronlund (cited by McInerney and McInerney, 2002, p. 14) our experience in introducing and teaching a new writing genre has been most successful when we have shared with the students the general learning outcomes for our writing focus and then broken these down into very specific objectives. Students and teacher discuss the learning outcomes with a focus on constructing meaning together. At CQS we have noticed that students experience success in learning a new writing genre when:

- they are introduced to it in small steps
- they are able to observe a teacher modelling the skill/concept being taught/used
- they are guided through the modelling process and/or may share the writing with the teacher an example of the task being explored (guided practice)
- discuss/articulate their ideas, knowledge and thinking processes about the skill/concept being focused on
- have their progress monitored
- receive feedback on the skill/concept being taught and then used
- they are provided with independent practice opportunities.

School-wide professional development

Our experiences at CQS have shown that when we approach staff professional development as a whole staff and we select a major focus for the year the greatest gains are made professionally by staff and that this is then reflected positively in the assessment results of our students. This conclusion has been borne out in our school-wide professional development in literacy as "classroom teaching is situated within a schooling context where school leadership and teachers are focused on raising student achievement" (Alton-Lee, 2003, p. 70). In order for a school to meet the needs of its students there had to be "total staff involvement with school improvement" (Mackenzie, 1983 cited by Manins, 2003, p. 4). At CQS this responsibility lay with all the staff members employed.

Staff on an on-going basis had to be committed to an interactive process of "collaborative consultation" (Spedding, 1996, cited by Manins, 2003 p. 9) where each staff member's different expertise, knowledge and experiences assisted in creating solutions to mutually agreed problems. This occurred when we began to implement both our reading comprehension and writing foci and as we worked to maintain them. Staff shared expertise and passions ensuring that we worked towards and reached our agreed goals.

At CQS a collective perspective across the school raised student achievement in reading comprehension and writing school-wide as we had incorporated the following points in our implementation process:

- a common approach across teachers
- intensive professional development to support the goal of a common approach
- agreement on the resources selected to ensure coherence with instructional goals
- on-going processes of, and structures for, teacher collaboration to support cross-school coherence
- teacher agreement about key instructional strategies

- teacher collaboration about appropriate achievement expectations, and
- channelling of community resources to support a core instructional programme.
    (Newmann, Smith, Allensworth and Bryk (2001) cited by Alton-Lee, 2003, p. 70)

Teachers made changes in their knowledge, beliefs and expectations. They modified and transformed their teaching practice which impacted positively on the learning outcomes for the students. This has been evidenced in the in-class observations of all teachers that Kerry and I undertook together.

Understanding difficulties

In analysing our reading assessment data since 2002 we have noted that many of the students not reading at their chronological age are students who have a non-English speaking background (NESB). In looking closely at this group of students we have also noted that they have not been at our school for four consecutive years. Research notes that these students cannot be compared with the general population until they have been immersed in the language of instruction for at least five years.

Our analysis has also highlighted that if students are not reading at their chronological age by the end of year 4 then the discrepancy compounds in each successive year. It is with this group in mind that we are beginning our school year (February 2008) targeting these students with an intensive reading programme.

Beyond literacy

Following our three year professional development focus on literacy, we agreed as a staff to focus our professional development in 2005 on the teaching of science and, more recently, thinking and questioning skills in 2006 and 2007. In doing so we maintained the following key features of our earlier professional development foci:

- the same model of school-wide professional development with all staff agreeing on the year's focus
- a model of professional development which was planned with a starting point from the experiences and knowledge of the less experienced members of staff in order to take everyone forward
- agreeing to limit our professional development foci for the year to give our major focus the necessary time and attention it requires ("a less is more" approach is what we've coined it)
- the action research model as the framework for our professional development focus including the gathering and analysing of student achievement data to ensure that we understand where are students actually are at at the start of a focus and to measure the gains during and following our focus
- a team approach to leading the professional development – using staff expertise within the school to provide overall leadership of the focus supported by outside experts/facilitators.

We firmly believe that the extensive change to teaching practice, based on professional development, research and analysis of our student assessment data, is a key feature at CQS. We are convinced that our school-wide approach to professional development and the focus on aiming for depth in teaching and learning theory and practice has resulted in the greatest gains for our students.

227

Notes

1   The Education Review Office (ERO) is a government department whose purpose is to evaluate and report publicly on the education and care of students in New Zealand schools and early childhood services.

In an Education Review ERO investigates and reports to boards of trustees, managers of early childhood education services and the Government on the quality of education provided for children and students in individual centres and schools.

Schools and early childhood services are reviewed on average once every three years. Reviews are undertaken more frequently where the performance of a school or centre is poor and there are risks to the education and safety of the students. ERO's reports on individual schools and early childhood services are freely available to the public.

2   A school's decile indicates the extent to which it draws its students from low socio-economic communities. Decile 1 schools are the 10 per cent of schools with the highest proportion of students from low socio-economic communities. Decile 10 schools are the 10 per cent of schools with the lowest proportion of these students.

3   'Syndicates' are groups of teachers at particular year levels. The junior syndicate comprises the teachers of years 0–4 students, and the senior syndicate teachers of years 5–8). At CQS we use the Māori word 'whānau' meaning family group as an alternative to 'syndicate'.

4   In New Zealand the academic year runs from February to December.

5   The New Zealand Curriculum Framework specifies the learning outcomes for all students in each of the curriculum areas. The achievement objectives for each curriculum area are set out in a number of levels, usually eight, to indicate progression and continuity of learning throughout schooling from year 1 to year 13. In any one class, students may be working at a range of levels, both in the different learning areas, and within a single learning area. It is not expected that all students of the same age will be achieving at the same level at the same time. It is anticipated that at years 7 and 8 the majority of students will be achieving at levels 3 and 4 of the curriculum. Teachers are encouraged to find the 'best fit' level in terms of consistent performance. To do so they should be reflecting on and using a range of assessment tools, observations, and samples of work.

References

Alton-Lee, A. (2003). *Quality Teaching for Diverse Students in Schooling: Best Evidence Synthesis*. Wellington: Ministry of Education.

AToL Assess to Learn seminar notes (2002), National Assessment Regional Seminar, Wellington, 11–12 April.

Brown, D. and Thomson, C. (2000). *Cooperative Learning in New Zealand Schools*. Palmerston North: Dunmore Press.

Clarke, S., Timperley, H., and Hattie, J., (2003). *Unlocking Formative Assessment*. Auckland: Hodder Moa Beckett.

Clyde Quay School Curriculum Plan for 2005 (unpublished).

Hall, A. (2001). The Professionalism and Teacher Ethics. In C. McGee and D. Fraser (eds), *The Professional Practice of Teaching* (pp. 273–300). Palmerston North: Dunmore Press.

Higgins, J. (2002). What Do Teachers Get Out of In-Class Modelling? In B. Webber (ed.), *SET: Research Information for Teachers* (2) (pp. 43–45). Wellington: New Zealand Council of Educational Research.

Lingard, B., and Mills, M. (2002). Teachers and School Reforms: Aligning the Message Systems. In B.Webber (ed.), *Teachers Make a Difference: What is the Research Evidence?* Conference Proceedings (pp. 43–61). Wellington: New Zealand Council of Educational Research.

McInerney, D. and McInerney V. (2002). *Educational Psychology: Constructing Learning*. Australia: Prentice Hall.

Manins, L. (2003). *TIES 11* (PowerPoint notes). Wellington College of Education: Wellington (Personal communication).

Ministry of Education (MOE), (2002). Exploring Effective Literacy Practice. In *Literacy Leadership in New Zealand Schools*. Wellington: Learning Media.

Ministry of Education (MOE), (2003). *Effective Literacy Practice in Years 1 to 4*. Wellington: Learning Media.

Ministry of Education (MOE), (2004). *The Effects of Curricula and Assessment on Pedagogical Approaches and on Educational Outcomes*. www.minedu.govt.nz.

Ministry of Education (MOE), (2006). *Effective Literacy Practice in Years 5 to 8*. Wellington: Learning Media.

Nuthall, G. (2002). Knowing What We Know and Need to Know About Effective Teaching. In B. Webber (ed.), *Teachers Make a Difference: What is the Research Evidence?* Conference Proceedings (pp. 63–92). Wellington: New Zealand Council of Educational Research.

Nuthall, G. and Alton-Lee, A. (1994). How Pupils Learn. *SET: Research Information for Teachers* (2) (pp. 1–8). Wellington: New Zealand Council of Educational Research.

Preece, A. (1995). Self Evaluation: making it matter. In A. Costa and B. Kallick (eds), *Assessment in the Learning Organisation: Shifting the Paradigm* (pp. 30–48). Alexandria, USA: ASCD Pub.

The Assessment Network (2005). www.nsac.ns.ca/cde/staff/lcj/development/prototype/definitions.htm. Accessed 1 September 2005.

Williams, C. and Leitch, R. (2005) Building Leadership Capability: What does that mean? How can it be done? *New Zealand Principal*, 20(2), p. 13.

17

Dyslexia
Overcoming the barriers of transition

Vicky Hunter

This chapter considers

- transition from primary school to secondary school
- transition from secondary school to further or higher education
- transition to the world of work
- transition focusing on student empowerment and self-advocacy.

Transition is a time of anxiety and stress for many people. For dyslexic students it can be a time of very high anxiety as the way they and others handle their dyslexia will affect the success of the transition. It is difficult to hide your dyslexia in a literate world and trying to do so in itself causes problems. Therefore it is vital that dyslexic students are given strategies that will enable them to meet the challenges of transition successfully.

Every transition for a dyslexic student involves three partners – the young person, his parents and the professionals. At different transitional stages the role of each will change and be of differing weight. But each of these three can have an impact on the success or otherwise of the transition. For that reason it is advisable to plan transition as this will help the significant people in the dyslexic person's life to anticipate the potential difficulties and try to minimise their effect.

Transition from primary to secondary school

For the parents of dyslexic students this is often a time of very high anxiety. The major thrust of all transition work is to alleviate anxieties and ensure as far as possible that the dyslexic student not only has his needs met, but both he and parents know they are being met.

In an ideal world staff from the secondary school would get to know the pupil from an early stage perhaps even a couple of years before transition. In the real world this is generally speaking harder to organise. If resources permit a support for learning teacher or a learning assistant might be able to go into the primary school class with the pupil and get to know his strengths, weaknesses and learning style(s).

At the very least the following strategies need to be put in place.

Review meetings

Primary schools often organise annual review meetings to include parents and professionals. It is important that relevant staff from the receiving high school are invited to and attend these meetings. As these are annual reviews they may well take place in the May/June of the year before transition and primary schools have to be alert to the need to forward plan not just for the last year of Primary but also for transition. A meeting held in the May/June prior to transition is really too late to allow for productive planning. A better time to hold these meetings is often the December/January of the last year in primary. Although it is important to have parents, primary staff and outside professionals present to give the receiving high school a picture of the pupil, there are also problems in this kind of meeting. Often it can become, understandably, a celebration of the success the pupil has achieved in primary school. Parents want to express appreciation of the work done by the primary and primary teachers often want to create a good impression of a pupil of whom they have become very fond. Outside professionals may in fact have had little to do with the pupil recently and are there essentially to update their own records. In this pleasant atmosphere it is sometimes difficult to get a true idea of the needs a pupil may present in high school. Of course, unfortunately the opposite situation may arise where the parents are not at all happy about the service that has been provided and the school cannot wait to pass their problem on to the high school. It is therefore important that secondary school staff do not expect to gain all the information they need just by attending review meetings. Staff have to liaise on a teacher to teacher basis, on a teacher to parent basis and on a teacher-to-pupil basis.

Teacher to teacher

Secondary staff need to liaise with both the classroom teacher and the support for learning teacher. It is also important to ensure that any member of senior management who has knowledge/records about the involvement of outside agencies ensures that this information is shared, either by attending the meeting or by ensuring relevant documentation is made available. It is very useful to hear a teacher's opinion of a pupil and anecdotal evidence has its place, but it is also vital that test scores, individualised plans, referrals to and reports from outside agencies are all made available. It is sometimes quite difficult to get a clear picture of a pupil who may behave differently in a small withdrawal group than in the classroom and teachers' own styles and attitudes can also cloud the picture.

A further benefit for secondary school support teachers visiting the primary is that they can learn about methodologies and resources that have benefit not only for the pupil being discussed but also about resources for other pupils with similar needs.

Teacher to pupil

It is very useful if a support for learning teacher from the secondary school can at least meet the pupil prior to transition. Explaining a bit about how support works in secondary school can be very reassuring and the teacher can get to know the pupil in the comfort zone of his primary class-room by talking to him about his work, looking at examples of work and possibly observing or working with the class.

Transition groups

Some secondary schools organise transition groups where pupils who are likely to find the transition difficult are given extra support. A good model is for the group to meet weekly for about six weeks before transition and to continue this group for about the first six weeks of secondary education. Topics covered include:

- Expectations and worries – from academic to bullying.
- Will the teachers know I'm dyslexic? Will I get into trouble for bad spelling?
- Can I use my laptop in class and/or for homework?
- Will I get my head flushed down the toilet?!

Secondary systems:

- subject department, learning support set-up, pastoral care set up
- how the timetable works
- how to find your way around
- what-ifs
- What do I do if I've forgotten my homework?
- What if I get lost? What if I am struggling?
- strategies
- planning your homework schedule, following a timetable, how to set up reminders at home – post-its, colour-coded folders, etc., phone a friend for homework.

Many schools have set up a programme where all new pupils come to the secondary school for some sort of visit late in the summer term – perhaps a few days of following the timetable and being in the class to alleviate the anxieties that could arise over the summer holidays waiting and wondering about classmates and teachers. Most dyslexic pupils may be quite happy with this standard approach, but for some the extra reinforcement of a transition group gives them a bit more confidence – and incidentally allows them to be the ones who know their way around when their non-dyslexic peers are just finding out. If no provision is made for a group, support teachers should consider some individualised approach such as a special visit possibly with a learning assistant from primary school to give support on the day of the visit, but also to be able to go over relevant points with the pupil once they are back in primary school.

The essence of all these strategies is to give the pupil confidence that his needs are acknowledged and will be addressed and to make sure he knows where to come if he is worried about anything.

Teacher to parent

One of the most stressful times for parents of dyslexic pupils is the time of transition to high school. They worry that their children will get lost both literally and metaphorically. They worry that they will not be able to find their way round school and they worry that all the different teachers will not be aware of their child's difficulties or will not take them into account. They worry that their children will not take homework down accurately, will not manage to keep up with reading, note-taking and copying tasks and will therefore be disadvantaged in assessments, course choices and ultimately in achieving their potential. They worry that teachers will not see beyond these difficulties to the ability underneath. They worry that staff will see them as worriers and write them off as over-anxious parents. It is important to reassure parents that their worries are genuine and understandable. It is also essential that any promises of support are in fact implemented once the pupil arrives at secondary school. The greatest advantage of parents and teacher meetings is that parents have a named person whom they can contact and to whom they are encouraged to communicate their concerns before these become apparently insurmountable. Secondary schools need to explain their systems and the sorts of support that might be available, but hopefully there is also room for individualised approaches to suit the needs of the pupils as they become evident.

Once pupils arrive in secondary school, support for learning and/or pastoral staff need to check out that the pupil has settled in and is having his needs met. Class teachers may need occasional reminders of the strategies required and possibly assistance to implement them. Any ICT requirements must be set up effectively and monitored. It is important that dyslexic pupils do not become invisible, possibly underachieving because they do not want to draw attention to themselves. Others, unfortunately, may become troublesome if they are overwhelmed by the secondary curriculum and it is important to step in quickly before this becomes entrenched. Hopefully the relationship established at the review meeting will mean that parents feel comfortable contacting secondary staff about any problems before they escalate into major problems.

With the above support in place dyslexic pupils should be able to make a successful transition to seconday school where they can fulfil their potential.

Transition from secondary school to further and higher education

Dyslexic students need extra support to enable them to plan the next steps after school. They have to consider what kind of career they wish to follow and what course or training will be appropriate. Some dyslexics want to forget about the difficulties of struggling with literacy and consider careers where their other strengths are valued. Many want the chance to follow their ambitions but in the knowledge that they may require a great deal of support to do so.

Early meetings with careers advisers are helpful in enabling senior pupils to look at their options and start planning the best way to meet their needs. School review meetings can be arranged where pupil, parent, careers advisers and representatives from college can share ideas and make plans to ease the transition to further education.

Students also have to start considering to what extent they want to disclose their dyslexia. This is a major issue and not one that has an easy answer. Much as we might wish that there was no discrimination against anyone with a disability it unfortunately remains true that in some situations an admission of dyslexia might lead to difficulties. Not all dyslexics are prepared to stand up against this and would rather just keep quiet. Some pioneering spirits will blaze a trail for dyslexia and make sure that educators and employers put in dyslexia friendly policies that help not just them but also other dyslexics too reserved to declare it.

Colleges and universities generally have disability offices where dyslexic students can seek advice and support. However, it is a very different situation from school as no one is going to come looking for you to check that you are getting notes down and keeping up to date with reading. Students have to be helped to develop independence skills while at school to prepare them for this adult environment. IT skills should be developed to a high standard to enable students to use IT in all their work. They should also have been encouraged to develop study and revision skills to a high level. Students will benefit greatly from having their own copies of core text books which they can annotate and highlight freely in order to reduce the burden of reading, rereading, identifying key points and then having to take notes. School should assist pupils in becoming independent learners who know their own learning styles and have developed effective strategies to address their needs.

Transition to the world of work

Once into the world of work a dyslexic adult has to decide how to handle his dyslexia – there is no parent or teacher there any longer to insist that provision is made. Whether he goes straight into work from school or whether he starts work after further or higher education, the same concerns need to be addressed. Adults with dyslexia have to work out what is best for them. One student known to the author has become an advocate for dyslexia in his workplace and makes submissions to management to make life easier for dyslexics – recognised or hidden – such as ensuring good spellchecking software is available for staff using the internal email system. Those who choose not to disclose can find themselves on training courses where they do not have enough time to read materials and therefore fail to understand the task or in work situations where their poor writing and spelling skills could be exposed. Hiding these problems leads to a great deal of workplace stress. School, parents and outside professionals have a large part to play in enabling young people to make this transition to adult life successfully. Teachers can help by talking through situations and issues that are likely to arise; students preparing to leave school can be greatly helped by being part of a dyslexic peer group who have similar problems and fears and who can share their concerns and strategies. Parents can help by understanding the pressures faced by their dyslexic children and offering sympathy tempered by a firm belief that they have developed effective strategies.

Transition to self-advocacy

One of the most important transitions is for a young person becoming an adult and taking ownership of his dyslexia. Dyslexia is not just a problem of literacy, it is also a problem of identity and self-esteem. It is important that the dyslexic person develops skills in self-advocacy. This may need some adult guidance and support and there is scope for this type of activity in a life skills programme.

Parents have often been very involved with their child's educational needs and it is a major step to let go. Parents have often had the experience of seeing their bright, chatty, articulate, happy toddler turn into an unhappy failing child shortly after starting school. From there on parents are very involved in their child's ability to address and handle his dyslexia. Some parents have had the painful experience of not being listened to by school, of feeling they have to fight to have their child's needs first recognised and then addressed, of feeling that there are not enough resources to enable their child to reach his potential. The child may have undergone a variety of tests both in school and by outside professionals. Some parents may take the opposite view, insisting that there is no such thing as dyslexia, their child is just lazy and needs to buckle down. Some may have a very happy experience where their child's needs are recognised, resources are put in place and parents are welcomed as partners in their child's education. Whatever the experience it will have affected the parent/child relationship and it will have affected how the child sees himself. Some children will feel well supported and accepted by home and school, some will wish their parents would leave them alone and stop bothering the school, some will be in denial of any problem and become disaffected and underachieving.

Children and young people have to be helped to develop a sense of identity that includes the acceptance of their dyslexia and the effect it is going to have on their life. Parents have a major role to play in this and need to learn how to step back from active involvement in making things happen into more of a role of supporter and encourager.

Colleges and universities often request an up-to-date assessment before making allowances for dyslexia students. This is not a decision to be taken lightly. The student has to understand that such testing will generally include scores indicating ability levels and they have to be ready to face these scores. For example, for a student who is mildly dyslexic but has worked really hard with excellent support from home and school to achieve highly, it may be disheartening to learn that overall ability lies merely in the average band. For a severely dyslexic pupil to learn he is well above average/gifted may stir up emotions of 'if only I weren't dyslexic'. A student should always talk through the reasons for undergoing the test and should understand what benefits or issues the results may bring. For some young people this is the stage when an assessment is incredibly helpful in helping them to understand the kinds of abilities and difficulties that have puzzled them for years and helping them to more fully understand what the term 'dyslexia' really means for them.

Throughout their working life dyslexic people will have to take account of their dyslexia and the effect it has on various tasks within their job remit. They will have to be creative in working round some problems and will have to be aware of who needs to know about their dyslexia and who can help. In personal life too dyslexia can intrude – how to tell a new boyfriend/girlfriend that you can't read too well or your spelling is pathetic is not always easy. And ultimately, the dyslexic may have to make the transition to being a parent with dyslexia and all the difficulties tied up with helping your dyslexic or non-dyslexic child with his homework.

If parents and professionals have helped the dyslexic through the various previous transitions, to have effective strategies, together with a strong sense of self worth, the adult will be able to take ownership of his lifelong dyslexia and manage it effectively.

Conclusion

Careful forward planning and monitoring is required for dyslexic students at the transition from primary to secondary school; from secondary school to further or higher education; from education to the world of work; and from being a child with dyslexia to being an adult with ownership of your own dyslexia. Although all transitions are challenging for dyslexic students, with thoughtful planning and support from parents and professionals in partnership these transitions can be effected successfully.

18

Overcoming the barriers to literacy
An integrated, contextual workshop approach

Jennifer Drysdale

This chapter

- introduces the concept of the workshop approach for the development of literacy skills
- describes key factors which will predict success in reading and writing and which can be identified in the early years
- describes situations where contextual assessment can yield practical information which can inform planning decisions
- explains what happens in a workshop session to remove barriers and support learning
- highlights the three core elements in workshop sessions: phonological awareness, semantic and syntactic knowledge, reading and responding to texts
- acknowledges the contribution of technology in supporting learning and providing scope for creativity.

The workshop for literacy is an effective approach for teaching core literacy skills, in which essential learning activities are embedded in current class topics and themes, thus ensuring that learning is stimulating and purposeful. At its core is contextual assessment; continuous, focused observation, which allows practitioners, during normal class work to recognise the barriers – cognitive, procedural and social – which might obstruct learning. These observations are used to inform planning, enabling practitioners to devise appropriate learning activities so that every learner can experience success. This creates an inclusive environment, allowing children with dyslexia to develop essential core skills successfully, within the same learning contexts as their peers.

A workshop for literacy

Imagine a workshop – a place where people come together to use new tools and to learn new skills. Imagine a rich kaleidoscope of words and pictures, a bright, inviting place where a wealth of 'hands-on,' multi-sensory language activities, call out to be sampled, engaged with and enjoyed. This is the workshop for literacy, a place where young apprentice readers come to learn. Activities are carefully planned to acknowledge learning preferences and to harness the creative skills and talents which learners bring; there is scope to use oral skills and artistic flair to embellish content. Activities are integrated with current class topics so that learning always has a purpose. Experiences are carefully scaffolded to ensure success. Emphasis is placed on phonological awareness; everyone participates in activities requiring the identification and manipulation of sounds in spoken words. Listening to and discussing stories fosters the development of rich oral vocabulary. This workshop is furnished with texts in every shape and form; on computer screens, audio tapes and MP3 players as well as books. Opportunities to write sit alongside opportunities to read. The inclusion of word games and puzzles, jokes and riddles, instructions for making things, books for facts and books for fiction, ensures that all kinds of language are widely experienced and subtle differences absorbed. A wide array of books with high literary merit has been carefully selected to help young learners gain access to a complex, magical, inner world where worthy role models are encountered, experiences enriched, thinking developed, values shaped, and a wide range of emotions explored in safety.

Before learners can benefit from participation in the workshop, their requirements must be recognised. Identification of skill development and learning preferences before they come, and continuous contextual assessment once involved, are vital means of profiling each learner's needs and are used to inform decisions on what should be selected from an extensive toolkit of approaches.

Early identification: factors which predict success in reading

To become a skilled reader, the young learner must create entirely new neurological circuitry connecting visual, auditory and motor systems at lightning speed (Wolf, 2008). Development of the skills within any one of these systems and the learner's ability to make neural connections at speed will affect success in learning to read.

Aspects of these developments are reflected in the behaviours of children at play in the nursery and early primary stages where, through focused observation, predictors of success with reading and writing can be recognised.

Key factors

Auditory and language skills

In a stimulating pre-school environment, most children will develop good oral language skills. They will listen attentively whilst enjoying stories or receiving information and talk clearly to retell stories sequentially, express ideas, exchange information and ask questions. They will recognise rhyme, enjoy inventing nonsense rhymes and may be able to make alliterative phrases. Marching to the pulse in singing games and clapping the syllables in each other's names will come easily. Although children should not all be expected to develop these skills in the same way or at the same rate, it is vitally important that, where there is significant difficulty or delay, additional opportunities to stimulate learning should be introduced and subsequent learning closely monitored to help determine whether the problem was due to lack of experience or maturation or the result of specific difficulty.

Vocabulary

Richly extended semantic knowledge and syntactic skill enable faster recognition of the printed word (Salmelin and Helenius, 2004). Children who come to school with a broad experience of literacy and an extensive oral vocabulary therefore have a huge advantage as beginning readers. Those whose oral vocabulary is limited are likely to find reading harder than their more fortunate peers (Vellutino *et al.* (2004). Clearly, the importance of stimulating early interest in words, asking searching questions about chosen activities and of devoting quality time to listening to and evaluating children's responses should not be overlooked.

Visual skill development and awareness of print

Visual discrimination and recall are core skills required for processing the fine detail in print. The ability to recognise and discriminate shapes, colours, patterns and symbols can be observed when children play board games, card games, build or create patterns with shapes and blocks. Speed of visual processing can be observed in the game of 'Snap', where opponents try to be first to recognise identical pairs of picture cards. 'Pelmanism', in which picture cards, spread out face down, are turned up for inspection one at a time and then replaced whilst players try to recall the position of matching pairs, will reveal how well a visual image can be held in short-term memory. Once children become aware of print in the environment and realise that print conveys meaning, it is likely that they will quickly begin to develop logographic awareness – the recognition of a word by some particular visual feature such as a distinctive letter formation (Frith, 1985). Observations of aspects of visual developments such as these should be included in the early profile.

Motor skill development and bilateral performance

Successful readers employ different areas on both sides of the brain to process written language (Wolf, 2008). The ability to perform cross lateral movements such as crawling and skipping shows whether bilateral, whole-brain processing is taking place. Watching how children coordinate movement on, over and around objects can reveal how well they plan, organise, control and execute a sequence of events.

Integration between systems

If reading with comprehension is to be accomplished, operation of the different skills described above must be integrated and work at speed described as 'automatic' (Wolf, 2008). It is necessary therefore to observe not only how accurately, but also how quickly a child can integrate sensory signals. Tasks such as naming colours or shapes demand the connection of an auditory response to a visual stimulus and the child who cannot perform such tasks at speed, is likely to experience difficulty in making sharp grapheme to phoneme correspondence.

Assessing key aspects of literacy in context

Contextual assessment provides a broad platform for observation yielding valuable information about learners' strengths as well as weaknesses across the curriculum.

Phonological awareness

Phonological awareness is the foundation upon which phonic knowledge is built. In the workshop, strong emphasis is placed on listening games where children learn to identify and segment units of sound in speech – words, syllables and phonemes. In the earliest stages they simply listen and respond orally. Later they might use counters to track phoneme clusters and mark specific sounds.

Important points can be observed whilst children are involved in everyday games and activities:

- Can they recognise the rime?
- Can they generate rhyme?
- Can they recognise alliteration?
- Can they generate alliteration?
- Can they identify the separate words in a spoken sentence?
- Can they identify single sounds in spoken words – initial/medial/final?
- Can they identify consonant clusters in spoken words?
- Can they identify long vowel sounds in spoken words?
- Can they manipulate sounds within words?
- Can they blend sounds smoothly together?

Grapheme/phoneme correspondence and phonic knowledge

Matching sounds to letters is a task that requires accurate connection between the visual and auditory systems; to be effective in reading, this connection must be made in the first milliseconds of visual perception. It is important however to recognise that grapheme to phoneme correspondence can become a mere 'labelling' exercise unless the child can also identify the function of each sound and recognise the part it plays within the spoken word. Observation of activities using magnetic letters will reveal how well this development is progressing. Important markers of progress are:

- Can children demonstrate sharp phoneme-grapheme correspondence?
- Can they select letters to represent the phonemes in spoken non-words?
- Can they select the correct letter to change 'mat' to 'sat,' 'sat' to 'sit,' and 'sit' to 'sip'?
- Can they find letters for some vowel digraphs?

Developing a mental lexicon

Broadly speaking, there are three stages of development through which every learner will progress when learning to read; the logographic stage where shapes or strong visual clusters are recognised, the alphabetic stage where words are processed by sounding out and blending and finally the orthographic stage where word recognition is so fast as to appear automatic. Many children will progress steadily through these stages, having stored necessary visual, phonological and semantic information to become skilled readers who can effortlessly retrieve words from a mental lexicon. Children with specific difficulties struggle to create a fast track to core vocabulary and often retain elements of logographic and alphabetic stages. This problem can be recognised when children

- confuse words with visual similarity but phonic difference, e.g. words with '-ppy' are all read as 'Floppy'
- look away from the text to 'find' rather than decode
- make semantic substitutions
- sound every letter of every word
- fail to break words into manageable 'chunks.'

239

Processing overload

Difficulty in acquiring literacy skills often coexists with poorly developed motor skills resulting in handwriting difficulty (Hill, 2001). The production of a piece of writing is cognitively demanding for anyone, involving as it does, sequential organisation, syntactic skill, semantic knowledge as well as spelling and correct letter formation. The dyslexic learner may experience some difficulty in any or all of these and where inordinate attention must be directed to the production of letter formations, processing overload is likely to occur. This often results in apparent inability to express knowledge and ideas in writing. Observation can help ascertain to what extent the problem is alleviated and expression is enhanced through the introduction of:

- acceptance of oral expression
- graphic planning
- scribing or ICT support.

Gathering evidence

Unless observations are recorded systematically over time and regularly evaluated, their full significance may not be recognised. It is helpful when planning topic work, to devise checklists prompting relevant observation to be used unobtrusively in particular contexts. Contextual assessment, the driving force behind effective learning and teaching, provides information which is essential for appropriate planning. It is the important backdrop to all that takes place in the workshop for literacy.

Welcome to the workshop

The Workshop for Literacy is an eclectic toolbox of approaches; it is not a specific programme. It is content free; it is never tied to a particular reading scheme. The way it operates can vary; it can be for the whole class, for groups or for individuals. At best, it is so embedded in everyday practice that it is indistinguishable from whatever else is happening in the classroom. At the other extreme, it can be 'showcased' by setting up resources in a special location such as a library, where teachers and pupils can come to sample and learn, to try new strategies and take back what works.

- The steps and strategies for skilled reading are modelled explicitly using concrete materials and practised by the young apprentice readers in multi-sensory activities until learning is internalised.
- Learning processes are illustrated and articulated to encourage development of meta-cognition.
- A session in the workshop will always include practice in three core elements: phonological awareness, semantic and syntactic knowledge, and reading unfamiliar texts.

Helping to remove barriers

For many children with dyslexia, the perception of failure and the need for different approaches, create barriers to learning which are harder to overcome than the actual weaknesses with reading or spelling. The workshop approach seeks both to remove such barriers and to support any weaknesses, by providing an inclusive environment where everyone contributes to the same curriculum and differentiated activities mean everyone can experience success.

240

Reliance on graded reading scheme material may provide the teacher with a useful progress marker, but often does little to help the learner who may be acutely aware that the level at which he is reading is well below that of his peers. This is likely to have a devastatingly negative impact on self-esteem In the workshop there are no levels, 'real' books, related to cross-curricular topics and read aloud by the teacher, provide a common starting point, shared by all learners.

Customised texts are then devised to meet different reading abilities, with paired and shared reading sessions (Topping, 1995) allowing children to experience different 'versions.' In this way a truly inclusive environment is created – everyone is effectively 'on the same book.' All kinds of texts can be included:

- stories
- poems
- instructions
- information.

User-friendly software allows practitioners to devise a variety of activities presented on-screen or in print, customised to provide differentiation and necessary 'overlearning.' These include:

- texts on-screen with auditory support
- stories rewritten using familiar vocabulary
- customised versions of stories with paragraphs well spaced or reduced amount of text on each page
- sentences to sequence
- cloze procedure.

Differentiation of outcomes is achieved by acceptance of a wide range of forms including oral, graphic and written presentations with ICT support where appropriate. It is important for morale, to develop a culture where individual learning preferences are respected and to ensure that all modes of presentation are received with equal value and none is perceived as being superior.

Supporting learning

The workshop offers activities in three core elements. The context of the activities is always directly related to a current theme:

1 working with sounds and letters
2 using words in sentences
3 reading and responding to texts.

Working with sound and letters

The workshop takes an eclectic approach to phonics. Although heavily weighted towards Synthetic Phonics, onset and rime and sound blending also feature. Learning is multi-sensory; as well as listening to identify speech sounds, children use mirrors to see the shape their lips make or close their eyes to focus on the 'feel' of lip and tongue position. Kinaesthetic learners enjoy tracing huge letter shapes using the 'rainbow' font on the interactive white board (IWB). Group teaching takes the form of working with magnetic letters and children learn to combine:

- consonant–vowel–consonant
- consonant blends – cc–v–c, c–v–cc, cc–v–cc
- digraphs.

Knowledge of morphemes is introduced in the earliest stages so that children understand how words are composed and are able to break down unfamiliar words into manageable 'chunks.'

When children understand the function of phonics and can combine letters to represent the single sounds they hear in spoken words, their ability in independent, personal writing is greatly enhanced. In the workshop, phonic worksheets are never used. Instead, children enjoy using phonics to write and are able from a very early stage to produce writing which they and their peers can enjoy reading. A boy, in the third term of P1, wrote the following sentence independently in response to the common provided starter, 'One day Humpty came to my house . . .'

*He had macroanay and **chips** and brod**ay** and it waz **deelish**.*

This sentence provides clear evidence of ability in phonemic tracking and digraph awareness; some words not spelled correctly, are good phonetic representations that can be read easily. This writing was valued by the peer group as a contribution to a wall display for the class theme of 'Nursery Rhyme Land' – a rewarding experience for its author.

Semantic knowledge: Using words in sentences

In the workshop there are opportunities for 'overlearning' of core vocabulary which is always presented in contexts, never in isolation, so that learners can draw upon meaning and emotion as well as phonic and visual cues to strengthen word recognition. High focus words can be practised in a variety of ways, including:

- breakthrough folders; a word bank of magnetic tiles which are assembled to construct sentences;
- clicker grids (Clicker 5) – software providing customised talking word banks;
- cloze procedure (Cloze –Pro) – software to generate sentences with missing words;
- key words are sorted into 'families' to draw attention to common letter patterns.

Children with word retrieval difficulties benefit from the introduction of word 'webs'. These display graphic representations of diverse features of a word – eg its colour, its function, how it is classified, what it is made from, where it is found, what sound it begins with – along with the written word itself. Forming links between a word and several different associated features helps to anchor the word more firmly and strengthens access to the mental lexicon

Reading texts

When children have limited sight vocabulary and a weakness in phonological processing, they often tend to become over-reliant on using context to predict meaning. The well-illustrated, richly contextual, 'top down' approach common to most core reading schemes today, can provide so much support that children with good oral vocabulary and a good grasp of syntax, are able to predict content without having processed much of the text. Dyslexic readers can often do this so well that an underlying core phonological weakness goes undetected until well through primary school and opportunities to develop decoding skills have been missed. In the workshop, new texts with fewer contextual cues are presented in every session, guiding readers to explore and practise a wider range of decoding skills. Key vocabulary is embedded in all new texts and related activities to provide 'overlearning' an essential step towards automaticity and fluent reading. A variety of methods is used to scaffold the reading experience, ensuring success and gradually developing confidence. Reading one-to-one with an adult who will prompt when appropriate, using text-to-audio software to cope with challenging words and engaging in paired reading activities are some of the measures used. Unobtrusive scaffolding, means that young readers learn to anticipate success and as confidence in their own ability grows, their enjoyment of reading is seen to flourish. The creation of opportunities to read aloud to appreciative audiences such as younger children, parent helpers or even to a specially trained and authorised dog, are effective ways to create a relaxed and pleasurable ethos in which frequent practice will be willingly undertaken.

Responding to texts

Visualisation

Children with dyslexia who have difficulty processing information may be failing to create mental imagery. In the workshop, children are encouraged to visualise their own pictures as they listen to stories or verbal descriptions without accompanying illustrations, and to describe and compare what they have imagined. This has been shown to lead to improvement in several skills areas (Bell, 1991) including

- imagination
- information processing
- prediction
- short term memory
- recognition of main points.

Higher order thinking and comprehension skills

Keith Stanovich has described 'Matthew effects' in the acquisition of reading (Stanovich, 1986); the reading rich will get richer and the poor get poorer. Children who become skilled readers realise deeper levels of cognitive development uniquely through their experiences of reading complex texts. Clearly those who struggle to read are denied this opportunity if their reading diet is restricted to the simple, prosaic language of reading primers. It is essential therefore, in the pursuit of holistic cognitive development, to enable every child to encounter a variety of gripping, stimulating and complex literature and to help them to comprehend and appreciate such texts. Access to harder texts can be supported through

- an adult reading aloud
- paired or shared reading
- software which reads and tracks as text is viewed on screen
- audio tapes/MP3 recording.

Too often in the early stages comprehension tasks are limited to simple, literal questions. Challenging questions, involving higher order thinking skills are introduced in the workshop right from the start. This includes:

- literal questions
- retelling the content or summarising the main points
- inferential reasoning
- evaluation and judgement of characters
- appreciation and emotional response to language and imagery.

Children with dyslexia often find skimming and scanning onerous and will tend to draw on their own background knowledge to answer questions rather than scrutinise the text. It is necessary to teach the importance of finding evidence. This can be supported if questions are examined before the text is read and if children are encouraged to highlight key words as they read.

Dyslexia is essentially a difficulty in processing information and for many learners the auditory signals from words and phrases fail to trigger sharp connections between ideas and concepts. Recording information graphically can help build better mental links. In the workshop, learners are encouraged when retelling, summarising or evaluating texts to use

- mind maps
- venn diagrams
- story boards
- tables.

Transparent learning

Where tasks are carefully planned and structured and activities are carried out with concrete resources, learning becomes transparent and valuable information about skill development is apparent in every activity. This means assessment never has to be conducted artificially; rather the learning task itself becomes an assessment opportunity.

Watching children working with magnetic letters reveals who has developed competence in phonemic tracking and who can perhaps select the appropriate letters yet lack the phonemic judgement to know where to place them. Similarly, observation of children composing sentences using Breakthrough or Clicker grids, gives insight into a range of knowledge:

- key words – sight vocabulary
- use of phonic cues to discriminate – e.g. went/want
- knowledge of morphemes – e.g. adding -ing and -ed
- one-to-one matching
- sentence construction/syntax
- word order
- punctuation.

Hands-on resources

A workshop by its very nature creates opportunities for practical endeavour and fosters emergent skills. This is exactly what the workshop for literacy sets out to achieve. Everything is 'hands-on' and learners are constantly urged to try something new. There is an emphasis on active learning; children arrange chunky magnetic letters, touch words on the IWB, respond to phonic tasks by moving on a 'dance mat.'

Given a word each, children in a group will sort themselves physically to represent a meaningful sentence or similarly put sentences in sequential order. Learners may make drawings, construct models or use a story board, to help process the information they wish to express.

Using technology

Many people have expressed concerns about the negative impact too much use of ICT can have on cognitive development – notably Maryanne Wolf (Wolf, 2008) and Susan Greenfield (Greenfield, 2008), yet there is no doubt that for dyslexic learners, ICT can be hugely beneficial. It can help both to support or bypass the difficulties they encounter and also to develop skill in areas of specific weakness. For most children it is extremely motivating, allowing them to work independently, at an appropriate pace and to produce a dignified end-product.

Editing

For children with poor motor skills, trying to read the scripts they have written is like trying to read without spectacles in a dimly lit room; they struggle so hard to make sense of their graphic scrawl that the task of re-reading for editing or for presentation, becomes impossible. Simply using any word processor to produce clear script, even where poor spelling remains a problem, enables most children to re-read comfortably and thus gain experience in the necessary tasks of editing and redrafting.

Spelling support

Clicker offers a split screen, encompassing a talking word bank in grid form and a talking word processor. This software enables teachers to produce customised, talking word banks quickly and easily, providing topic specific words to support spelling and written expression. Grids can also be devised to provide overlearning of key vocabulary to support reading.

CoWriter, a 'talking' predictive word bank, provides support for poor spellers but wider skill development also takes place implicitly. Because learners usually only require to identify the first 2–3 phonemes to find the target word, they focus positively on this task, exert much effort and are rewarded when their attempts trigger the correct word; phonological awareness has been developed, the development has been driven by the learner. The prediction list has to be scrutinised and the target word identified; because the target word is already in the learner's mind, in auditory form, the written form is more readily identified and neural pathways for word recognition are strengthened.

Reading support

Clicker comes with templates, making it easy to produce illustrated, talking books – customised versions of whatever is of current interest. Children can read and listen on screen, then print a copy to take away and enjoy.

WordTalk, text-to-audio software, can become the perfect 'reading buddy' – there is no 'loss of face' in asking a computer for help and it is always readily available. It is important to remember that many children who are dyslexic, will have comprehension and thinking skills which are developed well beyond their reading ability. These skills will not be challenged and further developed unless stimulating texts with complex syntax are explored. WordTalk can be

245

used to enable access to 'harder' texts, ensuring that able thinkers are not restricted to simple scripts.

2Create is used to make series of animated graphic slides telling a story in sequential steps. This calls for story-board planning, a very concrete way to help dyslexic learners arrange ideas sequentially. The text can be typed at the bottom of each screen or if there is a preference for oral expression, a voice- over recording can be added.

Early development of Keyboard skills – an investment for the future

TuxType and **2Type** provide games which develop keyboard awareness and typing skills.

Technology offers support to overcome almost any aspect of literacy difficulty. This support can only be accessed if learners are competent in using the keyboard and can respond intuitively to new software. In the workshop all children are encouraged to use the word processor as well as pencil and paper as soon as they learn to write words. Those with weak motor skills who struggle to form clear handwriting learn to type fluently as early as possible. Early training in keyboard skills is for many pupils a worthwhile investment which will pay dividends in the future.

Scope for children's creativity

Dyslexic children who struggle with analytic, left brain processing, often excel in right brain, artistic perceptions. Such abilities if directed to creative activities, can have a dynamic effect on learning. The wealth of opportunities presented by technology allows oral, artistic and musical abilities to be given full range in the production of multi–media presentations. The MP3 player allows radio networks to be set up and shared via an intranet across a cluster of schools, encouraging children with good oral skills to demonstrate knowledge and insights which they might struggle to express in writing.

The digital video camera offers scope for children to work collaboratively to produce a film and provides an experience where many talents other than reading and writing are seen to be necessary and valued. One child revealed highly developed skills in observation and recall of detail as well as the ability to 'sculpt' when he created beautiful plasticene figures – which seemed to 'grow' effortlessly from his hands – for a video animation. No one had noticed these talents before. Because the animation was an important part of the class topic, his contribution was highly valued by his peers and his self-esteem shot up accordingly.

Workshop for Literacy: A successful approach

The workshop has proved successful over several years and in different situations.

Focus on learners and how they learn has meant that from the earliest stage, appropriate activities have been introduced and the experience of failure avoided. As a result, children have anticipated success and become confident learners, eager to participate in new tasks.

Teachers have found that contextual assessment, using the very fabric of their own teaching has enabled them to recognise barriers of which they had been unaware.

Results have compared favourably with classes who did not participate; children in the workshop programme have developed skills to tackle reading and writing across the curriculum. In some cases, children with acquired helplessness have become independent, active learners who have taken pride in making worthwhile contributions along with their peers.

Parents have expressed appreciation when their children have been helped to overcome barriers; as one mother put it: 'He has gone from hating school, which I believe was because he was unable to read and participate with others, to now looking forward to going. And now he loves to read everything.' The most convincing evidence of success is that without exception, children who have experienced the workshop approach have become confident individuals who enjoy reading and writing.

References

Bell, N. (1991) *Visualising and Verbalising: for Language Comprehension and Thinking*. Paso Robles CA: Academy of Reading Publications.

Frith, U. (1985) Beneath the surface of developmental dyslexia. In K.E. Patterson, J.C. Marshall and M. Coltheart (eds), *Surface Dyslexia*, pp. 301–330. London: Erlbaum.

Greenfield, S. (2008) Reinventing us. *New Scientist, 198* (No 2656): pp. 48–49.

Hill, E.L. (2001) Non-specific nature of specific language impairment: a review of the literature with regard to concomitant motor impairments. *International Journal of Language and Communication Disorders, 36*: 149–171.

Salmelin, R. and Helenius, P. (2004). Functional Neuro-Anatomy of Impaired Reading in Dyslexia. *Scientific Studies of Reading, 8*(4): 257–272.

Stanovich, K.E. (1986) Matthew Effects in reading: some consequences of individual differences in the acquisition of literacy. *Reading Research Quarterly, 21*(4): 360–407.

Topping, K.J. (1995) *Paired Reading, Spelling and Writing: the Handbook for Teachers and Parents*. London and New York: Cassell.

Vellutino, F.R., Fletcher J. M., Snowling M. and Scanlon D. (2004) Specific reading disability (dyslexia): What have we learned in the past four decades? *Journal of Child Psychology and Psychiatry, 45* (1) 2–40.

Wolfe, M. (2008) *Proust and the Squid*. Cambridge: Icon Books.

Resources

Breakthrough to Literacy: Pearson Education, Ltd, Oxford UK.

Software

Clicker 5: Crick Software Northampton, UK.
Cloze Pro: Crick Software Northampton, UK.
CoWriter: Don Johnston Incorporated. donjohnston.co.uk.
WordTalk: Rod Macaulay TASSC Aberdeen. Free download.
2Create: 2Simple Software: London.
TuxType: Tux Typing GNU General Public License (GPL).
2Type: 2Simple Software: London.

19

The implications of students' perspectives on dyslexia for school improvement

Barbara Riddick

This chapter

- looks at the history and nature of listening to students perspectives on dyslexia
- examines the variety of sources from which dyslexic children's views on school have emerged
- discusses conceptual and practical issues related to eliciting children's perspectives
- voices children's views on a dyslexia friendly school initiative
- stresses the importance of linking children's and student's perspectives on dyslexia to school improvement.

History and nature of students' perspectives on dyslexia

Students' perspectives on dyslexia can been heard in both direct (face-to-face) and less direct ways. They can also be seen as on a continuum from informal to formal. A dyslexic child who makes a passing comment to a teacher about not wanting to read out loud is making a direct but informal comment. For younger children in particular, parents are important mediators, who as advocates for their children act as an indirect voice for their child. Riddick (1996) found that parents reported intervening when their children came home distressed or unhappy from school because of difficulties associated with their dyslexia. They would, for example, ask the school not to make their child read out loud in front of the class or would point out that their child had spent time learning the required spellings and was not being simply 'lazy'. Although parents have a vital contribution to make, it is important to be aware that they are not usually directly experiencing what happens in the classroom and they are dependent on what their children choose to tell them. When Riddick (1996) interviewed children about their experiences of dyslexia some children made it clear that they told their parents little about their school experiences even if they had been distressed or upset by them. It was interesting to see that parents and children rated problems at school in a different order, with children, for example, giving a higher rating to the problem of copying things down fast enough from the board. This perhaps reflects some of the day-to-day difficulties that dyslexic children face that are less obvious to parents and teachers. It was also the case that most older children reported being more selective in what they told their parents about their experiences at school.

Internationally there has been increasing emphasis on the need for a range of professionals to listen to parents' perspectives on their children's development and well-being. In the UK for, example, the second chapter of the special educational needs (SEN) *Code of Practice* (DfES, 2001) is devoted to working in partnership with parents. The Code emphasizes that parents should have a central role in the assessment of their children and in alongside their children be involved in planning of any additional support or development of any Individual Education Plans.

It could be argued that an early way in which the voices of children and adults with dyslexia were heard were through biographies, autobiographies and collections of interviews. In 1981 Susan Hampshire, a prominent television and film actor of the time, published her autobiography entitled *Susan's Story: My Struggle with Dyslexia*. In this she recounted some of her experiences of learning to read and write and some of the difficulties she encountered as a severe dyslexic. What she made clear was that literacy difficulties were not just a technical problem, but because of the social stigma attached to poor literacy lead to feelings of shame, embarrassment and unworthiness. She comments, for example, 'I desperately wanted to be liked and I assumed no one could like someone as stupid as me'. More positively she also demonstrated that coping strategies could be put in place such as learning her lines from audio tapes. None of this may seem very surprising now, but early contributions such as this were important in raising the profile of dyslexia, and in helping teachers and the public in general to have more understanding and sympathy for children who struggled with literacy difficulties. Several accounts in the early 1990s (Van de Stoel, 1990; Osmond, 1993; Edwards, 1994) started to indicate the range of practices in school that could demoralise or support dyslexic children in their learning. Like Hampshire's account they also underlined the marked social and emotional difficulties engendered by some of these learning experiences. They also made it clear that schools and teachers had a critical impact on the literacy development, wider learning and general well-being of dyslexic children. Such work was important in countering the negative stereo-type held by some educationalists, of parents of dyslexic children as neurotic, over-ambitious people who made excuses for their 'thick' and/or 'lazy' children. Although this chapter is focused on student's perspectives, as indicated earlier, some parents play an important role in helping children to articulate or have their views listened to. It has therefore been an important development that in the case of parents as well as children their views are seen as legitimate and worthy of consideration. The emphasis now placed on listening to students' and parents' views, combined with the increasing legitimisation of the term dyslexia, would suggest that children's perspectives should be playing an increasingly important role in bringing about school improvements.

Dyslexia students in further and higher education and successful adult dyslexics

Some children with dyslexia, despite their difficulties, have progressed on to further and higher education. With better identification and support in schools there has been a considerable increase in the number of declared dyslexics in further and higher education in the UK. There have been several studies which have researched the experiences of these students, and as part of these studies students have often commented on their experiences of school (Riddick *et al.*, 1997; Farmer *et al.*, Sterling 2002; Pollack, 2005). Much of what they have to say underlines and reinforces the experiences recounted by school-age children. What they can add is a long-term and developmental perspective on their experiences of schooling. With age and relative success in the academic system they can also articulate what aspects of schooling enabled them to be successful and what aspects of schooling acted as barriers. Views of this nature have added weight, credence and perspective to the experiences of school-age children. In particular they have illustrated how dyslexia impacts on the learning of even relatively successful students and the range of successful coping strategies students adopt to cope with these difficulties. Such accounts do underline the variability of school provision with both very supportive and very unsupportive experiences of schools and teachers re-counted. Many students and successful adults with dyslexia stress the importance of having at least one teacher who 'believed' in them and was willing to act as an advocate for them. Possibly with changes in school practices and a more dyslexia-friendly school environment children should feel supported by a range of teachers and the need for one key teacher who believes in them should be less prominent. The dyslexia-friendly school approach advocates that there should be at least one teacher with specialist dyslexia training in each school, it will be interesting to see if such teachers tend to take on this role or support their colleagues so that this becomes a collective responsibility. Some researchers have interviewed adult dyslexics who have not gone onto further or higher education (Macdonald, 2006) or have done so by less traditional routes (Pollak, 2005). This has given a wider and more representative perspective on dyslexic adults' recollections of school.

The role of voluntary organisations

Another important channel for the voice of children with dyslexia and their parents has been through voluntary organisations such as the British Dyslexia Association (BDA) in the UK and the International Dyslexia Association (IDA) in the USA. In the past when dyslexia was not recognised or treated as a legitimate construct by many schools, such organisations played an important role as pressure groups that argued for the legitimacy of dyslexia and campaigned for the kind of structured support and understanding that such children needed in school. As part of this process they distilled many of the experiences recounted to them by dyslexic children and their parents to articulate what needed changing within mainstream schools. Although such organisations were often keen to share their expertise with teachers in mainstream school, they were often treated with hostility or wariness. In the last 10 to 15 years this situation has changed and voluntary organisations are more likely to be seen as an important source of expertise to be utilised by mainstream provision. In the UK for example the SEN *Code of Practice* (DfES, 2001) stipulates that schools should develop positive relations with appropriate voluntary organisations and where possible draw on their expertise or collaborate with them. A prime example of this has been the Dyslexia Friendly Schools Pack (BDA, 2005a) developed as a result of a collaboration between the BDA and the Department for Education and Skills (DfES). The dyslexia-friendly schools approach is discussed in detail other chapters in this book, but in essence it provides a set of detailed guidelines for mainstream schools on the best way to support and educate dyslexic children (Riddick, 2006). It can be argued that students' perspectives have played an important part in shaping these guidelines. Recommending that teachers do not ask children to read out loud in front of the class unless they wish to do so, or marking separately for content and presentation of work, can be traced back to the many comments of distress or demoralisation made by dyslexic children about such practices. A 16-year-old severely dyslexic student in the Riddick (1995, 1996) interview study made the following comment. 'In lessons they make you read out all the time. My mum does complain but the school doesn't listen. They don't know how much it affects you. I think it like frightens you, it really frightens you. Being put through the trauma of it.' It is interesting to note that the BDA states it 'is the voice of dyslexic people. We aim to influence government and other institutions to promote a dyslexia friendly society' (BDA, 2008). A disadvantage from the perspective of such organisations is that they are not embedded within the school system and do not have the direct power to change policy and practice. However their relative independence means that they can act as a critical friend and as a powerful advocate and conduit for the views of individuals with dyslexia.

More recent research on dyslexic children's experiences of school

Johnson (2004) gathered the views of dyslexic children on the practices and attitudes of teachers who they thought made learning easy or difficult for them. Interestingly children's responses were very similar to those gathered by Riddick (1996) on the characteristics of the best and worst teachers they had encountered. Some of the positive qualities described by dyslexic children such as 'kind and helpful' or 'patient and approachable' may be with which ones most non-dyslexic children would identify. But because dyslexic children are, for example, more likely to need help or to need a teacher to be patient, such qualities are probably especially important to them. It may also be the case that teachers are more likely to display these qualities if they understand why a child is working slowly or appears to need additional support. What is unclear is how far teachers' understanding of dyslexia or literacy difficulties underpins their attitudes and behaviour. In a similar vein behaviours such as shouting a lot or getting angry if a child doesn't understand would probably be on most children's list of negatives. But again, dyslexic children, because of their literacy difficulties, are more likely to find themselves in the 'firing line' because, for example, their work is untidy or they haven't completed the task on time. Qualities more specific to their dyslexia were also mentioned by the majority of dyslexic children. The positives included giving them time to copy things down, not humiliating them in public for poor literacy and understanding their learning difference. Negative behaviours included not giving them time to copy things down, making them read out loud in front of the class, marking down for spelling, grammar and hand writing and humiliating them by asking for test scores in public. Secondary school children in particular found having too much to copy off the board a common problem, some also felt that they were undervalued because of their poor literacy and automatically put in bottom sets. One of the recommendations of the dyslexia-friendly school approach is that children should be put in the set or group commensurate with their cognitive ability and not their literacy level.

Children's voice and school improvement

Because dyslexic individuals are first and foremost part of the wider learning community it is important to consider more generic approaches and attitudes to listening to the voice of the learner.

At present much emphasis has been placed on the importance of children's or students' views on learning. This leads to three fundamental questions:

1 Why should we be interested in children's/students perspectives on learning?
2 How can we gain access to those perspectives?
3 What can we learn from those perspectives?

Why listen to children/students

The National Foundation for Educational Research (2008) in its section on school improve-ment makes the following observation.

Recent years have witnessed a growing commitment to including young people's voice in research, evaluation and consultation, the benefits of which have been widely reported. For example, seeking the views of children and young people and involving them in decision making is reported to improve services, improve decision making, enhance the democratic process, enhance young people's skills, promote their sense of responsibility, and empower and enhance their self-esteem.

The following list summarises some of the main reasons given for listening to the voice of the child/student about teaching and learning:

1 it democratises learning and involves children in the learning process
2 it is a crucial and integral part of any comprehensive and valid evaluation of educational practice
3 it can give more complex feedback which allows for more finely tuned improvements or alteration to policy and practice
4 it can heighten teacher/school understanding of children's difficulties and lead to more constructive attributions about their learning
5 it can help map out the range of responses children have to particular educational practices
6 it can sometimes highlight issues that may not have occurred to educationalists or indicate which issues are particularly important from the students' perspective.

What do we mean by the voice or perspective of the child/student?

As indicated in the introduction to this article there are questions about what exactly is meant by listening to the voice or perspective of the learner. It could be argued that at an informal and taken-for-granted level many teachers do listen to children as part of their every-day approach to teaching. Research suggests (Wade and Moore, 1993; Ruddock and Flutter, 2000) that individual teachers vary considerably in the extent to which they claim to consult children about their learning and the importance that they place on this. Wade and Moore asked the following question of teachers 'Do you regularly take account of pupils' views in either planning or providing learning experiences? If so, why? If not, why not?' They received replies from 76 primary school teachers and 48 secondary school teachers in both cases less than a third of teachers said that they did so. The figures may well have changed with time, but interesting accompanying information on teachers' reasons for their responses was provided. The major reason given by those teachers who did consult children was so they could teach more effectively, whereas one of the main reasons given for not doing so was that teachers saw no value in consulting children.

There is also the question as to how far listening to learners can be embedded into everyday teaching practices and how far additional or less embedded approaches are needed to supplement the day-to-day approach. A variety of direct and indirect methods can be used, ranging from school councils to individual interviews with children. Whereas some issues are well suited to public debate, other issues require much more privacy. Lewis and Lindsay (2000) have discussed the ethical issues involved in eliciting children's/students' views, especially in research studies or activities outside of ongoing classroom teaching. Particularly with younger children, the unequal power relation between adults and children has to be borne in mind. In some cases children may feel more comfortable with less direct methods such as anonymous questionnaires. Smith found in his large scale surveys of bullying (Whitney and Smith, 1993) that much higher rates of bullying were reported when children could fill in questionnaires anonymously. This indicates the importance of having a range of methods depending on what is being asked or enquired into and also on the age of the learners. Morrow (2001) found that when children were given a choice of how they would like to give their views, younger children (9–11 years of age) chose to draw and older children, especially girls, preferred to write. Wade and Moore (1993) in their research into the views of children with a range of SENs, used several techniques including informal group discussions, interviews, question-naires and a sentence completion task. The sentence completion task indicated that many children

- wished they could do better academically and physically
- viewed themselves negatively
- saw themselves as inferior to their peers
- felt shame and embarrassment at public reprimands
- dreaded or intensely disliked testing.

More recent approaches have involved children taking photographs of their school or making their own video diaries. With newer technologies audio and video clips have become a relatively common way of letting individuals give their view or perspective as part of an information or training package. In Scotland (Deponio, 2007) a DVD entitled *Dyslexia at Transition* has been compiled and a copy has been given to each school in Scotland with a follow-up road show. The DVD has numerous clips of dyslexic children talking about their experiences of schooling as well as clips of their parents and teachers. Although it could be argued that educationalists have asked the questions and compiled the DVD, the broad range of children interviewed and the level of detail and focus involved allows the complexity and variations in children's perspectives to be clearly illustrated. It is interesting that an initiative like this has the backing of the Scottish Government and demonstrates that student's perspectives are now seen as central to improvements in teaching and learning.

Who listens to the learners' perspectives?

Another question is who is doing the listening and what use are they likely to make of the information they are given by children. Although teachers have the advantage of an ongoing relationship with children and see them on a regular basis, they also have limited time and restraints on what they can feasibly change in response to children's comments. In Wade and Moore's (1993) research, two of the main reasons given by class teachers for not consulting children about their learning was that they said consultation was precluded by decisions taken above their head and that it was time-consuming. With more emphasis currently on listening to the perspective of learners (Ruddock and Flutter, 2000), this should have lessened but it is still the case that class teachers are constrained by a number of factors outside of their control. In other cases a child may be reluctant to reveal certain matters to their teacher or reluctant to be seen to directly question or criticize their teacher. Many children with special educational needs tend to receive much of their additional support from learning support assistants (LSAs). In some cases it is their learning support assistant who knows most about their views on learning. How far these can be passed onto the class teacher or fed into the school's plans for learning will depend on local factors such as the time allowed for LSAs to talk to teachers and to attend school in-service days, etc. Issues of confidentiality also arise, a child may wish an LSA to know something but not want it passed onto their class teacher.

Whose voice is listened to?

Another question in gaining children's/students' perspectives is what sort of sampling strategy will be adopted. Will all children/students in a given class, year or school be listened to or will a representative sample be consulted? In all cases the samples drawn upon or methods used to listen to children and students will depend on the particular issues to be addressed. A concern running through much of this is to ensure that all children are listened to and that less forthcoming or less confident children have their views taken into account. At a practical level in terms of eliciting students' perspectives there are questions about

- How often?
- How much?
- How is the sample chosen?
- How recorded?
- How is it acted upon?
- Is it embedded in school practice?
- How much time/effort will it take?

School improvement is based on a complex interaction of factors ranging from school leadership and management to the individual practices of classroom teachers. In order to consider how learners' perspectives can influence school policy and practice, a multi-faceted approach has to be adopted that can look at how students' perspectives can influence their learning experiences at many levels. To gain as full a picture as possible a complex patchwork of consultation on learners' perspectives is needed

ranging from external one-off funded research to ongoing teacher-led practices which are embedded within everyday school practices. It can be argued that in the case of dyslexia this has been gradually taking place and has involved an amalgam of activities including external interview and questionnaire studies as well as information via Individual Education Plans and Personal Learning Plans and various school and teacher consultation exercises.

Audits of dyslexia-friendly school practices

In the current climate of inclusion in the UK and elsewhere, there have been understandable attempts to document or audit specific policies and practices that it is assumed will lead to more positive educational outcomes for children with a range of needs. The Index for Inclusion (2002) which is linked to the special educational needs (SEN) *Code of Practice* (DfES, 2001) is a prime example of this. It sets out in detail the kinds of activities teachers and schools should be carrying out in order to improve their practices and ultimately create a more inclusive climate for all children. In a similar vein various more specific audit documents have been produced concentrating on more specific areas of SEN. Within the area of specific learning difficulty the BDA has produced a document which enables schools to audit how 'dyslexia friendly' their practice is. Some Local Authorities have produced their own versions of this, Durham Local Authority, for example (Coffield and O'Neil, 2004), produced a dyslexia- and dyspraxia-friendly school audit document. All these documents are filled in by education professionals. An important question is, how did the constructors of these audits know what items to include? What evidence were they basing their assumptions on about the validity of their audit documents? To put it plainly, how did they know what was good for children? In addition to the issue of what questions are asked in audit documents, there is also the issue of how educationalists respond to them. In some cases educationalists may feel that they should give the responses that others want to hear. In other cases educationalists may give their genuine observations but these will be shaped by the level of awareness and time which they have available to focus on individual children or practices. Humphrey (2002) found, for example, that although children with dyslexia in mainstream schools scored lower in their own self-ratings of various aspects of self-esteem, they were less likely to be seen as having low self-esteem by their teachers than similar children with dyslexia in specialist units. Various explanations could be given for this finding, Humphrey suggests that one of the most likely is that teachers in specialist dyslexia units are more aware of the impact of literacy difficulties on children's general well-being and approach to learning and the likely negative consequences for their self-esteem. Whole-school and class-level attempts to improve practice are to be applauded, but it is important that the opinions of students are included in this process.

Dyslexic children's views on a dyslexia friendly school approach

As a follow-up to the Durham LA dyslexia-friendly school initiative, we (Riddick, 2006; Coffield et al., 2008) decided to evaluate its impact from the point of view of both dyslexic and non-dyslexic children. Most people would argue that there is a continuum of children with literacy difficulties, from those who are clearly recognised as dyslexic to those with milder difficulties who are not formally recognised as dyslexic. The British Dyslexia Association suggests that many of the strategies recommended for dyslexic children are beneficial for the learning of most children. The sampling approach chosen allowed us to hear the views of a spectrum of children on the impact of a dyslexia-friendly school approach from their perspective. The questionnaire was designed to ask the children about a number of specific dyslexia-friendly strategies that were recommended for class teachers, such as being prepared to repeat instructions, making work sheets easy to follow by highlighting important information, and for primary school teachers providing literacy support materials such as word mats, alphabet strips, special dictionaries, etc. There were a number of examples of good practice, but it was clear that there were considerable variations in practice between classes and between schools. As well as questions on specific practices there were questions designed to gauge children's sense of well –being, and confidence in their own learning. For primary schools these included questions about statements such as:

- I am happy at school most of the time.
- I am proud of my work.
- I think my work is as good as everybody else's in the class.

Whereas 94 per cent of the dyslexic children in primary school said they were happy in school most of the time only 28 per cent thought their work was as good as everybody else's in the class. This may be linked to the fact that 54 per cent of dyslexic children reported getting lots of red marks in their exercise books, 21 per cent said that they did not have time to copy their homework down and 32 per cent said that they did not have time to finish their written work in class. In addition to this, 35 per cent of dyslexic children reported that they were required to read out loud in class even if they did not want to. It appears that even in schools that have signed up to a dyslexia-friendly approach there are variations in practice which may impact on how children see themselves as learners. A problem with having a prescribed set of practices (as teachers are all too aware) is that individual children vary in what they find helpful or unhelpful. Whereas most dyslexic children do not want to be asked to read out loud, one boy reported being offended that he was not asked to read out loud in class. In another case, two children in a class were embarrassed by attention or support from their teacher, whereas another boy in the same class wished that the teacher would pay him more attention. Much seems to depend on the overall atmosphere and context in which practices take place and the relationship that the child has with their teacher.

Final summary

This gets back to the question of how dyslexic children's and students' perspectives can best be accessed and acted upon to bring about school improvements. Is it best, for example, for teachers to be given a detailed list of recommended practices in the classroom or to read an autobiographical account of a child with dyslexia which may increase their empathy and understanding towards children who struggle with their literacy? How far should the focus be on individual classroom practice as opposed to wider school policies and opportunities for training? As indicated earlier in the chapter in reality a range of approaches are needed, but these need to be underpinned with the belief that children's/students' perspectives are valuable and have an important contribution to make. May (2005) notes that it is adults who set the agenda and often decide on the questions to ask about pupil perceptions. This links to a final point about what the ultimate purpose of gaining students' perspectives might be. Is it essentially to drive up standards in terms of formal assessment results, is it to empower students and give them a stronger sense of agency in their own learning, or is it really about improving children's general well-being and school experience? Educationalists are often caught in the tensions between a standards and an inclusion agenda and may wish to listen to students' views for a variety of reasons. For children with dyslexia, past accounts of unhappiness at school accompanied by low self-esteem scores (Riddick et al., 2002) has made improving their well-being and experience of school a priority and an important reason for listening to their perspectives. Equally concerning has been the lack of progress in reading and spelling age scores, and overall literacy performance for many dyslexic children with the knock-on effect of difficulty in fully accessing many areas of the curriculum. This again is an important reason for listening to the voices of dyslexic children on how best intensive literacy support can be provided and good curriculum access ensured. From a meta cognitive point of view we know that the more aware dyslexic children are of themselves as learners the more likely they are to develop effective coping strategies (Reid, 2005). It is important that we understand dyslexic children's perspectives on what helps them to develop awareness and effective coping strategies.

Some improvement has been made in all these areas but it is patchy to date and more work is needed on how best to integrate the diverse sources of information on children's perspectives on dyslexia.

References

British Dyslexia Association (BDA) (2001) *Dyslexia Friendly Schools Audit*. Reading: BDA.

British Dyslexia Association (BDA) (2005a) *Dyslexia Friendly Schools Pack*. Reading: BDA/DfES. Available online www.bdadyslexia.org.uk.

British Dyslexia Association (BDA) (2005b) *Achieving Dyslexia Friendly Schools* (5th edn). Oxford: Information Press.

British Dyslexia Association (BDA) (2008) *About Dyslexia: What is Dyslexia?* www.bdadyslexia.org.uk. (Retrieved 3 September 2008).

Coffield, M. and O'Neill, J. (2004) The Durham experience: promoting dyslexia and dyspraxia friendly schools. *Dyslexia, 10*(3): 253–264.

Coffield, M., Riddick, B., Barmby, P. and O'Neil, J. (2008) Dyslexia friendly primary schools, what can we learn from asking the pupils? In G. Reid, A. Fawcett, F. Manis and L. Siegel (eds) *Sage Handbook of Dyslexia*. London: Sage.

Department for Education and Skills (DfES) (2001) *Code of Practice on the Identification and Assessment of Special Educational Needs*. Nottingham: DfES Publications.

Deponio, P. (2007) *Dyslexia at Transition* (DVD). Edinburgh, Scotland: Dyslexia Scotland/Moray House School of Education. Available www.transition.org.

Edwards, J. (1994) *The Scars of Dyslexia*. London: Cassell.

Farmer, M., Riddick, B. and Sterling, C. (2002) *Dyslexia and Inclusion: Assessing and Supporting Students in Higher Education*. London: Whurr Publishers.

Humphrey, N. (2002) Teacher and pupil ratings of self-esteem in developmental dyslexia. *British Journal of Special Education, 29*(1): 29–36.

Johnson, M. (2004), Dyslexia-friendly schools: policy and practice. In G. Reid and A. Fawcett (eds) *Dyslexia in Context: Research, Policy and Practice*. London: Wiley.

Lewis, A. and Lindsay, G. (2000) *Researching Children's Perspectives*. Buckingham: Open University Press.

Macdonald, S. (2006) *Dyslexia, Slass and the Education System*. PhD thesis, Newcastle University.

May, H. (2005). Whose participation is it anyway? Examining the context of pupil participation in the UK. *British Journal of Special Education, 32*(1): 29–34.

Morrow, V. (2001) Using qualitative methods to elicit young people's perspectives on their environments. *Health Education Research*, 16(3): 255–268.

National Foundation for Educational Research (2008) Research into pupil engagement in building schools for the future. http://www.nfer.ac.uk/research-areas (Retrieved 26 March 2008).

Osmond, J. (1993) *The Reality of Dyslexia*. London: Cassell.

Pollak, D. (2005) *Dyslexia: The Self and Higher Education*. Stoke on Trent: Trentham Books.

Reid, G. (2005) *Learning Styles and Inclusion*. London: Sage.

Riddick, B. (1995) Dyslexia and development: an interview study. *Dyslexia, 1*(2): 63–74.

Riddick, B. (1996) *Living with Dyslexia: The Social and Emotional Consequences of Specific Learning Difficulties*. London: Routledge.

Riddick, B. (2006) Dyslexia friendly schools in the UK. *Topics in Language Disorders, 26*(2): 142–154.

Riddick, B., Farmer, M. and Sterling, C. (1997) *Students and Dyslexia: Growing Up With a Specific Learning Difficulty*. London: Whurr Publishers.

Riddick, B., Wolfe, J. and Lumsdon, D. (2002) *Dyslexia: A Practical Guide for Teachers and Parents*. London: David Fulton.

Ruddock, J. and Flutter, J. (2000) Pupil participation and pupil perspective: 'Carving a new order of experience'. *Cambridge Journal of Education, 30*(1):75–89.

Tresman, S. (2005) Dyslexia friendly LEAs and schools: the BDA quality mark initiative. *The Dyslexia Handbook 2005*. Reading: British Dyslexia Association.

Wade, B. and Moore, M. (1993) *Experiencing Special Education*. Buckingham: Open University Press.

Whitney, I. and Smith, P. (1993) A Survey of the nature and extent of bullying in junior/middle and secondary schools. *Educational Research, 35*(1): 625–638.

Van der Stoel, S. (1990) *Parents on Dyslexia*. Clevedon: Multilingual Matters.

257

Part 4

Identifying and meeting needs in further, higher education and the workplace

20

The development of protocols for assessment and intervention at university for students with dyslexia

Jay Kirkland

This chapter

- considers the driving principles to take into account when supporting dyslexic students in higher education
    - legislative
    - political
    - pedagogical
    - institutional
- considers challenges around developing protocols for assessing and intervening with dyslexic students
    - readiness of managerial and academic staff to engage
    - external agendas (economics) imposed by government
    - willingness of students to engage
- considers appropriate assessment and intervention with dyslexic students
    - purpose of assessment
    - feedback of diagnosis
    - and appropriate manner of intervention.

Driving principles

Legislative

One might well ask why anyone is still at the stage of considering the development of protocols for assessment and intervention at university for students with dyslexia. In 1995 the Disability Discrimination Act (which covers people with dyslexia in some circumstances) made it plain that those tasked with managing Higher Education in the UK had to make adjustments for disabled individuals to enable them to participate fully in all aspects of the educational process. Since 2001 the participation of post-16 students has increased significantly due to the legislative spur of the DDA. This at first gave disabled people the right to claim equality of provision then shifted in emphasis to impose a duty on institutions to provide equality of access to education in all its forms. It is also incumbent on institutions to measure the progress they make in improving outcomes for their disabled students and to publish their findings in their Disability Equality Schemes.

Political

Institutions, ranging from those with 'small specialist' status to larger, possibly more market driven institutions, are pressed by funding bodies to adhere to agendas set by Government. In 2003 the DfES white paper listed the following as key to maintaining and increasing institutional success:

- global competitiveness through graduate skills and research
- economic progress through a high skills workforce
- high quality in teaching and research
- greater engagement with communities outside campus through widening participation and knowledge transfer.

So while institutions can espouse principles providing a framework in which to develop protocol to assess and intervene with dyslexic students in HE they are still slaves to competing priorities, possibly imposed by external forces as well as internally.

Pedagogical

In line with requirements of the DDA and other recent equalities legislation, and the increasing recognition of the need to promote social diversity to achieve social justice there is growing awareness of, and interest in, inclusive pedagogy. Open University courses on inclusion for teaching staff in HE and the 10-year Teachability project that ran in Scotland until 2006 are two projects that have had a dramatic impact on the teaching practice of many lecturers in Scottish HEI, however this is still a challenging area for some.

Institutional

Institutions of course have their own priorities regarding how they fit in to a wider landscape. Institutions' strategic plans, action plans and objectives will influence the priorities of their schools, faculties and departments and how they prioritize how their resources are used. Evidence of why the development of protocol for assessing students with dyslexia should be a priority in HE may be requested by managers in order to justify decisions and expenditure.

Developing protocol for assessment

When developing protocol for assessing students with dyslexia in HE it is important that this takes account of students at different stages of their relationship with the institution. Assessment at pre-admission requires different consideration to that of assessment at the stage of transition to employment. Tensions however exist here as well. It must be established in advance what the purpose of any assessment is and it must be designed accordingly to:

- diagnose disability/specific learning difficulty
- establish initial competency
- inform the design of an individual support programme.

If assessment is designed to assess whether a student has a 'disability' such as dyslexia, ethical issues around confidentiality, data protection and, perhaps, what follow-up work will be appropriate may arise. People who are being assessed have the right to know the purpose of the assessment and whether and how the outcomes of the assessment will be shared with them and perhaps others.

If the assessment is to establish initial competencies this may conflict with disability equality legislation. Adjustments are not legally required to be made to competency standards however as discrimination can never be justified, competence standards must not be discriminatory in the first place and must be assessed in an inclusive way.

If the purpose of assessment is to assess a student's likely difficulty with learning and gauge the appropriate level of support then it must be designed with this in mind. To avoid requests for adjustments at the assessment stage, account might be taken of whether the assessment is to be oral or written, either by hand or by using a computer or other assistive technology. Are IT skills being tested or the ability to handwrite coherently under pressure of time? Is the assessment designed to enable analysis of errors in spelling, punctuation or grammar? Is the purpose of assessment to analyse the way in which the students have processed their task and presented it?

It is now a duty on HEIs to check with bodies representing the interests of people with impairments whether they are likely to experience any negative impact caused by the development of institutional practices, policies or procedures; this could equally apply to developing new protocols. In the interest of dyslexic people two points of reference might be the Scottish Accessible Information Forum and the British Dyslexia Association which both offer guidelines on producing accessible information in a variety of formats to dyslexic people.

Feedback on assessment

If managers of institutions are going to prioritize the assessment of students for dyslexia a further imperative will be to consider how assessment results are fedback to those being assessed and whose responsibility it will be to do this. Potential students and students newly diagnosed with dyslexia will have to come to terms with the exposure of their learning difficulties and possibly a new self identity encompassing the concept of having a 'disability'. They will perhaps require support to develop new learning and coping strategies and perhaps to master assistive technologies. Will counselling and disability related employability advice be made available? Will such students be provided with access to assistive technologies within the institution and specialist training or will this be facilitated to take place elsewhere? Managers of institutions will need to consider to what extent they will be able to make services and resources available.

Professional development

Given that dyslexic students will require strong organizational and time management skills (areas manifestly weaker for dyslexic people) to arrange support or develop new learning strategies alongside other study, work and social life demands, the additional pressure this creates for them is obvious. Consideration might be given as to how time spent developing alternative learning strategies and communication skills can be acknowledged and accounted for, perhaps even more radically accredited by institutions.

Developing protocol for intervention

Intervention can be targeted at those who have disclosed dyslexia, but not all students are willing to do this. Students who have been diagnosed dyslexic at an earlier stage in their education may have received some remedial tuition with varying degrees of success. They may have a negative impression of what 'support' means and initially avoid this as a course of action. They may have received support from parents or carers that disguised their difficulties and which is no longer available to them in the HE environment. For these reasons students sometimes do not ask for help until it is too late. It can be anticipated that there will be dyslexic students matriculated in HE institutions who have not disclosed their condition. By embedding support for dyslexic students throughout the institution from pre-admissions stage to post-graduation the need for intervention can be minimised.

Where inclusive pedagogy has not yet been fully embedded within institutions then intervention usually takes the form of additional support such as the provision of assistive technology and time and training to use it, adjustments to the manner in which learning outcomes are assessed or time given to attend additional one-to-one or small group support. This kind of intervention has added value to students. Skills developed can, when recognised, be reflected in their Personal Development Plans. Students can transfer their investment in time (spent developing new, effective 'coping strategies') or experience (managing support workers) into employment when they have graduated. Intervention might take the form of a 'light touch' whereby a staff member prompts to enable the student to consider the values of new skills they have developed to use assistive technology or manage tutors in a context wider than that of HE.

Conclusion

So, it can be seen that developing protocols for assessing and intervening with dyslexic students in HE is a challenging task. It requires an awareness of the effects of the driving principles (legislative, political, institutional and pedagogical) that influence how institutions develop. It requires a readiness of staff to accept that it is a priority to assess and intervene with dyslexic students in HE when there are many other competing priorities driven from both within and out with institutions and it requires an awareness of the ethical issues and resource implications of assessing and intervening with dyslexic students in HE. It requires confidence and a willingness from students to engage with policies, practices and procedures around assessment and intervention. Inevitably it will be a willingness from teaching staff to adopt inclusive teaching practice and embed equality of experience for all learners that will have the biggest impact on the learning experience of dyslexic students in HE. Whether this is stick driven (legislation) or carrot led (more resources given to academics to develop their teaching according to the principles of inclusive pedagogy) is the question, but a positive outcome could eliminate the need to assess and intervene with dyslexic students in HE.

21

Reading comprehension solutions for college students with dyslexia in an era of technology
An integrated approach

Noel Gregg and Manju Banerjee

This chapter

- integrates the literature related to the cognitive/metacognitive strategies necessary for success in comprehending printed text with research targeting the influence of digital reading across open (i.e., Internet) and closed (i.e., electronic text) learning environments specific to the college population with dyslexia
- establishes that the integration of both cognitive/metacognitive strategies and electronic tools (eTools) is essential for providing effective instruction and accommodations for college students with dyslexia
- explains that we use the term 'college students' in this chapter to be inclusive of adults attending many different types of postsecondary institutions (i.e., technical colleges, two-year colleges, four-year colleges, and graduate school).

Juan, a 17-year-old male, comes from a rural farming community where he was identified as demonstrating dyslexia and AD/HD in first grade. His verbal deficits (e.g., verbal working memory, phonemic awareness, orthographic processing, naming, and listening comprehension) lead to reading decoding and comprehension performance significantly below average. In addition, specific executive functioning deficits that co-occur with verbal language deficits influence his reading performance. Juan is currently struggling academically at a technical college. Several of the accommodations Juan is provided at his college include extra time during testing, electronic texts, and text-to-speech software.

Pat is a 21-year old African American student with a history of special education dating back to second grade. She is currently attending a four-year college. Her reading deficits in the areas of phonemic and orthographic awareness significantly limit her reading decoding abilities and provide support for the right to specific accommodations in the classroom and in testing situations. Several of her accommodations include extra time on tests that require reading, electronic texts and text-to-speech software.

For many adolescents and adults with dyslexia difficulties understanding print presents a substantial barrier and has a negative impact on secondary and postsecondary outcomes (Gregg,

2007). Juan and Pat provide us two very different reading profiles. While both of these individuals demonstrate difficulty comprehending printed text, the multiple factors influencing their reading underachievement are not identical. Therefore, interventions and accommo- dations must match their individual needs and interests. A variety of cognitive/metacognitive strategies and technology solutions are available to enable them both greater success at independently accessing meaning from print.

Reading comprehension strategies

Theories provide a framework for professionals to utilize as they attempt to interpret the dynamic reasons that contribute to a reader's success in extracting and constructing meaning from written text (Sweet and Snow, 2003). Unfortunately, a great deal of recent research with adolescent and adult readers with dyslexia is not grounded in theory. As noted by Faggella-Luby and Deschler (2008), "accelerated progress in the development and validation of powerful interventions may result if research and practitioners grounded their work in theory" (p. 74). Some scholars propose that the skills needed for reading comprehension are organized in a hierarchy ranging from higher-order skills to lower-order skills. Such theories of reading comprehension have been categorized as following along a continuum from top-down to bottom-up models. Researchers taking a more top-down perspective on the process of reading comprehension closely examine the relationship between the reader, the text, and the activity of reading (Galda and Beach, 2001; Sweet and Snow, 2003). Bottom-up models are used by professionals more interested in the specific cognitive and linguistic processes influencing the act of comprehending text (Kinstch, 1998; Perfetti et al., 1996). Such models purport that the reader extracts meaning from the print only after the lower-order processes, such as basic cognitive and linguistic processes involved in word decoding, have been completed. The RAND Reading Study Group (RRSG, 2002) in a recent review of the literature, public policy, and best practice encourage professionals to utilize both the top-down and bottom-up models to better understand how readers do or do not comprehend written text.

Researchers are currently directing a great deal of attention to better understanding the strategies accessed by readers during the process of comprehending printed text. Table 21.1 provides evidence-based support for the effectiveness of specific cognitive/metacognitive strategies for improving reading comprehension for adolescents and adults with and without dyslexia. Cognitive/metacognitive strategies are utilized by all readers whenever there is a breakdown of understanding during the process of comprehending text. According to Graesser (2007), a reading comprehension strategy is "a cognitive or behavioral action that is enacted under particular contextual conditions, with the goal of improving some aspect of compre- hension" (p. 6). He identifies three distinctive strategies essential to effective reading com- prehension performance which includes the reader's ability to: (a) set goals; (b) contract meaning at the local (word/sentence) and global (text) level; and (c) generate explanation (s) of why events occur. Adolescents and adults with dyslexia often demonstrate difficulty using the essential cognitive/metacognitive strategies necessary for successful reading performance (Faggella-Luby and Deshler, 2008).

Technology and reading comprehension

As a result of emerging technologies, a fundamental shift in how we define literacy and reading is being witnessed in school and at work. For college students with dyslexia, instructional technologies offer opportunities, as well as, challenges for today's technology-rich environment.

Table 21.1 Literature Supporting Reading Comprehension Strategies for Adolescents and Adults

Broad Strategy	Specific Strategy	Research SWOD	Research LD
Monitoring Comprehension	Generating questions Marking Key words Taking a test Recall text Self-regulating	Pressley and Ghatala (1990) King (1994) Thiede, Anderson, and Therriault (2003) King (2007) Rosenshine and Meister (1994)	Ellis, Deshler, and Schumaker (1989) Greenleaf, Schoenbach, Cziko, and Mueller (2001) Harmon, Hendrick, Wood, and Gress (2005) Lamb, Bibby, Wood, and Chapman (1996)
Preparing to Read	Generating questions Previewing Concept maps Identify purpose Setting goals	Palinescar and Brown (1984) Van den Broek, Lorch, Linderholm, and Gustafson (2001) Pressley (2000, 2002) Richardson and Morgan (2000) Jonnasen (2000) King (2007) Johnson and Glenberg (2007)	Malone, and Mastropieri (1991) Schumaker, Deshler, Alley, Warner, and Denton (1982) Schumaker, Deshler, Nolan, and Alley (1984) Clark, Deshler, Schumaker, Alley, and Warner (1984) Lenz (1990) Vaughn, Klinger, and Bryant (2001)
Interpreting meanings of words, sentences, and ideas in text	Generating questions Paraphrasing Chunking Marking Annotating Notetaking Predicting Close reading Text structure Rereading	McNamara (2004) Todaro, Magliano, Millis, Kirby McNamara (2006) Magliano and Millis (2003, 2007) Cain, Oakhill, Barnes, and Bryant Herrell and Jordan (2001)	Fritschmann (2006) Hock, Brasseur, Deshler (2008) Abrahamsen and Shelton (1989) Ellis (1992) Harmon, Hendrick, Wood, and Gress (2005) Roberts, Torgesen, Boardman, and Scammacca (2008)

Table 21.1 Continued

Broad Strategy	Specific Strategy	Research SWOD	Research LD
Going Beyond the Text	Generating questions Think aloud Paraphrasing Visualization Outside sources Elaborating	Beck and McKeown (2001) Pressley and Affleerback (1995) Kucan and Beck (1997) Stahl and Fairbanks (1986) Rosenshine, Meister, and Chapman (1996) Ericsson and Simon (1998) McNamara (2004) Glenberg, Jaworski, Rischal, and Levin (2007) Glenberg, Havas, Becker, and Rinck (2005)	Schumaker, Deshler, Alley, Warner and Denton (1982) Schumaker, Deshler, Nolan, and Alley (1984) Clark, Deschler, Schumaker, Alley, and Warner (1984) Lenz (1990)
Organize, Restructure and Synthesize	Generating questions Reading guides Summarization Graphic organizers	Vitale and Romance (2007) Hauser, Nukles, and Renkl (2006) Meyer and Poon (2001) Williams (2007) Caccamise, Franzke, Eckhoff, Kintsch, and Kintsch (2007) Wade-Stein, and Kintsch (2004) Chmiekewski and Kansereau (1998) Dansereau and Newbern (1997) Chang, Sung, and Cheng (2002) Romance and Vitale (2001)	Bulgren, Hock, Schumaker, and Deshler (1995) Brasseur, Hock, and Deshler (2008) Eberling–Penner (1999) Gajria and Salvia (1992) Malone and Mastropieri (1991) Vaughn, Klinger and Bryant (2001)

Notes:
1 McNamara *et al.* (2007) Broad Reading Comprehension Strategies
2 Research evidence supporting strategies for adolescents and adults without disabilities
3 Research evidence supporting strategies for adolescents and adults with learning disabilities

Shaped by national and global influences, historically held beliefs about literacy and reading are being called into question (Lewis and Fabos, 2005). The ability to decipher the printed word no longer holds supreme in the definition of literacy. Contemporary writing and studies on literacy suggests that literacy is multi-dimensional and changeable (Cope and Kalantzis, 2004; Lankshear and Knobel, 2003; Leu, 2005; Leu and Kinzer, 2000; Lewis and Fabos, 2005; New London Group, 2000), and representation of content in multi-media format (such as on the Internet and eText) makes reading a function of the technology within which it is hosted. According to Leu et al., (2004), a precise definition of new literacies may never be achieved given the continuously changing nature of technology, but there is no doubt that the Internet and other information and communication technologies (ICT) are shaping new theoretical perspectives on literacy. Although reading printed text may no longer be the sole yardstick of literacy, the ability to read and comprehend text is still the foundation for much of academic and work related success (Silver-Pacuilla et al., 2004). As reading in non-print based media becomes prolific, the need to understand the requirements and implications of alternative media become especially pertinent.

Reading and the Internet

Consider reading on the Internet. In 1994 the percentage of classrooms in the US with at least one computer with Internet access was 3 per cent; in 2002, it went up to 92 per cent (NCREL, 2003). This is an unprecedented adoption rate for any technology by schools in the U.S., including books (Leu et al., 2004). The Internet presents an enabling context that is different from that of text books, where enabling context refers to the affordances and invariance (i.e., elements that are fixed) by the medium. A book represents finite space; the Internet, on the other hand, is boundless. Reading on the Internet is guided by navigational decisions made by the individual at critical junctures, following an initial search and inquiry. On the Internet, decoding for comprehension includes decoding not only letters and words, but also the strategic use of color, meaning-bearing icons and animations, pictures, maps, graphs and charts that are not necessarily static, and hyperlinks that navigate to other texts and images (Leu, et al., 2004). In other words, comprehension and meaning is represented in multi-media format on the Internet which includes icons, animated symbols, audio, video, interactive images, virtual reality environments and more (Brunner and Tally, 1999).

The underlying cognitive processes that guide college students while reading printed text are different from those required for reading on the Internet, however, the exact nature of these differences are still unclear. In discussing what is new about online reading comprehension, Leu et al. (2007) talk about five specific skills that are unique to reading in open learning environments, namely: (a) identifying a question or search query which starts the reading process, (b) navigating and locating information to read, (c) critically evaluating the information, (d) synthesizing information (through the choices made about sites to visit and links to follow), and communicating the information. Two students, such as Juan and Pat, searching for information to read on an identical topic can end up reading two quite different texts on the Internet, with varying conclusions.

Knowledge of reading patterns and the cognitive/metacognitive processes that guide reading decisions on the Internet are emerging. Understanding of reading on the Internet is clearly in its nascent stages. The RAND Reading Study Group [RRSG] (2002) notes that "accessing the Internet makes large demands on individual's literacy skills; in some cases, this technology requires readers to have novel literacy skills, and little is known about how to analyze or teach those skills" (p. 4). Successful Internet reading experiences appear to require both similar and more complex applications of (a) prior knowledge sources; (b) inferential reasoning strategies; and (c) self-regulated reading processes (Coiro and Dobler, 2007), but awareness of such skills among students in general is still limited. Decision-making while reading online by college students with dyslexia is largely unknown.

Reading and eText

Technology is redefining traditional concepts of access to print for individuals such as Juan and Pat. Electronic text (eText) rather than print text is fast becoming the medium by which a large percentage of our society with or without dyslexia read. One can buy an eText of a book, newspaper, or magazine and have it auto-delivered wirelessly to your laptop or hand-held device in less than one minute. The process of reading is no longer solely defined by holding a book in one's hands and accessing meaning with one's eyes. However, little evidence-based research is available that identifies the cognitive demands that an eText format presents to a reader as compared to print formats during the comprehension of content. As eText is fast being integrated into the instruction and testing of adolescent readers, a better understanding of the cognitive processing demands is critical. Alternative media (alt media) is a term that refers to a variety of formats into which printed text is converted to eText for use with access computer technologies. To access e-text an individual can use assistive technologies (AT) such as text-to-speech (TTS) and many other electronic tools (eTools: highlighting, summarizing, etc.). However, electronic formats alone do not provide accessibility to print, but when they are used in conjunction with cognitive/metacognitive strategies the potential to make the world of print more available to college students with dyslexia significantly increases.

Profile of college students and technology

As the conceptual framework of literacy changes, competencies and skills that define literacy for college students are also altered (NCREL, 2003; Pew Research Center, 2007). A new generation of college students is emerging as a result of unprecedented growth in learning technologies in postsecondary education. The importance of technology in postsecondary education is not difficult to validate. Consider the following positions:

> The definition of student achievement must be broadened to include the 21st century skills that will be required for students to thrive in the future.
> (The CEO Forum on Education and Technology, 2001, p.1).

> The sheer magnitude of human knowledge, globalization, and the accelerating rate of change due to technology necessitates a shift in our children's education—from plateaus of knowing to continuous cycles of learning.
> (enGauge-21st Century Skills: Literacy in the Digital Age, 2003, p. 4).

Understanding the ways in which college students are adopting and using technologies is a necessary starting point for exploring the implications of technology mediated learning for students with reading disorders. Surveys and opinion polls of selected groups of college students indicate that:

- college students are by far the largest group of Internet users in the general population (Allen and Seaman, 2007);

270

- frequency of use of the Internet is high among teens and adolescents (ages 12–17), with 51 per cent reporting they use the Internet daily, and 24 per cent reporting using the Internet several times a day (Lenhart, 2007);
- a distinguishing characteristic of this generation of college students is use of real time technologies that allows them to interact synchronously via instant messaging and text messaging, and interact with people in new and unique ways (Pew Research Center, 2007);
- college students are the most active users of social networking sites such as Facebook, MySpace, MyYearBook, and Friendster and of those who use social networks, 48 per cent log onto the site several times a day (Lenhart, 2007);
- more than half (57 per cent) of adolescents who are Internet users are also media creators, that is, they have their own webpage or blog, and /or have posted their own creations, stories, photographs or videos online (Pew Internet and American Life Project, 2005);
- ownership of technologies is high among this population of students. In 2004, 45 per cent of online adolescents (ages 12–17) reported processing a cell phone, in 2006 the number was up to 68 per cent (Lenhart, 2007). In 2005, 52.8 per cent of undergraduate students reported owning a laptop computer; the number was up to 75.8 per cent in 2007 (ECAR Center for Applied Research, 2007).

College students today are more adept at using technology than any generation before them. Students use technologies in ways that blur the line between academic and non-academic uses of technology, while demonstrating skills and competencies that are unique to a technology-mediated learning environment. Yet, many students with learning disabilities and/or Attention Deficit Hyperactivity Disorder report a reduced level of comfort with instructional technologies (Parker and Banerjee, 2007). In following sections, we discuss what is known and what may still be largely speculative about skills and underlying processes that students engage in when reading with technology tools within a technology enabled learning environment, and the need to redefine access for college students with dyslexia given multiple perspectives on reading and literacy.

Profile of college students with dyslexia and technology

Use and ownership of technologies by students with disabilities is varied and reflects usage and adoption patterns that are different from those in the general population of postsecondary students. Much of what is known about technology and students with disabilities is based on information regarding assistive technologies (AT) and the role of AT in overcoming barriers to access. Assistive technology machines, equipment, and software serve to bridge the gap between students' current level of functioning and their expected level of academic proficiency. In this capacity, technology is primarily used as an augmentative device or tool that enables access.

The traditional view of technology for individuals with disabilities is that technology can extend an individual's physical and sensory capabilities (Norton and Wilburg, 1998), while allowing one to circumvent functional limitations due to the disability. For college students with dyslexia, like Pat, the most commonly used AT is printed text in audio format. The opportunity to listen to text being read out aloud makes it accessible to individuals with weak decoding skills and/or limited reading fluency. Students with dyslexia have traditionally used books in audio format available from audio book libraries or through a variety of optical character recognition (OCR) systems with speech synthesis/read back software (i.e., voice output systems that read back text displayed on a computer screen) and screen readers. Today, most computers come equipped with some form of audio capability.

Despite the acknowledged benefits of AT for students with disabilities (Anderson-Inman *et al.*, 1999; Goldberg and O'Neill, 2000; Hasselbring and Glaser, 2000), research suggests that individuals with disabilities are less than half as likely as their non-disabled peers to own a computer (Burghstahler, 2000), and are even less likely (one quarter as likely) to use the Internet (Kaye, 2000). According to Hitchcock and Stahl (2003), most of the technologies introduced in the last 25 years continue to be inaccessible to individuals with disabilities. Inaccessibility is often created by the design and infrastructure of institutional/educational technologies that can create hurdles for students with disabilities (National Council on Disability, 2000). The National Council on Disability report states that "the rapid acquisition of educational technology has not sufficiently addressed the needs of students with disabilities. Access for students with disabilities is just beginning to be identified as an important factor when purchasing educational technology" (p. 25).

Finding a sustainable solution to access at the postsecondary level is complex because of the need for synchronization among multiple players. According to Rowland (2000), true access requires coordination between key six participants: creators of browsers (e.g., *Internet Explorer, Netscape, America Online*), creators of assistive technologies (e.g., *JAWS, IBM HomePage Reader*), knowledge and skills of web designer (e.g., alt tags, captioning), creators of markup language editors (e.g., *Dreamweaver*), creators of course software (e.g., *WebCT, Black Board*), and knowledge and skills of the user (e.g., student). Accessibility is compromised if any one of these participants fails to recognize the needs of college students with dyslexia, or is not cognizant of the interconnectivity among multiple players. Thus, the newest version of an assistive technology device may not be accessible if features within the new product are not supported by the version of the browser being used. As long as the capabilities of one product are constrained by the limits of another, full accessibility cannot be achieved (Rowland, 2000).

According to a report by the National Council on Disability (2000), use and adoption of technology by individuals with dyslexia is often shaped by lack of trained professionals to evaluate the rapidly changing array of assistive technologies, difficulties in locating available AT, confusion about existing laws and policies regarding AT, inaccessible electronic and information technologies, gaps in laws and policies that fund AT, and the bureaucracy of public programs (National Council on Disability, 2000). Another less recognized inaccessibility shaping the technology profile of adults with dyslexia is their lack of fluency and familiarity with technologies other than AT that have become common in education and the workplace. Assistive technologies seek to accommodate and/or compensate functional limitations due to a disability, but they do not necessarily address the skills and capabilities needed for reading within a multimedia, multi-dimensional networked space. The Internet for example, continues to be a challenge for many students with dyslexia (Leu, 2005). A study by Parker and Banerjee (2007) found that students with LD and Attention Deficit Hyperactivity Disorder report significantly diminished experience with and/or exposure to online and technology blended courses compared to their non-disabled peers, despite similarities in age, gender, and GPA status. The study found statistically significant differences between students with and without LD and/or ADHD with respect to multi-tasking on the computer, Internet searches, and communication by email.

Integrating cognitive/metacognitive strategies and technology solutions for enhancing reading comprehension

McNamara *et al.* (2007) propose a framework for classifying reading comprehension strategies that we have chosen to use and modify as the theoretical framework guiding our discussion of reading comprehension in a digital world (see Figure 21.1). McNamara's work grew out of collaboration with the College Board to revise the English, Language, and Arts Standards for middle school through college-reading high school students. They organize the evidence-based cognitive/ metacognitive strategies essential to monitor reading comprehension within a four-pronged framework which includes the reader's ability to: (a) prepare to read; (b) go beyond the text; (c) organize, restructure, and synthesize the text; and (d) interpret the words, sentences, and ideas in the text. We adapted the McNamara model by integrating electronic tools (eTools) that support the cognitive/metacognitive strategies at each of these phases of the reading comprehension process. Unfortunately, the diversity of eTools, resources, and scaffolds in digital learning environments can be bewildering, particularly to college students with dyslexia who are typically parsimonious in the use of tools and strategies, digital or otherwise. In addition, most learning technology products that take advantage of the capabilities of digitalization are created by external designers, researchers, and education vendors. Such resources are costly and rarely available to college students for use across the numerous printed and electronic texts that they are required to read. Therefore, we will be discussing cognitive/metacognitive strategies and technology solutions to be hosted within a familiar digital environment (i.e., *Microsoft Word*) that is available at no cost to a student.

Lack of understanding the ways reading demands in a digital space can affect students with dyslexia is disconcerting given the technology mediated dimensions of education today. Technology alone is not the solution to enhancing the reading comprehension performance of adults with dyslexia. However, teaching cognitive/metacognitive reading strategies without

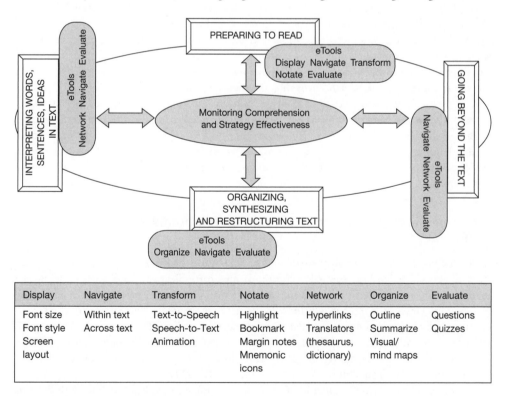

Display	Navigate	Transform	Notate	Network	Organize	Evaluate
Font size	Within text	Text-to-Speech	Highlight	Hyperlinks	Outline	Questions
Font style	Across text	Speech-to-Text	Bookmark	Translators	Summarize	Quizzes
Screen		Animation	Margin notes	(thesaurus,	Visual/	
layout			Mnemonic	dictionary)	mind maps	
			icons			

Figure 21.1 Cognitive strategies for enhancing reading comprehension with eTool

Source: adapted from McNamara *et al* (2007)

serious consideration of the digital reading world of today leaves many college students with dyslexia missing effective solutions for reading success.

Teaching students strategies for enhancing reading comprehension has been found to be effective for students with dyslexia (Gersten *et al.*, 2001; Swanson, 1999; Swanson and Hoskyn, 1998; Swanson and Sachse-Lee, 2000; Vaughn *et al.*, 2000). These strategies include the cognitive processes efficient readers employ when they read narrative and expository text and the metacognitive and self-regulatory strategies they use when they select, monitor, and evaluate their understanding of text (Deshler and Schumaker, 1988; Gersten *et al.,* 2001; Swanson, 1999; Swanson and Hoskyn, 1998; Torgesen *et al.*, 2007; Vaughn *et al.* 2000). Using the McNamara *et al.* (2007) broad strategies necessary for increasing the comprehension of text (Figure 21.1), we also listed in Table 21.1 research specific to the adolescent and adult population with dyslexia in which these strategies are supported by empirical-based evidence as effective for increasing reading performance.

However, little is known of the cognitive/metacognitive requirements of technology blended and/or web supported instructional platforms that are ubiquitous for secondary and postsecondary instruction. Lack of understanding of the ways reading demands in a digital space can affect college students with dyslexia is disconcerting given the technology mediated dimensions of education today. An exponential increase in the number of distance education course offerings by colleges, coupled with the use of multi-media technologies in the delivery and assessment of instruction, have changed the postsecondary landscape from just a decade ago. Reporting in 2000, authors of the National Reading Panel noted that the two most promising technology trends for supporting reading were hypertext capabilities of digitalization that allowed for linking of text to other online resources, and word processing that supported built-in learning tools, such as a thesaurus and dictionary. Technology in education has come a long way since the days of the computer as a compensatory assistive device for reading disorders. Traditional reading strategies and accommodations for college students with dyslexia may no longer be appropriate, adequate, or even accessible. Technology tools can make a significant difference for college students with dyslexia, and are no longer restricted to an "assistive" capacity (Rose and Meyer, 2000). Again, we stress the need for integrating the findings from recent studies pertaining to the effectiveness of specific cognitive/metacognitive reading comprehension strategies for the adolescent and adult population with dyslexia along with evidence-based research specific to the technologies and assistive technologies effective with this population.

Electronic tools to enhance the reading comprehension proficiency

In the area of reading, alternative media (alt media) and the software to access these formats (text-to-speech: TTS) are essential accommodations for college students with dyslexia. Alt media is a broad term that refers to a variety of formats into which printed text is converted (e.g., audio taped text, enlarged print, electronic text, Braille). The alt media used most commonly by college students with dyslexia are electronic text (eText) and audio files (Wolf and Lee, 2007). Electronic text is made available in machine-readable or computerized formats. The type of file that eText is converted into also has significant impact on the type of technologies and tools that integrate with it (e.g., ASCII, HTML).

Regardless of the alt media format, eText is not accessible for college students with dylsexia unless it is used in conjunction with TTS software. Optical character recognition software (OCR) is first used to convert scanned or bit-mapped images of text into machine-readable form. The text may then be saved on magnetic media (e.g., hard drives) or on optical media (e.g., CD-ROMs). Text converted by OCR software is then read by text-to-speech (TTS) software. TTS is a type of speech synthesis application that is used to create a spoken sound version of the eText on a computer or handheld device. TTS can enable the reading of computer display information for an adolescent or adult with LD, or it may simply be used to augment the reading of a text message. Anderson-Inman and Horney (2007) prefer the term "supported e-text" to refer to the integration of eText with assistive software. An important feature of alt media is its portability. Digital files can be delivered to adolescents or adults via email or internet portals and used in a variety of electronic and physical environments. Current advancements in technology now allow eText files to easily be downloaded not only to computers, but to hand-held devices such as phones, PDAs, or MP3 players to be read through specialized TTS software.

Research evidence to support the effectiveness of eText and TTS software for enhancing the reading performance of college students with dyslexia is currently limited in scope and depth (Gregg, 2009). However, even more disheartening is the fact that much of the TTS software cannot access or integrate with the various social media tools—from text messaging to blogging—that are essential to master for success in the school or workplace. To help illustrate why TTS software might be an important accommodation for individuals with decoding deficits, let's consider Pat's profile. Pat demonstrates strengths in learning, reasoning, and listening comprehension. Her significant problem reading appears to be the function of phonemic/orthographic awareness, and word fluency deficits. Therefore Pat's reading decoding problems appear to influence her ability to comprehend text in a timed situation. However, when the text is read-aloud, her strengths (e.g., reasoning, listening comprehension) help her circumvent her decoding problems. Pat appears to be an excellent candidate for using TTS software. Such software can read the text aloud to Pat and even simultaneously provide a highlighted synchronization of the text with audio feedback. Pat might even elect to download efiles onto her MP3 player (Ipod). An important feature of eText is its portability as digital files can be delivered to college students via email or internet portals and used in a variety of electronic and physical environments.

Reading comprehension underacheivement resulting from difficulties using cognitive/metacognitive strategies are often more difficult to accommodate than those deficits that are primarily a decoding issue. Read-alouds or extended time accommodations do not always effectively accommodate the learning needs of individuals struggling with the meaning of language such as Juan. For college students who also demonstrate AD/HD for whom executive processing deficits limit strategic thinking, organization, and revision, such accommodations might also be limited in their effectiveness. However, current technology advancements are providing professionals with more tools than ever before to help college students with language-based or executive functioning deficits to comprehend written text. Anderson-Inman and Horney (2007) developed a typology that professionals are encouraged to utilize in standardizing decisions surrounding the enhancement and modification of eText for individuals demonstrating print disabilities. However, as they note: "We know relatively little about how to construct and present electronic text in ways that have a consistently positive effect on student learning, especially when considering the diverse learning styles and needs of students with disabilities" (p. 155).

One promising technology software accommodation are embedded eText supports. For example, MacArthur and Haynes (1995) investigated eText versions of a 10th grade biology text in which the following embedded supports were evaluated: online notebook (notational resource), text-to-speech and links to definitions, highlighting, and summaries of text. Many of the embedded supports significantly helped readers with reading comprehension problems. Embedded supports used along with eText and text-to-speech software might be more effective than eText or text-to-speech alone for readers with dyslexia (Gregg, 2009). A growing body of research is providing strong validation for the effectiveness of embedded supports in enhancing reading comprehension for students with print disabilities (Anderson-Inman, 2004; Anderson-Inman and Horney, 2007; Anderson-Inman et al., 1994; Horney and Anderson-Inman, 1994, 1999). The National Center for Embedded eText (http://ncset.uoregon.edu/) website provides resources effective for adolescents or adults with LD or AD/HD demonstrating significant problems with reading comprehension.

Juan is an individual for whom embedded eText supports along with TTS software would enhance his ability to comprehend written text. His difficulties with working memory, vocabulary, and listening comprehension abilities indicate that processing verbal language is difficult for him. In addition, Juan demonstrates significant problems with decoding as a result of low phonemic and orthographic awareness. While TTS software will provide the text for him to hear, his difficulty with verbal language will still make understanding what is read to him a problem. Therefore, embedded supports to an eText file, such as links to definitions, highlighting, and summaries of text will allow him to gain meaning from the printed word. In addition, Juan can download such embedded eText on his MP3 player so that he would have immediate access to technical manuals while he is at school or in a work situation.

Redefining reading in multi media digital space

Although there is consensus that skills and competencies for reading, and even the definition of literacy is fundamentally altered by technology, less is known or agreed upon regarding differences in engagement and interaction between print-based and digital media. We lack adequate understanding to answer the query: "what are the cognitive and metacognitive processes used by proficient versus inefficient readers in a multi-media technology infused learning environment?" An attempt to decipher a response this question, however, is pertinent to the quest to understand reading and access to reading for college students with dyslexia, in today's digital, networked environment. Two sources of understanding serve as our starting point. One is recognition of the capabilities of digitalization and its effect on printed text, and two, emerging frameworks and paradigms for reading and new literacies.

Capabilities of digitalization

Digitalization affords a degree of interactivity and decision-making which can be simultaneously opportunistic and daunting. According to Rose and Meyer (2000), when text is digitized it becomes malleable (i.e., it can be transformed from one format to another). Digital information can be changed from text-to-speech, speech-to-text, static to animated, text-to-touch (e.g., refreshable Braille) and so on. The permanence inherent in print media is abandoned when text is converted to a digital format. Among others, digitalization makes possible the separation of content from display. On a computer screen, for instance, it is possible to keep content intact while varying in real time, the size of font, background-foreground color, spacing between lines, number of words on a line, amount of content on a single screen, screen density, and other features of legibility. Additionally, digitalization allows for user-directed extensions and enhancements to the content. Content can be enriched, buttressed, scaffolded, and embedded with tools and links that facilitate learning capabilities.

Text malleability

Printed text is the most common medium for reading in schools. Text in printed form consists largely of orthographic symbols, i.e., words, composed of phonemic graphemes, which in the Western culture, and is arranged horizontally from left to right. The defining characteristic of print is its stability (Kozma, 1994). Text that has been assigned to print cannot be altered by the reader. Reading of print follows an established linear progression which requires the reader to move in a pre-defined fashion (i.e., left to right) over symbols in order to derive meaning from the presenting context. The stability of the technology of print means that proficient reader can use established strategies to facilitate comprehension of the text. Readers can speed up (quickly scan) or slow down the pace at which they peruse the words, or go back to re-read something, with the knowledge that the order and format of word display will not have changed.

The introduction of graphics (i.e., pictures and diagrams) within the text changes somewhat the way students interact with printed text, but the stability of print remains. The cognitive effects of introducing graphics within a symbolic system are fairly well known. For instance, there is a large body of traditional research which suggests that pictures in combination with text generally increase recall, particularly for poor readers, if the graphics help to clarify or depict structural relationships mentioned in the text (Levie and Lentz, 1982; Schallert, 1980). Discussing the relationship between graphics and the text, Kozma (1994) notes that, "The stability of the medium allows the kind of serial, sequential, back-and-forth processing between specific information in the text and the components of pictures that facilitate the construction and elaboration of mental models." This permanence of printed information however, changes radically when text is presented in other media (such as television, video streaming, or audio) and embedded with tools and hyperlinks.

Malleability means that text can be transformed into alternative formats such as audio, visual, data, and animation, and such transformations can be achieved fairly easily by the reader with commercially available technology tools. Transformation of text into alternative media changes the rules of stability inherent to printed text. Constructing meaning through reading must then be considered in light of the reciprocity between the learner's cognitive resources and the capabilities of the given medium.

Text display

Digitalization of text makes possible real-time changes in the way the text is displayed. Such an observation is significant in light of research which suggests that visual display of text is positively associated with learning of online materials (Harrell, 1999; Ikegulu, 1998). A meta-analysis of studies on visual design of computer-based instruction by Lioa (1992) noted that screen display plays a crucial role in the comprehension and retention of online content. Display on a computer screen includes considerations of color, typography, spatial layout, and screen density. Given appropriate technologies, each of these elements can be manipulated by the reader to enhance engagement with the content (Geraci, 2002). Spatial layout helps to create a "visual gestalt or underlying pattern to the information that allows the learner to build a mental scheme for grouping and processing the lesson's content" (Geraci, 2002, p.69). However, it is important to note that guidelines for print publishing do not translate exactly onto a computer screen display. Screen display and the concept of navigation between text and screens on a computer are unique to digital text. Scrolling is a commonly required feature of screen display. Choi and Tinker (2002) found that "scrolling of reading passages on computer screens interferes with test taking behaviors of younger students. Providing page-up and page-down buttons in place of a vertical scroll bar may alleviate the interference that might have affected younger students" (p.

10). Interaction between screen display, screen navigation, and reading disorders is largely unknown.

Text enhancements

Once the permanence of printed text has been altered through digitalization, text can be embedded and linked with a variety of "features" that are designed to engage and extended learning. Hannafin et al., (1999) identify three broad categories of features—tools, resources, and scaffolds—that can be incorporated into what the authors describe as open learning environments (OLE). OLEs are learning environments where "The individual determines how to proceed based on his or her unique needs, perception, and experiences, distinguishes known from unknown, identifies resources available to support learning efforts, and formalizes and tests personal beliefs" (Hannafin et al., 1999, p.119). Reading on the Internet simulates reading text in digital format in an OLE. Borrowing this three structured categorization of features (from the authors) helps to understand the range of technology mediated text enhancements that are now a common part of most students' reading experience.

Electronic tools (eTools) provide the means to process and manipulate what a reader requires to comprehend printed or electronic text. Hanafin et al. (1999) identify three categories of eTools – (a) processing tools (i.e., tools that support cognitive processing), (b) manipulation tools (i.e., tools that allow one to test the validity of, or to explore, beliefs and theories), and (c) communication tools (i.e., tools that promote communication among learners). These eTools range from those that assist in seeking and locating information such as search engines and key search words to eTools that enable the learner to share ideas, promote a discourse and ask questions through e-mail and discussion boards. Scaffolds are supports that extend student learning. Insufficient background knowledge while reading on the Internet can instantly scaffolded by navigating to another site that offers an alternate explanation of a word or a topic.

Reading comprehension frameworks and digital learning environments

Aligned with the theory expressed earlier and empirical evidence of the effectiveness of strategy instruction for adolescent and adult readers with dyslexia (see Table 21.1), we suggest that professionals begin developing interventions that provide college students the cognitive/ metacognitive tools used to comprehend content presented in open (i.e., Internet) and closed (eText) digital learning environments. These interventions should provide college students with dyslexia strategies to help them select appropriate reading strategies, monitor comprehension effectiveness, and read eText in an effective and efficient manner. The four-pronged comprehension strategy framework developed by McNamara, et al. (2007) provides an empirical-based foundation for such interventions (see Figure 21.1). Furthermore, we strongly encourage professionals to provide college students with dyslexia opportunities and resources to become efficient with eTool solutions that can be used along with each of these essential cognitive/metacogntive reading strategies (see Figure 21.1). These tools should address displaying, navigating, notating, evaluating, transforming and organizing eText in a fashion that supports comprehension. As an example, we listed below the four broad strategies (Preparing to Read; Intepreting Words, Sentences, and Ideas in Text; Going Beyond Text; and Organizing, Synthesizing, and Restructuring Text) of the McNamara model with suggested eTools to enhance the comprehension of eText.

Preparing to Read

The Preparing to Read broad strategy is designed to acquaint the reader with activities that help organize cognitive processes and the reading material in preparation for reading (see Table 1 for specific strategies). The reader would then simultaneously learn and deploy eTools that support Preparing to Read strategies. Supporting eTools might include transforming eText and displaying text in user-friendly formats in order to facilitate the previewing process. For example, students may wish to enlarge the text by using a *zoom* feature, change from single to *double space* or using *dual screen display* for integrating additional documentation related to the text.

Interpreting Words, Sentences, and Ideas in Text

The Interpreting Words, Sentences, and Ideas in Text broad strategy is designed to equip students with cognitive cues to take when they encounter words, sentences, and ideas within the text that are unfamiliar or unknown (see Table 21.1 for specific strategies). Electronic tools that support vocabulary development include use of built-in eTools such as *e-thesaurus* and *e-dictionary*.

Going Beyond the Text

The Going Beyond the Text strategy is designed to facilitate a student's own understanding of the information that is read that help to record understanding (see Table 21.1 for specific strategies). Several eTools support locating main ideas and important details and then paraphrasing the information. These might include *highlighting* in color code and use of the *note-pad* or *margin notes* feature within a selected word processing program.

Organizing, Restructuring and Synthesizing Text

The purpose of the Organizing, Restructuring, and Synthesizing Text broad strategy is to help a reader pull together (synthesize) information that has been read (see Table 21.1 for specific strategies). Electronic tools to help organize and synthesize eText could be pulling together all "*note pad*" summarizations into a summary section in *split-screen* mode. A reader might also use electronic margin notes or "note pad" which can then be bookmarked by the student anywhere within the eText. Students can also be taught to create on-screen *outlines* and to navigate between outline mode and text mode.

Redefining accessibility for college students with dyslexia

As our understanding of learning and literacy changes, so must traditional perceptions of access and accommodations. Some accommodations may become redundant (such as a human reader) while new ones may need to be identified (Banerjee and Gregg, in press). It has long been recognized that learning technologies are inherently supportive of options and alternatives that can be built-in from the start rather than as retrofits or adaptations to the original environment (Hitchcock and Stahl, 2003). The creation of learning environments that seek to maximize usability by the largest number of users without the need for special adaptations or accommodations is embodied within the paradigm of universal design (Center for Universal Design, 1997; Pisha, and Coyne, 2001). An environment that supports multiple means of representation, expression, and engagement (as prescribed by universal design for learning) is the first step towards a move away from the traditional notion of accommodations as the only response to equal access (Rose and Meyer, 2002).

Online text supports provide essential tools for helping college students with dyslexia comprehend eText, but they do not guarantee success for students like Pat and Juan. The need to build familiarity and fluency with the cognitive/metacognitive strategies needed for reading within a technology mediated context is equally relevant. Current trends in learning technologies suggest that *access* for students with dyslexia must be visualized as *solutions* that prepare students for the digital postsecondary environment. Traditional concepts of accommodations need to be re-envisioned and expanded because of the opportunities presented by eTools, e-resources and built-in scaffolds. It would appear that solutions to access in the future must be guided by emerging definitions of literacy and the "tech sophistication" of today's average college student. Solutions to access must not only afford physical and/or cognitive entry into these new dimensions of technology mediated learning, but must also be considerate of the "usability" of such features by college students with dyslexia.

Investigation of the current technology mediated environment suggest that it may be time to consider yet another next step forward in the evolving view of *access* and accommodations for college students with dyslexia. The approach needs to be "solutions" drawn from multiple theoretical perspectives and empirical validation. In particular, *access* must not only provide the means and methods for equal participation, but must at the same time be: (a) efficient (i.e., competitive and not onerous), (b) ubiquitous (i.e., available any time, any place), (c) customizable (i.e., flexible enough to support individual needs), (d) intuitive (i.e., user-friendly), and (e) affordable (i.e., not so expensive as to be beyond the reach of the average college student). In other words, access must not only afford physical and cognitive entrée to the learning environment, but must also be "usable" by the individual with relative ease in variable settings. Access that is usable is one that offers *equal opportunity* without *unequal burden*. In this respect, the search for solution to access may lie in the opportunities afforded by learning technologies that are changing the postsecondary education landscape.

References

Abrahamsen, E.P. and Shelton, K.C. (1989). Reading comprehension in adolescents with learning disabilities: Semantic and syntactic effects. *Journal of Learning Disabilities, 22*(9), 569–572.

Allen, I. and Seaman, J. (2007). Online nation: Five years of growth in online learning. Retrieved May 13, 2008 from http://www.sloan-c.org/publications/survey/.

Anderson-Inman, L. (2004). Reading on the Web: making the most of digital Text. *Wisconsin State Reading Association Journal, 4*, 8–14.

Anderson-Inman, L. and Horney, M.A. (2007). Supported eText: Assistive technology through text transformations. *Reading Research and Practice, 14*, 153–160.

Anderson-Inman, L., Horney, M.A., Chen, D., and Lewin, L. (1994). Hypertext literacy: Observations from the Electro Text project. *Language Arts, 71*, 37–45.

Anderson-Inman, L., Knox-Quinn, C., and Szymanski, M. (1999). Computer supported studying: stories of successful transition to postsecondary education. *Career Development for Exceptional Individuals, 22* (2), 185–212.

Banerjee, M., and Gregg, N. (in press). Redefining accessibility in an era of alternative media for postsecondary students with learning disabilities. *Learning Disabilities: A Multidisciplinary Journal.*

Beck, I. and McKeown, M. (2001). Inviting students into the pursuit of meaning. *Educational Psychology Review*, 13, 225–241.

Brunner, C.B. and Tally, W. (1999). *The new media literacy handbook: An educator's guide to bringing new media into the classroom.* New York: Anchor Books.

Bulgren, J.A., Hock, M.F., Schumaker, J.B., and Deshler, D.D. (1995). The effects of instruction in a paired associates strategy on the information mastery performance of students with learning disabilities. *Learning Disabilities Research and Practice, 10*(1), 22–37.

Burgstahler, S. (2000). The role of technology in preparing youth with disabilities for postsecondary education and employment. Retrieved May 4, 2008 from http://jset.unlv.edu/18.4/burgstahler/first.html.

Caccamise, D., Frankzke, M., and Eckhoff, A., Kintsch, E., and Kintsch, W. (2007). Guided practice in technology-based summary writing. In D.S. McNamara (ed.). *Reading comprehension srategies: theories, interventions, and technologies* (pp. 375–396). New York: LEA.

Cain, K., Oakhill, J.V., Barnes, M.A., and Bryant, P.E. (2001). Comprehension skill, inference making ability and their relation to knowledge. *Memory* and *Cognition, 29,* 850–859.

Center for Universal Design. (1997). Environments and Products for all People. Raleigh: North Carolina State University, Center for Universal Design. Retrieved March 12, 2006, from http://www.design.ncsu.edu/cud/univ_design/ud.htm.

Chang, K., Sung, Y., and Chen, I. (2002). The effect of concept mapping to enhance text comprehension and summarization. *Journal of Experimental Education, 71,* 5–23.

Chmielewski, T. and Dansereau, D.F. (1998). Enhancing the recall of text: Knowledge mapping promotes implicit transfer. *Journal of Educational Psychology, 90,* 407–413.

Choi, S.W. and Tinkler, T. (2002, April). Evaluating comparability of paper-and pencil and computer-based assessment in a K–12 setting. Paper presented at the annual meeting of the National Council on Measurement in Education, New Orleans, LA.

Clark, F.L., Deshler, D.D., Schumaker, J.B., Alley, G.R., and Warner, M.M. (1984). Visual imagery and self-questioning: Strategies to improve comprehension of written material. *Journal of Learning Disabilities, 17*(3), 145–149.

Coiro, J. and Dobler, E. (2007). Exploring the online reading comprehension strategies used by sixth grade skilled readers to search for and locate information on the Internet. *Reading Research Quarterly, 42,* 214–57.

Cope, B. and Kalantzis, M. (2003). *Text-made text.* Melbourne, Australia: Common Ground.

Cope, B. and Kalantizis, M. (2004). Text-made Text. *E-Learning, 1*(2), 198–281. Retrieved November 11, 2008 from http://www.cgpublisher.com/ui/about/ui/Text-MadeTextELearning2004.pdf

Dansereau, D.F. and Newbern, D. (1997). Using knowledge map to enhance teaching. In W.E. Campbell and K.A. Smith (eds), *New Paradigms for College Teaching* (pp. 125–147). Edina, MN: Interaction Book.

Deshler, D.D. and Schumaker, J.B. (1988). An instructional model for teaching students how to learn. In J.L. Graden, J.E. Zins, and M.J. Curtis (eds), *Alternative Educational Delivery Systems: Enhancing Instructional Options for all Students* (pp. 391–411). Washington, DC: NASP.

Eberling-Penner, M.D. (1999). Planning the attack on content area reading: The effect of four metacognitive strategies on weak adolescent readers' confidence. (M.Ed. thesis, University of Manitoba, Canada.)

ECAR (2007). The ECAR study of undergraduate students and information technology. Retrieved May 2007 from http://connect.educause.edu/Library/ECAR/TheECARStudyofUndergradua/45075?time=1189954853

Ellis, E.S. (1992). *The Vocabulary Learning Strategy.* Lawrence, KS: Edge Enterprises.

Ellis, E.S., Deshler, D.D., Schumaker, J.B. (1989). Teaching adolescents with learning disabilities to generate and use task-specific strategies. *Journal of Learning Disabilities, 22*(2), 108–130.

enGauge (2003). Literacy in the digital age. Retrieved May 22, 2008 from www.ncrel.org/engauge.

Ericsson, K.A. and Simon, H.A. (1998). How to study thinking in everyday life: Contrasting think–aloud protocols with descriptions and explanations of thinking. *Mind, Culture,* and *Activity, 5, 178–186.*

Faggella-Luby, M.N. and Deshler, D. (2008). Reading comprehension in adolescents with LD: What we know; what we need to learn. *Learning Disabilities Research* and *Practice, 23*(2), 70–78.

Fritschmann, N.S. (2006). The effects of instruction in an inference strategy on the reading comprehension of adolescents with learning disabilities. (Ph.D. thesis, The University of Kansas.)

Gajria, M. and Salvia, J. (1992). The effects of summarization instruction on text comprehension of students with learning disabilities. *Exceptional Children, 58*(6), 508–516.

Galda, L. and Beach, R. (2001). Response to literature as a cultural activity. *Reading Research Quarterly, 36,* 64–73.

Geraci, M.G. (2002). Designing web-based instruction: A research review on color, typography, layout and screen density. Capstone report. University of Oregon.

Gersten, R., Fuchs, L.S., Williams, J.P., and Baker, S. (2001). Teaching reading comprehension strategies to students with learning disabilities: A review of research. *Review of Educational Research*, *71*, 279–320.

Glenberg, A.M., Havas, D., Becker, R., and Rinck, M. (2005). Grounding language in bodily states: The case for emotion. In R. Zwaan and D. Pecher (eds), *The Grounding of Cognition: The role of perception and action in memory, language, and thinking* (pp. 115–128). Cambridge, England: Cambridge University Press.

Glenberg, A.M., Jaworski, B., Rischal, M., and Levin ,J. (2007). What brains are for: Action, meaning, and reading comprehension. In D.S. McNamara (ed.), *Reading Comprehension Strategies: Theories, Interventions, and Technologies* (pp. 221–240). New York: LEA.

Goldberg, L.B.G. and O'Neill, L.M. (2000). Computer technology can empower students with learning disabilities. *Exceptional Parent*, *30*(7), 72–74.

Graesser, A.C. (ed.) (1993). Inference generation during text comprehension [Special issue]. *Discourse Processes*, *16* (1–2).

Graesser, A. (2007). An introduction to strategic reading comprehension. In D.S. McNamar (ed.), *Reading Comprehension Strategies: Theories, interventions, and technology* (pp. 2–21). New York: LEA.

Greenleaf, C.L., Schoenbach, R., Cziko, C., and Mueller, F.L. (2001). Apprenticing adolescent readers to academic literacy. *Harvard Educational Review*, *71*(1), 79–129.

Gregg, N. (2007). Underserved and underprepared: Postsecondary Learning Disabilities. *Learning Disabilities Research and Practice*, *22*(4), 219–228.

Gregg, N. (2009). *Assessing and Accommodating Adolescents and Adults with LD and AD/HD*. New York: Guilford Press.

Hannafin, M., Land, S., and Oliver, K. (1999). Open learning environments: Foundations, methods, and models. In C.M. Reigeluth (ed.), *Instructional-design Theories and Models: A New Paradigm of Instructional Theory* (pp. 115–140). Mahwah, NJ: Lawrence Erlbaum Associates.

Harmon, J.M., Hendrick, W.B., Wood, K.D., and Gress, M. (2005). Vocabulary Self-Selection: A Study of Middle-School Students' Word Selections from Expository Texts. *Reading Psychology*, *26*(3), 313–333.

Harrell, W. (1999). Effective monitor display design. *International Journal of instructional Media*, *26*(4), 447–458.

Hasselbring, T.S., and Glaser, C.H. (2000). Use of computer technology to help students with special needs. *Future of Children*, *10*(2), 102–22.

Hauser, S., Nuckles, M., and Renkl, A. (2006). Supporting concept mapping for learning from text. In S.A. Barab, K.E. Hay, and D.T. Hickey (eds), *Proceedings of the Seventh International Conference of the Learning Sciences* (pp. 243–249). Mahwah, NJ: Lawrence Erlbaum Associates, Inc.

Hitchcock, C. and Stahl, S. (2003). Assistive technology, universal design, Universal Design for Learning: Improved opportunities. *Journal of Special Education Technology*, *18*(4).

Hock, M.F., Brasseur, I.F. and Deshler, D.D. (2008). *Results from a randomized study comparing two high school reading intervention programs*. Lawrence, Kansas: The University of Kansas Center for Research on Learning.

Horney, M.A. and Anderson-Inman, L. (1994). The Electro Text Project: Hypertext reading patterns of middle school students. *Journal of Educational Multimedia and Hypermedia*, *3*, 71–91.

Horney, M. A. and Anderson-Inman, L. (1999). Supported text in electronic reading environments. *Reading and Writing Quarterly*, *15*, 127–168.

Ikegulu, P.R. (1998). *Effects of Screen Designs in CBI Environments*. Grambling, LA: Grambling State University.

Johnson-Glenberg, M.C. (2007). Web-based reading comprehension instruction: Three studies of 3D-Readers. In D.S. McNamara (ed.), *Reading Comprehension Strategies: Theories, interventions, and technologies* (pp. 293–324). New York: LEA.

Jonassen, D. H. (2000). *Computers as Mindtools for Schools: Engaging Critical Thinking* (2nd edn). Upper Saddle River, NJ: Prentice Hall.

Kaye, H.S. (2000). Disability and the digital divide. *Disability Statistics Abstract*. San Francisco, CA: Disability Statistics Center, University of California, San Francisco and Washington, DC: U.S. Department of Education National Institute on Disability and Rehabilitation Research.

King, A. (1994). Autonomy and question asking: The role of personal control in guided student-generated questioning. *Learning and Individual Differences*, *6*, 163–185.

King, A. (2007). Beyond literal comprehension: A strategy to promote deep understanding of text. In D.S. McNamara (ed.), *Reading Comprehension Strategies: Theories, interventions, and technologies* (pp. 267–290). New York: LEA.

282

Kinstch, W. (1998). *Comprehension: A Paradigm for Cognition*. Cambridge, England: Cambridge University Press.

Kucan, L. and Beck, I.L. (1997). Thinking aloud and reading comprehension research: Inquiry, instruction, and social interaction. *Review of Educational Research, 67*, 271–299.

Kozma, R.B. (1994). The influence of media on learning: The debate continues. Retrieved June 1, 2008 from http://www.ala.org/ala/aasl/aaslpubsandjournals/slmrb/editorschoiceb/infopower/selectkozma html.cfm.

Lankshear, C. and Knobel, M. (2003). *New Literacies: Changing knowledge and classroom learning*. Buckingham, UK: Open University Press.

Lamb, S.J., Bibby, P.A., Wood, D.J., and Leyden, G. (1998). An intervention programme for children with moderate learning difficulties. *The British Journal of Educational Psychology, 68*(4), 493–504.

Lenhart, A. (2007). A timeline for teens and technology. Retrieved April 11, 2008 from http://www.pewinternet.org.

Lenz, B.K. (1990). *The effects of a interpreting visual aids strategy on the performance of middle and high school students with learning disabilities*. Institute for Research on Learning Disabilities Research Report. The University of Kansas.

Lenz, B.K., Adams, G.L., Bulgren, J.A., Pouliot, N., and Laraux, M. (2007). Effects of curriculum maps and guiding questions on the test performance of adolescents with learning disabilities. *Learning Disability Quarterly, 30*(4), 235–244.

Leu, D.J. (2005). New literacies, reading research, and the challenges of change: A deictic perspective of our research worlds. Presidential address presented at the meeting of the National Reading Conference, Miami, Florida, November.

Leu, D.J. and Kinzer, C.K. (2000). The convergence of literacy instruction with networked technologies for information and communication. *Reading Research Quarterly, 35*(1), 108–127.

Leu, D.J., Kinzer, C.K., Coiro. J.L., and Cammack, D.W. (2004). Towards a theory of new literacies emerging from the Internet and other information and communication technologies. In R.B. Ruddell and N. Unrau (eds), *Theoretical models and processes of reading* (5th ed., pp. 1570–1613). Newark, DE: International Reading Association.

Leu, D. J., Jr., Zawilinski, L., Castek, J., Banerjee, M., Housand, B.C., Liu, Y., and O'Neil, M. (2007). What is new about the new literacies of online reading comprehension? In L.S. Rush, A.J. Eakle, and A. Berger (eds), *Secondary School Literacy: What research reveals for classroom practice* (pp. 37–68).Urbana, IL: National Council of Teachers of English.

Levie, W.H. and Lentz, R. (1982). Effects of textillustrations: A review of research. *Educational Communication and Technology Journal, 30*, 195–232.

Lewis, C. and Fabos, B. (2005). Instant messaging, literacies, and social identities. *Reading Research Quarterly, 40*(4), 470–501.

Liao, Y.K. (1992). Effects of computer-assisted instruction on cognitive outcomes: A meta-analysis. *Journal of Research on Computing in Education, 24*(3), 367–379.

MacArthur, C. and Haynes, J.B. (1995). Student assistant for learning from text (SALT): A hypermedia reading aid. *Journal of Learning Disabilities, 28*, 50–59.

McNamara, D.S., Ozuru, Y., Best, R., and O'Reilly, T. (2007). The 4-pronged comprehension strategy framework. In D.S. McNamara (ed.). *Reading Comprehension Strategies: Theories, Interventions, and Technologies* (pp.465–513). New York: LEA.

McNamara, D.S. (2004). SERT: Self-explanation reading training, *Discourse Processes, 38*, 1–30.

Magliano, J.P. and Millis, K.K. (2003). Assessing reading skill with a think-aloud procedure. *Cognition and Instruction, 3*, 251–283.

Magliano, J.P., Millis, K., Ozuru,Y., and McNamara, D.S. (2007). A multidimensional framework to evaluate reading assessment tools. In D.S. McNamara (ed.), *Reading Comprehension Strategies: Theories, Interventions, and Technologies* (pp.107–136). New York: LEA.

Malone, L.D. and Mastropieri, M.A. (1991). Reading comprehension instruction: summarization and self-monitoring training for students with learning disabilities. *Exceptional Children, 58*(3), 270–279.

Meyer, B.F. and Poon, L.W. (2001). Effects of structure strategy training and signaling on recall of text. *Journal of Educational Psychology, 93*, 141–159.

National Council on Disability (2000). Transition and postsecondary outcomes for youth with disabilities: Closing the gap to postsecondary education and employment. Retrieved April 20, 2008 from http://www.ncd.gov/newsroom/publications/2000/transition_11–01–00.htm.

National Reading Panel. (2000). Report of the National Reading Panel. *Teaching children to read: An evidence-based assessment of the scienfitif research literature on reading and its implications for reading instructions* (NHI Publication No. 00–4769). Washington, DC: U.S. Government Printing Office.

New London Group. (2000). A pedagogy of multiliteracies designing social futures. In B. Cope and M. Kalantzis (eds), *Multiliteracies: Literacy learning and the design of social futures* (pp. 9–37). London: Routledge.

North Central Regional Educational Laboratory (NCREL). (2003). 21st century skills: Literacy in the digital age. Retrieved 2 October, 2007 from http://www.ncrel.org/engauge/skills/skills.htm.

Norton, P. and Wilburg. K.M. (1998). *Teaching with Technology: Designing opportunities to learn* (2nd edn) (pp. 1–12). Belmont, CA: Wadsworth Publishing.

Palincsar, A.S. and Brown, A.L. (1984). Reciprocal teaching of comprehension fostering and monitoring activities. *Cognition and Instruction, 1*, 117–175.

Parker, D.R. and Banerjee, M. (2007). Leveling the digital playing field: Assessing the learning technology needs of college-bound students with LD and/or ADHD. *Assessment for Effective Intervention, 33*(1), 5–14.

Perfetti, C.A., Marron, M.A., and Foltz, P.W. (1996). Sources of comprehension failure: Theoretical perspectives and case studies. In C. Coroldi and J. Oakhill (eds), *Reading Comprehension Difficulties: Processes and intervention* (pp. 137–165). Mahwah, NJ: Lawrence Erlbaum.

Pew Internet and American Life Project (2002). The Internet goes to college: How students are living in the future with today's technology. Retrieved March 20, 2008 from http://www.pewinternet.org/.

Pew Internet and American Life Project (2005). Teens and Technology. Retrieved March 20, 2008 from http://www.pewinternet.org/pdfs/PIP_Teens_Tech_July2005web.pdf.

Pew Research Center for the People and the Press (2007). A portrait of "Generation Next". Retrieved June 10, 2008 from http://www.pewinternet.org/pdfs/PIP_Teens_Tech_July2005web.pdf

Pisha, B. and Coyne, P. (2001). Smart from the start: The promise of Universal Design for Learning. *Remedial and Special Education, 22*(4): 197–203.

Pressley, M. (2000). What should comprehension instruction be the instruction of? In M.L. Kamil, P.B. Mosenthal, P.D. Pearson, and R. Barr (eds), *Handbook of Reading Research: Volume III* (pp. 545–561). Mahwah, NJ: Lawrence Erlbaum.

Pressley, M. (2002). Metacognition and self-regulated comprehension. In A.E. Farstrup and S. Samuels (eds), *What Research Has to Say about Reading Instruction* (pp. 291–309). Newark, DE: International Reading Association.

Pressley, M. and Afflerbach, P. (1995). *Verbal Protocols of Reading: The nature of constructively responsive reading.* Mahwah, NJ: Lawrence Erlbaum.

Pressley, M. and Ghatala, E. (1990). Self-regulated learning: Monitoring learning from text. *Educational Psychologist, 25*, 19–33.

RAND Reading Study Group (RRSG). (2000). *Reading for Understanding: Towards an R&D program in reading comprehension.* Santa Monica, CA: RAND.

Richardson, J.S. and Morgan, R.F. (2000). *Reading to Learn in the Content Areas.* Belmont, CA: Wadsworth Publishing.

Roberts, G., Torgesen, J.K., Boardman, A., and Scammacca, N. (2008). Evidence-based strategies for reading instruction of older students with learning disabilities. *Learning Disabilities Research & Practice, 23*(2), 63–69.

Romance, N. R. and Vitale, M. R. (2001). Implementing an in-depth expanded science model in elementary schools: Multi-year findings, research issues, and policy implications. *International Journal of Science Education, 23,* 373–404.

Rosenshine, B. and Meister, C. (1994). Reciprocal teaching: A review of the research. *Review of Educational Research, 64*, 479–530.

Rosenshine, B., Meister, C., and Chapman, S. (1996). Teaching students to generate questions: A review of the intervention studies. *Review of Educational Research, 66*, 181–221.

Rose, D.H. and Meyer, A. (2000). *The Future is in the Margins: The Role of Technology and Disability in Educational Reform.* A report prepared for the U.S. Department of Education Office of Special Education Technology. Washington, DC: USDOE.

Rowland, C. (2000). Accessibility of the Internet in postsecondary education: Meeting the challenge. Retrieved April 25, 2008 from http://www.webaim.org/coordination/articles/meetchallenge.

Schallert, D. (1980). The role of illustrations in reading. In R. Spiro, B. Bruce, and W. Brewer (eds), *Theoretical Issues in Reading Comprehension.* Hillsdale, NJ: Lawrence Erlbaum.

Schumaker, J.B., Deshler, D.D., Alley, G.R., Warner, M.M., and Denton, P.H. (1982). MultiPass: A learning strategy for improving reading comprehension. *Learning Disability Quarterly, 5*, Summer, 295–304.

Schumaker, J.B., Deshler, D.D., Nolan, S.M. and Alley, G.R. (1984). *The Self-questioning Strategy.* Lawrence, KS: The University of Kansas.

Silver-Pacuilla, H., Ruedel, K. and Mistrett, M. (2004). A Review of Technology-Based Approaches for Reading Instruction: Tools for Research and Vendors. Retrieved September 30, 2005, from the Center for Implementing Technology in Education Web site: http://www.citeducation.org/math matrix/default.asp#.

Stahl, S. and Fairbanks, M. (1986). The effects of vocabulary instruction: A model based on meta-analysis. *Review of Educational Research, 56*, 72–110.

Swanson, H. L. (1999). Reading research for students with LD: A meta-analysis of intervention outcomes. *Journal of Learning Disabilities, 32*(6) 504–532.

Swanson, H.L. and Hoskyn, M. (1998). Experimental intervention research on students with learning disabilities: A meta-analysis of treatment outcomes. *Review of Educational Research, 68*(3), 277–321.

Swanson, H.L. and Sachse-Lee, C. (2000). A meta-analysis of single-subject-design intervention research for students with LD. *Journal of Learning Disabilities, 33*(2), 114–136.

Swanson, H.L., Carson, C., and Saches-Lee, C. M. (1996). A selective synthesis of intervention research for students with learning disabilities. *School Psychology Review, 25*(3), 370–391.

Sweet, A.P. and Snow, C.E. (2003). *Rethinking Reading Comprehension.* New York: Guilford.

The CEO Forum on School Technology and Readiness (2001). Key building blocks for student achievement in the 21st century. Retrieved June 13, 2008 from http://www.ceoforum.org/downloads/report4.pdf. http://www.ceoforum.org/downloads/report4.pdf.

Thiede, K.W., Anderson, M.C., and Therriault, D. (2003). Accuracy of metacognitive monitoring affects learning of texts. *Journal of Educational Psychology, 95*, 66–73.

Todaro, S., Magliano, J.P., Millis, K.K., Kurby, C.A., and McNamara, D.S. (2006). Understanding factors that influence the content and form of verbal protocols: The roles of the reader and text. Submitted.

Torgesen, J.K., Houston, D.D., Rissman, L.M., Decker, S.M., Roberts,G., Vaughn, S., Wexler, J., Francis, D.J., Rivera, M. O., and Lesaux, N. (2007). Academic literacy instruction for adolescents: A guidance document from the Center on Instruction. Portsmouth, NH: RMCResearch Corporation, Center on Instruction. Retrieved May 15, 2008 from http://www.ceteroninstruction.org/files/Academic per cent20Literacy.pdf.

Vaughn, S., Gersten, R., and Chard, D.J. (2000). The underlying message in LD intervention research: Findings from research syntheses. *Exceptional Children, 67*(1), 99–114.

Vaughn, S., Klinger, J.K., and Bryant, D.P. (2001). Collaborative strategic reading as a means to enhance peer-mediated instruction for reading comprehension and content area learning. *Remedial and Special Education, 22*(2), 66–74.

Van den Broek, P., Lorch, R.F., Jr., Linderholm, T., and Gustafson, M. (2001). The effects of readers' goals on inference generation and memory for texts. *Memory* and *Cognition, 29*, 1081–1087.

Vitale, M.R. and Romance, N.R. (2007). A knowledge-based framework for unifying content-area reading comprehension and reading comprehension strategies. In D.S. McNamara (ed.), *Reading comprehension strategies: Theories, interventions, and technologies* (pp.73–104). New York: LEA.

Wade-Stein, D. and Kintsch, E. (2004). Summary Street: Interactive computer support for writing. *Cognition and Instruction, 22*, 333–362.

Williams, J.P. (2007). Literacy in the curriculum: Integrating test structure and content area instruction. Vitale, M.R., and Romance, N.R. (2007). In D.S. McNamara (ed.), *Reading Comprehension Strategies: Theories, interventions, and technologies* (pp. 199–220). New York: LEA.

Wolf, G. and Lee, C. (2007). Promising practices for providing alternative media to postsecondary students with print disabilities. *Learning Disabilities Research and Practice, 22*, 256–264.

285

22

Dyslexia
Meeting the needs of employers and employees in the workplace

David McLoughlin and Carol Leather

This chapter

- discusses the issues facing both dyslexic employees and their employers, specifically:
    - the importance of disclosure
    - how employers can assist and support
    - how dyslexic individuals can help themselves.

Introduction

There are many reasons for acknowledging the difference dyslexic individuals can bring to any organisation. Valuing difference enables people to work best, facilitates their personal growth and leads to a more rewarding and productive environment. (Armstrong, 1999; Walker, 1994). There is no doubt that many organisations have adopted a positive approach to supporting dyslexic employees. Others have made provision more cynically, fulfilling their statutory obligations, probably to their loss.

The underlying philosophy of disability legislation, such as the United Kingdom Disability Discrimination Act (DDA), 1995, and the United States of America Americans with Disabilities Act (ADA), 1990, is inclusion. To achieve this both Acts place obligations on employers to make adjustments or accommodations for employees in recruitment, selection and on the job; the aim being to allow disabled employees to compete on a level playing field.

Although it is often assumed by advocacy and self-advocacy groups that hidden disabilities such as dyslexia are covered by the legislation this is not necessarily the case. The *DDA* (UK) defines a disabled person as someone who has a physical or mental impairment which has a substantial and long-term adverse effect on his ability to carry out normal day-to-day activity. The *ADA* (USA) defines a disability as a substantial limitation to one or more major life activities; the word substantial is common to both and suggests that many dyslexic individuals would not be covered. In law, however, each case is decided individually and recent judgments from the Employment Tribunals have accepted that 'severe dyslexia' should be considered a disability, and the need to have extra time to complete examinations when these are part of the promotion process constitutes a substantial day-to-day effect.

While the acknowledgement of the existence of dyslexia in the workplace has grown following the introduction of disability legislation, the understanding of its impact for dyslexic individuals themselves and employers is still limited. Performance issues and sometimes inappropriate action arise because of misunderstanding; there is a huge cost; there is personal cost to the individual and cost to the employers in terms of productivity.

The misunderstanding is partially due to the diversity of dyslexia itself; there is still controversy over the definition of it. Furthermore, it affects everyone differently: some dyslexic people are spectacularly successful; others are singularly unsuccessful; for some people it is a disability, for others a difference. Research in America (Gerber *et al.*, 1992; Spekman *et al.*, 1992) has considered the factors that contribute to success. Establishing 'goodness of fit' has been identified as one of the keys. (Gerber *et al.*, 1992, 1996). Achieving this involves the individual dyslexic through self-advocacy, the employer by making adjustments and professional tutor/coaches through advocacy and the provision of appropriate training.

Disclosing dyslexia

Self-advocacy starts with the process of disclosure. Accessing adjustments or accommodations inevitably requires that individuals tell employers that they are dyslexic. It is not until they do so that they can seek the protection of the legislation. Having done so obliges their employers accordingly, and if they fail to do so employees can seek recourse through Courts and Tribunals. A judicial outcome analysis has, however, shown that many disabled employees have been prevented from gaining the protection offered by legislation, with 63 per cent of Tribunal decisions favouring employers (Konur, 2007). This will contribute to the reluctance to disclose, dyslexic individuals feeling that the odds are stacked against them.

One of the ways in which the success of legislation and the understanding of dyslexia are reflected in society is therefore the disclosure rate; that is, the extent to which individuals feel comfortable about telling employers and colleagues that they are dyslexic. Research in the United States and Canada, as well as the United Kingdom has suggested that individuals with learning disabilities such as dyslexia are reluctant to reveal that they have a difficulty, despite the existence of the legislation that is supposed to prevent discrimination. The authors found that the majority of adults in the samples of individuals interviewed or asked to complete questionnaires did not ask for accommodations (adjustments) in the selection process did not tell their employers during an interview and did not ask for adjustments in the job. (Madaus *et al.*, 2002; Gerber and Price, 2003; Gerber *et al.*, 2004; Martin *et al.*, 2008). Some of the reasons given were:

- I never thought it would apply to work.
- I was afraid to be found out – they might have taken the job away.
- They would think I couldn't do the job.
- People would look down on you.
- I was embarrassed.
- I didn't think it was my place to ask for those things.
- I would feel like a burden if they gave me anything extra.
- I was worried about discrimination.

Several themes emerge from this research but fundamentally dyslexia is a much mis-understood syndrome. Although there is now greater recognition of the fact that it persists throughout life and that there are more dyslexic adults than there are dyslexic children, it is still perceived as something to do with education. Other themes and their corollary include:

- Dyslexia is a reading/spelling problem – dyslexic individuals and their employers still see dyslexia as an educational issue but literacy is often not the main difficulty facing people in the workplace.

- Dyslexic people are incompetent – many dyslexic people are however highly competent and successful and are able to contribute to society without good literacy skills.
- Dyslexic people need a lot of help – some do, some don't. Often they just need sympathetic and supportive managers and colleagues. When they do need help it should always suit the context and be task focused.
- Dyslexia is a source of embarrassment – because it is not well understood and because some dyslexic people have not been treated well by others despite their legal obligations. There is still a stigma associated with poor spelling, for example, and this one of the more obvious and exposing difficulties.
- Employers don't understand dyslexia – there is a need for awareness training and dyslexic individuals should be encouraged to explain things from their own perspective.
- There is a fear of discrimination – this is legitimate. And despite the provisions of the DDA and the ADA it is difficult to legislate for personality.

It should be no surprise therefore that many dyslexic people choose to keep it to themselves when they leave education and move in to employment, as well as in daily living.

Understanding dyslexia

The Internet has been a great boon to those seeking to understand themselves as well as those seeking to understand others. At the same time the plethora of information available can contribute to greater confusion rather than clarity, particularly in a field that lends itself to pop psychology and cottage industry. There are many definitions of dyslexia but most focus on the literacy difficulties experienced by children and the language used to describe dyslexia belongs to the world of education, particularly special education. The broader problems experienced during the adult years have not really been addressed.

Developments in experimental and neuro-psychology have demonstrated clearly that dyslexia is in information processing difference or difficulty, involving components of working memory. It has been described as a syndrome – a family of lifelong manifestations that show themselves in many other ways than poor reading (Miles *et. al.*, 1998). What dyslexic children and adults have in common is not their levels of literacy but the difficulty they have with the processing of verbal and written information. In the adult years this has an impact on:

- organisation – personal and at work
- time management – underestimating and overestimating
- social communication – word finding and word order
- writing – especially organising ideas
- spelling – particularly in context
- reading – often comprehension rather than accuracy
- maths – the procedures, including mental arithmetic.

It is perhaps the first two of these that are of greatest concern. They are obvious and can mask an individual's competencies. They can also be more difficult to resolve, whereas information technology can resolve many of the literacy and numeracy problems.

We need language and theory that are appropriate for the adult years and which address all of the above. Theory and definitions only reflect knowledge at a particular point in time and should be refined according to current developments. This has yet to be done and there is a need for much more research into dyslexia as it affects adults, particularly in the sphere that defines them most, that is, employment.

The impact of secondary characteristics such as lack of confidence and low self-esteem, as well as anxiety, must also be considered. These develop as a result of the experiences dyslexic people have in learning and work settings and interact negatively with the primary characteristics. For many not being able to forget negative experiences is more of a problem than being unable to remember new information. Secondary factors exacerbate the processing and literacy difficulties and this can lead to even greater misunderstanding. People become constrained by what they can't do rather than valued for what they can do.

Understanding dyslexia from the perspective of an individual starts with diagnostic assessment. This should be a process of evaluating abilities and explaining why certain tasks are difficult. The standard assessment conducted by psychologists and specialist training consultants usually includes measures of verbal ability, non-verbal ability, as well as memory and processing skills. The impact on literacy skills is also measured. It should be a positive experience and lead to better self-understanding. The result should be recommendations written in an appropriate format that are of value to both the employer and the dyslexic person. A subsequent and more specific work skills assessment can ensure that adjustments are relevant and practical.

What employers need to know

Dyslexia does present individuals with difficulties that extend beyond literacy and numeracy. It is much more than an educational issue and the information processing difficulty which characterises the syndrome persists throughout life. For those who have left formal education dyslexia might not be reflected as a learning difficulty but can undermine 'performance'. Employers need to understand it in its broadest context. In particular, it is important to acknowledge that it is transitions in life which can continue to undermine a dyslexic person's performance and highlight their difficulties. Transitions include:

- job redefinition
- change of job
- promotion
- from work back to training/education
- change of personnel.

It is often because dyslexic individuals have done well that their difficulties become obvious. They can be victims of their own success, particularly in a world where demands on paperwork have increased so much. Further, in employment people have less control of how they use their time and deadlines are less flexible. It is at times of transition when the development of skills, as well as using alternative means of dealing with tasks through compensation is especially important. Most dyslexic adults do not, however, require 'teaching', the best model for assisting them to develop the skills they need comes from coaching. The emphasis should always be on what they need to improve their performance in the short term, but anticipating what might be important in the future is essential so that change can become less challenging. Toscano (2006) has a suggested that coaching allows the individual being coached to take control of their actions and make the changes required to improve. Good practice in adult training and education always transfers control to the learner (Knowles, 1990). The coaching process would therefore seem to provide an ideal way of assisting dyslexic adults adapt and improve their performance, particularly because it focuses on transitions and change, as well as the development of skills that will facilitate this (McLoughlin and Kirwan, 2007).

Dyslexia can be described as a difficulty and can sometimes constitute a disability. In terms of supporting people it is best understood as a difference, especially in the way information is processed. Further, employers need to recognise that dyslexic people are not incompetent; they have 'abilities'. There are many dyslexic people working at high levels in all occupations; in business, public services, the professions, as well as design and technology. The achievements of iconic individuals have been promoted but there also those who are authors, script writers and journalists. Others are hard-working, conscientious and caring people who have persevered and demonstrated considerable resilience.

Dyslexic employees might need to work differently to their colleagues because of the way in which they process information. As people value 'sameness', this can make others feel uncomfortable, leading them to jump to ill-informed and inappropriate conclusions. Dyslexic people are different in the way they learn and work, but this should be seen as an important attribute. People feel valued when they believe that their difference has been taken into account and work best when they feel valued.

How employers can help

There many ways in which employers can help dyslexic individuals. They can start by arranging a work skills evaluation. This should look at the whole person, including their skills and abilities. It should be flexible, individualised and provide a wide variety of solutions and suggestions for skill development. Its resulting recommendations should facilitate progression and independence. Monitoring to consider changing circumstances needs to be incorporated.

A satisfactory evaluation should lead to adjustments or accommodations being made. They should lead to evidence-based adjustments; these are required to be 'reasonable' but this concept is contentious. What a dyslexic person might consider reasonable could be entirely unreasonable from an employer's perspective. Completely changing a job description to accommodate an individual can be unfair to colleagues and isolate the individual. Is it reasonable, for example, that the dyslexic member of staff is the only one who has their own office when everyone else, including managers, works in an open plan environment? There are certain underlying principles that can help. An adjustment can be considered reasonable if it:

- is based on documented individual needs – being dyslexic is not sufficient; specific issues to be addressed must be identified
- allows the most integrated experience possible – the underlying philosophy of the legislation is inclusion and adjustments should 'level the playing field' so that individuals are included. Too many adjustments can lead to exclusion
- does not compromise the essential requirements of the job – the key competencies should be identified so that it can be determined whether the individual has most of these. The impact dyslexia is likely to have and the extent to which reasonable adjustments make up for the difference must be considered
- does not pose a threat to personal or public safety – the risk to the individual, colleagues and the public are essential considerations
- does not impose an undue financial or administrative burden – supporting dyslexic individuals can often involve low cost interventions such as training, the provision of equipment and administrative support. Sometimes the cost can be too great, for example adapting an integrated IT system to incorporate a software package that is only to be used by one individual.

What organisations can do

There is a statutory requirement for employers to have a policy for employees who have disabilities. This should outline the procedures that enable people to access the support and adjustments they need. Some organisations take this further; arranging awareness training, making information available on intranet systems and distributing guidance notes throughout. It is usually the Human Resources department in conjunction with Occupational Health that are responsible for this.

The starting point for this support should be at the recruitment stage so that appropriate adjustments can be made. Both the employer and the individual need to have a good understanding of the demands of the job. In many cases extra time is given in selection tests. This is appropriate and enables people to get the job. Nevertheless, the demands of the job may not allow extra time and without follow-up support the capable employee can flounder, being unable to meet the immediate demands. Some dyslexic people need more time to adjust to new roles, procedures and routines even if they have worked in a similar role previously. Modifying expectations regarding the meeting of targets in performance appraisals can ensure that they have time to develop the skills and strategies they need to work at a level commensurate with their ability. Organisations can also provide helplines, support groups, advisors, and mentors both for the dyslexic individuals and their managers.

Often the above can suffice but employers can take the matter further if a dyslexic employee is still having trouble meeting targets. Current assessment by a specialist can, for example, lead to a greater understanding of individual need and assist in making the adjustments more relevant. Some individuals will need more assistance than others. Targeted individualised skill development training can lead to significant gains in performance. This often only needs to be short-term, but should be reviewed regularly, especially at times of transition. Information technology such as planning software, as well as text-to-speech and voice recognition software can provide immediate as well as long-term solutions. The latter can also help with the development of skills. Information technology is not, however, a panacea and its provision does not solve the problem. Further, some dyslexic people need individual training in its use if they are to make the best of it.

How dyslexic people can help themselves

Dyslexia has been described as a 'hidden disability'. One of the advantages of this is that dyslexic people 'look normal'. This can also be a disadvantage in that the problems encountered cannot readily be perceived. Dyslexic people do need to disclose and to advocate for themselves. Even the most supportive of employers will not have a great deal of expertise in providing for dyslexic people. It is individuals who need to become experts in how it affects them.

Professionals working with dyslexic people need to help them develop a good understanding of the nature of their difficulty, how it affects them and what they need to do about it, as well as know how others can help. It is particularly important that they are given the opportunity to talk about what they can do rather than what they cannot do, as well as how they function most effectively. Others need to know not just that a person is dyslexic, but that they:

- read thoroughly (not slowly)
- write carefully (not slowly)
- prefer to use a word processor (rather than have poor handwriting)
- like to have someone check over their work (because they are a perfectionist)
- like to be organised
- prefer written rather than verbal instructions.

One of the keys to a successful adult life is being able to disclose dyslexia in a constructive manner, providing solutions not problems, reflecting self-awareness and the ability to define oneself as more than one's disability (Goldberg *et al.*, 2003). Nevertheless, disclosure is a very complex process and there are risks as well as potential benefits (Gerber and Price, 2008).

To avoid discrimination, and ensure that they are properly understood, dyslexic people need to be able to explain what dyslexia is, how it affects them, the way in which they work best, and what an employer can do to assist them. This applies, during the process of selection and whilst in the job.

Good practice: an organizational case study

Although the DDA did not apply to police officers until 2004, in anticipation of this in 2003, the Metropolitan Police Service sought advice from dyslexia specialists as to how best to include potential and existing dyslexic police officers. This led to a three-pronged strategic approach:

- awareness training days throughout the whole organisation, particularly for management;
- training for the trainers of Hendon Police Training College;
- assessment of and one-to-one tuition for trainee police officers. The latter has included developing self-understanding, memory strategies, some spelling, effective use of pocket books, reading and revision techniques, strategies for knowledge examinations and scenario assessments. They have also been helped prepare for future challenges presented by street duty as well as report writing, supported by an Exit Report that includes recommendations for the future.

Initially the first and third aspects were adopted. Awareness training days were run and the students at Hendon Training College had access to assessment and one-to-one skills training. This was coordinated/promoted by the Skills To Achieve Results Team (START) Hendon. This is the team that provides studies skills help and support for any student who is experiencing difficulties. The dyslexic specialists carried out the assessments for those students who thought they might be dyslexic and provided the one-to-one tuition. This system was well accessed by students and over 200 were supported.

In 2006 it was felt that there was such a demand for this provision that it would be better to train police trainers to screen for dyslexia and be in a position to provide the more specialist support required by dyslexic students. This was promoted for two reasons; it would be more cost-effective, but more importantly it was thought that police officers involved in training had a much better idea of how dyslexia might impact on an individual's performance. They would be able to give targeted and appropriate support. The work of a police officer is complex, requiring multi-tasking such as taking notes at the scene of an incident, following procedures correctly in custody suites after making an arrest and dealing with paper-work generally. Some of the specialized roles require even more. As well as driving at speed, officers in rapid response units, for example, have to process a great deal of verbal information quickly. Understanding such demands enables trainers to make very specific and realistic recommendations.

The members of the START team now all undergo dyslexia specialist training. They are taught to screen students using the Dyslexia Adult Screening Test (DAST) and make recommendations about reasonable adjustments such as allowing extra time to complete training, as well as examinations and skills training. The advisors are also trained to carry out workplace consultation to support dyslexic officers already working in the field.

At present this provision of skills training is available for those in initial training and continues to the end of their probation period at Hendon, but it is hoped that it will extend across the whole organisation and already the START team is providing advice, support and awareness training to all areas of the service.

The Dyslexia Advisers Project has been very successful and the model is being considered by other police services. In addition to providing help which is enabling students to pass their examinations and work more effectively, there are other benefits; the awareness of dyslexia is improving and there is a far better understanding of its complex nature and impact on individuals. Unlike the situation in other organisations, disclosure is not mandatory but students at Hendon and serving police officers seem more willing to seek support. A greater number than expected have been assessed. Feedback from students suggests increased confidence, that they have a better idea how to learn and work and that they are more self-aware and analytical. Many express relief. If the disclosure rate is a reflection of the effectiveness of legislation and the understanding of dyslexia the Project can be considered a success.

Conclusion

There are dyslexic people working effectively in jobs representing the complete occupational spectrum. So many adults have achieved success in their personal and working lives that it must now be accepted that dyslexia is not an insurmountable barrier. Most are determined and hard working and just want to get on with their job. They are, however, different and need to be able to advocate for themselves in a constructive fashion, focusing on solutions which can often be quite simple, effective and benefit the whole organisation. Dealing with dyslexia can in fact be a creative experience for both employers and employees in that it is about problem solving.

Understanding, confidence and good communication are among the keys to success. Employers who understand dyslexia and create work environments in which dyslexic people can develop, grow and become increasingly successful will gain more than just the knowledge that they are fulfilling their statutory responsibilities.

References

Armstrong, M. (1999) A *Handbook of Human Resources Management Practice*. London: Kogan Page.

Gerber, P. and Price, L.A. (2003) Persons with learning disabilities in the workplace: what we know so far in the *Americans with Disabilities Act* era. *Learning Disabilities Research and Practice*, 18(2) 132–136.

Gerber, P.J. and Price, L.A. (2008) Self-disclosure and adults with learning disabilities: practical ideas about a complex process. *Learning Disabilities*, 15(1) 21–23.

Gerber, P.J., Ginsberg, R. and Reiff, H.B. (1992) Identifying alterable patterns in employment success for highly successful adults with learning disabilities. *Journal of Learning Disabilities* 25(8) 475–487.

Gerber, P.J., Reiff, H.B. and Ginsberg, R. (1996) Reframing the learning disabilities experience. *Journal of Learning Disabilities*, 29(1) 98–101.

Gerber, P., Price, L., Mulligan, R. and Shessel, I. (2004). Beyond transition: a comparison of the employment experiences of American and Canadian adults with LD. *Journal of Learning Disabilities*, 37(4), 283–291.

Goldberg, R., Higgins, E., Raskind, M. and Herman, K. (2003) Predictors of success in individuals with learning disabilities: A qualitative analysis of a 20-year longitudinal study. *Learning Disabilities Research and Practice*, 18(4), 222–236.

Knowles, M. (1990) *The Adult Learner: A Neglected Species*. Houston, TX: Gulf.

Konur, O. (2007) A judicial outcome analysis of the *Disability Discrimination Act*: a windfall for employers? *Disability and Society*, 22 (March), 187–204.

McLoughlin, D. and Kirwan, B.M. (2007) Coaching and Dyslexia in the Work Place. *Selection and Development Review*, 23(2), 3–7.

Madaus, J.W., Ruban, L.M., Foley, T.E., McGuire, J.M. and Ruban, L.M. (2002) Employment self-disclosure of postsecondary graduates with learning disabilities: rates and rationales. *Journal of Learning Disabilities*, 5(4), 364–369.

Martin, A., McLoughlin, D. and Leather, C.A. (2008) Pilot study of SpLD disclosure in the workplace. Seventh British Dyslexia Association International Conference, Harrogate, UK, March.

Miles, T.R., Haslum, M.N. and Wheeler, T.J. (1998) Gender ratio in dyslexia. *Annals of Dyslexia. 48,* 27–57.

Spekman, N.J., Goldberg, R.J. and Herman, K.L. (1992) Learning disabled children grow up. A search for factors related to success in the young adult years. *Learning Disabilities Research and Practice*, 7, 161–170.

Toscano, J. (2006) The case for coaching. *Selection and Development Review*, 22(2), 12–13.

Walker, B.A. (1994) Valuing differences: the concept and a model. In C. Mabey and P. Iles (eds), *Managing Learning*. London: Routledge, pp. 211–223.

Part 5

Diversity, culture and language

23

Dyslexia and foreign language learning

Elke Schneider

This chapter will answer the following questions:

- Why can learning a foreign language be difficult for individuals with dyslexia?
- What does research say about foreign language learning and dyslexia?
- Are some foreign languages easier to learn for individuals with dyslexia than others?
- Which foreign language teaching strategies are suitable for individuals with dyslexia?
- How can school administrators support foreign language learning for individuals with dyslexia?

With today's intercultural and multilingual demands on society and the job market, it becomes increasingly important to be able to speak, read and write in more than one language. Many cultures require children to learn not just one but several additional languages in school. When these languages are not used by the majority culture for daily routines, children learn a 'foreign language' such as native speakers of German learning French in German schools. When the language(s) are used by the majority culture outside the school setting, children learn a 'second language' (Saville-Troike, 2006). An example would be Luxembourg, where all children regardless of their first language background learn Letzeburgish, German, French, and English for daily use outside of the school premises.

To prepare children for the multilingual and multicultural society around them, many educational programs around the world start foreign languages in kindergarten or in early elementary grades because research continues to point out that the earlier one learns languages the easier it is (Romaine, 1995; Singleton, 1989). In such settings, foreign languages frequently taught are English, Spanish, French, Russian, and Arabic (Alfred *et al.*, 2006; Dutcher, 1995; Kuntz, 2001; Council of Europe Language Policy Division, 2007; Leewen, 2005). In addition, increasingly high school and university degrees contain foreign language requirements to better prepare students for multilingual and multicultural challenges in their future professions (Brod and Huber, 1996). When approximately every fifth person in the world is affected by some degree of a language learning disability called dyslexia (Wood and Richardson, 2002; Shaywitz, 2003), it is imperative that language educators and school administrators be aware of the difficulties dyslexia can cause with foreign language learning. Further, on the basis of such heightened awareness, it is essential to implement effective foreign language teaching strategies that meet the needs of students with dyslexia. Under such conditions, individuals with dyslexia have a realistic opportunity to succeed in learning a foreign language. Answers to the introductory questions provide information towards these goals.

Why can learning a foreign language be difficult for individuals with dyslexia?

Two main factors make foreign language learning difficult for individuals with dyslexia. The first is the nature of the disability itself; the second is the way that foreign languages are traditionally taught in public schools and at universities.

For decades, research has documented that individuals with dyslexia predominantly struggle with literacy tasks that involve print (Birsh, 2005; Henry, 2003; Shaywitz, 2003). These struggles include difficulties decoding, encoding, and comprehending print at the letter-sound, morpheme (prefixes, roots, suffixes with grammatical or semantic information), and syntax level. Writing coherent, well-structured texts without grammatical, conventional and spelling errors present challenges as well. Completing reading and writing tasks with appropriate fluency is another major issue for many students with dyslexia (Wolf and Bowers, 1999). Comprehensible note taking, legible handwriting, and effective study and test taking are additional common challenges for this population (Birsh, 2005; Henry, 2003; Shaywitz, 2003). Short-term memory problems also play a major part in students' poor written and oral language performance (Shaywitz, 2003; Siegel and Ryan, 1988, 1989). All of these difficulties are based on differences in how the brain processes literacy tasks into comprehensible information. Therefore, individuals with dyslexia will not outgrow their language processing difficulties. However, for many students with dyslexia multi-sensory structured and meta-cognitive language instruction (henceforth MSL) can lead to lasting, effective coping strategies (Shaywitz, 2003), and can open the door for a positive foreign language learning experience (for overview, see Schneider, 1999).

The instructional practices commonly used to teach foreign languages in schools are the second reason for which students with dyslexia do not succeed in foreign languages. These methods are insensitive to dyslexic students' needs for explicit, direct, and meta-cognitive instruction because they are based on theoretical concepts that do not consider significantly struggling learners. Foreign language teaching and research is still largely based on ideal foreign language learners who possess a natural *language acquisition device* and a *universal grammar* that allow them to succeed in learning other languages without great difficulties (Saville-Troike, 2006). Currently promoted instructional practices are based on the presumption that native and foreign language skills are best acquired through immersion and implicit instruction (Richards and Rodgers, 2001; Saville-Troike, 2006). Krashen's *Natural Approach* and Curran's *Communicative Approach* are examples of such foreign language teaching approaches (Krashen, 2003; Richards and Rodgers, 2001). Lack of personal motivation for and engagement in learning a foreign language as well as high test and performance anxiety have been commonly accepted explanations for significant foreign language learning difficulties (McIntyre and Gardner, 1991; Oxford, 1990; Omaggio-Hadley, 2000). Consequently, current foreign language teacher education programs do not prepare teachers adequately to meet the needs of dyslexic students. Research documenting the positive effect of MSL instruction on reading, writing, and spelling performance of students with dyslexia and other at-risk students has not been considered by the majority of foreign language educators (Mather *et al.*, 2001; McCutchen, *et al.*, 2002; McIntyre and Pickering, 2003). A small body of research and anecdotal references from foreign language educators report positive effects of MSL instruction in foreign language instruction as well. Examples of MSL use range from whole class to individualized one-on-one MSL teaching practices (Arries, 1999; Downey *et al.*, 2000; Sparks *et al.*, 1991; Schneider, 1999; Simon, 2000; Sparks and Miller, 2000).

What does research say about foreign language learning and dyslexia?

It was not until the 1970s that educators began to realize that severe difficulties in succeeding with foreign language requirements might not be explainable with affective issues alone. Harvard University councilor Dinklage (1971) was one of the first to raise the issue of a possible foreign language learning disability in severely struggling foreign language students. In the 1980s and 1990s, a few foreign language educators continued to raise awareness for the challenges of severely struggling foreign language learners suggesting different MSL practices to meet the needs of students with language processing difficulties in foreign languages (Demuth and Smith, 1987; Gajar, 1987; Sparks *et al.*, 1991; Pompian and Thum, 1988). Foreign and second language researchers Skehan (1986) and Spolsky (1989) stressed that intact linguistic processing skills in the mother tongue are essential prerequisites for success in a foreign or second language. These findings identify clear disadvantages for individuals with dyslexia because poor language processing skills define their disability. In the late 1980s, educational researchers Ganschow and Sparks discovered a phenomenon they termed the *Linguistic Coding Differences Hypothesis* (LCDH) in their research with high school and college foreign language learners (Ganschow and Sparks, 2000, 2001; Ganschow *et al.*, 1998; Sparks, 1995). Over 15 years of research about the LCDH have now documented that subtle or overt language processing difficulties in students' academic native language performance resurface when learning a foreign language. Difficulties in the mother tongue with spelling and punctuation, reading fluency and compre-hension, grammatically correct writing with complete sentences and correct subject–verb or noun–pronoun agreement are all problems that can recur in the foreign language. Research on the LCDH has identified poor phonological–orthographic processing (knowing how sounds of the language are presented in print and vice versa) as a cause for early experiences of failure in the foreign language. Difficulties with grammatical or more complex vocabulary structures may enable students to succeed initially; but once more complex oral and written performance in the foreign language is required, severe struggles seem unavoidable. The LCDH also documents severe difficulties with learning a foreign language not primarily being due to anxiety or lack of motivation in the first place, but rather such follow-up symptoms as poor linguistic proces-sing skills characteristic for dyslexia. While Ganschow, Sparks and their colleagues researched alphabetic foreign languages such as Spanish, German, and Latin, others gathered support for the LCDH with regard to English as a foreign language and nonalphabetic languages such as Hebrew and Japanese (Ben-Dror, Bentin, and Frost, 1995; Dufva and Voeten, 1999; Durkin; 2000; Service and Kohonen, 1995; Yamada and Banks, 1994; for a summary, see Schneider, 1999). Additionally, cross-linguistic research supports the LCDH with findings on the transfer of phonological–orthographic, syntactic, and semantic knowledge from the first language to additional languages. *Positive transfer* occurs when transfer of linguistic knowledge (pro-nunciation, grammar, vocabulary, handwriting, spelling) from one language leads to correct performance in the other language. When errors occur based on a transfer from the mother tongue to the new language, *negative transfer* has taken place. The weaker the linguistic knowledge of the first language, the more challenging it is to acquire the additional language (Durunoglu, 2002; Frith, 2007; Koda, 2005; Jackson-Maldonado, 2004; Saville-Troike, 2006).

When language processing difficulties transfer from one language to another, then teaching strategies that have been shown effective in remediating these difficulties in one language promise success in the foreign language. Based on this premise, over 15 years of research has found MSL instruction in the native language to be equally effective in foreign language learning contexts (Ganschow and Sparks, 2000, 1995; Ganschow et al., 1998; Sparks, 1995; Sparks and Ganschow 1993; Sparks, et al., 1998; Sparks et al., 2002). To date, this research has focused mainly on alphabetic languages such as German, Spanish, Latin, Italian, and French. MSL instruction with high school and college students included one-on-one, small group, and whole class MSL instruction (Downey et al., 2000; Hill et al., 1995; Schneider, 1999; Simon, 2000; Sparks and Miller, 2000; Sparks et al., 1996).

Are some languages easier to learn for individuals with dyslexia than others?

While to date no evidence-based answers are available for the question which foreign language might be more suitable for individuals with dyslexia than others, a number of steps can be taken to make an informed decision. First, parents, teachers, and administrators confronted with having to select a foreign language for students with dyslexia should gain a clear understanding of the individual students' linguistic strengths and weaknesses. Existing test data on reading, writing, spelling, and comprehension skills in the native language and personal specific interviews with the student help gain an understanding of first language processing skills. In addition, results from the Modern Language Aptitude test (Caroll and Sapon, 2002) or the Pimsleur Language Aptitude Battery (Pimsleur, 1966) provide information about a student's foreign language learning capabilities by assessing grammatical, vocabulary, and auditory-visual processing skills in samples of a variety of unfamiliar languages.

Next, the linguistic characteristics of foreign languages themselves have to be analyzed in relation to the students' identified strengths and weaknesses in areas such as letter-sound awareness, grammar, vocabulary retention, reading comprehension, decoding, spelling and writing abilities. Languages differ in degrees of complexity with regard to pronunciation, reading, and spelling patterns, sentence structures, tenses and moods, as well as grammatical endings. Languages also differ in word composition mechanisms, types and degrees of differences in print patterns between the mother tongue and the new language as well as differences between reading and writing directions are other aspects of challenge to consider (for a review see Grigorenko, 2002).

Both student and language factors should be considered before making an informed choice. The selected foreign language should place least stress on the student's language processing weaknesses and utilize any identified strengths. For instance, when phonological–orthographic weaknesses are dominant, a foreign language that has a fairly regular pronunciation and spelling system with few spelling and pronunciation choices such as Spanish, Italian, or German might be a good fit. Latin might be suitable for students who can handle syntactic challenges because Latin demands close attention to word endings that carry grammatical information. Also, the vocabulary is limited because Latin no longer expands like currently spoken languages. When sign language is accepted as a foreign language, individuals with dyslexia may do well because learning occurs primarily through kinesthetic–tactile communication. A third essential consideration factor is the foreign language teacher. The more the teacher is willing to adapt instruction and the more versed the teacher is in MSL strategies the more successful the learning experience for students with dyslexia. Specifics of MSL strategies are discussed next.

Which foreign language teaching strategies are beneficial for individuals with dyslexia?

Over 60 years of research have documented the effectiveness of MSL instruction for students with dyslexia in English as a native language resulting in over 20 different instructional programs. Examples are the Orton-Gillingham Approach, Alphabetic Phonics, the Slingerland Approach, The Wilson Program, the Hickey Program, and the Shelton Program (for a summary, see McIntyre and Pickering, 2003; Schneider, 1999). After over 15 years of research on MSL instruction, for the first time MSL strategies were included explicitly in a new high school foreign language curriculum for U.S. high school students of Spanish and French in 2005 (Ganschow and Sparks, 2005a,b; Schneider *et al.*, 2007). This demonstrates a heightened awareness in the twenty-first century for the need to include dyslexia-appropriate instructional practices in regular foreign language programs as well as an active interest by publishing companies in accommodations for this high incidence population.

MSL instruction in native and foreign languages applies the following eight principles:

1 Multisensory Students use all learning channels simultaneously, particularly the kinesthetic–tactile one, to utilize strong learning channels and to circumvent reliance on weak learning channels. Teachers guide students in age and skill-appropriate "see–say, and act/do" activities to make abstract concepts concrete. This, in turn, enhances memorization and retrieval skills.

2 Structured The teacher breaks content down into small steps and sequences tasks carefully from less to more complex to assure mastery. Instruction progresses to the next step only when students have mastered the previous ones.

3 Meta-cogitive The teacher models for students how and why certain procedures/rules are necessary for success in foreign language reading, writing, spelling, pronunciation, and listening. Through think-aloud activities, students understand and practice foreign language mechanisms. Think-alouds also tell the teacher informally to what degree students have comprehended new content and where more instructional support is necessary. Thus, metacognitve practice is an essential component of dynamic assessment (Lidz, 1991). Further, over time metacognitive practice enables students to self-identify and self-correct errors and decreases dependencies on teacher guidance.

4 Repetitive Students engage in multiple forms of multisensory structured practice because understanding a concept guarantees the ability to apply language concepts or study/test-taking strategies correctly. Teacher guidance is gradually reduced throughout repetitive practice to lead students to independence.

5 Explicit The teacher models concretely how to use certain language concepts to help the foreign language student understand the mechanisms that characterize appropriate use in the new language. Explicit instruction makes language concepts transparent that the student with dyslexia would otherwise not be able to realize. In the area of awareness about the pronunciation of print representations and vice versa, learners of an alphabetic language might learn the letter sounds and letter names of the alphabet. Students learning a logographic language such as Chinese might learn in what sequence to place the strokes of a logographic unit (e.g. for tree). Students learning a syllabic language such as Japanese might learn how to differentiate similar syllabic representations and how to pronounce them. Explicit instruction also includes the demonstration of a variety of self-correction, study and test-taking strategies as well as ways to decipher and understand graphs and charts that frequently provide relevant information about the foreign language in the students' foreign language books (e.g., grammar and vocabulary concepts and connotations).

6 Analytic-synthetic Through explicit instruction and practice, students who learn an alphabet language become versed in breaking words, syllables, sentences, and paragraphs apart to be able to analyze and understand their components. Students also learn how to synthesize these parts back together into meaningful whole units.

7 Diagnostic While students practice new language concepts, the teacher informally assesses the degree of understanding through dynamic assessment procedures. The teacher acts as a facilitator of learning who stimulates thinking and problem solving in the students through thought-provoking questions, gestures and other images (Lidz, 1991; Schneider and Ganschow, 2000).

8 Prescriptive The teacher adapts instructional procedures according to the diagnostic findings both during remaining class time and in preparation for subsequent lessons.

When implementing these MSL principles, foreign language teachers apply the following procedures (for further details, see Sparks *et al.*, 2002):

- Based on detailed task analysis, the teacher *rearranges the scope and sequence* of the curriculum presented in the foreign language book to ensure learning progression from less to more complex information (for examples, see Downey and Snyder, 2001; Schneider, 1999).
- Based on this task analysis, the teacher also breaks each new content into *carefully sequenced small working steps* and plans for explicit and comprehensible instruction through modeling and multiple meta-cognitive learning opportunities (for examples, see Schneider, 1999; Schneider and Crombie, 2003).
- To avoid confusion, new pronunciation, spelling, grammar or reading concepts are taught in sequences that *keep similar sounding or looking concepts* at least three to five lessons *apart*. For instance, German letter patterns {au} and {äu} would be taught several lessons apart because they look similar. Likewise, the short vowel pronunciation of English letters {e} and {a} would be taught several lessons apart because they carry a similar sound. Only when students have mastered the first concept in pronunciation, reading, and writing, the other similar one is taught. Such careful linguistic sequencing of content may require a shifting of existing curricula components or a division of chapter content that addresses many and similar concepts (for examples of a restructured commercial foreign language program, see Schneider, 1999).
- The more complex a language concept is the more *hands-on, color, and shape-coded materials* are necessary to help students with dyslexia understand and internalize them. Grammatical concepts such as conditionals, hypothetical statements, complex sentences with complex tenses, or subject–predicate agreement are more effectively taught, remembered and retrieved when learned with hands-on, color and shape-coded resources. The same is true for vocabulary concepts such as complex compounds, prefix–root–suffix patterns, words with multiple meanings, words with connotations that differ greatly from comparable words in the mother tongue, or polite and respectful expressions for unique foreign language contexts (e.g., condolences, illness, weddings, cultural celebrations). These materials allow the student with dyslexia to understand abstract language patterns through concrete hands-on learning while articulating out-loud why and how they master the task. Students need to see through color and shape-coding why and how specific grammatical, syntactic, and morphological patterns apply to the foreign language. For this purpose, students work with laminated paper strips, cards, or Lego blocks and combine language elements with sticky tack, tape, or magnetic devices either on their own or in small groups. Gradually, students are weaned off the shape and then the color support cues as they show

mastery of the concept at each progressive step (for more details, see Schneider, 1999; Schneider and Crombie, 2003; for MSL English grammar see Carraker, 2004, 2006).

- *Pronunciation practice* takes place through explicit, highly repetitive learning with all senses. Pronunciation and the formation of matching print patterns are directly linked. Students trace/write, see, and say letter sounds, or syllabic, or logographic patterns one at a time before these patterns are practiced in a variety of contexts that gradually increase in complexity. Students move from words and phrases to individual sentences and paragraphs. Teachers take time to model explicitly for students how to use their vocal apparati (vocal cords, tongue, teeth, lips) to produce the sounds of the foreign language, especially those sounds that are unfamiliar in the first language. Per pattern learned, students collect on summary sheets what helps them recall the pronunciation and spelling of the new letter, or syllabic or logographic pattern. Mnemonic devices might include personally meaningful illustrations and keywords in the native and foreign language.

- For *explicit vocabulary practice* the teacher models how and why words are composed in certain ways in the foreign language. Then students engage in extensive multi-sensory word composition practice based on current individual vocabulary knowledge. Students create their own words applying teacher-modeled vocabulary building mechanisms. They also use word and syllable cards to synthesize new words. The students practice integrating the piece into a variety of personally meaningful sentences or short poems. Acting out and illustrating differences in word meanings of same and similar looking words (e.g., meet/met; heat/seat, feed/feet, multiple meanings of the word 'trunk') and word connotations (e.g., the difference between cute, handsome, pretty) is part of multi-sensory vocabulary practice, as well. In the end, students create vocabulary resource or summary sheets on which they collect newly learned vocabulary building patterns and semantic differentiation issues with personally relevant illustrations and examples in the foreign and first language. Students keep these summary sheets (along with grammar and pronunciation/spelling summary sheets) in a language resource folder. Vocabulary resource sheets can contain productive word patterns. They may summarize word patterns for words with same prefixes, same roots or same suffixes. They may also present frequent compound patterns of words (e.g., noun + noun; adjective + adjective) or word construction mechanisms to turn verbs into nouns or adjectives (e.g., construct–construction–constructive) (for details, see Schneider, 1999; Schneider and Crombie, 2003).

- The teacher models for students how to develop *mnemonic devices* to remember and recall new pronunciation and spelling as well as grammar and vocabulary information. The use of color- and shape-coding as a mnemonic can help students with dyslexia memorize details about word gender, singular–plural, and case endings of vocabulary. It can also help students recall sentence structures and unusual pronunciations. Other mnemonic devices include the use of songs, gestures, acronyms, keywords in the native and/or foreign language, illustrations, and acting out language issues such as roles of direct versus indirect objects (for more details, see Mastropieri and Scruggs, 1991; Schneider, 1999; Schneider and Crombie, 2003; Sperber, 1989).

- The teacher builds *explicit study and test taking practice* into the curriculum. This includes explicit modeling and practicing of mnemonic devices to help students manage their weak short-term memory capacities. Songs, gestures, drawings, and other visual cues assist in improving memorization and recall skills. Providing study guides with visual cues and ideas how to create them independently is essential to help students become active, independent, and successful foreign language learners. Further, time management and organization of materials and learning routines are important components of study and test-

303

taking skills. (For additional discussion of strategies, see Schneider and Crombie, 2003; Mastropieri and Scruggs, 1991.)

■ Common *test accommodations* include extended time, taking the test in a distraction-free environment, receiving foreign language dictations in a one-on-one setting with repeated listening opportunities, and oral instead of written assessment of foreign culture, grammar, and vocabulary knowledge. 'Fill-in-the gap' assignments are kept to a minimum. If gap-filling assignments are used, word and/or picture banks are provided, especially in the initial stages of acquiring the foreign language (for more details, see Ganschow *et al.*, 1999; Schneider, 2000; Schneider and Crombie, 2003).

■ *Paring a stronger with a weaker student* for guided pair work to reinforce a language concept benefits both students, especially when *reciprocal teaching* is encouraged (Palincsar and Brown, 1984).

■ The teacher provides a *reliable, structured learning environment* that keeps anxiety and stress levels low. Beneficial are clear visuals for the sequence of classroom routines, and sharing of any reading materials for class prior to discussion in class. Other effective learning resources are tape recordings with authentic pronunciation samples of chapter vocabulary. Students can use these at their own pace and time without embarrassing themselves in front of their peers. Peers as note takers and the organization of study groups are additional practices to reduce stress and anxiety.

■ The teacher does *not call spontaneously* on the student with dyslexia during class activities that require quick oral or written performance without giving the student ample time to witness peers on the same task. This acknowledges respect to the impaired language processing skills characteristic of individuals with dyslexia.

■ Routine *individualized conferences* between teacher and student help monitor the learning progress and provide the student with opportunities to practice awareness of reflective thinking and speaking about specific areas of concern in a receptive environment. Such practice is essential to developing realistic self-advocacy skills for higher educational settings and the future profession. Research has shown that self-advocacy is an underdeveloped ability in the majority of individuals with dyslexia (Wehman, 2006; Wehmeyer, 1997).

For students who continue to display severe learning problems despite these instructional practices infused in the foreign language classroom, additional approaches are necessary. Among them are:

■ *Close collaboration* of the student, the classroom teacher, an additional MSL-trained tutor, and, if the student is underage, the student's parents/guardians. This helps monitor the effectiveness of specific teaching and learning strategies used. It also actively engages the struggling student in a tightly structured academic support system.

■ *Alternative foreign language learning opportunities* in separate MSL-based foreign language courses and foreign language substitution courses are alternatives described in the following section as they require substantial administrative support.

How can school administration support foreign language learning for individuals with dyslexia?

There are many ways in which school administration can actively support foreign language instruction that allows individuals with dyslexia to succeed. While mildly struggling foreign language learners may receive appropriate support without much administrative engagement, alternative foreign language learning opportunities for severely struggling learners are impossible without substantial administrative flexibility and support. The following suggestions have been implemented successfully in a number of American schools and universities. Because the severity of dyslexia plays an essential role in what constitutes an effective foreign language learning environment, administrators best provide support along a continuum of foreign language learning accommodations. As a team, educators and administrators routinely discuss viable foreign language learning options, collect data on the effectiveness of selected support models, and improve aspects as needed. Collected data may include written documentation of students' oral versus written performance on homework assignments, in-class assignments, and on tests with a variety of accommodations. They may also include structured interviews at certain intervals with the students themselves, their parents and tutors regarding the impact of specific interventions in test taking, study, and foreign language content. In accordance with Ganschow and Sparks' model of a continuum of foreign language learning accommodations (described in Ganschow et al., 1995), the following suggestions are organized from mild to most severe cases of dyslexia.

For students with milder forms of dyslexia and already well-developed study and test taking strategies, tutorial collaboration with a peer and routine support from the foreign language teacher (e.g., class notes, test topics ahead of time, extended test taking time) may suffice. Administrators can support these practices by encouraging faculty and students to engage in such practices and by providing rewards for collaborative work with struggling learners. Students with milder forms of dyslexia lacking well-developed study and test-taking skills may need additional professional tutoring outside of class that applies MSL strategies. Peers are not able to provide such specific support. Administrators can support such services by offering MSL tutor and teacher training on the school premises and by supporting individuals to receive MSL instructional expertise in inservices, at conferences, and through additional college coursework. Regional branches of the International Dyslexia Association (IDA) provide names of established MSL trainers and tutors in the area (see also internationally: www.interdys.org). While MSL teacher training is currently available primarily in English as a native language, research documents that the principles are easily and effectively transferable to other languages (for overview and details, see Schneider, 1999; Schneider and Crombie, 2003). For such pioneering work to spread and succeed, administrative support that encourages foreign language teachers to learn and experiment with new evidence-based instructional practices is essential.

When tutorial support and/or infusion of MSL strategies in regular foreign language instruction, as described under the previous question, does not lead to significant improvement for the student with dyslexia, more intense intervention steps are necessary. One option is to offer a specific MSL foreign language class for severely struggling foreign language learners. Such a course typically contains no more than eight to ten students and progresses at a considerably slower pace to guarantee mastery of content through intense MSL practice (Arries, 1999; Ashe, 1997; Sparks et al., 1991; Sparks and Miller, 2000). Students remain in this class until the foreign language requirement is completed or until they have grasped the basic new concepts of pronunciation, spelling, reading, writing, and grammar of the foreign language to a degree that enables them to succeed in subsequent mainstream foreign language classes. Completing an entire two-year foreign language requirement in a separate MSL class might take three to four years (for more details, see Demuth and Smith, 1987; Downey and Snyder, 2001; Hill et al., 1995). Without administrative support that allows for flexible schedules, encourages alternative course model implementation, and finances teacher training and purchase of MSL materials, these forms of alternative foreign language instruction are impossible. Administrative minds need to come to terms with the fact that fair learning opportunities for all students, including the many students with dyslexia, calls for alternative, differentiated instructional practices in different class models.

Another option to complete a foreign language requirement might be to allow severely struggling students to take a foreign language course in the country where the foreign language is spoken and where they can live with native speakers to acquire at least oral proficiency in the foreign language along with authentic experiences of another culture. School administrators can support fundraising events so that a small group of individuals can take advantage of such an opportunity during the summer or a semester abroad. Investigating reliable international foreign language exchange programs is another way administrators can add benefits to the school's learning opportunities.

College students may opt for completing a foreign language course requirement in a summer intensive course when no other course requirements exist. Students with severe forms of dyslexia are advised to receive MSL tutorial support during such intense three-to-six week foreign language courses that cover content of a 15-week course. Effective study and test taking strategies are essential for successful completion of a foreign language requirement in an intensive course.

A final solution for students with language processing difficulties so severe that passing a foreign language requirement presents an insurmountable stumbling block, despite accommodations described in this chapter, is a foreign language substitution. Instead of taking a foreign language, students learn about cultural diversity issues of another country in their native language by taking courses about art, history, politics, and literature of the other culture. Schools and universities with a foreign-language substitution option state qualification procedures and courses in their governance documents. Usually, a school-based learning assistance director helps determine the eligibility for substitutions based on official documentation of a learning disability (for details, see Block et al., 1995; Ganschow et al., 2000; Philips et al., 1991; Shaw, 1999). In a survey conducted by Ganschow et al., (2000), over 80 students taking foreign language substitution courses at a Midwestern university in the U.S. validated not only the reality of their insurmountable struggles in high school and college foreign language courses despite above-average personal investment; they also stressed that the foreign language substitution courses allowed them to become better prepared global citizens because they could concentrate on culture- and diversity-sensitive content without being distracted by foreign language demands (Ganschow et al., 2000). While not a viable option in countries that require multilingual education (e.g., Luxembourg, Switzerland, many former British, French, and Dutch colonies in Africa and the Far East), foreign language substitutions present an important option to consider in predominantly monolingual countries (e.g. U.S., France, Spain, Austria, Italy, Mexico). Overall, the success of any of the described foreign language learning accommodations and modifications can only be successful with consistent school administrative support.

In this chapter, several suggestions for alternative instructional procedures have been presented to help students with dyslexia succeed in learning a foreign language. Positive results depend on a number of factors. The most essential factor to consider is the severity of the student's disability and the specific language processing areas most affected by the disability (letter-sound processing, pronunciation, grammar, and/or vocabulary, fluency, memory). This information is essential in selecting a suitable foreign language and learning model. Another influential factor is the student's personal commitment to and investment in learning the foreign language. Without the students' serious commitment, no instructional adaptations and learning models can lead to success. On the other hand, without skilled MSL instruction in a foreign language, the student with dyslexia will fail to succeed as responses from over 90 college students at a Midwestern midsize university document (Ganschow *et al.*, 2000). When such multifaceted and substantial adaptations are necessary to meet the needs of students with dyslexia in foreign language classes, administrative support is a final crucial component. While current research does not provide specific answers as to which foreign languages are more suitable than others for students with dyslexia, research does provide solid evidence for the effectiveness of MSL-based foreign language instruction. When students, their parents, and teachers, as well as administration collaborate effectively, individuals with dyslexia receive a realistic opportunity to succeed in another language and learn about multicultural issues.

References

Alfred, G., Byram, M., and Fleming, M. (eds) (2006). *Education for Intercultural Citizenship: Concepts and comparisons*. Clevedon, UK: Multilingual Matters.

Arries, J. (1999). Learning disabilities and foreign languages: A curriculum approach to the design of inclusive courses. *Modern Language Journal, 83*, 98–110.

Ashe, A.C. (1997). Latin for special needs students: Meeting the challenge of students with learning disabilities. In R.A. LaFluer (ed.), *Latin for the 21st century* (pp. 237–250). Glenview, IL: Scott Foresman-Addison Wesley.

Ben-Dror, I., Bentin, S., and Frost, R. (1995). Semantic, phonological, and morphologic skills in reading disabled and normal children: Evidence from perception and production of Hebrew speakers. *Reading Research Quarterly, 30*, 876–893.

Birsh, J. (2005). *Multisensory teaching of basic language skills*. Baltimore, MD: Brookes Publishing.

Birsh, J. (2006). What is multisensory structured language instruction? In M. Henry and P. Hook (eds), A look at multisensory structured language instruction. *Perspectives, 32*, (4), 15–20.

Block, L., Brinckerhoff, B., and Tureba, C. (1995). Options and accommodations in mathematics and foreign language for college students with learning disabilities. *Higher Education and the Handicapped (HEATH), 14* (2/3), 1–5.

Brod, R., and Huber, B. (1996). The MLA survey of foreign language entrance and degree requirements 1994–1995. *ADFL Bulletin, 28* (1), 35–43.

Carraker, S. (2004). *Multisensory grammar and written composition*. Houston, TX: Neuhaus Publications.

Carraker, S. (2006). Teaching the structure of language through seeing, hearing and doing. In M. Henry, and P. Hook (eds), A look at multisensory structured language instruction. *Perspectives, 24*, (4), 24–28.

Carroll, J.B., and Sapon, S. M. (2002). *Modern Language Aptitude Test Manual (MLAT)*. North Bethesda, MD: Second Language Testing.

Council of Europe Language Policy Division (2007). *From linguistic diversity to plurilingual educaton. Guide for the development of language education policies*. Strasbourg, Language Policy Division. Council of Europe, Retrieved on 3–21–08 from www.coe.int/lang.

Demuth, K., and Smith, N. (1987). The foreign language requirement: An alternative program. *Foreign Language Annals, 20*, 67–77.

Dinklage, K. (1971). Inability to learn a foreign language. In G. Baine and C. McArthur (eds), *Emotional problems of the student* (pp. 185–206). New York: Appleton-Century-Crofts.

Downey, D., and Snyder, L. (2001). Curricular accommodations for college students with language learning disabilities. *Topics in Language Disorders, 21*(2), 55–67.

Downey, D., Snyder, L., and Hill, B. (2000). College students with dyslexia: Persistent linguistic deficits and foreign language learning. *Dyslexia, 6*, 101–111.

Dufva, M., and Voeten, M. (1999). Native language literacy and phonological memory as prerequisites for learning English as a foreign language. *Applied Psycholinguistics, 202*, 329–348.

Durgunoglu, A. (2002). Crosslinguistic transfer in literacy development and implications for language learners. *Annals of Dyslexia, 52*, 189–204.

Durkin, C. (2000). Dyslexia in bilingual children: Does recent research assist identification? *Dyslexia, 6*, 248–267.

Dutcher, N. (1995). *Overview of foreign language education in the United States*. Washington DC: Center for Applied Linguistics. Retrieved on 3–21–08 from http://www.ncela.gwu.edu/pubs/resource/foreign.htm.

Frith, U. (2007). *The effect of orthography on reading and reading problems*. Samuel Orton Memorial Lecture at the International Dyslexia Association, Dallas, TX.

Gajar, A.H. (1987). Foreign language disabilities: The identification of predictive and diagnostic variables. *Journal of Learning Disabilities*, *20* (6), 327–30.

Ganschow, L., and Sparks, R. (1995). Effects of direct instruction in phonology on the native skills and foreign aptitude of at-risk foreign language learners. *Journal of Learning Disabilities*, *28*, 107–120.

Ganschow, L., and Sparks, R. (2000). Reflections on foreign language study for students with language learning problems: Research, issues, and challenges. *Dyslexia*, *6*, 87–100.

Ganschow, L., and Sparks, R. (2001). Learning difficulties and foreign language learning: A review of research and instruction. *Language Teaching*, *34*, 79–98.

Ganschow, L., and Sparks, R. (2005a). Inclusion in the French classroom. In J.-P. Valette and R.M. Valette (eds), *Discovering French Nouveau! Texas Teacher's Edition* (pp. T52–T55). Evanston, IL: McDougall Littell.

Ganschow, L., and Sparks, R. (2005b). Inclusion in the Spanish classroom. In Gahala, E., *et al.* (eds), *En Espanol Texas Teacher's Edition* (pp. T50–T53). Evanston, IL: McDougall Littell.

Ganschow, L., Sparks, R., and Schneider, E. (1995). Learning a foreign language: Challenges for students with language learning difficulties. *Dyslexia: International Journal of the British Dyslexia Association*, *1*, 75–95.

Ganschow, L., Philips, L., and Schneider, E. (2000). Experiences with the University foreign language requirement: Voices of students with learning disabilities. *Learning Disabilities. A Multidisciplinary Journal*, *10*, (3), 111–128.

Ganschow, L., Sparks, R., and Javorksy, J. (1998). Foreign language learning difficulties: A historical perspective. *Journal of Learning Disabilities*, *31*, 248–258.

Grigorenko, E. L. (2002). Foreign language acquisition and language-based learning disabilities. In P. Robinson (ed.), *Individual differences and instructed language learning* (pp. 95–112). Philadelphia, PA: John Benjamins Publishing.

Henry, M. (2003). *Unlocking literacy: Effective decoding and spelling instruction*. Baltimore, MD: Paul Brookes.

Henry, M., and Hook, P. (2006). A look at multisensory structured language instruction. *Perspectives*, *24*(4), entire volume.

Hill, B., Downey, D., Sheppard, M., and Williamson, V. (1995). Accommodating the needs of students with severe language learning difficulties in modified foreign language classes. In G. K. Crouse, P. J. Campana, and M. H. Rosenbusch (eds), *Broadening the frontiers of foreign language education* (pp. 46–56). Selected Papers from the 1995 Central States Conference. Lincolnwood, IL: National Textbook.

Jackson-Maldonado, D. (2004). Verbal morphology and vocabulary in monolinguals and emergent bilinguals. In B. Goldstein (ed.), *Bilingual language development and disorders in Spanish-English speaking speakers* (pp. 131–162). Baltimore, MD: Paul Brookes.

Koda, K. (2005). *Insights into second language reading. A cross-linguistic approach*. Cambridge Applied Linguistics. New York: Cambridge University Press.

Krashen, S. (2003). *Explorations in language acquisition and use*. Portsmouth, NH: Heinemann.

Kuntz, P. (2001). *African languages at the K-12 level*. Retrieved on 3–18–08 from http://www.cal.org/resources/digest/kuntz001.html.

Leewen, van, E. C. (2005). *Sprachenlernen als Investition in die Zukunft*. Tübingen, Germany: Gunter Narr Verlag.

Lidz, C. S. (1991). *A practitioner's guide to dynamic assessment*. New York: Guilford Press.

McCutchen, D., Abbott, R., Green, L., Beretvas, S., Cox, S., Potter, N., Quiroga, T., and Gray A. (2002). Beginning literacy: Links among teacher knowledge, teacher practice, and student learning. *Journal of Learning Disabilities*, *35*, 69–86.

McIntyre, C., and Pickering, J. (2003). *Clinical studies of multisensory structured language education. For students with dyslexia and related disorders*. Salem, OR: IMSLEC.

MacIntyre, P., and Gardner, R. (1991). Language anxiety: Its relationship to other anxieties and to processing in the native and second languages. *Language Learning*, *41*, 513–534.

Mastropieri, M., and Scruggs, T. (1991). *Teaching students ways to remember: Strategies for learning mnemonically*. New York: Brookline Books.

Mather, N., Boss, C., and Babur, N. (2001). Perceptions and knowledge of preservice and inservice educators about early reading instruction. *Journal of Learning Disabilities*, *34*, 472–482.

Moats, L. (1995). *Spelling development, disability and instruction*. Timonium, MD: York Press.

Omaggio-Hadley, A. (2000). *Teaching language in context*. Boston, MA: Heinle and Heinle.

Oxford, R. (1990). *Language Learning strategies: What every teacher should know*. Boston, MA: Heinle and Heinle.

Palincsar, A.S., and Brown, A.L. (1984). Reciprocal teaching of comprehension fostering and monitoring activities. *Cognition and Instruction, 1,* 117–175.

Philips, L., Ganschow, L., and Anderson, R. (1991). The college foreign language requirement: An action plan for alternatives. *NACADA (National Academic Advising Association) Journal, 11,* 51–56.

Pimsleur, P. (1966). *The Pimsleur language aptitude battery.* New York: Harcourt Brace Jovanovich.

Pompian, N., and Thum, C. (1988). Dyslexic/learning disabled students at Dartmouth College. *Annals of Dyslexia, 38,* 276–284.

Richards, J., and Rodgers, T. (2001). *Approaches and methods in language teaching.* Cambridge Language Teaching Library. New York: Cambridge University Press.

Romaine, S. (1995). *Bilingualism* (2nd edn). London, UK: Blackwell.

Saville-Trioke, M. (2006*). Introducing second language acquisition.* New York: Cambridge University Press.

Schneider, E. (1999). *Multisensory structured metacognitive instruction: An approach to teaching a foreign language to at-risk students.* Frankfurt, Germany: Peter Lang Verlag.

Schneider, E., and Crombie, M. (2003). *Dyslexia and foreign language learning.* London: David Fulton Publishers.

Schneider, E., and Ganschow, L. (2000). Dynamic assessment and instructional strategies for learners who struggle to learn a foreign language. *Dyslexia. International Journal of Research and Practice, 6,* 72–82.

Schneider, E. Ganschow, L., Sparks, R., and Miller, K. (2007). Identifying and teaching learners with special needs. In R. McCarthy (ed.), *Best Practices Tool Kit ¡Avanza! ¡Avençemos!* (pp. A35-A42). Boston, MA: McDougal Littell, Houghton Mifflin Division.

Service, E., and Kohonen, V. (1995). Is the relationship between phonological memory and foreign language learning accounted for by vocabulary acquisition? *Applied Psycholinguistics, 16,* 155–172.

Shaw, R. (1999). The case for course substitutions as reasonable accommodation for students with foreign language learning difficulties. *Journal of Learning Disabilities, 32,* 320–328.

Shaywitz, S. (2003). *Overcoming dyslexia.* New York: Alfred Knopf Publishers.

Siegel, L., and Ryan, E. (1988). Development of grammatical-sensitivity, phonological, and short-term memory skills in normally achieving and learning disabled children. *Developmental Psychology, 24,* 28–37.

Siegel, L., and Ryan, E. (1989). Development of working memory in normally achieving and subtypes of learning disabled children. *Child Development, 60,* 973–980.

Simon, C.S. (2000). Dyslexia and learning a foreign language: A personal experience. *Annals of Dyslexia, 50,* 155–187.

Singleton, D. (1989). *Language acquisition. The age factor.* Clevedon, UK: Multilingual Matters.

Skegan, P. (1986) The role of foreign language learning aptitude in a model of school learning. *Language Testing, 3,* 188–221.

Sparks, R. (1995). Examining the linguistic coding differences hypothesis to explain individual differences in foreign language learning. *Annals of Dyslexia, 45,* 187–214.

Sparks, R., Artzer, M., Patton, J., Ganschow, L., Miller, K., Hordubay, D., and Walsh, G. (1998). Benefits of multisensory language instruction for at-risk learners: A comparison study of high school Spanish students. *Annals of Dyslexia, 48,* 239–270.

Sparks, R., and Ganschow, L. (1993). The effects of a multisensory structured language approach on the native and foreign language aptitude skills of high-risk, foreign language learners: A follow-up study. *Annals of Dyslexia, 43,* 193–216.

Sparks, R., Ganschow, L., Kenneweg, S., and Miller, K. (1991). Using Orton-Gillingham methodologies to teach a foreign language to learning disabled/dyslexic students: Explicit teaching of phonology in a second language. *Annals of Dyslexia, 41,* 96–118.

Sparks, R., Ganschow, L., Fluharty, K., and Little, S. (1996). An exploratory study of the effects of Latin on the native language skills and foreign language aptitude of students with and without learning disabilities. *Classical Journal, 91,* 165–184.

Sparks, R., and Miller, K. (2000). Teaching a foreign language using multisensory structured language techniques to at-risk learners: A review. *Dyslexia. International Journal of Research and Practice, 6,* 124–132.

Sparks, R., Schneider, E., and Ganschow, L. (2002). Teaching foreign (second) languages to at-risk learners: Research and practice. In J.A. Hammadou-Sullivan (ed.), *Literacy and the second language learner* (pp. 55–84). Greenwich, CT: Information Age.

Sperber, H. (1989). *Mnemotechniken im Fremdsparchenunterricht mit Schwerpunkt, Deutsch als Fremdsprache.* Vol. 9 Studien Deutsch. Munich, Germany: Iudicium Verlag.

Spolsky, B. (1989). *Conditions for second language learning.* Oxford, UK: Oxford University Press.

Wehman, P. (2006). *Life beyond the classroom: Transition strategies for young people with disabilities*. Baltimore, MD: Paul Brookes.

Wehmeyer, M. (1997). *Teaching self-determination to students with disabilities: Basic skills for successful transition*. Baltimore, MD: Paul Brookes.

Wolf, M., and Bowers, P. G. (1999). The double-deficit hypothesis for the developmental dyslexias. *Journal of Educational Psychology, 91*(3), 1–24.

Wood, C., and Richardson, A. (2002). Defining dyslexia. In C. Wood, and Richardson, A. (eds), *Challenging psychological issues. Book 2* (pp. 229–235). Milton Keynes, UK: The Open University.

Yamada, J., and Banks, A. (1994). Evidence for and characteristics of dyslexia among Japanese children. *Annals of Dyslexia, 64*, 105–119.

24

Reading and dyslexia in Arabic

Abdessatar Mahfoudhi, Gad Elbeheri and John Everatt

This chapter

- provides the reader with an overview of the research conducted on typically achieving and reading disabled/dyslexic Arabic speakers
- reports on studies focusing on phonological, orthographic and morphological processing
- suggests that focusing on the word level literacy may not be the most productive way of assessing variations in literacy acquisition in the Arabic language
- comments on the role of sociolinguistic factors in predicting variability in Arabic literacy learning
- identifies gaps in the literature to encourage further research on reading development and specific reading disorders among Arabic-speaking children and adults.

Introduction

Reading research in general has been centered on three major areas (cf. Perfetti *et al.*, 2001): lexical processing, sentence processing and text comprehension. In order to consider its relevance to developmental dyslexia, this work needs to be looked at from the perspective of developmental research investigating changes in literacy levels over time and the cognitive predictors of those levels. Such research can be used to attempt to explain individual differences in literacy acquisition that are due to cognitive/neurological factors, and thereby support the identification of likely causes of literacy learning problems or dyslexia. The present discussion, therefore, will focus on this area of work performed in the Arabic language. However, in Arabic, while there is research on literacy development and predictors of lexical processing, research on text comprehension and sentence processing is scarce. Therefore, word level literacy will, of necessity, form the focus of the work reported in this chapter. This may not be a major problem if dyslexia is viewed as based around problems with acquiring word reading and spelling (see British Psychological Society, 1999). However, a point that this chapter will cover is that there are specific features of the Arabic language/orthography that mean that focusing simply on word level literacy may not be the most productive way of assessing variations in literacy acquisition.

Features of the Arabic language: factors to consider

Arabic is one of the major languages in the world. UNESCO statistical reports put Arabic as roughly joint second (along with English and Spanish, but behind Mandarin) in terms of the number of individuals reporting it as their first language. These statistics suggest that it is the main language of communication for more than 300 million individuals. In addition to this, the written form of Arabic is experienced by many more peoples around the world in the form of religious texts (particularly the Quran). Indeed, the written form of Arabic has a special function in representing a standard form of Arabic (Modern Standard Arabic or MSA), which provides a common language across the Arab world. The diversity and geographical separation of countries where Arabic is spoken has led to a variety of versions (local forms or dialects) being used, which means that the local language used by an individual may not be understood that well by another individual from another part of the Arab world. Hence MSA is the common language of communication across the Arab world and the written form represents this common language. Since acquiring good skills in MSA may occur during schooling, the learning of the written form, therefore, can be argued to provide a route to support understanding across the Arab-speaking countries, as well as its role in its cultural expression. However, despite the potential significance of written text in cultural and religious aspects of Arabic life, there are still a large number of individuals who cannot formally read (potentially some 9 per cent of the world's illiterate individuals live in the Arab world). Hence, it is an important language to consider in terms of literacy acquisition and factors that may be related to literacy learning problems. Clearly, problems related to formal schooling explain a large part of the number of individuals without functioning literacy skills. However, work that also looks at individual differences in acquisition from the perspective of cognitive-developmental factors that are often associated with dyslexia may also help explain weaknesses in literacy acquisition, and the present chapter provides a focus for this consideration.

In addition to its importance as a world language and the need to support literacy learning, Arabic has some interesting features that may mean that investigations of Arabic literacy acquisition may give us important leads with which to understand literacy problems in general. One is the variation between the spoken and written forms of the language; i.e., the local version of Arabic versus MSA, as explained above. Further research on the effects of this divergence is clearly needed; though we will touch on this topic again below. A second is the different written forms that an Arabic reader may experience. Arabic has a highly regular/ transparent orthography when presented in the marked or vowelized form of the writing system (in this respect, it is similar to most other Semitic languages, such as Hebrew). A regular/transparent orthography is one where there is a relatively simple relationship between the written form and the language sounds that it represents: i.e., there is close to a one-to-one correspondence between graphemes and phonemes. In other orthographies (English is the best example), this correspondence is less transparent, meaning that a letter may represent several sounds, and a particular sound may be represented by several different letters. However, the Arabic language is based on a highly derivational morphological system. Once learning of the basic association between written and verbal form has taken place, the emphasis of the written form is on meaning, which is primarily conveyed by morphological components. Hence, despite languages such as Arabic having a highly regular orthography when fully marked (or fully vowelized), this form of the orthography is rarely used in most literary texts read by the more experienced reader (the exception, most likely, being religious texts). Once beyond initial schooling grades, the Arabic child is likely to experience text in which short vowel markers are removed, leading to an orthography that is opaque in its relationship between letters and sounds, and to texts that contain a large number of homographic words (i.e., words that look alike but which represent different concepts and are pronounced differently). Such non-vowelized text needs to be read 'in context'. This means that an adult or child experiencing such writings will have to decipher the context within which a word is written, such as the meaning of words around the homograph or the general theme of the passage, to be able to understand the meaning of the word and even pronounce that word correctly. Hence, Arabic word processing may rely on sentence processing or text comprehension to a larger extent than found in some other languages (even English) – for example, Abbott (2006) concluded that Arabic speakers self-refer to different strategies when reading compared to Chinese speakers. Further research on sentence or text level processes would be recommended.

However, there has been a reasonable amount of work conducted on typically achieving students in the Arab world. This work has either concentrated on phonological development (e.g., Amayreh and Dyson, 1998; Hamdan and Amayreh, 2007), reading development stages/models (e. g., Azzam, 1993; Taouk and Coltheart, 2004) or correlates of reading and spelling (e.g., Abu-Rabia, 1995; Abu-Rabia, 1997a, 1997b, 1997c; Abu-Rabia, 1998; Abu-Rabia, 2007; Abu-Rabia et al., 2003; Abu-Rabia and Siegel, 1995; Al-Mannai and Everatt, 2005; Elbeheri and Everatt, 2007; Ibrahim et al., 2007; Salim, 2005), and although the results highlight the importance of phonological, morphological and orthographic processing in Arabic reading and spelling development, further studies are required to understand the underlying skills needed to become a skilled Arabic reader/speller, as well as to understand at what stages of development such skills become critical.

Given the significance of these three factors (phonology, morphology and orthography), the following overview will consider these as the basis of the discussion of the work undertaken. However, the potential importance of the difference between the spoken and written forms of Arabic means that this will also provide a focus for the coverage of the literature. Together, these topics should provide a basis for understanding cognitive-developmental literacy learning problems amongst Arabic learners.

Phonological processing

The dominant causal theory in the English language dyslexia literature is that the word-level literacy learning problems found amongst dyslexic populations are due to deficits in phonological processing – i.e., those processes primarily involved in the identification, storage, manipulation and production of sound forms. Such processes may be critical in the ability to translate a written letter string into an appropriate pronunciation. Given its importance in the dyslexia literature, and its role as a predictor of word-level literacy in many languages (see Goulandris, 2003; Smythe et al., 2004; Snowling, 2000; Stanovich, 1988), it is hardly surprising to find that investigations of phonological processing, and its role in reading development among typical and non-typical (dyslexic) groups, have been undertaken in a number of studies in Arabic. For example, Abu-Rabia (1995) found that dyslexic Arabic readers (aged 8–11), diagnosed on the basis of their performance in measures of isolated word reading, performed significantly worse than normal readers in various language tests, but not in terms of visual-based task scores. Such findings led Abu-Rabia (1995) to conclude that phonological processing, syntactic awareness and working memory were highly related to reading ability; a conclusion similar to that proposed for English (e.g., Siegel and Ryan, 1988). Somewhat similar findings were reported by Salim (2005), who compared the reading performance of 60 typical readers with 60 reading disabled learners (ages 9–11) in Amman, Jordan. This study identified significant differences between the two groups in all twelve subtests of the Illinois Test of

313

Psycholinguistic Abilities, but the difference was greatest in the subtests of sound blending, auditory completion, visual sequential memory and grammar completion, again implicating phonological processes as well as memory and syntactic awareness.

Abu-Rabia et al. (2003) compared the performance of reading disabled Arabic learners with both age-matched and reading-level matched peers in tests of phonological and orthographic processing as well as measures of syntax, morphological awareness, working memory and visual memory. Results of this study showed that the reading disabled group did worse than both control groups on phonological awareness tasks. Indeed, the most severe deficiencies amongst the reading disabled group were found for measures of phonological awareness, in contrast to their relative strengths in orthographic processing.

Similar evidence for dyslexics performing worse than reading level matched controls was identified by Abu-Rabia (1995) in a spelling and reading error analysis. The large number of errors made of a semantic dys-phonetic type amongst the dyslexics was attributed by Abu-Rabia to problems with phoneme to grapheme conversion, which leads the dyslexic to guessing pronunciations and/or spellings. Such effects have been found amongst English language dyslexics and have been interpreted as due to weak phonological skills leading to problems with conversion between letters and sounds (see Snowling, 2000). The importance of appropriate grapheme–phoneme relationships for learning Arabic was also identified in the work of Azzam (1993) who examined the reading and spelling errors of Arabic children in a primary school in Abu Dhabi, United Arab Emirates. This study found evidence of incorrect sound–symbol associations amongst young learners – which may be consistent with the conclusions above. However, this work also identified omissions and additions of letters as major errors in the word level literacy work of these children, and there was evidence of inappropriate sound–symbol associations involving context sensitive rules amongst the spelling errors.

In a cross-sectional study examining the spelling errors of Arabic native learners in Israel (grades 1–9) who were learning Arabic in addition to Hebrew from grade 3, Abu-Rabia and Taha (2006) found that phonetic spelling errors (as defined by Snowling et al., 1996) stay with the child till grade 9. Unlike Azzam (1993) who found a developmental pattern in the number of errors, Abu-Rabia and Taha (2006) found that these phonemic errors were fairly stable across grades leading them to argue that this is different from theories of spelling development based on Latin orthographic systems (e.g., Frith, 1985) in which children are thought to move to an orthographic stage after initial learning via an alphabetic phase. Abu-Rabia and Taha interpret the large number of phonological errors as evidence that the Arabic learner tends to rely on their phonological/decoding/alphabetic skills for longer than would be predicted based on the Frith (and related) model (although contrast this with the conclusions of Taouk and Coltheart, 2004, for similarities between Arabic and English in reading acqusition stages). Abu-Rabia and Taha explained that this might be a specific effect within Arabic, due to the complex phonology and orthography of Arabic. However, an alternative reason that the authors propose is the interference of the phonology of the spoken variety with literary Arabic (see also Saiegh-Haddad, 2003; and Abu-Rabia and Taha, 2004). We will return to both these points below.

The Abu-Rabia et al. (2003) study also identified phonological awareness as the strongest predictor of the variation in reading levels, with morphological awareness as a close second. The importance of phonological processing measures as predictors of Arabic literacy levels was also noted by Al-Mannai and Everatt (2005) who examined predictors of literacy development (word reading aloud and spelling) among grade 1 through grade 3 Arabic-speaking learners in Bahrain. Regression analysis indicated that pseudo-word reading was the best predictor of variability, with a rhyme awareness task also strongly predicting variation in literacy levels – again consistent with the need to use phonological and letter-sound decoding processing skills.

The importance of phonological measures as a potential predictor of reading ability levels amongst fourth and fifth graders in Egypt led Elbeheri and Everatt (2007) to conclude that reading Arabic, like English, depends to a large extent on phonological processing skills. Such evidence was used by Elbeheri *et al.* (2006) to propose that models of English literacy acquisition, and literacy learning difficulties (particularly the phonological deficit viewpoint), could be applicable to understanding the same processes in Arabic. However, these authors also argue that further research is necessary to allow firm conclusions to be made given that variations from predictions based on English language models were identified. These were reasoned as potentially related to specific orthographic and/or morphological features of Arabic.

Orthographic/morphological factors

The Arabic written form may be described as complex for the beginning reader/writer. The seemingly arbitrary combination of shapes, dots and marks, with the positioning of dots or marks (either above or below the shapes, and sometimes even within a shape) distinguishing different letters or grammatical rules, can make for a difficult spatial recognition process. However, the Arabic orthography is further complicated by the feature that letter shapes can vary dependent on their positioning at the beginning, middle or end of a word. Hence, the Arabic child needs to be able to recognize several different forms of the same letter (and the same sound). This may be akin to an English child having to learn the difference between lower case and upper case letters, as well as a different cursive form of the same letter. However, for the Arabic child reading text, differing forms will occur regularly, potentially in most words in a sentence, and the text is always cursive, meaning that most (though not all) letters will be joined. Whereas an English child will experience mainly distinct lower case letters in their reading texts, the Arabic child will experience only cursive text with letter shapes varying dependent on position within the word and all marks being included or not depending on the level of the text. Additionally, there are some letters in Arabic (one-way connectors) that do not join to both letters around them, meaning that a space in Arabic text does not necessarily indicate a word boundary; it is the size of the space that distinguishes a word boundary from a one-way connector within a word. As such, recognizing an individual feature, such as a letter or a letter combination, within Arabic text may be a more complex process than doing the same thing in English. Potentially consistent with this complexity argument, Ibrahim *et al.* (2002) found that when biliterate children were given a trail-making task, in which participants had to serially order letters while matching them with numbers, the Arabic orthography condition was significantly slower than a Hebrew orthography condition, even though Arabic was the first language, and Hebrew a second language, of the individuals tested, and both orthographies being derived from the same Semitic background. These findings led the authors to argue that the complexity of the Arabic orthography makes it difficult to process. Additionally, Elbeheri and Everatt (2007) found that a word chains task (in which participants had to indicate word boundaries in a random series of Arabic written words from which the spaces between words had been removed) was highly related to reading levels amongst Egyptian primary school children, and this relationship was larger than the analogous correlations for the phonological and decoding measures in the study.

Clearly, orthographic complexity may be a second explanation for the problems experienced by Arabic children in reading tasks, and may explain the decoding problems amongst poor readers covered in the previous section. Such problems may not be due to phonological deficits, but rather to problems processing the Arabic orthography. However, the relationship between literacy and phonology found when using verbal phonological tasks seems to argue for a phonological effect and, hence, any influence of orthographic complexity may be an additional hurdle for the Arabic child when learning letter-sound decoding. This may be particularly the case when the transition between vowelized and non-vowelized forms is encountered. For example, Abu-Rabia (1999, 2001) investigated the influence of using vowelized and non-vowelized variations of the Arabic script among second- and sixth-grade children and adults and found that the vowelized form of the Arabic script tended to increase the levels of reading comprehension shown by these Arabic readers. Making the link between letters and sounds simply may improve reading skills, even for skilled/adult readers. Although, in a later study, Abu-Rabia (2007) examined the reading skills of typical and dyslexic Arabic native readers (grades 3, 6, 9 and 12) and found that vowelization (either within words or at the end of words as a measure of syntactic knowledge) was not a predictor of reading accuracy or reading comprehension. Further research is needed to determine the effects of orthographic complexity and vowelization on literacy skills, potentially involving additional letter identification or discrimination tasks. However, it would also be surprising to find that experience did not affect the influence of vowelization on reading comprehension levels – and whether text comprehension is assessed by reading aloud versus silent reading may be a further factor to consider.

Whereas Abu-Rabia (2007) did not find vowelization predictive of Arabic reading amongst dyslexic and control children, there was an effect of morphology. Along with spelling ability, the identification and/or production of morphological units was generally predictive of reading (both accuracy and comprehension) in both groups across the grade range studied. Therefore, morphology, rather than orthographic effects, may be the reason why studies have found differing effects from that predicted by English language data. Indeed, studies contrasting Arabic orthography and morphology and their influence on reading (particularly word processing) among typically achieving Arabic speakers are reasonably numerous. For example, a number of studies have investigated whether the effects of orthography in lexical processing are distinct from morphology. Boudelaa and Marslen-Wilson (2004) examined whether vowels had a priming role and, therefore, a morphemic status as proposed in McCarthy's (1981) prosodic morphology. However, they did not find any facilitation of word recognition due to vocalic overlap between primes and targets. Additionally, Boudelaa and Marslen-Wilson (2001) examined the effect of morphemic root and pattern, as well as semantic and orthographic factors, in different stages of the recognition process using two masked priming lexical decision experiments. The results indicated that morphological priming was distinct from orthographic and semantic factors. Boudelaa and Marslen-Wilson (2005), found that, in contrast to morphology and semantics effects, orthographic priming seems to emerge at a different processing point (based on the time between prime and target presentation, referred to as stimulus onset asynchrony or SOA). Boudelaa and Marslen-Wilson (2001, 2005) and Mahfoudhi (2007) also found that priming by morphological units was significantly different to that of orthographic/phonological controls. Overall, these data argue for morphology and orthographic influences on word processing to be treated somewhat independently in models of Arabic reading ability.

Diglossia

A number of studies have investigated various sociolinguistic factors as a way of predicting variability in Arabic literacy learning. In particular, the issue of the disparity between spoken Arabic (the language of communication at home) and the written Arabic of the books that form a large part of the children's school work has been a focus of research in this area. Almost all available studies suggest that exposure to Modern Standard Arabic (MSA), the language of literacy, is beneficial for reading. For example, Abu-Rabia (2000) examined the effect of exposure to literary Arabic (MSA) in preschool on the reading comprehension of first and second graders. In comparison to a control group who were exposed to spoken Arabic (their spoken variety), those exposed to literary Arabic performed significantly better in reading comprehension. Iraqi (1990; cited in Abu-Rabia, 2000) examined the effect of reading literary stories to kindergarten students as compared with reading stories in the spoken dialect on listening comprehension of literary texts and on oral communicative skills in literary Arabic. The results showed a significant advantage in both tests for those who were read stories in literary Arabic after five months of such intervention.

Such studies of what is sometimes referred to as diaglossia suggest that the difference between literary and spoken Arabic is significant enough to affect reading skills. Therefore, given this difference between normal spoken form and written Arabic, letter-sound decoding strategies may not be as effective as might be predicted if the child has not had enough experience of literary Arabic. Similarly, the normal finding in the field, that there is a reciprocal relationship between literacy acquisition and phonological processing skills, may not apply as clearly in Arabic. In Arabic, the association between literacy and phonology may depend on the level of exposure to MSA. Indeed, those not regularly exposed to MSA prior to schooling may have to learn the literary Arabic as if it were a second language. Ibrahim and colleagues (Ibrahim, 2006; Ibrahim and Aharon-Peretz, 2005) have taken this a stage further and argued that MSA should be considered as a second language for Arabic learners, with distinct lexica for the two forms. For example, Eviatar and Ibrahim (2000) examined whether exposure to literary Arabic of Palestinian kindergarten and first grade students would lead to the rise of meta-linguistic awareness that is common in bilinguals by comparing them to Russian–Hebrew bilinguals of the same age. The results showed that the Arabic learners performed similar to the bilinguals in obtaining higher scores on awareness tasks; i.e., the Arabic learners were showing evidence of phonologically related skills akin to that expected of second language learners.

However, diaglossia may have negative as well as positive effects. The potential negative effects of the difference between spoken and written forms have formed a fairly unique Arabic feature of research into literacy acquisition. For example, differences in phoneme and syllable structure between the spoken and written Arabic have been found to interfere with performance on phonemic awareness and pseudo-word reading tasks among pre-school and first-grade learners (Saiegh-Haddad, 2003). In another study, Saiegh-Haddad (2005) tested first grade Arabic speakers on their ability to process MSA phonemes, which were not within the spoken vernacular of children, versus phonemes that were familiar to the children from their spoken language. Both phoneme isolation and discrimination for the MSA phonemes were more challenging than that for the phonemes within the spoken language of the children, consistent with the view that learning MSA may be a particular challenge for Arabic learners. Interestingly, though, these phonological tasks were not directly predictive of performance on a vowelized decoding task; a finding that needs further clarification to determine how an Arabic child may be accomplishing pseudo-word reading.

Summary and implications for research

Much of the research evidence suggests that many of the processes that support the acquisition of reading amongst Arabic-speaking children are similar to those identified in other languages, particularly English, the most researched language. These findings seem to indicate the importance of phonological processing in both Arabic and English literacy acquisition and, therefore, provide the potential for a cross-language framework on which to distinguish those with literacy acquisition problems (e.g., dyslexics) from those who are likely to progress at normal rates in literacy classes. However, the data on Arabic also diverges, in certain respects, from predictions based on English language models. The effects of diaglossia, the complexity of the orthography and its variation between vowelized and non-vowelized forms, as well as the potential importance of morphology, all seem to show some evidence of unique effects in Arabic that are worthy of further investigation and explanation.

There is a need for further studies on younger populations and readers with reading difficulties to determine whether the findings from typical adult readers (from which much of the work on word recognition processes has been derived) can be used to inform models of Arabic reading acquisition and dyslexia – longitudinal studies from pre-school would be highly informative. Similarly, the focus on word processing has meant that reading comprehension research seems to be somewhat neglected in Arabic, and studies investigating sentence parsing as a subcomponent of reading comprehension would be most welcome. As for the studies on text comprehension that have been conducted so far in Arabic, most are concerned with what has been understood of the text, while processes the reader utilizes when building an understanding, or mental image, of the text (e.g., van Dijk and Kintsch, 1983; Kintsch, 1998) have been rarely attempted in Arabic. Moreover, the role of syntax in reading Arabic has not been studied, which is surprising given its potential relationship to morphology and that this may play an important role in sentence level processing. The fact that syntax can be represented by marks attached to letter shapes in Arabic also makes it an interesting feature to consider when investigating orthographic complexity. Indeed, the interaction between orthography, morphology and syntactic awareness in comprehension processes, as well how these might influence single word processing during text reading seem a highly profitable area of research. Reading in context would seem to be an important feature of skill development in Arabic and, therefore, the processes that need to be acquired for this to happen smoothly require further investigation. How this might be supported by appropriate teaching programmes would also be a useful line of research.

In addition to the above, there is a need for fundamental research that is relevant for reading/dyslexia work; namely, the linguistic development (lexical, phonological and syntactic) of children in their local varieties. There is a need to investigate the various types of difficulties Arabic-speaking monolingual individuals face, and it would seem beneficial to compare reading development amongst bilingual/multilingual Arabic populations to further investigate the effects of diaglossia.

References

Abbott, M.L. (2006). ESL reading strategies: Differences in Arabic and Mandarin speaker test performance. *Language Learning*, 56, 633–670.

Abu-Rabia, S. (1995). Learning to read in Arabic: Reading, syntactic, orthographic and working memory skills in normally achieving and poor Arabic readers. *Reading Psychology*, 16, 351–394.

Abu-Rabia, S. (1997a). The need for cross-cultural considerations in reading theory: The effects of Arabic sentence context in skilled and poor readers. *Journal of Research in Reading*, 20, 137–147.

Abu-Rabia, S. (1997b). Reading in Arabic orthography: The effects of vowels and context on reading accuracy of poor and skilled Arabic native readers in reading paragraphs, sentences, and isolated words. *Journal of Psycholinguistic Research*, 26, 465–482.

Abu-Rabia, S. (1997c). Reading in Arabic orthography: The effect of vowels and context on reading accuracy of poor and skilled native Arabic readers. *Reading and Writing*, 9, 65–78.

Abu-Rabia, S. (1998). Reading Arabic texts: Effects of text type, reader type and vowelization. *Reading and Writing: An Interdisciplinary Journal*, 10, 105–119.

Abu-Rabia, S. (1999). The effect of Arabic vowels on the reading comprehension of second- and sixth-grade native Arab children. *Journal of Psycholinguistic Research, 28*, 93–101.

Abu-Rabia, S. (2000). Effects of exposure to literary Arabic on reading comprehension in a diaglossic situation. *Reading and Writing, 13*, 147–157.

Abu-Rabia, S. (2001). The role of vowels in reading Semitic scripts: Data from Arabic and Hebrew. *Reading and Writing, 14*, 39–59.

Abu-Rabia, S. (2007). The role of morphology and short vowelization in reading Arabic among normal and dyslexic readers in grades 3, 6, 9, and 12. *Journal of Psycholinguistic Research, 36*, 89–106.

Abu-Rabia, S. and Siegel, L.S. (1995). Different orthographies different context effects: The effects of Arabic sentence context in skilled and poor readers. Reading Psychology 16, 1–19.

Abu-Rabia, S. and Taha, H. (2004). Reading and spelling error analysis of native Arabic dyslexic readers. *Reading and Writing, 16*, 651–689.

Abu-Rabia, S. and Taha, H. (2006). Phonological errors predominate in Arabic spelling across grades 1–9. *Journal of Psycholinguistic Research, 35*, 167–188.

Abu-Rabia, S., Share, D. and Mansour, M.S. (2003). Word recognition and basic cognitive processes among reading-disabled and normal readers in Arabic. *Reading and Writing, 16*, 423–442.

Al-Mannai, H. and Everatt, J. (2005). Phonological processing skills as predictors of literacy amongst Arabic speaking Bahraini school children. *Dyslexia, 11*, 269–291.

Amayreh, M. and Dyson, A. (1998). The acquisition of Arabic Consonants. *Journal of Speech, Language and Hearing Research, 41*, 642–53.

Azzam, R. (1993). The nature of Arabic reading and spelling errors of young children. *Reading and Writing,* 5, 355–385.

Boudelaa, S. and Marslen-Wilson, W.D. (2001). Morphological units in the Arabic mental lexicon. *Cognition, 81*, 65–92.

Boudelaa, S. and Marslen-Wilson, W.D. (2004). Abstract morphemes and lexical representation: The CV-skeleton in Arabic. *Cognition, 92*, 271–303.

Boudelaa, S. and Marslen-Wilson, W.D. (2005). Discontinuous morphology in time: Incremental masked priming in Arabic. *Language and Cognitive Processes, 20*, 207–260.

British Psychological Society (1999). *Dyslexia, Literacy and Psychological Assessment.* Report of a Working Party of the Division of Educational and Child Psychology of the British Psychological Society. Leicester: British Psychological Society.

Elbeheri, G. and Everatt, J. (2007). Literacy ability and phonological processing skills amongst dyslexic and non-dyslexic speakers of Arabic. *Reading and Writing, 20*, 273–294.

Elbeheri, G., Everatt, J., Reid, G. and Al Mannai, H. (2006). Dyslexia Assessment in Arabic. *Journal of Research in Special Educational Needs*, 6, 143–152.

Eviatar, Z. and Ibrahim, R. (2000). Bilingual is as bilingual does: metalinguistic abilities of Arabic-speaking children. *Applied Psycholinguistics, 21*, 451–471.

Frith, U. (1985). Beneath the surface of developmental dyslexia. In K.E. Patterson, J.C. Marashall and M. Coltheart (eds), *Surface Dyslexia* (pp. 301–330). London: Lawrence Erlbaum Associates.

Goulandris, N. (ed.) (2003). *Dyslexia in Different Languages: Cross Linguistic comparisons.* London: Whurr Publishers Ltd.

Hamdan, J.M. and Amayreh, M.M. (2007). Consonant profile of Arabic-speaking school-age children in Jordan. *Folia Phoniatrica et Logopaedica, 59*, 55–64.

Ibrahim, R. (2006). Morpho-phonemic similarity within and between languages: A factor to be considered in processing Arabic and Hebrew. *Reading and Writing, 19*, 563–586.

Ibrahim, R. and Aharon-Peretz, J. (2005). Is literary Arabic a second language for native Arab speakers? Evidence from a semantic priming study. *Journal of Psycholinguistic Research, 34*, 51–70.

Ibrahim, R., Eviatar, Z. and Aharon-Peretz, J. (2002). The characteristics of Arabic orthography slow its processing. *Neuropsychology, 16*, 322–326.

Ibrahim, R., Eviatar, Z. and Aharon-Peretz, J. (2007). Metalinguistic awareness and reading performance: A cross language comparison. *Journal of Psycholinguistic Research, 36*(4), 297–317.

Kintsch, W. (1998). *Comprehension: A Paradigm for Cognition.* Cambridge: Cambridge University Press.

McCarthy, J.J. (1981). A prosodic theory of non-concatenative morphology. *Linguistic Inquiry, 12*, 373–418.

Mahfoudhi, A. (2007). Roots and patterns in Arabic lexical processing. In E. Benmamoun (ed.), *Perspectives on Arabic Linguistics XIX.* Amsterdam: Benjamins.

Perfetti, C., van Dyke, J. and Hart, L. (2001). The psycholinguistics of basic literacy. *Annual Review of Applied Linguistics, 21*, 127–149.

319

Saiegh-Haddad, E. (2003). Linguistic distance and initial reading acquisition: The case of Arabic diaglossia. *Applied Psycholinguistics*, 24, 431–451.

Saiegh-Haddad, E. (2005). Correlates of reading fluency in Arabic: Diaglossic and orthographic factors. *Reading and Writing*, *18*, 559–582.

Salim, S. (2005). *Diagnosing dyslexia in a sample in the Capital district in Jordan* (in Arabic). A paper presented at the 'Special Education Conference', Jordon, 26–27 April 2005.

Siegel, L.S. and Ryan, E.B. (1988). Development of grammatical sensitivity, phonological, and short-term memory skills in normally achieving and learning children. *Developmental Psychology*, *24*, 28–37.

Smythe, I., Everatt, J. and Salter, R. (eds) (2004). *The International Book of Dyslexia*, 2nd edition. London: Wiley and Sons.

Snowling, M. (2000). *Dyslexia*, 2nd edition. Oxford: Blackwell.

Snowling, M.J., Goulandris, N. and Defty, N. (1996). A longitudinal study of reading development in dyslexic children. *Journal of Educational Psychology*, *88*, 653–669.

Stanovich, K.E. (1988). Explaining the difference between the dyslexic and the garden-variety poor reader: The phonological-core variable-difference model. *Journal of Learning Disabilities*, *21*, 590–612.

Taouk, M. and Coltheart, M. (2004). The cognitive processes involved in learning to read Arabic. *Reading and Writing*, *17*, 27–57.

van Dijk, T.A. and Kintsch, W. (1983). *Strategies of Discourse Comprehension*. New York: Academic Press.

Acknowledgements

United Nations Development Programme, Kuwait
Centre for Child Evaluation and Teaching, Kuwait
University of Surrey, United Kingdom

25

Reading and reading disabilities in Spanish and Spanish–English contexts

Charles W. Haynes, Angela Ayre,
Brad Haynes and Abdessatar Mahfoudhi

This chapter

- examines reading acquisition and reading difficulties in Spanish
- studies the above in the context of bilingual Spanish English language learners
- explores the structure of spoken and written Spanish and how it can influence the way that children acquire basic reading skills in Spanish
- investigates the first language factors that influence literacy outcomes when Spanish-speaking children learn to read in English
- discusses the most effective ways to teach literacy skills to Spanish English-language learners.

Introduction

In this chapter, we examine reading acquisition and reading difficulties, first in monolingual Spanish speakers and then in the context of bilingual Spanish English-language learners in the U.S. There are good reasons for these foci. Spanish is the third most common world language, spoken by 330 to 400 million native speakers (Gordon, 2005; Niño-Murcía *et al.*, 2008). In addition, population literacy levels in Spanish exert significant influence over the economies of Spain, as well as those of most South American, Central American and Caribbean countries. The status of foundational language and literacy skills in Spanish additionally influences the well-being of citizens of the United States (U.S.), where Spanish is spoken by approximately 10 to 13 per cent of the population and is the second most frequently used language in that country (Shin and Bruno, 2003). In US schools, children learning English as an additional language – the vast majority of whom are Spanish-speaking English-language learners – lag behind their monolingual English-speaking peers in reading performance (U.S. Department of Education, 2005, 2007). Understanding reading acquisition and reading disabilities in Spanish as well as Spanish–English contexts is therefore of interest internationally as well as in the U.S.

This chapter explores three key questions:

1 How does the structure of spoken and written Spanish influence the way that children acquire basic reading skills in Spanish and, similarly, what factors predict children's reading failure?

2 What first language factors influence literacy outcomes when Spanish-speaking children learn to read in English?

3 What appear to be the most effective ways to teach literacy skills to Spanish-speaking English-language learners?

Linguistic aspects of Spanish and their relationships to reading acquisition and reading failure

In this first section we examine the structural and lexical characteristics of spoken and written Spanish, with emphases on phonological, orthographic and morphological features. We then examine dyslexia and related reading difficulties as they manifest in Spanish and structurally similar languages. Because English is heavily researched and offers relevant contrasts, we will often elucidate features of Spanish through comparisons with English.

What are the historical roots and characteristics of Spanish and which features of Spanish are most salient to literacy learning? Spanish is a Romance language with geographical roots in the Iberian Peninsula. It is closely related to Portuguese, as well as to Italian and French. In addition, many Spanish words are derived from Arabic (e.g., ¡Ojalá!–Law-sha-Allah = God grant; aceite –az-zayt = oil; naranja–naaranja = orange); this lexical sharing stems historically from the Berber and Arab presence between 700–1500 A.D. in areas that now include much of Spain and Portugal. Spanish shares with English systems of Latin cognates (e.g, edificio ↔ edifice, nacion↔nation, naturaleza↔nature), a phenomenon we will revisit in our discussion of instructional needs of Spanish-English ELLs. The spread of Spanish to South and Central Americas, as well as to the Caribbean derives largely from Spain's colonial occupation of those areas during the fifteenth through nineteenth centuries (for a detailed history of Spanish, see Penny, 2002).

Sound–symbol factors: Spanish compared with English

Reading is influenced to varying degrees by a given language's speech sounds (phonology) and written symbols (orthography), as well as how those sounds and symbols are processed mentally (phonological and orthographic processing).[1] Key phonological and orthographic factors that influence word-level reading and reading fluency in Spanish are the simplicity of phoneme–grapheme (sound-to-symbol) correspondence as well as the syllabic structure of the language (Seymour, Aro and Erskine, 2003). At the phoneme (individual speech sound) level, Spanish is parsimonious relative to English. In contrast with the approximately 39 phonemes of English (+/- 15 distinctive vowel sounds and +/- 24 consonantal sounds), Spanish has approximately 24 (5 distinct vowel sounds, 19 consonant sounds). Because dialectal and pronunciation differences contribute to both phonemic and allophonic (subtle differences in pronunciation of the same phoneme) variation within languages, we stress the term "approximate." The relative succinctness of the phonemic inventory of Spanish streamlines the quantity of sounds that the learner must match with letters.

With respect to their orthographies, both English and Spanish have 26 graphemes (letters). These orthographies can be analyzed according to their "transparency"—the degree to which they adhere to the alphabetic principle of one-to-one match between sound and grapheme (e.g., Seymour *et al.*, 2003). According to this metric, the orthography of Spanish is highly transparent: its 24 phonemes can be represented by 26 individual graphemes and three digraphs (ch, ll, rr). There are few exceptions to the alphabetic principle—for example, /s/ can be spelled with c as in centavo (cent) or s as in sentir (to feel), or the c can make the sound /k/ as in cuaderno (notebook) or /s/ as in conocer (to be aquainted with). In sum, the child learning to read Spanish encounters a highly predictable system for reading or spelling.

In contrast with Spanish, English is highly opaque, or inconsistent in its grapheme to phoneme correspondences. In many cases, an individual English letter has multiple possible pronunciations and a given sound can be spelled with several different letters. For example, in most dialects of U.S. English, the sound /sh/ can be spelled with sh as in ship, ti as in nation, su as in insurance, ci as in ancient, ch as in charlatan, and sch as in mensch. With respect to sound symbol relationships for spelling alone, the approximate 39 phonemes of English can be represented by literally hundreds of graphemes or grapheme combinations. The larger phoneme inventory of English, combined with the extraordinarily high number of options for representing phonemes, complicates the English learner's choices for sound-symbol reading and spelling.

At the syllable level, Spanish has a tendency towards consonant–vowel (CV) syllables which are often simple in structure, containing few consonant blends, for example, "machaca" (CV–CV–CV, "crushed"), "conocido" (CV–CV–CV–CV, "known"), "camino" (CV–CV–CV, "road"). In contrast, English tends towards a variety of syllable structures with numerous consonant blends, for example: "splay" (CCCV), "imp" (VCC), "cramps" (CCVCCC).

Cognitive–linguistic predictors of reading in Spanish

Regardless of the differences in sound structure between Spanish and English, within both languages, there is robust agreement about the capacity of phonological skills to predict early literacy skills. In preschool children, emergent literacy skills (letter naming, recognizing sounds of letters) are predicted by:

- phonological awareness of speech sounds, including sound blending, sound-matching, and deletion of sounds from words (elision)
- phonological memory for nonwords—pseudo-words that have no meaning but are phonetically consistent
- phonological memory for words and sentences.

The same phonological skills have been shown to predict Spanish and English readers' word recognition skills in early grade school (Anthony et al., 2006; Adams, 1990; Jiménez et al., 2000; Jiménez, 1997). While Goswami (1999) has suggested that onset-rime[2] awareness varies in different languages as a function of orthographic transparency, phonemic awareness remains a strong predictor of early word recognition skills across orthographies.

Seymour and colleagues (2003) examined the combined effects of orthographic transparency and syllabic complexity on beginning reading in a variety of European languages, and found that children learning English took twice as long to develop word recognition skills as did children learning in Spanish and other transparent languages, like Finnish and Italian. The authors concluded that, "the delayed acquisition of foundation literacy skills in . . . English can be interpreted as a combined effect of syllabic complexity and of orthographic depth" (p. 167). They hypothesized that when the orthographic depth of a language is shallow (i.e., transparent, as with Spanish), word recognition occurs via a single, symbol-to-sound decoding, or "phonological recoding" route. When a certain threshold for orthographic depth is exceeded, as with a deep, or opaque, symbol system like English, two routes must be employed: the phonological recoding route and in addition an orthographic, or "lexical" route which codes syllabic and morphemic shape.[3] Seymour and colleagues postulate that it is this need to use two

323

routes for word recognition in a deep orthography that halves reading efficiency, and thus doubles the time children need to learn foundational reading skills. While a single sound–symbol decoding route model for Spanish is attractive in its efficiency, we next explore how the speed of early reading interacts with morphological structures to complicate early reading development in Spanish.

The term "morphology" refers to meaningful parts of words, such as prefixes, roots and affixes. Within respect to noun phrase, verb phrase and pronoun morphology, Spanish is significantly more inflected than English and much of this structural richness of Spanish morphology derives from the latter's historic Latin roots (Anderson and Centeno, 2007; Penny, 2002). In the area of noun phrase morphology, for example, suffixed marking of gender occurs more frequently in Spanish (e.g., feminine: doctora = "doctor," hermana = "sister," novia = "girlfriend"; masculine: doctor, hermano, novio) than in English (e.g., princess–prince, bachelorette–bachelor; heroine–hero). In another contrast with English, most Spanish articles and demonstratives must agree with the noun in both number and gender (e.g. la novia–el novio; las novias–los novios; este doctor–esta doctora; estos doctores – estas doctoras). In English, neither articles nor demonstratives denote gender, and while number is denoted by demonstratives (this dog – these dogs, that picture – those pictures) and the article "a"/"an" (a cup, an apple), the highly frequent article "the" is number neutral (the apple – the apples).

In the area of verb phrase morphology, the system of Spanish verb endings is highly complex and, much as with conjugation of verbs in Latin, morphological endings of regular verbs typically vary according to person (first-person, second-, third-), number (singular versus plural), infinitive form ("thematic vowel": -ar, -er, -ir), mood (indicative, subjunctive, imperative), as well as tense/aspect (past, present, future; imperfect, perfect). With respect to pronoun morphology, Spanish varies significantly from English in the use of enclitics, pronouns that are attached to the end of verbs. While object pronouns are free standing in English (for example: "Give it (the chair) to me!"), they are often joined to the ends of verbs in Spanish ("Dámela!"; Da = give, me = me, la = it) (see Anderson and Centeno, 2007, pp. 16–26.)

Morphology and reading speed in Spanish

There is evidence that the rich morpho-syllabic complexity of Spanish influences the strategies that children employ when they read contributes to reading speed deficits in Spanish. As noted previously, Seymour and colleagues (2003) theorized that learning foundational reading skills in a shallow orthography such as Spanish or Italian occurs rapidly due to children's reliance on a single (grapheme–phoneme) route for reading. While this may be true for the first and second grade readers studied by Seymour and colleagues, the work of other researchers suggests a complementary, developmentally compatible view of foundational literacy learning in Spanish. According to this more comprehensive perspective, children's early sound–symbol efficiency reading in the shallow orthography of Spanish causes them to encounter longer and morphologically more complex words early in the process of learning to read. In order to overcome the inefficiency of letter-by-letter reading, they adopt a strategy of reading words at the morpho-syllabic level. Jiménez and Guzmán's (2003) efficacy study of decoding versus meaning approaches to teaching word recognition supports this interpretation. They found that first and second grade children who received sound–symbol instruction were much faster on a lexical decision task than were students who received the meaning based approach. Within the code instructed groups, second graders performed significantly faster on the word-naming task than did first graders. These findings suggest that automaticity of decoding occurs early as a function of sound-symbol instruction within a transparent orthography and that this automaticity is associated with accelerated "acquisition of sublexical correspondences" (p.75).

In a study of Italian, a language with a shallow orthography and syllable structure similar to Spanish, Burani *et al.* (2002) examined second- and third-grade children's reading of nonwords alone versus nonwords with morphemes embedded (roots and derivational suffixes) and found that children read the nonwords with morpheme constituents more quickly and more accurately. Their finding is consistent with the view that in shallow orthographies like those of Italian and Spanish, orthographic knowledge at a level above that of the phoneme is important for aiding reading speed (Jiménez, 2002). Recent support for this theory comes from Davies *et al.* (2007), who studied accuracy and speed of word recognition in Spanish-speaking grade school children in the third to fifth grades and found a positive relationship between orthographic 'neighborhood' size (number of words that can be generated by replacing a single letter of the given word) and participants' reading speed.[4] Davies and colleagues' finding further supports the hypothesis that developmental differences in reading speed in Spanish are closely tied to orthographic (i.e., morpho-syllabic) knowledge about words.[5]

Morphological processing may play a key role in the difficulties of Spanish-speaking learners with dyslexia, otherwise typically developing children who exhibit extraordinary difficulties most often with word recognition, reading fluency and spelling. Numerous studies of Spanish-speaking children with dyslexia have shown that, while impairments in phonological awareness and accuracy of nonword decoding are clearly evident, deficits in reading speed are more pronounced and are indeed a hallmark of dyslexia in Spanish (e.g., Serrano and Defior, 2008; Davies, Cuetos and Glez-Seijas, 2007; Jiménez and Hernández, 2000). Davies and colleagues (2007) studied Spanish-speaking persons with dyslexia who were reading at the third grade level. These participants showed deficits in speed relative to age-matched controls and their reading difficulties were linked more to deficits in morphological reading skills than to inaccurate sound-symbol decoding.

Jiménez and Ramírez (2002) contribute additional support for the hypothesis that Spanish speed deficits may lie more in difficulties with orthographic reading than in sound-symbol decoding. In a study of dyslexia subtypes in Spanish, they examined reaction times (RTs) to nonwords versus familiar words in a sample of 89 Spanish-speaking dyslexic third graders and compared these children's performance to that of age-matched controls. Dyslexic children with significantly longer RTs in response to nonwords were deemed "phonological dyslexics" (PDs) and children with greater delays in response to familiar words were termed "surface dyslexics" (SDs). They found that their proportions of "pure" SDs relative to pure PDs in their Spanish dyslexics was higher (20.2 per cent SDs vs. 4.4 per cent PDs) than had been found in studies of English dyslexics by Castles and Coltheart in 1993 (15.1 per cent PDs vs. 7 per cent SDs) and by Manis and colleagues in 1996 (9.8 per cent PDs vs. 9.8 per cent SDs). These data support the hypothesis that problems with rapid recognition of aspects of word shape—morpho-syllabic recognition—contribute more to dyslexia in Spanish at the third grade level and beyond than do difficulties with accuracy of sound-symbol decoding.

To recap, the findings converge to support the view that word recognition accuracy is less problematic in Spanish than English due in part to the former's comparatively parsimonious and highly regular orthography as well as simple syllable structure. Although longitudinal studies of reading development in Spanish are needed to confirm the changing contributions of the dual routes to reading in Spanish, cross-sectional and correlational studies suggest an intriguing developmental progression in which the phonological recoding, or sound-symbol, route plays a key role in the earliest phase of learning to read (preschool through grade 2), with the shallow orthography of Spanish facilitating a comparatively rapid rate of decoding acquisition. From around second or third grade on, a direct, or orthographic route for reading, necessitated by the increasingly morpho-syllabic strategies brought on by the rapid advance of early sound-symbol reading, appears to make gradually larger contributions to rate of reading in Spanish. The characteristics of dyslexia in Spanish are consistent with this conclusion. Core deficits in phonological skills (phonemic awareness, sound-symbol decoding) are problematic as they are in English, but proportionally, difficulties in reading speed are the predominant characteristic of dyslexia in Spanish and again appear to be related at least in part to rate of morpho-syllabic recognition.

Intervention for dyslexia in Spanish

Intervention studies of monolingual Spanish learners are sparse. In a study of code-oriented (sound-symbol) versus meaning oriented instruction of word recognition, Jiménez and Guzman (2003) found that children in the first and second grades who were taught with a sound-symbol approach demonstrated significantly faster reaction times on lexical decision tasks and inferred that sound-symbol instruction increased the automaticity of children's sublexical analytical skills.

In a follow-up study of children with reading disabilities, Jiménez and colleagues (2007) employed a computer-based remediation to further explore the effects on word-level reading of teaching using different sizes of sub-lexical unit. The researchers compared and contrasted the effects of four conditions for reading training—whole-word, syllable, onset-rime and phoneme—in a controlled study of 89 Spanish-speaking children. Given the previous findings regarding contributions to word recognition of phoneme-level awareness as well morpho-syllabic recognition speed in Spanish, Jiménez and colleagues hypothesized that the groups who received phoneme- and syllable-level training would show greater gains in word decoding than would the whole-word and onset-rime groups. Participants were identified by teachers and met the study's criteria of falling below the twenty-fifth percentile on a standardized measure of nonword reading. A computer systematically presented orthographic and digitized speech for words in units corresponding to the training condition (whole-word, syllable, onset-rime, phoneme). After 15 training sessions, participants in the phoneme and syllable conditions showed greater gains in their word and pseudo-word reading skills than did the onset-rime and whole-word groups. Given that an optimal number of interventions sessions is 30 to 40, it is not surprising that the students did not show transfer to reading comprehension (Torgesen *et al.*, 2001, as cited in Jiménez at al, 2007). While these studies add to our knowledge regarding intervention for accuracy and automaticity of word recognition, they do not address decoding fluency, the greatest area of need for struggling readers in Spanish. More intervention research in Spanish is needed, particularly studies that examine methods for enhancing automaticity of morpho-syllabic recognition and for extending that skill to improving the contextual reading efficiency of students with dyslexia.

Reading, reading disabilities and reading intervention in Spanish-speaking English-language learners

We now focus on reading acquisition and reading difficulties in Spanish-speaking English-language learners (SpELLs) in the U.S.; first we acknowledge the larger societal context, and after that explore diagnostic factors that can help to guide cross-linguistic prediction of reading difficulties. Our focus then shifts to studies of the efficacy of reading interventions for SpELLs, and we conclude with summary implications for practitioners as well as researchers.

Acknowledgment of the societal context of Spanish-speaking English-language learners

While the main focus of this chapter is on cognitive and linguistic factors in reading and dyslexia, it is critical to interject in this discussion the significant influences of economic and social context on SpELLs' reading acquisition. When literacy variables are factor analyzed in studies of adult and child literacy attainment, socio–cultural factors such as conditions at home and school conditions, as well as literacy environment emerge as highly influential (e.g., Samuelsson and Lundberg, 1996). As noted previously, SpELLs comprise the largest minority language group in the U.S.; as of the 2000 Census, five and one half million English-language learners attended U.S. public schools and of these, 80 per cent were Hispanic (McCardle *et al.*, 2005). For these SpELLs as a group, a wide gap exists between their literacy performance and that of their monolingual English-speaking peers. For example, in 2003, fourth grade reading test scores from the U.S. National Assessment of Educational Progress (NAEP) revealed that children living in homes where English is the only language spoken showed a 22–29 point scale score advantage over children "who lived in homes where a language other than English was always used" (National Center for Educational Statistics, 2003, as cited in August *et al.*,2005, p. 50). Despite the passage in the U.S. of the No Child Left Behind Act of 2001 (U.S. Department of Education, 2001) and corresponding implementation of Reading First Initiative's requirements for research-based methodologies for reading intervention, English-language learners (ELLs) display persisting patterns of underperformance, with 70 per cent of both fourth grade and eighth grade ELLs performing below basic levels of proficiency in reading, compared with 30 per cent and 24 per cent underperformance respectively for fourth grade and eighth grade monolinguals (U.S. Department of Education, 2007).

The roots of the persistent reading lag for ELLs in general and SpELLs in particular lie in part in the socio-economic context of the U.S., where the income and educational levels of Spanish-speaking English-language learners' parents are often lower than those of parents of monolingual English-speaking children. As a result SpELLs often have less access to literacy-rich environments in either Spanish or English compared to monolingual English speaking peers (e.g., Vernon-Feagans *et al.*, 2001). Given SpELLs' noteworthy lags in acquiring basic literacy skills, diagnostic and instructional recommendations for SpELLs should reflect knowledge about the individual's family literacy levels as well as environment and in addition should include strategies for supporting parent involvement and accessing needed resources. In the following section, our focus returns to cognitive and linguistic factors as we examine first language (L1) and second language (L2) relationships in Spanish-speakers learning to read in English.

L1 predictors of L2 reading in Spanish-speaking English-language learners

As noted previously, a research consensus indicates that phonological awareness is closely related to monolingual reading skills development in a range of languages with highly varied orthographies (e.g., Goswami, 2002; Kobayashi *et al.*, 2005; National Institute of Child Health and Human Development, 2000; Wimmer, 1993). Within SpELLs and other English-language learners, what is the role of L1 or L2 phonological awareness in predicting L2 prereading and reading skills? A number of studies indicate that for both Spanish-speaking ELLs and ELLs whose L1 is other than Spanish, *phonological awareness* (PA) skills transfer from L1 to L2. For example, Dickinson *et al.* (2004) examined deletion detection and rhyming performance in bilingual preschool children and found evidence of cross-linguistic transfer of PA. Meta-phonological skills such as rhyme awareness have been shown to transfer in non-alphabetic languages as well, even when L1 reading instruction occurs in a non-alphabetic orthography such as Chinese (e.g., Gottardo *et al.*, 2001).

With respect to L1 predictors of L2 *word recognition*, L1 phonological awareness, coupled with rapid retrieval (as measured by rapid automatic naming, or RAN), print knowledge, and word reading have been identified as predictors of English word reading skills in SpELL beginning readers. In a study of bilingual Spanish- and English-speaking first graders of low socioeconomic status, Durgunoglu *et al.*, (1993) found that Spanish PA predicted word reading both within and across languages and that Spanish PA and word recognition were significantly related to English word and pseudoword reading skills. This pattern of prediction has been replicated several times for SpELLs' first as well as second grade word recognition skills (Genesse and Geva, 2006, p.186; Quiroga *et al.*, 2002; Gottardo *et al.*, 2008).

In a longitudinal study that followed SpELLs from kindergarten through grade 2, Manis *et al.*, (2004) examined the effects of one-and-a-half years of Spanish literacy training that begins in kindergarten and is followed by transition to English literacy instruction in the second grade. They found that kindergarten Spanish print knowledge was the strongest cross-language predictor of second-grade English letter and word identification. In addition, kindergarten Spanish PA and RAN also contributed unique variance to the children's second-grade English letter and word identification. It is not surprising that first-grade English PA performance, which involves the same phoneme system as does English word recognition, accounted for more variance than did any Spanish language predictor of second grade English letter and word identification. Páez and Rinaldi (2006) followed children from kindergarten through first grade and arrived at similar findings. In addition, they found that kindergarten Spanish word-reading performance accounted for 10 per cent of the variation in the English word reading scores of first grade ELLs. Gottardo and colleagues (2008) examined first grade L2 English predictors of second-grade English reading performance and as has been found in English-speaking monolinguals, performance on English phonological measures like pseudoword repetition, phonological awareness, and rapid retrieval (RAN) predicted second grade word attack and word identification.

Bialystok *et al.*, (2005) examined first-grade word reading skills in Spanish–English, Hebrew–English and Cantonese–English language learners exposed to reading instruction in both L1 and L2. The researchers found strong correlations between L1 and L2 non-word reading skills in Spanish–English and Hebrew-English learners, while this relationship was relatively weak in Cantonese–English learners. The authors concluded that the alphabetic orthographies of Spanish and Hebrew may facilitate transfer of skills to English.

Given the above research regarding L1 factors associated with L2 phonological awareness and word recognition skills in ELLs, what factors predict L2 performance in the area of *reading fluency* (text level speed and accuracy)? Remarkably little research exists regarding development of text level reading fluency in SpELLs in particular and in ELLs in general. The most widely cited study of L2 reading fluency provides us with parallel findings from languages other than Spanish. Geva and Zadeh's (2006) study of second-grade English-language learners whose native languages included Cantonese, Punjabi, Tamil, and Portuguese, focused on L2 English predictors of L2 reading fluency. Their study also included a control group of L1 English readers. The researchers found that rapid retrieval of letter names (RAN), PA and word reading performance in English predicted both word-level automaticity and text-level reading efficiency in English. These results are comparable to patterns of prediction seen in studies of monolingual English learners, however, Geva and Zadeh found differences between their ELL and native English-speaking group.

Overall, children in Geva and Zadeh's ELL group demonstrated faster letter naming speed (RAN) and word-level reading than did monolingual English readers. In addition, when children in both groups (L2 English versus L1 English) were further subdivided into those with high versus low efficiency (fluency) scores and "poor decoders," the "high efficient" ELL readers demonstrated better PA than did "high efficient" L1 English readers. In contrast, L1 English "low efficient" readers and "poor decoders" outperformed the ELL "low efficient" and "poor decoder" groups in measures of English PA.

In a study of SpELLs in bilingual classrooms in grades 1–5, Ramírez and Shapiro (2007) employed reading fluency probes in Spanish at the beginning of the school year and found that fluency performance in Spanish predicted fluency performance in English at the end of the year, which supports the view that, for children who have received literacy schooling in L1, basic reading skills facilitate speed and accuracy of text level reading in L2. While the above studies of fluency in ELLs are instructive, replication and elaboration of these findings are needed.

As has been found in monolingual learners, linguistic context (syntactic and discourse structures) appear to aid reading fluency in bilingual children when reading in their first language; however, the facilitative effect of context across languages appears to be weak. Geva and Zadeh (2006) found that context enhanced English reading performance in ELLs as well as in monolingual English speakers; however, children in the ELL group benefited less from context than did native English speaking peers when reading in English. This finding suggests that beginning readers' English oral language proficiency may be related to ELLs' English text level fluency, but its role is small. Geva and Zadeh further clarify that, when children read texts judged to be at or just below their level of oral proficiency—in line with texts read fluently in Chall's stage two, oral proficiency does not significantly affect performance (Chall, 1996, as cited in Geva and Zadeh, 2006, p.51). Research with more demanding texts characteristic of Chall's (1983) stage 3, or Learning to Read, which include longer, less familiar words and more complex concepts, may require additional cognitive resources and reduce comprehension.

To this point, we have discussed L1 and L2 predictors of phonological awareness, word recognition and text level fluency in SpELLs and other English-Language Learners. In the following section, we examine L1 and L2 predictors of *reading comprehension*.

Reading comprehension in SpELLs

Findings of studies of reading comprehension in SpELLs and other English-language learners are similar to results of studies of reading comprehension in monolingual children. In beginning reading, where the focus is on learning to read text that represents very simple language, English phonological awareness and RAN are strongly related to English reading comprehension (Manis *et al.*, 2004), while vocabulary and sentence processing skills become stronger predictors of reading comprehension skills in upper grade school when children are using reading as a vehicle to learn.

Manis and colleagues (2004) examined Spanish and English print knowledge, phonological awareness, and expressive language in K-2 SpELLs. Of the Spanish measures, kindergarten print knowledge was the strongest predictor of second grade English reading comprehension. When grade one measures of English and Spanish print knowledge, PA, RAN and expressive language were all entered into regression analyses, the final regression equation showed that first grade English PA, RAN and expressive language were significant predictors of second grade English passage reading comprehension. In comparison to PA and RAN, however, expressive language

329

accounted for a much smaller percentage of unique variance. First grade English phonological awareness was the strongest predictor of second grade English reading comprehension.

With respect to reading comprehension in the upper grade school years, Proctor and colleagues (2005) conducted a four-year longitudinal study of SpELLs, and identified predictors of fourth-grade reading comprehension similar to those found in studies of monolingual children. SpELLs' oral language skills (listening comprehension and vocabulary knowledge) in English were found to predict more variance in English reading comprehension than did English pseudo word recognition and word level decoding automaticity.

In a reanalysis of the above data, Proctor and colleagues (2006) found that initial language of instruction and assessment had a predictably strong effect on reading comprehension performance: English oral language proficiency and reading comprehension scores were highest for fourth graders initially receiving reading instruction in English, while Spanish oral language proficiency and reading comprehension scores were highest for those initially receiving reading instruction in Spanish. When Proctor and colleagues controlled for effects of language instruction, knowledge of English vocabulary, English listening comprehension and English alphabetic knowledge, they found that only one percent of the variance in SpELLs' English reading comprehension scores was accounted for by English word reading fluency and Spanish vocabulary knowledge. While the contribution of Spanish vocabulary to English reading comprehension was minimal in this study, research examining the relationship between L1 vocabulary knowledge and L2 English reading comprehension is sparse and further study is warranted.

Taken together, the above studies of phonological awareness, word recognition, and reading fluency suggest a picture of changing relationships between L1 and L2 literacy predictors in SpELLs. These patterns of prediction have implications for the diagnostic measures we employ to identify children at risk for failing in different component reading skills. With respect to phonologically related skills, L1 phonological awareness and sound-symbol decoding skills predict English L2 performance in those basic reading skills.

With respect to reading fluency, studies are sparse, but the patterns appear to be as follows: L1 reading fluency predicts acquisition of L2 reading fluency, and within L2 English, RAN for letters, PA and word reading performance in English predicted both word-level automaticity and text-level reading efficiency at least at the second grade level. SpELLs' abilities to make use of linguistic context enhance their fluency within L1 or L2, but transfer of fluency skills across languages appears to be weak and the contributions of English L2 oral language proficiency to fluency, at least at the second grade level, appear to be small.

In the earliest grades, where the focus is on learning to decode accurately and then fluently, L2 English phonological awareness and RAN are strongly related to L2 English reading comprehension, and as children move into the upper grades where they are required to read texts containing longer words, new knowledge and more complex sentence structures, English L2 vocabulary and sentence processing skills become stronger predictors of English reading comprehension. L1 Spanish vocabulary skills appear to contribute negligibly to L2 English reading comprehension, however, and additional research in this area is needed. These cross-linguistic patterns in SpELLs' literacy learning are supported by Farnia and Geva's (2008) yet unpublished large-scale longitudinal study of developmental interrelationships between reading fluency and reading comprehension in Grade K-6 ELLs and monolingual English learners.

The above findings regarding diagnostic predictors of L1 and L2 reading performance have implications for which skills to teach and when to teach them. We now turn to studies that have explored the efficacy of different methods for teaching English reading skills to Spanish-speaking English-language learners.

Effective reading instruction for Spanish-speaking English-language learners

In 2000, the U.S. National Reading Panel (National Institute of Child Health and Human Development, 2000) reported their influential syntheses of efficacy studies in the areas of phonological awareness, phonics, reading fluency, vocabulary and reading comprehension for L1 monolingual English learners. Given recurrent National Assessment of Educational Progress (NAEP) (e.g., U.S. Dept. of Education, 2005, 2007) reports documenting persisting literacy failure in ELLs, many researchers have examined the efficacy of extending research-based methods to reading instruction for ELLs. Because Spanish-speaking English-language learners comprise the largest segment of ELLs in the U.S., much of the intervention research has targeted this group. In this section, we examine representative evidence of which methods appear to work best for improving SpELLs' literacy skills.[6]

Vaughn and colleagues (2005; Mathes *et al.*, 2007) tested methods for teaching beginning reading and oral language development to at-risk first graders whose home language was Spanish. Two groups of struggling readers were targeted, one group whose core literacy instruction was in English, and one whose instruction was in Spanish. The English and Spanish interventions shared the following, systematic, explicit emphases:

- phonemic awareness training of discrimination, segmentation and blending;
- letter knowledge instruction that couples graphemic and phonological awareness as well as teaches to automaticity;
- direct teaching of word attack skills, with emphases on developing automaticity of both sound–symbol and syllable-level decoding for regular words and efficient identification of irregular words;
- repeated readings of text to promote text-level reading fluency;
- comprehension strategy instruction, such as activation of prior knowledge, prediction, recalling what has been read and sequencing the recollection, identification of story grammar structure (e.g., setting, characters, initiating event, response, plan, actions, resolution);
- highly consistent, scripted vocabulary activities including: a) teachers selecting and defining key vocabulary used in directions, phonemic awareness and phonics exercises, as well as reading fluency texts; b) students defining the same vocabulary words, inferring their meaning from context, and c) using the words in sentences. In addition, read-alouds, accompanied by teacher-scaffolded discussion of key vocabulary and story retellings by students, supported students' understanding and use of oral vocabulary (2005, pp. 59–65).

While the Spanish and English interventions followed the general pattern above, the following adaptations of Spanish instruction were implemented based on research regarding the Spanish language:

- Syllable reading instruction emphasized accurate automatic decoding of CV and CVC syllable shapes with systematic introduction of diphthongs and consonant clusters.
- Word recognition emphases were first on syllable-by-syllable reading and then on blending syllables into words, with words incrementally increasing in syllable length. Automaticity at each level was stressed.

Participants came from a school district in Texas where schools were already teaching the majority of students to read at acceptable levels, as determined by state mandated assessments.

Only children identified as at risk for reading failure based on a screening battery of early reading skills were included in the study. Treatment and control groups were employed for studying the Spanish and English interventions. Children were taught in small groups of three to five students and received approximately 40 minutes of instruction daily for a total of approximately 120 sessions during the school year. We mention these implementation details, because in addition to the actual focus of a reading treatment, the frequency, intensity and duration of intervention has repeatedly been identified as a key to achieving successful literacy outcomes for children with reading disabilities (Torgesen *et al.*, 2001).

With respect to results of Vaughn and colleagues' (2005) Spanish intervention, the treatment group significantly outperformed the comparison group in phonological awareness, oral language, word attack and reading fluency. These differences did not carry over to measures of English spoken and written language achievement.

For the English intervention, significant differences favoring the treatment group were found in composite phonological processing (combination of phonological awareness, memory, and retrieval speed), word attack and reading comprehension, while differences were not found in oral language performance. The researchers did not report differences in performance on Spanish outcome measures (Vaughn *et al.*, 2005, pp. 59–65).

The findings have been replicated with other groups of first graders, and again, cross-language transfer of skills outcomes was not observed at this developmental level (Mathes *et al.*, 2007). Mathes and colleagues suggested that the lack of transfer may have been due to the fact that children's initial language skills in Spanish were significantly below average. This interpretation is consistent with Geva and Zadeh's (2006) observation that transfer may be contingent on the level of L1 cognitive and linguistic capacity and skills. The combined results indicate that Spanish-speaking first grade children with reading difficulties, whether they are learning to read English or Spanish, benefit from small-group, explicit, systematic instruction with characteristics similar to those that have been proven effective with typically developing and reading disabled monolingual English speakers.

Our literature search for research examining the efficacy of systematic reading instruction for struggling SpELL readers above the first grade level revealed a sparse number of studies, all of which had significant methodological flaws. Longitudinal, structurally sound studies are needed that examine the effects of systematic instruction in grades two and beyond. As we suggested previously, texts for the earliest grades are written to help children acquire and apply reading skills to access what they already know, while texts for middle and upper grade school contain increasingly less frequent and morphologically more complex vocabulary, new concepts, more complex sentence structures, and a richer variety of narrative and discourse structures. An additional challenge posed in designing reading instruction for SpELLs with reading disabilities, is that, if they have not achieved basic decoding and decoding fluency by grade three, it is more difficult to narrow the reading achievement gap between them and their typically developing peers (Torgesen *et al.*, 2001).

Summary observations

In this chapter, we have explored key studies examining reading, reading difficulties and reading intervention in native Spanish-speaking as well as bilingual Spanish-English learners. Predictors of learning to read in Spanish and English share similar features, with phonological skills, most notably phonological awareness, playing a key role in supporting word recognition. Nevertheless, reading in Spanish is influenced by unique structural characteristics of the language. Its transparent orthography and comparatively simple syllable structure facilitates rapid learning of basic word recognition skills in comparison to English. Spanish learners, in response to early encounters with long, morphologically rich words, acquire morpho-syntactic reading skills that critically influence reading fluency. For L1 English readers with phonological deficits associated with dyslexia, reading deficits are usually evident at the level of word recognition accuracy, while in L1 Spanish readers, dyslexia is more often evidenced by deficits in reading speed.

At the early grade school level, systematic explicit instruction at the phoneme and syllable levels has been shown to enhance L1 Spanish learners' word recognition skills. In the future, research is needed that elaborates the nature of morpho-syllabic reading in Spanish learners, and examines interventions for enhancing reading speed, perhaps via enhanced automaticity of morpheme recognition. Also, additional research is needed that explores the efficacy of reading intervention for native Spanish learners at middle and upper grade school levels.

With respect to bilingual Spanish-speaking English-language learners (SpELLs), the cross-linguistic research reviewed in this chapter has practical diagnostic implications for forecasting their L2 English reading outcomes. If a diagnostician wishes to select tests for predicting SpELLs' *word-level reading* in English, promising measures to consider employing would be L1 Spanish phonological awareness, rapid retrieval (RAN), print knowledge and word reading. Candidate L2 English areas to consider for predicting English word recognition skills include speech perception and phonological awareness in English. While the findings for SpELLs in grades K–2 indicate that L2 English vocabulary measures are minimally useful for predicting L2 English word recognition, more research is needed the capacity of L2 vocabulary to predict L2 word recognition in the reading-to-learn phase (~grades three to six).

With respect to L1 Spanish predictors of L2 *reading fluency*, measures of reading fluency in Spanish can help to predict reading fluency in English. With respect to L2 predictors of L2 fluency, phonological awareness, rapid retrieval of letters (RAN), and word-level reading would appear to be diagnostically useful. L1 Spanish measures for predicting L2 *reading comprehension* include Spanish print knowledge (Manis *et al.*, 2004) and to a minimal extent, Spanish vocabulary (Proctor *et al.*, 2006). L2 English tests that predict L2 reading comprehension are phonological awareness (particularly in beginning readers), rapid retrieval (RAN), with L2 oral language proficiency (listening comprehension and vocabulary knowledge) best predicting reading comprehension in readers who are in middle and upper grade school. More research remains to be done on the role of L1 Spanish vocabulary in L2 word recognition and reading comprehension, particularly in the middle and upper grade school years. In general, more cross-linguistic research is needed in order to better understand SpELLs' reading in grades 3–6.

While reading intervention efficacy research on SpELLs has largely focused on instruction in grades one to two, within those constaints, there is robust evidence indicating that systematic explicit instruction of phonological awareness, sound-symbol decoding, reading fluency, vocabulary and reading comprehension results in significant improvements in these skills. With respect to SpELLs learning to read in Spanish, modifications of phonological awareness and phonics instruction to respect the syllabic characteristics of the language have proven effective. As is the case with the intervention research on monolingual Spanish readers, additional efficacy research is needed examining the effects of methods for teaching morphological recognition, including its effects on reading speed and reading comprehension in grades three to five.

Notes

1 See Chapter 11 by Mahfoudhi and Haynes in this book, for a detailed discussion of relationships between phonology, phonological awareness, and reading.

2   *Onset* refers to the consonant sound initiating a syllable, and *rime* refers to the vowel or vowel plus consonant sounds that follow within the syllable.

3   See Meyer *et al.* (1974) for a classic review of single versus dual routes for word recognition.

4   See Perea and Carreiras, 1998, for an in-depth discussion of neighborhood frequency effects on word recognition.

5   The fact that morphologically similar words such as "damos" (we give), "hablamos" (we talk), and "andamos" (we walk) would technically fall in different 'neighborhoods' suggests that Davies and colleagues' findings of a neighborhood effect might be even more noteworthy if the definitional criteria were expanded.

6   For a comprehensive meta-analysis and summary of biliteracy efficacy studies, see August and Shanahan, 2006.

References

Adams, M.J. (1990). *Beginning to read: Thinking and learning about print.* Cambridge, MA: MIT Press.

Anderson, R. and Centeno, J. (2007). Contrastive analysis between Spanish and English. In J. Centeno, R. Anderson, and L. Obler (eds), *Communication disorders in Spanish speakers.* Multilingual Matters LTD: Toronto, 11–33.

Anthony, J.L., Williams, J.M., McDonald, R., Corbitt-Schindler, D., Carlson, C. and Francis, D. (2006). Phonological processing and emergent literacy in Spanish-speaking preschool children, *Annals of Dyslexia, 56*(2), 239–270.

August, D. and Shanahan, T. (2006). *Developing literacy in second-language learners: Report of the national literacy panel on language-minority children and youth.* Mahwah, NJ: Lawrence Erlbaum Associates.

August, D., Carlo, M., Dressler, C. and Snow, C. (2005). The critical role of vocabulary development for English language learners. *Learning Disabilities Research* and *Practice, 20*(1), 50–57.

Bialystok, E., Luk, G. and Kwan, E. (2005). Bilingualism, biliteracy, and learning to read: Interactions among languages and writing systems. *Scientific Studies of Reading, 9,* 43–61.

Burani, C., Marcolini, S. and Stella, G. (2002). How early does morpho-lexical reading develop in readers of a shallow orthography? *Brain and Language, 81,* 568–586.

Castles, A. and Coltheart, M. (1993). Varieties of developmental dyslexia, *Cognition, 47,* 149–180, as cited in Jiménez and Ramirez (2002).

Chall, J.S. (1983). *Stages of reading development.* New York: McGraw-Hill.

Chall, J.S. (1996). *Stages of reading development.* 2nd Edition. Orlando, FL: Harcourt Brace. As cited in Geva and Zadeh (2006).

Davies, R., Cuetos, F. and Glez-Seijas, R.M. (2007). Reading development and dyslexia in a transparent orthography: A survey of Spanish children, *Annals of Dyslexia, 57,* 179–198.

Dickinson, D.K., McCabe, A., Clark-Chiarelli, N. and Wolf, A. (2004). Cross-language transfer of phonological awareness in low-income Spanish and English bilingual preschool children. *Applied Psycholinguistics, 25,* 323–347.

Durgunoglu, A.Y., Nagy, W.E., and Hancin-Bhatt, B.J. (1993). Cross-language transfer of phonological awareness. *Journal of Educational Psychology, 85,* 453–465.

Farnia, F. and Geva, E. (2008). A longitudinal examination of the reciprocal relations between reading fluency and reading comprehension in monolingual and ESL students. Presentation at Society for the Scientific Study of Reading, Ashville, NC, July 10.

Genesee, F. and Geva, E. (2006). Cross-linguistic relationships in working memory, phonological processes, and oral language. In D. August and T. Shanahan (eds), *Developing literacy in second-language learners: Report of the national literacy panel on language-minority children and youth.* Mahwah, NJ: Lawrence Erlbaum Associates, 169–177.

Geva, E. and Zadeh, Z. (2006). Reading efficiency in native English-speaking and English-as-a-second-language children: The role of oral proficiency and underlying cognitive-linguistic processes. *Scientific Studies of Reading, 10,* 31–57.

Gordon, R. (2005). *Ethnologue: Languages of the world,* 15th edn. Summer Institute for Linguistics: Dallas, Texas.

Goswami, U. (1999). The relationship between phonological awareness and orthographic representation in different orthographies. In M. Harris and G. Hatano (eds), *Learning to read and write: A cross-linguistic perspective.* Cambridge: Cambridge University Press, 51–70.

Goswami, U. (2002). Phonology, reading development, and dyslexia: A cross-linguistic perspective. *Annals of Dyslexia*, *52*, 141–163.

Gottardo, A., Yan, B., Siegel, L. S. and Wade-Woolley, L. (2001). Factors related to English reading performance in children with Chinese as a first language: More evidence of cross-language transfer of phonological processing. *Journal of Educational Psychology*, *93*, 530–542.

Gottardo, A., Collins, P., Baciu, I. and Gebotys, R. (2008). Predictors of grade 2 word reading from grade 1 variables in Spanish-speaking children: Similarities and differences. *Learning Disabilities Research* and *Practice*, *23*(1), 11–24.

Gunn, B., Biglan, A., Smolkowski, K. and Ary, D. (2000). The efficacy of supplemental instruction in decoding skills for Hispanic and non-Hispanic students in early elementary school. *The Journal of Special Education*, *34*(2), 90–103.

Jiménez, J.E. (1997). A reading-level design study of phonemic processes underlying reading disabilities in a transparent orthography. *Reading and Writing: An Interdisciplinary Journal*, *9*, 23–40.

Jiménez, J.E., and Ramírez, G. (2002). Identifying subtypes of reading disability in the Spanish language. *The Spanish Journal of Psychology*, *5*(1), 3–19.

Jiménez, J.E. and Hernández-Valle, I. (2000). Word identification and reading disorders in the Spanish language. *Journal of Learning Disabilities*, *32*, 267–275.

Jiménez, J.E. and Guzmán, R. (2003). The influence of code-oriented versus meaning-oriented approaches to reading instruction on word recognition in the Spanish language. *International Journal of Psychology*, *38*(2), 65–78.

Jiménez, J.E. (2002). Reading disabilities in a language with a transparent orthography. In E. Witrock, A.D. Frederici and T. Lachman (eds.), *Basic functions of reading language and learning disability*. Dordrecht: Kluwer Academic Publishers, 251–264.

Jiménez, J.E., Álvarez, C., Estévez, A. and Hernández-Valle, I. (2000). Onset-rime units in visual word recognition in Spanish normal readers and children with reading disabilities. *Learning Disabilities Research* and *Practice*, *15*, 135–141.

Jiménez, J.E., Hernández-Valle, I., Ramírez, G., Ortiz, M.R., Rodrigo, M., Estévez, A., O'Shanahan, I., García, E. and Trabaue, M.L. (2007). Computer-based remediation for reading disabilities: The size of spelling-to-sound unit in a transparent orthography. *The Spanish Journal of Psychology*, *10*(1), 52–67.

Kobayashi, M., Haynes, C., Macaruso, P., Hook, P. and Kato, J. (2005). Effects of mora deletion, nonword repetition, rapid naming, and visual search performance on beginning reading in Japanese. *Annals of Dyslexia*, *55*, 105–127.

Linan-Thompson, S., Bryant, D.P., Dickson, S.V. and Kouzekanani, K. (2005). Spanish literacy instruction for at-risk kindergarten students. *Remedial and Special Education*, *26*(4), 236–244.

McCardle, P., Mele-McCarthy, J. and Leos, K. (2005). English language learners and learning disabilities: Research agenda and implications for practice. *Learning Disabilities Research and Practice*, *20*, 68–78.

Manis, F.R., Seidenberg, M.S., Doi, L.M., McBride-Chang, C. and Petersen, A. (1996). On the bases of two subtypes of developmental dyslexia. *Cognition*, *58*, 157–195, as cited in Jiménez and Ramírez (2002).

Manis, F.R., Lindsey, K.A., and Bailey, C.E. (2004). Development of reading in grades K-2 in Spanish-speaking English-language learners. *Learning Disabilities Research* and *Practice*, *19*, 214–224.

Mathes, P.G., Pollard-Durodola, S.D., Cárdenas-Hagan, E., Linan-Thompson, S. and Vaughn, S. (2007). Teaching struggling readers who are native Spanish speakers: What do we know? *Language, Speech and Hearing Services in the Schools*, *38*, 260–271.

Meyer, D.E., Schvaneveldt, R.W. and Ruddy, M.G. (1974). Functions of graphemic and phonemic codes in visual word-recognition. *Memory and Cognition*, *2*(2), 309–321.

National Center for Educational Statistics (2003). *The nation's report card*. Retrieved September 7, 2004 from http://nces.ed.gov/nationsreportcard, as cited by August, Carlo, Dressler and Snow (2005).

National Institute of Child Health and Human Development (2000). *Report of the National Reading Panel. Teaching children to read: An evidence-based assessment of the scientific research literature on reading and its implications for instruction*. Reports of the subgroup. Washington, DC: U.S. Government Printing Office.

Niño-Murcía, M., Godenzzi, J.C. and Rothman, J. (2008). Spanish as a world language: The interplay of globalized localization and localized globalization, International *Multilingual Research Journal*, *2*(1), 48–66.

Páez, M. and Rinaldi, C. (2006). Predicting English word reading skills for Spanish-speaking students in first grade. *Topics in Language Disorders*, *26*, 338–350.

335

Penny, R. (2002). A history of the Spanish language. Cambridge University Press: Cambridge, UK.

Perea, M. and Carreiras, M. (1998). Effects of syllable frequency and syllable neighborhood frequency in visual word recognition. Journal of Experimental Psychology: Human Perception and Performance, 24(1), 134–144.

Proctor, C.P., Carlo, M., August, D. and Snow, C. (2005). Native Spanish-speaking children reading in English: Toward a model of comprehension. Journal of Educational Psychology, 97, 246–256.

Proctor, C.P., August, D., Carlo, M. and Snow, C. (2006). The intriguing role of Spanish language vocabulary knowledge in predicting English reading comprehension. Journal of Educational Psychology, 98, 159–169.

Quiroga, T., Lemos-Britton, Z., Mostafapour, E., Abbott, R.D. and Berninger, V.W. (2002). Phonological awareness and beginning reading in Spanish speaking ESL first graders: Research into practice. Journal of School Psychology, 40, 85–111.

Ramírez, R.D. and Shapiro, E.S. (2007). Cross-language relationship between Spanish and English oral reading fluency among Spanish-speaking English language learners in bilingual education classrooms. School Psychology, 44(8), 795–806.

Samuelsson, S. and Lundberg, I. (1996). The impact of environmental factors on components of reading and dyslexia. Annals of Dyslexia, 53(1), 201–217.

Serrano, F. and Defior, S. (2008). Dyslexia speed problems in a transparent orthography, Annals of Dyslexia, 58(1), 81–95.

Seymour, H.K.S., Aro, M. and Erskine, J.M. (2003). Foundation literacy acquisition in European orthographies. British Journal of Psychology, 94, 143–174.

Shin, H. and Bruno, R. (2003). Language use and English-speaking ability: 2000 (Census 2000 Brief, Series C2KBR-29). Washington, DC: U.S. Bureau of the Census.

Torgesen, J., Alexander, A.W., Wagner, R. K., Rashotte, C.A., Voeller, K.S. and Conway, T. (2001). Intensive remedial instruction for children with reading disabilities: Immediate and long-term outcomes of two instructional approaches. Journal of Learning Disabilities, 34, 33–58.

US Department of Education (2001). No child left behind act of 2001, accessed August 8, 2007 at http://www.ed.gov/policy/elsec/leg/esea02/index.html.

US Department of Education (2005). National assessment of educational progress (NAEP): The nation's report card: Reading 2005 (NAEP), Institute of Education Sciences, National Center for Education Statistics, accessed July 25, 2008 at http://nces.ed.gov/pubsearch/ pubsinfo.asp?pubid=2006451.

US Department of Education (2007). National assessment of educational progress (NAEP): The nation's report card: Reading 2007 (NAEP), Trends in Achievement Levels by Race/Ethnicity, accessed August 8, 2008 at http://nationsreportcard.gov/reading_2007/data.asp.

Vaughn, S., Mathes, P.G., Linan-Thompson, S. and Francis, D. (2005). Teaching English language learners at risk for reading disabilties to read: Putting research to practice. Learning Disabilities Research and Practice, 20(1), 58–67.

Vernon-Feagans, L., Hammer, C.S., Miccio, A. and Manlove, E. (2001). Early language and literacy skills in low-income African American and Hispanic children. In S. Neuman and D. Dickinson (eds), Handbook of early literacy research, New York: Guilford Press, 192–210.

Wimmer, H. (1993). Characteristics of developmental dyslexia in a regular writing system. Applied Psycholinguistics, 14, 1–33.

Acknowledgements

C. Haynes—MGH Institute of Health Professions, Boston; Center for Child Evaluation and Teaching (CCET), Kuwait City, Kuwait

A. Ayre—Massachusetts General Hospital, Boston, Massachusetts, U.S.A

B. Haynes—Fulbright Fellowship Program, Temuco, Chile

A. Mahfoudhi—United Nations Development Program and Center for Child Development and Teaching, Kuwait City, Kuwait

26

Responsive approaches to literacy learning within cultural contexts

Mere Berryman and Janice Wearmouth

This chapter

- takes a socio-cultural approach to exploring students' literacy learning at school
- examines the difficulties they experience.

Summary Points

- Dyslexia is commonly understood as an explanation of difficulties in literacy when seen through a cognitive psychology lens. This level of explanation accounts for difficulties in aspects of literacy acquisition related to the processing of data. It lends itself less easily to aspects related to other important aspects of literacy acquisition that are provided by the top-down and semantic aspects of the interactive models. Explanations that relate to culture are thus ignored.
- Research shows the benefits to literacy learning that accrue when schools work to address issues of cultural understandings between themselves and their home communities. By understanding, respecting and seeking to include the potential of students and their home communities, and collaborating on literacy learning tasks and contexts, literacy values and practices that are evident in different cultural communities can be recognised and affirmed and improvements in students' literacy achievements can occur.

Introduction

This chapter takes a socio-cultural approach to exploring students' literacy learning at school and, conversely, the difficulties they experience. Socio-cultural theories of human learning (Vygotsky, 1978; Bruner, 1996) point to the importance of understanding the relationships and interactions between students and their teachers and subsequently between schools and their home communities. Socio-cultural theories of learning stem from the core idea that intellectual and social development are interdependent from birth. As babies, children begin to communicate, understand, relate and interact through active engagement with others in the social and cultural contexts of their own families and homes. These social and cultural contexts provide the values, beliefs and behaviours that will shape learners' understandings and the way in which they make sense of the new situations in which they will find themselves, and how they will respond in those situations.

Dyslexia in context

Dyslexia is often understood as poor literacy achievement from a cognitive psychology perspective. As such it has relevancy within an information-processing domain of explanation. In other words it is useful in explaining aspects of literacy acquisition that refer specifically to the processing of data. It is important to examine which aspects these might be, which aspects lend themselves less easily to an information-processing approach and the salience of these aspects to students' literacy acquisition overall.

Two contrasting models are commonly proposed in relation to the reading process and learning to read (Reid, 1998). The *bottom-up* model suggests that readers attend first to the visual features of text, such as the letters in the words. Reader identify the symbols, connect them with sounds and then they move on to consider the meaning of the printed words. In this model of the reading process, learning to read is data-driven and requires first focusing on symbol-sound relationships, on phonics and alphabetic knowledge, before making sense of the text. On the other hand, the *top-down* model is driven by the reader's active search for meaning. The reader anticipates the meaning of text before checking how the available syntactic and graphic cues fit with the meaning. A third, more interactive, model (Stanovich, 2000; McNaughton, 2002) suggests that readers use information simultaneously from different levels. They do not necessarily begin with the graphics (bottom-up) or with meaning (top-down) to make sense of reading but that during the development of reading skills, readers may at times rely more heavily on some levels than they do on others.

A cognitive, information-processing model relates to the processes in the bottom-up model and, in one part, to the interactive model. Being constrained to explanations of information-processing alone, however, provides us with little power to understand or explain other important aspects of literacy acquisition that are provided by the top-down and semantic aspects of the interactive models. Explanations that relate to culture are thus ignored. Adopting a socio-cultural view enables cultural aspects of the barriers to literacy to be examined, understood and, potentially, addressed effectively.

A socio-cultural view, with its emphasis on the role of the more experienced and skilled other in supporting the individual child's learning within the Zone of Proximal Development (Vygotsky, 1978; Glynn *et al.*, 2006) also allows for a focus on bottom-up aspects of literacy acquisition to be acknowledged. A skilled knowledgeable tutor will pick up on the nature of the individual student's difficulties *naturally* as it were, and will use multi-sensory methods of encouraging the development of phonemic and phonological awareness, word accuracy, spelling, and so on. Accurate identification of difficulties related to the way the learner processes information and also a sensitive awareness of the wide range of experiences that students bring with them when they come to school can, together, make an important contribution to students' literacy acquisition at school and also to addressing difficulties they experience.

Worldview and culture

Our view of the world is patterned on the traditional experiences, belief systems and ways of thinking in which we are raised. These conceptualisations and patterns of life extend from the past and are inherent in the beliefs, narratives, symbols and logic that form a people's *worldview* (Marsden, 2003). Our worldview forms the central system of 'conceptions of reality to which members of a culture assent and from which stems their values system' (Marsden and Henare, 1992, p. 3). People's perceptions of reality, what they regard as actual, probable and possible, are thus conceptualized according to what they perceive reality to be (Wearmouth *et al.*, 2005).

From our worldview comes our culture. The concept of culture is often used by various groups to identify and define themselves and to differentiate themselves from others. In this regard, culture may be defined by the relationships, interactions and icons within which specific groups of people engage with over time. Quest Rapuara (1992), for example, provides a definition of culture that encapsulates both responsive (how we think, relate and interact) and appropriate (cultural iconography) elements, often associated with culture:

> Culture is what holds a community together, giving a common framework of meaning. It includes how people communicate with each other, how we make decisions, how we structure our families and who we think is important. It expresses our values towards land and time and our attitudes towards work and play, good and evil, reward and punishment.
>
> Culture is preserved in language, symbols and customs and celebrated in art, music, drama, literature, religion and social gatherings. It constitutes the collective memory of the people and the collective heritage which will be handed down to future generations.
>
> (p.7)

People who participate in a shared culture may have common aspirations and interests, often meeting together to share in their activities and experiences. Cultural contexts in which children are reared, while also involving these qualities, are also characterised by a close and enduring interconnectedness with family and other group members, and an ongoing sharing of values, beliefs and lifestyles through a commonly understood language. Cultural contexts such as these have a very important and ongoing role in influencing young people's ability to make sense of and understand their world. In this sense, culture may also be linked with membership to a particular ethnic group (Glynn and Bishop, 1995) or class.

Bruner (1996) proposes that the way the human mind has developed and works is linked to 'a way of life where "reality" is represented by a symbolism shared by members of a cultural community in which a technical-social way of life is both organised and construed in terms of that symbolism' (p. 3). In turn this shared symbolism is 'conserved, elaborated and passed on to succeeding generations who, by virtue of this transmission, continue to maintain the culture's identity and way of life' (Bruner, 1996, p. 3). Patterns of life that extend from the past are inherent in discourse and metaphor, in logic and narrative. Communications such as these provide evidence to interpret the understandings and intention of a particular group of people (Bruner, 1990). Bruner (1990) suggests:

> . . . it is culture, not biology, that shapes human life and the human mind, that gives meaning to action by situating its underlying intentional states in an interpretive system. It does this by imposing the patterns inherent in the culture's symbolic systems – its language and discourse modes, the forms of logical and narrative explication, and the patterns of mutually dependent communal life.
>
> (p.34)

In this regard, Walker (1978) suggests that the messages or cultural imperatives must be defined by the cultural groups themselves and thus clearly signposted if they are to be better understood. Given this challenge it is useful to consider that different people may be viewing the same thing or listening to the same discourse, but defining and interpreting it from a different worldview and cultural perspective. This can be especially problematic when the culture into which the child is born and raised for much of their first years, is different from the culture of the school.

Home-based learning

Vygotsky (1962) contends that all mental processes have social origins. One's sense of words is rooted in one's experiences with others. Certainly most babies are able to have their needs satisfied by communicating their emotions to those around them, long before they can talk. From their immersion in largely home-based, social contexts from birth, they appear to use these first forms of communication and learn language in a natural and easy way. From what they feel, hear, and see, and how others respond to them, babies actively begin to make sense of their world and to communicate their own ideas to those around them (Glynn *et al.*, 2006). People they know talk to them, talk about them and talk to others. Everyday sounds from these interactions, from music and from other sources, are often a part of their very first intellectual and social experiences:

> Any function in the child's development appears twice, on two planes. First it appears on the social plane, and then on the psychological plane. First it appears between people as an interpsychological category, and then within the child as an intrapsychological category. This is equally true with regard to voluntary attention, logical memory, the formation of concepts, and the development of volition.
>
> (Vygotsky, 1981, p. 163)

The young child's thought development begins through interpersonal experiences and negotiation with parents or caregivers and family members at home, and this then begins to be internalised into intrapersonal understanding. Vygotsky (1962) suggests that, 'at about the age of two the curves of development of thought and speech, till then separate, meet and join to initiate a new form of behaviour' (p. 43).

In this way, young children experience activities with others and soon begin to learn to internalise these experiences by symbolising them in words in their communications with those around them. Likewise, the interpersonal dimension is crucial if learning to read and write is seen as understanding and communicating meaning in the form of text, and seen as being done in company with others, with caregivers and siblings in the home then teachers and peers at school.

Even while we are very young, the cultural contexts within which we grow up and the people with whom we engage begin to shape our ability to organise meaning in ways that we can communicate with others. 'Thought development is determined by language' (Vygotsky, 1962, p.51) and in turn, this is developed by linguistic skills and socio-cultural experiences (Smith, and Elley, 1997). Cognitive development steadily evolves within communities when the reality of individual experiences is represented by symbolism such as verbal or written language being shared amongst its people, and where the community's way of life is organised and understood through this shared symbolism (Bruner, 1996). Talking therefore, is an essential intellectual and social skill that is shaped by how we think and forms part of how we learn to communicate with others and continue to make sense of the world by using other forms of shared symbolism such as reading and writing.

Links to home culture

If we take the view that literacy begins and is mediated from birth by, for example, parents, siblings, carers, relatives and other community members, then, as Street (1995) suggests, we are more likely to appreciate the wide and varied forms of literacy that students may bring with them to school, other than school-sanctioned literacy activities alone. By the same token, schools that acknowledge this view are in a good position to understand and benefit from a wider range of mediators who can support the literacy development of students who experience difficulties other than school staff alone (Gregory, 1998; Gregory, 2004a, b; Gregory *et al.*, 2005 a, b). The attitude of schools to the role of parents, families and community members, as prime educators of children, is therefore of great importance. This perspective highlights the importance of schools' responsibilities to prepare themselves more effectively for the literacy understandings that students bring with them from home rather than continuing to advocate predominantly for children and families to prepare themselves for the literacy activities of the school. This is especially important for students from diverse cultures who may come to school from backgrounds rich in literacy activities that may be quite different from the literacy activities and attitudes to learning that are common in schools. The two examples below (Berryman, unpublished) show how this has implications for both the pedagogies that schools employ and the curriculum to which they relate.

The first example relates to a five-year-old who had learned from experiences within her own family and culture prior to going to school that effective learning occurs through active participation. Good learners question, examine, try things out, contribute their own thinking, and present their attempts to decode and encode written alphabetic symbols to others for feedback. This five-year-old also knew that *not knowing* was an important and acceptable part of learning in general, and literacy learning in particular. By her fifth week of formal schooling, however, she had learned new school-related lessons about learning. She had learned that learners who were quiet and who sat up were far more valued, that the teacher's questions were the only really important questions in the classroom and that, more often than not, these questions had either a correct or an incorrect answer. She quickly learned that the correct answers were valued most, it was important for learners not to ask questions and that learning is a fairly risky business.

The way in which schools view learning can be even more problematic when both the culture and the language of the home are different from that of the school. The second example refers to another five-year-old, who could speak English but had been raised also to speak her own indigenous language at home and in her cultural community whose practices included traditional songs and chants. Many of these were accompanied by actions which she had also learned, often performing both the songs and actions alongside other members of her family and extended family. This child was asked by her teacher at school if she would recite a nursery rhyme. The young girl appeared to think about it for a while, only to be prompted by the teacher with, 'Any one will do' and then by her peers, 'Don't you even know "Mary had a little lamb"?' Unable to perform she hung her head in silence, perhaps retreating into her own world to make sense of what was happening. Here was a girl who had grown up hearing and learning, through informal modelling, long and often complex traditional chants and songs in her own language. She did not know 'Mary had a little lamb'. However, the teacher had not realised that what she was asking this student to do might well have been outside her cultural experience, or, just as importantly, that within this learner's experience there were other alternatives to be equally valued. After a number of other *tests* in which this student was found to be similarly lacking, the teacher concluded that this child came with few literacy experiences and was unable to contribute to the lesson. Perhaps she needed a hearing test and might even require speech language therapy. Thus her profile as a literacy learner began to emerge in deficit terms.

Both of these students had supportive families and the skills and confidence to question these experiences. There are many other students who may not cope as easily with these sorts of

341

experiences. Many teachers from the majority school-culture may fail to recognise the full implications of their own cultural expectations and assumptions that they place, perhaps unwittingly, on students from minority cultures. They may not understand the influence that their own culture and attitude plays in this. For some students, experiences such as these can lead to ongoing assumptions, incorrect diagnosis and remedial programmes on the part of well meaning teachers and lack of self-esteem, self doubt and a pathway to ongoing failure for the student. There is no possibility of making sense of what bears no relation to one's own ways of making sense of things. Unfamiliarity with local culture, customs and language on entering school can result in complete bewilderment and an inability to understand the expectations and norms of the literacy curriculum. Gregory (1996, p. 33) notes, for example, how 'Tony' arrived at school, aged four years and ten months, with an 'eye for detail' and a 'disciplined and structured approach to reading from his Chinese school'. In his Chinese school he had been 'given an exercise book where he had to divide the page into columns and practise ideographs over and over again until they are perfect' (Gregory, 1996, p. 32). The carefully and clearly delineated and constrained tasks set by the previous teacher contrasted sharply with the range of personal choice given to 'Tony' and his classmates in the mainstream classroom in Northampton, England. His aimless wandering around the classroom while peers chose activities for themselves indicated that he appeared unable to cope with the non-realisation of his expectations about what school should be about.

The way in which a lack of understanding can feel threatening to oneself and can lead to feelings of anxiety or hostility is illustrated by an inmate of a UK prison who recalls in relation to his own school experiences, 'a cocktail of . . . um . . . conflicts there all the time' as he tried to cope with the expectations of a mainstream London school that conflicted with those of home:

> I was weak in certain subjects, like English mainly, because I tend to write the way I speak. I'm born here, my parents are from the West Indies. I am in an English school I had to cope with the different . . . criteria because at home it was like a cross between Caribbean where we tend to speak more Patois or broken English. School was like trying to do it faithfully . . . You get to learn . . . how important language is for you to fit . . . and then, like . . . I might get homework to do and I'll ask my dad and he will say no, it's done this way, which is, their schooling was from the old grammar, and it's always a conflict and I would always believe what my father had said because he was a father figure . . . Yes, and then it was completely wrong, and eventually you get frustrated, and I am not going to do this, and you just sort of throw it out.
>
> (Wearmouth, 1997)

Links to social status

There is much anecdotal evidence to suggest teacher expectations are sometimes based on assumed causal links between a child's ethnicity or culture and their capacity or willingness to learn (Rubie-Davies et al., 2006). This often extends to expectations of students who belong to a different social class also. Early research by Brophy and Good (1974) for example, examined a number of studies that investigated treatment of students by teachers, according to students' socio-economic status. They found that teachers related more easily to students from higher social classes and even overestimated their ability as compared to students from lower-class homes. In addition, the types of interactions that teachers were having with students of higher social class were more positive and facilitative when compared to other students. Brophy and Good (1974) also found that once students were grouped (according to their perceived *ability*) they were rarely given an opportunity to move, despite their potential or actual measured ability. Brophy and Good (1974) thus concluded that, 'socioeconomic status predicts both teachers' perceptions of their children and their treatment of them in the classroom' (p. 9).

Nieto (1994) goes so far as to suggest that teachers' expectations of their students are a reflection of deeply ingrained, wider societal and ideological values. In this regard, research by Weinstein et al. (2004) adds to a growing body of American literature that suggests that teachers' expectations contribute to the ethnic achievement gap. This literature contends that teachers expect more from their European American and Asian American students than from their African American and Latino peers (Baron et al., 1985) and indeed provide higher quality instruction to students from whom they expect more. Students receiving the higher quality instruction internalise the high expectations, become motivated and achieve in line with these expectations (Weinstein and Middlestadt, 1979). On the other hand, students receiving the low teacher expectations become concerned with the stereotypical response and are increasingly susceptible to negative expectancy effects (McKown, and Weinstein, 2002, 2003; Steele, 1997). African American elementary students were found to be most vulnerable to negative teacher expectation effects (Jussim et al., 2002).

Similar findings emerged from a New Zealand study by St. George (1983) who investigated teachers' perceptions of 90, Year 5 Polynesian (Māori and Pacific Islands' students were combined) and Pākehā students in five classrooms across four different schools. A point bi-serial correlation was undertaken between teachers' ratings of these students, on a series of attributes. Results showed that teachers perceived Polynesian students less favourably than Pākehā (non-Māori) in terms of their engagement and participation in class. Further, despite the fact that teachers had not always met the parents or visited the homes of these students, they perceived Polynesian students as coming from homes with poor parental attitudes to school and less stimulating home environments. More than half of the Polynesian students were designated to the low expectation group, while only one quarter of the Pākehā students were similarly designated. In this study, class observations revealed that while student ethnicity appeared to have little effect on patterns of interactions between teachers and students, differences were experienced according to the *expectation group* (high, middle and low) into which students were located. This was significant, given that more than half of the Polynesian students were in the low expectation group. This study found that teachers interacted differently with students from the high and low expectation groups. It was noted, for example, that students in the high expectation group received significantly less criticism. While standardized achievement results matched students to the three different expectation groups, it was suggested that these results could have been attributed to the different expectations, relationships and interactions experienced by students in each of the expectation groups. St. George (1983) concluded that a shift away from the stereotyped perceptions about factors that were beyond the control of the teacher, such as perceived attitudes about parents, home environments and cultural differences between the child and the school, would likely improve outcomes.

A more recent study by Timperley (2003) summarised teachers' expectations of students, prior to and after professional development around literacy. Participants in this study believed that the causes of low literacy achievement for their Year 3 students were due to poor student skills upon entry to school and the amount of time teachers had to teach these early skills. Guided by the researcher, these teachers developed a list of 25 skills considered to be essential prior to school entry. Forty new entrant students were tested on their mastery of these skills and teachers were then asked to estimate the percentage of skills accomplished by students. One teacher estimated mastery at 70 per cent to 80 per cent of skills, while the remaining teachers estimated much lower at 30 per cent to 40 per cent of the skills. Actual results revealed that average percentage of skills mastered was in fact 74 per cent. By looking at actual achievement of students it was found that the one teacher, who had estimated higher skill mastery, achieved the highest reading outcomes for students. Timperley's study indicated that there was a connection between low literacy achievement of students and low teacher expectations. One way that low teacher expectations impacted upon students was in teachers providing students with reading materials and instruction, at difficulty levels that were far too low.

Similar findings have emerged from a more recent study by Rubie-Davies et al. (2006). This study involved 21 primary school teachers at twelve Auckland schools and was concerned with their expectations for their students' achievement in reading. The actual reading achievement of 540 students from the beginning of the year and again from the end of the year was compared with both teachers' expectations and teachers' judgements for the end of year reading achievement of these students. This study found that teachers' expectations for Māori students were lower than their expectations for Pacific, Asian and New Zealand European students. Not only were teacher expectations lower for Māori, their expectations were significantly lower than the actual achievement of Māori students. Achievement levels at the beginning of the year showed that there was no statistically significant difference between the actual achievement of Māori students and any other ethnic group. The group of Māori students was shown to be on par with all other groups. Interestingly, by the end of the year, despite teachers previously judging Pacific students to be achieving at similar levels to Asian and New Zealand European students, the achievement levels of both Māori and Pacific students were significantly below that of their Asian and New Zealand European counterparts. However, effect size gains for reading achievement were lower for Māori than any other group.

Links between home and school

Many studies have shown that home culture, background and socio-economic status impacts upon schooling or that teachers' expectations vary according to the ethnic and cultural background of their students. Whatever the case, a re-examination of the large data sets of the Smithfield (1994) and Progress at School (1991) studies by Harker (2007) points us in a potentially more useful direction. Harker concludes that:

> [i]t is clear from the data presented here that any uni-causal explanation based on socio-economic circumstances is inadequate to explain ethnic differences . . . The most likely explanation would seem to lie in the interaction between school environments and the values, attitudes, motivations that underpin the school 'culture' and the culture of the home and community environments and the values, attitudes and motivations on which they are based.
>
> (p. 17)

Harker (2007) further suggests that:

> [w]hile it is important (even necessary) for the family and community culture of the students to be understood and supported by schools, it is also important (even necessary) for the culture of the school to be understood and supported by families and communities.
>
> (p. 17)

Therefore, a better understanding of the relationships and interactions between both of these groups can lead to a better understanding of the variation in achievement and more

344

importantly, help to identify solutions to problems of educational disparities. Timperley (2003) contends that raising 'expectations appears to be fundamental to reducing disparities between the highest and lowest achieving students in New Zealand classrooms' (p. 86). Alton–Lee (2003), however, notes that high expectations alone are inadequate for enhancing educational outcomes. Effective teaching is also required. In this regard Sleeter (2005) provides another important challenge:

> [i]t is true that low expectations for students of color and students from poverty [stricken] communities, buttressed by taken-for-granted acceptance of the deficit ideology, has been a rampant and persistent problem for a long time . . . therefore, empowering teachers without addressing the deficit ideology may well aggravate the problem.
>
> (p. 2)

The basic assumption behind deficit ideologies appears to be that the student (their culture and home experience) is the problem, and that in order to achieve, the student must be changed or improved in some way (Bishop, *et al.,* 2003). A survey of teachers conducted by Morgan and Morris (1999) found that 62 per cent of teachers' responses ascribed student failure to 'something to do with the pupil or his or her home background', while 'something to do with me, the teacher' was found amongst only 18 per cent of the response statements (p.68). Similar patterns of blame and denial of teachers taking responsibility for students lack of success were found by Bishop *et al.* (2003), Prochnow and Kearney (2002) and Phillips *et al.* (2001).

Responding to the way that some teachers tend to ascribe failure to the child and/or family background rather than to inappropriate pedagogy, can be extremely difficult. The discourses associated with an assumption of deficit in the learner and/or family often support long-standing societal norms (Nieto, 1994) and are used to help shape educational policies that, in turn, provide guidelines for practice that are self-justifying, and circular, and often very difficult for educators to change (Shields *et al.,* 2005). Bishop *et al.* (2003) identified that when teachers believed that the deficits of children and their home environments or the school were the primary causes of student failure in schools, then teachers found it extremely problematic to offer additional responses to improving students' achievement and parents felt powerless to contribute. However, supporting teachers to focus on that they have some control, that is, what goes on in their own classrooms, is an important first step.

Culturally responsive pedagogy of relations

Classroom contexts for learning that are responsive to cultural differences among students and where the pedagogy is based on relationships of care and high expectations for learning were described in Bishop *et al.* (2003) as where we:

> create learning relationships within classrooms wherein learners' culturally generated sense-making processes are used in order that they may successfully participate in classroom interactions.
>
> (p. 7)

Such relationships privilege students' prior learning experiences and thus their sense-making processes are seen as acceptable and legitimate. Where students' experiences and what they know forms an important foundation of the relationships and interaction patterns that are in the classroom learning contexts, teachers and students are able to work in ways where new knowledge is collaboratively co-created. In this way, Bishop *et al.* (2003) suggest that learners can be co-enquirers who:

> interact and exchange notes and take part in the whole process of learning from goal setting to assessment and evaluation. Learning is to be seen as active, close to real-life, problem-based, integrated, critically reflective, creative, and life-long.
>
> (p. 7)

When teachers give students' home cultures a central position within the pedagogy of the classroom, student learning is more effective because the learning of new concepts is linked to prior knowledge emanating from outside the classroom. This approach provides a positive response to Alton-Lee's (2006) finding that 'substantial amounts of classroom time, is wasted because the instructional experiences do not match children's memory processes' (p. 618). The greater the distance between the world of the teacher and that of the child, the greater importance culturally responsive pedagogies can potentially have. Bishop (2003) further suggests that when there is a cultural mismatch between the teacher and the student it must be the teacher who makes the cognitive adjustment.

The implications of this discussion, for enabling all children to engage in literacy learning activities in the social context of classroom reading, include:

- The need for teachers to learn of the literacy practices taking place in their pupils' lives outside school;
- The need to find strategies to build on strengths that each of the children in the group bring to school;
- The need to make school interpretations of literacy explicit to children and their families.

(adapted from Gregory, 1996, p. 45)

On-going research examines how literacy achievement can be improved by changing teachers' attitudes and developing culturally responsive pedagogies in classrooms, and also by greater collaboration with literacy initiatives between schools and their home communities. This chapter now examines four studies such as this, three from New Zealand and one from Australia.

Literacy improvements within culturally responsive pedagogies

Research by Bishop *et al.* (2007) mentioned previously, tested the impact of working with a wide range of teachers across all curriculum areas in Years 9 and 10 to embed culturally responsive pedagogies in their classrooms as a means to raising the achievement of Māori students. The project had begun in 2001 by talking with Maori secondary school students and other participants in their education about barriers to, and facilitators of, their educational achievement. According to the majority of Māori students who were interviewed in each of the schools it was teachers' perceptions of Māori students that were particularly problematic. The students themselves suggested solutions around the kinds of relationships, interactions and strategies that would help teachers to facilitate Māori students' engagement with their learning. From these student narratives, the project developed an 'Effective Teaching Profile' which identifies understandings and practices with the potential to support Māori students to achieve to their potential in mainstream classrooms. When this effective teacher profile was applied in a professional development process with teachers from a number of secondary schools, the classroom results supported the conclusion that the students' suggestions were valid.

Bishop *et al.* (2006) have summarised some of the achievement of both Māori and non–Māori students in schools included in the Te Kotahitanga project as follows:

In 2005 Te Kotahitanga entered into the second year of using the Essential Skills Assessment to measure student literacy achievement . . . For the second consecutive year results revealed there was a statistically significant improvement in student literacy achievement scores for both Maori and non-Maori students. For both years the strength of these differences was above the threshold of what we would expect by natural maturation during the school year.

(Slavin and Fashola, 1998)

These findings revealed that in 2005 Maori students continued to have statistically significant improvements in literacy achievement scores. At the same time non-Māori students had similar gains. In particular, these findings revealed that Maori students in the lower third stanine, who are the students of greatest concern, had the largest significant gains over the year.

(Bishop and Berryman, 2006, p. 21)

Given the educational significance of these results, the researchers were able to conclude that the difference between the pre- and post-test scores for these students was beyond what might be expected during a school year's natural growth in literacy. While researchers concede that other variables may have influenced this change over time, teachers and students interviewed in this report (Bishop, *et al.,* 2007), suggest that the development of more effective relationships with students and the establishment of culturally responsive pedagogies in their classrooms, meant that many of these students were now more confident and able to use all of the skills and knowledge that they brought with them into their classrooms. Students also understood that teachers and peers had both become important mediators of their learning and held high expectations of them as learners. Thus a significant shift was shown for Years 9 and 10 Māori students working with teachers involved in the project.

'Picking up the pace'

An earlier study by Phillips *et al.* (2001) that also examined the impact of the understandings and expectations of teachers, delivered concentrated professional development in literacy instruction to groups of early childhood and new entrant teachers working with students from culturally diverse and low socioeconomic communities. Over 90 percent of the children from these communities were from Māori and/or Pacific Island homes. Like Bishop *et al.* (2007), this professional development also challenged teachers' ideas and expectations about the learning development of their students and the subsequent emergence of students' literacy skills. It also challenged teachers to develop expertise in their profession and thus be more effective teachers. In so doing the training enhanced teachers' ideas about literacy learning, it raised their expectations of their students, and developed their teaching expertise and practice.

This research, titled *Picking up the Pace*, referred to the urgency and speed needed to reach the expected level of literacy progress that students should be achieving at this stage. Pace also referred to the students' actual progress and teachers' need to pick up from this actual point if progress was to be made. Finally pace referred to the teachers themselves and their need to pick up the pace in their own practice, in order to be more effective literacy instructors. Researchers believed that teachers would be able to *pick up* the expected rate of literacy progress for these students, with early and accelerated learning techniques. Traditionally these students have been left behind the majority of their peers in ways that impact detrimentally on overall, progressive levels of achievement at school. In order to close the achievement gaps between themselves and their peers and guarantee development in literacy across a broader front, researchers aimed for students to be under way with literacy learning as soon after their entry to school as possible whilst also receiving the most effective literacy instruction. Consequently, researchers worked to improve literacy instruction in both early childhood centres and primary schools and also develop common understandings about effective transitions in both of these settings.

With early childhood teachers, researchers focused on reading to children, guided writing, and telling and retelling stories. This involved learning about the most effective conditions under which these activities could produce a range of essential literacy learning outcomes. They also worked to manage students' transition to school more effectively. For the primary teachers, intensive professional development aimed to change teachers' literacy misconceptions and improve pedagogies. Teachers were supported to reach a greater alignment between their students' expertise on arrival at school and the early literacy instruction they provided. This involved teachers developing in-depth understandings of language, literacy, and learning in order to think and practise in ways that enhanced children's opportunities to acquire literacy in their classrooms. Specifically teachers learned to:

- develop a greater awareness of the behaviours that signal students' understanding of tasks, thereby developing a greater awareness of the relevance of experience and strengths in language and literacy with which students come to school;
- observe students' reading and writing behaviours in specific and focused ways in order to build on from students' strengths;
- help students make connections between their own diverse communities and experiences to school literacy experiences;
- help students to monitor their own reading and writing behaviours.

Some of the professional development involved teachers from both early childhood and primary settings. A wide range of early literacy and language assessments were used to compare the progress of these students over six-monthly intervals.

Results showed that students who came from the targeted early childhood settings entered school with significantly higher scores on conventional measures of literacy and language than other groups of children entering these schools at five. In school settings, the intervention accelerated students' progress over the first six months of school and despite some having gained low scores in the language and literacy measures on entry to school (those in the main from non targeted early childhood centres), significant gains were shown across a broad range of literacy measures for baseline groups when compared to a non-intervention group. The substantial lift in the reading and writing achievement of students in this study indicate that by changing teachers' expectations of their Māori and Pacific Island students, 'low rates of progress in literacy are neither inevitable nor unchangeable in low decile[1] schools. Educators working in these environments can help bring children up to speed – to expected levels of achievement' (Phillips *et al.*, 2001, p. 10).

Reading to learn in Murdi Paaki

Educational outcomes for Australia's indigenous students also highlight the urgent need to develop more effective educational strategies if the disparity of outcomes between indigenous

348

and their non-indigenous students is to be challenged and addressed (Koop, and Rose, 2008; Rose, 2004). In-service training, designed to address this need, has been developed and is being used in a number of indigenous and mainstream Australian schools in New South Wales. This training utilises the *Reading to Learn* programme (Rose *et al.*, 1999) which aims to improve the literacy outcomes of indigenous students by providing opportunities for teachers from these communities to improve the language skills of their students in order to develop their reading skills and subsequently improve their own writing and spelling skills.

The *Reading to Learn* approach works from an assumption that gaps in students' achievement are understood as being the responsibility of the school, rather than a problem that is located at the level of individual cognitive ability. Teachers are trained to provide differing degrees of scaffold (Bruner, 1986) or support to the student.

Reading to Learn begins as a top-down strategy with a focus on meaning, using fiction and non-fiction texts at challenging and age appropriate levels. Teachers are trained to provide students with explicit support to read texts at a level beyond that which they could read independently. Once students are familiar with the meaning of the texts, the focus shifts to consider the structure of language in the text, its organisation and sequence. This includes consideration of spelling, wording and letters. The ultimate goal is to support students to use the newly acquired literacy and language features in order to read and write new texts more independently.

Rather than being seen as a traditional remedial programme with teachers focusing only on students' literacy problems, *Reading to Learn* focuses on scaffolding students' literacy learning by modelling the correct answers and rewarding students when they respond in kind. In this way new language and literacy learning is part of the social and cultural contexts in which students engage (Vygotsky, 1978). Through strategic guidance and scaffolding by their teachers, high levels of initial support are able to be gradually reduced as students develop new skills and are able to complete increasingly challenging tasks with greater levels of independence.

This study (Koop, and Rose, 2008), working across 17 schools in the Murdi Paaki region of New South Wales, Australia, is aimed at providing indigenous students with the literacy skills needed to engage successfully at all levels of schooling. These schools are provided with in- class tutors who are trained to support classroom teachers and ensure accountability to the Reading to Learn, programme. Teacher expectations are made explicit to the learners who are supported, through the scaffolding process, to buy in to the interactive teaching and learning support with which they are being provided. Teachers report that students develop confidence and competence in literacy and develop literacy skills that are far broader than being able to read, write and spell. Students develop an educational platform that enables them to access, 'the academic "ways of speaking and thinking" that are necessary for educational success' (Koop and Rose, 2008, p. 43). In this way their learning is accelerated and students are able to catch up with their more advanced peers.

Home school literacy partnerships in second language settings

Tape-assisted reading

Given the past colonisation of Māori within the New Zealand education system, many of today's indigenous, Māori parents, while keen for their children to become literate in Māori, do not have the Māori language competencies or confidence to assist their children learning to read in Māori immersion settings. Given the increasing availability of high-quality reading materials in Māori, and the need to focus on the range of competencies, of students and their families, especially those with limited language and literacy skills, there appeared to be benefits from exploring reading support strategies that could be implemented at home as well as at school, and also by parents with limited Māori language themselves.

To this end, a series of 100 Māori language stories, covering eight reading levels from within the Ngā Kete Kōrero Māori language reading framework (Ngā Kete Kōrero Framework Team, 1996) were read onto tapes by fluent native speakers, including elders. Previous research had demonstrated that because of the phonemic regularity of the Māori language, measures of children's reading competence based on accuracy and fluency alone tended to over-estimate levels of reading comprehension (Ngā Kete Kōrero Framework Team, 1995). Therefore, two comprehension activities were prepared to accompany each book and tape. This involved a set of two cloze cards, and a three-level guide, guiding readers in their understanding of the text. Together, the tape resources and the comprehension activities provided opportunities for teachers to monitor students' reading and for students to self-manage (initiate, monitor and record) their own reading progress within and across reading texts. They also provided specific activities for school staff and family members at home to engage in and support students' learning to read in Māori.

In 2006, a literacy project that aimed to raise the reading achievement of Māori students in two New Zealand bilingual schools was conducted using this tape-assisted reading resource for students learning to read in the Māori language (Berryman and Woller, 2007). In School 1 students were encouraged to use the resources with family members for two terms in their homes, while in School 2 the programme was maintained in the school for two terms.

Both schools managed to complete two terms of approximately ten weeks each, in programme. In each school, the same researcher was able to conduct assessments prior to the intervention and after two consecutive terms of being in programme. Effect sizes were calculated on reading levels for students in both schools. The results indicate that, for students reading at the lowest levels in both schools, shifts in book level from baseline to the end of the second ten weeks of programme were of statistical significance and that they were also much larger than typical. Importantly, further analysis of data showed that, improvements in book levels for students from both schools did not compromise improvements in reading fluency, reading rates and reading comprehension, which in the main were maintained or improved.

These results indicate the worth of oral language tasks, in collaboration with competent speakers of Māori, such as those providing the oral reading models of texts and then monitoring through appropriate levels of difficulty. Providing readers with regular opportunities to *match* a competent oral/aural reading model with specific visual information in the context of meaningful texts appeared to be highly beneficial. This is especially so, when it is followed up with students, either in one-to-one or in small group contexts, predicting the likely outcomes of story lines on the basis of prior knowledge and experience, or, identifying new vocabulary items, language structures and talking about what this means, as is provided by this tape resource and the collaborative method employed for its implementation. Students working mainly in the home setting with family members from School 1, showed similar levels of progress to those who worked mainly in the school setting from School 2.

This research underscores the critical role of similar resources, utilised in both the home and school settings as a key to collaborating across both of these settings in order to address the challenge of boosting second language learners' reading and comprehension of written texts in other settings.

Conclusion

A comprehensive explanation of, and effective responses to, difficulties in literacy experienced by students in schools requires both:

- accurate identification of difficulties related to the way the learner processes information, and
- a sensitive awareness of the wide range of experiences that students bring with them when they come to school.

Together, these have the potential to make an important contribution to students' literacy acquisition at school and also to addressing difficulties they experience.

The way in which schools respond to family culture and background and the kind of teacher–student and home–school relationships that exist can serve to include or alienate the very students, parents, families and communities that schools seek to serve. Embedded within the particular discourses, approaches and strategies of schools are a variety of preconceptions about the abilities and rights of students, parents, families and communities, from a diversity of backgrounds and cultures, to support the literacy development of their children (Dale, 1996; Wearmouth, 2004). Schools must recognise these preconceptions and assumptions in order to negotiate more effective home–school literacy initiatives. Research shows the benefits to literacy learning that accrue when schools work to address issues of cultural understandings between themselves and their home communities as well as difficulties experienced by students in the processing of information related to a bottom-up approach. Thus schools will be able to harness all available resources to address difficulties in literacy development effectively and help to maintain the 'broad-based' instruction (Wragg *et al.*, 1998) required to support all children's literacy development.

Notes

1   All New Zealand schools are given a decile weighting based on socioeconomic status of the communities in which they are situated, thus attracting additional needs-based funding.

References

Alton-Lee, A. (2003). *Quality Teaching for Diverse Students in Schooling: Best Evidence Synthesis*. Wellington, New Zealand: Ministry of Education.

Alton-Lee, A. (2006). How teaching influences learning: Implications for educational researchers, teachers, teacher educators and policy makers. *Teaching and Teacher Education*, 22, 612–626.

Baron, R. M., Tom, D. Y. and Cooper, H. M. (1985). Social class, race, and teacher expectations. In J. B. Dusek (ed.), *Teacher Expectancies* (pp. 251–270). Hillsdale, NJ: Erlbaum.

Berryman, M. and Woller, P. (2007). *RÅPP: Tape-assisted reading to support students' literacy in Māori in two bilingual schools*. SET (2), 19–23. Wellington: NZCER.

Bishop, R. (2003). Changing power relations in education: Kaupapa Maori messages for 'mainstream' education in Aotearoa/New Zealand. *Comparative Education*, *39*(2), 221–238.

Bishop, R. and Berryman, M. (2006). *Culture Speaks: Cultural relationships and classroom learning*. Wellington, New Zealand: Huia

Bishop, R., Berryman, M., Tiakiwai, S. and Richardson, C. (2003). *Te Kotahitanga: Experiences of year 9 and 10 Māori students in mainstream classrooms. Final Report to the Ministry of Education*. Wellington, New Zealand: Ministry of Education.

Bishop, R., Berryman, M., Cavanagh, T., Teddy, L. and Clapham, S. (2006). *Te Kōtahitanga Phase 3: Establishing a culturally responsive pedagogy of rlations in mainstream secondary school classrooms*. Wellington, New Zealand: Ministry of Education.

Bishop, R., Berryman, M., Powell, A. and Teddy, L. (2007). *Te Kotahitanga: Improving the educational achievement of Māori students in mainstream education Phase 2: Towards a whole school approach*. Report to the Ministry of Education. Wellington, New Zealand: Ministry of Education.

Brophy, J. E. and Good, T. L. (1974). *Teacher–student relationships: Causes and consequences*. New York: Rinehart and Winston.

Bruner, J. (1986). *Actual Minds, Possible Worlds*. Cambridge, MA: Harvard University Press.

Bruner, J. (1990). *Acts of Meaning*. Cambridge, MA: Harvard University Press.

Bruner, J. (1996). *The Culture of Education*. Cambridge, MA: Harvard University Press.

Dale, N. (1996). *Working with Families of Children with Special Needs: Partnership and practice*. London: Routledge.

Glynn, T. and Bishop, R. (1995). Cultural Issues in Educational Research: A New Zealand Perspective. *He Pukenga Kōrero, 1*(1), (pp. 37–43).

Glynn, T., Wearmouth, J. and Berryman, M. (2006). *Supporting Students with Literacy Difficulties: A Responsive approach*. Maidenhead: Open University Press/McGraw-Hill Education.

Gregory, E. (1996) *Making Sense of a New World*. London: Paul Chapman.

Gregory, E. (1998) Siblings as mediators of literacy in linguistic minority communities. *Language and Education, 12*(1), 33–54.

Gregory, E. (2004a) 'Bridges to literacy'. In M. Nind, K. Sheehy and K. Simmons (eds), *Inclusive Education: Learners and Learning Contexts* (pp. 263–280). London: David Fulton.

Gregory, E. (2004b) Invisible teachers of literacy: collusion between siblings and teachers in creating classroom cultures. *Literacy* (July), 97–105.

Gregory, E., Long, S. and Volk, D. (2004a). A sociocultural approach to learning. In E. Gregory, S. Long and D. Volk (eds), *Many Pathways to Literacy: Young children learning with siblings, grandparents, peers and communities* (pp. 6–20). New York and London: Routledge Falmer.

Gregory, E., Williams, A., Baker, D. and Street, B. (2004b). Introducing literacy to four year olds: Creating classroom cultures in three schools. *Journal of Early Literacy Learning, 4*(1), 85–107.

Harker, R. (2007). *Ethnicity and school achievement: Some data to supplement the Biddulph* et al. *(2003)* Best Evidence Synthesis: Secondary analysis of the Progress at School and Smithfield (1994) data sets for the iterative Best Evidence Synthesis Programme. Wellington, New Zealand: Ministry of Education.

Jussim, L., Eccles, J. S. and Madon, S. (1996). Social perception, social stereotypes and teacher expectations: accuracy and the quest for the powerful self-fulfilling prophecy. In M. P. Zanna (ed.), *Advances in Experimental Social Psychology* (Vol. 28, pp.281–388). New York: Academic Press.

Koop, C. and Rose, D. (2008). Reading to learn in Murdi Paaki: Changing outcomes for indigenous students. *Literacy Learning: The Middle Years, 16*(1), 41–46.

Marsden, M. (2003). *The Woven Universe: Selected Writings of Rev. Māori Marsden*. Edited by T. C. Royal. Published by The Estate of Rev. Māori Marsden. Masterton: Printcraft '81 Ltd.

Marsden, M. and Henare, T. (1992). *Kaitiakitanga: A definitive introduction to the holistic world view of the Māori*. Wellington, New Zealand: Ministry of the Environment.

McKown, C. and Weinstein, R. S. (2002). Modeling the role of child ethnicity and gender in children's differential response to teacher expectations. *Journal of Applied Social Psychology, 32*, 159–184.

McKown, C and Weinstein, R.S. (2003). The development and consequences of stereotype-consciousness in middle childhood. *Child Development, 74* (2), 498–515.

McNaughton, S. (2002). *Meeting of Minds*. Wellington, New Zealand: Learning Media.

Morgan, C. and Morris, G. (1999). *Good Teaching and Learning: Pupils and teachers speak*. Buckingham: Philadelphia Open University Press.

Nash, R. (1993). *Succeeding Generations: Family resources and access to education in New Zealand*. Auckland, New Zealand: Oxford University Press.

Ngā Kete Kōrero Framework Team (1995). *Final Report to Te Puni Kōkiri*. Wellington, New Zealand: Ministry of Māori Development.

Ngā Kete Kōrero Framework Team, (1996). *Ngā Kete Kōrero Framework Teacher Handbook: A framework for organising junior Māori reading texts*. Wellington, New Zealand: Ministry of Māori Development, and Huia Publishers.

Nieto, S. (1994). Lessons from students on creating a chance to dream. *Harvard Educational Review, 64*(4), 392–426.

Phillips, G., McNaughton, S. and MacDonald, S. (2001). *Picking up the Pace: Effective literacy interventions for accelerated progress over the transition into decile 1 schools*. Wellington, New Zealand: Ministry of Education.

Prochnow, J. and Kearney, A. (2002). Barriers to including students with difficult behaviour: What are we really saying? Paper presented at the New Zealand Association for Research in Education, Palmerston North, December.

Quest Rapuara (1992). *Cultural Identity: Whakamana tangata.* Wellington, New Zealand: Quest Rapuara, the Career Development and Transition Education Service.

Reid, G. (1998). *Dyslexia: A Practitioner's Handbook.* Chichester: Wiley

Rose, D. (2004). Sequencing and pacing of the hidden curriculum: How indigenous children are left out of the chain. In J. Muller, A. Morais and B. Davies (eds), *Reading Bernstein, Researching Bernstein*, pp. 91–107. London: RoutledgeFalmer.

Rose, D., Gray, B. and Cowey, W. (1999). Scaffolding reading and writing for indigenous children in school. In P. Wignell (ed.), *Double Power: English literacy and indigenous education.* Melbourne: Languages Australia.

Rubie-Davies, C., Hattie, J. and Hamilton, R. (2006). Expecting the best for students: Teacher expectations and academic outcomes. *British Journal of Educational Psychology*, 76, 429–444.

Shields, C. M., Bishop, R. and Mazawi, A. E. (2005). *Pathologising Practices: The impact of deficit thinking on education.* New York: Peter Lang Publishing.

Slavin, R. E. and Fashola, O. S. (1998). *Show Me the Evidence: Proven and promising programs for America's schools.* Thousand Oaks, CA: Corwin.

Sleeter, C. (2005). *Un-Standardizing Curriculum: Multicultural teaching in the standards-based classroom.* New York: Teachers College Press.

Smith, J. and Elley, W. (1997). *How Children Learn to Write.* New Zealand: Longman.

St. George, A. (1983). Teacher expectations and perceptions of Polynesian and Pakeha pupils and the relationship to classroom behaviour and school achievement. *British Journal of Educational Psychology*, 53, 48–59.

Stanovich, K. (2000). *Progress in Understanding Reading: scientific foundations and new frontiers.* London: The Guilford Press.

Steele, C. M. (1997). A threat in the air: How stereotypes shape intellectual identity and performance. *American Psychologist*, 52, 613–629.

Street, B. (1995). *Social Literacies: Critical approaches to literacy development, ethnography, and education.* Cambridge: Cambridge University Press.

Timperley, H. (2003). School improvement and teachers' expectations of student achievement. *New Zealand Journal of Educational Studies*, 38(1), 73–88.

Vygotsky, L. S. (1962). *Thought and Language.* Cambridge, MA: MIT Press.

Vygotsky, L. S. (1978). *Mind in Society: The development of higher psychological processes.* London: Harvard University Press.

Vygotsky, L. S. (1981). The instrumental method in psychology. In J.V. Wersch (ed.), *The Concept of Activity in Soviet Psychology* (pp. 3–35). New York: MR Sharpe.

Walker, R. (1978). The relevance of Maori myth and tradition. In M. King, (ed.), *Tihe mauri ora aspects of Maoritanga* (pp. 19–32). New Zealand: Methuen.

Wearmouth, J. (1997). Prisoners' perspectives on what constitutes a 'good' education. Paper presented to the British Psychological Society Annual Conference (Education Section), Warwick, England.

Wearmouth, J. (2004). Issues in addressing children's difficulties in literacy development through family-school partnerships. *Curriculum Journal*, 15(1), 5–18.

Wearmouth, J., Glynn, T. and Berryman, M. (2005). *Perspectives on Student Behaviour in Schools: Exploring theory and developing practice.* London: Routledge Falmer.

Weinstein, R. S. and Middlestadt, S. E. (1979). Student perceptions of teacher interactions with male high and low achievers. *Journal of Educational Psychology*, 71 (4), 421–431.

Weinstein, R. S., Gregory, A. and Strambler, M. J. (2004). Intractable self-fulfilling prophecies fifty years after. *Brown v. Board of Education. American Psychologist*, 59 (6), 511–520.

Wragg, E. C., Wragg, C. M., Haynes, G. S. and Chamberlain, R. P. (1998). *Improving Literacy in the Primary School.* London: Routledge.

Index